KU-472-249

The American Express
International Traveller's Pocket
FRENCH
Dictionary and Phrase Book

Collins/Mitchell Beazley

List of abbreviations

abbrev	–	abbreviation	*num*	–	numeral
adj	–	adjective	*pl*	–	plural
adv	–	adverb	*pref*	–	prefix
art	–	article	*prep*	–	preposition
conj	–	conjunction	*pron*	–	pronoun
excl	–	exclamation	*vi*	–	intransitive verb
f	–	feminine noun	*vr*	–	reflexive verb
m	–	masculine noun	*vt*	–	transitive verb
n	–	noun	*vt/i*	–	transitive/intransitive verb

The asterisk * denotes an irregular verb, to which the reader is referred in the list of irregular verbs in the grammar section.

Cross-reference letter keys occur in brackets after main section headings. Phrases are numbered in sequence following each main heading. Phrase words are cross-referenced in the English-French dictionary section by letter and number to their relevant phrases. An *f* after the number indicates that the cross-reference applies also to the subsequent phrase(s).

Collins Publishers

Editor
Lorna Sinclair
with
Nicholas Rollin
Rosemary C. Milne
Christiane Cooper
Assistant Editors
Susan Dunsmore
Valerie McNulty
Lesley Robertson
Managing Editor
Richard H. Thomas

Mitchell Beazley Publishers

Editors
James Hughes
Christopher McIntosh
Designer
Philip Lord
Executive Art Editor
Douglas Wilson
Production
Julian Deeming

Edited by William Collins Sons & Co Ltd
and by Mitchell Beazley International Ltd
Designed by Mitchell Beazley International Ltd
87-89 Shaftesbury Avenue
London W1V 7AD
© Mitchell Beazley Publishers 1983
© William Collins Sons & Co Ltd 1983

All rights reserved
ISBN 0 85533 463 0

No part of this work may be reproduced or utilized in any form by any means, electronic or mechanical, including photocopying, recording or by any information storage and retrieval system, without the prior written permission of the publisher.

Typeset by Coats Dataprint Ltd, Inverness

Printed in Great Britain by William Collins Sons & Co Ltd, Glasgow

Contents

Pronunciation

English spelling gives only an approximate idea of the French sounds, which can be learned only by listening to the French themselves. The table below lists the closest English equivalents to sounds that English speakers may find particularly difficult.

The French vowel sound in such words as *tu*, *du*, *vue*, or *rue*, (shown in the table as *ōō*) has no English equivalent, although many people can't distinguish it from the sound in *roue* or *bout* (*roo*, *boo*). It may be formed by pursing the lips and then trying to say *ee*.

Vowels followed by the letters *n* or *m*, such as *an*, *em*, *on*, etc., are sometimes nasalized, especially when they occur at the end of words. Here the sound is similar to that at the end of *restaurant*. To make these sounds, breathe out slightly through the nose as you pronounce the vowel shown in the pronunciation. These sounds are shown here by the addition of the symbol *ñ* to the closest vowel sound, e.g. *añ*, *oñ*.

The letter *e* in French is often very weak, rather like the English *a* in *above* or *o* in *position*. This is shown as *uh* in the table.

The letter *j* is indicated as *zh* and pronounced like the *s* in English words such as *television* or *measure*, as is the letter *g* in certain cases (see the table).

In French, the letter *r* is always pronounced, unlike some forms of English where it is almost silent. The sound is produced in the throat by rolling the uvula (rather as in gargling), but you can also use a rolled tongue-tip *r*, as many French speakers do.

The pronunciations shown here should be taken at face value. The reader should be on his guard against pronunciations that look like an actual English word: for instance, *poste* is shown as *post* (not *pôst*), and therefore it rhymes more closely with *lost* than with *most*!

How to Pronounce French

French spelling	Closest English sound	Shown here by	Example
a, à	intermediate between *f*a*t* and *f*a*ther*	a	chat *sha*, là *la*
a, â	*f*a*ther*	ah	pas *pah*, mât *mah*
ai, e, é	pl*a*y	ay	quai *kay*, mes *may*, été *ay-tay*
ai, e, è, ê	s*e*t	e/eh	chaise *shez*, mets *meh*, père *pehr*, même *mem*
i, y	m*ee*t or *y*et	ee y	vide *veed*, cycle *see-kluh* pied *pyay*
o	p*o*t, US th*ou*ght	o	bol *bol*
o, au, eau	b*oa*t	ō	trop *trō*, faux *fō*, seau *sō*
ou	b*oo*t	oo	bout *boo*
u	see text above	ōō	rue *rōō*
eu, œu	th*u*d	u/uh	pleut *pluh*, cœur *kur*
e	*a*bove	uh	le *luh*
euil(le), ueil	u of th*u*d + y of *y*acht	uhy	feuille *fuhy*, recueil *ruh-kuhy*
oi, oy	s*ua*ve	wa(h)	mois *mwah*, voyage *vwa-yazh*
ail	b*uy*	ye	travail *tra-vye*
ain/aim, ein, in/im	see text above	añ	pain *pañ*, frein *frañ*, impair *añ-pehr*
an/am, en/em, on/om	see text above	oñ	plan *ploñ*, temps *toñ*, mon *moñ*
un/um	see text above	uñ	lundi *luñ-dee*
gn	compa*ni*on	ny	rognon *ro-nyoñ*
g (*before* e, i), j	mea*s*ure	zh	rouge *roozh*, gilet *zhee-lay*, joue *zhoo*
ch	*sh*ut	sh	chat *sha*
h	silent		haché *a-shay*
qu	*c*ar	k	quel *kel*
th	*t*ime	t	thé *tay*

Introduction

The French language

French is the mother tongue of more than 80 million people in various parts of the world, including just over 54 million in France itself. Millions more speak it as a second tongue. It is a language of great elegance, used with equal grace by poets, diplomats and chefs. To use it is one of the great joys of visiting a French-speaking country. This book will help you to do so.

How the book works

This is a combined phrase book and dictionary, designed primarily for the needs of the traveller. It enables you to find easily and quickly just the phrase you need, whether you are buying a suit or trying to tell a garage mechanic what is wrong with your car. The French is accompanied in all cases by an instant guide to pronunciation.

Many of the phrases listed consist of a basic group of words which can be linked up with different subsidiary words to produce variations, in the way that a power tool can be fitted with extensions. With phrases of this kind the basic "tool" is shown on one side and the "extension" on the other, with a dash in between; alternative extensions are either indicated by an oblique stroke or shown on the line below. A further stock of extensions is found in the dictionary section at the back of the book, and this serves also as an index to the phrases.

Here is an example. If you look up the word "toll" in the dictionary, you will find "le péage" and a cross-reference letter to Section T (Travel). Cross-reference numbers indicate the number of the phrase within each section of the phrase book. So the cross-reference in the dictionary will lead you to the kind of phrase you may need in using this word. In this way you will soon be able to express yourself with flexibility and confidence, and what you learn from this book can open the door to the whole French language.

Understanding what you hear

This book not only tells you what to say but also helps you to interpret some of the things that will be said to you. For example, the section on "Finding the way" anticipates the sort of directions you may be given. But to understand what you hear it is necessary to attune your ear to sounds and intonations that may be unfamiliar. You should realize, for example, that when the French ask a question they very often do so by making a statement in a questioning tone, as in *ça va*? ("How are you?" or "Is that all right?"). So read, listen, learn and practise. Even a limited competence in French will bring you great satisfaction as you travel. *Bon voyage!*

Basic Equipment (B)

Here are some of the words and phrases which make up the basic coinage of French and which it is useful to have in your pocket for a wide variety of situations. You would be well advised to read through this whole section before starting your trip. If you can memorize any of it, so much the better.

Some essentials

Yes
Oui
wee

No
Non
noñ

Please
S'il vous plaît
seel voo pleh

Thank you
Merci
mehr·see

You're welcome
De rien, je vous en prie
duh ree·añ, zhuh voo zoñ pree

No thank you
Non merci
Noñ mehr·see

You are very kind/I am very grateful
Vous êtes très gentil(le)/
Je suis très reconnaissant(e)
*voo zet treh zhoñ·teey/
zhuh swee treh
ruh·ko·neh·soñ(·soñt)*

Greetings and general exchanges

Bear in mind that the French are rather formal when they address each other. They are sparing in their use of the familiar "tu" (you) – you should use this only when you are speaking to someone you know really well. The normal form of *you* is "vous". The French also use "Monsieur", "Madame" and "Mademoiselle" a great deal.

    Let us say you are greeting a Madame Grenier whom you do not know, or whom you may have met only two or three times before. The usual form is "Bonjour Madame", not just "Bonjour", or "Bonjour Madame Grenier". Similarly, if you are meeting someone called Jean whom you know well, you should say "Bonjour Jean". Remember also that handshaking is normal when greeting and taking leave, and is not restricted to the first meeting.

1   Good morning/afternoon   *(to a man)*
                Bonjour — Monsieur
          boñ·zhoor — *muh·syuh*
                       (to a lady)
                       — Madame
                       — *ma·dam*
                       (to a girl)
                       — Mademoiselle
                       — *ma·duh·mwa·zel*

2 Good evening
Bonsoir
boñ·swar

3 Good night
Bonne nuit
bon nwee

4 Hello
Bonjour/Bonsoir
boñ·zhoor/boñ·swar

5 Hello *(by telephone)*
Allô
a·lô

6 Goodbye
Au revoir
ô ruh·vwar

7 How do you do?
Enchanté(e)
oñ·shoñ·tay

8 I'm very glad to meet you
Enchanté(e) de faire votre connaissance
oñ·shoñ·tay duh fehr vo·truh ko·neh·soñs

9 See you soon
À bientôt
a byañ·tô

10 See you later *(in the day)*
À tout à l'heure
a too ta lur

11 **What's your name?**
Comment vous appelez-vous?
ko·moñ voo za·puh·lay·voo

12 **My name is . . .**
Je m'appelle . . .
zhuh ma·pel . . .

13 **How are you?**
Comment allez-vous? (*formal*)
ko·moñ ta·lay·voo
Ça va? (*informal*)
sa va

14 **I'm very well, thank you**
Très bien, merci
treh byañ, mehr·see

15 **I'm sorry/I beg your pardon**
Pardon
par·doñ

16 **Excuse me**
Excusez-moi
ek·skoo·zay·mwah

17 **That's all right/It doesn't matter**
Ce n'est pas grave/Ça ne fait rien
suh neh pa grav/sa nuh feh ree·añ

18 **With pleasure**
Avec plaisir
a·vek play·zeer

19 **Just a minute**
Un instant
uñ nañ·stoñ

20 **What did you say?**
Comment?
ko·moñ

21 **I understand**
Je comprends
zhuh koñ·proñ

22 **I don't understand**
Je ne comprends pas
zhuh nuh koñ·proñ pa

23 **Do you understand?**
Vous comprenez?
voo koñ·pruh·nay

24 **I don't speak French**
Je ne parle pas français
zhuh nuh parl pa froñ·seh

25 **I don't speak French very well**
Je ne parle pas très bien français
zhuh nuh parl pa treh byañ froñ·seh

26 **Please repeat that**
Vous voulez bien répéter?
voo voo·lay byañ ray·pay·tay

27 **Please speak more slowly**
Parlez plus lentement, s'il vous plaît
par·lay plōō loñt·moñ seel voo pleh

28 **Could you please write that down?**
Voulez-vous bien écrire ça?
voo·lay·voo byañ ay·kreer sa

29 **Do you speak English?**
Parlez-vous anglais?
par·lay·voo oñ·gleh

30 **I am English**
Je suis Anglais(e)
zhuh swee zoñ·gleh(·glez)

31 **I am American**
Je suis Américain(e)
zhuh swee za·may·ree·kañ (·ken)

32 **I don't mind**
Ça m'est égal
sa meh tay·gal

33 **Agreed, quite so/Fine**
D'accord
da·kor

34 **Isn't it? Don't you agree?**
N'est-ce pas?
nes pa

35 **Do you follow?**
Vous comprenez?
voo koñ·pruh·nay

36 **Really?**
Vraiment?
vray·moñ

37 **That's true**
C'est vrai
seh vray

38 **You are right**
Vous avez raison
voo za·vay ray·zoñ

Common questions and statements

Many of the things you will need to ask and say will involve the following groups of words. You will notice that many questions begin with, or include, the words, "Est-ce que . . ." (pronounced *es kuh*) added to a verb: for example, "Est-ce que vous avez . . .?" ("Do you have . . .?" or literally "Is it that you have . . .?"). But it is usually possible, as an alternative, to use the verb and pronoun themselves, turned around so as to make a question. For example, in this case you could say simply: "Avez-vous . . .?". Even more simply, the French often ask a question by making a statement in a questioning tone, as in "Ça va?" (literally: "It goes?" — "How are you?" or "Is that all right?").

39 **Do I have to/Ought I to . . .**
Est-ce que je dois . . .?
es kuh zhuh dwah . . .

40 **Do you have . . .?**
Vous avez . . .? *or*
    Avez-vous . . .?
voo za·vay . . . a·vay·voo . . .

41 **Is it necessary to . . .?**
Faut-il . . .?
fō·teel . . .

42 **How much/many?**
Combien?
koñ·byañ

43 **How often?**
Combien de fois?
koñ·byañ duh fwah

44 **How long will that take?**
Combien de temps est-ce que cela prendra?
koñ·byañ duh toñ es kuh suh·la proñ·dra

45 **Where is . . . ?**
Où est . . . ?
oo eh . . .

46 **Where are . . . ?**
Où sont . . . ?
oo soñ . . .

47 **Here is/are . . .**
Voici . . .
vwa·see . . .

48 **There is/are . . .**
Voilà . . .
vwa·la . . .

49	**How do you say . . .**	**— in French?**
	Comment dit-on . . .	— en français?
	ko·moñ dee·toñ . . .	— *oñ froñ·seh*
50	**I need**	**— a doctor**
	Il me faut	— un médecin
	eel muh fō	— *uñ mayt·sañ*
51	**I want**	**— a cup of coffee**
	Je voudrais	— une tasse de café
	zhuh voo·dreh	— *ōōn tas duh ka·fay*
52	**I want**	**— to go to Paris**
	Je veux	— aller à Paris
	zhuh vuh	— *a·lay a pa·ree*
53	**I would like**	**— a glass of wine**
	Je voudrais	— un verre de vin
	zhuh voo·dreh	— *uñ vehr duh vañ*
54	**May I**	**— borrow your pen?**
	Est-ce que je peux	— emprunter votre stylo?
	es kuh zhuh puh	— *oñ·pruñ·tay vo·truh stee·lō*
55	**Do you mind if**	**— I open the window?**
	Ça ne vous dérange pas que	— j'ouvre la fenêtre?
	sa nuh voo day·roñzh pa kuh	— *zhoo·vruh la fuh·neh·truh*

56 **I mean that . . .**
Je veux dire que . . .
zhuh vuh deer kuh . . .

57 **What is this/that?**
Qu'est-ce que c'est?
kes kuh seh

58 **What time is it?**
Quelle heure est-il?
kel ur eh·teel

59 **(At) what time?**
À quelle heure?
a kel ur

60 **Is there any charge?**
C'est payant?
seh pay·yoñ

61 **Could you come with me please?**
Vous pourriez venir avec moi?
voo poo·ree·ay vuh·neer a·vek mwah

62 **What's the matter?**
Qu'est-ce qu'il y a?
kes keel ee a

63 **What does that mean?**
Qu'est-ce que ça veut dire?
kes kuh sa vuh deer

General problems and requests

64 **Can you help me please?**
Est-ce que vous pouvez m'aider, s'il vous plaît?
es kuh voo poo·vay may·day seel voo pleh

65 **I've made a mistake**
Je me suis trompé(e)
zhuh muh swee troñ·pay

66 **Whom should I see about this?**
A qui dois-je m'adresser à ce sujet?
a kee dwa·zhuh ma·dreh·say a suh sōō·zhe

67 We need someone who can speak English
Il nous faut quelqu'un qui parle anglais
eel noo fô kel·kuñ kee parl oñ·gleh

68 Please repeat that
Voulez-vous répéter s'il vous plaît?
voo·lay·voo ray·pay·tay seel voo pleh

69   We are — in a hurry
            Nous sommes — pressés
            noo som — preh·say

70   Can you do it for me — at once?
      Est-ce que vous pouvez
            me faire ça — immédiatement?
      es kuh voo poo·vay
      muh fehr sa — ee·may·dyat·moñ
                  — by Wednesday?
                  — avant mercredi?
                  — a·voñ mehr·kruh·dee

71   The machine — has broken down
        La machine — est en panne
        la ma·sheen — eh toñ pan

72   I have broken — the switch/the glass
        J'ai cassé — le bouton de contact/le verre
        zhay ka·say — luh boo·toñ duh koñ·takt/luh vehr

73   I have spilled — the water/the wine
        J'ai renversé — l'eau/le vin
   zhay roñ·vehr·say — lô/luh vañ

74   I have forgotten — my glasses/my key
        J'ai oublié — mes lunettes/ma clef
        zhay oo·blee·ay — may lōō·net/ma klay

75   I have left my bag — in the plane/in the bus
        J'ai laissé mon sac — dans l'avion/dans le bus
        zhay leh·say moñ sak — doñ la·vyoñ/doñ luh bōōs

76 I wish to leave a message for Mr Smith
Je voudrais laisser un message pour M. Smith
zhuh voo·dreh leh·say uñ meh·sazh poor muh·syuh Smith

77 Is there a message/letter for me?
Il y a un message/une lettre pour moi?
eel ee a uñ meh·sazh/ōōn leh·truh poor mwah

78 Go away!
Allez-vous en!
a·lay·voo zoñ

Travel   (T)

General

1   I'm leaving — tomorrow
             Je pars — demain
             zhuh par — duh·mañ
                  — on Thursday
                  — jeudi
                  — zhuh·dee

2 How long will the train/flight be delayed?
Le train/l'avion arrivera avec combien de temps de retard?
luh trañ/la·vyoñ a·ree·vuh·ra a·vek koñ·byañ duh toñ duh ruh·tar

3   I've missed — my train
        J'ai manqué — mon train
        zhay moñ·kay — moñ trañ
                 — my flight
                 — mon vol
                 — moñ vol

4   At what time is the next — train?
      A quelle heure est
         le prochain — train?
      a kel ur eh luh
        pro·shañ — trañ

At what time is the next — flight?
A quelle heure est
le prochain — vol?
a kel ur eh luh
pro·shañ — vol
— bus?
— autobus?
— *ō·tō·bōōs*

5 I am a member of the American Express party travelling to Marseilles
Je suis du groupe American Express et nous allons à Marseille
zhuh swee dōō groop American Express ay noo za·loñ za mar·say

6 **My party has left without me**
Mon groupe est parti sans moi
moñ groop eh par·tee soñ mwah

7 **I have lost the rest of my party**
J'ai perdu les autres membres du groupe
zhay pehr·dōō lay zō·truh moñ·bruh dōō groop

8 Where do I change — for Marseilles?
Où est la correspondance — pour Marseille?
oo eh la ko·reh·spoñ·doñs — poor mar·say

9 Could you please — keep my seat for me?
Voulez-vous — me garder ma place?
voo·lay·voo — muh gar·day ma plas
— keep an eye on my luggage for a few moments
— surveiller mes bagages quelques instants
— *sōōr·vay·yay may ba·gazh kel·kuh zañ·stoñ*

Arrival and departure

10 Here is — my passport
Voici — mon passeport
vwa·see — moñ pas·por
— my driving licence
— mon permis de conduire
— *moñ pehr·mee duh koñ·dweer*

11 **My wife and I are on a joint passport**
Ma femme et moi sommes sur le même passeport
ma fam ay mwah som sōōr luh mem pas·por

12 **Our children are on this passport**
Nos enfants sont sur ce passeport
nō zoñ·foñ soñ sōōr suh pas·por

13 I am staying for — two weeks
Je reste — deux semaines
zhuh rest — duh suh·men

14 I am staying at — the Hôtel de France
Je loge à — l'Hôtel de France
zhuh lozh a — lō·tel duh froñs

15 **I have nothing to declare**
Je n'ai rien à déclarer
zhuh nay ree·añ a day·kla·ray

16 **I have the usual allowance of cigarettes and liquor**
J'ai en cigarettes et en alcool les quantités autorisées (pour le règlement des douanes)
zhay oñ see·ga·ret ay oñ nal·kol lay koñ·tee·tay ō·tō·ree·zay poor luh reh·gluh·moñ day dwan

17 **Those are my personal belongings**
Ce sont des effets personnels
suh soñ day zeh·feh pehr·so·nel

18 **I represent Universal Chemicals**
Je représente Universal Chemicals
zhuh ruh·pray·zoñt Universal Chemicals

19 **I am looking for the representative of Alpha Engineering**
Je cherche le représentant de Alpha Engineering
zhuh shehrsh luh ruh·pray·zoñ·toñ duh Alpha Engineering

20 He/she was due to meet me here
    Il/elle devait me rencontrer ici
    eel/el duh·veh muh roñ·koñ·tray ee·see
21 The people I was to meet have not turned up
    Les personnes que je devais rencontrer ne sont pas venues
    lay pehr·son kuh zhuh duh·veh roñ·koñ·tray nuh soñ pa vuh·nōō

Luggage

22   Please take these bags — to platform 9
            Portez ces valises — jusqu'au quai neuf, s'il vous plaît
            por·tay say va·leez — zhōō·skó kay nuf, seel voo pleh
                               — to a taxi
                               — jusqu'à un taxi, s'il vous plaît
                               — *zhōō·ska uñ tak·see, seel voo pleh*
23   My luggage — has not arrived
            Mes bagages — ne sont pas arrivés
            may ba·gazh — nuh soñ pa za·ree·vay
24 Where is the luggage from
                     the flight — from London?
    Où sont les bagages du vol — de Londres?
    oo soñ lay ba·gazh dōō vol — duh loñ·druh
25 Is there a left-luggage office (baggage room)?
    Est-ce qu'il y a une consigne?
    es keel ee a ōōn koñ·seen·yuh
26   Are there any — porters?
    Est-ce qu'il y a des — porteurs?
    es keel ee a day — por·tur
                         — luggage trolleys (carts)?
                         — chariots à bagages?
                         — *sha·ree·ō za ba·gazh*
27 That bag is not mine
    Ça, ce n'est pas ma valise
    sa, suh neh pa ma va·leez
28 Where is my other bag?
    Où est mon autre valise?
    oo eh moñ nō·truh va·leez
29 The contents of that bag are fragile
    Le contenu de ce sac est fragile
    luh koñ·tuh·nōō duh suh sak eh fra·zheel
30 I wish to have my luggage sent on ahead
    Je voudrais expédier mes effets en bagages non accompagnés
    *zhuh voo·dreh zek·spay·dee·ay may zeh·feh oñ ba·gazh noñ
    na·koñ·pan·yay*
31 I sent a suitcase in advance. Where do I pick it up?
    J'ai expédié une valise en bagages non accompagnés. Où est-ce que
    je la récupère?
    *zhay ek·spay·dee·ay ōōn va·leez oñ ba·gazh noñ na·koñ·pan·yay. oo
    es kuh zhuh la ray·kōō·pehr*
32 That case is specially insured
    J'ai contracté une assurance particulière pour cette valise
    zhay koñ·trak·tay ōōn a·sōō·roñs par·tee·kōō·lee·ehr poor set va·leez
33 I want to leave these bags in the left-luggage office (baggage room)
    Je désire laisser ces valises à la consigne
    zhuh day·zeer leh·say say va·leez a la koñ·seen·yuh
34   I shall pick them up — this evening/tomorrow
    Je les reprendrai — ce soir/demain
    zhuh lay ruh·proñ·dray — suh swar/duh·mañ
35 How much is it per suitcase?
    C'est combien par valise?
    seh koñ·byañ par va·leez
36 What time do you close?
    A quelle heure fermez-vous?
    a kel ur fehr·may·voo

Airport and flight inquiries

37 Where do I get the bus — for Charles de Gaulle airport?
Où est-ce qu'on prend le bus — pour l'aéroport Charles de Gaulle?

oo es koñ proñ luh bōōs — poor la·eh·rō·por sharl duh gōl
— for the centre of town?
— pour le centre-ville?
— *poor luh soñ·truh·veel*

38 I wish to check in my luggage — for the Air France flight to Lyon
Je voudrais enregistrer mes bagages — pour le vol Air-France en destination de Lyon

*zhuh voo·dreh
zoñ·ruh·zhee·stray
may ba·gazh — poor luh vol ehr·froñs oñ
deh·stee·na·syoñ duh lee·oñ*

39 Where is the departure/arrival board?
Où est le tableau des départs/arrivées?
oo eh luh ta·blō day·par/za·ree·vay

40 At what time will the flight be called?
A quelle heure ce vol sera-t-il annoncé?
a kel ur suh vol suh·ra·noñ·say

41 Which gate do I go to?
A quelle porte est-ce que je dois me présenter?
a kel port es kuh zhuh dwah muh pray·zoñ·tay

42 Is there a snack bar/duty-free shop in the departure lounge?
Est-ce qu'il y a un buffet/un magasin hors-taxe dans la salle des départs?
es keel ee a uñ bōō·feh/uñ ma·ga·zañ or·taks doñ la sal day day·par

43 Will a meal be served on the plane?
On nous sert un repas à bord?
oñ noo sehr uñ ruh·pa a bor

44 What are weather conditions like for the flight?
Quelles sont les conditions météorologiques pendant la durée du vol?
kel soñ lay koñ·dee·syoñ may·tay·o·ro·lo·zheek poñ·doñ la dōō·ray dōō vol
(for answers see "The weather" under Making conversation, p.68)

45 Can I change my seat?
Est-ce que je peux prendre une autre place?
es kuh zhuh puh proñ·druh ōōn ō·truh plas
I should like to be — nearer the front/the window
Je voudrais être — plus à l'avant/près de la fenêtre
zhuh voo·dreh zeh·truh — plōō za la·voñ/preh duh la fuh·neh·truh

46 I suffer from airsickness
Je suis toujours malade en avion
zhuh swee too·zhoor ma·lad oñ na·vyoñ

47 I should like to speak to the airport police
Je voudrais m'adresser au service de la Police de l'air
zhuh voo·dreh ma·dreh·say ō sehr·vees duh la po·lees duh lehr

48 I am meeting somebody arriving on a flight from Madrid
Je viens chercher quelqu'un qui a pris un vol au départ de Madrid
zhuh vyañ shehr·shay kel·kuñ kee a pree uñ vol ō day·par duh ma·dreed

49 At what time do you expect the flight from Madrid to arrive?
A quelle heure est attendu l'avion au départ de Madrid?
a kel ur eh ta·toñ·dōō la·vyoñ ō day·par duh ma·dreed

Trains

The French railway system is on the whole well run and efficient. The trains are fast and reliable and the long-distance ones very comfortable.

Here are some things you will probably need to say during the course of
your journey, and a few pointers to help you understand the system.

Inquiring

At the information desks of larger stations you will be given a numbered
ticket and must wait until your number is flashed before you can make
your inquiry. At smaller stations you can go straight to the desk.

50	Where is — the ticket office/information office?
	Où est — le guichet/le bureau des renseignements?
	oo eh — luh gee·sheh/luh bōō·rō day roñ·sen·suh·moñ
	— the timetable board?
	— le tableau des horaires?
	— luh ta·blō day zo·rehr
51	I want to go to Nice — tomorrow/next Wednesday
	Je veux aller à Nice — demain/mercredi prochain
	zhuh vuh za·lay a nees — duh·mañ/mehr·kruh·dee pro·shañ

52 What are the times of trains between 8 a.m. and noon?
Quels sont les horaires des trains entre huit heures du matin et midi?
kel soñ lay zo·rehr day trañ oñ·truh wee tur dōō ma·tañ ay mee·dee

53 Which is the fastest train?
Quel est le train le plus rapide?
kel eh luh trañ luh plōō ra·peed

54 Could I see a timetable, please?
Est-ce que je peux consulter un indicateur?
es kuh zhuh puh koñ·sōōl·tay uñ nañ·dee·ka·tur

55 When does the next/last train to Tours leave?
Le prochain/dernier train de Tours part à quelle heure?
luh pro·shañ/dehrn·yay trañ duh toor par a kel ur

56 Do I have to change?
Est-ce qu'il faut changer?
es keel fō shoñ·zhay

57 What time does the train arrive?
Le train arrive à quelle heure?
luh trañ a·reev a kel ur

Tickets and reservations

An extra charge is imposed on certain express trains, known as *rapides*
(the term *express* refers to an ordinary fast train). Children under ten pay
half and those under four travel free. Trains have first-class and
second-class compartments. At the entrance to the platform you will see
the sign "N'oubliez pas de composter votre billet" (Do not forget to
cancel your ticket). You should insert it in the machine provided. For
overnight travel you can reserve a sleeper (wagon-lit *va·goñ·lee*) or a
couchette, which is a simple berth with blankets in a compartment shared
by several passengers.

58	A one-way/return ticket to Nice — second-class/first-class
	Un aller/aller-retour pour Nice — en deuxième/en première
	uñ na·lay/na·lay·ruh·toor poor nees — oñ duhz·yem/oñ pruhm·yehr

59 A child's return to Nice
Un aller-retour enfant pour Nice
uñ na·lay·ruh·toor oñ·foñ poor nees

60 He is under ten
Il a moins de dix ans
eel a mwañ duh dee zoñ

61   I would like to book a seat — on the 10:30 to Calais
Je voudrais réserver une
place — dans le train de dix heures trente
de Calais

zhuh voo·dreh ray·zehr·vay
ōōn plas — *doñ luh trañ duh dee zur troñt duh*
ka·leh
— by the window
— près de la fenêtre
— *preh duh la fuh·neh·truh*
— in a smoking/non-smoking
compartment
— dans un compartiment fumeur/
non-fumeur
— *doñ zuñ koñ·par·tee·moñ*
fōō·mur/noñ·fōō·mur

62 I would like a sleeper/couchette on the 22:00 to Lyon
Je voudrais un wagon-lit/une couchette dans le train de vingt-deux
heures de Lyon
zhuh voo·dreh zuñ va·goñ·lee/zōōn koo·shet doñ luh trañ duh
vañt·duh zur duh lee·oñ

Station and journey

63 Which platform do I go to for
the Nice train?
Le train de Nice part de quel
quai?
luh trañ duh nees par duh kel
keh
64 Is this the right platform for
Nice?
Est-ce que c'est bien le quai
pour le train de Nice?
es kuh seh byañ luh keh poor
luh trañ duh nees
65 Is this the Nice express?
Est-ce que c'est bien le rapide
pour Nice?
es kuh seh byañ luh ra·peed
poor nees
66 Is there a dining car/buffet
(club) car?
Est-ce qu'il y a un
wagon-restaurant/buffet?
es keel ee a uñ va·goñ
res·tō·roñ/bōō·feh
67 When do we get to Nice?
On arrive à Nice à quelle
heure?
oñ na·reev a nees a kel ur
68 Do we stop at Lyon?
Est-ce qu'on arrête à Lyon?
es koñ na·ret a lee·oñ
69 Is this a through train?
Est-ce que c'est un train
direct?
es kuh seh tuñ trañ dee·rekt
70 Where do I have to change for
Toulon?
Où faut-il changer pour
Toulon?
oo fō·teel shoñ·zhay poor
too·loñ

71 Is this seat taken?
Est-ce que cette place est
occupée?
es kuh set plas eh to·kōō·pay
72 This is my seat
C'est ma place
seh ma plas
73 Can you help me with my
bags, please?
Pouvez-vous m'aider avec mes
valises, s'il vous plaît?
poo·vay·voo may·day a·vek
may va·leez, seel voo pleh
74 May I open/shut the window?
Puis-je ouvrir/fermer la
fenêtre?
pwee·zhuh oov·reer/fehr·may
la fuh·neh·truh
75 This is a non-smoking
compartment
C'est un compartiment
non-fumeur
seh tuñ koñ·par·tee·moñ
noñ·fōō·mur
76 Are we in Lyon yet?
Est-ce que nous sommes
arrivés à Lyon?
es kuh noo som za·ree·vay a
lee·oñ
77 Are we on time?
Est-ce que nous sommes à
l'heure?
es kuh noo som za lur

Buses and subways

Most towns and cities are well covered by bus routes. You can pay as you
enter or save money by buying a book of tickets (*carnet*) or a tourist pass

(billet touristique). Paris and Lyon also have subway *(métro)* systems, and the bus and métro tickets are interchangeable. You cancel *(composter)* your ticket as you enter the bus or pass through the métro turnstile. The métro has two classes and smoking is not allowed. Paris also has a fast suburban service, the RER. If you want to transfer from one to the other for a short journey ask for a "billet combiné" *(bee·yeh koñ·bee·nay).*

78	Which bus goes to — the Louvre?	
	C'est quel autobus pour — le Louvre?	
	seh kel ō·tō·bōōs poor — luh loo·vruh	
79	Does this bus go — to the Opéra?	
	Est-ce que ce bus va — à l'Opéra?	
	es kuh suh bōōs va — a lo·pay·ra	
80	Where should I change?	
	Je dois changer où?	
	zhuh dwah shoñ·zhay oo	
81	And then what number do I take?	
	Et alors, qu'est-ce que je dois prendre comme numéro d'autobus?	
	ay a·lor, kes kuh zhuh dwah proñ·druh kom nōō·may·rō dō·tō·bōōs	
82	Should I get out at the next stop for — the Grand Palais?	
	Est-ce qu'il me faut descendre à l'arrêt suivant pour — le Grand-Palais?	
	es keel muh fō deh·soñ·dra la·reh swee·voñ poor — luh groñ·pa·leh	
83	I want to go — to St Denis	
	Je veux aller — à St Denis	
	zhuh vuh za·lay — a sañ duh·nee	
84	How many tickets do I need?	
	Il me faut combien de tickets?	
	eel muh fō koñ·byañ duh tee·keh	
85	A seven-day tourist ticket, please	
	Un billet touristique pour sept jours, s'il vous plaît	
	uñ bee·yeh too·ree·steek poor set zhoor, seel voo pleh	
86	Can you let me off at the right stop?	
	Pouvez-vous me dire où descendre?	
	poo·vay·voo muh deer oo deh·soñ·druh	
87	How much is the fare to the city centre?	
	C'est combien jusqu'au centre-ville?	
	seh koñ·byañ zhōō·skō soñ·truh·veel	
88	How long does it take to get to the Odéon?	
	On met combien de temps pour aller à l'Odéon?	
	oñ meh koñ·byañ duh toñ poor a·lay a lo·day·oñ	

Taxis

Taxis can be ordered by telephone, picked up at a rank or hailed (provided you are not within 50 metres of a rank). Many drivers will not accept more than three passengers, but some can be induced to do so for a tip on top of the normal one of 12–15 percent. Beware of pirate drivers offering "first-class" *(première classe)* rides. The easiest way to tell the driver where you are going is just to state your destination and add "s'il vous plaît" *(seel voo pleh* – please). But you may also need some of the following phrases:

89	Can you order me a taxi?	
	Vous pouvez me demander un taxi?	
	voo poo·vay muh duh·moñ·day uñ tak·see	
90	Where can I get a taxi?	
	Où est-ce que je vais trouver un taxi?	
	oo es kuh zhuh vay troo·vay uñ tak·see	
91	Take me to — this address, please	
	Conduisez-moi à — cette adresse, s'il vous plaît	
	koñ·dwee·zay·mwah a — set a·dres, seel voo pleh	

92   How much is the taxi fare — to Charles de Gaulle airport?
     C'est combien pour aller
                en taxi — à l'aéroport Charles de Gaulle?
     seh koñ·byañ pour a·lay
                oñ tak·see — a la·eh·rō·por sharl duh gōl

93 Please drive us around the town
     Vous voulez bien nous faire faire un petit tour de la ville
     voo voo·lay byañ noo fehr fehr uñ puh·tee toor duh la veel

94 Would you put the luggage in the boot (trunk)?
     Pouvez-vous mettre ces bagages dans le coffre?
     poo·vay·voo meh·truh say ba·gazh doñ luh ko·fruh

95 I'm in a hurry
     Je suis pressé
     zhuh swee preh·say

96 Please wait here for a few minutes
     Attendez ici quelques minutes, s'il vous plaît
     a·toñ·day ee·see kel·kuh mee·nōōt seel voo pleh

97 Turn right/left, please
     Tournez à droite/gauche, s'il vous plaît
     toor·nay a drwat/gōsh, seel voo pleh

98 Stop here, please
     Arrêtez ici, s'il vous plaît
     a·reh·tay ee·see, seel voo pleh

99 How much is that?
     C'est combien?
     seh koñ·byañ

100 Keep the change
     Gardez la monnaie
     gar·day la mo·neh

Motoring

Although the more crowded towns can be hectic for the driver, motoring in France is usually a pleasant experience. You may, however, be confused by the system of "priority from the right" (*priorité à droite*), which means that you have to give way to someone emerging from a side road or entering a roundabout that you are already on. The system does not apply on major roads classed as "protected ways" (*passages protégés*), but elsewhere watch out for the *priorité à droite* signs. If you yourself are entering from the right, beware of drivers who disobey the rule. Speed limits are 60 km/h in towns, 90 km/h on ordinary roads, 110 on dual carriageways or main roads and 130 km/h on autoroutes (see conversion table, p.76).

Renting a car

101 A hired car should be ready for me
     Une voiture de location devrait être à ma disposition
     ōōn vwa·tōōr duh lo·ka·syoñ duh·vreh teh·truh a ma
     dees·po·zee·syoñ

102 I arranged it through the Speed-Link fly-drive service
     Ce sont les services avion-auto de la Speed-Link qui s'en sont
     occupés
     suh soñ lay sehr·vees a·vyoñ·ō·tō duh la Speed-Link kee soñ soñ
     to·kōō·pay

103   I want to rent a car — for driving myself
     Je voudrais louer une voiture — sans chauffeur
     zhuh voo·dreh loo·ay ōōn
                vwa·tōōr — *soñ shō·fur*
                      — with a chauffeur
                      — avec chauffeur
                      — *a·vek shō·fur*

104   I want it for — five days
     Je la voudrais pour — cinq jours
     zhuh la voo·dreh poor — *sañk zhoor*

105	What is the charge — per day/per week?	

105   What is the charge — per day/per week?
         C'est combien — par jour/par semaine?
         seh koñ·byañ — par zhoor/par suh·men

106   Do you have a car that is — larger/cheaper?
         Avez-vous une voiture — plus grande/moins chère?
         a·vay·voo zōōn vwa·tōōr — plōō groñd/mwañ shehr

107   Is there a mileage charge?
         Est-ce qu'on paie au kilomètre?
         es koñ pay ō kee·lō·meh·truh

108   My wife/my husband will be driving as well
         Ma femme/mon mari conduira également
         ma fam/moñ ma·ree koñ·dwee·ra ay·gal·moñ

109   I should like comprehensive insurance
         Je voudrais une assurance tous-risques
         zhuh voo·dreh zōōn a·sōō·roñs too·reesk

110   Must I return the car here?
         Faut-il ramener la voiture ici?
         fō·teel ra·muh·nay la vwa·tōōr ee·see

111   I should like to leave the car in Nice
         Je voudrais laisser la voiture à Nice
         zhuh voo·dreh leh·say la vwa·tōōr a nees

112   I should like the car delivered to my hotel
         Pourriez-vous m'amener la voiture à l'hôtel?
         poo·ree·ay·voo ma·muh·nay la vwa·tōōr a lō·tel

113   Please show me how to operate the controls
         Pourriez-vous me montrer comment fonctionnent les commandes?
         poo·ree·ay·voo muh moñ·tray ko·moñ foñk·syon lay ko·moñd

114   Please explain the car documents
         Vous voulez m'expliquer à quoi correspondent les différents papiers
         de la voiture
         voo voo·lay mek·splee·kay a kwa ko·res·poñd lay dee·fay·roñ
         pap·yay duh la vwa·tōōr

Parking

In big towns parking can be a headache. In many areas there are parking meters; in others known as blue zones (*zones bleues*) you must display a special disk (*disque de stationnement*), which you can get from hotels, garages and tourist offices. If you are lucky there will be a multi-storey car park. Otherwise you can settle for a street away from the centre, but beware of ones marked *stationnement abusif* (parking obstructive) – if you park here your vehicle will be towed away. There are also streets where parking is allowed on one side only, on certain days.

115   Where can I park?
      Où puis-je stationner?
      oo pwee·zhuh sta·syo·nay

116   Can I park here?
      Puis-je stationner ici?
      pwee·zhuh sta·syo·nay ee·see

117   Are you leaving?
      Vous partez?
      voo par·tay

118   Is there a car park (parking lot) nearby?
      Est-ce qu'il y a un parking près d'ici?
      es keel ee a uñ par·king preh dee·see

119   What time does the car park (parking lot) close?
      Le parking ferme à quelle heure?
      luh par·king fehrm a kel ur

120   How much does it cost per hour?
      C'est combien de l'heure?
      seh koñ·byañ duh lur

121   How long can I leave the car here?
      Combien de temps puis-je laisser la voiture en stationnement ici?
      koñ·byañ duh toñ pwee·zhuh leh·say la vwa·tōōr oñ sta·syon·moñ ee·see

122   I will only be a few minutes
      Je reviens tout de suite
      zhuh ruh·vyañ too duh sweet

123   Do I need a parking disk?
      Est-ce que je dois mettre le disque?
      es kuh zhuh dwah meh·truh le deesk

124   Where can I get a parking disk?
      Où est-ce que je peux me procurer un disque?
      oo es kuh zhuh puh muh pro·kōō·ray uñ deesk

125 Do I need parking lights?
    Je dois mettre les feux de position?
    zhuh dwah meh·truh lay fuh duh po·zee·syoñ

Road conditions

French roads are for the most part well maintained and relatively trouble-free. If you use the motorways (*autoroutes*) you will periodically have to pay a toll (*péage*) except on toll-free sections near large towns. These many-lane roads are superb, but using minor routes does not necessarily mean slow going. The main problems you are likely to meet are peak traffic in summer and heavy snow if you are on a winter sports trip, in which case studded snow tyres or chains may be compulsory. Excellent alternative routes on minor roads are signposted with green arrows (*flèches vertes*). In towns you will encounter the usual problems of congestion, one-way systems, dead ends, and so on.

126 Is there a route that avoids the traffic?
    Y a-t-il un itinéraire qui permette d'éviter la circulation?
    ee a·teel uñ nee·tee·nay·rehr kee pehr·met day·vee·tay la seer·kōō·la·syoñ

127 Is there a shortcut/detour?
    Y a-t-il un raccourci/détour?
    ee a·teel uñ ra·koor·see/ day·toor

128 Is the traffic heavy?
    Est-ce que les routes sont encombrées?
    es kuh lay root soñ toñ·koñ·bray

129 What's causing this hold-up?
    Ce bouchon est provoqué par quoi?
    suh boo·shoñ eh pro·vo·kay par kwa

130 When will the road be clear?
    La route sera dégagée quand?
    la root suh·ra day·ga·zhay koñ

131 What is the speed limit?
    La vitesse est limitée à combien?
    la vee·tes eh lee·mee·tay a koñ·byañ

132 Is there a toll on this highway?
    Est-ce qu'il y a un péage sur cette autoroute?
    es keel ee a uñ pay·yazh sōōr set ō·tō·root

133 Is the road to Chamonix snowed up?
    Est-ce que la route de Chamonix est enneigée?
    es kuh la root duh sha·mo·nee eh toñ·neh·zhay

134 Is the pass open?
    Est-ce que le col est ouvert?
    es kuh luh kol eh too·vehr

135 Do I need studded tyres/chains?
    Est-ce qu'il faut des pneus à clous/des chaînes?
    es keel fō day pnuh za kloo/day shen

Road signs

The following are road signs commonly seen in France

136 Aire (de repos)
    Motorway lay-by ahead

137 Autoroute
    Motorway

138 Autres directions
    Other destinations

139 Centre-ville
    Town centre

140 Chaussée déformée
    Uneven surface

141 Dégustation gratuite
    Free wine-tasting (in wine growing areas)

142 Déviation
    Detour

143 Entrée interdite
    No entry

144 Passage à niveau
    Level crossing

145 Passage protégé
    It means that you are on a major road and have right of way at an approaching junction

146 Péage
    Toll point (all motorways in France are toll roads except near major towns)

147 Priorité à droite
    Give way to traffic from right

148 Ralentir
    Slow down

149 Rappel
    Literally, "reminder" – that a previous sign (e.g. speed limit) still applies

150	Route barrée Road closed off	154	Toutes directions All destinations
151	Sortie de secours Emergency exit	155	Un train peut en cacher un autre One train may conceal another
152	Stationnement interdit, Défense de stationner No parking	156	Verglas Ice on road
153	Stationnement toléré Parking allowed		

Fuel

Petrol (*essence*) comes in two grades: *ordinaire* (2 star) and the higher-octane and more expensive *super* (4 star). Diesel fuel is also used. See conversion tables (p.76) for fuel quantities and tyre pressures.

157   15 litres — of 2 star
             Quinze litres — d'ordinaire
             kañz lee·truh — dor·dee·nehr

                     — of 4 star
                     — de super
                     — *duh sōō·pehr*

                     — of diesel fuel
                     — de diesel
                     — *duh dee·ay·zel*

158 50 francs' worth, please
     Pour cinquante francs, s'il vous plaît
     poor sañ·koñt froñ, seel voo pleh

159 Fill her up, please
     Le plein, s'il vous plaît
     luh plañ, seel voo pleh

160   Check — the oil
                   Vérifiez — l'huile
            vay·ree·fee·ay — lweel

                     — the water
                     — l'eau
                     — *lō*

                     — the tyre pressure
                     — la pression des pneus
                     — *la preh·syoñ day pnuh*

161 The pressure is 1·3
     La pression est de un virgule trois
     la preh·syoñ eh duh uñ veer·gōōl trwah

162 I want some distilled water
     Je voudrais de l'eau distillée
     zhuh voo·dreh duh lō dee·stee·lay

163 Could you clean the windscreen (windshield)?
     Pourriez-vous faire le pare-brise?
     poo·ree·ay·voo fehr luh par·breez

164 Could you put some water in the windscreen washer?
     Pourriez-vous remplir le lave-glace?
     poo·ree·ay·voo roñ·pleer luh lav·glas

165 Can I pay by credit card?
     Vous acceptez les règlements sur carte de crédit?
     voo zak·sep·tay lay reh·gluh·moñ sōōr kart duh kray·dee

166 Is there a lavatory/a telephone here?
     Il y a des toilettes/un téléphone ici?
     eel ee a day twa·let/uñ tay·lay·fon ee·see

Breakdowns and repairs

167   My car — has broken down
              Ma voiture — est en panne
         ma vwa·tōōr — eh toñ pan

                     — won't start
                     — ne veut pas démarrer
                     — *nuh vuh pa day·ma·ray*

168 There is something wrong with my car
     Il y a quelque chose qui ne va pas à ma voiture
     eel ee a kel·kuh shōz kee nuh va pa a ma vwa·tōōr

169 I wish to telephone for emergency road service
Je voudrais téléphoner à un service de dépannage
zhuh voo·dreh tay·lay·fo·nay a uñ sehr·vees duh day·pa·nazh

170 Can you send — a mechanic?
Pouvez-vous envoyer — un mécanicien?
poo·vay·voo zoñ·vwa·yay — uñ may·ka·nee·syañ
— a breakdown van (tow truck)?
— une dépanneuse?
— *ōōn day·pa·nuz*

171 Can you — take me to the nearest garage?
Pouvez-vous — m'emmener au garage le plus
proche?
*poo·vay·voo — moñ·muh·nay ō ga·razh luh plōō
prosh*
— give me a tow?
— me remorquer?
— *muh ruh·mor·kay*
— give me a push?
— pousser la voiture?
— *poo·say la vwa·tōōr*
— give me a can of petrol, please?
— me donner un bidon d'essence,
s'il vous plaît?
— *muh do·nay uñ bee·doñ deh·soñs
seel voo pleh*

172 Can you find the trouble?
Pouvez-vous trouver ce qui ne va pas?
poo·vay·voo troo·vay suh kee nuh va pa

173 I have run out of petrol
Je suis en panne d'essence
zhuh swee zoñ pan deh·soñs

174 This is broken
C'est cassé
seh ka·say

175 It's making a funny noise/smell
Il y a un drôle de bruit/une drôle d'odeur
eel ee a uñ drōl duh brwee/ōōn drōl do·dur

176 The brakes — have something wrong with them
Les freins — marchent mal
lay frañ — marsh mal

177 The windscreen (windshield)
wipers — are not working
Les essuie-glace — ne fonctionnent pas
lay zeh·swee·glas — nuh foñk·syon pa

178 I need — a new fan belt
Il me faut — une nouvelle courroie de
ventilateur
*eel muh fō — tōōn noo·vel koor·wa duh
voñ·tee·la·tur*

179 Can you replace — the exhaust pipe?
Est-ce que vous pouvez
remplacer — le pot d'échappement?
*es kuh voo poo·vay
roñ·pla·say — luh pō day·shap·moñ*

180 My windscreen (windshield) has shattered
Mon pare-brise est cassé
moñ par·breez eh ka·say

181 I have a flat tyre
J'ai une crevaison
zhay ōōn kruh·veh·zoñ

182 The battery is dead
La batterie est à plat
la ba·tuh·ree eh ta pla

183 The engine is overheating
Le moteur chauffe
luh mo·tur shōf

184 There is a leak in the radiator
Il y a une fuite dans le radiateur
eel ee a ōōn fweet doñ luh ra·dya·tur

185 I have blown a fuse
C'est un fusible qui est grillé
seh tuñ foo·zee·bluh kee eh gree·yay

186 There is a bad connection
Il y a un mauvais contact
eel ee a uñ mo·veh koñ·takt

187 I have lost the ignition key
J'ai perdu la clé de contact
zhay pehr·doo la klay duh koñ·takt

188 Is it serious?
C'est grave?
seh grav

189 How long will it take to repair it?
La réparation prendra combien de temps?
la ray·pa·ra·syoñ proñ·dra koñ·byañ duh toñ

190 Do you have the parts?
Est-ce que vous avez les pièces de rechange?
es kuh voo za·vay lay pyes duh ruh·shoñzh

191 Can you repair it for the time being?
Est-ce que vous pouvez le réparer provisoirement?
es kuh voo poo·vay luh ray·pa·ray pro·veez·war·moñ

192 Can I have an itemized bill for my insurance company?
Est-ce que je peux avoir une facture détaillée pour ma compagnie d'assurances?
es kuh zhuh puh za·vwar oon fak·toor day·tye·yay poor ma koñ·pan·yee da·soo·roñs

Accidents and the police

The police in France are vigilant and have the power to impose on-the-spot fines. But they are on the whole well-mannered and helpful. If you have dealings with them about an accident or a driving offence, behave in a calm and reasonable manner, and they will do likewise. See also Emergencies (p.67).

193 I'm very sorry, officer
Je suis désolé, monsieur
zhuh swee day·zo·lay, muh·syuh

194 I am a foreigner
Je suis étranger (étrangère)
zhuh swee zay·troñ·zhay (zay·troñ·zhehr)

195 I did not see the sign
Je n'ai pas vu le panneau
zhuh nay pa voo luh pa·nō

196 I did not know about that regulation
Je ne connaissais pas ce règlement
zhuh nuh ko·neh·seh pa suh reh·gluh·moñ

197 I did not understand the sign
Je n'ai pas compris le panneau
zhuh nay pa koñ·pree luh pa·nō

198 Here is my driving licence
Voilà mon permis
vwa·la moñ pehr·mee

199 How much is the fine?
La contravention est de combien?
la koñ·tra·voñ·syoñ eh duh koñ·byañ

200 I was driving at 80 km/h (50 mph) (see conversion tables, p.76)
Je roulais à quatre-vingts kilomètres à l'heure
zhuh roo·leh za ka·truh·vañ kee·lō·meh·tra lur

201 He/she was too close
Il/elle me suivait de trop près
eel/el muh swee·veh duh trō preh

202 I did not see him/her
Je ne l'ai pas vu(e)
zhuh nuh lay pa voo

203 He was driving too fast
Il conduisait trop vite
eel koñ·dwee·zeh trō veet

204 He did not stop
Il ne s'est pas arrêté
eel nuh seh pa za·reh·tay

205 He did not give way (yield)
Il n'a pas respecté la priorité
eel na pa res·pek·tay la pree·o·ree·tay

206 He stopped very suddenly
Il s'est arrêté brusquement
eel seh ta·reh·tay brōōs·kuh·moñ

207 He swerved
Il a donné un coup de volant
eel a do·nay uñ koo duh vo·loñ

208 The car turned without signalling
L'automobiliste n'a pas mis son clignotant pour tourner
lo·to·mo·bee·leest na pa mee soñ kleen·yo·toñ poor toor·nay

209 He ran into me
Il m'est rentré dedans
eel meh roñ·tray duh·doñ

210 He overtook me on a bend (passed me on a curve)
Il m'a dépassé dans un virage
eel ma day·pa·say doñ zuñ vee·razh

211 His car number (license number) was ...
Le numéro minéralogique était ...
luh noo·may·rō mee·nay·ra·lo·zheek ay·teh ...

212 The road was wet
La route était mouillée
la root ay·teh moo·yay

213 I skidded
J'ai dérapé
zhay day·ra·pay

214 My brakes failed
Mes freins ont lâché
may frañ zoñ la·shay

215 I could not stop in time
Je n'ai pas pu m'arrêter à temps
zhuh nay pa pōō ma·reh·tay a toñ

216 I have run over a dog/cat
J'ai écrasé un chien/un chat
zhay ay·kra·zay uñ shyañ/uñ sha

217 Do I need to report it?
Dois-je le signaler?
dwa·zhuh luh seen·ya·lay

218 What is your name and address?
Quel est votre nom et votre adresse?
kel eh vo·truh noñ ay vo·tra·dres

219 What is your insurance company?
Quelle est votre compagnie d'assurances?
kel eh vo·truh koñ·pan·yee da·sōō·roñs

220 We should call the police
Nous devrions appeler la police
noo duh·vree·oñ za·puh·lay la po·lees

221 Will you please be a witness?
Acceptez-vous d'être témoin?
ak·sep·tay·voo deh·truh tay·mwañ

222 Do you admit responsibility?
Est-ce que vous vous reconnaissez coupable?
es kuh voo voo ruh·ko·neh·say koo·pa·bluh

223 Could we settle in cash now?
Pourrions-nous régler tout de suite l'affaire en payant en espèces?
poo·ree·oñ·noo ray·glay too duh sweet la·fehr oñ pay·yoñ oñ nes·pes

Finding the way (F)

Questions

The simplest way to get directions is just to say where you want to go and add "please", as you would with a taxi driver. For example, "Where is the cathedral?" would be "La cathédrale, s'il vous plaît". Here are some other phrases that you may need.

1 I have lost my way
J'ai perdu mon chemin
zhay pehr·dōō moñ shuh·mañ

2 How do I get to this address?
Comment est-ce que je vais à cette adresse?
ko·moñ tes kuh zhuh vay za set a·dres

3 Where is — the station/the cathedral?
Où est — la gare/la cathédrale?
oo eh — la gar/la ka·tay·dral
Where are — the toilets?
Où sont — les toilettes?
oo soñ — lay twa·let

4 I would like to go — to the town centre
Je voudrais aller — au centre-ville
zhuh voo·dreh za·lay — ō soñ·truh·veel

5 We are looking for — the Tourist Information Office
Nous cherchons — le syndicat d'initiative
noo shehr·shoñ — luh sañ·dee·ka dee·nee·sya·teev

6 Can you tell me the way — to the castle?
Pouvez-vous m'indiquer le chemin — du château?
poo·vay·voo mañ·dee·kay luh shuh·mañ — dōō shah·tō

7 Can you show me on the map?
Est-ce que vous pouvez me montrer sur la carte?
es kuh voo poo·vay muh moñ·tray sōōr la kart

8 Where is the nearest post office?
Où est la poste la plus proche?
oo eh la post la plōō prosh

9	Is there a service station	— near here?
	Est-ce qu'il y a une	
	station-service	— dans les environs?
	es keel ee a ōōn sta·syoñ	
	sehr·vees	— *doñ lay zoñ·vee·roñ*
10	Is this the right way	— to the museum?
	C'est bien le chemin	— du musée?
	seh byañ luh shuh·mañ	— *dōō mōō·zay*
11	Is it far	— to Montmartre?
	Est-ce que c'est loin	— Montmartre?
	es kuh seh lwañ	— *moñ·mar·truh*
12	How far is it to	— Brussels?
	Bruxelles	— est à quelle distance?
	brōō·sel	— *eh ta kel dee·stoñs*

13 How long does it take to get there?
Combien de temps faut-il pour y aller?
koñ·byañ duh toñ fō·teel poor ee a·lay

14 Can one walk there?
Est-ce qu'on peut y aller à pied?
es koñ puh tee a·lay a pyay

15 Is there a bus that goes there?
Est-ce qu'il y a un bus pour y aller?
es keel ee a uñ bōōs poor ee a·lay

16	Which road do I take	— for Bordeaux?
	Je prends quelle route	— pour Bordeaux?
	zhuh proñ kel root	— *poor bor·dō*
17	Do I turn here	— for Reims?
	Est-ce que je tourne ici	— pour Reims?
	es kuh zhuh toorn ee·see	— *poor rañs*
18	Which is the best route	— to Nîmes?
	Quelle est la meilleure route	— pour aller à Nîmes?
	kel eh la may·yur root	— *poor a·lay a neem*

19 Which is the most scenic route?
Quelle est la route la plus pittoresque?
kel eh la root la plōō pee·to·resk

20	How do I get back on to	— the autoroute?
	Comment puis-je rejoindre	— l'autoroute?
	ko·moñ pwee·zhuh	
	ruh·zhwañ·druh	— *lō·tō·root*

21 Where does this road go to?
Où va cette route?
oo va set root

22 Will we arrive by this evening?
Est-ce que nous arriverons avant ce soir?
es kuh noo za·ree·vuh·roñ a·voñ suh swar

Answers

These are the key phrases of the answer you will receive when you ask
for directions. In this case the French is given first, with the English
below.

23	Vous allez — tout droit
	voo za·lay — too drwa
	You go — straight ahead
	— à droite
	— *a drwat*
	— right
	— à gauche
	— *a gōsh*
	— left
	— jusqu'à . . .
	— *zhōō·ska . . .*
	— as far as . . .
24	Tournez — à droite
	toor·nay — a drwat
	Turn — right

	Tournez	— à gauche
	toor·nay	— *a gōsh*
	Turn	— **left**
25	Continuez tout droit	— vers . . .
	kon·tee·nōō·ay too drwa	— *vehr* . . .
	Keep going straight ahead	— **towards** . . .
		— jusqu'à ce que . . .
		— *zhōō·ska suh kuh* . . .
		— **until** . . .
26	Prenez	— la direction de . . .
	pruh·nay	— *la dee·rek·syoñ duh* . . .
	Take	— **the road for** . . .
		— la première à droite
		— *la pruhm·yehr a drwat*
		— **the first (road) on the right**
		— la deuxième à gauche
		— *la duhz·yem a gōsh*
		— **the second (road) on the left**
27	Traversez	— la rue
	tra·vehr·say	— *la rōō*
	Cross	— **the street**
28	Franchissez	— le passage à niveau
	froñ·shee·say	— *luh pa·sazh a nee·vō*
	Cross over	— **the level crossing**
		— le pont
		— *luh poñ*
		— **the bridge**
29	C'est	— tout près d'ici
	seh	— *too preh dee·see*
	It's	— **not far from here**
		— au croisement
		— *ō krwaz·moñ*
		— **at the junction (intersection)**
		— à côté du théâtre
		— *a kō·tay dōō tay·a·truh*
		— **next to the theatre**
		— après les feux
		— *a·preh lay fuh*
		— **after the traffic lights**
		— en face de l'église
		— *oñ fas duh lay·gleez*
		— **opposite the church**
		— par là
		— *par la*
		— **over there**
		— au coin de la rue
		— *ō kwañ duh la rōō*
		— **at the corner**

Money (M)

General

1	**How much is that**	— **altogether?**
	C'est combien	— en tout?
	seh koñ·byañ	— *oñ too*
2	**How much is it**	— **to get in?**
	C'est combien	— l'entrée?
	seh koñ·byañ	— *loñ·tray*
		— **for a child?**
		— pour un enfant?
		— *poor uñ noñ·foñ*
		— **per person?**
		— par personne?
		— *par pehr·son*

How much is it — per kilo?
C'est combien — le kilo?
seh koñ·byañ — luh kee·lō

3 Is there any extra charge?
Est-ce qu'il y a un supplément?
es keel ee a uñ sōō·play·moñ

4 Is the tip/tax included?
Le service est compris?/La TVA est comprise?
luh sehr·vees eh koñ·preella tay·vay·a eh koñ·preez

5 Is there a discount for — a group?
Est-ce qu'il y a une réduction
pour — un groupe?
es keel ee a ōōn
ray·dōōk·syoñ poor — uñ groop?
— students?
— les étudiants?
— *lay zay·tōō·dyoñ*
— senior citizens?
— le troisième âge?
— *luh trwaz·yem azh*

6 Can you give me a discount of 10 percent?
Pouvez-vous m'accorder une réduction de 10 pour cent?
poo·vay·voo ma·kor·day ōōn ray·dōōk·syoñ duh dee poor·soñ

7 How much of a discount can you give me?
Qu'est-ce que vous pouvez m'accorder comme réduction?
kes kuh voo poo·vay ma·kor·day kom ray·dōōk·syoñ

8 Can you give me an estimate of the cost?
Pouvez-vous me donner un état estimatif du coût?
poo·vay·voo muh do·nay uñ nay·ta es·tee·ma·teef dōō koo

9 Do I have to pay a deposit?
Dois-je verser des arrhes?
dwa·zhuh vehr·say day zar

10 Do I pay in advance or later?
Est-ce que je paie d'avance ou après?
es kuh zhuh pay da·voñs oo a·preh

11 Can I pay in instalments?
Est-ce que je peux payer en plusieurs versements?
es kuh zhuh puh pay·yay oñ plōō·zyur vers·moñ

12 Do you accept traveller's cheques?
Est-ce que vous acceptez les chèques de voyage?
es kuh voo zak·sep·tay lay shek duh vwa·yazh

13 I wish to pay by credit card
Je désire payer avec une carte de crédit
zhuh day·zeer pay·yay a·vek ōōn kart duh kray·dee

14 May I have — an itemized bill?
Pouvez-vous me donner — la note détaillée?
poo·vay·voo muh do·nay — la not day·tye·yay
— a receipt?
— un reçu?
— *uñ ruh·sōō*

15 You have given me the wrong change
Vous vous êtes trompé dans la monnaie
voo voo zet troñ·pay doñ la mo·neh

16 That's too much for me
C'est trop cher pour moi
seh trō shehr poor mwah

17 I have no money
Je n'ai pas d'argent
zhuh nay pa dar·zhoñ

18 I do not have enough money
Je n'ai pas assez d'argent
zhuh nay pa za·say dar·zhoñ

19 That's all, thank you
Merci, c'est tout
mehr·see, seh too

20 Can you change a 50-franc note — into 5-franc pieces?
Pouvez-vous changer un billet de cinquante francs — en pièces de cinq francs?
poo·vay·voo shoñ·zhay uñ bee·yeh duh sañ·koñt froñ — oñ pyes duh sañk froñ

Can you change a 50-franc
note — into 1-franc pieces?
Pouvez-vous changer un
billet de cinquante francs — en pièces d'un franc?
poo-vay-voo shoñ-zhay uñ
bee-yeh duh sañ-koñt froñ — oñ pyes duñ froñ

21 Can you give me some small change?
Est-ce que vous avez de la petite monnaie?
es kuh voo za-vay duh la puh-teet mo-neh

Banks and exchange offices

Banks are usually open from about 9:00 to about 16:00 and most close for lunch, but hours vary considerably, especially outside large towns. Some small banks open on Saturday instead of Monday, but most are closed Saturday and Sunday. You can also change money at hotels, large stores and, of course, *bureaux de change*, but the rate of exchange there tends to be less favourable. Exchange offices at airports and major railway stations stay open at night and over the weekend. Remember that you need your passport when changing money. Traveller's cheques issued by major firms are widely accepted, as are personal cheques from Eurocheque banks.

22 Will you change — these traveller's cheques?
Est-ce que vous pouvez me
changer — ces chèques de voyage?
es kuh voo poo-vay muh
shoñ-zhay — say shek duh vwa-yazh
— these notes?
— ces billets?
— *say bee-yeh*

23 What is the exchange rate for — sterling/dollars?
À combien est — la livre sterling/le dollar?
a koñ-byañ eh — la lee-vruh ster-ling/luh do-lar

24 I would like to withdraw 500 francs
Je voudrais retirer 500 francs
zhuh voo-dreh ruh-tee-ray sañ soñ froñ

25 I would like to cash a cheque with my Eurocheque card
Je voudrais retirer de l'argent avec ma carte Eurochèque
zhuh voo-dreh ruh-tee-ray duh lar-zhoñ a-vek ma kart uh-rō-shek

26 I would like to obtain a cash advance with my credit card
Je voudrais retirer de l'argent avec ma carte de crédit
zhuh voo-dreh ruh-tee-ray duh lar-zhoñ a-vek ma kart duh kray-dee

27 What is your fee?
Vous prenez combien de commission?
voo pruh-nay koñ-byañ duh ko-mee-syoñ

28 Can you contact my bank to arrange for a transfer of funds?
Est-ce que vous pouvez contacter ma banque pour arranger un transfert de fonds?
es kuh voo poo-vay koñ-tak-tay ma boñk poor a-roñ-zhay uñ troñs-fehr duh foñ

29 I have an account with the Bank of X in London/New York
J'ai un compte à la Banque X à Londres/à New York
zhay uñ koñt a la boñk X a loñ-druh/New York

30 I have made an arrangement with this bank
J'ai pris les dispositions nécessaires auprès de cette banque pour retirer de l'argent
zhay pree lay dees-po-zee-syoñ nay-seh-sehr ō-preh duh set boñk poor ruh-tee-ray duh lar-zhoñ

31 I wish to make an arrangement with this bank
Je voudrais prendre avec cette banque les dispositions nécessaires pour retirer de l'argent
zhuh voo-dreh proñ-druh a-vek set boñk lay dees-po-zee-syoñ nay-seh-sehr poor ruh-tee-ray duh lar-zhoñ

32 I would like to speak to the manager
Je voudrais parler au directeur
zhuh voo-dreh par-lay ō dee-rek-tur

Accommodation (A)

Hotel reservations and inquiries

Hotels are officially grouped into categories of 1, 2, 3 and 4 stars, plus a small category of world-class luxury hotels marked by 4 stars and an "L". At the other end of the scale you can stay at one of the *relais routiers* (primarily for truck drivers but of a good standard) or, in country areas, in a *logis de France*. Most hotels can handle a reservation or inquiry in English, but if you want to take no chances, this section contains some things you might wish to say by letter or telephone, or at the reception desk. Most of the replies will be self-explanatory, but one to be prepared for is "Nous sommes complets" (we are full). You should also know the terms "demi-pension" (bed, breakfast and evening meal) and "pension complète" (full board).

1   Dear Sir
    Monsieur
    muh·syuh

2   I wish to stay in Tours from
    ... to ...
    Je souhaite rester à Tours du
      ... au ...
    zhuh swet res·tay a toor dōō
      ... ō ...
    — with my wife
    — avec ma femme
    — *a·vek ma fam*
    — with my family
    — avec ma famille
    — *a·vek ma fa·meey*

3   I wish to stay for three nights
    Je veux rester trois nuits
    zhuh vuh res·tay trwah nwee

4   Can you provide — a single room with toilet and shower/bath?
    Est-ce que vous auriez — une chambre pour une personne avec wc et douche/bain?
    es kuh voo zō·ree·ay — *ōōn shoñ·bruh poor ōōn pehr·son a·vek doo·bluh·vay·say ay doosh/bañ*
    — a room with twin beds
    — une chambre avec lits jumeaux
    — *ōōn shoñ·bruh a·vek lee zhōō·mō*
    — a double room with a bed for a child
    — une chambre pour deux personnes avec un lit pour un enfant
    — *ōōn shoñ·bruh poor duh pehr·son a·vek uñ lee poor uñ noñ·foñ*
    — a suite with living room, bedroom, bath and toilet
    — un appartement privé avec living-room, chambre à coucher, salle de bain et wc
    — *uñ na·par·tuh·moñ pree·vay a·vek lee·ving-room, shoñ·bra koo·shay, sal duh bañ ay doo·bluh·vay·say*

5   I should like a room — that is quiet
    Je voudrais une chambre — tranquille
    zhuh voo·dreh zōōn shoñ·bruh — *troñ·keel*

I should like a room — with a view
Je voudrais une chambre — avec un beau point de vue
zhuh voo·dreh zōōn
shoñ·bruh — *a·vek uñ bō pwañ duh vōō*
— on the ground/first floor
— au rez-de-chaussée/au premier
étage
— *ō ray·duh·shō·say/ō pruh·myehr*
ay·tazh
— with a TV/radio
— avec télévision/radio
— *a·vek tay·lay·vee·zyoñ/ra·dyō*

6 **Please send me a brochure of your hotel**
Veuillez m'envoyer un dépliant de l'hôtel
vuhy·yay moñ·vwa·yay uñ day·plee·oñ duh lō·tel

7 **Yours faithfully**
Veuillez agréer Monsieur mes salutations distinguées
vuhy·yay za·gray·yay muh·syuh may sa·lōō·ta·syoñ dees·tañ·gay

8 **How much is the room per night?**
Quel est le prix de la chambre à la journée?
kel eh luh pree duh la shoñ·bruh a la zhoor·nay

9 **Is breakfast/tax included?**
Le petit déjeuner est-il compris/Les taxes sont-elles comprises dans
le prix?
luh puh·tee day·zhuh·nay eh·teel koñ·pree/lay taks soñ·tel koñ·preez
doñ luh pree

10   How much is it — with breakfast?
C'est combien — avec le petit déjeuner?
seh koñ·byañ — *a·vek luh puh·tee day·zhuh·nay*
— with breakfast and evening meal?
— en demi-pension?
— *oñ duh·mee·poñ·syoñ*
— with all meals?
— en pension complète?
— *oñ poñ·syoñ koñ·plet*

11 **Do you have a swimming pool/sauna?**
Vous avez une piscine/un sauna?
voo za·vay zōōn pee·seen/zuñ sō·na

12 **Can you suggest another hotel that might have a vacancy?**
Pourriez-vous m'indiquer un autre hôtel qui ait une chambre libre?
poo·ree·ay·voo mañ·dee·kay uñ nō·trō·tel kee eh tōōn shoñ·bruh
lee·bruh

Checking in and out

13 **I've reserved a room in the name of Smith**
J'ai réservé une chambre au nom de Smith
zhay ray·zehr·vay ōōn shoñ·bruh ō noñ duh Smith

14 **Can I see the room, please?**
Est-ce que je peux voir la chambre?
es kuh zhuh puh vwar la shoñ·bruh

15   The room is too — small/noisy
La chambre est trop — petite/bruyante
la shoñ·bruh eh trō — *puh·teet/brwee·yoñt*

16 **When will the room be ready?**
Quand est-ce que la chambre sera prête?
koñ tes kuh la shoñ·bruh suh·ra pret

17 **Where is the bathroom/toilet?**
Où est la salle de bain?/Où sont les toilettes?
oo eh la sal duh bañ/oo soñ lay twa·let

18 **I want to stay an extra night**
Je voudrais rester une nuit supplémentaire
zhuh voo·dreh res·tay ōōn nwee sōō·play·moñ·tehr

19 **We shall be leaving at 9 o'clock tomorrow morning**
Nous partirons à 9 heures demain matin
noo par·tee·roñ za nuh vur duh·mañ ma·tañ

20   **By what time do we have to vacate the room?**
A kel ur duh-von-noo kee-tay la shon-bruh
À quelle heure devons-nous quitter la chambre?

21   **I would like the bill, please**
la not, seel voo pleh
La note, s'il vous plaît

22   **Can I pay by credit card?**
es kuh zhuh puh pay-yay a-vek ma kart duh kray-dee
Est-ce que je peux payer avec ma carte de crédit?

23   **Do you accept traveller's cheques?**
voo zak-sep-tay — lay shek duh vwa-yazh
Vous acceptez — les chèques de voyage?

— **American Express cards/cheques?**
— les cartes American Express/
les chèques?
lay kart American Express/lay shek

24   **Could you have my luggage brought down/sent
on?**
Est-ce que vous pourriez
faire — descendre/suivre mes bagages?
es kuh voo poo-ree-ay fehr — deh-son-druh/swee-vruh may
ba-gazh

25   **Could you have any letters/messages forwarded?**
Voulez-vous faire suivre mon courrier/les messages?
voo-lay voo fehr swee-vruh mon koo-ree-ay/lay meh-sazh

Service and practical needs

26   **What time is breakfast/lunch?**
À quelle heure servez-vous — le petit déjeuner/le déjeuner?
a kel ur sehr-vay-voo — luh puh-tee day-zhuh-nay/luh
day-zhuh-nay

27   **Can we have breakfast in our room, please?**
Est-ce que nous pourrions avoir le petit déjeuner dans notre
chambre, s'il vous plaît?
es kuh noo poo-ree-on za-vwar luh puh-tee day-zhuh-nay don no-truh
shon-bruh, seel voo pleh

28   **Where can I park the car?**
Où est-ce que je peux garer la voiture?
oo es kuh zhuh puh ga-ray la vwa-toor

29   **What time does the hotel close?**
L'hôtel ferme à quelle heure?
lo-tel fehrm a kel ur

30   **Is there a lift (elevator)?**
Est-ce qu'il y a un ascenseur?
es keel ee a un na-son-sur

31   **Can I drink the tap water?**
Est-ce que l'eau du robinet est potable?
es kuh lo doo ro-bee-neh eh po-ta-bluh

32   **Please call me at 8 o'clock**
Réveillez-moi à huit heures, s'il vous plaît
ray-vay-ay-mwah a wee tur seel voo pleh

33   **Can I leave these for safekeeping?**
Est-ce que je peux déposer ces affaires dans votre coffre?
es kuh zhuh puh day-po-zay say za-fehr don vo-truh ko-fruh

34   **Can I have my things back from the safe?**
Est-ce que je peux récupérer les affaires que j'ai déposées dans votre
coffre?
es kuh zhuh puh ray-koo-pay-ray lay za-fehr kuh zhay day-po-zay
don vo-truh ko-fruh

35   **Can I — make a telephone call from here?**
Est-ce que je peux — téléphoner d'ici?
— tay-lay-fo-nay dee-see

— **send a telex message from here?**
— envoyer un message par télex
d'ici?
— on-vwa-yay un meh-sazh par
tay-leks dee-see

36 **Are there any letters/messages for me?**
Est-ce qu'il y a des lettres/des messages pour moi?
es keel ee a day leh·truh/day meh·sazh poor mwah

37 **I should like a private room — for a conference/cocktail party**
Pourriez-vous mettre à ma disposition une salle — de conférence/de réception?
poo·ree·ay·voo meh·tra ma dees·po·zee·syon oon sal — duh kon·fay·rons/duh ray·sep·syon

38 **I am expecting a Monsieur Fouquet**
J'attends un certain Monsieur Fouquet
zha·ton zun sehr·tan muh·syuh foo·keh

39 **Could you call me when he arrives?**
Vous voudrez bien m'appeler quand il arrivera?
voo voo·dray byan ma·puh·lay kon teel a·ree·vuh·ra

40 **Is the voltage 220 or 110?**
C'est du 220 ou du 110?
seh doo duh·son·van oo doo son·dees

41 **Can I have — my key?**
Est-ce que je peux avoir — ma clef?
es kuh zhuh puh za·vwar — ma klay

— **some soap?**
du savon?
doo sa·von

— **some towels?**
des serviettes?
day sehr·yet

— **some note paper?**
du papier à lettres?
doo pap·yay a leh·truh

— **an ashtray?**
un cendrier?
un son·dree·ay

— **another blanket?**
encore une couverture?
on·kor oon koo·vehr·toor

— **another pillow?**
encore un oreiller?
on·kor un no·ray·yay

42 **Where is the socket for my electric razor?**
Où est la prise pour mon rasoir?
oo eh la preez poor mon raz·wahr

43 **I cannot open the window**
Je ne peux pas ouvrir la fenêtre
zhuh nuh puh pa zoo·vreer la fuh·neh·truh

44 **The air conditioning/the heating is not working**
L'air conditionné/le chauffage ne marche pas
lehr kon·dee·syo·nay/luh sho·fazh nuh marsh pa

45 **I cannot turn the heating off**
Je ne peux pas éteindre le chauffage
zhuh nuh puh pa zay·tan·druh luh sho·fazh

46 **I want to turn the heating up/down**
Je veux mettre plus/moins de chauffage
zhuk vuh meh·truh plOOs/mwan duh sho·fazh

47 **The lock is broken**
La serrure est cassée
la seh·roor eh ka·say

48 **There is no hot water**
Il n'y a pas d'eau chaude
eel nee a pa do shod

49 **The washbasin is dirty**
Le lavabo est sale
luh la·va·bo eh sal

50 **The plug is broken**
La bonde est cassée
la bond eh ka·say

51 **There is no toilet paper**
Il n'y a pas de papier hygiénique
eel nee a pa duh pap·yay ee·zhee·ay·neek

52 Do you have a laundry room?
Est-ce que vous avez une lingerie?
es kuh voo za·vay zōōn lañ·zhuh·ree

53 I want to iron some clothes
Je voudrais repasser des vêtements
zhuh voo·dreh ruh·pa·say day vet·moñ

54 I want some clothes ironed
Je voudrais faire repasser des vêtements
zhuh voo·dreh fehr ruh·pa·say day vet·moñ

55 Thank you, we enjoyed our stay very much
Merci beaucoup, nous avons fait un excellent séjour
mehr·see bō·koo, noo za·voñ feh tuñ nek·say·loñ say·zhoor

Rented houses

56 We have arranged to rent a house through your agency
Nous avons loué une maison par votre agence
noo za·voñ loo·ay ōōn meh·zoñ par vo·tra·zhoñs

57 Here is our reservation
Voici notre réservation
vwa·see no·truh ray·zehr·va·syoñ

58 We need two sets of keys
Nous avons besoin de deux jeux de clés
noo za·voñ buh·zwañ duh duh zhuh duh klay

59 Will you show us around?
Pouvez-vous nous faire visiter la maison?
poo·vay·voo noo fehr vee·zee·tay la meh·zoñ

60 Which is the key for this door?
Quelle clé ouvre cette porte?
kel klay oo·vruh set port

61 Is the cost of electricity included in the rental?
Est-ce que la note d'électricité est comprise dans la location?
es kuh la not day·lek·tree·see·tay eh koñ·preez doñ la lo·ka·syoñ

62 Where is the electricity mains switch?
C'est où pour couper l'électricité?
seh too poor koo·pay lay·lek·tree·see·tay

63 Where is the water mains stopcock?
C'est où pour couper l'eau?
seh too poor koo·pay lō

64 Where is the water heater?
Où est le chauffe-eau?
oo eh luh shōf·ō

65 Please show me how this works
Montrez-moi comment ça marche, s'il vous plaît
moñ·tray·mwah ko·moñ sa marsh, seel voo pleh

66 How does the heating work?
Comment marche le chauffage?
ko·moñ marsh luh shō·fazh

67 When does the maid come?
Quand vient la femme de ménage?
koñ vyañ la fam duh may·nazh

68 Is there any spare bedding?
Est-ce qu'il y a de la literie en supplément?
es keel ee a duh la lee·tuh·ree oñ sōō·play·moñ

69 Where can I contact you if there are any problems?
Où est-ce que je peux vous contacter s'il y a des problèmes?
oo es kuh zhuh puh voo koñ·tak·tay seel ee a day pro·blem

70 The stove does not work
La cuisinière ne marche pas
la kwee·zee·nyehr nuh marsh pa

71 Where are the dustbins?
Où sont les poubelles?
oo soñ lay poo·bel

72 Is there a spare gas cylinder?
Est-ce qu'il y a une bouteille à gaz de rechange?
es keel ee a ōōn boo·tay a gaz duh ruh·shoñzh

73 Where can we get logs for the fire?
Où est-ce qu'on peut obtenir des bûches pour faire du feu?
oo es koñ puh top·tuh·neer day bōōsh poor fehr dōō fuh

74 I can't open the windows
Je ne peux pas ouvrir les fenêtres
zhuh nuh puh pa zoo·vreer lay fuh·neh·truh

75 We can't get any water
Nous n'avons pas d'eau
noo na·voñ pa dō

76 The toilet won't flush
La chasse d'eau ne marche pas
la shas dō nuh marsh pa

77 The pipe is blocked
Le tuyau est bouché
luh twee·yō eh boo·shay

78 A fuse has blown
Un plomb a sauté
uñ ploñ a sō·tay

79 There is a gas leak
Il y a une fuite de gaz
eel ee a ōōn fweet duh gaz

80 I need somebody to repair this
J'ai besoin de quelqu'un pour réparer ça
zhay buh·zwañ duh kel·kuñ poor ray·pa·ray sa

Camping

Camping in France is a very sophisticated activity, with campers bringing lots of home comforts with them. There are many official camping sites, graded from 1 star to 4 star, many with excellent facilities. It helps if you have an International Camping Carnet. If you can't find a site, the local *syndicat d'initiative* may be able to help. Never camp without permission in fields or on common land, as penalties are severe.

81 Is there anywhere for us to camp near here?
Est-ce que nous pouvons camper quelque part dans les environs?
es kuh noo poo·voñ koñ·pay kel·kuh par doñ lay zoñ·vee·roñ

82 Have you got a site for our tent?
Est-ce qu'il y a un emplacement pour notre tente?
es keel ee a uñ noñ·plas·moñ poor no·truh toñt

83 May we camp on your land?
Est-ce que nous pouvons camper sur votre terrain, s'il vous plaît?
es kuh noo poo·voñ koñ·pay sōōr vo·truh teh·rañ, seel voo pleh

84 This site is very muddy
Ce terrain est très boueux
suh teh·rañ eh treh boo·uh

85 Could we have a more sheltered site?
Est-ce que nous pourrions avoir un endroit plus abrité?
es kuh noo poo·ree·oñ za·vwar uñ noñ·drwa plōō za·bree·tay

86 May we put our caravan (trailer) here?
Est-ce que nous pouvons mettre notre caravane ici?
es kuh noo poo·voñ meh·truh no·truh ka·ra·van ee·see

87 Is there a shop on the site?
Est-ce qu'il y a un magasin dans le camp?
es keel ee a uñ ma·ga·zañ doñ luh koñ

88 Can I have a shower?
Est-ce que je peux prendre une douche?
es kuh zhuh puh proñ·drōōn doosh

89 Where is the drinking water?
Où est l'eau potable?
oo eh lō po·ta·bluh

90 Where are the toilets and washroom?
Où sont les toilettes et les lavabos?
oo soñ lay twa·let ay lay la·va·bō

91 Where can we buy ice?
Où peut-on acheter de la glace?
oo puh·toñ ash·tay duh la glas

92 Where can we wash our dishes/our clothes?
Où peut-on faire la vaisselle/la lessive?
oo puh·toñ fehr la veh·sel/la leh·seev

93 Is there another campsite near here?
Est-ce qu'il y a un autre terrain de camping près d'ici?
es keel ee a uñ nō·truh teh·rañ duh koñ·ping preh dee·see

94 Are there any washing machines?
Est-ce qu'il y a des machines à laver?
es keel ee a day ma·sheen za la·vay

95 We need to buy a new gas cylinder
Il nous faut acheter une nouvelle bouteille de butagaz
eel noo fō tash·tay ōōn noo·vel boo·tay duh bōō·ta·gaz

96 I would like to move my tent
Je voudrais changer d'endroit
zhuh voo·dreh shoñ·zhay doñ·drwah

Eating out   (E)

A trip to France is an invitation to good eating. You may wish to treat
yourself to some top-quality restaurants, but remember that the more
modest ones are often equally memorable — order a simple omelette in a
small bistro, and it will be cooked and served with style and care.
Set-price menus are often good value, but beware of *menus touristiques*
in places obviously catering to tourists, where the standards are not likely
to be high for customers who are only passing through. The best
recommendation is the presence of the French themselves. The menu
guide on p.34 will help you decide what to eat. Don't miss the
opportunity to sample local specialities. If you have your family with you,
see Children, p.62.

General

1   **Do you know** — a good restaurant?
Est-ce que vous connaissez — un bon restaurant?
es kuh voo ko·neh·say — *uñ boñ reh·stō·roñ*
                             — a restaurant specializing in
                                Provençal dishes?
                             — un restaurant qui a comme
                                spécialité la cuisine provençale?
                           — *uñ reh·stō·roñ kee a kom*
                                spay·sya·lee·tay la kwee·zeen
                                pro·voñ·sal

2 I would like to reserve a table — for two people
Je voudrais réserver une
                           table — pour deux personnes
zhuh voo·dreh ray·zehr·vay
                 ōōn ta·bluh — *poor duh pehr·son*
                                — for 8 o'clock
                                — pour huit heures
                                — *poor wee tur*

3 I have reserved a table in the name of . . .
J'ai réservé une table au nom de . . .
zhay ray·zehr·vay ōōn ta·bluh ō noñ duh . . .

4   Do you have a quiet table — by the window/on the terrace?
Est-ce que vous avez une
                table tranquille — près de la fenêtre/sur la terrasse?
es kuh voo za·vay ōōn ta·bluh
                 troñ·keel — *preh duh la fuh·neh·truh/sōōr la*
                                teh·ras

5 Is it possible to have a private room?
Est-ce qu'on pourrait avoir une pièce séparée?
es koñ poo·reh ta·vwar ōōn pyes say·pa·ray

6 It is for a business lunch/dinner
C'est pour un déjeuner/un dîner d'affaires
seh poor uñ day·zhuh·nay/uñ dee·nay da·fehr

7 Monsieur Lenoir is expecting me
Monsieur Lenoir m'attend
muh·syuh luh·nwar ma·toñ

8 **The menu, please**
   La carte, s'il vous plaît
   la kart, seel voo pleh

Menu guide

In most restaurants you either order *à la carte* or take the set menu (*le menu*). Usually there will be a *plat du jour* (dish of the day) made from ingredients bought fresh the same morning. In some restaurants there will be *spécialités de la maison* (specialities of the house). You will be given bread automatically with your meal. Every region of France has its own special dishes, and the list of variations is endless. Listing the French first, we give here some of the standard and better-known dishes along with a few of the more unusual ones.

Hors d'œuvres, vegetables and main dishes

Assiette anglaise Plate of assorted cold cuts

Aubergines farcies Stuffed aubergines (eggplants)

Bifteck see Steak

Blanquette de veau Stewed veal in a white sauce

Bœuf bourguignon Beef stew with red wine

Bœuf en daube Beef casserole

Bouillabaisse A speciality of Marseille, a soup/stew made with fish and shellfish

Bourride Provençal Provençal mixed fish soup

Canard à l'orange Roast duck stuffed with orange and served with an orange and wine sauce

Canard rôti Roast duck

Carottes Vichy Carrots cooked in sugar and butter

Cassoulet A stew of beans with pork or mutton and sausages

Cèpes marinés Boletus mushrooms marinaded in oil, garlic, herbs and spices

Champignons à la grecque Mushrooms served in oil, wine and herbs

Choucroûte garni Sauerkraut garnished with assorted pork meats and boiled potatoes

Confit d'oie Goose cooked and preserved in its own fat

Coq au vin Chicken cooked in red wine

Coquilles Saint-Jacques Scallops served in their shells

Côtelettes de veau Veal cutlets

Côtes de porc Pork chops

Coulibiac de saumon Salmon sautéed with onion and mushrooms, and baked in pastry

Crudités Assortment of raw vegetables (grated carrots, sliced tomatoes, etc) served as an hors d'œuvre

Cuisses de grenouille frites Frogs' legs covered in egg and breadcrumbs and sautéed

Entrecôte grillée Grilled rib steak

Épaule d'agneau Shoulder of lamb

Escargots à la bourguignonne Snails in garlic butter sauce

Faisan rôti Roast pheasant

Filet de sole meunière Sole cooked in butter and served with lemon

Filets de sole normande Sole in white wine with mushrooms, oysters and shrimps

Gigot d'agneau rôti Roast leg of lamb

Homard à l'armoricaine Lobster sautéed with shallots, tomatoes, white wine; brandy is sometimes added

Jambon de Bayonne Raw, cured ham (from the Pays Basque)

Lapin chasseur Rabbit cooked with white wine and herbs

Macédoine de légumes Mixture of diced vegetables

Morue Provençale Cooked salt cod with tomatoes, onions, olives, capers, garlic and olive oil

Moules marinières Mussels in white wine

Œufs à l'alsacienne Poached eggs in a paprika sauce, served on a goose liver mousse

Œufs brouillés Scrambled eggs

Œufs pochés Poached eggs

Œufs à la poêle Fried eggs

Perdreau rôti Roast partridge

Pintadeau Guinea fowl

Piperade Cooked tomatoes and pimentos with an omelette mixture added

Pommes (de terre) allumettes Matchstick potatoes

Pommes (de terre) à l'anglaise Boiled potatoes

Pommes dauphine Potato balls covered in very light pastry and deep fried

Pommes frites (or just frites) Chips (French fries)

Pommes rissolées Small round potatoes cooked in deep fat

Pommes sautées Boiled potatoes, sliced then fried

Pommes vapeur Steamed potatoes

Potée Vegetable broth

Pot au feu A soup, almost a stew, made from beef and vegetables

Poule au riz Boiled chicken and rice

Poulet basquaise Chicken pieces cooked with tomatoes, peppers, mushrooms, diced ham and white wine

Poulet rôti Roast chicken

Râble de lièvre Roast saddle of hare

Ragoût de veau Stewed veal

Ratatouille niçoise Onions, green peppers, courgettes (zucchini), aubergine (eggplant), garlic and tomatoes stewed together. Very good cold

Ris de veau au beurre noir Sweetbreads in brown butter sauce

Rognons sautés madère Sautéed kidneys in madeira sauce

Rôti de bœuf Roast beef

Rôti de porc Roast pork

Salade niçoise Many variations on a famous theme: the basic ingredients are green beans, anchovies, black olives, green peppers

Soupe à l'oignon Onion soup, usually served with a crisp chunk of French bread in the dish with grated cheese piled on top

Steak au poivre Steak with peppercorns

Steak tartare Minced raw steak, mixed with raw egg, chopped onion, tartare or Worcester sauce, parsley, capers

Tomates farcies Stuffed tomatoes

Tomates à la provençale Grilled tomatoes steeped in garlic

Tournedos Rossini Tournedos on fried bread with goose liver and truffles on top

Tripes à la mode de Caen Tripe with vegetables, herbs, cider and calvados

Veau sauté Marengo Veal cooked in a casserole with white wine, garlic and mushrooms

---

Cheeses

The cheese course normally comes straight after the main dish in France, while the wine is still on the table.

Bleu de Bresse One of the milder blue-veined cheeses with a soft mottled texture

Brie Soft and creamy, one of the best-known French cheeses

Camembert Probably the best-known cheese of all. Soft and well-flavoured, it is pungent when fully ripened

Cantal Semihard, fairly strong-flavoured cheese

Chèvre Goat's milk cheese: it comes in many varieties and shapes

Comté A hard cheese from Jura, with a tangy taste

Emmenthal From Switzerland, but also made in France, a hard

cheese with larger holes than *Gruyère*, often used in cooking

Gruyère A hard Swiss cheese with a delicate flavour

Petit Suisse Small pots of rich creamy soft cheese, usually eaten with sugar

Pont-l'évêque Softish, mature, square-shaped cheese

Roquefort Blue-veined cheese made from ewe's milk. Rich and pungent with a crumbly texture

Saint Paulin Large round cheese made from rich cow's milk

Tomme aux raisins Semisoft cheese covered with grape pips

Desserts

Baba au rhum Sweet, spongy, yeast cake soaked in a rum-flavoured syrup

Beignets de pommes Apple fritters

Bombe favorite Chestnut ice cream filled with apricot mousse and flavoured with rum

Clafoutis Pastry or batter pudding filled with black cherries

Crème caramel Caramel custard

Crème renversée Caramelized custard

Crêpes Pancakes

Gauffres Waffles

Glace Ice cream

au café
coffee

au chocolat
chocolate

au praliné
almonds and burnt sugar crushed up when cold

à la vanille
vanilla

Tarte aux fraises Strawberry tart

Tarte aux pommes Apple tart

Yaourt Yogurt—often eaten as a dessert in France

Wines

France has tens of thousands of individual winemakers, merchants and wholesalers. The French drink large amounts of wine. To them it is an everyday commodity, to be taken about as seriously as the soap or sugar it stands next to on the supermarket shelf. This attitude can, paradoxically, make good French wines more expensive in France than abroad, while everyday ones are much cheaper.

Official wine categories are based on geography. The more closely defined the area the wine comes from, the better the wine is likely to be. Thus Bordeaux is a basic quality, St-Emilion and Médoc good-quality districts within it, and St-Estephe a highly rated village in the Médoc.

The top category is Appellation d'Origine Contrôlée (AOC). Vins Délimités de Qualité Supérieure (VDQS) are from second-rank areas, often improving, and below that again are Vins de Pays (not to be confused with *vin du pays*, which simply means the local wine of wherever you are). Many wines are not categorized at all. In a shop or restaurant these would be sold as *vin ordinaire* (ordinary wine) or *vin de table* (table wine). Some *vins ordinaires* are very drinkable, others decidedly not.

If you just want any inexpensive wine that is reasonably palatable just ask for *un vin en carafe* (a carafe of wine) or *en pichet* (in a jug), and specify whether you want *rouge* (red), *blanc* (white) or *rosé* (pink). But if you prefer to choose from the wine list, below are some of the names that you may come across. Unless otherwise stated, the wines listed come in both red and white. Vintages may be included. A non-vintage wine is not necessarily a bad one, and may be more reliable than the product of a poor year. Red wines (except basic Beaujolais and *Vins de Pays*) can often be better with age. Whites (except the best of them) are usually drunk young.

Alsace A region yielding dry, fruity, aromatic white wines similar to those of Germany

Anjou A group of Loire wines, including a rosé

Armagnac An area famous for its brandy, the main rival to Cognac

Barsac A sweet, white wine, akin to Sauternes

Beaujolais Large region yielding light, fruity wines to be drunk young

Beaune Classic middle-rank wine from Burgundy

Bergerac An improving area inland from Bordeaux

Blanc de blancs Any white wine made from white grapes only

Blanquette de Limoux Dry, sparkling white wine from southwest France

Bordeaux The region producing claret (red), and dry and sweet white wines, all of which vary from the basic to the top-class. The great wines, named after the châteaux where they are made (such as Lafite-Rothschild, Mouton-Rothschild, Latour and Margaux), are rare and expensive in France. The *petits châteaux*, often rated "cru bourgeois", are better value

Bourgogne The basic wine of Burgundy

Bourgueil Light, fruity, deep-coloured red from the Loire

Chablis Dry, white Burgundy

Chambertin Powerful red Burgundy. It ages well

Champagne Sparkling white or rosé wine. The real thing, bearing the word "Champagne", is made in that region by the classic champagne method. It is much imitated elsewhere, but not yet equalled

Château Theoretically this implies a wine from a single vineyard, but the term has no legal force. To be sure it is not a blend, look for *mise en bouteille au château* (château-bottled)

Châteauneuf-du-Pape Full-bodied red wine from the Rhône

Cognac The most famous of the brandy-producing areas

Côtes (or Coteaux) This word, meaning "hillsides", usually implies a wine superior to those from the vineyards on the plain. For example Côtes de Beaune and Côtes du Rhône are both good-quality wines from the Beaune and Rhône areas

Gewürztraminer Spicy white wine from Alsace

Mâcon A sound, ordinary wine from Burgundy

Médoc The principal red wine area of Bordeaux

Muscadet A dry white wine from the Lower Loire

Pouilly-Fuissé White Burgundy, light and dry

Pouilly-Fumé Spicy dry white Loire wine

Sancerre Dry, delicate white Loire wine

Sauternes A strong, fruity, sweet white wine

Ordering wine

---

9 **May we see the wine list, please?**
On pourrait avoir la liste des vins?
oñ poo·reh ta·vwar la leest day vañ

10 **Can you recommend a good local wine?**
Vous pourriez nous conseiller un bon vin du pays?
voo poo·ree·ay noo koñ·say·yay uñ boñ vañ dōō pay·yee

11 **Was this a good year?**
C'est une bonne année?
seh tōōn bon a·nay

12 **A bottle/carafe of house wine**
Une bouteille/une carafe de vin maison
ōōn boo·tay/ōōn ka·raf duh vañ meh·zoñ

13 **Another bottle/half bottle, please**
Une autre bouteille/une demi-bouteille s'il vous plaît
ōōn ō·truh boo·tay/ōōn duh·mee·boo·tay seel voo pleh

14 **Would you bring another glass, please?**
Vous voulez bien nous apporter un autre verre?
voo voo·lay byañ noo za·por·tay uñ nō·truh vehr

15 **What liqueurs do you have?**
Qu'est-ce que vous avez comme digestifs?
kes kuh voo za·vay kom dee·zhes·teef

Ordering the meal and paying

16   Do you have a set menu?
Avez-vous un menu?
a-vay-voo zuñ muh-nōō

     I will take the set menu — at 75 francs
     Je prendrai le menu — à 75 francs
     zhuh proñ-dray luh muh-nōō — a swa-soñt-kañz froñ

17   What would you recommend?
Qu'est-ce que vous nous conseillez?
kes kuh voo noo koñ-say-yay

18   How is this dish cooked?
Comment prépare-t-on ce plat?
ko-moñ pray-par-toñ suh plah

19   Do you have a local speciality?
Avez-vous une spécialité du pays?
a-vay-voo zōōn spay-see-a-lee-tay dōō pay-yee

20   I'll take that
Je prendrai cela
zhuh proñ-dray suh-la

21   We will begin — with onion soup
     Nous commencerons — par une soupe à l'oignon
     noo ko-moñ-suh-roñ — par ōōn soop a lo-nyoñ

22   I will have — steak and chips (French fries)
     Je prendrai — un steak-frites
     zhuh proñ-dray — uñ stayk-freet

23   I like it — very rare
     Je le voudrais — bleu
     zhuh luh voo-dreh — bluh
     — rare
     — saignant
     — *sen-yoñ*
     — medium rare
     — à point
     — *a pwañ*
     — well done
     — bien cuit
     — *byañ kwee*

24   Are vegetables included?
Est-ce que les légumes sont compris?
es kuh lay lay-gōōm soñ koñ-pree

25   Is this cheese very strong?
Est-ce que ce fromage est très fort?
es kuh suh fro-mazh eh treh for

26   This is not what I ordered
Ce n'est pas ce que j'ai commandé
suh neh pa suh kuh zhay ko-moñ-day

27   Does the fish come with anything else?
Le poisson vous le servez garni?
luh pwa-soñ voo luh sehr-vay gar-nee

28   That is for — me
     C'est pour — moi
     seh poor — mwah
     — him/her
     — lui/elle
     — *lwee/el*

29   Some more — bread/water, please
     Encore — du pain/de l'eau, s'il vous plaît
     oñ-kor — dōō pañ/duh lō, seel voo pleh

30   Could I have some butter?
Du beurre, s'il vous plaît
dōō bur, seel voo pleh

31   What is this called?
Ça s'appelle comment?
sa sa-pel ko-moñ

32 **This is very salty**
C'est très salé
seh treh sa·lay

33 **I wanted cheese**
Je voulais du fromage
zhuh voo·leh dōō fro·mazh

34 **Have you forgotten the soup?**
Avez-vous oublié la soupe?
a·vay·voo zoo·blee·ay la soop

35 **This is cold**
C'est froid
seh frwah

36 **This is very good**
C'est très bon
seh treh boñ

37 **I'll have a dessert**
Je prendrai un dessert
zhuh proñ·dray uñ deh·sehr

38 **Could I have a salad instead of the cheese course?**
Est-ce que je pourrais avoir de la salade au lieu du fromage?
es kuh zhuh poo·reh za·vwar duh la sa·lad ō lyuh dōō fro·mazh

39 **What do you have for dessert?**
Qu'est-ce que vous avez comme dessert?
kes kuh voo za·vay kom deh·sehr

40 **What cheeses do you have?**
Qu'est-ce que vous avez comme fromage?
kes kuh voo za·vay kom fro·mazh

41 **Nothing else, thank you — just coffee**
C'est tout, merci — du café seulement
seh too, mehr·see — dōō ka·fay sul·moñ

42 **Waiter, could we have the bill, please?**
Garçon, l'addition s'il vous plaît
gar·soñ, la·dee·syoñ seel voo pleh

43 **We are in a hurry**
Nous sommes pressés
noo som preh·say

44 **Is the tip included?**
Le service est compris?
luh sehr·vees eh koñ·pree

45 **There seems to be a mistake here**
Il y a une erreur je crois
eel ee a ōōn eh·rur zhuh krwah

46 **What is this item?**
A quoi cela correspond-il?
a kwa suh·la ko·res·poñ·teel

47 **The meal was excellent**
Le repas était excellent
luh ruh·pah ay·teh tek·say·loñ

Phrases you will hear

48 Deux couverts?
duh koo·vehr
A table for two?

49 Vous avez réservé?
voo za·vay ray·zehr·vay
Did you make a reservation?

50 Vous avez choisi?
voo za·vay shwa·zee
Are you ready to order?

51 Et avec ça?
ay a·vek sa
What would you like with it?

52 Et pour suivre?
ay poor swee·vruh
And to follow?

53 Qu'est-ce que vous voulez comme boisson/dessert?
kes kuh voo voo·lay kom bwa·soñ/deh·sehr
What would you like to drink/for dessert?

Cafés and bars

The French café is a civilized institution where people go not just to eat
and drink but for many other reasons: to seek a quiet corner, to meet
friends or to sit on the terrace and watch the world go by. Many cafés
double as restaurants where you can buy anything from a coffee to a full
meal, and most serve at least light snacks as well as tea, coffee, soft
drinks and alcohol.

Cafés are often convenient places to telephone from (see p.54). Many
also display a red, diamond-shaped "Tabac" sign, meaning they are
licensed to sell cigarettes, tobacco and stamps. When you order a drink
all you need to say is "un/une . . . , s'il vous plaît" (*uñ/ōōn . . . , seel voo
pleh*), e.g. "un cognac, s'il vous plaît" (a brandy, please), but you can if
you wish say "un verre de . . ." (*uñ vehr duh . . . a glass of . . .*). Here are
some of the standard café orders.

Alcohol

54 **A glass of red/white wine**
   Un vin rouge/blanc
   uñ vañ roozh/bloñ

55   **A glass of beer — on draught**
                      Une bière *or* un demi — pression
                      ōōn bee·ehr or uñ duh·mee — preh·syoñ

56 **A bottle of beer**
   Une bière en bouteille
   ōōn bee·ehr oñ boo·tay

57 **A whisky**
   Un whisky
   uñ wee·skee

58 **A brandy**
   Un cognac
   uñ koñ·yak
   (or, to be different, un
   armagnac *uñ nar·man·yak*
   or un marc *uñ mark*)

59 **A martini**
   Un martini
   uñ mar·tee·nee

Other alcoholic drinks you might like to try include *pastis* (*pa·stees*), an
aniseed drink taken with water and ice, and *kir* (*keer*), a refreshing
mixture of white wine and *cassis* (*ka·sees*) (blackcurrant liqueur)

Coffee, tea and chocolate

If you just ask for *un café* (a coffee) you will be given a small cup of black
coffee. If you want a large cup you have to ask for *un grand café* (*uñ groñ
ka·fay*). Otherwise, you may wish to ask for the following:

60 **Coffee with milk**
   Café au lait
   ka·fay ō leh

61 **Coffee with cream**
   Café-crème (although this
   usually means just coffee
   with milk)
   ka·fay·krem

62 **Tea with lemon**
   Thé au citron
   tay ō see·troñ

63 **Tea with milk**
   Thé au lait
   tay ō leh

64 **Hot chocolate**
   Chocolat chaud
   sho·ko·la shō

65 **Herbal tea**
   Tisane
   tee·zan

Soft drinks

One of the most popular and refreshing of these is *citron pressé* (*see·troñ
preh·say*) (the juice of a freshly squeezed lemon, served with water and
sugar). Sweetened fruit cordials (*sirops — see·rō*) are also drunk a great
deal. You might, for example, ask for one flavoured with mint (*une
menthe — ōōn moñt*), strawberry (*une fraise — ōōn frez*) or pomegranate
(*une grenadine — ōōn gruh·na·deen*). Other soft drinks include:

66 Orange juice
   Jus d'orange
   zhōō do·roñzh

67 Grapefruit juice
   Jus de pamplemousse
   zhōō duh poñ·pluh·moos

68 Pineapple juice
   Jus d'ananas
   zhōō da·na·na

69 Apricot juice
   Jus d'abricot
   zhōō da·bree·kō

70 A Coke/Pepsi
   Un Coca-Cola/Pepsi-Cola
   uñ ko·ka·ko·la/pep·see·ko·la

71 Mineral water
   Eau minérale
   ō mee·nay·ral
   This comes in effervescent
   (*gazeuse — ga·zuz*) and still
   (*non-gazeuse — noñ·ga·zuz*)
   varieties.

Snacks

For breakfast or with midmorning coffee, try a *croissant* (*krwa·soñ*) (light
pastry in a crescent shape). Another typically French snack dish is *un
croque-monsieur* (*uñ krok·muh·syuh*) (a toasted ham and cheese open
sandwich). The following are more familiar snacks:

72 A cheese sandwich
   Un sandwich au fromage
   uñ soñd·weech ō fro·mazh

73 A ham sandwich
   Un sandwich au jambon
   uñ soñd·weech ō zhoñ·boñ

74 A pâté sandwich
   Un sandwich au pâté
   uñ soñd·weech ō pa·tay

75 A salami sandwich
   Un sandwich au saucisson
   uñ soñd·weech ō sō·see·soñ

Note that all these sandwiches will be served on crisp French bread split
open lengthways, and not on the soft bread usual in other countries.

76 Potato crisps
   Des chips
   day sheep

77 A hard-boiled egg
   Un œuf dur
   uñ nuf dōōr

78 Ham and egg
   Un œuf au jambon
   uñ nuf ō zhoñ·boñ

Leisure   (L)

Sightseeing

When you arrive in a town and require some general information about it
you should inquire at the local Tourist Information Office (*syndicat
d'initiative — sañ·dee·ka dee·nee·sya·teev*). Here are some of the phrases
you might wish to use there as well as in the street and at museums,
churches and other sights.

1 Excuse me, can you tell me . . .?
   Pardon Monsieur/Madame/Mademoiselle, vous pourriez me
   dire . . .?
   *par·doñ muh·syuh/ma·dam/ma·duh·mwa·zel, voo poo·ree·ay muh
   deer . . .*

2 What are the most important things to see here?
   Qu'est-ce qu'il ne faut pas manquer de voir ici?
   kes keel nuh fō pa moñ·kay duh vwar ee·see

3   Where is — the main square?
                           Où se trouve — la Grand'Place?
                           oo suh troov — la groñ·plas

4   Do you have — a guidebook to the town/area
                                         (in English)?
                           Avez-vous — un guide touristique de la
                                        ville/région (en anglais)?
                           *a·vay·voo — uñ geed too·ree·steek duh la
                                        veel/ray·zhoñ (oñ noñ·gleh)*
                                      — a map of the town?
                                      — un plan de la ville?
                                      — *uñ ploñ duh la veel*

Do you have — an audio-guide to the museum?
Avez-vous — un guide-audio du musée?
a·vay·voo — uñ geed·ō·dyō dōō mōō·zay

5   Are there any — local festivals?
Est-ce qu'il y a des — fêtes locales?
es keel ee a day — fet lo·kal

6   Is there — a guided tour of the town/castle?
Est-ce qu'il y a — une visite guidée de la ville/du château?
es keel ee a — ōōn vee·zeet gee·day duh la veel/ dōō shah·tō

7   Is there a one-day excursion to Chartres?
On peut aller en excursion à Chartres en une journée?
oñ puh ta·lay oñ neks·kōōr·syoñ a shar·truh oñ ōōn zhoor·nay

8   When does the tour begin?
A quelle heure commence la visite guidée?
a kel ur ko·moñs la vee·zeet gee·day

9   How long does it last?
Ça dure combien de temps?
sa dōōr koñ·byañ duh toñ

10   Where is the point of departure?
Où est le point de départ?
oo eh luh pwañ duh day·par

11   Is there an English-speaking guide?
Est-ce qu'il y a un guide qui parle anglais?
es keel ee a uñ geed kee parl oñ·gleh

12   What is this building?
Qu'est-ce que c'est, ce bâtiment?
kes kuh seh, suh bah·tee·moñ

13   Can we go in?
Est-ce que nous pouvons entrer?
es kuh noo poo·voñ zoñ·tray

14   What time does the museum/château open?
A quelle heure ouvre le musée/le château?
a kel ur oo·vruh luh mōō·zay/luh shah·tō

15   What is the admission charge?
L'entrée, c'est combien?
loñ·tray, seh koñ·byañ

16   Can one go to the top?
Est-ce qu'on peut monter jusqu'en haut?
es koñ puh moñ·tay zhōō·skoñ ō

17   Is one allowed to take photos — with flash/tripod?
Est-ce qu'on peut prendre des photos — avec flash/pied?
es koñ puh proñ·druh day fō·tō — a·vek flash/pyay

18   Where can one buy — slides?
Où peut-on acheter — des diapos?
oo puh·toñ nash·tay — day dee·a·pō
— postcards?
— des cartes postales?
— *day kart pos·tal*
— reproductions?
— des reproductions?
— *day ruh·pro·dōōk·syoñ*

Beach, country and sports

Changing rooms as well as beach and sports items can often be rented on the main beaches, although sometimes only on private sections which you have to pay to enter. French lifeguards hoist the following flags: red = unsafe; orange = unsafe, but lifeguards present; green = safe.

19   Is it safe to swim here?
Est-ce qu'il est prudent de nager ici?
es keel eh prōō·doñ duh na·zhay ee·see

20   Is the water warm/cold?
L'eau est chaude/froide?
lō eh shōd/frwad

21 Can you recommend a quiet beach?
Est-ce que vous connaissez une plage tranquille?
es kuh voo ko·neh·say ōōn plazh troñ·keel

22 Where can we change?
Où sont les vestiaires?
oo soñ lay veh·stee·ehr

23   Can I rent — a deck chair?
     Est-ce que je peux louer — un transat?
      es kuh zhuh puh loo·ay — uñ troñ·za?
                         — a sunshade?
                         — un parasol?
                         — uñ pa·ra·sol
                         — a sailing boat?
                         — un voilier?
                         — uñ vwal·yay
                         — a rowing boat?
                         — une barque?
                         — ōōn bark
                         — a motorboat?
                         — un bateau à moteur?
                         — uñ ba·tō a mo·tur

24   Is it possible to go — sailing?
  Est-ce qu'il est possible de
                    faire — de la voile?
    es keel eh po·see·bluh duh
                     fehr — duh la vwal
                         — water-skiing?
                         — du ski nautique?
                         — dōō skee nō·teek
                         — surfing?
                         — du surf?
                         — dōō sōōrf
                         — wind surfing?
                         — de la planche à voile?
                         — duh la ploñsh a vwal
                         — scuba diving?
                         — de la plongée sous-marine?
                         — duh la ploñ·zhay soo·ma·reen

25 What sports can one take part in here?
Quels sports peut-on pratiquer ici?
kel spor puh·toñ pra·tee·kay ee·see

26 Is there a swimming pool?
Est-ce qu'il y a une piscine?
es keel ee a ōōn pee·seen

27   Where can I play — tennis?
  Où est-ce que je peux jouer — au tennis?
  oo es kuh zhuh puh zhoo·ay — ō teh·nees
                         — golf?
                         — au golf?
                         — ō golf

28   Is it possible to go — riding?
  Est-ce qu'il est possible de
                    faire — du cheval?
    es keel eh po·see·bluh duh
                     fehr — dōō shuh·val
                         — gliding?
                         — du vol à voile?
                         — dōō vol a vwal

29 Can I go fishing?
Est-ce que je peux aller à la pêche?
es kuh zhuh puh za·lay a la pesh

30 Can I rent the equipment?
Est-ce que je peux louer le matériel?
es kuh zhuh puh loo·ay luh ma·tay·ree·el

31 Do you know of any interesting walks?
Est-ce que vous connaissez des promenades intéressantes à faire?
es kuh voo ko·neh·say day pro·muh·nad añ·tay·reh·soñt a fehr

32 Do you have a footpath map of the area?
Vous avez un topoguide de la région?
voo za·vay uñ to·po·geed duh la ray·zhoñ

33 **Are conditions good for — skiing?**
Les conditions sont bonnes
pour faire — du ski?
*lay koñ·dee·syoñ soñ bon
poor faire — dōō skee*

— **sailing?**
— de la voile?
— *duh la vwal*

34 **Are there any picnic areas near here?**
Est-ce qu'il y a des aires de pique-nique près d'ici?
es keel ee a day zehr duh peek·neek preh dee·see

35 **What is the name of that bird/flower?**
Quel est le nom de cet oiseau/cette fleur?
kel eh luh noñ duh set wa·zō/set flur

36 **Is there any interesting wildlife in this area?**
La faune de la région est-elle intéressante?
la fōn duh la ray·zhoñ eh·tel añ·tay·reh·soñt

Entertainment and night life

37 **How can we find out about local entertainment?**
Où peut-on se renseigner sur les distractions dans la région?
oo puh·toñ suh roñ·sen·yay sōōr lay dee·strak·syoñ doñ la ray·zhoñ

38 **Where can one go — to hear jazz/folk music?**
Où est-ce qu'on pourrait aller — écouter du jazz/de la musique
folklorique?
*oo es koñ poo·reh ta·lay — ay·koo·tay dōō jaz/duh la
mōō·zeek folk·lo·reek*

— **to dance?**
— danser?
— *doñ·say*

— **to see a floor show?**
— voir un spectacle de cabaret?
— *vwar uñ spek·ta·kluh duh
ka·ba·reh*

39 **Are there — any films in English?**
Est-ce qu'il y a — des films en anglais?
es keel ee a — day feelm zoñ noñ·gleh

— **any good night clubs/discos?**
— des night clubs/discos
convenables?
— *day night club/dee·skō
koñ·vuh·na·bluh*

— **any good concerts?**
— de bons concerts?
— *duh boñ koñ·sehr*

40 **Have you any seats — for Wednesday evening?**
Vous avez des places libres — pour mercredi soir?
voo za·vay day plas lee·bruh — poor mehr·kruh·dee swar

41 **I should like to reserve — a box**
Je voudrais réserver — une loge
zhuh voo·dreh ray·zehr·vay — ōōn lozh

— **two seats in the balcony/
orchestra stalls**
— deux balcons/orchestres
— *duh bal·koñ/zor·keh·struh*

42 **What is being performed?**
Qu'est-ce qu'on donne?
kes koñ don

43 **Who is singing/playing?**
Qui est-ce qui chante/joue?
kee es kee shoñt/zhoo

44 **How long does the performance last?**
Le spectacle dure combien de temps?
luh spek·ta·kluh dōōr koñ·byañ duh toñ

45 **Where can one buy a programme?**
Où est-ce qu'on peut acheter un programme?
oo es koñ puh tash·tay uñ pro·gram

                 Is there — an interval?
                 Il y a — un entracte?
                 eel ee a — uñ noñ·trakt
                 — a buffet/bar?
                 — un buffet/un bar?
                 — *uñ bōō·feh/uñ bar*

47 **When does the performance/floor show begin?**
A quelle heure commence la représentation/le spectacle de variétés?
a kel ur ko·moñs la ruh·pray·zoñ·ta·syoñ/luh spek·ta·kluh duh va·ree·ay·tay

48 **How much do the drinks cost?**
C'est combien pour les boissons?
seh koñ·byañ poor lay bwa·soñ

49 **Is there a minimum/cover charge?**
Il y a un minimum à payer/un couvert à payer?
eel ee a uñ mee·nee·mum a pay·yay/uñ koo·vehr a pay·yay

Gambling

It is not for nothing that so many gambling stories and films are set in the great casinos of France and Monaco. And you don't need to be a gambler to know the familiar cries of the croupier: "Faites vos jeux" (place your bets) and "Rien ne va plus" (no more bets). Without entering in detail into the language of gambling, we include here some of the phrases you might need in a casino.

50 **What is the minimum/maximum stake?**
Quelle est la mise minimum/maximum?
kel eh la meez mee·nee·mum/mak·see·mum

51 **Where can I cash my chips?**
Où puis-je échanger mes jetons?
oo pwee·zhuh ay·shoñ·zhay may zhuh·toñ

52 **Must one be a member to play here?**
Est-ce qu'il faut être membre pour pouvoir jouer ici?
es keel fō teh·truh moñ·bruh poor poo·vwar zhoo·ay ee·see

53 **Am I allowed to tip the croupier?**
Est-ce que j'ai le droit de donner quelque chose au croupier?
es kuh zhay luh drwah duh do·nay kel·kuh shōz ō kroop·yay

54 **This person is cheating**
Cette personne triche
set pehr·son treesh

55 **Excuse me, you have picked up my stake/winnings**
Excusez-moi, mais vous avez pris ma mise/mes gains
ek·skōō·zay·mwah, meh voo za·vay pree ma meez/may gañ

56 **Where is the cashier's counter (cage)?**
Où est la caisse?
oo eh la kes

57 **Do you have a blackjack/pontoon table here?**
Est-ce que vous avez une table de blackjack/vingt-et-un?
es kuh voo za·vay ōōn ta·bluh duh blackjack/vañ·tay·uñ

58 **I double (*in backgammon*)**
Je contre
zhuh koñ·truh

59 **May I have my passport back, please?**
Vous pouvez me rendre mon passeport, s'il vous plaît?
voo poo·vay muh roñ·druh moñ pas·por, seel voo pleh

Shopping   (s)

General

---

1 **What time do you open/close?**
Vous ouvrez/fermez à quelle heure?
voo zoo·vray/fehr·may a kel ur

2 **One of these, please**
  Un de ceux-là, s'il vous plaît
  uñ duh suh·la, seel voo pleh

3 **Two of those, please**
  Deux de ceux-là, s'il vous plaît
  duh duh suh·la, seel voo pleh

4 **How much does that cost?**
  Ça coûte combien?
  sa koot koñ·byañ

5 **I am willing to pay up to 3,000 francs**
  Je veux bien mettre jusqu'à 3.000 francs
  zhuh vuh byañ meh·truh zhōō·ska trwa meel·froñ

6   **I should like (to buy) — some presents**
       Je voudrais (acheter) — des cadeaux
       zhuh voo·dreh (zash·tay) — day ka·dō

7   **Do you sell — sunglasses?**
       Vendez-vous — des lunettes de soleil?
       voñ·day·voo — day lōō·net duh so·lay

8   **Do you have any — pencils?**
       Est-ce que vous avez des — crayons?
       es kuh voo za·vay day — kray·yoñ

9   **I need — some suntan oil**
       Il me faut — de l'huile solaire
       eel muh fō — duh lweel so·lehr

10 **Do you sell duty-free goods?**
  Vous vendez des produits hors-taxe?
  voo voñ·day day pro·dwee or·taks

11   **Where is — the shoe department?**
       Où est — le rayon des chaussures?
       oo eh — luh ray·yoñ day shō·sōōr
       — the food department?
       — le rayon d'alimentation?
       — luh ray·yoñ da·lee·moñ·ta·syoñ

12   **Can I see — the hat in the window?**
       Puis-je voir — le chapeau en vitrine?
       pwee·zhuh vwar — luh sha·pō oñ vee·treen
       — that hat over there?
       — ce chapeau-là?
       — suh sha·pō·la

13 **No, the other one**
  Non, l'autre
  noñ, lō·truh

14   **Have you anything — cheaper?**
       Avez-vous quelque chose — de moins cher?
       a·vay·voo kel·kuh shōz — duh mwañ shehr
       — secondhand?
       — de seconde main?
       — duh suh·goñd mañ

15 **I need a gadget for . . .**
  J'ai besoin d'un truc pour . . .
  zhay buh·zwañ duñ trōōk poor . . .

16 **Can you show me how it works?**
  Vous voulez bien me montrer comment ça fonctionne?
  voo voo·lay byañ muh moñ·tray ko·moñ sa foñk·syoñ

17   **Have you got — a larger one?**
       Est-ce que vous en avez — un plus grand?
       es kuh voo zoñ na·vay — uñ plōō groñ
       — a smaller one?
       — un plus petit?
       — uñ plōō puh·tee

18 **I'm just looking**
  Je regarde seulement
  zhuh ruh·gard sul·moñ

19   **I'm looking for — a blouse**
       Je cherche — un chemisier
       zhuh shehrsh — uñ shuh·meez·yay

20 **I like this one**
  J'aime celui-ci
  zhem suh·lwee·see

21 I don't like it
    Je ne l'aime pas
    zhuh nuh lem pa
22   I'll take — this one
                 Je prendrai — celui-ci
         zhuh proñ·dray — suh·lwee·see
                              — that one
                              — celui-là
                              — *suh·lwee·la*
                              — the other one
                              — l'autre
                              — *lō·truh*
23 Please wrap it
    Est-ce que vous pouvez me l'emballer, s'il vous plaît?
    es kuh voo poo·vay muh loñ·ba·lay, seel voo pleh
24 There's no need to wrap it, thank you
    Inutile de l'emballer, merci
    ee·nōō·teel duh loñ·ba·lay, mehr·see
25 Can I have a plastic bag?
    Un sac en plastique, s'il vous plaît
    uñ sak oñ pla·steek, seel voo pleh
26 How much would it cost to send it to England/America?
    Ça coûterait combien pour l'envoyer en Angleterre/Amérique?
    *sa koo·tuh·reh koñ·byañ poor loñ·vwa·yay oñ noñ·gluh·tehr/
    na·may·reek*
27 Please send it to this address
    Expédiez-le à cette adresse, s'il vous plaît
    ek·spay·dyay·luh a set a·dres, seel voo pleh
28 Please pack it carefully
    Emballez-le avec soin, s'il vous plaît
    oñ·ba·lay·luh a·vek swañ, seel voo pleh

Food and drink

France boasts countless small family-run food shops and market stalls, as
well as sometimes gigantic and often well-stocked supermarkets. Some of
the categories may be unfamiliar. For example, you will notice that,
besides the general butchers, there are specialists in different types of
meat products, such as the *marchand de volaille* (poultry dealer), the
triperie (selling tripe, liver, kidneys and other offal), the *boucherie
chevaline* (horse butcher) and the *charcuterie* (for meat pies, pâté, etc).
In choosing wine you would do well to refer to the wines section under
"Eating out" (p.36). Frequently there is a returnable deposit (*consigne*)
on each bottle. A word also about weights. A kilo is just over two
pounds, and half a kilo is frequently referred to as *une livre* (a pound).
For smaller and intermediate weights you would normally ask for x
number of grams (*grammes*) or possibly slices (*tranches* pronounced:
troñsh).
  The French place great importance on what they eat and drink, and
this makes shopping for food in France great fun. Be adventurous and try
unfamiliar things if you want to get the best out of it.

29   Where can I find — a baker/butcher?
          Où est-ce qu'il y a — une boulangerie/une boucherie?
          *oo es keel ee a — ōōn boo·loñ·zhuh·ree/ōōn
                              boo·shuh·ree*
30 What sort of cheese/butter do you have?
    Qu'est-ce que vous avez comme fromage/beurre?
    kes kuh voo za·vay kom fro·mazh/bur
31   I would like — a kilo of apples
                   Je voudrais — un kilo de pommes
           zhuh voo·dreh — uñ kee·lō duh pom
                              — half a kilo of tomatoes
                              — un demi-kilo (*or* une livre) de
                                tomates
                              — *uñ duh·mee·kee·lō (or ōōn
                                lee·vruh) duh to·mat*

	I would like	— a quarter kilo of sugar
	Je voudrais	— deux cents cinquante grammes de sucre
	zhuh voo·dreh	— *duh soñ sañ·koñt gram duh sōō·kruh*
		— 100 grams of ground coffee
		— cent grammes de café moulu
		— *soñ gram duh ka·fay moo·lōō*
		— five slices of ham
		— cinq tranches de jambon
		— *sañk troñsh duh zhoñ·boñ*
		— half a dozen eggs
		— six œufs
		— *see zuh*

32 **A packet of salt, please**
Un paquet de sel, s'il vous plaît
uñ pa·keh duh sel, seel voo pleh

33 **A tin of peas**
Une boîte de pois
ōōn bwat duh pwah

34 **A litre of milk**
Un litre de lait
uñ lee·truh duh leh

35 **A bottle of wine**
Une bouteille de vin
ōōn boo·tay duh vañ

36 **Two pork chops**
Deux côtes de porc
duh kōt duh por

37 **A joint of lamb**
Un rôti d'agneau
uñ rō·tee dan·yō

38 **I would like enough for two people**
Donnez-m'en pour deux personnes
do·nay·moñ poor duh pehr·son

39 **Shall I help myself?**
Je peux me servir?
zhuh puh muh sehr·veer

Chemist

In France a chemist is just that, and often does not sell toiletries and photographic equipment, for which there are special shops. A pharmacy, marked by a green cross sign, will diagnose minor ailments and sell the appropriate medicines. Many pharmacies sell homeopathic as well as allopathic remedies.

40 | I want something for | — a headache |
	Je voudrais quelque chose pour	— le mal de tête
	zhuh voo·dreh kel·kuh shōz poor	— *luh mal duh tet*
		— insect bites
		— les piqûres d'insectes
		— *lay pee·kōōr dañ·sekt*
		— chapped skin
		— les gerçures
		— *lay zhehr·sōōr*
		— a cold
		— le rhume
		— *luh rōōm*
		— a cough
		— la toux
		— *la too*
		— hay fever
		— le rhume des foins
		— *luh rōōm day fwañ*
		— a sore throat
		— le mal de gorge
		— *luh mal duh gorzh*
		— sunburn
		— un coup de soleil
		— *uñ koo duh so·lay*
		— toothache
		— une rage de dents
		— *ōōn razh duh doñ*
		— an upset stomach
		— le mal de ventre
		— *luh mal duh voñ·truh*

I want something for — insomnia
Je voudrais quelque chose
pour — l'insomnie
zhuh voo·dreh kel·kuh shōz
poor — lañ·som·nee

41 **How many do I take?**
J'en prends combien?
zhoñ proñ koñ·byañ

42 **How often do I take them?**
Combien de fois par jour faut-il les prendre?
koñ·byañ duh fwah par zhoor fō·teel lay proñ·druh

43 **Are they safe for children to take?**
Est-ce que les enfants peuvent en prendre?
es kuh lay zoñ·foñ puv toñ proñ·druh

44 **Could I see a selection of perfume/toilet water?**
Vous voulez bien me montrer ce que vous avez en parfums/
eaux de toilette?
voo voo·lay byañ muh moñ·tray suh kuh voo za·vay oñ par·fuñ/
ō duh twa·let

45 **I would like something with a floral scent**
Je voudrais quelque chose qui sente la fleur
zhuh voo·dreh kel·kuh shōz kee soñt la flur

46 **May I smell/try it, please?**
Vous permettez que je le sente/l'essaye?
voo pehr·meh·tay kuh zhuh luh soñt/leh·say

Cameras and film

47 I need film — **for this camera**
J'ai besoin d'un film — pour cet appareil-photo
zhay buh·zwañ duñ feelm — *poor set a·pa·ray·fō·tō*
— **for this cine-camera**
— pour cette caméra
— *poor set ka·may·ra*

48 I want — **a 35 mm black and white film**
Je voudrais — une pellicule noir et blanc 24 x 35
zhuh voo·dreh — *ōōn peh·lee·kōōl nwar ay bloñ*
vañ·ka·truh troñt·sañk
— **a fast/slow film**
— un film rapide/lent
— *uñ feelm ra·peed/loñ*
— **a colour print film**
— une pellicule couleur sur papier
— *ōōn peh·lee·kōōl koo·lur sōōr*
pap·yay
— **a colour slide film**
— une pellicule couleur pour
diapositives
— *ōōn peh·lee·kōōl koo·lur poor*
dee·a·po·zee·teev
— **batteries for the flash**
— des piles pour le flash
— *day peel poor luh flash*

49 **Can you develop this film, please?**
Est-ce que vous pouvez développer ce film, s'il vous plaît?
es kuh voo poo·vay day·vuh·lo·pay suh feelm, seel voo pleh

50 **I would like two prints of this one**
Je voudrais deux exemplaires de cette photo
zhuh voo·dreh duh zeg·zoñ·plehr duh set fō·tō

51 **When will the photographs be ready?**
Quand est-ce que les photos seront prêtes?
koñ tes kuh lay fō·tō suh·roñ pret

52 **I would like this print enlarged**
Je voudrais un agrandissement de cette photo
zhuh voo·dreh zuñ na·groñ·dees·moñ duh set fō·tō

53 **There is something wrong with my camera**
Mon appareil-photo marche mal
moñ na·pa·ray·fō·tō marsh mal

54 The film is jammed
Le film est bloqué dans l'appareil
luh feelm eh blo·kay doñ la·pa·ray

55 I would like to buy a camera — with single-lens reflex
Je voudrais un appareil — reflex mono-objectif
zhuh voo·dreh zuñ na·pa·ray — ruh·fleks mo·nō·op·zhek·teef

— **with a built-in light meter**
— avec cellule incorporée
— *a·vek seh·lōōl añ·kor·po·ray*

— **with instant developing**
— avec développement instantané
— *a·vek day·vuh·lop·moñ añ·stoñ·ta·nay*

56 I need — a flash attachment
Il me faut — un flash
eel muh fō — uñ flash

— **a close-up/wide-angle lens**
— un téléobjectif/un objectif grand angulaire
— *uñ tay·lay·op·zhek·teef/uñ nop·zhek·teef groñ toñ·gōō·lehr*

— **a camera case**
— un boîtier
— *uñ bwat·yay*

Clothes and shoes

57 I am looking for — a dress
Je cherche — une robe
zhuh shersh — ōōn rob

— **a sweater**
— un pull
— *uñ pōōl*

58 I would like something — informal
Je voudrais quelque chose — de tout simple
zhuh voo·dreh kel·kuh shōz — duh too sañ·pluh

— **for evening wear**
— d'habillé pour le soir
— *da·bee·yay poor luh swar*

— **for a cocktail party**
— pour un cocktail
— *poor uñ kok·tel*

59 Can you please show me some — sun dresses?
Voudriez-vous me montrer des — robes bain de soleil?
voo·dree·ay·voo muh moñ·tray day — rob bañ duh so·lay

— **silk shirts?**
— chemises en soie?
— *shuh·meez oñ swah*

60 I would like to have a suit/pair of shoes made to measure
Je voudrais me faire faire un costume/une paire de chaussures sur mesure
zhuh voo·dreh muh fehr fehr uñ kos·tōōm/ōōn pehr duh shō·sōōr sōōr muh·zōōr

61 I would prefer — a dark material
Je préfère — un tissu foncé
zhuh pray·fehr — uñ tee·sōō foñ·say

— **a natural fibre**
— une fibre naturelle
— *ōōn fee·bruh na·tōō·rel*

62 I take (a continental) size 40
Je porte du quarante
zhuh port dōō ka·roñt

63 I take (a continental) shoe size 40
Je chausse du quarante
zhuh shōs dōō ka·roñt

64 Can you measure me?
Pouvez-vous prendre mes mesures?
poo·vay·voo proñ·druh may muh·zōōr

65 Do you have this — in blue?
Est-ce que vous l'avez — en bleu?
es kuh voo la·vay — oñ bluh

66 What is the material?
C'est fait en quoi?
seh feh oñ kwa

67 I like — this one
J'aime — celui-ci
zhem — suh·lwee·see
— that one there
— celui-là
— *suh·lwee·la*
— the one in the window
— celui qui est en vitrine
— *suh·lwee kee eh toñ vee·treen*

68 May I see it in the daylight?
Puis-je le regarder au jour?
pwee·zhuh luh ruh·gar·day ō zhoor

69 May I try it on?
Est-ce que je peux l'essayer?
es kuh zhuh puh leh·say·yay

70 Where are the dressing rooms?
Où sont les cabines d'essayage?
oo soñ lay ka·been deh·say·yazh

71 I would like a mirror
Je voudrais une glace
zhuh voo·dreh zōōn glas

72 I like it
J'aime ça
zhem sa

73 I don't like it
Je n'aime pas ça
zhuh nem pa sa

74 I prefer the blue one
Je préfère le bleu
zhuh pray·fehr luh bluh

75 It does not suit me
Ça ne me va pas
sa nuh muh va pa

76 It does not fit
Ce n'est pas la taille
suh neh pa la tye

77 It is too — tight
C'est trop — serré
seh trō — seh·ray
— small
— petit
— *puh·tee*
— big
— grand
— *groñ*

78 Can you — alter it?
Vous pouvez — le retoucher?
voo poo·vay — luh ruh·too·shay
— take it in?
— le reprendre?
— *luh ruh·proñ·druh*
— let it out?
— lâcher la couture?
— *lah·shay la koo·tōōr*

79 I'd like one — with a zip
J'en voudrais un — avec fermeture éclair
zhoñ voo·dreh zuñ — a·vek fehrm·tōōr ay·klehr
— without a belt
— sans ceinture
— *soñ sañ·tōōr*

80 **Is this all you have?**
C'est tout ce que vous avez?
seh toos kuh voo za·vay

81 **I'll take it**
Je le prends
zhuh luh proñ

82 **Is it washable?**
Est-ce que c'est lavable?
es kuh seh la·va·bluh

83 **Will it shrink?**
Est-ce que ça rétrécit au lavage?
es kuh sa ray·tray·see ō la·vazh

84 **Must it be dry-cleaned?**
Est-ce qu'il faut le nettoyer à sec?
es keel fō luh neh·twa·yay a sek

Jewellers, silversmiths and watchmakers

85	Have you any —	antique/modern jewellery?
	Vous avez des —	bijoux anciens/modernes?
	voo za·vay day —	*bee·zhoo zoñ·syañ/mo·dehrn*
86	I am a collector of —	silverware/brooches
	Je collectionne —	l'argenterie/les broches
	zhuh ko·lek·syon —	*lar·zhoñ·tuh·ree/lay brosh*
87	Could you show me a selection of your —	rings/watches?
	Vous voulez me montrer ce que vous avez comme —	bagues/montres?
	voo voo·lay muh moñ·tray suh kuh voo za·vay kom —	*bag/moñ·truh*

88 **What precious stone is this?**
C'est quoi comme pierre précieuse?
seh kwa kom pyehr prays·yuz

89 **Is this solid gold/silver?**
C'est de l'or/de l'argent massif?
seh duh lor/duh lar·zhoñ ma·seef

90 **Is it gold-/silver-plated?**
C'est plaqué or/argent?
seh pla·kay or/ar·zhoñ

91	Can you repair —	this watch/necklace?
	Vous pouvez me réparer —	cette montre/ce collier?
	voo poo·vay muh ray·pa·ray —	*set moñ·truh/suh kol·yay*

Books, newspapers, postcards and stationery

If you want a newspaper, you will get it at a newsstand, *un kiosque à journaux*, while stationery is generally sold along with books in a *librairie-papeterie*. Some major foreign newspapers are available on the larger stands, sometimes a day or two late outside Paris.

92	Have you any —	English/American newspapers?
	Vous avez des —	journaux anglais/américains?
	voo za·vay day —	*zhoor·nō zoñ·gleh/za·may·ree·kañ*
		— postcards?
		— cartes postales?
		— *kart pos·tal*
93	I would like —	some notepaper
	Je voudrais —	du papier à lettres
	zhuh voo·dreh —	*dōō pap·yay a leh·truh*
		— some envelopes
		— des enveloppes
		— *day zoñ·vuh·lop*
		— some padded envelopes
		— des enveloppes matelassées
		— *day zoñ·vuh·lop ma·tuh·la·say*
		— a ball-point pen
		— un stylo à bille
		— *uñ stee·lō a beey*

	I would like —	a pencil
	Je voudrais —	un crayon
	zhuh voo-dreh —	*uñ kray-yoñ*
94	I need —	some airmail stickers/envelopes
	Il me faut —	des étiquettes/des enveloppes "par avion"
	eel muh fó —	*day zeh-tee-ket/day zoñ-vuh-lop par a-vyoñ*
		— some adhesive tape
		— du Scotch
		— *dōō skotch*
95	Do you sell —	English paperbacks?
	Est-ce que vous vendez —	des livres de poche anglais?
	es kuh voo voñ-day —	*day lee-vruh duh posh oñ-gleh*
		— street maps?
		— des plans de la ville?
		— *day ploñ duh la veel*
96	Have you a postcard —	of the Arc de Triomphe?
	Vous avez une carte postale —	de l'Arc de Triomphe?
	voo za-vay ōōn kart pos-tal —	*duh lark duh tree-oñf*

Tobacconist

Although there are some little shops whose main business is selling tobacco, a *café-tabac*, that is a café with a red "Tabac" sign outside, is the easiest place to buy it. British and American brands of cigarettes are often available at a price along with the stronger French varieties.

97 A packet of . . ., please
    Un paquet de . . ., s'il vous plaît
    uñ pa-keh duh . . ., seel voo pleh

    — with filter tip
    — avec filtre
    — *a-vek feel-truh*
    — without filter
    — sans filtre
    — *soñ feel-truh*

98 Have you got any American/English brands?
    Est-ce que vous avez des cigarettes américaines/anglaises?
    es kuh voo za-vay day see-ga-ret za-may-ree-ken/zoñ-glez

99 A pouch of pipe tobacco
    Du tabac pour pipe
    dōō ta-ba poor peep

100 Some pipe cleaners
    Des cure-pipe
    day kōōr-peep

101 A box of matches
    Une boîte d'allumettes
    ōōn bwat da-lōō-met

102 A cigar
    Un cigare
    uñ see-gar

103 A cigarette lighter
    Un briquet
    uñ bree-keh

104 A gas (butane) refill
    Une recharge de briquet
    ōōn ruh-sharzh duh bree-keh

Presents and souvenirs

105 I am looking for a present for — my wife/husband
    Je cherche un cadeau pour — ma femme/mon mari
    zhuh shehrsh uñ ka-dó poor — *ma fam/moñ ma-ree*

106 I would like to pay between 100 and 200 francs
    Je voudrais mettre entre 100 et 200 francs
    zhuh voo-dreh meh-truh oñ-truh soñ ay duh soñ froñ

107 Can you suggest anything?
    Qu'est-ce que vous me proposez?
    kes kuh voo muh pro-pó-zay

108 Have you anything suitable for a ten-year-old girl/boy?
    Auriez-vous quelque chose pour une fille/un garçon de dix ans?
    ó-ree-ay-voo kel-kuh shōz poor ōōn feey/uñ gar-soñ duh dee zoñ

109   Do you have something — made locally?
Auriez-vous quelque chose — de fabrication locale?
ō·ree·ay·voo kel·kuh shōz — *duh fa·bree·ka·syoñ lo·kal*
— handmade?
— fait-main?
— *feh·mañ*
— unusual?
— qui sorte de l'ordinaire?
— *kee sort duh lor·dee·nehr*

Services and everyday needs (Sn)

Post office

Post offices are marked by a sign with a blue swallow on a white disc or by the letters PTT, and are open Monday to Friday 08:00–19:00, Saturday 08:00–12:00. Stamps can also be bought in *café-tabacs*, hotels and newsagents, and from coin-operated vending machines, painted yellow. Post boxes are also yellow and marked *boîte aux lettres*. Mail can be addressed *poste restante* to any post office, and collected on payment of a small fee and proof of identity. Allow 3–4 days for mail from abroad to reach France.

1   How much is a letter — to Britain?
C'est combien pour envoyer
une lettre — en Grande-Bretagne?
seh koñ·byañ poor
oñ·vwa·yay ōōn leh·truh — *oñ groñd·bruh·tan·yuh*
— to the United States?
— aux États-Unis?
— *ō zay·ta·zōō·nee*

2 Six 2-franc stamps, please
Six timbres à deux francs, s'il vous plaît
see tañ·bra duh froñ, seel voo pleh

3   I would like six stamps for
postcards/letters — to Britain
Je voudrais six timbres pour
cartes postales/lettres — à envoyer en Grande-Bretagne
zhuh voo·dreh see tañ·bruh
poor kart pos·tal/leh·truh — *a oñ·vwa·yay oñ*
groñd·bruh·tan·yuh
— to the United States
— à envoyer aux États-Unis
— *a oñ·vwa·yay ō zay·ta·zōō·nee*

4   I want to send — this parcel
Je voudrais expédier — ce colis
zhuh voo·dreh
zek·spay·dee·ay — *suh ko·lee*
— a telegram
— un télégramme
— *uñ tay·lay·gram*

5 A telegram form, please
Un formulaire pour télégramme, s'il vous plaît
uñ for·mōō·lehr poor tay·lay·gram, seel voo pleh

6 When will it arrive?
Quand est-ce qu'il arrivera?
koñ tes keel a·ree·vuh·ra

7 I want to send this by registered mail
Je voudrais envoyer cela en recommandé
zhuh voo·dreh zoñ·vwa·yay suh·la oñ ruh·ko·moñ·day

8 I am expecting a letter *poste restante*
J'attends une lettre en poste restante
zha·toñ ōōn leh·truh oñ post res·toñt

Telephoning

The simplest but most expensive way to telephone is from your hotel, but otherwise you will have to use a public telephone, found in post offices and cafés as well as on pavements. Most telephones take 50c, 1f, 2f and 5f coins, although some older phones in cafés may only take tokens (*jetons* pronounced: *zhuh·toñ*) bought at the bar. All numbers are of six figures, written in three groups of two (except in Paris, which has a first group of three), and a two-figure prefix for the district (not used in local calls). When using this district code you must prefix it with 16 to get a line. In telephone booths the coin is inserted before dialling, coins being refunded if you hang up without getting through. The ringing signal is a shrill intermittent tone, while the engaged signal is less shrill and more rapid. For international calls, either use the code if the place can be dialled direct, or dial 19 then 33 33 for the international operator. (For numerals, see p.72.)

Phrases you will use

9 Hello
Allô
a·lô

10 This is Peter Williams
Peter Williams à l'appareil
Peter Williams a la·pa·ray

11 Can I speak to Madame Renard?
Je voudrais parler à Madame Renard
zhuh voo·dreh par·lay a ma·dam ruh·nar

12 I would like to make a phone call to Britain/America
Je voudrais téléphoner en Grande-Bretagne/Amérique
zhuh voo·dreh tay·lay·fo·nay oñ groñd·bruh·tan·yuh/ na·may·reek

13 The number I want is ...
Je voudrais le ...
zhuh voo·dreh luh ...

14 I wish — to make a reversed charge call
Je voudrais — téléphoner en PCV
zhuh voo·dreh — tay·lay·fo·nay oñ pay·say·vay
— to make a person-to-person call
— téléphoner avec préavis
— *tay·lay·fo·nay a·vek pray·a·vee*

15 What is the dialling code for Lyon/Los Angeles?
Quel est l'indicatif pour Lyon/Los Angeles?
kel eh lañ·dee·ka·teef poor lee·oñ/Los Angeles

16 Would you write it down for me, please?
Vous voulez bien me le mettre par écrit?
voo voo·lay byañ muh luh meh·truh par ay·kree

17 Could you put me through to (international) directory inquiries?
Vous voudriez me passer les renseignements (internationaux)?
voo voo·dree·ay muh pa·say lay roñ·sen·yuh·moñ (añ·tehr·na·syo·nô)

18 Which booth do I use?
C'est quelle cabine?
seh kel ka·been

19 May I use the phone, please?
Est-ce que je peux me servir du téléphone?
es kuh zhuh puh muh sehr·veer dōō tay·lay·fon

20 Do I need a token?
Il me faut un jeton?
eel muh fô tuñ zhuh·toñ

21 Can I have three tokens, please?
Est-ce que je peux avoir trois jetons?
es kuh zhuh puh za·vwar trwah zhuh·toñ

22 I have a crossed line (bad connection)
Il y a d'autres personnes sur la ligne
eel ee a dô·truh pehr·son sōōr la leen·yuh

23 We have been cut off
Nous avons été coupés
noo za·voñ zay·tay koo·pay

24 How much does it cost to telephone California?
C'est combien pour téléphoner en Californie?
seh koñ·byañ poor tay·lay·fo·nay oñ ka·lee·for·nee

25 Is there a cheap rate?
Y a-t-il un tarif réduit?
ee a-teel uñ ta-reef ray-dwee

26 **What is the time now — in Hong Kong?**
Quelle heure est-il en ce
moment — à Hong Kong?
kel ur eh-teel oñ suh mo-moñ — a ong-kong

27 I cannot get through
Je n'arrive pas à obtenir la communication
zhuh na-reev pa za op-tuh-neer la ko-mōō-nee-ka-syoñ

28 Can I check this number/code?
Je voudrais vérifier le numéro/l'indicatif
zhuh voo-dreh vay-ree-fee-ay luh nōō-may-rō/lañ-dee-ka-teef

29 **Do you have a directory — for Marseilles?**
Vous avez l'annuaire — pour Marseille?
voo za-vay la-nōō-ehr — poor mar-say

Phrases you will hear

30 Qui est à l'appareil?
kee eh ta la-pa-ray
Who is speaking?

31 Je vous passe Madame Renard
zhuh voo pas ma-dam ruh-nar
I am putting you through to Madame Renard

32 Ne quittez pas
nuh kee-tay pa
Hold the line

33 J'essaie d'obtenir votre communication
zheh-say dop-tuh-neer vo-truh ko-mōō-nee-ka-syoñ
I am trying to connect you

34 La ligne est occupée
la leen-yuh eh to-kōō-pay
The line is engaged (busy)

35 Veuillez rappeler
vuhy-yay ra-puh-lay
Please try later

36 Ce numéro est en dérangement
suh nōō-may-rō eh toñ-day-roñzh-moñ
This number is out of order

37 Je n'arrive pas à avoir ce numéro
zhuh na-reev pa za a-vwar suh nōō-may-rō
I cannot obtain this number

38 Demandeur, parlez
duh-moñ-dur, par-lay
Please go ahead

The hairdresser

39 I'd like to make an appointment
Je voudrais prendre rendez-vous
zhuh voo-dreh proñ-druh roñ-day-voo

40 **I want — a cut**
Je voudrais — une coupe
zhuh voo-dreh — ōōn koop
— a blow-dry
— un brushing
— *uñ bruh-shing*

41 A trim, please
Recoupez-moi un peu les cheveux, s'il vous plaît
ruh-koo-pay-mwah uñ puh lay shuh-vuh, seel voo pleh

42 **I want my hair — fairly short**
Coupez-moi les cheveux — assez courts
koo-pay-mwah lay shuh-vuh — a-say koor
— not too short
— pas trop courts
— *pa trō koor*
— short and curly
— courts, et frisez-les
— *koor, ay free-zay-lay*
— layered
— en dégradé
— *oñ day-gra-day*

43 I want a fringe
Faites-moi une frange
fet-mwah ōōn froñzh

44	Take more off — the front
	Recoupez — devant
	ruh·koo·pay — duh·voñ
	— the back
	— derrière
	— *deh·ree·ehr*
45	Not too much off — the sides
	Pas trop dégagé — sur les côtés
	pa trō day·ga·zhay — sōōr lay kō·tay
	— the top
	— sur le dessus
	— *sōōr luh duh·sōō*
46	I would like a parting — in the centre
	Je voudrais une raie — au milieu
	zhuh voo·dreh zōōn reh — ō mee·lyuh
	— on the left
	— à gauche
	— *a gōsh*
	— on the right
	— à droite
	— *a drwat*
47	I'd like — a perm
	Je voudrais — une permanente
	zhuh voo·dreh — ōōn pehr·ma·noñt
	— a curly perm
	— une permanente bouclée
	— *ōōn pehr·ma·noñt boo·klay*
	— a shampoo and set
	— un shampooing mise en plis
	— *uñ shoñ·pwañ meez oñ plee*
	— my hair tinted
	— une coloration
	— *ōōn ko·lo·ra·syoñ*
	— my hair streaked
	— des mèches
	— *day mesh*

48 The water is too hot/cold
   L'eau est trop chaude/froide
   lō eh trō shōd/frwad

49 The dryer is too hot/cold
   Le séchoir est trop chaud/froid
   luh sesh·wahr eh trō shō/frwa

50	I'd like — a conditioner
	Je voudrais — une crème démêlante
	zhuh voo·dreh — ōōn krem day·meh·loñt
	— hair spray
	— de la laque
	— *duh la lak*

51 That's fine, thank you
   C'est très bien, merci
   seh treh byañ, mehr·see

Repairs and technical jobs

If you want something fixed in France, from a lock to a waste pipe, and you don't know how to contact a specialist, you can make use of one of the general *dépannage* (repair) firms which provide a range of experts. The following list tells you how to describe some of the things for which you might need specialist help during your stay (cars are dealt with on p.19, clothes on p.58).

52 Where can I get this repaired?
   Où est-ce que je peux faire réparer ça?
   oo es kuh zhuh puh fehr ray·pa·ray sa

53 I am having trouble with — the heating/plumbing
   J'ai des ennuis avec — le chauffage/la tuyauterie
   zhay day zoñ·nwee a·vek — luh shō·fazh/la twee·yō·tuh·ree

54 This is — broken
   C'est — cassé
   seh — ka·say

This is — not working
C'est — en panne
seh — *oñ pan*
— damaged
— endommagé
— *oñ·do·ma·zhay*
— blocked
— bouché
— *boo·shay*
— torn
— déchiré
— *day·shee·ray*

55   There is — a leak in the pipe/roof
Il y a — une fuite au tuyau/à la toiture
eel ee a — *ōōn fweet ō twee·yō/a la twa·tōōr*
— a gas leak
— une fuite de gaz
— *ōōn fweet duh gaz*

56 Would you have a look at this, please?
Est-ce que vous pouvez y regarder, s'il vous plaît?
es kuh voo poo·vay zee ruh·gar·day, seel voo pleh

57   Can you repair — my suitcase?
Est-ce que vous pouvez
réparer — ma valise?
es kuh voo poo·vay
ray·pa·ray — *ma va·leez*

58   Can you — resole these shoes?
Pouvez-vous — ressemeler ces chaussures?
poo·vay·voo — *ruh·suh·muh·lay say shō·sōōr*
— get it working again?
— le dépanner?
— *luh day·pa·nay*

59 Have you got a replacement part?
Est-ce que vous avez une pièce de rechange?
es kuh voo za·vay ōōn pyes duh ruh·shoñzh

60 When will it be ready?
Quand est-ce que cela sera prêt?
koñ tes kuh suh·la suh·ra preh

61 Can you do it quickly?
Est-ce que vous pouvez le faire rapidement?
es kuh voo poo·vay luh fehr ra·peed·moñ

62 I would like a duplicate of this key
Je voudrais un double
zhuh voo·dreh zuñ doo·bluh

63   I have lost — my key
J'ai perdu — ma clé
zhay pehr·dōō — *ma klay*

64 I have locked myself out
La clé est à l'intérieur et je ne peux pas rentrer
la klay eh ta lañ·tay·ree·ur ay zhuh nuh puh pa roñ·tray

65 Can you open the door?
Pourriez-vous ouvrir la porte?
poo·ree·ay·voo zoo·vreer la port

66 The fuse for the lights has blown
Les plombs ont sauté
lay ploñ oñ sō·tay

67 There is a loose connection
Il y a un mauvais contact
eel ee a uñ mo·veh koñ·takt

68 Sometimes it works, sometimes it doesn't
Quelquefois ça marche, quelquefois ça ne marche pas
kel·kuh·fwah sa marsh, kel·kuh·fwah sa nuh marsh pa

Laundry, dry cleaners and clothes-mending

A dry cleaner's is called either *une teinturerie* (*tañ·tōō·ruh·ree*) or *un pressing* — pronounced as in English — (the former implies that a mending and alteration service is also provided). Sometimes it is combined with *une blanchisserie* (*bloñ·shee·suh·ree* — laundry), which will usually provide fairly quick service. A launderette is *une laverie automatique* (la·vree ō·tō·ma·teek).

69	Will you —	clean this skirt?
	Pouvez-vous —	nettoyer cette jupe?
	poo·vay·voo —	neh·twa·yay set zhōōp
	—	press these trousers?
	—	repasser ce pantalon?
	—	ruh·pa·say suh poñ·ta·loñ
	—	wash and iron these shirts?
	—	laver et repasser ces chemises?
	—	la·vay ay ruh·pa·say say shuh·meez
	—	wash these clothes?
	—	laver ces affaires?
	—	la·vay say za·fehr

70	This stain is —	grease/ink
	Ceci, c'est une tache —	de graisse/d'encre
	suh·see, seh tōōn tash —	duh gres/doñ·kruh

71 **Can you get this stain out?**
Vous pourriez faire partir cette tache?
voo poo·ree·ay fehr par·teer set tash

72 **This fabric is delicate**
C'est un tissu délicat
seh tuñ tee·sōō day·lee·ka

73 **When will my things be ready?**
Quand est-ce que mes affaires seront prêtes?
koñ tes kuh may za·fehr suh·roñ pret

74 **I need them in a hurry**
Je les voudrais assez rapidement
zhuh lay voo·dreh a·say ra·peed·moñ

75 **Is there a launderette nearby?**
Est-ce qu'il y a une laverie automatique près d'ici?
es keel ee a ōōn la·vree ō·tō·ma·teek preh dee·see

76 **Can I have my laundry done?**
Est-ce que vous pouvez me laver ce linge?
es kuh voo poo·vay muh la·vay suh lañzh

77 **Where can I get clothes repaired?**
Où est-ce que je peux faire réparer des vêtements?
oo es kuh zhuh puh fehr ray·pa·ray day vet·moñ

78 **Can you do invisible mending?**
Vous savez faire du stoppage?
voo sa·vay fehr dōō sto·pazh

79 **Do you think you could repair this?**
Vous sauriez me réparer ça?
voo sō·ree·ay muh ray·pa·ray sa

80	Could you —	sew this button back on?
	Vous pourriez —	recoudre ce bouton?
	voo poo·ree·ay —	ruh·koo·druh suh boo·toñ
	—	mend this tear?
	—	réparer cet accroc?
	—	ray·pa·ray set a·krō
	—	replace this zip?
	—	remplacer la fermeture éclair?
	—	roñ·pla·say la fehrm·tōōr ay·klehr
	—	turn up/let down the hem?
	—	raccourcir/rallonger l'ourlet?
	—	ra·koor·seer/ra·loñ·zhay loor·leh

Police and legal matters

81 **I wish to call the police**
Je veux appeler la police
zhuh vuh za·puh·lay la po·lees

82 **Where is the police station?**
Où est le poste de police?
oo eh luh post duh po·lees

83	I should like to report —	a theft
	Je voudrais signaler —	un vol
	zhuh voo·dreh seen·ya·lay —	uñ vol

	I should like to report — the loss of a camera
	Je voudrais signaler — la perte d'un appareil-photo
	zhuh voo·dreh seen·ya·lay — la pehrt duñ na·pa·ray·fō·tō
84	Someone has broken into — my car/my room
	Quelqu'un s'est introduit
	dans — ma voiture/ma chambre par effraction
	kel·kuñ seh tañ·tro·dwee
	doñ — ma vwa·tōōr/ma shoñ·bruh par eh·frak·syoñ
85	Someone has stolen — my wallet
	On a volé — mon portefeuille
	oñ na vo·lay — moñ port·fuhy
86	My insurance company requires me to report it
	Ma compagnie d'assurances exige que la police soit informée
	ma koñ·pan·yee da·sōō·roñs eg·zeezh kuh la po·lees swa tañ·for·may
87	I have lost — my passport
	J'ai perdu — mon passeport
	zhay pehr·dōō — moñ pas·por
88	My son is lost
	Mon fils a disparu
	moñ fees a dees·pa·rōō
89	I wish *or* I demand — to see a lawyer
	Je demande — à voir un avocat
	zhuh duh·moñd — a vwar uñ na·vo·ka
90	Where is the British/American Consulate?
	Où est le Consulat britannique/américain?
	oo eh luh koñ·sōō·la bree·ta·neek/a·may·ree·kañ

Worship

France is mainly Roman Catholic, but all other main denominations and religions are well represented, especially in the larger cities.

91	Where is there — a Catholic church?
	Où y a-t-il — une église catholique?
	oo ee a·teel — ōōn ay·gleez ka·to·leek
	— a Protestant church?
	— un temple?
	— *uñ toñ·pluh*
	— a synagogue?
	— une synagogue?
	— *ōōn see·na·gog*
	— a mosque?
	— une mosquée?
	— *ōōn mos·kay*
92	What time is the service?
	L'office est à quelle heure?
	lo·fees eh ta kel ur
93	I'd like to see — a priest
	Je voudrais voir — un prêtre
	zhuh voo·dreh vwar — uñ preh·truh
	— a minister
	— un pasteur
	— *uñ pas·tur*
	— a rabbi
	— un rabin
	— *uñ ra·bañ*
94	Is there one — who speaks English?
	Est-ce qu'il y en a un — qui parle anglais?
	es keel ee oñ na uñ — kee parl oñ·gleh
95	Could you hear my confession — in English?
	Est-ce que je peux me confesser — en anglais?
	es kuh zhuh puh muh koñ·feh·say — oñ noñ·gleh

Business matters   (Bm)

Making appointments (see also Telephoning, p.54)

1   My name is George Baker — of Universal Chemicals
    Je m'appelle George Baker — des Universal Chemicals
    zhuh ma·pel George Baker — day Universal Chemicals
2   Here is my card
    Voici ma carte
    vwa·see ma kart
3   Could I see/speak to your — managing director/buyer?
    Est-ce que je peux voir/parler
    à votre — directeur général/chef des achats?
    es kuh zhuh puh vwar/par·lay
    a vo·truh — dee·rek·tur zhay·nay·ral/shef day
    za·sha
4   He/she is expecting me to telephone
    Il/elle attend un coup de téléphone de moi
    eel/el a·toñ uñ koo duh tay·lay·fon duh mwah
5   Could you put me through to Monsieur Leblanc?
    Vous pourriez me passer Monsieur Leblanc?
    voo poo·ree·ay muh pa·say muh·syuh luh·bloñ
6   Is Monsieur Leblanc in?
    Monsieur Leblanc est là?
    muh·syuh luh·bloñ eh la
7   Is his assistant/secretary there?
    Son adjoint/sa secrétaire est là?
    soñ nad·zhwañ/sa suh·kray·tehr eh la
8   When will he/she be back?
    Quand est-ce qu'il/qu'elle sera rentré(e)?
    koñ tes keel/kel suh·ra roñ·tray
9   I have an appointment with Monsieur Leblanc
    J'ai un rendez-vous avec Monsieur Leblanc
    zhay uñ roñ·day·voo a·vek muh·syuh luh·bloñ
10 I would like to make an appointment with Monsieur Leblanc
    Je voudrais prendre rendez-vous avec Monsieur Leblanc
    zhuh voo·dreh proñ·druh roñ·day·voo a·vek muh·syuh luh·bloñ
11 I am free on Thursday between 9:00 and 11:00
    Je suis libre jeudi de 9 heures à 11 heures
    zhuh swee lee·bruh zhuh·dee duh nuv ur a oñz ur
12 Shall we say 10:00?
    Alors 10 heures, ça vous convient?
    a·lor dee zur, sa voo koñ·vyañ

Practicalities and fieldwork

13 I am on a business trip to France
    Je suis en voyage d'affaires en France
    zhuh swee zoñ vwa·yazh da·fehr oñ froñs
14 I wish to hire — a secretary/a typist
    Je voudrais engager — une secrétaire/une dactylo
    zhuh voo·dreh oñ·ga·zhay — ōōn suh·kray·tehr/ōōn dak·tee·lō
    — a conference room
    — une salle de conférence
    — *ōōn sal duh koñ·fay·roñs*
15 Where can I get photocopying done?
    Où est-ce que je peux faire faire des photocopies?
    oo es kuh zhuh puh fehr fehr day fō·tō·ko·pee
16 Can I send a telex from here?
    Est-ce que je peux envoyer un télex d'ici?
    es kuh zhuh puh zoñ·vwa·yay uñ tay·leks dee·see
17 My firm specializes in — agricultural equipment
    Mon entreprise se spécialise
    dans — le matériel agricole
    mon noñ·truh·preez suh
    spay·see·a·leez doñ — luh ma·tay·ree·el a·gree·kol

18   I wish — to carry out a market survey
       Je voudrais — faire une étude de marché
     zhuh voo·dreh — fehr ōōn ay·tōōd duh mar·shay
             — to test the French market for this
                product
             — tester le marché français pour ce
                produit
             — *tes·tay luh mar·shay froñ·seh poor*
                suh pro·dwee

19 My firm is launching an advertising/sales campaign
Mon entreprise lance une campagne de publicité/de ventes
moñ noñ·truh·preez loñs ōōn koñ·pan·yuh duh pōō·blee·see·tay/duh voñt

20 Have you seen our catalogue?
Avez-vous vu notre catalogue?
a·vay·voo vōō no·truh ka·ta·log

21 Can I send our sales representative to see you?
Je peux vous envoyer notre représentant de commerce?
zhuh puh voo zoñ·vwa·yay no·truh ruh·pray·zoñ·toñ duh ko·mehrs

22 I will send you a letter/telex with the details
Je vous enverrai les détails par lettre/par télex
zhuh voo zoñ·veh·ray lay day·tye par leh·truh/par tay·leks

23   Can I see — a sample of your product?
         Puis-je voir — un échantillon de votre produit?
      pwee·zhuh vwar — uñ nay·shoñ·tee·yoñ duh vo·truh
                 pro·dwee
               — a selection of your goods?
               — un choix de vos articles?
            — *uñ shwah duh vō zar·tee·kluh?*

24 Can I have a copy of this document/brochure?
Est-ce que je peux avoir un exemplaire de ce document/de cette
   brochure?
es kuh zhuh puh za·vwar uñ neg·zoñ·plehr duh suh do·kōō·moñ/duh set bro·shōōr

25 Can you give me an estimate of the cost?
Pouvez-vous me donner un état estimatif du coût?
poo·vay·voo muh do·nay uñ nay·ta es·tee·ma·teef dōō koo

26 What percentage of the cost is transportation?
Les frais de transport rentrent pour quelle part dans le coût?
lay freh duh troñs·por roñ·truh poor kel par doñ luh koo

          What is the average cost — of a pocket calculator?
          Quel est le coût moyen — d'une calculatrice de poche?
       kel eh luh koo mwa·yañ — dōōn kal·kōō·la·trees duh posh

27 What is the wholesale/retail price?
Quel est le prix de gros/de détail?
kel eh luh pree duh grō/duh day·tye

28 What is the rate of inflation in France?
Quel est le taux d'inflation en France?
kel eh luh tō doñ·fla·syoñ oñ froñs

29 How high are current interest rates?
Quels sont les taux d'intérêt actuels?
kel soñ lay tō doñ·tay·reh ak·tōō·el

30 How is this project being financed?
Comment est financé ce projet?
ko·moñ eh fee·noñ·say suh pro·zheh

31 It's a pleasure to do business with you
C'est un plaisir de traiter affaires avec vous
seh tuñ pleh·zeer duh treh·tay a·fehr a·vek voo

Children   (c)

Travelling with children abroad presents its own special problems. We have therefore grouped together here certain phrases that parents may need in a variety of situations.

1   Do you have — a special children's menu?
       Est-ce que vous avez — un menu spécial pour enfants?
     es kuh voo za·vay — uñ muh·nōō spay·syal poor oñ·foñ

2   Do you serve — half portions for children?
          Servez-vous — des demi-portions pour enfants?
          sehr·vay·voo — day duh·mee·por·syoñ poor oñ·foñ

3 Can you warm this bottle for me?
  Voulez-vous me réchauffer ce biberon?
  voo·lay·voo muh ray·shō·fay suh bee·buh·roñ

4 Have you got a highchair?
  Avez-vous une chaise haute?
  a·vay·voo ōōn shez ót

5   Do you operate — a baby-sitting service?
          Vous assurez — un service de baby-sitting?
          voo za·sōō·ray — uñ sehr·vees duh bay·bee·see·ting
                    — a day nursery?
                    — une crèche?
                    — ōōn kresh

6 Do you know anyone who will baby-sit for us?
  Est-ce que vous connaissez quelqu'un qui pourrait garder nos
    enfants?
  es kuh voo ko·neh·say kel·kuñ kee poo·reh gar·day nō zoñ·foñ

7 We shall be back at 11
  Nous rentrons à onze heures
  noo roñ·troñ za oñz ur

8 She goes to bed at 8
  Elle se couche à huit heures
  el suh koosh a wee tur

9 Are there any organized activities for the children?
  Est-ce qu'il y a des activités organisées pour les enfants?
  es keel ee a day zak·tee·vee·tay zor·ga·nee·zay poor lay zoñ·foñ

10   Is there — a playground?
          Est-ce qu'il y a — une cour?
          es keel ee a — ōōn koor
                  — an amusement park?
                  — un parc d'attractions?
                  — uñ park da·trak·syoñ

11 Have you got a cot (crib) for our baby?
  Avez-vous un petit lit pour notre bébé?
  a·vay·voo uñ puh·tee lee poor no·truh bay·bay

12 Can my son sleep in our room?
  Est-ce que mon fils peut dormir dans notre chambre?
  es kuh moñ fees puh dor·meer doñ no·truh shoñ·bruh

13 Are there any other children in the hotel?
  Est-ce qu'il y a d'autres enfants dans l'hôtel?
  es keel ee a dō·truh zoñ·foñ doñ lō·tel

14 How old are your children?
  Quel âge ont vos enfants?
  kel azh oñ vō zoñ·foñ

15 My son is 9 years old
  Mon fils a neuf ans
  mon fees a nuh voñ

16 My daughter is 15 months old
  Ma fille a quinze mois
  ma feey a kañz mwah

17 Where can I feed my baby?
  Où est-ce que je peux allaiter mon bébé?
  oo es kuh zhuh puh za·lay·tay moñ bay·bay

18 I need some disposable nappies (diapers)
  J'ai besoin de couches en cellulose
  zhay buh·zwañ duh koosh oñ seh·lōō·lōz

Illness and disability   (I)

The disabled

1   I suffer from — a weak heart/asthma
          Je suis — cardiaque/asthmatique
          zhuh swee — kar·dyak/ast·ma·teek

2   Do you have — facilities for the disabled?
Est-ce que vous avez — des installations spéciales pour les handicapés?
es kuh voo za·vay — *day zañ·sta·la·syoñ spay·syal poor lay oñ·dee·ka·pay*

— a toilet for the disabled?
— des toilettes spéciales pour les handicapés?
— *day twa·let spay·syal poor lay oñ·dee·ka·pay*

3 Is there a reduced rate for disabled people?
Vous avez un tarif réduit pour les handicapés?
voo za·vay uñ ta·reef ray·dwee poor lay oñ·dee·ka·pay

4 I am unable to — climb stairs
Je ne suis pas capable de — monter les escaliers
zhuh nuh swee pa ka·pa·bluh duh — *moñ·tay lay zes·kal·yay*

— walk very far
— marcher très loin
— *mar·shay treh lwañ*

5 Can you supply a wheelchair?
Vous pouvez mettre à ma disposition un fauteuil roulant?
voo poo·vay meh·tra ma dees·po·zee·syoñ uñ fō·tuhy roo·loñ

6 Does your lift accommodate a wheelchair?
Est-ce qu'un fauteuil roulant pourra rentrer dans l'ascenseur?
es kuñ fō·tuhy roo·loñ poo·ra roñ·tray doñ la·soñ·sur

Doctors and hospitals

If a visit to a doctor is necessary, you will have to pay on the spot. Check before your visit whether a doctor is *conventionné* (subject to a scale of charges fixed by the state) or *non-conventionné* (free to charge as he wishes, usually very expensive). Some of the cost of medical treatment is repayable under reciprocal EEC agreements for British and Irish visitors (form E111 should be obtained before departure and taken with you), but proper accident and medical insurance is still advisable. Ambulances also have to be paid for, and there is no central number for you to dial. The emergency operator will tell you the numbers.

Preliminary

7 I need a doctor
J'ai besoin d'un docteur
zhay buh·zwañ duñ dok·tur

8 I feel ill
Je ne me sens pas bien
zhuh nuh muh soñ pa byañ

9 Can I have an appointment with the doctor?
Est-ce que je peux avoir un rendez-vous avec le docteur?
es kuh zhuh puh za·vwar uñ roñ·day·voo a·vek luh dok·tur

10 I would like a general checkup
Voudriez-vous me faire un bilan de santé
voo·dree·ay·voo muh fehr uñ bee·loñ duh soñ·tay

11 I would like to see — a skin specialist
Je voudrais consulter — un dermatologue
zhuh voo·dreh koñ·sōōl·tay — *uñ dehr·ma·to·log*

— an eye specialist
— un oculiste
— *uñ no·kōō·leest*

In the event of an accident

12 There has been an accident
Il y a eu un accident
eel ee a ōō uñ nak·see·doñ

13 Call an ambulance
Appelez une ambulance
a·puh·lay ōōn oñ·bōō·loñs

14 Get a doctor
Allez chercher un docteur
a·lay shehr·shay uñ dok·tur

15 He is unconscious
Il a perdu connaissance
eel a pehr·dōō ko·neh·soñs

16 **He is in pain**
Il a mal
eel a mal

17 **She has been seriously injured**
Elle est sérieusement blessée
el eh say·ree·uz·moñ bleh·say

18 **She has been badly hurt**
Elle s'est fait très mal
el seh feh treh mal

19 **I have cut myself**
Je me suis coupé
zhuh muh swee koo·pay

20 **He has burned himself**
Il s'est brûlé
eel seh broo·lay

21 **I have had a fall**
Je suis tombé
zhuh swee toñ·bay

22 **He has been stung**
Il s'est fait piquer
eel seh feh pee·kay

23 **She has been bitten**
Elle a été mordue
el a ay·tay mor·doo

24 **I have hurt — my arm/my leg**
Je me suis fait mal — au bras/à la jambe
zhuh muh swee feh mal — ō bra/a la zhoñb

25 **I have broken my arm**
J'ai le bras cassé
zhay luh bra ka·say

26 **He has dislocated his shoulder**
Il s'est démis l'épaule
eel seh day·mee lay·pōl

27 **She has sprained her ankle**
Elle s'est foulé la cheville
el seh foo·lay la shuh·veey

28 **I have pulled this muscle**
J'ai une élongation de ce muscle
zhay ōōn ay·loñ·ga·syoñ duh suh mōō·skluh

Symptoms, conditions and treatment

29 **There is a swelling here**
C'est enflé ici
seh toñ·flay ee·see

30 **It is inflamed here**
C'est enflammé ici
seh toñ·fla·may ee·see

31 **I have a pain here**
J'ai une douleur ici
zhay ōōn doo·lur ee·see

32 **I find it painful — to walk/breathe**
Ça me fait mal — quand je marche/quand je respire
sa muh feh mal — koñ zhuh marsh/koñ zhuh reh·speer

33 **I have — a headache/a sore throat**
J'ai — mal à la tête/mal à la gorge
zhay — mal a la tet/mal a la gorzh

34 **I have a high temperature**
J'ai beaucoup de température
zhay bō·koo duh toñ·pay·ra·tōōr

35 **I can't sleep**
Je ne dors pas
zhuh nuh dor pa

36 **I have sunstroke**
J'ai eu une insolation
zhay ōō ōōn añ·so·la·syoñ

37 My stomach is upset
J'ai l'estomac dérangé
zhay les·to·ma day·roñ·zhay

38 I feel nauseous
J'ai envie de vomir
zhay oñ·vee duh vo·meer

39 I think I have food poisoning
Je crois que c'est une intoxication alimentaire
zhuh krwah kuh seh tōōn añ·tok·see·ka·syoñ a·lee·moñ·tehr

40 I have vomited
J'ai vomi
zhay vo·mee

41 I have diarrhoea
J'ai la diarrhée
zhay la dee·a·ray

42 I am constipated
Je suis constipé
zhuh swee koñ·stee·pay

43 I feel faint
Je sens que je vais m'évanouir
zhuh soñ kuh zhuh vay may·va·nweer

44 I am allergic — to penicillin/to cortisone
Je suis allergique — à la pénicilline/à la cortisone
zhuh swee za·lehr·zheek — a la pay·nee·see·leen/a la kor·tee·zon

45 I have high blood pressure
J'ai de la tension
zhay duh la toñ·syoñ

46 I am a diabetic
Je suis diabétique
zhuh swee dee·a·bay·teek

47 I am taking these drugs
Je prends ces médicaments
zhuh proñ say may·dee·ka·moñ

48 Can you give me a French prescription for them?
Est-ce que vous pouvez me donner des médicaments équivalents?
es kuh voo poo·vay muh do·nay day may·dee·ka·moñ zay·kee·va·loñ

49 I am pregnant
Je suis enceinte
zhuh swee zoñ·sañt

50 I am on the pill
Je prends la pilule
zhuh proñ la pee·lōōl

51 My blood group is...
Mon groupe sanguin est...
moñ groop soñ·gañ eh...

52 I don't know my blood group
Je ne connais pas mon groupe sanguin
zhuh nuh ko·neh pa moñ groop soñ·gañ

53 Must I stay in bed?
Est-ce que je dois rester au lit?
es kuh zhuh dwah res·tay ō lee

54 Will I be able to go out tomorrow?
Est-ce que je pourrai sortir demain?
es kuh zhuh poo·ray sor·teer duh·mañ

55 Will I have to go to the hospital?
Est-ce que je dois aller à l'hôpital?
es kuh zhuh dwah za·lay a lo·pee·tal

56 Here is my E111 form
Voici mon formulaire britannique de sécurité sociale
assurance-maladie
*vwa·see moñ for·mōō·lehr bree·ta·neek duh say·kōō·ree·tay so·syal
a·sōō·roñs·ma·la·dee*

57 How do I get reimbursed?
Comment est-ce que je me fais rembourser?
kom·oñ es kuh zhuh muh feh roñ·boor·say

Dentists

58 I need to see the dentist
    Il faut que je voie le dentiste
    eel fō kuh zhuh vwa luh doñ·teest

59 I have a toothache
    J'ai mal aux dents
    zhay mal ō doñ

60 It's this one
    C'est celle-ci
    seh sel·see

61 I've broken a tooth
    J'ai une dent de cassée
    zhay ōōn doñ duh ka·say

62 The filling has come out
    Le plombage est parti
    luh ploñ·bazh eh par·tee

63 Will you have to take it out?
    Est-ce qu'il faudra l'arracher?
    es keel fō·dra la·ra·shay

64 Are you going to fill it?
    Est-ce que vous allez la plomber?
    es kuh voo za·lay la ploñ·bay

65 That hurts
    Ça fait mal
    sa feh mal

66 Please give me an anaesthetic
    Faites-moi une piqûre pour insensibiliser, s'il vous plaît
    fet·mwah ōōn pee·kōōr poor añ·soñ·see·bee·lee·zay, seel voo pleh

67 My gums hurt
    Mes gencives sont douloureuses
    may zhoñ·seev soñ doo·loo·ruz

68 My dentures are broken
    Mon dentier est cassé
    mon doñ·tyay eh ka·say

69 Can you repair them?
    Est-ce que vous pouvez le réparer?
    es kuh voo poo·vay luh ray·pa·ray

Emergencies and accidents   (Ea)

Hopefully you will not need the following phrases, but it is better to know them, as they could make a difference in a critical situation. For a medical emergency, see also p.64.

1 Help!
   Au secours!
   ō suh·koor

2 Stop!
   Arrêtez!
   a·reh·tay

3 Stop thief!
   Au voleur!
   ō vo·lur

4 There has been an accident
   Il y a eu un accident
   eel ee a ōō uñ nak·see·doñ

5 A fire has broken out
   Un incendie s'est déclaré
   uñ nañ·soñ·dee seh day·kla·ray

6   I have been — robbed/attacked
                          J'ai été — victime d'un vol/d'une agression
                          zhay ay·tay — veek·teem duñ vol/dōōn a·greh·syoñ

7 Where is the nearest telephone/hospital?
   Où se trouve le téléphone/l'hôpital le plus proche?
   oo suh troov luh tay·lay·fon/lo·pee·tal luh plōō prosh

8   Call — a doctor
           Appelez — un médecin
       a·puh·lay — *uñ mayt·sañ*
              — an ambulance
              — une ambulance
              — *ōōn oñ·bōō·loñs*
              — the police
              — la police
              — *la po·lees*
              — the fire brigade
              — les sapeurs-pompiers
              — *lay sa·pur·poñ·pyay*

9 This is an emergency
   C'est une urgence
   seh tōōn ōōr·zhoñs
10 It is urgent
   C'est urgent
   seh tōōr·zhoñ
11 Please hurry
   Dépêchez-vous, je vous en conjure
   day·peh·shay·voo, zhuh voo zoñ koñ·zhōōr
12 My address is . . .
   Voici mon adresse . . .
   vwa·see moñ na·dres . . .

Making conversation   (Mc)

Topics

The weather

1   It's — hot/cold
           Il fait — chaud/froid
         eel feh — *shō/frwah*
2   Is it going — to be a nice day?
   Est-ce qu'il va — faire beau?
      es·keel va — *fehr bō*
                — to rain?
                — pleuvoir?
                — *pluh·vwar*

3 It's a lovely day
   Il fait beau
   eel feh bō
4 It's raining
   Il pleut
   eel pluh
5 It's windy
   Il fait du vent
   eel feh dōō voñ
6 It's snowing
   Il neige
   eel nezh
7 It's foggy
   Il fait du brouillard
   eel feh dōō broo·yar
8 What is the temperature?
   Quelle est la température?
   kel eh la toñ·pay·ra·tōōr
9 Is the water warm?
   Est-ce que l'eau est chaude?
   es kuh lō eh shōd
10 When is high tide?
   La marée haute est à quelle heure?
   la ma·ray ōt eh ta kel ur
11 It's a clear night
   La nuit est claire
   la nwee eh klehr

National and regional characteristics

This is an endlessly fruitful source of material for conversation. Here are some of the points that might be raised.

12 My country has a population of . . .
    La population de mon pays est de . . .
    la po·pōō·la·syoñ duh moñ pay·yee eh duh . . .

13 The country has a high/low standard of living
    Le niveau de vie dans le pays est élevé/n'est pas élevé
    luh nee·vō duh vee doñ luh pay·yee eh tay·luh·vay/neh pa zay·luh·vay

14 The country has a high/low cost of living
    Le coût de la vie dans le pays est élevé/n'est pas élevé
    luh koo duh la vee doñ luh pay·yee eh tay·luh·vay/neh pa zay·luh·vay

15 The pace of life is fast/slow
    On y vit à un rythme lent/accéléré
    oñ nee vee a uñ reet·muh loñ/ak·say·lay·ray

16 The way of life is traditional
    On a gardé les traditions
    oñ na gar·day lay tra·dee·syoñ

17 The way of life is rapidly changing
    La façon de vivre change rapidement
    la fa·soñ duh vee·vruh shoñzh ra·peed·moñ

18   The people are — friendly/hardworking
                  Les gens sont — sympathiques/travailleurs
                  lay zhoñ soñ — sañ·pa·teek/tra·vye·yur

19 Is it customary in France for acquaintances to use first names?
    Est-ce qu'il est dans les usages de s'appeler par le prénom en France?
    es keel eh doñ lay zōō·zazh duh sa·puh·lay par luh pray·noñ oñ froñs

20 What sports are popular in France?
    Quels sports sont populaires en France?
    kel spor soñ po·pōō·lehr oñ froñs

21 How does the French educational system work?
    Comment fonctionne l'Enseignement en France?
    ko·moñ foñk·syon loñ·seh·nyuh·moñ oñ froñs

22 Where did you spend your holidays last year?
    Où avez-vous passé vos vacances l'année dernière?
    oo a·vay·voo pa·say vō va·koñs la·nay dehrn·yehr

23 Did you like it there?
    Ça vous a plu, là-bas?
    sa voo za plōō la·ba

24 What region do you come from?
    De quelle région êtes-vous?
    duh kel ray·zhoñ et·voo

25   What is the climate like — in the Auvergne?
             Comment est le climat — en Auvergne?
             ko·moñ eh luh klee·ma — oñ nō·vehrn·yuh

26 What are the people like?
    Comment sont les gens?
    ko·moñ soñ lay zhoñ

27 Is the region prosperous?
    C'est une région prospère?
    seh tōōn ray·zhoñ pros·pehr

28 Is the region unspoiled?
    La région est restée intacte?
    la ray·zhoñ eh res·tay añ·takt

29 Do you know the country around Reims?
    Vous connaissez la campagne des environs de Reims?
    voo ko·neh·say la koñ·pan·yuh day zoñ·vee·roñ duh rañs

30 The wine/food in the Dordogne is wonderful
    Les vins sont/la cuisine est formidable(s) en Dordogne
    lay vañ soñ/la kwee·zeen eh for·mee·da·bluh oñ dor·don·yuh

31 What are its main agricultural products?
    Quels sont les produits agricoles principaux?
    kel soñ lay pro·dwee za·gree·kol prañ·see·pō

32 **Where is its commercial/administrative centre?**
Où est le centre commercial/administratif?
oo eh luh soñ·truh ko·mehr·see·al/ad·mee·nee·stra·teef

33 **Chartres is a beautiful town**
Chartres est une belle ville
shar·truh eh tōōn bel veel

34 **Have you ever been to Nice?**
Vous êtes déjà allé a Nice?
voo zet day·zha a·lay a nees

35 **The best time to go to the Côte d'Azur is in the summer/the spring**
Le meilleur moment pour aller sur la Côte d'Azur c'est l'été/le
printemps
*luh may·yur mo·moñ poor a·lay sōōr la kôt da·zōōr seh lay·tay/luh
prañ·toñ*

Breaking the ice

Here are a few stock questions and answers that tend to be exchanged by
people who meet casually (see also Greetings and General Exchanges,
p.6).

36   Do you mind if — I sit here?
     Ça ne vous dérange pas
            que — je m'asseye ici?
  sa nuh voo day·roñzh pa
            kuh — zhuh ma·say ee·see*
               — I smoke?
               — je fume?
               — *zhuh fōōm*

37   Can I — offer you a cigarette?
     Je peux — vous offrir une cigarette?
     zhuh puh — voo zo·freer ōōn see·ga·ret
               — buy you a drink?
               — vous offrir un verre?
               — *voo zo·freer uñ vehr*

38 **May I introduce myself?**
Permettez-moi de me présenter
pehr·meh·tay·mwah duh muh pray·soñ·tay

39 **Are you French?**
Vous êtes Français(e)?
voo zet froñ·seh(·sez)

40 **Are you Belgian/Swiss?**
Vous êtes Belge/Suisse?
voo zet belzh/swees

41 **I am English**
Je suis Anglais(e)
zhuh swee zoñ·gleh(·glez)

42 **I live in New York/London**
J'habite New York/Londres
zha·beet New York/loñ·druh

43 **Is this your first visit to Paris?**
C'est la première fois que vous venez à Paris?
seh la pruh·myehr fwah kuh voo vuh·nay a pa·ree

44 **This is my third visit**
C'est la troisième fois que je viens ici
seh la trwa·zyem fwah kuh zhuh vyañ zee·see

45 **Have you been here long?**
Il y a longtemps que vous êtes ici?
eel ee a loñ·toñ kuh voo zet zee·see

46 **I have been here two days**
Je suis ici depuis deux jours
zhuh swee zee·see duh·pwee duh zhoor

47 **Are you staying long?**
Vous allez rester longtemps?
voo za·lay res·tay loñ·toñ

48 **I am staying for two weeks**
Je vais rester deux semaines ici
zhuh vay re·stay duh suh·men ee·see

49 Where are you staying?
Où logez-vous?
oo lo·zhay·voo

50 I am staying at the Hôtel de France
Je suis à l'Hôtel de France
zhuh swee za lō·tel duh froñs

51 What is your job?
Qu'est-ce que vous faites dans la vie?
kes kuh voo fet doñ la vee

52   I am — a businessman
           Je suis — homme d'affaires
        zhuh swee — *zom da·fehr*
                    — a student
                    — étudiant(e)
                    — *zay·tōō·dyoñ(t)*

53 Have you visited England/America?
Vous êtes déjà allé en Angleterre/Amérique?
voo zet day·zha a·lay oñ noñ·gluh·tehr/na·may·reek

54   What do you think — of the country?
           Que pensez-vous — du pays?
        kuh poñ·say voo — *dōō pay·yee*
                    — of the people?
                    — des gens?
                    — *day zhoñ*
                    — of the food?
                    — de la cuisine?
                    — *duh la kwee·zeen*

55 Are you married?
Vous êtes marié?
voo zet ma·ree·ay

56 Do you have any children?
Vous avez des enfants?
voo za·vay day zoñ·foñ

57   Would you like — to go out with me this evening?
          Voulez-vous — sortir avec moi ce soir?
        voo·lay·voo — *sor·teer a·vek mwah suh swar*
                    — to have dinner/lunch with me?
                    — manger avec moi ce soir/ce midi?
                    — *moñ·zhay a·vek mwah suh swar/suh mee·dee*
                    — to go to the cinema/theatre with me?
                    — aller au cinéma/au théâtre avec moi?
                    — *a·lay ō see·nay·ma/ō tay·a·truh a·vek mwah*
                    — to show me something of your city?
                    — me montrer un peu votre ville?
                    — *muh moñ·tray uñ puh vo·truh veel*

58 I would be delighted to meet — your fiancé(e)
       Je serais ravi de faire la connaissance de — votre fiancé(e)
    zhuh suh·ray ra·vee duh fehr la ko·neh·soñs duh — *vo·truh fee·oñ·say*

Reference (R)

The alphabet

The French alphabet is the same as the English. In the following table the names of the letters are given phonetically, and each letter forms the initial of a personal name printed on the right. This is a standard system for clarification, which might be used, for example, when a word is being spelled out over the telephone.

A	for	Anatole	N	for	Nicolas
a		*a·na·tol*	*en*		*nee·kō·la*
B		Berthe	O		Oscar
bay		*behrt*	*ō*		*os·kar*
C		Célestin	P		Pierre
say		*say·les·tañ*	*pay*		*pyehr*
D		Désiré	Q		Quintal
day		*day·zee·ray*	*kōō*		*kañ·tal*
E		Eugène	R		Raoul
uh		*uh·zhen*	*ehr*		*ra·ool*
F		François	S		Suzanne
ef		*froñ·swah*	*es*		*sōō·zan*
G		Gaston	T		Thérèse
zhay		*gas·toñ*	*tay*		*tay·rez*
H		Henri	U		Ursule
ash		*oñ·ree*	*ōō*		*ōōr·sōōl*
I		Irma	V		Victor
ee		*eer·ma*	*vay*		*veek·tor*
J		Joseph	W		William
zhee		*zhō·zef*	*doo·bluh·vay*		*weel·yam*
K		Kléber	X		Xavier
ka		*klay·behr*	*eeks*		*zav·yay*
L		Louis	Y		Yvonne
el		*loo·ee*	*ee·grek*		*ee·von*
M		Marcel	Z		Zoé
em		*mar·sel*	*zed*		*zō·ay*

Numbers

Cardinal numbers

0 zéro	13 treize	50 cinquante
zay·rō	*trez*	*sañ·koñt*
1 un	14 quatorze	60 soixante
uñ	*ka·torz*	*swa·soñt*
2 deux	15 quinze	70 soixante-dix
duh	*kañz*	*swa·soñt·dees*
3 trois	16 seize	80 quatre-vingts
trwah	*sez*	*ka·truh·vañ*
4 quatre	17 dix-sept	90 quatre-vingt-dix
ka·truh	*dee·set*	*ka·truh·vañ·dees*
5 cinq	18 dix-huit	100 cent
sañk	*deez·weet*	*soñ*
6 six	19 dix-neuf	110 cent dix
sees	*deez·nuf*	*soñ dees*
7 sept	20 vingt	200 deux cents
set	*vañ*	*duh soñ*
8 huit	21 vingt-et-un	1,000
weet	*vañ·tay·uñ*	mille
9 neuf	22 vingt-deux	*meel*
nuf	*vañ·duh*	2,000
10 dix	23 vingt-trois	deux mille
dees	*vañ·trwah*	*duh meel*
11 onze	30 trente	1,000,000
oñz	*troñt*	un million
12 douze	40 quarante	*uñ meel·yoñ*
dooz	*ka·roñt*	

Ordinal numbers

1st	11th	20th
premier, première	onzième	vingtième
pruhm·yay,	*oñz·yem*	*vañt·yem*
pruhm·yehr	12th	21st
2nd	douzième	vingt et unième
deuxième	*dooz·yem*	*vañ·tay·ōōn·yem*
duz·yem	13th	22nd
3rd	treizième	vingt-deuxième
troisième	*trez·yem*	*vañ·duz·yem*
trwahz·yem	14th	23rd
4th	quatorzième	vingt-troisième
quatrième	*ka·torz·yem*	*vañ·trwahz·yem*
ka·tree·em	15th	30th
5th	quinzième	trentième
cinquième	*kañz·yem*	*troñt·yem*
sañk·yem	16th	40th
6th	seizième	quarantième
sixième	*sez·yem*	*ka·roñt·yem*
seez·yem	17th	50th
7th	dix-septième	cinquantième
septième	*dee·set·yem*	*sañ·koñt·yem*
set·yem	18th	100th
8th	dix-huitième	centième
huitième	*deez·weet·yem*	*soñt·yem*
weet·yem	19th	1,000th
9th	dix-neuvième	millième
neuvième	*deez·nuv·yem*	*meel·yem*
nuv·yem		
10th		
dixième		
deez·yem		

Other numerical terms

a half	10 percent	five times
un demi	dix pour cent	cinq fois
uñ duh·mee	*dee poor soñ*	*sañk fwah*
a quarter	a dozen	the last (one)
un quart	une douzaine	le dernier, la dernière
uñ kar	*ōōn doo·zen*	*luh dehrn·yay, la*
a third	half a dozen	*dehrn·yehr*
un tiers	une demi-douzaine	
uñ tyehr	*ōōn duh·mee doo·zen*	

Time

In reply to the question "quelle heure est-il?" (*kel ur eh·teel*: what time is it?) you will hear "il est" (*eel eh*: it is) followed by the number. If the time is on the hour, say ten o'clock, the answer will be "dix heures" (*deez ur*: 10 hours). The 24-hour clock is often used. Otherwise, to indicate a.m. you add "du matin" (*dōō ma·tañ*: in the morning), and for p.m., "de l'après-midi" (*duh la·preh·mee·dee*: in the afternoon) or "du soir" (*dōō swar*: in the evening). The only exceptions are noon (midi *mee·dee*) and midnight (minuit *mee·nwee*). Times in between the hours follow a pattern similar to the English one. Here are some examples.

Nine o'clock a.m./p.m.
Neuf heures du matin/du soir
nuh vur dōō ma·tañ/dōō swar
9:05
Neuf heures cinq
nuh vur sañk
9:15
Neuf heures quinze *or* Neuf heures et quart
nuh vur kañz or *nuh vur ay kar*

9:30
Neuf heures trente *or* Neuf heures et demie
nuh vur troñt or *nuh vur ay duh-mee*
9:40
Dix heures moins vingt (literally, ten hours minus twenty)
dee zur mwañ vañ
9:45
Dix heures moins le quart
dee zur mwañ luh kar

The same sequence using the 24-hour clock, and assuming it is p.m., would be:

9:00	9:30
Vingt-et-une heures	Vingt-et-une heures trente
vañ-tay-ōōn ur	*vañ-tay-ōōn ur troñt*
9:05	9:40
Vingt-et-une heures cinq	Vingt-et-une heures quarante
vañ-tay-ōōn ur sañk	*vañ-tay-ōōn ur ka-roñt*
9:15	9:45
Vingt-et-une heures quinze	Vingt-et-une heures quarante-cinq
vañ-tay-ōōn ur kañz	*vañ-tay-ōōn ur ka-roñt-sañk*

Here are some other useful phrases connected with time:

tonight	after three o'clock	in half an hour
ce soir	après trois heures	dans une demi-heure
suh swar	*a-preh trwah zur*	*doñ zōōn duh-mee-ur*
at night	nearly five o'clock	soon
la nuit	presque cinq heures	bientôt
la nwee	*pres-kuh sañk ur*	*byañ-tō*
in the morning	at about one o'clock	early
le matin	vers une heure	de bonne heure
luh ma-tañ	*vehr ōōn ur*	*duh bon ur*
this afternoon	in an hour's time	late
cet après-midi	dans une heure	tard
set a-preh-mee-dee	*doñ zōōn ur*	*tar*
before midnight	two hours ago	
avant minuit	il y a deux heures	
a-voñ mee-nwee	*eel ee a duh zur*	

The calendar

Sunday	yesterday	January
dimanche	hier	janvier
dee-moñsh	*ee-yehr*	*zhoñ-vee-ay*
Monday	today	February
lundi	aujourd'hui	février
luñ-dee	*ō-zhoor-dwee*	*fay-vree-ay*
Tuesday	tomorrow	March
mardi	demain	mars
mar-dee	*duh-mañ*	*mars*
Wednesday	spring	April
mercredi	le printemps	avril
mehr-kruh-dee	*luh prañ-toñ*	*a-vreel*
Thursday	summer	May
jeudi	l'été	mai
zhuh-dee	*lay-tay*	*may*
Friday	autumn (fall)	June
vendredi	l'automne	juin
voñ-druh-dee	*lō-ton*	*zhwañ*
Saturday	winter	July
samedi	l'hiver	juillet
sam-dee	*lee-vehr*	*zhwee-yeh*
on Friday	in spring	August
vendredi	au printemps	août
voñ-druh-dee	*ō prañ-toñ*	*oot*
next Tuesday	in summer	September
mardi prochain	en été	septembre
mar-dee pro-shañ	*oñ nay-tay*	*sep-toñ-bruh*

October	in June	next week
octobre	au mois de juin	la semaine prochaine
ok·to·bruh	*ō mwah duh zhwañ*	*la suh·men pro·shen*
November	July 6	last month
novembre	le six juillet	le mois dernier
no·voñ·bruh	*luh see zhwee·yeh*	*luh mwah dehrn·yay*
December		
décembre		
day·soñ·bruh		

Public holidays

New Year's Day	January 1
Good Friday	(Switzerland only)
Easter Monday	
Labour Day	May 1 (not Switzerland)
Ascension Day	
Whit Monday	
Bastille Day	July 14 (France only)
National Holiday	July 21 (Belgium only)
Assumption	August 15 (not Switzerland)
All Saints' Day	November 1 (not Switzerland)
Armistice Day	November 11 (not Switzerland)
Christmas Day	December 25
St Stephen's Day	December 26 (not France)

If you are travelling in Switzerland, it is worth remembering that each canton has its own local holidays.

Abbreviations

Cie or Co.	Compagnie (company)
h.	heure (o'clock)
M.	Monsieur (Mr)
Mlle.	Mademoiselle (Miss)
MM.	Messieurs (Messrs)
Mme.	Madame (Mrs)
M^o	Métro (underground)
NF	Nouveaux francs (new francs)
PTT	Postes télégraphes téléphones (French Post Office)
RER	Réseau express régional (fast suburban train service)
RATP	Régie autonome des transports parisiens (Paris Transport Organization)
RN	Route nationale (national trunk road)
SA	Société anonyme (limited company)
SNCF	Société nationale des chemins de fer français (French railways)
s.v.p.	s'il vous plaît (please)
TVA	Taxe sur la valeur ajoutée (Value Added Tax, VAT)

Signs and notices (see also Road signs p.18)

Accès aux quais	Baignade interdite	Défense de marcher
This way to the trains	No swimming	sur les pelouses
À louer	Caisse (*in shop*)	Keep off the grass
For rent, for hire	Pay here	Dégustation
Appuyez	Caisse (*in bank*)	Sampling (*of wine,*
Push	Cashier	*oysters, etc*)
Arrêt	Chaud (C)	En panne
Stop (*for bus etc*)	Hot	Out of order
Ascenseur	Complet	Entrée interdite
Lift (elevator)	Full	No entry
Attention	Dames	Entrée gratuite *or*
Be careful	Ladies	libre
À vendre	Défense de fumer	Admission free
For sale	No smoking	

French	English	French	English	French	English
Fermé		Messieurs		Réservé	
Closed		**Gentlemen**		**Reserved**	
Froid (F)		Ne pas toucher		Service compris	
Cold		**Do not touch**		**Tip included**	
Fumeurs		Non-fumeurs		Service non compris	
Smokers		**Nonsmokers**		**Tip not included**	
Gendarmerie		Occupé		Soldes	
Police		**Engaged**		**Sale**	
Hommes		Ouvert		Sonnez	
Gentlemen		**Open**		**Ring**	
Libre		Peinture fraîche		Sortie	
Vacant		**Wet paint**		**Exit**	
Libre-service		Poussez		Sortie de secours	
Self-service		**Push**		**Emergency exit**	
Maintenez le		Prière d'attendre		Syndicat d'initiative	
loqueteau levé –		**Please wait**		**Tourist information**	
l'ouverture des portes		Privé		**office**	
est automatique		**Private**		Tirez	
Lift the handle – the		Renseignements		**Pull**	
doors open		**Information**			
automatically					

Conversion tables

In the tables for weight and length, the central figure may be read as either a metric or a traditional measurement. So to convert from pounds to kilos you look at the figure on the right, and for kilos to pounds you want the figure on the left.

feet		metres	inches		cm	lbs		kg
3.3	1	0.3	0.39	1	2.54	2.2	1	0.45
6.6	2	0.61	0.79	2	5.08	4.4	2	0.91
9.9	3	0.91	1.18	3	7.62	6.6	3	1.4
13.1	4	1.22	1.57	4	10.6	8.8	4	1.8
16.4	5	1.52	1.97	5	12.7	11	5	2.2
19.7	6	1.83	2.36	6	15.2	13.2	6	2.7
23	7	2.13	2.76	7	17.8	15.4	7	3.2
26.2	8	2.44	3.15	8	20.3	17.6	8	3.6
29.5	9	2.74	3.54	9	22.9	19.8	9	4.1
32.9	10	3.05	3.9	10	25.4	22	10	4.5
			4.3	11	27.9			
			4.7	12	30.1			

°C	0	5	10	15	17	20	22	24	26	28	30	35	37	38	40	50	100
°F	32	41	50	59	63	68	72	75	79	82	86	95	98.4	100	104	122	212
Km	10	20	30	40	50	60	70	80	90	100	110	120					
Miles	6.2	12.4	18.6	24.9	31	37.3	43.5	49.7	56	62	68.3	74.6					

Tyre pressures

lb/sq in	15	18	20	22	24	26	28	30	33	35
kg/sq cm	1.1	1.3	1.4	1.5	1.7	1.8	2	2.1	2.3	2.5

Fuel

UK gallons	1.1	2.2	3.3	4.4	5.5	6.6	7.7	8.8
litres	5	10	15	20	25	30	35	40
US gallons	1.3	2.6	3.9	5.2	6.5	7.8	9.1	10.4

Basic French Grammar

NOUNS AND ARTICLES

Gender

This is one of the basic differences between French and English. In French, all nouns are either masculine or feminine. In English we say 'a/the wall' or 'a/the table', but in French it is '*un/le mur*' or '*une/la table*', reflecting the fact that *mur* is masculine and *table* is feminine.

Gender is nearly always unpredictable, and it simply has to be learned along with each new word you acquire. However, nouns referring to female people and animals are, largely, feminine, and for males they are masculine. We say 'largely' because there are some exceptions, e.g. *le professeur* (the teacher) can refer to either a man or a woman.

In the plural, the French definite article is *les*, regardless of gender, e.g. 'the walls', '*les murs*'; 'the tables', '*les tables*'. Equally, for all nouns in the singular beginning with a vowel or a silent *h*, *le* and *la* become *l'*, e.g. *l'air*, *l'hôtel*.

Definite article: Masculine singular — *le, l'* (before a vowel)
masculine plural — *les*
feminine singular — *la, l'* (before a vowel)
feminine plural — *les*

Indefinite article: masculine — *un* / feminine — *une*

In the plural, *s* is usually added to the word, as in English. But words ending in *-au*, *-eau*, *-eu* and some in *-ou* add *x* in the plural. Hence: *les tables*, the tables; *les couteaux*, the knives.

If a noun already ends in *s*, *x* or *z* in the singular, it does not change in the plural, e.g. *le nez*, *les nez* (the noses). Nouns ending in *-al* usually change this ending to *-aux*, e.g. *le cheval*, *les chevaux* (the horses). All exceptional plural endings are clearly shown in the French-English dictionary section.

Use of articles

In almost all cases where 'the' is not used in English, the article must be used in French. For instance:

apples are good this year   *les pommes sont bonnes cette année*
salmon is expensive   *le saumon est cher*
France is beautiful   *la France est belle*
he likes skiing   *il aime le ski*

A (à) + le/les, de + le/les

When the articles *le* and *les* are preceded by the prepositions *à* (at, to) or *de* (from, of) they are contracted thus:

$à + le = au$ $de + le = du$
$à + les = aux$ $de + les = des$

This does not apply to *à la* and *de la* which remain two separate words.

Du (du), de la, de l', des = some, any

e.g. some bread   *du pain*   some cream   *de la crème*
some ink   *de l'encre*   some apples   *des pommes*

These forms are used as in:

I should like some bread   *je voudrais du pain*
have you any apples?   *avez-vous des pommes?*

However, in a negative sentence only the word *de* is used meaning 'any':

I haven't any bread   *je n'ai pas de pain*
haven't you any apples?   *vous n'avez pas de pommes?*

ADJECTIVES

Position

Adjectives generally *follow* the noun in French

un plat délicieux   a *delicious* dish
une robe verte   a *green* dress

Among which as a general rule *precede* the noun are some very common adjectives:

grand (big)   *gros* (big)   *haut* (high)   *long* (long)   *petit* (small)   *vieux* (old)   *jeune* (young)   *bon* (good)   *mauvais* (bad)   *joli* (pretty)   *beau* (beautiful)   *nouveau* (new)   *ancien* (old)

Agreement

The adjective has to 'agree' in number (singular or plural) and in gender (masculine or feminine) with its noun. To make an adjective feminine, *e* is added to the masculine (unless the masculine form already ends in *e*) and for the plural *s* or *x* is added as for nouns. There are exceptions and these are clearly shown in the English-French dictionary section, e.g. the layout *doux, douce* in the dictionary means the masculine form is *doux* and the feminine *douce*. Where a third form is shown it is the plural form, e.g. *mon, ma, mes* (see also below — possessive adjectives).

Some examples:

Masculine singular	Feminine singular	Masculine plural	Feminine plural
*le **grand** arbre	la **grande** maison	les **grands** arbres	les **grandes** maisons
*le livre **bleu**	la porte **bleue**	les livres **bleus**	les portes **bleues**
le **bon plat	la **bonne** surprise	les **bons** plats	les **bonnes** surprises
le **beau garçon	la **belle** fille	les **beaux** garçons	les **belles** filles

* 'regular' adjectives   ** 'irregular' adjectives

Possessive adjectives ('my', 'his', 'her', etc.)

Like all adjectives, these must agree in number and gender with the noun they qualify, *not* with the gender of the owner. Thus it is *son chapeau* (= *his* or *her* hat), *sa montre* (= *his* or *her* watch) and *ses enfants* (= *his* or *her* children).

	with a masculine noun	with a feminine noun	with a plural noun of either gender
my	*mon*	*ma*	*mes*
your (*familiar form*)	*ton*	*ta*	*tes*
his/her/its	*son*	*sa*	*ses*
our	*notre*	*notre*	*nos*
your	*votre*	*votre*	*vos*
their	*leur*	*leur*	*leurs*

Demonstrative adjectives ('this', 'that')

These follow the same pattern as the possessives, having a separate form for masculine and feminine nouns, and a form for all plural nouns:

  ce bureau   this/that office
  cette fille   this/that girl
  ces stylos   these/those pens

The distinction between 'this' and 'that' is often not made, but if you want to be precise, the suffixes *-ci* and *-là* are added to the noun:

  ce garçon-ci   this boy   *ce garçon-là*   that boy
  ces pommes-ci   these apples   *ces pommes-là*   those apples

PRONOUNS

Personal pronouns

Subject	Direct object	Indirect object	in stressed position	Reflexive
SINGULAR				
1st person				
je (I)	*me, m' (me)*	*me, m', moi (to me)*	*moi (me)*	*me, m'*
2nd person				
tu (you)	*te, t' (you)*	*te, t', toi (to you)*	*toi (you)*	*te, t'*
3rd person (*m*)				
il (he/it)	*le, l' (him/it)*	*lui (to him/it)*	*lui (him/it)*	*se, s'*
3rd person (*f*)				
elle (she/it)	*la, l' (her/it)*	*lui (to her/it)*	*elle (her/it)*	*se, s'*
PLURAL				
1st person				
nous (we)	*nous (us)*	*nous (to us)*	*nous (us)*	*nous*
2nd person				
vous (you)	*vous (you)*	*vous (to you)*	*vous (you)*	*vous*
3rd person (*m*)				
ils (they)	*les (them)*	*leur (to them)*	*eux (them)*	*se, s'*
3rd person (*f*)				
elles (they)	*les (them)*	*leur (to them)*	*elles (them)*	*se, s'*

Notes

1) As all nouns are either masculine or feminine in French, the pronoun reflects the gender of nouns in French, so that *il* has the meaning 'he' or 'it', and *elle* can also refer to feminine things as well as people. This also applies, of course, to the plural *ils* and *elles*, and to all other 3rd person pronouns.
2) The forms *m'*, *t'*, *l'* and *s'* are used when the following word begins with a vowel.
3) The forms shown in the fourth column ('in stressed position') are used
  — following prepositions
  e.g. *avec moi* 'with me'   *après vous* 'after you'
  — if standing alone
  e.g. *Qui est-ce?* — *Moi*   'Who's there? Me'

4) Reflexive pronouns are used with reflexive verbs, shown in the dictionary section with **se** (or **s'**) preceding the infinitive. The reflexive pronoun has the value of 'oneself', e.g.:

se laver	**to wash oneself**
je me lave	I wash myself
tu te laves	you wash yourself
il/elle se lave	he/she washes him/herself
nous nous lavons	we wash ourselves
vous vous lavez	you wash yourselves
ils/elles se lavent	they wash themselves

Sometimes the value of 'oneself' is not reflected in the English translation, but if the French verb is given with **se**, you must use the appropriate form of the pronoun, e.g.

se lever	'to get up'	*je **me** lève**	I get up
se souvenir	'to remember'	*nous **nous** souvenons**	we remember

*For appropriate forms of the verbs see the section on verb conjugations.

Order of personal pronouns

1) The direct object pronoun *precedes* the verb (unlike in English, where it follows the verb):

   *il **le** fait*   he does *it*   *vous **m'**aidez*   you help *me*

Only in commands does the direct object pronoun *follow* the verb:

   *faites-**le*** do it   *aidez-**nous*** help us

Note the use of the stressed form of *me* (> *moi*) in this position (see the table of Personal Pronouns above). This also applies to the second person singular (*te* > *toi*) e.g. *lève-toi* 'get up'.

2) When both a direct and indirect object pronoun are used before the same verb the order is that of *person* (i.e. 1st person before 2nd person, and 2nd before 3rd):

   *il **me** le donne*   he gives it to me
   *vous **nous** le dites*   you say it to us

If the pronouns are of the same person the order is *direct before indirect*:

   *je **le** lui donne*   I give it to him
   *je **le** leur donne*   I give it to them

But if the pronouns come after the verb (i.e. in commands) the direct object pronoun always precedes the indirect:

   *donnez-**le**-lui* give it to him   *dites-**le**-moi* say it to me

Demonstrative pronouns

These are words meaning 'the one/ones' (as in 'the one in the window'), 'this (one)' and 'that (one)', 'these' and 'those', and are as follows:

   Masculine singular: *celui* / Masculine plural: *ceux*
   Feminine singular: *celle* / Feminine plural: *celles*

Possessive pronouns ('mine', 'his', etc.)

These also depend on the number and gender of the noun described (and not on the sex of the 'possessor' — *cf* the possessive adjectives, above):

	with a masculine noun	with a feminine noun	with a masculine plural noun	with a feminine plural noun
mine	*le mien*	*la mienne*	*les miens*	*les miennes*
yours (*familiar*)	*le tien*	*la tienne*	*les tiens*	*les tiennes*
his/hers/its	*le sien*	*la sienne*	*les siens*	*les siennes*
ours	*le nôtre*	*la nôtre*	*les nôtres*	*les nôtres*
yours	*le vôtre*	*la vôtre*	*les vôtres*	*les vôtres*
theirs	*le leur*	*la leur*	*les leurs*	*les leurs*

Example:

   A qui est-ce? — (C'est) le mien/la mienne
   Whose (literally: to whom) is it? — (It's) mine

Note that for this particular usage it is easier to avoid using the possessive pronoun and to say simply: *c'est à moi* (= literally, 'it is to me').

ADVERBS

These are usually formed by adding **-ment** to the feminine form of the adjective:

   fort (masculine) — *forte* (feminine) — *fortement* (adverb)
   large (masculine) — *large* (feminine) — *largement* (adverb)

If the masculine form of the adjective ends in **-ent** or **-ant**, the adverb is formed by adding **-emment** or **-amment** in place of the ending:

   patient — *patiemment*   *bruyant* — *bruyamment*

VERBS

Verb conjugations

The verb tables below give ending patterns for the 'regular' verbs. A separate list provides patterns for all the irregular verbs marked with an asterisk in the dictionary section of this book. Only four tenses are set out in this short grammar section, as you will rarely need any tense but the present, the imperfect, the future and the perfect.

Tenses

1) *Present*

There is no equivalent of the 'progressive' *-ing* form of English (e.g. I am read*ing*). This sense of 'being in the process of doing' is rendered by the simple present tense. Hence:

je mange = I eat *Or* I am eating

2) *Past*

Past actions are shown by the perfect or imperfect tense in French. The *perfect* tense is formed by the use of *avoir* ('to have'), plus the past participle (see table)

e.g. *donner*: *j'ai donné*   I gave, I have given

vous avez donné   you gave, you have given

Some verbs expressing the concepts of 'motion' or 'becoming' take *être* instead of *avoir* in the perfect tense. The main ones of these are: *aller, arriver, descendre, devenir, entrer, monter, mourir, naître, partir, rester, retourner, revenir, sortir, tomber, venir*.

Similarly, all reflexive verbs in French are conjugated with *être*:

e.g. *se mettre* (to begin): *je me suis mis* (I began)

For actions in the past which happened at a specific point in time, French always uses the *perfect* tense, which corresponds to our structure 'to have done'. This applies even when in English we would use a simple past tense:

I *did* it yesterday   *je l'ai fait hier* (literally: I *have done* it ...)

he *saw* him   *il l'a vu* (literally: he *has seen* him)

The French perfect is also used where this tense is used in English:

I *have seen* him   *je l'ai vu*   he *has done* it   *il l'a fait*

The *imperfect* tense in French is used only for an action or state in the past without definite limits in time, or for habitual actions in the past. It is a simple tense, whereby endings are added to the verb stem (see table)

il était malade   he *was* ill

nous habitions Londres pendant la guerre   we *lived* in London during the war

j'allais au bureau à 9 heures   I *went* (= used to go) to the office at 9

3) *Future*

Largely used as its English counterpart, the future tense endings (see table) are added to the infinitive form of the verb (for exceptions, see the table of irregular verbs).

Regular verb conjugations

The table below shows how to conjugate regular verbs ending in *-er*, *-ir* or *-re* in the infinitive (the form given in the dictionary), in all the tenses you will need for basic communication. For all other regular verbs with these endings (i.e. those NOT marked with an asterisk in the dictionary) remove the infinitive ending and add the endings shown.

INFINITIVE		
parler	*finir*	*rendre*

PRESENT		
je parle	*je finis*	*je rends*
tu parles	*tu finis*	*tu rends*
il/elle parle	*il/elle finit*	*il/elle rend*
nous parlons	*nous finissons*	*nous rendons*
vous parlez	*vous finissez*	*vous rendez*
ils/elles parlent	*ils/elles finissent*	*ils/elles rendent*

FUTURE		
je parlerai	*je finirai*	*je rendrai*
tu parleras	*tu finiras*	*tu rendras*
il/elle parlera	*il/elle finira*	*il/elle rendra*
nous parlerons	*nous finirons*	*nous rendrons*
vous parlerez	*vous finirez*	*vous rendrez*
ils/elles parleront	*ils/elles finiront*	*ils/elles rendront*

IMPERFECT		
je parlais	*je finissais*	*je rendais*
tu parlais	*tu finissais*	*tu rendais*
il/elle parlait	*il/elle finissait*	*il/elle rendait*
nous parlions	*nous finissions*	*nous rendions*
vous parliez	*vous finissiez*	*vous rendiez*
ils/elles parlaient	*ils/elles finissaient*	*ils/elles rendaient*

PERFECT*

j'ai parlé	*j'ai fini*	*j'ai rendu*
tu as parlé	*tu as fini*	*tu as rendu*
il/elle a parlé	*il/elle a fini*	*il/elle a rendu*
nous avons parlé	*nous avons fini*	*nous avons rendu*
vous avez parlé	*vous avez fini*	*vous avez rendu*
ils/elles ont parlé	*ils/elles ont fini*	*ils/elles ont rendu*

*If a verb takes *être* in the perfect instead of *avoir* as shown here, the verb form is the same but the relevant part of *être* replaces that of *avoir* (see *être* in the table below) e.g. *je suis allé* etc.

Irregular verb forms
PATTERNS FOR ALL VERBS MARKED WITH AN ASTERISK IN THE DICTIONARY

1) 'Semi-irregular' verbs. Some verbs are only 'irregular' in a predictable way:

letter(s) affected	change to	environment	example
c, g	ç, ge	before o, a	*manger — nous mangeons* *placer — nous plaçons*
l, t e	ll, tt è	before the endings e, es, ent and throughout the future tense	*appeler — j'appelle, ils appelleront* *jeter — je jette, ils jetteront* *acheter — j'achète, ils achèteront*
é	è	before the endings e, es, ent	*espérer — j'espère, ils espèrent*

2) Truly irregular verbs. The irregular forms shown below are: *1)* the present tense in full *2)* the first person of the future tense *3)* the first person of the imperfect tense *4)* the past participle, used with '*avoir*' or '*être*' to give the perfect tense. For the future and imperfect tenses, use the form shown but alternate the endings as in the table of regular verbs with the first person ending given here. For all other verbs marked with an asterisk in the dictionary and not covered in 1 above, refer to the verb in the table with an identical ending e.g. for *promettre* see *mettre*; for *cuire* see *conduire*.

acquérir *1) acquiers, acquiers, acquiert, acquérons, acquérez, acquièrent*
2) acquerrai 3) acquérais 4) acquis

aller *1) vais, vas, va, allons, allez, vont 2) irai 3) allais 4) allé*

asseoir (s') *1) assieds, assieds, assied, asseyons, asseyez, asseyent 2) assiérai*
3) asseyais 4) assis

avoir *1) ai, as, a, avons, avez, ont 2) aurai 3) avais 4) eu*

battre *1) bats, bats, bat, battons, battez, battent 2) battrai 3) battais*
4) battu

boire *1) bois, bois, boit, buvons, buvez, boivent 2) boirai 3) buvais*
4) bu

bouillir *1) bous, bous, bout, bouillons, bouillez, bouillent 2) bouillirai*
3) bouillais 4) bouilli

conduire *1) conduis, conduis, conduit, conduisons, conduisez, conduisent*
2) conduirai 3) conduisais 4) conduit

connaitre *1) connais, connais, connaît, connaissons, connaissez,*
connaissent 2) connaîtrai 3) connaissais 4) connu

coudre *1) couds, couds, coud, cousons, cousez, cousent 2) coudrai*
3) cousais 4) cousu

courir *1) cours, cours, court, courons, courez, courent 2) courrai*
3) courais 4) couru

croire *1) crois, crois, croit, croyons, croyez, croient 2) croirai*
3) croyais 4) cru

croître *1) croîs, croîs, croît, croissons, croissez, croissent 2) croîtrai*
3) croissais 4) crû

cueillir *1) cueille, cueilles, cueille, cueillons, cueillez, cueillent*
2) cueillerai 3) cueillais 4) cueilli

devoir *1) dois, dois, doit, devons, devez, doivent 2) devrai 3) devais*
4) dû

dire *1) dis, dis, dit, disons, dites, disent 2) dirai 3) disais 4) dit*

dissoudre 1) dissous, dissous, dissout, dissolvons, dissolvez, dissolvent 2) dissoudrai 3) dissolvais 4) dissous

dormir see *partir*

écrire 1) écris, écris, écrit, écrivons, écrivez, écrivent 2) écrirai 3) écrivais 4) écrit

être 1) suis, es, est, sommes, êtes, sont 2) serai 3) étais 4) été

exclure 1) exclus, exclus, exclut, excluons, excluez, excluent 2) exclurai 3) excluais 4) exclu

faire 1) fais, fais, fait, faisons, faites, font 2) ferai 3) faisais 4) fait

falloir 1) faut 2) faudra 3) fallait 4) fallu (used in 3rd person singular only)

fuir 1) fuis, fuis, fuit, fuyons, fuyez, fuient 2) fuirai 3) fuyais 4) fui

joindre 1) joins, joins, joint, joignons, joignez, joignent 2) joindrai 3) joignais 4) joint

lire 1) lis, lis, lit, lisons, lisez, lisent 2) lirai 3) lisais 4) lu

mentir see *sentir*

mettre 1) mets, mets, met, mettons, mettez, mettent 2) mettrai 3) mettais 4) mis

moudre 1) mouds, mouds, moud, moulons, moulez, moulent 2) moudrai 3) moulais 4) moulu

mourir 1) meurs, meurs, meurt, mourons, mourez, meurent 2) mourrai 3) mourais 4) mort

mouvoir 1) meus, meus, meut, mouvons, mouvez, meuvent 2) mouvrai 3) mouvais 4) mû

naître 1) nais, nais, naît, naissons, naissez, naissent 2) naîtrai 3) naissais 4) né

offrir see *ouvrir*

ouvrir 1) ouvre, ouvres, ouvre, ouvrons, ouvrez, ouvrent 2) ouvrirai 3) ouvrais 4) ouvert

paraître 1) parais, parais, paraît, paraissons, paraissez, paraissent 2) paraîtrai 3) paraissais 4) paru

partir 1) pars, pars, part, partons, partez, partent 2) partirai 3) partais 4) parti

peindre 1) peins, peins, peint, peignons, peignez, peignent 2) peindrai 3) peignais 4) peint

plaindre see *peindre*

plaire 1) plais, plais, plaît, plaisons, plaisez, plaisent 2) plairai 3) plaisais 4) plu

pleuvoir 1) pleut 2) pleuvra 3) pleuvait 4) plu (used in 3rd person singular only)

pourvoir 1) pourvois, pourvois, pourvoit, pourvoyons, pourvoyez, pourvoient 2) pourvoirai 3) pourvoyais 4) pourvu

pouvoir 1) peux, peux, peut, pouvons, pouvez, peuvent 2) pourrai 3) pouvais 4) pu

prendre 1) prends, prends, prend, prenons, prenez, prennent 2) prendrai 3) prenais 4) pris

prévoir see *pourvoir*

recevoir 1) reçois, reçois, reçoit, recevons, recevez, reçoivent 2) recevrai 3) recevais 4) reçu

résoudre 1) résous, résous, résout, résolvons, résolvez, résolvent 2) résoudrai 3) résolvais 4) résolu

rire 1) ris, ris, rit, rions, riez, rient 2) rirai 3) riais 4) ri

rompre 1) romps, romps, rompt, rompons, rompez, rompent 2) romprai 3) rompais 4) rompu

savoir 1) sais, sais, sait, savons, savez, savent 2) saurai 3) savais 4) su

sentir 1) sens, sens, sent, sentons, sentez, sentent 2) sentirai 3) sentais 4) senti

servir *1) sers, sers, sert, servons, servez, servent 2) servirai 3) servais 4) servi*

sortir *1) sors, sors, sort, sortons, sortez, sortent 2) sortirai 3) sortais 4) sorti*

souffrir see *ouvrir*

suffire *1) suffis, suffis, suffit, suffisons, suffisez, suffisent 2) suffirai 3) suffisais 4) suffi*

suivre *1) suis, suis, suit, suivons, suivez, suivent 2) suivrai 3) suivais 4) suivi*

taire *1) tais, tais, tait, taisons, taisez, taisent 2) tairai 3) taisais 4) tu*

tenir *1) tiens, tiens, tient, tenons, tenez, tiennent 2) tiendrai 3) tenais 4) tenu*

traire *1) trais, trais, trait, trayons, trayez, traient 2) trairai 3) trayais 4) trait*

vaincre *1) vaincs, vaincs, vainc, vainquons, vainquez, vainquent 2) vaincrai 3) vainquais 4) vaincu*

valoir *1) vaux, vaux, vaut, valons, valez, valent 2) vaudrai 3) valais 4) valu*

venir *1) viens, viens, vient, venons, venez, viennent 2) viendrai 3) venais 4) venu*

vivre *1) vis, vis, vit, vivons, vivez, vivent 2) vivrai 3) vivais 4) vécu*

voir *1) vois, vois, voit, voyons, voyez, voient 2) verrai 3) voyais 4) vu*

vouloir *1) veux, veux, veut, voulons, voulez, veulent 2) voudrai 3) voulais 4) voulu*

FRENCH–ENGLISH DICTIONARY

à *a prep* to/at; **aller* à Londres** *a·lay a loñ·druh* to go to London; **à l'école** *a lay·kol* to/at school; **au Portugal** *ō por·tōō·gal* to/in Portugal; **à 30 kilomètres** *a 30 kee·lo·meh·truh* 30 kilometres away; **100 kilomètres à l'heure** *100 kee·lo·meh·truh a lur* 100 km per hour; **à gauche/droite** *a gōsh/drwat* on/to the left/right; **à 4 heures** *a 4 ur* at 4 o'clock; **jeter* quelque chose à quelqu'un** *zhuh·tay kel·kuh shōz a kel·kuñ* to throw something at someone; **au mur** *ō mōōr* on the wall; **à la télévision** *a tay·lay·vee·zyoñ* on television; **l'homme au parapluie** *lom ō pa·ra·plwee* the man with the umbrella; **c'est à vous** *seh ta voo* it's your turn

abat-jour *a·ba·zhoor m* lampshade
abbaye *a·bay·ee f* abbey
abcès *ap·seh m* abscess
abdomen *ab·do·men m* abdomen
abeille *a·bay f* bee
abîmer *a·bee·may vt* damage; spoil
aboiement *a·bwah·moñ m* bark (of dog)
abolir *a·bo·leer vt* abolish
abonné(e) *a·bo·nay m/f* subscriber; **être* abonné(e) à** *eh·truh a·bo·nay a* subscribe to (periodical)
abonnement *a·bon·moñ m* subscription (to periodical)
aboyer *a·bwah·yay vi* bark
abréviation *a·bray·vya·syoñ f* abbreviation
abri *a·bree m* shelter
abricot *ab·ree·kō m* apricot
s'abriter *sa·bree·tay vr* shelter
abrupt(e) *a·brōōpt adj* abrupt (slope)
absent(e) *ap·soñ(·soñt) adj* absent; **absent(e) de chez soi** *ap·soñ(t) duh shay swah* away from home
absentéisme *ap·soñ·tay·eez·muh m* absenteeism
absolu(e) *ap·so·lōō adj* absolute
absorbant(e) *ap·sor·boñ(·boñt) adj* absorbent
absorber *ap·sor·bay vt* absorb (fluid); **absorber une firme** *ap·sor·bay ōōn feerm* to take over a firm
absorption *ap·sorp·syoñ f* takeover
s'abstenir* *sap·stuh·neer vr* abstain (in voting)
abstrait(e) *ap·streh(·stret) adj* abstract
absurde *ap·sōōrd adj* absurd
absurdités *ap·sōōr·dee·tay fpl* nonsense
acajou *a·ka·zhoo m* mahogany
accélérateur *ak·say·lay·ra·tur m* accelerator
accélérer* *ak·say·lay·ray vi* speed up; accelerate
accent *ak·soñ m* emphasis; accent; **l'accent circonflexe** *ak·soñ seer·koñ·fleks* circumflex (accent); **l'accent aigu** *ak·soñ ay·gōō* acute (accent); **l'accent grave** *ak·soñ grav* grave (accent); **l'accent sur quelque chose** *lak·soñ sōōr kel·kuh shōz* emphasis on something
accentuer *ak·soñ·tōō·ay vt* emphasize (syllable etc)
acceptable *ak·sep·ta·bluh adj* reasonable (price)

acceptation *ak·sep·ta·syoñ f* acceptance
accepter *ak·sep·tay vt* accept
accès *ak·seh m* access; fit (seizure)
accessible *ak·seh·see·bluh adj* accessible
accessoires *ak·seh·swahr mpl* accessories
accident *ak·see·doñ m* accident
accidentel(le) *ak·see·doñ·tel adj* accidental
accidentellement *ak·see·doñ·tel·moñ adv* by accident
acclamer *a·kla·may vt* cheer
accompagner *a·koñ·pa·nyay vt* accompany; **accompagner quelqu'un à la gare** *a·koñ·pa·nyay kel·kuñ a la gar* to see someone off at the station; **accompagner quelqu'un à la maison** *a·koñ·pa·nyay kel·kuñ a la meh·zoñ* to see someone home
accord *a·kor m* agreement; understanding; **être* d'accord avec quelqu'un** *eh·truh da·kor a·vek kel·kuñ* to agree with somebody; **se mettre* d'accord sur** *suh meh·truh da·kor sōōr* to agree on (price); **ne pas être* d'accord avec quelqu'un** *nuh pa zeh·truh da·kor a·vek kel·kuñ* to disagree with somebody; **nous étions tous d'accord** *noo zay·tyoñ toos da·kor* we were unanimous
accorder *a·kor·day vt* tune (instrument); grant (wish)
accotement *a·kot·moñ m* verge; **l'accotement stabilisé** *a·kot·moñ sta·bee·lee·zay* hard shoulder
accrocher *a·kro·shay vt* hang
s'accroître* *sa·krwah·truh vr* increase; accrue
accueil *a·kuhy m* welcome
accueillir* *a·kuh·yeer vt* greet; welcome
accumuler *a·kōō·mōō·lay vt* accumulate
accusation *a·kōō·za·syoñ f* accusation; charge
accusé de réception *a·kōō·zay duh ray·sep·syoñ m* receipt (for parcel)
accuser *a·kōō·zay vt* accuse
achat *a·sha m* purchase; **l'achat en gros** *a·sha oñ grō* bulk buying; **les achats** *a·sha* shopping; **faire* des achats** *fehr day za·sha* to go shopping
acheter* *ash·tay vt* buy; purchase
acheteur *ash·tur m* buyer
acheteuse *ash·tuhz f* buyer
achevé(e) *ash·vay adj* complete
achever* *ash·vay vt* complete
acide *a·seed adj* sour (sharp) □ *m* **l'acide** *a·seed* acid
acier *a·syay m* steel
acné *ak·nay m* acne
acompte *a·koñt m* down payment; deposit
acquérir* *a·kay·reer vt* acquire
acquisition *a·kee·zee·syoñ f* acquisition
acquitté(e) *a·kee·tay adj* paid
acrylique *a·kree·leek adj* acrylic
acte *akt m* act (of play); **l'acte de décès** *akt duh day·seh* death certificate; **l'acte de naissance** *akt duh nay·soñs* birth certificate
acteur *ak·tur m* actor

actif ak·teef m assets (financial) □ adj
actif(ive) ak·teef(·teev) active (energetic)
action ak·syon f share (finance); action; les **actions privilégiées** ak·syon pree·vee·lay·zhyay preference shares
actionnaire ak·syo·nehr m/f shareholder; investor
activité ak·tee·vee·tay f activity; en activité on nak·tee·vee·tay active (volcano)
actualité ak·tōō·a·lee·tay f current events; les **actualités** lay zak·tōō·a·lee·tay the news
actuel(le) ak·tōō·el adj present
adapter a·dap·tay vt adapt
addition ad·dee·syon f addition; check (bill)
additionner a·dee·syo·nay vt add (up) (numbers)
adjoint(e) ad·zhwan(·zhwant) m/f deputy (second-in-command)
administration ad·mee·nee·stra·syon f administration; civil service
admirer ad·mee·ray vt admire
adolescent(e) a·do·leh·son(·sont) m/f teenager
adopter a·dop·tay vt adopt
adresse a·dres f skill; address
adresser a·dre·say vt address (letter)
Adriatique a·dree·a·teek f Adriatic (Sea)
adulte a·dōōlt m/f adult; devenir* adulte duh·vuh·neer a·dōōlt to grow up; pour adultes poor a·dōōlt adult (movie etc)
aérer* a·eh·ray vt air (room, clothes)
aérien(ne) a·eh·ryan(·ryen) adj overhead (railway)
aérodynamique a·eh·ro·dee·na·meek adj streamlined (car)
aérogare a·eh·ro·gar f terminal
aéroglisseur a·eh·ro·glee·sur m hovercraft
aéroport a·eh·ro·por m airport
s'affaiblir sa·feh·bleer vr weaken
affaire a·fehr f case (lawsuit); affair (matter); deal; l'homme d'affaires om da·fehr businessman; la femme d'affaires fam da·fehr businesswoman; les affaires a·fehr business (dealings, work); belongings; pour affaires poor a·fehr on business; faire* des affaires avec quelqu'un fehr day za·fehr a·vek kel·kun to do business with someone
affamé(e) a·fa·may adj hungry; être* affamé(e) e·truh a·fa·may starve
affecter a·fek·tay vt affect
affection a·fek·syon f affection
affectueusement a·fek·tōō·uhz·mon adv love from (on letter)
affectueux(euse) a·fek·tōō·uh(·uhz) adj affectionate
affiche a·feesh f poster; notice
affranchissement a·fron·shees·mon m postage
affréter* a·fray·tay vt charter (plane, bus)
affreux(euse) a·fruh(·fruhz) adj awful
africain(e) a·free·kan(·ken) adj African
Afrique a·freek f Africa
Afrique du Sud a·freek dōō sōōd f South Africa
agacer* a·ga·say vt annoy
âge azh m age (of person); quel âge avez-vous? kel azh a·vay·voo how old are you?; entre deux âges on·truh duh zazh middle-aged

âgé a·zhay adj aged; elderly; plus âgé(e) plōō za·zhay senior (in age)
agence a·zhons f agency (office); l'agence de voyages a·zhons duh vwah·yazh travel agency
agenda a·zhan·da m diary
s'agenouiller sa·zhuh·noo·yay vr kneel
agent a·zhon m agent; l'agent de police a·zhon duh po·lees policeman; l'agent de voyages a·zhon duh vwah·yazh travel agent; l'agent maritime a·zhon ma·ree·teem shipping agent; l'agent de change a·zhon duh shonzh stockbroker; l'agent immobilier a·zhon ee·mo·bee·lyay estate agent; l'agent de la sûreté a·zhon duh la sōōr·tay detective
agile a·zheel adj agile
agir a·zheer vi work (medicine); act (behave); il s'agit de eel sa·zhee duh it's a question of
agité(e) a·zhee·tay adj rough (sea)
agneau a·nyō m lamb
agrafe a·graf f staple; hook and eye
agrafeuse a·gra·fuhz f stapler
agrandir a·gron·deer vt enlarge
agrandissement a·gron·dees·mon m enlargement; extension (building)
agréable a·gray·a·bluh adj pleasant; sweet (smell); nice (place, holiday)
agréer a·gray·ay vt accept; veuillez agréer mes salutations distinguées vuh·yay za·gray·yay may sa·lōō·ta·syon dee·stan·gay yours faithfully; je vous prie d'agréer l'expression de mes sentiments distingués zhuh voo pree da·gray·yay lek·spreh·syon duh may son·tee·mon dee·stan·gay yours truly
agréments a·gray·mon mpl amenities
agresser a·greh·say vt attack
agressif(ive) a·greh·seef(·seev) adj aggressive
agricole a·gree·kol adj agricultural
agriculture a·gree·kōōl·tōōr f agriculture
aide ed f help
aider ay·day vt help; ça ne nous aide pas sa nuh noo zed pah it's of no benefit (to us)
aigle eh·gluh m eagle
aigu(ë) ay·gōō adj sharp; high (pitch, voice)
aiguille ay·gwee f needle; hand (of clock); l'aiguille à tricoter ay·gwee a tree·ko·tay knitting needle
ail eye m garlic
aile ehl f wing
d'ailleurs dye·yur adv besides (moreover)
aimable ay·ma·bluh adj pleasant (person)
aimant eh·mon m magnet
aimer ay·may vt love; like; j'aimerais mieux aller au cinéma zheh·muh·reh myuh za·lay ō see·nay·ma I'd rather go to the cinema; j'aimerais un... zheh·muh·reh zun I should like a...; aimeriez-vous un café? ay·muh·ryay voo zun ka·fay would you like a cup of coffee?; aimer faire quelque chose ay·may fehr kel·kuh shōz to like doing something; j'aimerais bien y aller zheh·muh·reh byan ee a·lay I'd love to go; j'aimerais y aller zheh·muh·reh zee a·lay I'd like to go
aîné(e) ay·nay adj elder; eldest
ainsi an·see adv thus (in this way)
air ehr m tune; air; look (appearance); il a l'air malade eel a lehr ma·lad he

appears ill; **en plein air** *oñ plen ehr* open-air; **de plein air** *duh plen ehr* outdoor

airbus *ehr·bŏŏs m* air bus

aire de stationnement *ehr duh sta·syon·moñ f* lay-by; **l'aire de services** *ehr duh sehr·vees* service area

ajournement *a·zhoor·nuh·moñ m* adjournment

ajouter *a·zhoo·tay vt* add

ajusté(e) *a·zhŏŏs·tay adj* tight (*clothes*)

alarme *a·larm f* alarm (*signal, apparatus*)

alarmer *a·lar·may vt* alarm

album *al·bum m* album

alcool *al·kol m* alcohol; **l'alcool à brûler** *al·kol a brŏŏ·lay* methylated spirits

alcoolique *al·ko·leek m/f* alcoholic

alcoolisé(e) *al·ko·lee·zay adj* alcoholic (*drink*); **non alcoolisé(e)** *noñ al·ko·lee·zay* soft

alcôve *al·kŏv f* alcove

Alger *al·zhay m* Algiers

Algérie *al·zhay·ree f* Algeria

algérien(ne) *al·zhay·ryañ(·ryen) adj* Algerian

algues *alg fpl* seaweed

aliment *a·lee·moñ m* food

alimentation *a·lee·moñ·ta·syoñ f* grocery shop

Allah *a·lah m* Allah

allée *a·lay f* gangway (*passage*); drive (*driveway*)

Allemagne *al·ma·nyuh f* Germany; **en Allemagne** *oñ nal·ma·nyuh* in/to Germany

Allemagne de l'Est *al·ma·nyuh duh lest f* East Germany

Allemagne de l'Ouest *al·ma·nyuh duh lwest f* West Germany

allemand *al·moñ m* German □ *adj* **allemand(e)** *al·moñ(·moñd)* German; **il est Allemand** *eel eh tal·moñ* he's German; **elle est Allemande** *el eh tal·moñd* she's German

aller* *a·lay vi* go; **nous allons à la plage** *noo za·loñ za la plazh* we are going to the beach; **nous sommes allés à Paris** *noo som za·lay a pa·ree* we have been to Paris; **comment est-ce que nous y allons?** *ko·moñ es·kuh noo zee a·loñ* how do we get there?; **aller* bien** *a·lay byañ* to be well; **ce chapeau vous va** *suh sha·pō voo va* that hat suits you; **ça va sa va** it's OK; **comment allez-vous?** *ko·moñ ta·lay·voo* how are you?; **comment ça va?** *ko·moñ sa va* how are you getting on?; **je vais le faire** *zhuh veh luh fehr* I'm going to do it; **aller* acheter** *a·lay ash·tay* to go and buy; **allez-y!** *a·lay·zee* go ahead!; **allons-y** *a·loñ·zee* let's go; **s'en aller*** *soñ na·lay* to go away; **aller* de X à Y** *a·lay duh X a Y* to range from X to Y; **est-ce que ça ira?** *es·kuh sa ee·ra* will it do? (*be enough*); **aller* bien avec** *a·lay byañ a·vek* to match; **ça me va** *sa muh va* it fits (me); **ceci va avec votre robe** *suh·see va a·vek vo·truh rob* this goes with your dress

aller (simple) *a·lay sañ·pluh m* single ticket

allergie *a·lehr·zhee f* allergy

allergique à *a·lehr·zheek a adj* allergic to

alliage *a·lee·azh m* alloy

alliance *a·lyoñs f* wedding ring; alliance

allocation *a·lo·ka·syoñ f* allowance (*state payment*)

s'allonger* *sa·loñ·zhay vr* lie down

allouer *a·loo·ay vt* allocate (*funds*)

allumage *a·lŏŏ·mazh m* ignition (*car*)

allumé(e) *a·lŏŏ·may adj* on (*light, radio*)

allumer *a·lŏŏ·may vt* turn on; light (*fire, cigarette*); **allumer les phares** *a·lŏŏ·may lay far* to light up (*car*); **allumer la lumière** *a·lŏŏ·may la lŏŏ·myehr* to put on the light

allumette *a·lŏŏ·met f* match

allure *a·lŏŏr f* pace (*speed*)

allusion *a·lŏŏ·zyoñ f* reference; **faire* allusion à** *fehr a·lŏŏ·zyoñ a* refer to (*allude to*)

alors *a·lor adv* then

aloyau *a·lwah·yō m* sirloin

Alpes *alp fpl* Alps; **des Alpes** *day zalp* alpine

alphabet *al·fa·beh m* alphabet

alpinisme *al·pee·neez·muh m* mountaineering; **faire* de l'alpinisme** *fehr duh lal·pee·neez·muh* to go mountaineering

alternateur *al·tehr·na·tur m* alternator (*in car*)

altitude *al·tee·tŏŏd f* altitude

aluminium *a·lŏŏ·mee·nyum m* aluminium, aluminum

amalgamation *a·mal·ga·ma·syoñ f* amalgamation

amande *a·moñd f* almond; **la pâte d'amandes** *paht da·moñd* almond paste

amarrer *a·ma·ray vt* moor

amateur *a·ma·tur m* amateur

ambassade *oñ·ba·sad f* embassy

ambassadeur *oñ·ba·sa·dur m* ambassador

ambitieux(euse) *oñ·bee·syuh(·syuhz) adj* ambitious

ambition *oñ·bee·syoñ f* ambition

ambulance *oñ·bŏŏ·loñs f* ambulance

âme *ahm f* soul

amélioration *a·may·lyo·ra·syoñ f* improvement

améliorer *a·may·lyo·ray vt* improve; **s'améliorer** *sa·may·lyo·ray* improve

amende *a·moñd f* fine

amener* *a·muh·nay vt* bring (*person*)

amer *a·mehr adj* bitter

amère *a·mehr adj* bitter

américain(e) *a·may·ree·kañ(·ken) adj* American; **il est Américain** *eel eh ta·may·ree·kañ* he's American; **elle est Américaine** *el eh ta·may·ree·ken* she's American

Amérique *a·may·reek f* America; **l'Amérique du Nord** *a·may·reek dōō nor* North America

Amérique du Sud *a·may·reek dōō sŏŏd f* South America

Amérique latine *a·may·reek la·teen f* Latin America; **d'Amérique latine** *da·may·reek la·teen* Latin American

améthyste *a·may·teest f* amethyst

ami(e) *a·mee m/f* friend; **la petite amie** *puh·teet a·mee* girlfriend; **le petit ami** *puh·tee ta·mee* boyfriend; **entre amis** *oñ·tra·mee* informal (*party*)

amiante *a·myoñt f* asbestos

amical(e) *a·mee·kal adj* friendly

amidon *a·mee·doñ m* starch

amortir *a·mor·teer vt* absorb (*shock*)

amortisseur *a·mor·tee·sur m* shock absorber

amour *a·moor m* love

amoureux(euse) *a·moo·ruh(·ruhz) adj* in love

ampère *oñ·pehr m* amp

ample *oñ·pluh adj* loose (*clothing*)

amplificateur *oñ·plee·fee·ka·tur m* amplifier

ampoule *oñ·pool f* light bulb; blister (*on skin*); **l'ampoule de flash** *oñ·pool duh flash* flashbulb

amusant(e) *a·mōō·zoñ(·zoñt) adj* funny

amuse-gueule *a·mōōz·gul m* appetizer

amuser *a·mōō·zay vt* amuse; entertain; **s'amuser** *sa·mōō·zay* to enjoy oneself; **nous nous sommes bien amusés** *noo noo som byañ a·mōō·zay* we had a lovely time

an *oñ m* year; **tous les ans** *too lay zoñ* yearly

analyse *a·na·leez f* analysis

analyser *a·na·lee·zay vt* analyse

analyste-programmeur *a·na·leest·pro·gra·mur m/f* systems analyst

ananas *a·na·na m* pineapple

ancêtre *oñ·seh·truh m* ancestor

anchois *oñ·shwah m* anchovy

ancien(ne) *oñ·syañ(·syen) adj* old; former

ancre *oñ·kruh f* anchor

andouille *oñ·doo·yuh f* type of sausage

âne *an m* donkey

anémique *a·nay·meek adj* an(a)emic

anesthésique *a·nes·tay·zeek m* an(a)esthetic

ange *oñzh m* angel

angine *oñ·zheen f* tonsillitis

anglais *oñ·gleh m* English; **en anglais** *oñ noñ·gleh* in English

anglais(e) *oñ·gleh(·glez) adj* English; **il est Anglais** *eel eh toñ·gleh* he's English; **elle est Anglaise** *el eh toñ·glez* she's English

Angleterre *oñ·gluh·tehr f* England

angora *oñ·go·ra m* angora (*fabric*)

anguilles *oñ·geey f pl* eels

animal *a·nee·mal m* animal; **les animaux sauvages** *a·nee·mō sō·vazh* wildlife

animé(e) *a·nee·may adj* busy (*place*)

année *a·nay f* vintage; year (*as duration*); **l'année budgétaire** *a·nay bōōd·zheh·tehr* fiscal year

annexe *a·neks f* enclosure (*in letter*)

anniversaire *a·nee·vehr·sehr m* anniversary; birthday

annonce *a·noñs f* advertisement (*in small ads*); **faire* paraître une annonce pour trouver une secrétaire** *fehr pa·reh·truh ōōn a·noñs poor troo·vay ōōn suh·kray·tehr* to advertise for a secretary

annoncer* *a·noñ·say vt* announce

annuaire *a·nōō·ehr m* directory; **l'annuaire des téléphones** *a·nōō·ehr day tay·lay·fon* telephone directory

annuel(le) *a·nōō·el adj* annual; yearly

annuler *a·nōō·lay vt* cancel

anorak *a·ra·rak m* anorak

anormal(e) *a·nor·mal adj* unnatural

anse *oñs f* handle (*of cup*)

Antarctique *oñ·tark·teek m* Antarctic

antenne *oñ·ten f* mast (*radio*); aerial; antenna

antérieur(e) *oñ·tay·ree·ur adj* earlier

antibiotique *oñ·tee·byo·teek m* antibiotic

antidater *oñ·tee·da·tay vt* backdate

antigel *oñ·tee·zhel m* antifreeze

antihistaminique *oñ·tee·ee·sta·mee·neek m* antihistamine

antiquaire *oñ·tee·kehr m/f* antique dealer

antiquité *oñ·tee·kee·tay f* antique

antiseptique *oñ·tee·sep·teek m* antiseptic

août *oo m* August

apéritif *a·pay·ree·teef m* aperitif

apparaître* *a·pa·reh·truh vi* appear

appareil *a·pa·ray m* appliance; **l'appareil acoustique** *a·pa·ray a·koos·teek* hearing aid

appareil-photo *a·pa·ray·fo·tō m* camera

apparemment *a·pa·ra·moñ adv* apparently

appartement *a·par·tuh·moñ m* apartment; flat

appartenir* à *a·par·tuh·neer a vi* belong to

appât *a·pah m* bait (*in fishing*)

appel *a·pel m* call; **l'appel en préavis** *a·pel oñ pray·a·vee* person-to-person call

appeler* *a·puh·lay vt* call; **appelez-moi demain** *a·puh·lay·mwah duh·mañ* ring me tomorrow; **faire* appeler** *fehr a·puh·lay* to page; **s'appeler*** *sa·puh·lay* to be called; **comment vous appelez-vous?** *ko·moñ voo za·play voo* what is your name?; **je m'appelle Paul** *zhuh ma·pel Paul* my name is Paul

appendicite *a·pañ·dee·seet f* appendicitis

appétit *a·pay·tee m* appetite

applaudir *a·plo·deer vi* clap

applaudissements *a·plō·dees·moñ mpl* applause

apporter *a·por·tay vt* bring (*thing*)

apprécier *a·pray·see·ay vt* appreciate

apprendre* *a·proñ·druh vt* learn; teach; **apprendre quelque chose à quelqu'un** *a·proñ·druh kel·kuh shōz a kel·kuñ* to teach someone something; **j'apprends le français à l'école** *zha·proñ luh froñ·seh a lay·kol* I'm taking French at school

apprenti(e) *a·proñ·tee m/f* apprentice

apprivoisé(e) *a·pree·vwah·zay adj* tame (*animal*)

approbation *a·pro·ba·syoñ f* approval

approcher *a·pro·shay vi* approach (*season*); **s'approcher** *sa·pro·shay* approach (*person*); **s'approcher d'un endroit** *sa·pro·shay duñ noñ·drwah* to approach a place

approprié(e) *a·pro·pree·ay adj* suitable; proper (*appropriate*)

approuver *a·proo·vay vt* approve of

approximatif(ive) *a·prok·see·ma·teef (·teev) adj* approximate

appui-tête *a·pwee·tet m* headrest

appuyer sur *a·pwee·yay sōōr vt* push; **s'appuyer contre quelque chose** *sa·pwee·yay koñ·truh kel·kuh shōz* to lean against something; **appuyez sur le bouton** *a·pwee·yay sōōr luh boo·toñ* press the button

après *a·preh adv* afterward(s) □ *prep* after; **c'est après le coin** *seh ta·preh luh kwañ* it's round the corner; **après que** *a·preh kuh* after; **le service après-vente** *sehr·vees a·preh·voñt* after-sales service; **après notre départ** *a·preh no·truh day·par* after we had left

après-demain *a·preh·duh·mañ adv* the day after tomorrow

après-midi *a·preh·mee·dee m* afternoon; **de l'après-midi** *duh la·preh·mee·dee* p.m.

aquarium *a·kwa·ryum m* aquarium

Arabe *a·rab m/f* Arab □ *adj* **arabe** *a·rab* Arabic □ *m* **l'arabe** *a·rab* Arabic

arachide *a·ra·sheed* f groundnut

araignée *a·reh·nyay* f spider

arbitre *ar·bee·truh* m referee (*sports*); umpire

arbre *ar·bruh* m tree; **l'arbre de Noël** *ar·bruh duh no·el* Christmas tree; **l'arbre à cames** *l'ar·bra kam* camshaft

arbrisseau *ar·bree·sō* m shrub

arc-en-ciel *ark·oñ·syel* m rainbow

architecte *ar·shee·tekt* m architect

architecture *ar·shee·tek·tōōr* f architecture

Arctique *ark·teek* m Arctic

ardoise *ar·dwaz* f slate

arête *a·ret* f ridge; bone (*of fish*)

argent *ar·zhoñ* m money; silver (*metal*); **payer quelque chose en argent comptant** *pay·yay kel·kuh shōz oñ nar·zhoñ koñ·toñ* to pay cash for something; **un bracelet en argent** *uñ bras·leh oñ nar·zhoñ* a silver bracelet; **faire° de l'argent** *fehr duh lar·zhoñ* to make money; **l'argent de poche** *l'ar·zhoñ duh posh* pocket money

argenterie *ar·zhoñ·tree* f silver (*ware*)

argentin(e) *ar·zhoñ·tañ(·teen) adj* Argentine

Argentine *ar·zhoñ·teen* f Argentina

argile *ar·zheel* f clay

argot *ar·gō* m slang

arithmétique *a·reet·may·teek* f arithmetic

arme *arm* f weapon; **l'arme à feu** *arm a fuh* firearm

armé(e) *ar·may adj* armed (*person*)

armée *ar·may* f army; **l'armée de l'air** *ar·may duh lehr* air force

armes *arm* fpl arms

armoire *ar·mwar* f cupboard

arracher *a·ra·shay* vt pull out; tear off; **se faire° arracher une dent** *suh fehr a·ra·shay ōōn doñ* to have a tooth taken out

arranger° *a·roñ·zhay* vt arrange (*flowers, furniture*)

arrêt *a·reh* m stopping; **l'arrêt facultatif** *a·reh fa·kōōl·ta·teef* request stop; **l'arrêt d'autobus** *a·reh dō·tō·bōōs* bus stop

arrêter *a·reh·tay* vt switch off (*engine*); stop; arrest; **s'arrêter** *sa·reh·tay* stop; **arrêter de faire quelque chose** *a·reh·tay duh fehr kel·kuh shōz* to stop doing something; **la voiture s'est arrêtée** *la vwah·tōōr set a·reh·tay* the car stopped

arrière *a·ryehr adj* rear (*wheel*); **faire° marche arrière** *fehr marsh a·ryehr* to back the car □ m **l'arrière** *a·ryehr* back; **en arrière** *oñ na·ryehr* backwards; **regarder en arrière** *ruh·gar·day oñ na·ryehr* to look behind

arriéré *a·ree·eh·ray* m arrears; **avoir° de l'arriéré dans ses paiements** *a·vwahr duh la·ree·eh·ray doñ say pay·moñ* to be in arrears with a payment

arriéré(e) *a·ree·eh·ray adj* backward (*child*)

arrière-plan *a·ryehr·ploñ* m background

arrivée *a·ree·vay* f arrival

arriver *a·ree·vay* vi happen; arrive; **quand est-ce que le train doit arriver?** *koñ tes·kuh luh trañ dwah a·ree·vay* when is the train due?; **arriver à faire quelque chose** *a·ree·vay a fehr kel·kuh shōz* to manage to do something; **qu'est-ce qui lui est arrivé?** *kes·kee lwee eh ta·ree·vay* what happened to him?; **arriver à** *a·ree·vay a*

to reach (*arrive at*); **vous y arrivez?** *voo zee a·ree·vay* can you manage?

arrondissement *a·roñ·dees·moñ* m district (*administrative*)

art *ar* m art

artère *ar·tehr* f artery; main road

arthrite *art·reet* f arthritis

artichaut *ar·tee·shō* m artichoke

article *ar·tee·kluh* m item; article (*in newspaper*); **les articles de toilette** *ar·tee·kluh duh twah·let* toiletries

articulation *ar·tee·kōō·la·syoñ* f joint (*of body*); **l'articulation des phalanges** *ar·tee·kōō·la·syoñ day fa·loñzh* knuckle

artificiel(le) *ar·tee·fee·syel adj* man-made; artificial

artisan *ar·tee·zoñ* m craftsman

artiste *ar·teest* m/f artist

as *ahs* m ace (*cards*)

ascenseur *a·soñ·sur* m elevator; lift

asiatique *a·zya·teek adj* Asian

Asie *azee* f Asia

asperge *a·spehrzh* f asparagus

asperger° *a·spehr·zhay* vt sprinkle

aspirateur *a·spee·ra·tur* m vacuum cleaner

aspirine *a·spee·reen* f aspirin

assaisonnement *a·seh·zon·moñ* m seasoning; dressing (*salad*)

assassin *a·sa·sañ* m killer

assassiner *a·sa·see·nay* vt murder

assemblée *a·soñ·blay* f meeting

s'asseoir° *sa·swahr* vr sit down; **asseyez-vous!** *a·say·yay·voo* sit down!

assez *a·say adv* quite (*fairly*); rather; **assez grand(e)** *a·say groñ (groñd)* big enough; **assez bon(ne)** *a·say boñ (bon)* fair (*average*) □ *pron* enough; **j'en ai assez** *zhoñ nay a·say* I have enough; I'm tired of it; **assez de temps** *a·say duh toñ* enough time; **assez de livres** *a·say duh lee·vruh* enough books

assiette *as·yet* f plate

assignation *a·see·nya·syoñ* f summons

assis(e) *a·see(·seez) adj* sitting

assistant(e) social(e) *a·see·stoñ(·stoñt) so·syal* m/f social worker

assister à *a·sees·tay a* vt attend (*meeting etc*)

association *a·so·sya·syoñ* f association; society

associé(e) *a·so·syay* m/f associate; partner (*in business*)

assorti(e) *a·sor·tee adj* assorted; matching

assortiment *a·sor·tee·moñ* m assortment

assurance *a·sōō·roñs* f insurance; **l'assurance tous-risques** *a·sōō·roñs too reesk* comprehensive insurance; **la compagnie d'assurances** *koñ·pan·yee da·sōō·roñs* insurance company

assurance-vie *a·sōō·roñs·vee* f life insurance

assuré(e) *a·sōō·ray adj* confident; insured

assurer *a·sōō·ray* vt insure; **ce train assure la correspondance avec le train de 16.45** *suh trañ a·sōō·ra la ko·res·poñ·doñs a·vek luh trañ duh 16.45* this train connects with the 16.45; **s'assurer contre quelque chose** *sa·sōō·ray koñ·truh kel·kuh shōz* to insure against something

asthme *as·muh* m asthma

astucieux(euse) *a·tōō·syuh(·syuhz) adj* shrewd

atelier *a·tuh·lyay* m workshop

Athènes *a·ten* f Athens

athlète *at·let* m/f athlete

Atlantique *at·loñ·teek* m Atlantic Ocean

atlas *at·las* m atlas

atout *a·too* m trump (*cards*); **prendre* avec l'atout** *proñ·dra·vek la·too* trump

attache *a·tash* f clip; tow-bar (*on car*)

attacher *a·ta·shay* vt bind (*tie*); fasten; attach; **attachez vos ceintures** *a·ta· shay vo sañ·tōōr* fasten seat belts; **attacher un chien à un poteau** *a·ta·shay uñ shyañ a uñ po·tō* to tie a dog to a post

attaque *a·tak* f attack

attaque d'apoplexie *a·tak da·po·plek· see* f stroke

attaquer *a·ta·kay* vt attack; **s'attaquer à** *sa·ta·kay a* tackle (*problem*)

atteindre* *a·tañ·druh* vt reach

attendre *a·toñ·druh* vi wait; **faire* attendre quelqu'un** *fehr a·toñ·druh kel· kuñ* to keep someone waiting □ vt attendre *a·toñ·druh* wait for; **attendre avec impatience** *a·toñ·druh a·vek añ·pa·syoñs* to look forward to; **elle attend un bébé** *el a·toñ uñ bay·bay* she's expecting a baby

attention *a·toñ·syoñ* excl look out; **faites attention!** *fet a·toñ·syoñ* be careful!; **attention à la marche** *a·toñ·syoñ a la marsh* mind the step

atterrir *a·tay·reer* vi land (*plane*)

atterrissage *a·tay·ree·sazh* m landing (*of plane*); **l'atterrissage en catastrophe** *a·tay·ree·sazh oñ ka·tas·trof* crash-landing; **l'atterrissage forcé** *a· tay·ree·sazh for·say* emergency landing

attitude *a·tee·tōōd* f attitude

attraper *a·tra·pay* vt catch; trick

attribuer *a·tree·bōō·ay* vt allocate (*duties*)

au = **à** + **le**

aube *ōb* f dawn

auberge *ō·berzh* f inn; **l'auberge de jeunesse** *ō·berzh duh zhuh·nes* youth hostel

aubergine *ō·behr·zheen* f aubergine; eggplant

aucun(e) *ō·kuñ(·kōōn)* pron none; no, not any

au-delà de *ō·duh·lah duh* prep beyond

au-dessus *ō·duh·sōō* adv above; **au-dessus de ses moyens** *ō·duh·sōō duh say mwah·yañ* beyond his means; **la maison est au-dessus de la vallée** *la meh·zoñ eh tō·duh·sōō duh la va·lay* the house is above the valley; **au-dessus vous voyez...** *ō·duh·sōō voo vwah·yay*, you can see...

audio-visuel(le) *ō·dyō·vee·zōō·el* adj audio-visual

augmentation *ōg·moñ·ta·syoñ* f rise (*in prices, wages*); raise; growth (*in amount etc*); increase

augmenter *ōg·moñ·tay* vt/i increase □ vt boost (*sales*) □ vi rise (*prices*)

au gratin *ō gra·tañ* adj au gratin

aujourd'hui *ō·zhoor·dwee* adv today

au revoir *ō·ruh·vwahr* excl goodbye

aussi *ō·see* adv also; too; as well; **moi aussi** *mwah ō·see* so do I; **lui aussi** *lwee ō·see* so is he; **aussi grand que** *ō·see groñ kuh* as big as

Australie *os·tra·lee* f Australia

australien(ne) *os·tra·lyañ(·lyen)* adj Australian; **il est Australien** *eel eñ tos·tra·lyañ* he's Australian; **elle est Australienne** *el eh tos·tra·lyen* she's Australian

autant *ō·toñ* adv so much; **autant que**

ō·toñ kuh as much/many as; **pour autant que je sache** *poor ō·toñ kuh zhuh sash* as far as I know

autel *ō·tel* m altar

auteur *ō·tur* m author; writer

authentique *ō·toñ·teek* adj genuine

autobus *ō·tō·bōōs* m bus; **le service d'autobus** *sehr·vees dō·tō·bōōs* bus service

automatique *ō·tō·ma·teek* adj automatic □ m **l'automatique** *ō·tō·ma· teek* S.T.D.

automatiquement *ō·tō·ma·teek·moñ* adv automatically

automatisation *ō·tō·ma·tee·za·syoñ* f automation

automatiser *ō·tō·ma·tee·zay* vt computerize (*system*)

automne *ō·ton* m autumn; fall (*season*)

automobiliste *ō·tō·mō·bee·leest* m/f motorist

autoroute *ō·tō·root* f motorway, freeway; **l'autoroute à péage** *ō·tō·root a pay·yazh* toll motorway

auto-stop *ō·tō·stop* m hitchhiking; **faire* de l'auto-stop** *fehr duh lō·tō· stop* hitchhike

autostoppeur *ō·tō·sto·pur* m hitchhiker

autostoppeuse *ō·tō·sto·puhz* f hitchhiker

autour *ō·toor* adv around; **nous étions assis autour de la table** *noo zay·tyoñ za·see zō·toor duh la ta·bluh* we sat round the table; **regarder autour de soi** *ruh·gar·day ō·toor duh swah* to look around; **aller* autour du monde** *a·lay ō·toor dōō moñd* to go around the world

autre *ō·truh* adj other □ m/f **l'autre** *ō· truh* the other; **l'autre jour** *lō·truh zhōōr* the other day; **je voudrais voir une autre chemise** *zhuh voo·dreh vwahr ōōn ō·truh shu·meez* I want to see another shirt; **lequel?** - **l'un ou l'autre** *luh·kel* - *luñ oo lō·truh* which one? - either; **l'autre sexe** *lō·truh seks* the opposite sex; **autre chose** *ō· truh shōz* something else

autrefois *ō·truh·fwah* adv once (*formerly*)

autrement *ō·truh·moñ* adv otherwise

Autriche *ō·treesh* f Austria

autrichien(ne) *ō·tree·shyañ(·shyen)* adj Austrian; **il est Autrichien** *eel eñ tō· tree·shyañ* he's Austrian; **elle est Autrichienne** *el eh tō·tree·shyen* she's Austrian

aux = **à** + **les**

en aval *oñ na·val* adv downstream

avalanche *a·voñ·say* vi gain (*clock*) □ vt/i advance; **ma montre avance** *ma moñ·truh a·voñs* my watch is fast

avant *a·voñ* adv, prep before; **avant que** *a·voñ kuh* before; **nous y serons avant 4 heures** *noo zee suh·roñ a·voñ 4 ur* we'll be there by 4 o'clock; **avant de me coucher** *a·voñ duh muh koo·shay* before I go to bed □ m, n **avant** *a·voñ* front; **à l'avant** *a la·voñ* at the front; **en avant** *oñ na·voñ* for-

avalanche *a·va·loñsh* f avalanche

avaler *a·va·lay* vt swallow

avance *a·voñs* f advance (*loan*); **vous arrivez en avance** *voo za·ree·vay oñ na·voñs* you're early; **en avance sur les autres** *oñ na·voñs sōōr lay zō·truh* ahead of the others; **à l'avance, d'avance** *a la·voñs, d'a·voñs* in advance; **faire* des projets à l'avance** *fehr day pro·zhay za la·voñs* to plan ahead

avancer *a·voñ·say* vi gain (*clock*) □ vt/i advance; **ma montre avance** *ma moñ·truh a·voñs* my watch is fast

ward(s); **trop en avant** *trō poñ na·voñ* too far forward

avantage *a·voñ·tazh m* advantage; benefit

avant-hier *a·voñ·tyehr adv* the day before yesterday

avant-première *a·voñ·pruh·myehr f* preview

avant-propos *a·voñ·pro·pō m* introduction (in book)

avare *a·var adj* mean (miserly)

avarié(e) *a·va·ryay adj* off (meat)

s'avarier *sa·va·ryay vr* go bad

avec *a·vek prep* with

avenir *a·vuh·neer m* future; **à l'avenir** *a la·vuh·neer* in future

aventure *a·voñ·tōōr f* adventure

avenue *a·vuh·nōō f* avenue

averse *a·vehrs f* shower (rain)

avertir *a·vehr·teer vt* inform; warn

avertisseur *a·vehr·tee·sur m* horn; alarm

aveugle *a·vuh·gluh adj* blind (person)

aviation *a·vya·syoñ f* aviation; flying

avion *a·vyoñ m* plane; aircraft; **voyager* en avion** *vwah·ya·zhay oñ na·vyoñ* fly; **par avion** *par a·vyoñ* by air; by plane; by air mail; **aimer l'avion** *ay·may la·vyoñ* to like flying; **l'avion à réaction** *a·vyoñ na ray·ak·syoñ* jet (plane)

aviron *a·vee·roñ m* oar; rowing (sport); **faire* de l'aviron** *fehr duh la·vee·roñ* row

avis *a·vee m* opinion; advice note; **changer* d'avis** *shoñ·zhay da·vee* to change one's mind; **avec avis de réception** *a·vek a·vee duh ray·sep·syoñ* by recorded delivery; **à mon avis** *a moñ na·vee* in my opinion

avocat *a·vo·ka m* avocado (pear); barrister; lawyer

avoine *a·vwahn f* oats

avoir* *a·vwahr vt* have; **j'ai faim** *zhay fañ* I am hungry

avoué *a·voo·ay m* attorney; solicitor

avouer *a·voo·ay vt* confess

avril *a·vreel m* April

B

baby-sitter *bay·bee·see·tehr m* baby-sitter

bac *bak m* ferry

baccara *ba·ka·rah m* baccarat

bacon *ba·koñ m* bacon

badminton *bad·meen·ton m* badminton

bagages *ba·gazh mpl* luggage; **les bagages à main** *ba·gazh a mañ* hand-luggage

bagarre *ba·gar f* fight

bague *bag f* ring (on finger); **la bague de fiançailles** *bag duh fee·yoñ·sye* engagement ring

baguette *ba·get f* stick of (French) bread

baguettes *ba·get fpl* chopsticks

baie *bay f* berry; bay (on coast)

se baigner *suh bay·nyay vr* bathe; **aller* se baigner** *a·lay suh bay·nyay* to go swimming

baignoire *bay·nwahr f* bath (tub)

bail *bye m* lease

bâiller *bye·yay vi* yawn

bain *bañ m* bath

baiser *beh·zay m* kiss

baisse *bes f* fall (decrease); reduction (in price)

baisser *beh·say vi* fall (prices etc) □ *vt* turn down (heat, etc); reduce (price)

bal *bal m* ball; dance

balai *ba·lay m* broom; **le balai à laver** *ba·lay a la·vay* mop

balance *ba·loñs f* scales (for weighing); **la balance des paiements** *la ba·loñs day pay·moñ* balance of payments; **la balance commerciale** *ba·loñs ko·mehr·syal* balance of trade

balancer* *ba·loñ·say vt* swing; **se balancer*** *suh ba·loñ·say* swing

balançoire *ba·loñ·swahr f* swing

balayer *ba·lay·yay vt* sweep (floor)

balcon *bal·koñ m* circle (in theatre); balcony; **le premier balcon** *pruh·myay bal·koñ* dress circle; **le dernier balcon** *dehr·nyay bal·koñ* gallery

baleine *ba·len f* whale

balle *bal f* bullet; ball; **la balle de golf** *bal duh golf* golf ball

ballet *ba·lay m* ballet

ballon *ba·loñ m* balloon; ball (inflated)

balustrade *ba·lōōs·trad f* rail (on bridge, balcony)

bambou *boñ·boo m* bamboo

banane *ba·nan f* banana

banc *boñ m* bench (seat); **le banc de sable** *boñ duh sa·bluh* sandbank

bande *boñd f* strip (stripe, length); gang; **la bande de magnétoscope** *boñd duh man·yay·to·skop* videotape; **la bande sonore** *boñd so·nor* sound track; **la bande magnétique** *boñd ma·nyay·teek* magnetic tape; **la bande médiane** *boñd may·dyan* central reservation

bandit armé *boñ·dee ar·may m* gunman

banlieue *boñ·lyuh f* suburbs; outskirts; **de banlieue** *duh boñ·lyuh* suburban

banlieusard(e) *boñ·lyuh·zar(·zard) m/f* commuter

bannière *ba·nyehr f* banner

banque *boñk f* bank (finance); **la banque d'affaires** *boñk da·fehr* merchant bank; **la banque de données** *boñk duh do·nay* data bank, data base

banquet *boñ·kay m* banquet; feast

banquier *boñ·kyay m* banker

baptême *ba·tem m* baptism

baptiste *bap·teest adj* Baptist

bar *bar m* saloon; bar

barbe *barb f* beard

barbecue *bar·buh·kōō m* barbecue

barboter *bar·bo·tay vi* splash; paddle

barème *ba·rem m* scale

barman *bar·man m* barman; bartender

barrage routier *ba·razh roo·tyay* road block

barre *bar f* bar (rod)

barrer *ba·ray vt* block; cross; cross out

barrière *ba·ryehr f* barrier; fence

bas *bah m* bottom (of page, list); stocking; **en bas** *oñ bah* below; downstairs; **vers le bas** *vehr luh bah* downward(s); **du bas** *dōō bah* bottom

bas(se) *ba (bas) adj* low; **c'est la marée basse** *seh la ma·ray bas* the tide is out

bascule *bas·kōōl f* seesaw

basculeur de phares *bas·kōō·lur duh far m* dip-switch

base *bahz f* basis; base; **de base** *duh bahz* basic

base-ball *bays·bol m* baseball

baser *bah·zay vt* base

basket-ball *bas·ket·bol m* basketball

bassin *ba·sañ m* pond (artificial)

bataille *ba·tye f* battle

bateau *ba·tō m* boat; ship; **le bateau de plaisance** *ba·tō duh play·zoñs* pleas-

ure boat; **le bateau à moteur** ba·tō a
mo·tur motorboat
bâtiment bah·tee·moñ m building
bâton bah·toñ m stick
bâtonnet glacé ba·to·nay gla·say m
popsicle
batterie ba·tree f battery (in car)
battre* ba·truh vt beat; break (record);
se battre* suh ba·truh fight
bavardage ba·var·dazh m gossip
bavarder ba·var·day vi gossip
bazar ba·zar m general store
beau bō adj handsome, beautiful;
lovely; fine (weather); **au beau fixe** ō
bō feeks settled; **il fait beau** eel feh
bō the weather's fine
beaucoup bō·koo pron, adv much;
beaucoup de lait bō·koo duh leh
plenty of milk; much/a lot of milk;
beaucoup de gens bō·koo duh zhoñ
many/a lot of people; **je l'aime beaucoup** zhuh lem bō·koo I like it very
much; **je n'en ai pas beaucoup** zhuh
noñ nay pah bō·koo I haven't very
much; **beaucoup mieux** bō·koo myuh
much better; **beaucoup plus grand**
bō·koo plōō groñ much bigger; **vous
en avez beaucoup?** voo zoñ na·vay
bō·koo have you got much?; **pas
beaucoup** pah bō·koo not much
beau-fils bō·fees m son-in-law; stepson
beau-frère bō·frehr m brother-in-law
beau-père bō·pehr m father-in-law;
stepfather
beauté bō·tay f beauty
bébé bay·bay m baby
bêcher beh·shay vt dig (ground)
beige bayzh adj beige
beignet beh·nyeh m fritter; doughnut
belle bel adj beautiful; lovely; fine
(weather)
belle-fille bel·feey f daughter-in-law;
stepdaughter
belle-mère bel·mehr f mother-in-law;
stepmother
belle-sœur bel·sur f sister-in-law
bénéfice bay·nay·fees m profit; benefit
bénéficiaire bay·nay·fee·syehr m/f
payee
Bénélux bay·nay·lōōks m Benelux
bénir bay·neer vt bless
béquille bay·keey f crutch
berceau behr·sō m cradle
bercer* ber·say vt rock
berline behr·leen f saloon (car)
besoin buh·zwañ m need; **avoir* besoin
de** av·wahr buh·zwañ duh need; **vous
n'avez pas besoin de venir** voo na·vay
pa buh·zwañ duh vuh·neer you
needn't come
bétail bay·tye m cattle
bête bet adj stupid
bêtises bay·teez fpl rubbish (nonsense)
béton bay·toñ m concrete; **en béton** oñ
bay·toñ concrete
betterave bet·rahv f beetroot
beurre bur m butter
biberon bee·buh·roñ m bottle (baby's)
Bible bee·bluh f Bible
bibliothèque bee·blyo·tek f library
bicyclette bee·see·klet f bicycle; **faire*
de la bicyclette** fehr duh la bee·see·
klet to cycle; to go cycling
bidet bee·deh m bidet
bien byañ adv well; right; good; **eh
bien!** ay byañ well!; **jouer bien au
golf** zhoo·ay byañ ō golf to be good
at golf; **bien sûr** byañ sōōr of course;
il va bien eel va byañ he's all right
(safe, fit); **être* bien faite** eh·truh
byañ fet to have a nice figure; **très**

bien! treh byañ (that's) fine! □ m **les
biens d'équipement** byañ day·keep·
moñ capital goods; **le lait vous fait
du bien** luh leh voo feh dōō byañ
milk is good for you; **ça vous fera du
bien** sa voo fuh·ra dōō byañ it'll do
you good
bien que byañ kuh conj although; **bien
que vous pensiez...** byañ kuh voo
poñ·syay though you may think...
bientôt byañ·tō adv soon; shortly
bienvenu(e) byañ·vuh·nōō adj welcome
bière byehr f beer; **la bière brune** byehr
brōōn bitter; **la bière blonde** byehr
bloñd lager; **la bière à la pression**
byehr a la preh·syoñ draft beer;
draught beer
bifteck beef·tek m steak
bifurcation bee·fōōr·ka·syoñ f fork (in
road)
bigoudi bee·goo·dee m curler (for hair)
bijou bee·zhoo m jewel; **les bijoux** bee·
zhoo jewellery; **les bijoux (de) fantaisie** bee·zhoo (duh) foñ·tay·zee costume jewellery
bijoutier bee·zhoo·tyay m jeweller
bikini bee·kee·nee m bikini
bilan bee·loñ m balance sheet
bilingue bee·lañg adj bilingual
billard bee·yar m billiards
bille beey f marble (ball)
billet bee·yeh m ticket; note (bank
note); **le billet de banque** bee·yeh duh
boñk bank note; **un billet de
deuxième classe** uñ bee·yeh duh duz·
yem klas a second class ticket; **le
billet aller-retour** bee·yeh a·lay·ruh·
toor return ticket; **le billet simple**
bee·yeh sañ·pluh one-way ticket
biologie bee·o·lo·zhee f biology
bis bees m encore; **bis!** bees encore!
biscuit bees·kwee m biscuit; cracker
bizarre bee·zar adj strange
blaireau bleh·rō m shaving brush
blâmer blah·may vt blame
blanc bloñ m breast (of poultry) □ adj
blanc bloñ white; blank; **le chèque en
blanc** shek oñ bloñ blank cheque;
laissez en blanc s'il vous plaît leh·say
oñ bloñ seel voo pleh please leave
blank
blanche bloñsh adj white; blank
blanchisserie bloñ·shee·suh·ree f laundry (place)
blazer bla·zehr m blazer
blé blay m wheat
blessé(e) bleh·say adj injured
blesser bleh·say vt injure; offend; **se
blesser** suh bleh·say to hurt oneself
blessure bleh·sōōr f injury; wound
bleu(e) bluh adj blue; very rare
(steak); **bleu marine** bluh ma·reen
navy blue □ m **le bleu** bluh bruise
bleus de travail bluh duh tra·vye mpl
overalls
bloc blok m block; pad (notepaper)
blocage des salaires blo·kazh day sa·
lehr m wage freeze
blond(e) bloñ (bloñd) adj fair (hair);
blond(e)
bloquer blo·kay vt block (road); **se
bloquer** suh blo·kay jam (machine);
bloquer le passage blo·kay luh pa·
sazh to be in the way
blouse blooz f overall; smock
blouson bloo·zoñ m jerkin
bocal bo·kal m jar
bock bok m glass of beer
bœuf buhf m beef
boire* bwahr vt drink; **buvez donc**

quelque chose! *bōō·vay doňk kel·kuh shōz* have a drink!

bois *bwah m* wood; **en bois** *oň bwah* wooden

boisson *bwah·soň f* drink

boîte *bwaht f* can (*container*); box; **la boîte postale** *bwaht pos·tal* P.O. Box; **la boîte aux lettres** *bwaht ō leh·truh* letter box; mailbox; **la boîte de nuit** *bwaht duh nwee* night club; **la boîte à gants** *bwaht a goň* glove compartment; **la boîte de vitesse** *bwaht duh vee·tes* gearbox; **la boîte d'allumettes** *bwaht da·lōō·met* matchbox; **en boîte** *oň bwaht* canned

boiter *bwah·tay vi* limp

bol *bol m* bowl (*for food*); basin (*dish*)

bombe *boňb f* bomb; aerosol

bon *boň m* token; voucher; **le bon de commande** *boň duh ko·moňd* order-form

bon(ne) *boň (bon) adj* good; right; **bon marché** *boň mar·shay* cheap; **les épinards sont bons pour la santé** *lay zay·pee·nar soň boň poor la soň·tay* spinach is good for you; **à quoi bon?** *a kwah boň* what's the point?

bonbon *boň·boň m* sweet; **le bonbon à la menthe** *boň·boň a la moňt* mint

bonde *boňd f* plug (*for basin etc*)

bondé(e) *boň·day adj* crowded

bonheur *bon·ur m* happiness

bonhomme de neige *bo·nom duh nezh m* snowman

bonjour *boň·zhoor excl* hullo; good morning/afternoon

bonne *bon adj see* **bon**

bonnet *bo·neh m* cap; **le bonnet de bain** *bo·neh duh baň* bathing cap

bonsoir *boň·swahr excl* good evening

boom *boom m* boom (*economic*)

bord *bor m* border; verge; edge; **à bord** *a bor* on board (*ship, plane*); **aller* à bord** *a·lay a bor* to go aboard; **à bord du bateau** *a bor dōō ba·tō* aboard the ship; **le bord de la mer** *bor duh la mehr* seaside; **le bord du trottoir** *bor dōō tro·twahr* curb

bordeaux *bor·dō adj* maroon

bordure *bor·dōōr f* border

borne *born f* terminal (*electricity*)

bosse *bos f* bump (*lump*); dent; hump (*on road*)

botte *bot f* boot; bunch; **la botte de caoutchouc** *bot duh ka·oot·shoo* wellington boot

bottin *bo·taň m* directory

bouche *boosh f* mouth

bouchée *boo·shay f* bite (*of food*)

boucher *boo·shay vt* block (*pipe*); plug □ *m* **le boucher** *boo·shay* butcher

boucherie *boo·shuh·ree f* butcher's (*shop*)

bouchon *boo·shoň m* stopper; cork (*of bottle*); top; tailback

boucle *boo·kluh f* curl; buckle; loop; **la boucle d'oreille** *boo·kluh do·ray* earring

boudin *boo·daň m* black pudding

boue *boo f* mud

bouée *boo·ay f* buoy; **la bouée de sauvetage** *boo·ay duh sōv·tazh* lifebelt; life preserver

boueux(euse) *boo·uh(·uhz) adj* muddy (*water*)

bouger* *boo·zhay vt/i* move

bougie *boo·zhee f* candle; sparking plug

bouillir* *boo·yeer vi* boil; **faire* bouillir** *fehr boo·yeer* boil

bouilloire *boo·yuh·wahr f* kettle

bouillon *boo·yoň m* stock (*for soup etc*)

bouillotte *boo·yot f* hot-water bottle

boulanger *boo·loň·zhay m* baker

boulangerie *boo·loň·zhuh·ree f* bakery

boule *bool f* ball; bowl; **les boules** **Quiès** *bool kyes* earplugs; **la boule de neige** *bool duh nezh* snowball

bouleau *boo·lō m* birch (*tree*)

boulette *boo·let f* dumpling

bouquet *boo·kay m* bunch (*of flowers*)

bourbon *boor·boň m* bourbon

bourgeois(e) *boor·zhwah(·zhwahz) adj* middle-class

bourgeon *boor·zhoň m* bud

Bourse *boors f* stock market; stock exchange; **la bourse** *boors* grant (*to student*)

boussole *boo·sol f* compass

bout *boo m* end (*of street, table*); tip

bouteille *boo·tay f* bottle; **la bouteille thermos** *boo·tay tehr·mos* vacuum flask

boutique *boo·teek f* shop

bouton *boo·toň m* button; switch; spot (*pimple*); knob; **le bouton de col** *boo·toň duh kol* collar stud; **le bouton de manchette** *boo·toň duh moň·shet* cuff link

bouton-pression *boo·toň·pre·syoň m* press-stud

boxe *boks f* boxing

boycotter *boy·ko·tay vt* boycott

bracelet *bras·lay m* bracelet

braisé(e) *breh·zay adj* braised

brancard *broň·kar m* stretcher

branche *broňsh f* branch (*of tree*)

brancher *broň·shay vt* plug in

branlant(e) *broň·loň(·loňt) adj* loose (*stone*)

branler *broň·lay vi* wobble (*chair etc*)

braquer *bra·kay vt* point (*gun*); aim (*gun etc*); **braquer un fusil sur quelqu'un** *bra·kay uň fōō·zee sōōr kel·kuň* to aim a gun at someone

bras *brah m* arm (*of person*)

brasserie *bra·suh·ree f* brewery

break *brek m* station wagon; estate (*car*)

bref *bref adj* brief

bretelle *bruh·tel f* strap; **sans bretelles** *soň bruh·tel* strapless; **les bretelles** *bruh·tel* braces; **la bretelle d'accès** *bruh·tel dak·seh* slip-road

brève *brev adj* brief

brevet d'invention *bruh·vay daň·voň·syoň m* patent

bricolage *bree·ko·lazh m* do-it-yourself

bride *breed f* bridle

bridge *bridge m* bridge (*game*)

brillant(e) *bree·yoň(·yoňt) adj* shiny; bright; brilliant

briller *bree·yay vi* shine; **faire* briller** *fehr bree·yay* polish (*metal*); **le soleil brille** *luh so·lay breey* the sun is out

brindille *braň·deey f* twig

brioche *bree·osh f* brioche

brique *breek f* brick

briquet *bree·keh m* cigarette lighter

brise *breez f* breeze

briser *bree·zay vt* smash

briseur de grève *bree·zur duh grev m* strike-breaker

britannique *bree·ta·neek adj* British; **il est Britannique** *eel eh bree·ta·neek* he's British; **elle est Britannique** *el eh bree·ta·neek* she's British

broche *brosh f* brooch; spit (*for roasting*)

brochette *bro·shet f* skewer; kebab

brocoli *bro·ko·lee m* broccoli

brodé(e) *bro·day adj* embroidered
broderie *bro·duh·ree f* embroidery
bronchite *broñ·sheet f* bronchitis
bronzage *broñ·zazh m* suntan
bronze *broñz m* bronze □ *adj* **bronzé(e)**
 broñ·zay sun-tanned
bronzer *broñ·zay vi* tan (*in sun*)
brosse *bros f* brush; la brosse à cheveux *bros a shuh·vuh* hairbrush; la
brosse à dents *bros a doñ* toothbrush; la brosse à ongles *bros a oñ·
gluh* nailbrush
brosser *bro·say vt* brush
brouette *broo·et f* wheelbarrow
brouillard *broo·yar m* fog; il y a du
brouillard *eel ya doo broo·yar* it's
foggy
brouiller *broo·yay vt* mix up
brouillon *broo·yoñ m* draft (*rough outline*)
bruine *brōō·een f* drizzle
bruit *brwee m* noise; on dirait le bruit
d'une voiture *oñ dee·reh luh brwee
dōōn vwah·tōōr* it sounds like a car
brûler *brōō·lay vt* burn; brûler un feu
rouge *brōō·lay uñ fuh roozh* to go
through a red light; je me suis brûlé
le bras *zhuh muh swee brōō·lay luh
brah* I've burnt my arm
brûlure *brōō·lōōr f* burn; les brûlures
d'estomac *brōō·lōōr des·to·ma* heartburn
brume *brōōm f* mist
brumeux(euse) *brōō·muh(·muhz) adj*
misty
brun(e) *bruñ (brōōn) adj* brown; dark
(*hair*); brun roux *bruñ roo* tan
brushing *bruh·sheeng m* blow-dry
brusque *brōōsk adj* abrupt (*person*);
sharp (*bend*)
brut(e) *brōōt adj* gross (*before deductions*); pretax (*profit*); raw (*unprocessed*); crude (*oil etc*)
brutal(e) *brōō·tal adj* brutal
Bruxelles *brōō·sel f* Brussels
bruyant(e) *brwee·yoñ(·yoñt) adj* noisy
bûche *bōōsh f* log (*of wood*)
budget *bōōd·zhay m* budget
buffet *bōō·fay m* buffet; sideboard
buisson *bwee·soñ m* bush
bulbe *bōōlb m* bulb
bulldozer *bōōl·dô·zehr m* bulldozer
bulle *bōōl f* bubble
bulletin *bōōl·tañ m* bulletin; le bulletin
météorologique *bōōl·tañ may·tay·o·
ro·lo·zheek* weather forecast; le bulletin de consigne *bōōl·tañ duh koñ·
see·nyuh* baggage check
bungalow *buñ·ga·lō m* bungalow
bureau *bōō·rō m* desk (*in office*); office; study (*room*); le bureau central
bōō·rō soñ·tral head office; le bureau
des objets trouvés *bōō·rō day zob·
zhay troo·vay* lost property office; le
bureau de poste *bōō·rō duh post* post
office; le bureau de réception *bōō·rō
duh ray·sep·syoñ* reception desk
buste *bōōst m* bust
but *bōō m* goal; purpose; aim (*intention*); à but lucratif *a bōō lōō·kra·
teef* profit-making
butagaz *bōō·ta·gaz m* Calor gas

C

ça *sa pron* that; oui, c'est ça *wee seh sa*
yes, that's right; qu'est-ce que c'est
que ça? *kes·kuh seh kuh sa* what is
that?
cabane *ka·ban f* hut
cabas *ka·ba m* shopping bag

cabine *ka·been f* cabin (*in ship*); cubicle; la cabine téléphonique *ka·been
tay·lay·fo·neek* telephone booth
cabinet *ka·bee·neh m* office; les cabi-
nets *ka·bee·neh* toilet; le cabinet de
consultation *ka·bee·neh duh koñ·
sōōl·ta·syoñ* doctor's office; consulting room
câble *kah·bluh m* cable
cacahuète *ka·ka·wet f* peanut
cacao *ka·ka·ō m* cocoa
cachemire *kash·meer m* cashmere
cacher *ka·shay vt* hide; se cacher *suh·
ka·shay* hide
cachet *ka·shō m* dungeon
cactus *kak·tōōs m* cactus
cadavre *ka·da·vruh m* body (*corpse*)
cadeau *ka·dō m* gift; le cadeau de mariage *ka·dō duh ma·ree·azh* wedding
present
cadenas *kad·na m* padlock
cadre *ka·druh m* frame (*of picture*);
executive; les cadres moyens *ka·druh
mwah·yañ* middle management
café *ka·fay m* coffee; café; le café noir
ka·fay nwahr black coffee; le café au
lait *ka·fay ō leh* white coffee; le café
en poudre *ka·fay oñ poo·druh* instant coffee
cafétéria *ka·fay·tay·rya f* cafeteria
cafetière *kaf·tyehr f* coffeepot
cage *kazh f* cage
cagnotte *ka·nyot f* pool (*game*)
cahier *ka·yay m* notebook
caille *kye f* quail
caillou *kye·yoo m* pebble
caisse *kes f* crate; case (*of wine*);
checkout (*in store*); cashdesk; till; la
caisse d'emballage *kes doñ·ba·lazh*
packing case; la caisse de retraite *kes
duh ruh·tret* pension fund; la caisse
d'épargne *kes day·par·nyuh* savings
bank
caissier *keh·syay m* cashier; teller
caissière *keh·syehr f* cashier; teller
calcium *kal·syum m* calcium
calcul *kal·kōōl m* calculation
calculatrice *kal·kōō·la·trees f* calculator
calculer *kal·kōō·lay vt* calculate
caleçon de bain *kal·soñ duh bañ m*
swimming trunks
calendrier *ka·loñ·dryay m* calendar
caler *ka·lay vi* stall (*car engine*)
call-girl *kol·geerl f* call girl
calmant *kal·moñ m* painkiller; tranquillizer
calme *kalm m* peace (*calm*) □ *adj* calm
calorie *ka·lo·ree f* calorie
cambrioleur *koñ·bree·o·lur m* burglar
caméra *ka·may·ra f* camera (*TV*);
cine-camera
camion *ka·myoñ m* truck, lorry; le camion de déménagement *ka·myoñ
duh day·may·nazh·moñ* removal van
camion-citerne *ka·myoñ·see·tehrn m*
tanker (*truck*)
camionnette *ka·myo·net f* van
campagne *koñ·pa·nyuh f* country (*not
town*); countryside; campaign; à la
campagne *a la koñ·pa·nyuh* in the
country; la campagne de publicité
koñ·pa·nyuh duh pōō·blee·see·tay
publicity campaign; la campagne de
presse *koñ·pa·nyuh duh pres* press-
campaign
camper *koñ·pay vi* camp; aller* camper *a·lay koñ·pay* to go camping
camping *koñ·ping m* camping;
camp(ing) site
Canada *ka·na·da m* Canada

canadien(ne) *ka·na·dyañ(·dyen)* adj
Canadian; **il est Canadien** *eel eh ka·na·dyañ* he's Canadian; **elle est Canadienne** *el eh ka·na·dyen* she's Canadian
canal *ka·nal* m canal
canapé *ka·na·pay* m sofa; canapé
canard *ka·nar* m duck
canasta *ka·na·sta* f canasta
cancer *koñ·sehr* m cancer
candidat(e) *koñ·dee·da(·dat)* m/f candidate
canif *ka·neef* m penknife; pocketknife
caniveau *ka·nee·vô* m gutter (*in street*)
canne *kan* f cane; walking stick; **la canne à pêche** *kan a pesh* fishing rod
cannelle *ka·nel* f cinnamon
canon *ka·noñ* m gun
canot *ka·nô* m boat; **le canot pneumatique** *ka·nô pnuh·ma·teek* dinghy (*inflatable*); **le canot de sauvetage** *ka·nô duh sôv·tazh* lifeboat (*from shore*)
cantine *koñ·teen* f canteen
cantique *koñ·teek* m hymn
caoutchouc *ka·oot·shoo* m rubber (*material*)
capable *ka·pa·bluh* adj capable; **capable de** *ka·pa·bluh duh* capable of
cape *kap* f cape
capitaine *ka·pee·ten* m captain; **le capitaine de port** *ka·pee·ten duh por* harbo(u)r master
capital *ka·pee·tal* m capital (*finance*)
capitale *ka·pee·tal* f capital (*city*)
capitalisme *ka·pee·ta·leez·muh* m capitalism
capitaliste *ka·pee·ta·leest* m/f capitalist
capitaux *ka·pee·tô* mpl capital
capot *ka·pô* m bonnet (*of car*)
capsule *kap·sôôl* f capsule
capturer *kap·tôô·ray* vt capture
capuchon *ka·pôô·shoñ* m hood
car *kar* m coach □ conj because
caractère *ka·rak·tehr* m character
carafe *ka·raf* f carafe; decanter
caramel *ka·ra·mel* m toffee; caramel
carat *ka·ra* m carat
caravane *ka·ra·van* f caravan
carbone *kar·bon* m carbon; sheet of carbon paper; carbon copy
carburateur *kar·bôô·ra·tur* m carburet(t)or
cardigan *kar·dee·goñ* m cardigan
caresser *ka·reh·say* vt pat; stroke; cuddle
cargaison *kar·geh·zoñ* f cargo; shipment
carnaval *kar·na·val* m carnival
carnet *kar·neh* m notebook; diary; book (*of stamps, tickets*); **le carnet de chèques** *kar·neh duh shek* chequebook
carotte *ka·rot* f carrot
carré *ka·ray* m square □ adj **carré(e)** *ka·ray* square; **un mètre carré** *uñ meh·truh ka·ray* a square metre
carreau *ka·rô* m diamonds (*cards*); tile (*on floor, wall*); **à carreaux** *a ka·rô* check(er)ed
carrefour *kar·foor* m intersection (*of roads*); crossroads
carrelet *ka·ruh·lay* m plaice
carrière *ka·ryehr* f career; quarry
carte *kart* f map (*of country*); chart (*map*); card; menu; **la carte postale** *kart pos·tal* postcard; **la carte de Noël** *kart duh no·el* Christmas card; **la carte des vins** *kart duh vañ* wine list; **la carte à jouer** *kart a zhoo·ay* playing card; **la carte de vœux** *kart*

duh vuh greetings card; **la carte grise** *kart greez* logbook (*of car*); **la carte d'abonnement** *kart da·bon·moñ* season ticket; **la carte verte** *kart vehrt* green card; **la carte de crédit** *kart duh kray·dee* credit card; **la carte d'identité** *kart dee·doñ·tee·tay* identity card; **jouer aux cartes** *zhoo·ay ô kart* to play cards; **à la carte** *a la kart* à la carte
cartel *kar·tel* m cartel
carter *kar·tehr* m sump
carton *kar·toñ* m cardboard; carton; box; **le carton ondulé** *kar·toñ oñ·dôô·lay* corrugated paper
cartouche *kar·toosh* f cartridge (*for gun*)
cas *kah* m case (*instance*); **en cas de** *oñ kah duh* in case of; **en tout cas** *oñ too kah* in any case
caserne *ka·zehrn* f barracks; **la caserne de pompiers** *ka·zehrn duh poñ·pyay* fire station
cash-flow *kash·flô* m cash flow
casier *ka·zyay* m rack; locker
casino *ka·zee·nô* m casino
casque *kask* m helmet; **le casque protecteur** *kask pro·tek·tur* crash helmet; **le casque à écouteurs** *kask a ay·koo·tur* headphones
casquette *kas·ket* f cap (*hat*)
casse-croûte *kas·kroot* m snack
casser *ka·say* vt break; **se casser** *suh ka·say* break; **se casser le bras** *suh ka·say luh brah* to break one's arm
casserole *kas·rol* f pot (*for cooking*); saucepan
casse-tête *kas·tet* m puzzle
cassette *ka·set* f cassette; cartridge (*of tape*); **la cassette vidéo** *ka·set vee·day·ô* videocassette
cassis *ka·sees* m blackcurrant
catalogue *ka·ta·log* m catalog(ue)
cathédrale *ka·tay·dral* f cathedral
catholique *ka·to·leek* adj catholic
cauchemar *kosh·mar* m nightmare
cause *kôz* f cause; **à cause de** *a kôz duh* because of
causer *kô·zay* vt cause
caution *kô·syoñ* f bail (*for prisoner*); security (*for loan*); deposit (*for key etc*); **sous caution** *soo kô·syoñ* on bail
cave *kav* f cellar; **la cave à vin** *kav a vañ* wine cellar
caverne *ka·vehrn* f cave
caviar *ka·vyar* m caviar(e)
ce *suh* adj this; that; **qu'est-ce que c'est?** *kes kuh seh* what's that?; **qui est-ce?** *kee es* who's that?; **c'est à dire...** *seh ta deer* that is (to say)...; **c'est ce que je veux** *seh suh kuh zhuh vuh* this is what I want; **ce garçon-là** *suh gar·soñ la* that boy; **c'est à 5 kilomètres** *seh ta 5 kee·lo·me·truh* it's 5 kilometres
ceci *suh·see* pron this
céder* *say·day* vi give in □ vt **céder* la priorité** *say·day la pree·o·ree·tay* to yield (*to traffic*)
cédille *say·deey* f cedilla
cèdre *seh·druh* m cedar
C.E.E. *say·uh·uh* f E.E.C.
ceinture *sañ·tôôr* f belt (*for waist*); **la ceinture de sécurité** *sañ·tôôr duh say·kôô·ree·tay* safety belt
célan *say·loñ* m pilchard
célèbre *say·leh·bruh* adj famous
célébrer* *say·lay·bray* vt celebrate
céleri *say·luh·ree* m celery
céleri-rave *say·luh·ree·rav* m celeriac

célibataire *say·lee·ba·tehr adj* single (*not married*) □ **le célibataire** *say·lee·ba·tehr* bachelor

celle *sel pron* the one

celle-ci *sel·see pron* this one

celle-là *sel·la pron* that one

celles *sel pron* the ones

celles-ci *sel·see pron* these

celles-là *sel·la pron* those

cellophane *seh·lo·fan f* cellophane

cellule *seh·lōōl f* cell

Celsius *sel·syōōs adj* Celsius

celui *suh·lwee pron* the one

celui-ci *suh·lwee·see pron* this one

celui-là *suh·lwee·la pron* that one

cendre *son·druh f* ash (*cinders*)

cendrier *son·dree·ay m* ashtray

censé *son·say adj* supposed

cent *sent m* cent □ *num* cent *son* hundred; **cent quatre-vingt-cinq** *son ka·truh·van·sank* a hundred (and) eighty five; **cent personnes** *son pehr·son* a hundred people

centaine *son·ten f* about a hundred; **des centaines de livres** *day son·ten duh le·vruh* hundreds of books

centenaire *son·tuh·nehr m* centenary

centième *son·tyem adj* hundredth

centigrade *son·tee·grad adj* centigrade

centilitre *son·tee·lee·truh m* centilitre

centimètre *son·tee·meh·truh m* centimetre

central *son·tral m* exchange (*telephone*)

central(e) *son·tral adj* central

central téléphonique *son·tral tay·lay·fo·neek m* telephone exchange

centre *son·truh m* centre; **le centre de Chicago** *luh son·truh duh shee·ka·gō* downtown Chicago; **le centre médical** *son·truh may·dee·kal* clinic; **le centre ville** *son·truh veel* city centre; **le centre commercial** *son·truh ko·mehr·syal* shopping centre; **le centre de sports et loisirs** *son·truh duh spor ay lwah·zeer* leisure centre

cependant *suh·pon·don adv* however

cerceau *sehr·sō m* hoop

cercle *sehr·kluh m* circle; ring

cercueil *sehr·kuhy m* coffin

céréale *say·ray·al f* cereal

cérémonie *say·ray·mo·nee f* ceremony

cerf *sehr m* deer

cerf-volant *sehr·vo·lon m* kite

cerise *suh·reez f* cherry

cerisier *suh·ree·zee·ay m* cherry tree

certain(e) *sehr·tañ(·ten) adj* definite; sure; certain; **c'est certain qu'il est malade** *seh sehr·tañ keel eh ma·lad* he's definitely ill □ *pron* **certains d'entre eux étaient...** *sehr·tañ don·truh ay·teh* some (of them) were...

certainement *sehr·ten·mon adv* definitely; certainly

certificat *sehr·tee·fee·ka m* certificate

cérumen *say·rōō·men m* wax (*in ear*)

cerveau *sehr·vō m* brain

cervelle *sehr·vel f* brains (*as food*)

ces *say adj* those; these; **ces garçons-là** *say gar·son·la* those boys; **ces femmes-ci** *say fam·see* these women

sans cesse *sons ses adv* continuously

cesser *seh·say vt/i* stop

cette *set adj* this; that; **cette femme-là** *set fam·la* that woman

ceux *suh pron* the ones

ceux-ci *suh·see pron* these

ceux-là *suh·la pron* those

chacun(e) *sha·kuñ(·kōōn) pron* each; everyone; **chacun d'entre eux** *sha·kuñ don·truh* each of them

chagrin *sha·grañ m* grief

chaîne *shen f* range (*of mountains*); chain; channel (*TV*); **la chaîne hi-fi** *shen ee·fee* hi-fi

chaîne de montage *shen duh mon·tazh f* assembly line

chair *shehr f* flesh

chaise *shez f* chair; **la chaise longue** *shez long* deckchair; **la chaise haute** *shez ōt* highchair

châle *shahl m* shawl; wrap

chalet *sha·leh m* chalet

chaleur *sha·lur f* heat

chaloupe *sha·loop f* launch; **la chaloupe de sauvetage** *sha·loop duh sōv·tazh* lifeboat (*on ship*)

chambre *shon·bruh f* bedroom; room (*in hotel*); lodgings; **une chambre pour une personne** *ōōn shon·bruh poor ōōn pehr·son* a single room; **la chambre pour deux personnes** *shon·bruh poor duh pehr·son* double room; **la chambre à coucher** *shon·bruh a koo·shay* bedroom; **la Chambre de Commerce** *shon·bruh duh ko·mehrs* Chamber of Commerce; **la chambre d'enfants** *shon·bruh don·fon* nursery; **la chambre d'amis** *shon·bruh da·mee* guest-room

chameau *sha·mō m* camel

champ *shon m* field; **le champ de foire** *shon duh fwahr* fairground; **le champ de courses** *shon duh koors* racecourse

champagne *shon·pa·nyuh m* champagne

champignon *shon·pee·nyon m* mushroom

champion *shon·pyon m* champion

championne *shon·pyon f* champion

chance *shons f* luck; **avoir* de la chance** *a·vwahr duh la shons* to be lucky; **il a de fortes chances de...** *eel a duh fort shons duh* he has a good chance of...; **bonne chance!** *bon shons* good luck!

chancelier *shon·suh·lyay m* chancellor (*in Germany, Austria*)

change *shonzh m* exchange

changement *shon·zhuh·mon m* change (*transformation*); **un changement de temps** *shon·zhuh·mon duh ton* a change in the weather

changer* *shon·zhay vt* alter; **changer* de** *shon·zhay duh* change (*substitute*); **changer* de vêtements** *shon·zhay duh vet·mon* to change one's clothes; **changer* de train à Marseille** *shon·zhay duh trañ a mar·say* to change trains at Marseilles; **se changer*** *suh shon·zhay* change

chanson *shon·son f* song; **la chanson folklorique** *shon·son folk·lo·reek* folk song

chant *shon m* hymn; singing; **le chant de Noël** *shon duh no·el* carol

chanter *shon·tay vt/i* sing

chantier *shon·tyay m* building site; roadworks; **le chantier naval** *shon·tyay na·val* shipyard

chapeau *sha·pō m* hat; **le chapeau de soleil** *sha·pō duh so·lay* sun-hat; **le chapeau melon** *sha·pō muh·lon* bowler hat

chapelle *sha·pel f* chapel

chapitre *sha·pee·truh m* chapter

chaque *shak adj* each; every

charbon *shar·bon m* coal

char d'assaut *shar da·sō m* tank (*military*)

charge *sharzh f* load

chargé(e) *shar·zhay adj* tight (*schedule*)

charger* *shar·zhay vt* load; charge (*battery*); **je m'en charge** *zhuh moñ sharzh* leave it to me

chargeur *shar·zhur m* cartridge (*for camera*)

chariot *sha·ryō m* trolley; **le chariot à bagages** *sha·ryō a ba·gazh* luggage trolley

charmant(e) *shar·moñ(·moñt) adj* charming

charme *sharm m* charm

charpentier *shar·poñ·tyay m* carpenter

charrette *sha·ret f* cart

charrue *sha·rōō f* plough

charter *shar·tehr m* charter flight

chasse *shas f* hunting; shooting

chasse-neige *shas·nezh m* snowplough, snowplow

chasser *sha·say vt* hunt

châssis *shah·see m* chassis

chat *sha m* cat

châtaigne *shah·teh·nyuh f* chestnut

châtain *shah·tañ adj* brown (*hair*)

château *shah·tō m* castle; mansion

chatouiller *sha·too·yay vt* tickle

chaud(e) *shō (shōd) adj* warm; hot; **il fait chaud aujourd'hui** *eel feh shō ō·zhoor·dwee* it's warm/hot today; **j'ai chaud** *zhay shō* I'm warm/hot

chauffage *shō·fazh m* heating; **le chauffage central** *shō·fazh soñ·tral* central heating

chauffe-eau *shōf·ō m* water heater; immersion heater

chauffer *shō·fay vi* overheat (*engine*)

chauffeur *shō·fur m* chauffeur; driver

chaussée *shō·say f* carriageway (*of road*)

chaussette *shō·set f* sock

chaussure *shō·sōōr f* shoe; **la chaussure de ski** *shō·sōōr duh skee* ski boot

chauve *shōv adj* bald

chauve-souris *shōv·soo·ree f* bat (*animal*)

chef *shef m* chef; chief; head; leader; **le chef d'orchestre** *shef dor·kes·truh* conductor; **le chef de train** *shef duh trañ* guard (*on train*)

chef-d'œuvre *shay·duh·vruh m* masterpiece

chef du personnel *shef dōō pehr·so·nel m* personnel manager

chemin *shuh·mañ m* path; lane (*in country*); track; **le chemin de fer** *shuh·mañ duh fehr* railroad, railway; **par chemin de fer** *par shuh·mañ duh fehr* by rail; **demander le chemin de Paris** *duh·moñ·day luh shuh·mañ duh pa·ree* to ask the way to Paris

cheminée *shuh·mee·nay f* fireplace; mantelpiece; chimney

chemise *shuh·meez f* shirt; **la chemise de nuit** *shuh·meez duh nwee* nightdress

chemiserie *shuh·mee·zuh·ree f* gentlemen's outfitters

chemisier *shuh·mee·zyay m* blouse

chêne *shen m* oak

chèque *shek m* cheque, check; **le chèque de voyage** *shek duh vwah·yazh* travel(l)er's cheque

chèque-cadeau *shek·ka·dō m* gift token

chequier *shek·yay m* cheque book

cher (chère) *shehr adj* dear; **Cher Monsieur Smith** *shehr muh·syuh Smith* Dear Mr. Smith

chercher *shehr·shay vt* look for; look

up (*word*); search for; **aller*** **chercher** *a·lay shehr·shay* to go and fetch; **j'irai vous chercher à la gare** *zhee·ray voo shehr·shay a la gar* I'll meet you at the station (*go to get*)

chéri(e) *shay·ree m/f* darling

cheval *shuh·val m* horse; **faire*** **du cheval** *fehr dōō shuh·val* to go horseriding; **le cheval de course** *shuh·val duh koors* racehorse

cheveu *shuh·vuh m* hair (*single strand*)

cheveux *shuh·vuh mpl* hair

cheville *shuh·veey f* ankle

chèvre *sheh·vruh f* goat

chevreau *shuh·vrō m* kid (*leather*)

chewing-gum *shwing·gum m* chewing gum

chez *shay prep* at the house of; **rentrer chez soi** *roñ·tray shay swah* to go home

chicorée *shee·ko·ray f* chicory (*for coffee*); endive (*curly*)

chien *shyañ m* dog

chiffon *shee·foñ m* rag

chiffre *shee·fruh m* figure; number; **le chiffre d'affaires** *shee·fruh da·fehr* turnover (*money*)

Chili *shee·lee m* Chile

chimie *shee·mee f* chemistry

chimique *shee·meek adj* chemical

Chine *sheen f* China

chinois(e) *shee·nwah m* Chinese □ *adj* chinois(e) *shee·nwah(·nwahz)* Chinese; **il est Chinois** *eel eh shee·nwah* he's Chinese; **elle est Chinoise** *el eh shee·nwahz* she's Chinese

chips *sheeps fpl* crisps

chirurgie *shee·rōōr·zhee f* surgery (*operation*); **la chirurgie esthétique** *shee·rōōr·zhee es·tay·teek* cosmetic surgery

chirurgien *shee·rōōr·zhee·añ m* surgeon

choc *shok m* shock; bump (*knock*)

chocolat *sho·kō·la m* chocolate; **le chocolat à croquer** *sho·kō·la a kro·kay* plain chocolate; **le chocolat au lait** *sho·kō·la ō leh* milk chocolate

chœur *kur m* choir

choisir *shwah·zeer vt* pick; choose

choix *shwah m* range (*variety*); choice

cholestérol *ko·le·stay·rol m* cholesterol

chômage *shō·mazh m* unemployment; **mis(e) au chômage** *mee (meez) ō shō·mazh* redundant (*worker*); **en chômage** *oñ shō·mazh* unemployed

chômeurs *shō·mur mpl* the unemployed

chose *shōz f* thing

chou *shoo m* cabbage; **les choux de Bruxelles** *shoo duh brōō·sel* Brussels sprouts

choucroute *shoo·kroot f* sauerkraut

chou-fleur *shoo·flur m* cauliflower

chou-rave *shoo·rav m* kohlrabi

chrétien *kray·tyañ m* Christian

chrétienne *kray·tyen f* Christian

chrome *krōm m* chrome

chronomètre *kro·nō·meh·truh m* stop watch

chrysanthème *kree·zoñ·tem m* chrysanthemum

chuchoter *shōō·sho·tay vi* whisper

chute *shōōt f* fall

chute d'eau *shōōt dō f* waterfall

Chypre *shee·pruh f* Cyprus

cible *see·bluh f* target

ciboulette *see·boo·let f* chives

cicatrice *see·ka·trees f* scar

se cicatriser *suh see·ka·tree·zay vr* heal (*wound*)

cidre *see·druh* m cider
ciel *syel* m sky
cigare *see·gar* m cigar
cigarette *see·ga·ret* f cigarette
cil *seel* m eyelash
cime *seem* f peak (*of mountain*)
cimetière *seem·tyehr* m cemetery; graveyard; churchyard
cinéma *see·nay·ma* m cinema
cinq *sañk* num five
cinquante *sañ·koñt* num fifty
cinquième *sañ·kyem* adj fifth
cintre *sañ·truh* m coat hanger
cirage *see·razh* m polish (*for shoes*)
circonscription *seer·koñ·skreep·syoñ* f precinct (*administrative area*)
circonstances *seer·koñ·stoñs* fpl circumstances
circuit *seer·kwee* m circuit (*electric*)
circulation *seer·kōō·la·syoñ* f traffic (*cars*)
circuler *seer·kōō·lay* vi move (*traffic*)
cire *seer* f polish (*for floor*); wax
cirer *see·ray* vt polish
cirque *seerk* m circus
ciseaux *see·zō* mpl scissors
citation *see·ta·syoñ* f quotation (*passage*)
cité *see·tay* f city; estate (*housing*)
citer *see·tay* vt quote (*passage*)
citron *see·troñ* m lemon; **le citron vert** *see·troñ vehr* lime (*fruit*)
civilisation *see·vee·lee·za·syoñ* f civilization
clair(e) *klehr* adj clear (*distinct*); light (*bright, pale*)
claque *klak* f slap
claquement *klak·moñ* m bang (*of door*)
claquer *kla·kay* vi flap (*sail*) □ vt/i slam
classe *klas* f grade; class
classeur *kla·sur* m filing cabinet; file
classique *kla·seek* adj classical
clause *klōz* f clause (*in contract*)
clé *klay* f spanner; key
clef *klay* f key; **la clef de contact** *klay duh koñ·takt* ignition key
client(e) *klee·oñ(·oñt)* m/f guest (*at hotel*); client; customer
cligner des yeux *klee·nyay day zyuh* vi blink
clignoteur *klee·nyo·tur* m indicator
climat *klee·ma* m climate
climatisation *klee·ma·tee·za·syoñ* f air-conditioning
climatisé(e) *klee·ma·tee·zay* adj air-conditioned
clin d'œil *klañ duhy* m wink
clochard(e) *klo·shar(·shard)* m/f tramp
cloche *klosh* f bell
cloison *klwah·zoñ* f partition (*wall*); **sans cloisons** *soñ klwah·zoñ* open-plan
clou *kloo* m stud; nail (*metal*); **le clou de girofle** *kloo duh zhee·ro·fluh* clove
clouer *kloo·ay* vt nail
clown *kloon* m clown
club *klub* m club (*society*); **le club de golf** *klub duh golf* golf club
coche *kosh* f tick (*mark*)
cocher *ko·shay* vt tick (*mark*)
cochon *ko·shoñ* m pig
cocktail *kok·tel* m cocktail; **le cocktail de crevettes** *kok·tel duh kruh·vet* prawn cocktail
cocotte *ko·kot* f casserole (*dish*)
cocotte-minute *ko·kot·mee·nōōt* f pressure cooker
code *kod* f code; **le code de la route**

kod duh la root Highway Code; **mettre* en code** *meh·troñ kod* dip (*headlights*); **le code postal** *kod pos·tal* post-code; zip code
codéine *ko·day·een* f codeine
cœur *kur* m heart; **hearts** (*cards*); **par cœur** *par kur* by heart
coffre *ko·fruh* m boot, trunk (*in car*)
coffre-fort *ko·fruh·for* m strongbox; safe
cognac *ko·nyak* m cognac; brandy
cogner *ko·nyay* vt bump; **se cogner la tête** *suh ko·nyay la tet* to bang one's head
se coiffer *suh kwah·fay* vr do one's hair
coiffeur *kwah·fur* m hairdresser; barber
coiffeuse *kwah·fuhz* f hairdresser; dressing table
coiffure *kwah·fōōr* f hair-style
coin *kwañ* m corner (*of streets*)
coïncidence *ko·añ·see·doñs* f coincidence
coïncider *ko·añ·see·day* vi coincide
col *kol* m pass (*in mountains*); collar; **le col roulé** *kol roo·lay* polo neck
colère *ko·lehr* f anger; **se mettre* en colère** *suh meh·troñ ko·lehr* to lose one's temper; **en colère** *oñ ko·lehr* angry (*person*); **être* en colère contre quelqu'un** *eh·troñ ko·lehr koñ·truh kel·kuñ* to be angry with someone
colique *ko·leek* f colic; diarrh(o)ea
collaborer *ko·la·bo·ray* vi collaborate
collant *ko·loñ* m tights; panty hose
colle *kol* f glue; paste
collectionner *ko·lek·syo·nay* vt collect (*stamps etc*)
collège *ko·lezh* m college
collègue *ko·leg* m/f colleague
coller *ko·lay* vt stick; glue
collier *kol·yay* m necklace; collar (*for dog*)
colline *ko·leen* f hill
collision *ko·lee·zyoñ* f collision; crash; **avoir* une collision avec sa voiture** *a·vwahr ōōn ko·lee·zyoñ a·vek sa vwah·tōōr* to crash one's car; **entrer en collision** *oñ·tray oñ ko·lee·zyoñ* to collide
colombe *ko·loñb* f dove
colonne *ko·lon* f column; **la colonne vertébrale** *ko·lon vehr·tay·bral* spine (*backbone*); **la colonne de direction** *ko·lon duh dee·rek·syoñ* steering column
combat *koñ·ba* m fight
combien *koñ·byañ* adv how much/many; **combien de gens?** *koñ·byañ duh zhoñ* how many people?; **combien de temps?** *koñ·byañ duh toñ* how long?; **combien y a-t-il jusqu'à...?** *koñ·byañ ee·a·teel zhōōs·ka* how far is it to...?; **le combien sommes-nous aujourd'hui?** *luh koñ·byañ som·noo ō·zhoor·dwee* what's the date today?
combinaison *koñ·bee·neh·zoñ* f suit (*astronaut, diver*); slip (*underskirt*)
combustible *koñ·bōōs·tee·bluh* m fuel
comédie *ko·may·dee* f comedy
comédienne *ko·may·dyen* f actress
comic *ko·meek* m comic
comique *ko·meek* m comedian
comité *ko·mee·tay* m committee
commande *ko·moñd* f order (*for goods*)
commander *ko·moñ·day* vt order (*goods, meal*); commander de nou-

veau *ko·moñ·day duh noo·vō* reorder

commandes *ko·moñd* fpl controls

commanditaire *ko·moñ·dee·tehr m* backer

comme *kom prep, conj* like; comme je *kom see* as if, as though; il est arrivé comme nous partions *eel et a·ree·vay kom noo par·tyoñ* he arrived as we left; faites comme je vous dis *fet kom zhuh voo dee* do as I say; comme il dormait *kom eel dor·meh* as he was asleep (*because*)

commencement *ko·moñ·suh·moñ m* beginning

commencer* *ko·moñ·say vt/i* begin □ *vi* open (*play*)

comment *ko·moñ adv* how; comment est-ce qu'on dit "dog" en français? *ko·moñ es·koñ dee dog oñ froñ·seh* what's the French for "dog"?; comment est-ce? *ko·moñ es* what's it like?; comment? *ko·moñ* pardon?; comment est-ce que ça s'appelle? *ko·moñ es·kuh sa sa·pel* what's it called?

commerçant(e) *ko·mehr·soñ(·soñt) m/f* trader

commerce *ko·mehrs m* commerce; business; trade; faire* le commerce de quelque chose *fehr luh ko·mehrs duh kel·kuh shōz* to deal in something

commercial(e) *ko·mehr·syal adj* commercial

commercialisé(e) *ko·mehr·sya·lee·zay adj* commercialized (*resort*)

commettre* *ko·meh·truh vt* commit (*crime*)

commissariat de police *ko·mee·sa·ree·a duh po·lees m* police station

commission *ko·mee·syoñ f* commission; errand; message

commode *ko·mod adj* convenient

commun(e) *ko·muñ(·mōōn) adj* common

communication *ko·mōō·nee·ka·syoñ f* communication; mettre* quelqu'un en communication *meh·truh kel·kuñ oñ ko·mōō·nee·ka·syoñ* to put someone through (*on phone*); obtenir* la communication *op·tuh·neer la ko·mōō·nee·ka·syoñ* to get through; je n'ai pas pu avoir la communication *zhuh nay pa pōō a·vwahr la ko·mōō·nee·ka·syoñ* I couldn't get through; la communication urbaine *ko·mōō·nee·ka·syoñ ōōr·ben* local call; la communication interurbaine *ko·mōō·nee·ka·syoñ añ·tehr·ōōr·ben* trunk-call

communiquer *ko·mōō·nee·kay vi* communicate

communiste *ko·mōō·neest m/f* Communist □ *adj* Communist

compagnie *koñ·pa·nyee f* firm; la compagnie d'aviation *koñ·pa·nyee da·vya·syoñ* airline; la compagnie de navigation *koñ·pa·nyee duh na·vee·ga·syoñ* shipping company

comparer *koñ·pa·ray vt* compare; comparer quelque chose avec quelque chose *koñ·pa·ray kel·kuh shōz a·vek kel·kuh shōz* to compare something with something

compartiment *koñ·par·tee·moñ m* compartment (*on train*); le compartiment non-fumeur *koñ·par·tee·moñ noñ·fōō·mur* nonsmoker

compassion *koñ·pa·syoñ f* sympathy

compatissant(e) *koñ·pa·tee·soñ(·soñt) adj* sympathetic

compatriote *koñ·pa·tree·yot m* fellow countryman

compensation *koñ·poñ·sa·syoñ f* compensation

compétence *koñ·pay·toñs f* ability

compétent(e) *koñ·pay·toñ(·toñt) adj* competent

compétition *koñ·pay·tee·syoñ f* competition

complet(ète) *koñ·pleh(·plet) adj* full up (*bus etc*); complet *koñ·pleh* no vacancies (*hotel sign*)

complètement *koñ·plet·moñ adv* completely

complexe *koñ·pleks adj* complex

compliment *koñ·plee·moñ m* compliment

compliqué(e) *koñ·plee·kay adj* elaborate; complicated

comportement *koñ·port·moñ m* behavio(u)r

se comporter *suh koñ·por·tay vr* behave

composer *koñ·pō·zay vt* compose; dial (*number*)

compositeur *koñ·po·zee·tur m* composer

compote *koñ·pot f* stewed fruit

compréhension *koñ·pray·oñ·syoñ f* understanding

comprendre* *koñ·proñ·druh vt* understand; comprise; nous croyons comprendre que... *noo krwah·yoñ koñ·proñ·druh kuh* we understand that...

comprimé *koñ·pree·may m* tablet (*medicine*)

compris(e) *koñ·pree(·preez) adj* including; service compris *sehr·vees koñ·pree* inclusive of service; ...non compris *noñ koñ·pree* exclusive of...

comptabilité *koñ·ta·bee·lee·tay f* accountancy

comptable *koñ·ta·bluh m/f* accountant

compte *koñt m* account; les comptes chèques postaux *koñt shek po·stō* giro (*post office*); le compte de dépôt *koñt duh day·pō* deposit account; le compte courant *koñt koo·roñ* current account, checking account; le compte en banque *koñt oñ boñk* bank account; travailler à son compte *tra·vye·yay a soñ koñt* to be self-employed

compter *koñ·tay vt* count (*objects, people*); comptez 10 minutes pour y aller *koñ·tay 10 mee·nōōt poor ee a·lay* allow 10 minutes to get there; compter jusqu'à 10 *koñ·tay zhōōs·ka 10* to count up to 10; compter sur *koñ·tay sōōr* to rely on (*person*)

compteur *koñ·tur m* speedometer; meter; le compteur kilométrique *koñ·tur kee·lō·may·treek* ≈ milometer; couper le courant/l'eau au compteur *koo·pay luh koo·roñ/lō ō koñ·tur* to turn the electricity/water off at the mains

comptoir *koñ·twahr m* bar; counter

comté *koñ·tay m* county

concerner *koñ·sehr·nay vt* concern; en ce qui concerne *oñ suh kee koñ·sern* regarding

concert *koñ·sehr m* concert; le concert pop *koñ·sehr pop* pop concert

concessionnaire *koñ·seh·syo·nehr m* distributor (*commercial*); le concessionnaire Renault *koñ·seh·syo·nehr ruh·nō* the Renault agent

concierge *koñ·syerzh m/f* porter (*doorkeeper) □ m le concierge *koñ·syerzh* janitor

conciliateur *koñ·see·lee·a·tur m* trouble-shooter (*political*)

concombre *koñ·koñ·bruh m* cucumber

concours *koñ·koor m* contest; aid

concurrent(e) *koñ·kōō·roñ(·roñt) m/f* competitor; contestant; **une firme concurrente** *ōōn feerm koñ·kōō·roñt* a rival firm

condamner *koñ·da·nay vt* condemn

condiments *koñ·dee·moñ mpl* condiments

condition *koñ·dee·syoñ f* condition; **à condition que... a** *koñ·dee·syoñ koñ·dee·syoñ ruh·keez* poor qualify for (*grant etc*); **sous condition** *soo koñ·dee·syoñ* on approval

conducteur *koñ·dōōk·tur m* driver; **le conducteur débutant** *koñ·dōōk·tur day·bōō·toñ* learner(-driver)

conductrice *koñ·dōōk·trees f* driver

conduire* *koñ·dweer vt* steer (*car*); drive (*car etc*); **savez-vous conduire?** *sa·vay·voo koñ·dweer* do you drive?; **conduire* quelqu'un à la gare** *koñ·dweer kel·kuñ a la gar* to take someone to the station

conduite *koñ·dweet f* driving; steering; behaviour; **la conduite à gauche** *koñ·dweet a gōsh* left-hand drive; **la conduite intérieure** *koñ·dweet añ·tay·ryur* saloon (*car*)

de confection *duh koñ·fek·syoñ adj* ready-made (*clothes*)

conférence *koñ·fay·roñs f* lecture; conference

confesser *koñ·feh·say vt* confess; **se confesser** *suh koñ·feh·say* confess

confession *koñ·feh·syoñ f* confession

confiance *koñ·fyoñs f* confidence (*trust*); **de confiance** *duh koñ·fyoñs* reliable (*person*); **la confiance en** *koñ·fyoñs oñ* confidence in; **avoir* confiance en** *a·vwahr koñ·fyoñs oñ* to trust

confidence *koñ·fee·doñs f* confidence

confidentiel(le) *koñ·fee·doñ·syel adj* confidential

confirmer *koñ·feer·may vt* confirm

confiserie *koñ·feez·ree f* confectionery

confiseur *koñ·fee·zur m* confectioner

confit d'oie *koñ·fee dwah m* conserve of goose

confiture *koñ·fee·tōōr f* jam; preserve(s); **la confiture d'oranges** *koñ·fee·tōōr do·roñzh* marmalade

conflit *koñ·flee m* conflict

confondre *koñ·foñ·druh vt* confuse; **confondre quelque chose avec quelque chose d'autre** *koñ·foñ·druh kel·kuh shōz a·vek kel·kuh shōz dō·truh* to confuse one thing with another

confort *koñ·for m* comfort (*ease*)

confortable *koñ·for·ta·bluh adj* comfortable

confus(e) *koñ·fōō(·fōōz) adj* confused (*muddled*)

congé *koñ·zhay m* leave (*holiday*); **un jour de congé** *uñ zhoor duh koñ·zhay* a day off

congélateur *kon·zhay·la·tur m* freezer; deepfreeze

congelé(e) *koñ·zhuh·lay adj* frozen (*food*)

congeler* *koñ·zhuh·lay vt* freeze (*food*)

congère *koñ·zhehr f* snowdrift

connaissance *ko·neh·soñs f* knowledge; acquaintance; **reprendre* connaissance** *ruh·proñ·druh ko·neh·soñs* to come round (*recover*); **faire* la connaissance de** *fehr la ko·neh·soñs duh* to meet (*make acquaintance of*)

connaisseur *ko·neh·sur m* connoisseur

connaître* *ko·neh·truh vt* know

conscience *koñ·syoñs f* conscience

consciencieux(euse) *koñ·syoñ·syuh (·syuhz) adj* conscientious; thorough (*work*)

conscient(e) *koñ·syoñ(·syoñt) adj* conscious

conseil *koñ·say m* advice; **le conseil d'administration** *koñ·say dad·mee·nee·stra·syoñ* board (*of directors*); **le conseil municipal** *koñ·say mōō·nee·see·pal* corporation (*of town*); council

conseiller *koñ·say·yay vt* advise; **conseiller à quelqu'un de faire quelque chose** *koñ·say·yay a kel·kuñ duh fehr kel·kuh shōz* to advise someone to do something

conséquence *koñ·say·koñs f* consequence

conservateur *koñ·sehr·va·tur adj* conservative

conservatoire *koñ·sehr·va·twahr m* academy of music

conservatrice *koñ·sehr·va·trees adj* conservative

conserve *koñ·sehrv f* canned food; **en conserve** *oñ koñ·sehrv* canned

conserver *koñ·sehr·vay vt* keep; **le lait ne se conserve pas bien** *luh leh nuh suh koñ·sehr·vay pah byañ* milk doesn't keep very well

considérer *koñ·see·day·ray vt* consider

consigne *koñ·see·nyuh f* deposit; left luggage office

consister en *koñ·sees·tay oñ vi* consist of

consommateur *koñ·so·ma·tur m* consumer

consommation *koñ·so·ma·syoñ f* consumption; drink; **les biens de consommation** *byañ duh koñ·so·ma·syoñ* consumer goods

consommatrice *koñ·so·ma·trees f* consumer

consommé *koñ·so·may m* consommé; **le consommé à la tortue** *koñ·so·may a la tor·tōō* turtle soup

constipé(e) *koñ·stee·pay adj* constipated

construction *koñ·strōōk·syoñ f* building

construire* *koñ·strweer vt* construct; build

consul *koñ·sōōl m* consul

consulat *koñ·sōō·la m* consulate

consultant *koñ·sōōl·toñ m* consultant

consulter *koñ·sōōl·tay vt* consult; refer to

contact *koñ·takt m* contact; **en contact avec** *oñ koñ·takt a·vek* in touch with; **se mettre* en contact avec** *suh met·troñ koñ·takt a·vek* to contact

contacter *koñ·tak·tay vt* contact

contagieux(euse) *koñ·ta·zhyuh (·zhyuhz) adj* infectious; contagious

container *koñ·tay·nehr m* container (*for shipping etc*)

contemporain(e) *koñ·toñ·po·rañ(·ren) adj* contemporary

contenir* *koñ·tuh·neer vt* hold; contain

content(e) *koñ·toñ(·toñt) adj* content(ed); pleased; **j'ai été content**

d'apprendre... *zhay ay·tay koñ·toñ da·proñ·druh* I was glad to hear...

contenu *koñ·tuh·nōō* m contents

contester *koñ·tes·tay* vt dispute (*fact*)

continent *koñ·tee·noñ* m continent; mainland

continental(e) *koñ·tee·noñ·tal* adj continental

continu(e) *koñ·tee·nōō* adj continuous

continuel(le) *koñ·tee·nōō·el* adj continual

continuer *koñ·tee·nōō·ay* vi continue; continuer de faire *koñ·tee·nōō·ay duh fehr* to continue to do

contraceptif *koñ·tra·sep·teef* m contraceptive

contractuel(le) *koñ·trak·too·el* m/f traffic warden

contraire *koñ·trehr* m opposite; au contraire *ō koñ·trehr* on the contrary

contrat *koñ·tra* m contract

contravention *koñ·tra·voñ·syoñ* f fine; parking ticket

contre *koñ·truh* prep against; versus

contrebande *koñ·truh·boñd* f contraband; passer en contrebande *pa·say oñ koñ·truh·boñd* smuggle

contremaître *koñ·truh·meh·truh* m foreman

contre-plaqué *koñ·truh·pla·kay* m plywood

contribuer *koñ·tree·bōō·ay* vi contribute

contrôle *koñ·trōl* m check; le contrôle radar *koñ·trōl ra·dar* radar trap

contrôler *koñ·trō·lay* vt check (*passport, ticket*)

contrôleur *koñ·trō·lur* m inspector (*of tickets*)

conurbation *ko·nōōr·ba·syoñ* f conurbation

convaincre* *koñ·vañ·kruh* vt convince

convalescence *koñ·va·leh·soñs* f convalescence

convenable *koñ·vuh·na·bluh* adj decent (*moral*); suitable (*fitting*); proper (*respectable*)

convenances *koñ·vuh·noñs* fpl etiquette

convenir* *koñ·vuh·neer* vi be suitable; est-ce que jeudi vous convient? *es· kuh zhuh·dee voo koñ·vyañ* does Thursday suit you?; est-ce que ça convient? *es·kuh sa koñ·vyañ* will it do? (*be suitable*); les œufs ne me conviennent pas *lay zuh nuh muh koñ·vyen pa* eggs disagree with me

convenu(e) *koñ·vuh·nōō* adj agreed

conversation *koñ·vehr·sa·syoñ* f conversation

conviction *koñ·veek·syoñ* f conviction

coopérative *kō·o·pay·ra·teev* f cooperative

coopérer* *kō·o·pay·ray* vi co-operate

Copenhague *ko·pen·hag* f Copenhagen

copie *ko·pee* f copy

copier *ko·pyay* vt copy

copropriété *kō·pro·pree·ay·tay* f joint ownership

coq *kok* m cock(erel); le coq de bruyère *kok duh brōō·yehr* grouse

coque *kok* f cockle; à la coque *a la kok* soft boiled (*egg*)

coqueluche *kok·lōōsh* f whooping cough

coquetier *kok·tyay* m egg cup

coquillage *ko·kee·yazh* m shell

coquille *ko·keey* f shell; la coquille Saint-Jacques *ko·keey sañ·zhak* scallop

cor *kor* m corn (*on foot*)

corail *ko·rye* m coral

corbeille *kor·bay* f basket; la corbeille à papier *kor·bay a pa·pyay* waste paper basket

corde *kord* f string (*of instrument*); rope; cord; la corde à linge *kord a lañzh* clothesline

cordial *kor·dyal* m cordial

corne *korn* f horn (*of animal*)

cornemuse *kor·nuh·mōōz* f (bag)pipes

cornet *kor·nay* m cornet; cone (*for ice cream*)

cornichon *kor·nee·shoñ* m gherkin

corps *kor* m body

correct(e) *ko·rekt* adj correct; proper

correctement *ko·rek·tuh·moñ* adv properly

correction *ko·rek·syoñ* f correction

correspondance *ko·res·poñ·doñs* f connection (*train etc*); correspondence (*mail*); acheter* quelque chose par correspondance *ash·tay kel·kuh shōz par ko·res·poñ·doñs* to buy something by mail order

correspondant(e) *ko·res·poñ·doñ (·doñt)* m/f pen pal

corriger* *ko·ree·zhay* vt correct

corroder *ko·ro·day* vt corrode

corrompu(e) *ko·roñ·pōō* adj corrupt

corruption *ko·rōōp·syoñ* f corruption

Corse *kors* f Corsica

corset *kor·seh* m corset

cosmétiques *kos·may·teek* mpl cosmetics

cosmopolite *kos·mo·po·leet* adj cosmopolitan

costume *kos·tōōm* m costume (*theatrical*); suit (*men's*); le costume national *kos·tōōm na·syoñ·nal* national dress

cote *kot* f odds (*in betting*)

côte *kōt* f coast; hill; rib

côté *kō·tay* m side; mettre* de côté *meh·truh duh kō·tay* to save (*money*); des deux côtés *day duh kō·tay* on either side; à côté de *a kō·tay duh* beside; je l'ai vu de l'autre côté de la rue *zhuh lay vōō duh lō·truh kō·tay duh la rōō* I saw him (from) across the road

Côte d'Azur *kōt da·zōōr* f Riviera

côtelette *kōt·let* f cutlet; la côtelette de porc *kōt·let duh por* pork chop

cotisation *ko·tee·za·syoñ* f subscription (*to club*)

coton *ko·toñ* m cotton (*fabric*); le coton hydrophile *ko·toñ ee·dro·feel* absorbent cotton; cotton wool

cou *koo* m neck

couche *koosh* f diaper; nappy; layer; la fausse couche *fōs koosh* miscarriage

couche-culotte *koosh·koo·lot* f plastic covered nappy

coucher *koo·shay* vt put to bed; on peut coucher 3 personnes dans l'appartement *oñ puh koo·shay 3 pehr·son doñ la·par·tuh·moñ* the apartment sleeps three; se coucher *suh koo·shay* to go to bed; lie down; aller* se coucher *a·lay suh koo·shay* to go to bed

couchette *koo·shet* f berth; couchette; bunk

coude *kood* m bend (*in pipe, wire etc*); elbow; faire* un coude *fehr uñ kood* to bend

coudre* *koo·druh* vi sew

couette *kwet* f continental quilt

couler *koo·lay* vi sink; run (*liquid*);

flow; **faire* couler** *fehr koo·lay* to turn on (*water*); **couler à flots** *koo·lay a flō* pour

couleur *koo·lur* f colo(u)r; suit (*cards*); **de couleur** *duh koo·lur* colo(u)red (*person*)

couloir *koo·lwahr* m corridor

coup *koo* m stroke; shot (*from gun*); hit; blow; **à coup sûr** *a koo sōōr* without fail; **le coup de soleil** *koo duh so·lay* sunburn (*painful*); **le coup d'état** *koo day·ta* coup d'état; **le coup de téléphone** *koo duh tay·lay·fon* phone-call; **le coup de pied** *koo duh pyay* kick; **donner un coup de pied à** *do·nay uñ koo duh pyay a* to kick; **le coup d'œil** *koo duhy* glance; **jeter* un coup d'œil à** *a zhuh·tay uñ koo duhy a* to glance at

coupable *koo·pa·bluh* adj guilty

coupe *koop* f goblet; dish; cup (*trophy*); **la coupe de cheveux** *koop duh shuh·vuh* haircut (*style*)

coupé *koo·pay* m coupé (*car*) □ adj **coupé(e)** *koo·pay* off (*machine*)

couper *koo·pay* vt cut; blend; dilute; **se faire* couper les cheveux** *suh fehr koo·pay lay shuh·vuh* to get one's hair cut; **se couper** *suh koo·pay* to cut oneself

couple *koo·pluh* m couple (*persons*)

couplet publicitaire *koo·pleh pōōb·lee·see·tehr* m jingle (*advertising*)

coupon *koo·poñ* m coupon

coupure *koo·pōōr* f cut; **la coupure de courant** *koo·pōōr duh koo·roñ* power cut

cour *koor* f court (*law*); courtyard; **la cour de récréation** *koor duh ray·kray·a·syoñ* playground; **la cour de ferme** *koor duh fehrm* farmyard

courage *koo·razh* m courage

courageux(euse) *koo·ra·zhuh(·zhuz)* adj brave

couramment *koo·ra·moñ* adv fluently

courant *koo·roñ* m power (*electricity*); current; **le courant d'air** *koo·roñ dehr* draught, draft

courant(e) *koo·roñ(·roñt)* adj common; standard; current

courbe *koorb* f curve

courber *koor·bay* vt bend; **se courber** *suh koor·bay* bend

courge *koorzh* f marrow (*vegetable*); squash (*gourd*)

courgettes *koor·zhet* fpl courgettes

courir* *koo·reer* vi run (*person, animal*); **courir* après quelqu'un** *koo·reer a·preh kel·kuñ* to run after someone

couronne *koo·ron* f crown

couronnement *koo·ro·nuh·moñ* m coronation

courrier *koo·ryay* m mail; post

courroie *koor·wah* f strap; **la courroie de ventilateur** *koor·wah duh voñ·tee·la·tur* fanbelt

cours *koor* m lesson; course; rate; **le cours intensif** *koor añ·toñ·seef* crash course; **en cours de réparation** *oñ koor duh ray·pa·ra·syoñ* under repair

course *koors* f race (*sport*); errand; **les courses** *koors* the races; **la course de taureaux** *koors duh to·rō* bullfight; **faire* une course** *fehr ōōn koors* to run an errand; **faire* les courses** *fehr lay koors* to go shopping; **les courses de chevaux** *koors duh shuh·vō* horseracing

court *koor* m court (*tennis etc*)

court(e) *koor (koort)* adj short; **à court terme** *a koor tehrm* short term; **être* à court de quelque chose** *eh·truh a koor duh kel·kuh shōz* to be short of something

court de tennis *koor duh teh·nees* m tennis court

courtier *koor·tyay* m broker

cousin(e) *koo·zañ(·zeen)* m/f cousin

coussin *koo·sañ* m cushion

coussinets *koo·see·neh* mpl bearings (*in car*)

coût *koo* m cost; **le coût de la vie** *koo duh la vee* cost of living

couteau *koo·tō* m knife

coûter *koo·tay* vt cost; **combien ça coûte?** *koñ·byañ sa koot* how much is it?

coûteux(euse) *koo·tuh(·tuhz)* adj expensive

coutume *koo·tōōm* f custom

couture *koo·tōōr* f seam; sewing

couvent *koo·voñ* m convent; monastery

couvercle *koo·vehr·kluh* m top; lid

couvert *koo·vehr* m cover charge; place setting; **mettre* le couvert** *meh·truh luh koo·vehr* to set the table

couverts *koo·vehr* mpl cutlery

couverture *koo·vehr·tōōr* f blanket; cover; wrapper (*paper*); **la couverture chauffante** *koo·vehr·tōōr shō·foñt* electric blanket

couvrir* *koo·vreer* vt cover

crabe *krab* m crab

cracher *kra·shay* vi spit

craie *kray* f chalk

crampe *kroñp* f cramp

crâne *krahn* m skull

craquement *krak·moñ* m crack (*noise*)

cravache *kra·vash* f crop (*whip*)

cravate *kra·vat* f (neck)tie

crawl *krol* m crawl (*swimming*)

crayon *kray·yoñ* m pencil; **le crayon de couleur** *kray·yoñ duh koo·lur* crayon

créance *kray·oñs* f debt

créancier *kray·oñ·syay* m creditor

créancière *kray·oñ·syehr* f creditor

crèche *kresh* f day nursery

crédit *kray·dee* m credit; **à crédit** *a kray·dee* on credit; **faire* crédit à quelqu'un** *fehr kray·dee a kel·kuñ* to give somebody credit

créditer *kray·dee·tay* vt credit; **créditer le compte de quelqu'un de F5000** *kray·dee·tay luh koñt duh kel·kuñ duh F5000* to credit F5000 to someone's account

créer *kray·ay* vt create

crème *krem* f cream; coffee with milk; **la crème pour les mains** *krem poor lay mañ* hand cream; **la crème anglaise** *krem oñ·glez* custard; **la crème pour le visage** *krem poor luh vee·zazh* face cream; **la crème aigre** *krem eh·gruh* sour(ed) cream; **la crème fouettée** *krem foo·eh·tay* whipped cream; **la crème à raser** *krem a ra·zay* shaving cream; **la crème de menthe** *krem duh moñt* crème de menthe

crémerie *kray·muh·ree* f dairy (*store*)

crémeux(euse) *kray·muh(·muz)* adj creamy (*texture*)

crêpe *krep* f pancake

crêperie *kreh·puh·ree* f pancake shop/restaurant

crépon de coton *kray·poñ duh ko·toñ* m seersucker

crépuscule *kray·pōōs·kōōl* m dusk

cresson *kreh·soñ* m watercress

Crète *kret f* Crete

creuse *kruhz adj* hollow

creuser *kruh·zay vt* dig (*hole*)

creux *kruh adj* hollow

crevaison *kruh·veh·zoñ f* puncture

crevé(e) *kruh·vay adj* flat (*deflated*)

crever* *kruh·vay vt/i* burst

crevette *kruh·vet f* shrimp; **la crevette rose** *kruh·vet rōz* prawn

cri *kree m* cry; shout

cric *kreek m* jack (*for car*)

crier *kree·yay vi* scream; shout

crime *kreem m* crime

criminel(le) *kree·mee·nel adj* criminal

crise *kreez f* crisis; **la crise cardiaque** *kreez kar·dyak* heart attack

cristal *kree·stal m* crystal (*glass*)

critique *kree·teek f* criticism; review

critiquer *kree·tee·kay vt* criticize

crochet *kro·sheh m* hook

crocodile *kro·ko·deel m* crocodile

crocus *kro·kōōs m* crocus

croire* *krwahr vt* believe; **je crois que oui** *zhuh krwah kuh wee* I expect so; **croire* en** *krwahr oñ* to believe in

croisière *krwah·zyehr f* cruise; **faire* une croisière** *fehr ōōn krwah·zyehr* to go on a cruise

croissance *krwah·soñs f* growth

croissant *krwah·soñ m* croissant

croix *krwah f* cross

croque-monsieur *krok·muh·syuh m* toasted ham and cheese sandwich

croquette *kro·ket f* croquette

croquis *kro·kee m* sketch (*drawing*); **faire* un croquis de** *fehr uñ kro·kee duh* sketch

croupier *kroo·pyay m* croupier

croustillant(e) *kroos·tee·yoñ(·yoñt) adj* crisp

croûte *kroot f* crust; scab

croûton *kroo·toñ m* crouton

cru(e) *krōō adj* raw (*uncooked*) □ *m* **un vin de grand cru** *uñ vañ duh groñ krōō* a vintage wine

cruche *krōōsh f* jug; pitcher

cruel(le) *krōō·el adj* cruel

Cuba *kōō·ba m* Cuba

cubain(e) *kōō·bañ(·ben) adj* Cuban

cube *kōōb m* cube

cube-flash *kōōb·flash m* flashcube

cueillir* *kuh·yeer vt* pick (*flower*)

cuiller *kwee·yehr f* spoon; **la cuiller à dessert** *kwee·yehr a deh·sehr* dessert-spoon; **la cuiller à café** *kwee·yehr a ka·fay* teaspoon; **la cuiller à soupe** *kwee·yehr a soop* tablespoon; soup-spoon

cuillerée *kwee·yuh·ray f* spoonful; **la cuillerée à soupe** *kwee·yuh·ray a soop* tablespoonful

cuir *kweer m* leather; **le cuir chevelu** *kweer shuh·vuh·lōō* scalp; **le cuir verni** *kweer vehr·nee* patent leather

cuire* *kweer vt/i* cook; **faire* cuire** *fehr kweer* cook

cuisine *kwee·zeen f* cooking; cuisine; kitchen

cuisinier *kwee·zee·nyay m* cook

cuisinière *kwee·zee·nyehr f* cook; cooker; **la cuisinière à gaz** *kwee·zee·nyehr a gaz* gas cooker

cuisse *kwees f* thigh; **les cuisses de grenouille** *kwees duh gruh·noo·yuh* frogs legs; **la cuisse de poulet** *kwees duh poo·leh* chicken leg

cuit(e) *kwee (kweet) adj* done (*cooked*); **tout cuit(e)** *too kwee(t)* ready-cooked

cuivre *kwee·vruh m* copper (*metal*); **le cuivre jaune** *kwee·vruh zhōn* brass

cul-de-sac *kōō·duh·sak m* cul-de-sac

culotte *kōō·lot f* pants (*women's*)

culpabilité *kōōl·pa·bee·lee·tay f* guilt

cultiver *kōōl·tee·vay vt* cultivate

culture *kōōl·tōōr f* culture; **la culture générale** *kōōl·tōōr zhay·nay·ral* general knowledge

curieux(euse) *kōō·ryuh(·ryuhz) adj* funny (*strange*); curious

curry *kōō·ree m* curry

cuvette *kōō·vet f* bowl (*for washing*)

cyclisme *see·klees·muh m* cycling

cycliste *see·kleest m/f* cyclist

cyclomoteur *see·klō·mo·tur m* moped

cygne *see·nyuh m* swan

cylindre *see·lañ·druh m* cylinder

D

d'abord *da·bor adv* at first

d'accord *da·kor adv* O.K., okay (*agreement*)

dactylo *dak·tee·lō m/f* typist

dactylographié(e) *dak·tee·lo·gra·fyay adj* typewritten

daim *dañ m* suede

dame *dam f* lady; queen (*in cards*); **les dames** *dam* draughts

Danemark *dan·mark m* Denmark

danger *doñ·zhay m* danger

dangereux(euse) *doñ·zhuh·ruh(·ruhz) adj* dangerous

danois *da·nwah m* Danish □ *adj* danois(e) *da·nwah(·nwahz)* Danish; **il est Danois** *eel eh da·nwah* he's Danish; **elle est Danoise** *el eh da·nwahz* she's Danish

dans *doñ prep* into; in; **il sera de retour dans 2 jours** *eel suh·ra duh ruh·toor doñ 2 zhoor* he'll be back in 2 days; **dans le train** *doñ luh trañ* on the train

danse *doñs f* dance; dancing; **la danse folklorique** *doñs folk·lo·reek* folk dance

danser *doñ·say vi* dance

date *dat f* date (*day*)

datte *dat f* date (*fruit*)

de *duh prep* from; of; **de Londres** *duh loñ·druh* from London; **de 8 heures** *duh 8 ur* from 8 o'clock; **la voiture de Mary** *lā vwa·tōōr duh Mary* Mary's car; **des pommes** *day pom* some apples; **du pain** *dōō pañ* some bread; **avez-vous du pain?** *a·vay voo dōō pañ* have you any bread?; **rouge de colère** *roozh duh ko·lehr* red with anger; **rempli(e) d'eau** *roñ·plee dō* filled with water; **tomber d'un mur** *toñ·bay duñ mōōr* to fall off a wall; **pour 50 francs d'essence** *poor 50 froñ deh·soñs* 50 francs worth of petrol/gas; **de pierre** *duh pyehr* made of stone; **un de mes amis** *uñ duh may za·mee* a friend of mine; **3 d'entre eux** *3 doñ·truh* 3 of them; **la clé de ma chambre** *la klay duh ma shoñ·bruh* the key to my room

dé *day m* dice

déballer *day·ba·lay vt* unpack (*clothes*)

débarcadère *day·bar·ka·dehr m* landing stage

débarquer *day·bar·kay vi* land (*from ship*)

débat *day·ba m* debate

débit *day·bee m* debit; **porter £50 au débit de quelqu'un** *por·tay £50 ō day·bee duh kel·kuñ* to debit £50 to someone's account

déboucher *day·boo·shay vt* clear (*pipe*)

debout *duh·boo* adv standing; upright;
être* debout *eh·truh duh·boo* to
stand; **se mettre* debout** *suh meh·
truh duh·boo* to stand up
début *day·bōō* m beginning
débutant(e) *day·bōō·toñ(·toñt)* m/f beginner
décaféiné(e) *day·ka·fay·ee·nay* adj decaffeinated
décapotable *day·ka·po·ta·bluh* f convertible (*car*)
décapsuleur *day·kap·sōō·lur* m bottle
opener
décembre *day·soñ·bruh* m December
décennie *day·seh·nee* f decade
décent(e) *day·soñ(·soñt)* adj decent
(*respectable*)
décevoir* *day·suh·vwahr* vt disappoint
décharge *day·sharzh* f shock (*electric*);
la décharge publique *day·sharzh pōō·
bleek* dump (*for rubbish*)
décharger *day·shar·zhay* vt unload
déchirer *day·shee·ray* vt tear; rip; **se
déchirer** *suh day·shee·ray* tear, rip
déchirure *day·shee·rōōr* f tear
décider *day·see·day* vt decide (on);
être* décidé à faire quelque chose *eh·
truh day·see·day a fehr kel·kuh shōz*
to be determined to do something;
décider de faire quelque chose *day·
see·day duh fehr kel·kuh shōz* to decide to do something; **se décider** *suh
day·see·day* to make up one's mind;
decide (*between alternatives*)
décimal(e) *day·see·mal adj* decimal
décimale *day·see·mal* f decimal
décision *day·see·zyoñ* f decision
déclaration *day·kla·ra·syoñ* f statement
déclarer *day·kla·ray* vt state; declare;
rien à déclarer *ryañ na day·kla·ray*
nothing to declare
décollage *day·ko·lazh* m takeoff (*of
plane*)
décoller *day·ko·lay* vi take off (*plane*)
décolleté *day·kol·tay* m low neck; **le
décolleté en V** *day·kol·tay oñ vay* V-
neck
décommander *day·ko·moñ·day* vt cancel (*appointment*)
décongeler* *day·koñ·zhuh·lay* vt defrost (*food*)
décorations *day·ko·ra·syoñ* fpl decorations
décorer *day·ko·ray* vt decorate
découper *day·koo·pay* vt carve (*meat*)
découragé(e) *day·koo·ra·zhay* adj discouraged
découvert *day·koo·vehr* m overdraft
découverte *day·koo·vehrt* f discovery
découvrir* *day·koo·vreer* vt uncover;
discover; find out
décrire* *day·kreer* vt describe
déçu(e) *day·sōō* adj disappointed
déduire* *day·dweer* vt deduct
défaillance *day·fye·yoñs* f failure
(*mechanical*)
défaire* *day·fehr* vt unpack (*case*); unfasten; undo; unwrap; untie
défaite *day·fet* f defeat
défaut *day·fō* m fault; defect
défectueux(euse) *day·fek·tōō·uh(·uhz)*
adj imperfect; faulty; defective
défendre *day·foñ·druh* vt defend; forbid; **défendre à quelqu'un de faire
quelque chose** *day·foñ·dra kel·kuñ
duh fehr kel·kuh shōz* to forbid
someone to do something
défense *day·foñs* f defence; **défense de
fumer** *day·foñs duh fōō·may* no
smoking

déficit *day·fee·see* m deficit
défilé *day·fee·lay* m parade
déflation *day·fla·syoñ* f deflation
dégager* *day·ga·zhay* vt clear (*road*)
dégâts *day·ga* mpl damage
dégeler* *day·zhuh·lay* vi thaw (*frozen
food*); **faire* dégeler** *fehr day·zhuh·
lay* thaw
dégivrer *day·zhee·vray* vt defrost (*refrigerator*); de-ice
dégoût *day·goo* m disgust
dégoûté(e) *day·goo·tay* adj disgusted
degré *day·gray* m degree (*unit of
measurement*)
déguisé(e) *day·gee·zay* adj in disguise;
in fancy dress
déguisement *day·geez·moñ* m disguise;
fancy dress
dehors *day·or* adv outside; outdoors;
en dehors de *oñ duh·or duh* apart
from; **au dehors (de)** *ō duh·or duh*
outside
déjà *day·zha* adv already
déjeuner *day·zhuh·nay* m lunch; **le petit déjeuner** *puh·tee day·zhuh·nay*
breakfast
délégation *day·lay·ga·syoñ* f delegation
délégué(e) *day·lay·gay* m/f delegate;
le/la délégué(e) syndical(e) *day·lay·
gay sañ·dee·kal* shop steward
déléguer* *day·lay·gay* vt delegate
délibéré(e) *day·lee·bay·ray* adj deliberate
délicat(e) *day·lee·ka(·kat)* adj delicate;
dainty
délicieux(euse) *day·lee·syuh(·syuhz)*
adj delicious
déloyal(e) *day·lwah·yal* adj unfair
(*competition*)
demain *duh·mañ* adv tomorrow
demande *duh·moñd* f request; application (*for job*); demand (*for goods*);
faire* une demande d'emploi *fehr
ōōn duh·moñd doñ·plwah* to apply
for a job
demander *duh·moñ·day* vt/i ask □ vt
claim (*lost property, baggage*); de-
mander l'heure à quelqu'un *duh·
moñ·day lur a kel·kuñ* to ask
someone the time; **demander quelque chose** *duh·moñ·day kel·kuh shōz*
to ask for something; **demander le
prix** *duh·moñ·day luh pree* to ask the
price; **se demander si...** *suh duh·
moñ·day see* to wonder whether...;
ça demande un grand effort *sa duh·
moñd uñ groñ tef·for* it takes a lot of
effort
démangeaison *day·moñ·zheh·zoñ* f
itch
démanger* *day·moñ·zhay* vi itch
démarreur *day·ma·rur* m starter (*in
car*)
démêler *day·meh·lay* vt untangle; **la
crème démêlante** *krem day·meh·loñt*
conditioner (*for hair*)
déménager* *day·may·na·zhay* vi move
house
se démener* *suh day·muh·nay* vr
struggle
demi(e) *duh·mee* adj, m/f half; **une
demi-douzaine** *ōōn duh·mee·doo·zen*
a half dozen; **une demi-heure** *ōōn
duh·mee·ur* half an hour; **trois kilomètres et demi** *trwah kee·lo·meh·tray
duh·mee* three and a half kilometers;
à demi ouvert *a duh·mee oo·vehr*
half open; **un demi de bière** *uñ duh·
mee duh byehr* a pint of beer
demi-finale *duh·mee·fee·nal* f semifinal

demi-frère *duh·mee·frehr m* step-brother

demi-heure *duh·mee·ur f* half-hour

demi-pension *duh·mee·pon·syoñ f* half board

demi-sœur *duh·mee·sur f* stepsister

démission *day·mee·syoñ f* resignation

démissionner *day·mee·syo·nay vi* resign

demi-tarif *duh·mee·ta·reef m* half-fare

demi-tour *duh·mee·toor m* U-turn *(in car)*

démodé(e) *day·mo·day adj* old-fashioned

démonstration *day·moñ·stra·syoñ f* demonstration; **faire* une démonstration de** *fehr ōōn day·moñ·stra·syoñ duh* demonstrate *(appliance etc)*

de nouveau *duh noo·vō adv* again

dense *doñs adj* dense *(fog etc)*

dent *doñ f* tooth

dentelle *doñ·tel f* lace

dentier *doñ·tyay m* dentures

dentifrice *doñ·tee·frees m* toothpaste

dentiste *doñ·teest m/f* dentist

déodorant *day·ō·do·roñ m* deodorant

dépanneuse *day·pa·nuhz f* breakdown van

départ *day·par m* departure

dépasser *day·pa·say vt* exceed; **il m'a dépassé en courant** *eel ma day·pa·say oñ koo·roñ* he ran past me; **il a dépassé la quarantaine** *eela day·pa·say la ka·roñ·ten* he's past forty

se dépêcher *suh day·peh·shay vr* hurry; **dépêchez-vous!** *day·peh·shay voo* hurry up!; be quick!

dépendre *day·poñ·druh vi* depend; **ça dépend** *sa day·poñ* it depends; **dépendre de** *day·poñ·druh duh* to depend on

dépenser *day·poñ·say vt* spend *(money)*

dépenses *day·poñs fpl* expenditure; outgoings

en dépit de *oñ day·pee duh prep* in spite of

dépliant *day·plee·yoñ m* brochure

déplier *day·plee·ay vt* unfold

déposer *day·pō·zay vt* deposit *(money)*; lay down; **déposer son bilan** *day·pō·zay soñ bee·loñ* to go into liquidation; **déposer en banque** *day·pō·zay oñ boñk* to bank; **se déposer** *suh day·pō·zay* to settle *(wine)*

dépôt *day·pō m* deposit; depot

dépression nerveuse *day·preh·syoñ nehr·vuhz f* nervous breakdown

déprimé(e) *day·pree·may adj* depressed *(person)*

depuis *duh·pwee prep* since; **depuis quand êtes-vous ici?** *duh·pwee koñ et·voo zee·see* how long have you been here?; **il est là depuis ce temps-là** *eel eh la duh·pwee suh toñ·la* he's been there ever since; **je suis là depuis 4 heures** *zhuh swee la duh·pwee 4 ur* I've been here since 4 o'clock; **depuis que nous sommes arrivés** *duh·pwee kuh noo som za·ree·vay* since we arrived

déranger* *day·roñ·zhay vt* disturb *(interrupt)*; **cela vous dérange si ...?** *suh·la voo day·roñzh see* do you mind if ...?

dérapage *day·ra·pazh m* skid

déraper *day·ra·pay vi* skid

dérive *day·reev f* centreboard; **aller* à la dérive** *a·lay a la day·reev* to drift *(boat)*

dernier(ère) *dehr·nyay(·nyehr) adj* last; **la semaine dernière** *la suh·men dehr·nyehr* last week; **en dernier** *oñ dehr·nyay* last; **les dernières nouvelles** *lay dehr·nyehr noo·vel* the latest news

dérouter *day·roo·tay vt* reroute

derrière *deh·ryehr m* bottom *(of person)*; back □ *prep, adv* behind; **derrière le mur** *deh·ryehr luh mōōr* behind the wall; **de derrière** *duh deh·ryehr* rear

des = de + les

dès *deh prep* from; since; **dès ce moment-là** *deh suh mo·moñ·lah* from then on

désaccord *day·za·kor m* disagreement

désagréable *day·za·gray·a·bluh adj* unpleasant

désapprouver *day·za·proo·vay vt* disapprove of

désarçonner *day·zar·so·nay vt* throw *(rider)*

désastre *day·zas·truh m* disaster

désavantage *day·za·voñ·tazh m* disadvantage □ *adj* **désavantagé(e)** *day·za·voñ·ta·zhay* at a disadvantage

descendre *deh·soñ·druh vt/i* come/go down; get/take down

description *deh·skreep·syoñ f* description

désert *day·zehr m* desert

désespéré(e) *day·zes·pay·ray adj* desperate

déshabiller *day·za·bee·yay vt* undress; **se déshabiller** *suh day·za·bee·yay* undress

désinfectant *day·zañ·fek·toñ m* disinfectant

désinfecter *day·zañ·fek·tay vt* disinfect

désintéresser *day·zañ·tay·reh·say vt* buy out *(partner etc)*

désir *day·zeer m* wish; desire

désirer *day·zee·ray vt* want

désobéir à *day·zo·bay·yeer a vt* disobey

désobéissant(e) *day·zo·bay·ee·soñ (·soñt) adj* disobedient

désolé(e) *day·zo·lay adj* sorry; **je suis désolé mais je ne peux pas le faire** *zhuh swee day·zo·lay meh zhuh nuh puh pah luh fehr* I'm afraid I can't do it

désordre *day·zor·druh m* mess; muddle; **faire* du désordre** *fehr dōō day·zor·druh* to make a mess; **en désordre** *oñ day·zor·druh* in a muddle; untidy *(room)*

desserré(e) *deh·seh·ray adj* loose *(knot, screw)*

dessert *deh·sehr m* dessert; pudding

dessin *deh·sañ m* design; drawing; **le dessin humoristique** *deh·sañ ōō·mō·rees·teek* cartoon; **le dessin animé** *deh·sañ a·nee·may* cartoon *(animated)*

dessinateur *deh·see·na·tur m* draftsman; draughtsman

dessiner *deh·see·nay vt* design; draw *(picture)*

dessous *duh·soo adv* underneath; **c'est en dessous** *seh toñ duh·soo* it's underneath; **mettre* sa valise en dessous de la chaise** *meh·truh sa va·leez oñ duh·soo duh la shez* to put one's case beneath the chair; **ma chambre est en dessous de la sienne** *ma shoñ·bruh eh toñ duh·soo duh la syen* my room is below his; **au dessous (de)** *ō duh·soo (duh)* below

dessous-de-plat *duh·soo·duh·pla m* table-mat

dessous-de-verre *duh·soo·duh·vehr m* mat (*under a glass*)

dessus *duh·sŏō m* top □ *adv* on top; **en/au dessus (de)** *oñ/ō duh·sŏō (duh)* above

destination *des·tee·na·syoñ f* destination; **à destination de** *a des·tee·na·syoñ duh* bound for

destiner *deh·stee·nay vt* intend

détacher *day·ta·shay vt* untie; **se détacher** *suh day·ta·shay* to come off

détail *day·tye m* detail; **vendre quelque chose au détail** *voñ·druh kel·kuh shōz ō day·tye* to sell something retail; **en détail** *oñ day·tye* in detail; **le prix de détail** *pree duh day·tye* retail price

détaillant *day·tye·yoñ m* retailer

détaillé(e) *day·tye·yay adj* detailed; itemized (*bill etc*)

se détendre *suh day·toñ·druh vr* relax

détente *day·toñt f* relaxation

détergent *day·tehr·zhoñ m* detergent

déterminé(e) *day·tehr·mee·nay adj* determined

déterrer *day·teh·ray vt* dig up

détester *day·tes·tay vt* hate

détonation *day·to·na·syoñ f* bang (*of gun etc*)

détoner *day·to·nay vi* bang (*gun etc*)

détour *day·toor m* detour; **faire* un détour** *fehr uñ day·toor* to make a detour

détourner *day·toor·nay vt* hijack; divert (*traffic*)

détresse *day·tres f* distress

détruire* *day·trweer vt* destroy

dette *det f* debt; **avoir* des dettes** *a·vwahr day det* to be in debt

deux *duh num* two; **couper quelque chose en deux** *koo·pay kel·kuh shōz oñ duh* to cut something in half; **les deux filles** *lay duh feey* both girls; **les deux** *lay duh* both; **tous (toutes) les deux** *too (toot) lay duh* both (of them)

deuxième *duh·zyem adj* second; **de deuxième classe** *duh duh·zyem klas* second-class; **le deuxième étage** *duh·zyem ay·tazh* second floor

deux-pièces *duh·pyes m* two-piece

dévaliser *day·va·lee·zay vt* rob

dévaluation *day·va·lŏō·a·syoñ f* devaluation

dévaluer *day·va·lŏō·ay vt* devalue (*currency*)

devant *duh·voñ m* front (*foremost part*) □ *prep, adv* in front (of); **s'asseoir* devant** *sa·swahr duh·voñ* to sit in front; **de devant** *duh duh·voñ* front

développement *day·vuh·lop·moñ m* development; **le pays en voie de développement** *pay·yee oñ vwah duh day·vuh·lop·moñ* developing country

développer *day·vuh·lo·pay vt* develop; **se développer** *suh day·vuh·lo·pay* expand (*business*); develop

devenir* *duh·vuh·neer vi* become; **devenir* professionnel(le)** *duh·vuh·neer pro·feh·syo·nel* to turn professional; **devenir* fatigué(e)** *duh·vuh·neer fa·tee·gay* to get tired

déviation *day·vya·syoñ f* diversion

dévier *day·vyay vt* divert

deviner *duh·vee·nay vt* guess

devis *duh·vee m* quotation (*price*)

devises étrangères *duh·veez ay·troñ·zhehr fpl* foreign currency

dévisser *day·vee·say vt* unscrew

devoir *duh·vwahr m* duty (*obligation*); **les devoirs** *duh·vwahr* homework

devoir* *duh·vwahr vt* owe (*money*); **il me doit £5** *eel muh dwah £5* he owes me £5 □ *vi* **il doit le faire** *el dwah luh fehr* she has to do it; **vous devez venir** *voo duh·vay vuh·neer* you must come; **je devrais le faire** *zhuh duh·vreh luh fehr* I ought to do it; **il devrait gagner** *eel duh·vreh ga·nyay* he ought to win; **nous devrions l'acheter** *noo duh·vryoñ lash·tay* we should buy it; **vous devriez le faire aujourd'hui** *voo duh·vree·ay luh fehr ō·zhoor·dwee* you're supposed to do it today

diabète *dya·bet m* diabetes

diabétique *dya·bay·teek m/f* diabetic

diagnostic *dya·gno·steek m* diagnosis

diagonal(e) *dya·go·nal adj* diagonal

diagramme *dya·gram m* diagram

dialecte *dya·lekt m* dialect

diamant *dya·moñ m* diamond

diamètre *dya·meh·truh m* diameter

diapositive *dya·po·zee·teev f* slide (*photo*)

diarrhée *dya·ray f* diarrh(o)ea

dicter *deek·tay vt* dictate (*letter*)

dictionnaire *deek·syo·nehr m* dictionary

diesel *dyeh·zel m* diesel

dieu *dyuh m* god; **Dieu** *Dyuh* God

différence *dee·fay·roñs f* difference

différent(e) *dee·fay·roñ(·roñt) adj* different; **différent de** *dee·fay·roñ duh* different from

différer* *dee·fay·ray vt* delay (*postpone*)

difficile *dee·fee·seel adj* difficult

difficulté *dee·fee·kŏōl·tay f* difficulty

difforme *dee·form adj* deformed

diffuser *dee·fŏō·zay vt* broadcast (*on radio*)

digital(e) *dee·zhee·tal adj* digital

digue *deeg f* dike; jetty

dilater *dee·la·tay vt* expand; **se dilater** *suh dee·la·tay* expand

diluer *dee·lŏō·ay vt* dilute

dimanche *dee·moñsh m* Sunday; **le dimanche de Pentecôte** *dee·moñsh duh poñt·kōt* Whitsunday

dimensions *dee·moñ·syoñ fpl* dimensions; size

diminuer *dee·mee·nŏō·ay vt* decrease

dinde *dañd f* turkey

dîner *dee·nay m* dinner; dinner party

diplomate *dee·plo·mat m* diplomat; trifle (*dessert*)

diplôme *dee·plōm m* diploma; **le diplôme universitaire** *dee·plōm ŏō·nee·vehr·see·tehr* degree

diplômé(e) *dee·plō·may adj* qualified

dire* *deer vt* say; tell; **dire* des bêtises** *deer day beh·teez* to talk nonsense; **dire* à quelqu'un de faire quelque chose** *deer a kel·kuñ duh fehr kel·kuh shōz* to tell someone to do something

direct(e) *dee·rekt adj* direct; **le train direct** *trañ dee·rekt* through train

directement *dee·rekt·moñ adv* directly; **aller* directement à la maison** *a·lay dee·rekt·moñ a la meh·zoñ* to go straight home

directeur *dee·rek·tur m* manager; headmaster; governor (*of institution*); director (*of firm*); principal (*of school etc*); **le directeur commercial** *dee·rek·tur ko·mehr·syal* sales manager; **le directeur de banque** *dee·rek·*

tur duh boǹk bank manager; **le directeur du marketing** *dee·rek·tur dōō mar·ke·ting* marketing manager; **le directeur général** *dee·rek·tur zhay·nay·ral* managing director, M.D.

direction *dee·rek·syoǹ f* management; direction

directives *dee·rek·teev fpl* instructions

directrice *dee·rek·trees f* manageress; headmistress; principal (*of school etc*)

diriger* *dee·ree·zhay vt* steer; run (*a business, country*)

discipline *dee·see·pleen f* discipline

disc-jockey *deesk·jo·kay m* disc jockey

disco *dees·kō f* disco(thèque)

discours *dees·koor m* speech (*oration*)

discret(ète) *dees·kreh(·kret) adj* discreet

discrimination *dees·kree·mee·na·syoǹ f* discrimination

discuter *dees·kōō·tay vt* discuss; **discuter de quelque chose** *dees·kōō·tay duh kel·kuh shōz* to talk something over

disloquer *dees·lo·kay vt* dislocate

disparaître* *dees·pa·reh·truh vi* disappear; **mon portefeuille a disparu** *moǹ port·fuhy a dees·pa·rōō* my wallet is missing

disparu(e) *dees·pa·rōō adj* missing

disponible *dees·po·nee·bluh adj* available

dispositif *dees·po·zee·teef m* device

dispute *dees·pōōt f* argument; dispute

se disputer *suh dees·pōō·tay vr* argue; quarrel; **se disputer avec quelqu'un** *suh dees·pōō·tay a·vek kel·kuǹ* to quarrel with somebody

disqualifier *dees·ka·lee·fyay vt* disqualify

disque *deesk m* record; disc; **le disque de stationnement** *deesk duh sta·syon·moǹ* parking disc

dissoudre* *dee·soo·druh vt* dissolve; **se dissoudre*** *suh dee·soo·druh* dissolve

distance *dees·toǹs f* distance

distant(e) *dees·toǹ(·toǹt) adj* distant

distillerie *dees·teel·luh·ree f* distillery

distinct(e) *dees·taǹ(·taǹkt) adj* distinct (*clear*)

distinguer *dees·taǹ·gay vt* distinguish; **distinguer quelque chose de quelque chose** *dees·taǹ·gay kel·kuh shōz duh kel·kuh shōz* to distinguish something from something

distraire* *dees·trehr vt* distract

distribuer *dees·tree·bōō·ay vt* distribute; deliver (*mail*)

distributeur *dees·tree·bōō·tur m* distributor (*in car*); **le distributeur automatique** *dees·treeb·bōō·tur ō·tō·ma·teek* vending machine

distribution *dees·tree·bōō·syoǹ f* distribution; delivery (*of mail*)

divan *dee·voǹ m* divan

divers(e) *dee·vehr(·vehrs) adj* various

diversifier *dee·vehr·see·fyay vi* diversify

dividende *dee·vee·doǹd m* dividend

diviser *dee·vee·zay vt* divide; **diviser 8 par 4** *dee·vee·zay 8 par 4* to divide 8 by 4

divorce *dee·vors m* divorce □ *adj* divorcé(e) *dee·vor·say* divorced

dix *dees num* ten

dix-huit *deez·weet num* eighteen

dixième *dee·zyem adj* tenth

dix-neuf *deez·nuhf num* nineteen

dix-sept *dees·set num* seventeen

dix-septième *dees·seh·tyem adj* seventeenth

dock *dok m* dock

docteur *dok·tur m* doctor

document *do·kōō·moǹ m* document

doigt *dwah m* finger; **le doigt de pied** *dwah duh pyay* toe

dollar *do·lar m* dollar

domaine *do·men m* property; estate

domicile *do·mee·seel m* home (*address*)

dommage *do·mazh m* damage; **quel dommage!** *kel do·mazh* what a pity!; **les dommages-intérêts** *do·mazh·zaǹ·tay·reh* damages

don *doǹ m* gift (*ability*); donation (*money*); **faire* don de** *fehr doǹ duh* donate (*funds*)

donc *doǹk adv* so

données *do·nay fpl* data

donner *do·nay vt* give; give away; **donner quelque chose à quelqu'un** *do·nay kel·kuh shōz a kel·kuǹ* to give someone something; **donnez-le-moi** *do·nay·luh·mwah* give it to me; **donner quelque chose à quelqu'un** *do·nay kel·kuh shōz a kel·kuǹ* to hand someone something

donneur *do·nur m* dealer (*cards*)

dont *doǹ pron* whose; **l'homme dont le fils** *lom doǹ luh fees* the man, whose son

doré(e) *do·ray adj* golden

dormir* *dor·meer vi* sleep

dortoir *dor·twahr m* dormitory (*room*)

dos *dō m* back

dose *dōz f* dose

dossier *dō·syay m* file; back (*of chair*)

douane *dwan f* customs; **exempté de douane** *eg·zoǹ·tay duh dwan* duty-free (*goods*)

douanier *dwa·nyay m* customs officer

double *doo·bluh adj* double; **un double whisky** *uǹ doo·bluh wees·kee* a double whisky; **coûter le double** *koo·tay luh doo·bluh* to cost double

doubler *doo·blay vt* pass, overtake (*car*); double

doublure *doo·blōōr f* lining; **sans doublure** *soǹ doo·blōōr* unlined

douce *doos adj* gentle; soft; mild

doucement *doo·suh·moǹ adv* quietly; gently

douche *doosh f* shower (*bath*)

doué(e) *doo·ay adj* gifted

douleur *doo·lur f* pain

douloureux(euse) *doo·loo·ruh(·ruhz) adj* sore; painful

doute *doot m* doubt; **sans doute** *soǹ doot* no doubt; **sans aucun doute** *soǹ zō·kuǹ doot* without (*a*) doubt

douter de *doo·tay duh vt* doubt; **j'en doute** *zhoǹ doot* I doubt it

douteux(euse) *doo·tuh(·tuhz) adj* doubtful

Douvres *doo·vruh m* Dover

doux *doo adj* gentle; soft; mild

douzaine *doo·zen f* dozen; **4 douzaines d'œufs 4** *doo·zen duh* 4 dozen eggs

douze *dooz num* twelve

douzième *doo·zyem adj* twelfth

drainer *dreh·nay vt* drain (*land*)

dramatique *dra·ma·teek adj* dramatic

drap *dra m* sheet

drapeau *dra·pō m* flag

dresser *dreh·say vt* draw up (*document*); train (*dog*); pitch (*tent*)

drogue *drog f* drug

droit *drwah adv* straight (*shoot, write etc*) □ *m* **le droit** *drwah* right (*entitlement*); **les droits d'auteur** *drwah dō·*

tur copyright; **les droits de douane** *drwah dwan* customs duty
droit(e) *drwah (drwaht) adj* right (*not left*); straight
droite *drwaht f* right (*right-hand side*); **à droite** *a drwaht* on the right; **tourner à droite** *toor·nay a drwaht* to turn right
droitier(ère) *drwah·tyay(·tyehr) adj* right-handed
drôle *drōl adj* funny (*amusing*)
dû (due) *dōō adj* due (*owing*)
duc *dōōk m* duke
dumping *duñ·peeng m* dumping (*of goods*)
dune *dōōn f* dune
dur(e) *dōōr adj* tough (*meat etc*); hard; hard-boiled
durer *dōō·ray vi* last; **le programme dure combien de temps?** *luh pro·gram dōōr koñ·byañ duh toñ* how long is the programme?
duvet *dōō·veh m* down (*fluff*)
dynamique *dee·na·meek adj* dynamic (*person*)
dynamo *dee·na·mō f* dynamo

E

eau *ō f* water; **l'eau de toilette** *ō duh twah·let* toilet water; **l'eau-de-vie** *ō duh·vee* brandy; **l'eau de Cologne** *ō duh ko·lo·nyuh* eau-de-Cologne; **l'eau du robinet** *ō dōō ro·bee·neh* tap-water; **l'eau de Javel** *ō duh zha·vel* bleach; **l'eau potable** *ō po·ta·bluh* drinking water; **l'eau distillée** *ō dees·tee·lay* distilled water; **l'eau minérale** *ō mee·nay·ral* mineral water
éblouir *ay·bloo·eer vt* dazzle
ébouillanter *ay·boo·yoñ·tay vt* scald
écaille *ay·kye f* scale (*of fish*); flake
écarlate *ay·kar·lat adj* scarlet
à l'écart de *a lay·kar duh prep* away from
échalote *ay·sha·lot f* shallot
échange *ay·shoñzh m* exchange
échanger* *ay·shoñ·zhay vt* exchange; **échanger* quelque chose contre quelque chose** *ay·shoñ·zhay kel·kuh shōz koñ·truh kel·kuh shōz* to exchange something for something
échangeur *ay·shoñ·zhur m* interchange (*on roads*)
échantillon *ay·shoñ·tee·yoñ m* sample (*of goods*)
s'échapper *say·sha·pay vr* escape (*person*) □ *vi* **échapper** *ay·sha·pay* escape (*liquid, gas*)
écharde *ay·shard f* splinter (*wood*)
écharpe *ay·sharp f* scarf; sling (*for arm*)
échec *ay·shek m* failure
échecs *ay·shek mpl* chess
échelle *ay·shel f* ladder; scale (*on map, thermometer*); run (*in stocking*)
écho *ay·kō m* echo
échouer *ay·shoo·ay vi* fail; **échouer à** *ay·shoo·ay a* fail (*exam*)
éclaboussement *ay·kla·boos·moñ m* splash
éclabousser *ay·kla·boo·say vt* splash
éclair *ay·klehr m* éclair; flash of lightning
éclairage *ay·kleh·razh m* lighting; **l'éclairage au néon** *ay·kleh·razh ō nay·oñ* strip-lighting
éclairer *ay·kleh·ray vt* light up
éclatement *ay·klat·moñ m* blow-out
éclater *ay·kla·tay vi* burst; explode
éclisse *ay·klees f* splint

écluse *ay·klōōz f* lock (*in canal*)
écœurant(e) *ay·kuh·roñ(·roñt) adj* sickly (*cake etc*)
école *ay·kol f* school; **l'école primaire** *ay·kol pree·mehr* primary school, grade school
économie *ay·ko·no·mee f* economy (*of country*); economics; **les économies** *ay·ko·no·mee* savings
économique *ay·ko·no·meek adj* economic; economical (*use, method*); **peu économique** *puh ay·ko·no·meek* uneconomical
économiser *ay·ko·no·mee·zay vt* save
économiste *ay·ko·no·meest m/f* economist
écorce *ay·kors f* peel (*of orange, lemon*); bark (*of tree*)
écorcher *ay·kor·shay vt* graze (*skin*)
écorchure *ay·kor·shōōr f* graze
Écossais(e) *ay·ko·seh(·sez) m/f* Scot; **il est Écossais** *eel eh tay·ko·seh* he's Scottish; **elle est Écossaise** *el eh tay·ko·sez* she's Scottish □ *adj* **écossais(e)** *ay·ko·seh(·sez)* Scottish; **une jupe écossaise** *ōōn zhōōp ay·ko·sez* a tartan skirt
Écosse *ay·kos f* Scotland
écouter *ay·koo·tay vi* listen □ *vt* listen to
écouteur *ay·koo·tur m* receiver (*telephone*)
écran *ay·kroñ m* screen (*TV, movie*)
écraser *ay·kra·zay vt* crush; run over
écrevisse *ay·kruh·vees f* crawfish, crayfish (*freshwater*)
écrire *ay·kreer vt/i* write □ *vt* spell (*in writing*); **écrire* en caractères d'imprimerie** *ay·kreer oñ ka·rak·tehr dañ·pree·mree* to print (*write in block letters*)
par écrit *par ay·kree adv* in writing
écriture *ay·kree·tōōr f* writing
s'écrouler *say·kroo·lay vr* collapse
écureuil *ay·kōō·ruhy m* squirrel
écurie *ay·kōō·ree f* stable
écusson *ay·kōō·soñ m* badge (*of cloth*)
eczéma *eg·zay·ma m* eczema
édifice *ay·dee·fees m* building
éditeur *ay·dee·tur m* publisher
édition *ay·dee·syoñ f* edition
éditrice *ay·dee·trees f* publisher
édredon *ay·druh·doñ m* eiderdown; quilt
éducation *ay·dōō·ka·syoñ f* education
effacer* *ay·fa·say vt* rub out; wipe off
effet *eh·feh m* effect; **prendre* effet** *proñ·dreh·feh* to take effect
efficace *eh·fee·kas adj* effective (*remedy etc*); efficient
effondrement *eh·foñ·druh·moñ m* slump
s'effondrer *seh·foñ·dray vr* collapse
effort *eh·for m* effort
effrayer *eh·fray·yay vt* frighten
effronté(e) *eh·froñ·tay adj* cheeky
égal(e) *ay·gal adj* even; equal; **cela m'est égal** *suh·la meh tay·gal* I don't mind; I don't care
également *ay·gal·moñ adv* equally; too
églefin *ay·gluh·fañ m* haddock
église *ay·gleez f* church
égoïste *ay·go·eest adj* selfish
égout *ay·goo m* drain
égoutter *ay·goo·tay vt* drain (*vegetables*); **laisser s'égoutter** *leh·say say·go·tay* drip-dry
égouttoir *ay·goo·twahr m* drainboard, draining-board; rack (*for dishes*)
Égypte *ay·zheept f* Egypt

égyptien(ne) *ay·zheep·syañ(·syen)* adj Egyptian

élastique *ay·las·teek* m elastic; elastic band

élection *ay·lek·syoñ* f election; **les élections législatives** *ay·lek·syoñ lay·zhee·sla·teev* general election

électricien *ay·lek·tree·syañ* m electrician

électricité *ay·lek·tree·see·tay* f electricity

électrique *ay·lek·treek* adj electric(al)

électronique *ay·lek·tro·neek* adj electronic □ **l'électronique** *ay·lek·tro·neek* electronics

électrophone *ay·lek·tro·fon* m record-player

élégant(e) *ay·lay·goñ(·goñt)* adj stylish; smart; elegant

élément *ay·lay·moñ* m unit (of machinery, furniture); element

éléphant *ay·lay·foñ* m elephant

élève *ay·lev* m/f pupil

élevé(e) *ay·luh·vay* adj high (price, temperature)

élever* *ay·luh·vay* vt bring up; raise (family); **ça s'élève à F400** *sa say·lev a F400* it amounts to F400

éliminatoire *ay·lee·mee·na·twahr* f heat (sports)

éliminé(e) *ay·lee·mee·nay* adj out (team, player)

élire* *ay·leer* vt elect

elle *el* pron she; her; it; **c'est elle** *seh tel* it's her

elle-même *el·mem* pron herself

elles *el* pron they; them

elles-mêmes *el·mem* pron themselves

éloigné(e) *ay·lwañ·nyay* adj distant; **le (la) plus éloigné(e)** *luh (la) plōō zay·lwañ·nyay* the farthest

émail *ay·mye* m enamel

emballage *oñ·ba·lazh* m packing (material)

emballer *oñ·ba·lay* vt pack (goods); rev (engine); **emballer un paquet** *oñ·ba·lay uñ pa·kay* to wrap up a parcel

embardée *oñ·bar·day* f swerve; **faire* une embardée** *fehr ōōn oñ·bar·day* to swerve

embargo *oñ·bar·gó* m embargo

embarquement *oñ·bar·kuh·moñ* m boarding; **la carte d'embarquement** *kart doñ·bar·kuh·moñ* boarding pass

embarquer *oñ·bar·kay* vi embark

embêter *oñ·beh·tay* vt bother

embouteillage *oñ·boo·tay·yazh* m traffic jam; hold-up (traffic)

embrasser *oñ·bra·say* vt embrace; kiss; **s'embrasser** *soñ·bra·say* to kiss (each other)

embrayage *oñ·bray·yazh* m clutch (of car)

émeraude *ay·muh·rōd* f emerald

émeute *ay·muht* f riot

émigrer *ay·mee·gray* vi emigrate

émission *ay·mee·syoñ* f program(me) (radio, TV); issue (of stocks); broadcast

emmêler *oñ·may·lay* vt tangle

emménager* *oñ·may·na·zhay* vi move in

emmener* *oñ·muh·nay* vt take; **emmener* quelqu'un au théâtre** *oñ·muh·nay kel·kuñ ō tay·ah·truh* to take someone out to the theatre; **emmener* quelqu'un en ville** *oñ·muh·nay kel·kuñ oñ veel* to give someone a ride into town

émotion *ay·mō·syoñ* f emotion

émoussé(e) *ay·moo·say* adj blunt (knife)

empêcher *oñ·peh·shay* vt prevent; **empêcher quelqu'un de faire quelque chose** *oñ·peh·shay kel·kuñ duh fehr kel·kuh shōz* to stop someone doing something

empereur *oñ·puh·rur* m emperor

empire *oñ·peer* m empire

emploi *oñ·plwah* m use; job; employment

employé(e) *oñ·plwah·yay* m/f employee; **l'employé(e) de bureau** *oñ·plwah·yay duh bōō·rō* clerk (in office); office worker

employer *oñ·plwah·yay* vt use; employ (worker)

employeur *oñ·plwah·yur* m employer

empoisonnement *oñ·pwah·zon·moñ* m poisoning

emporter *oñ·por·tay* vt take (away); **à emporter** *a oñ·por·tay* take-away (food); carry-out

emprunt *oñ·pruñ* m loan

emprunter *oñ·pruñ·tay* vt borrow; **emprunter quelque chose à quelqu'un** *oñ·pruñ·tay kel·kuh shōz a kel·kuñ* to borrow something from someone

en *oñ* pron some; any; of it/them; **il en restait un peu** *eel oñ res·teh tuñ puh* some (of it) was left □ prep in; to; by; **en bois** *oñ bwah* made out of wood; **en français** *oñ froñ·seh* in French; **en mai** *oñ may* in May; **il l'a fait en 2 jours** *eel la feh oñ 2 zhoor* he did it in 2 days; **en ville/France** *oñ veel/froñs* in/to town/France; **en train/voiture** *oñ trañ/vwah·tōōr* by train/car

encaisser *oñ·keh·say* vt cash

enceinte *oñ·sañt* adj pregnant

enchanté(e) *oñ·shoñ·tay* adj delighted

enchère *oñ·shehr* f bid

encore *oñ·kor* adv still (up to this time); yet; **encore plus vite** *oñ·kor plōō veet* even faster; **encore une fois** *oñ·kor ōōn fwah* once more; **encore de** *oñ·kor duh* more; **encore du fromage** *oñ·kor dōō fro·mazh* more cheese; **encore du monde** *oñ·kor dōō moñd* more people; **encore une bière s'il vous plaît** *oñ·kor ōōn byehr seel voo pleh* another beer please; **est-ce qu'il y a encore de la soupe?** *es·keel ya oñ·kor duh la soop* is there any more soup?

encouragement *oñ·koo·razh·moñ* m encouragement

encre *oñ·kruh* f ink

encyclopédie *oñ·see·klo·pay·dee* f cyclop(a)edia

endive *oñ·deev* f endive (smooth)

endives *oñ·deev* fpl chicory (vegetable)

endormi(e) *oñ·dor·mee* adj asleep; **être* profondément endormi(e)** *eh·truh pro·foñ·day·moñ oñ·dor·mee* to be fast asleep

endosser *oñ·dō·say* vt endorse (document)

endroit *oñ·drwah* m the right side (of cloth etc); place; spot (locality)

énergie *ay·nehr·zhee* f energy

énergique *ay·nehr·zheek* adj energetic

enfant *oñ·foñ* m/f child; **un enfant unique** *uñ oñ·foñ ōō·neek* an only child; **le/la petit(e)** *puh·tee (·teet) oñ·foñ* grandchild

enfin *oñ·fañ* adv at last

enflé(e) *oñ·flay* adj swollen

enfler *oñ·flay* vi swell (up) (limb etc)

enflure *oñ·flōōr* f swelling (lump)

enfoncer* oñ·foñ·say *vt* push in

engager* oñ·ga·zhay *vt* engage; **s'engager* à faire** soñ·ga·zhay a fehr to undertake to do

engin spatial oñ·zhañ spa·syal *m* spacecraft

engourdi(e) oñ·goor·dee *adj* numb

enjeu oñ·zhuh *m* stake (*in gambling*)

enlever(e) oñ·luh·vay *vt* remove; take off (*clothes*); take away

ennemi(e) eh·nuh·mee *m/f* enemy

ennui oñ·nwee *m* nuisance; trouble; **les ennuis de moteur** oñ·nwee duh mo·tur engine trouble; **avoir* des ennuis** a·vwahr day zoñ·nwee to be in trouble

ennuyer oñ·nwee·yay *vt* bother (*annoy*); **je m'ennuie** zhuh moñ·nwee I'm bored

ennuyeux(euse) oñ·nwee·yuh(·yuhz) *adj* boring; dull; **c'est ennuyeux** seh toñ·nwee·yuh it's a nuisance

énorme ay·norm *adj* enormous

enregistrer oñ·ruh·zhee·stray *vt* record (*sound*); register (*luggage*); check in

enrouler oñ·roo·lay *vt* roll up (*newspaper etc*); wind

enseignement oñ·seh·nyuh·moñ *m* education

enseigner oñ·seh·nyay *vt* teach

ensemble oñ·soñ·bluh *adv* together □ *m* **l'ensemble** oñ·soñ·bluh ensemble (*clothes*)

ensoleillé(e) oñ·so·lay·yay *adj* sunny

ensuite oñ·sweet *adv* then

entasser oñ·ta·say *vt* pile up

entendre oñ·toñ·druh *vt/i* hear; **je ne vous entends pas** zhuh nuh voo zoñ·toñ pa I can't hear (you); **on n'entend rien sur la ligne** oñ noñ·toñ ryañ sōōr la lee·nyuh the line is dead (*phone*)

entendu oñ·toñ·dōō *adv* all right (*yes*)

enterrement oñ·tehr·moñ *m* funeral

enterrer oñ·teh·ray *vt* bury

enthousiasme oñ·too·zyaz·muh *m* enthusiasm

enthousiaste oñ·too·zyast *adj* enthusiastic; keen (*swimmer, reader*)

entier(ère) oñ·tyay(·tyehr) *adj* whole (*complete*)

entorse oñ·tors *f* sprain

entourer oñ·too·ray *vt* surround

entracte oñ·trakt *m* interval (*in performance*)

entrain oñ·trañ *m* liveliness; **plein(e) d'entrain** plañ (plen) doñ·trañ lively

entraînement oñ·tren·moñ *m* training (*for sports*)

entraîner oñ·treh·nay *vt* pull along; **s'entraîner** soñ·treh·nay train (*sportsman*)

entre oñ·truh *prep* between; **est-ce que l'un d'entre vous sait chanter?** es·kuh luñ doñ·truh voo seh shoñ·tay can any of you sing?; **lequel (laquelle) d'entre vous?** luh·kel (la·kel) doñ·truh voo which one of you?

entrecôte oñ·truh·kōt *f* rib steak

entrée oñ·tray *f* entry; entry (*way in*); admission; hall; entrance; **le prix d'entrée** pree doñ·tray admission fee

entrepôt oñ·truh·pō *m* warehouse; store

entreprendre* oñ·truh·proñ·druh *vt* undertake

entrepreneur oñ·truh·pruh·nur *m* contractor

entreprise oñ·truh·preez *f* venture; undertaking; enterprise; project;

l'entreprise privée oñ·truh·preez pree·vay private enterprise

entrer oñ·tray *vi* come in; enter; go in; **ça n'entre pas** sa noñ·truh pa it won't go in; **entrer dans** oñ·tray doñ to enter (*room*)

entretien oñ·truh·tyañ *m* talk (*conversation*); upkeep; maintenance

entrevue oñ·truh·vōō *f* interview

enveloppe oñ·vuh·lop *f* envelope

envelopper oñ·vuh·lop·pay *vt* wrap

envers oñ·vehr *prep* toward; **son attitude envers les autres** soñ na·tee·tōōd oñ·vehr lay zō·truh his attitude towards others □ *m* **l'envers** oñ·vehr the wrong side; **à l'envers** a loñ·vehr upside down; back to front; inside out; **mettre* quelque chose à l'envers** meh·truh kel·kuh shōz a loñ·vehr to turn something upside down etc.

envie oñ·vee *f* envy; **avoir* envie de quelque chose** a·vwahr oñ·vee duh kel·kuh shōz to want something; **j'ai envie d'une bière** zhay oñ·vee doon byehr I feel like a beer; **avoir* envie de faire** a·vwahr oñ·vee duh fehr to feel like doing

envier oñ·vyay *vt* envy

envieux(euse) oñ·vee·yuh(·vyuhz) *adj* envious

environ oñ·vee·roñ *adv* around; about

environs oñ·vee·roñ *mpl* surroundings

envoi oñ·vwah *m* remittance; consignment; **l'envoi recommandé** oñ·vwah ruh·ko·moñ·day certified mail

envoyer oñ·vwa·yay *vt* send; **envoyer quelque chose par voie de terre** oñ·vwah·yay kel·kuh shōz par vwah duh tehr to send something surface mail; **envoyer par la poste** oñ·vwah·yay par la post to mail

épais(se) ay·peh(·pes) *adj* thick; **peu épais(se)** puh ay·peh(·pes) thin (*liquid*)

épaisseur ay·peh·sur *f* thickness; **3 mètres d'épaisseur** 3 meh·truh day·peh·sur 3 metres thick

épaule ay·pōl *f* shoulder

épave ay·pav *f* wreck (*ship*)

épée ay·pay *f* sword

épi de maïs ay·pee duh ma·ees *m* corn-on-the-cob

épice ay·pees *f* spice

épicé(e) ay·pee·say *adj* spicy

épicerie ay·pee·suh·ree *f* grocery shop; **l'épicerie fine** ay·pee·suh·ree feen delicatessen

épicier ay·pee·syay *m* grocer

épidémie ay·pee·day·mee *f* epidemic

épilepsie ay·pee·lep·see *f* epilepsy

épinards ay·pee·nar *mpl* spinach

épingle ay·pañ·gluh *f* pin; **l'épingle de nourrice** ay·pañ·gluh duh noo·rees safety pin; **l'épingle de sûreté** ay·pañ·gluh duh sōōr·tay safety pin

épingler ay·pañ·glay *vt* pin

éplucher ay·plōō·shay *vt* peel

épluchure ay·plōō·shōōr *f* peel

éponge ay·poñzh *f* sponge

éponger* ay·poñ·zhay *vt* mop

époque ay·pok *f* age (*era*); **d'époque** day·pok period (*furniture*)

épouser ay·poo·zay *vt* marry

épousseter* ay·poos·tay *vt* dust (*furniture*)

épouvantable ay·poo·voñ·ta·bluh *adj* terrible

épreuve ay·pruhv *f* proof; print (*photographic*); **mettre* à l'épreuve** meh·tra lay·pruhv to test (*ability*)

épuisé(e) ay·pwee·zay *adj* sold out; exhausted; worn-out (*person*); out of stock; out of print

équateur *ay·kwa·tur m* equator

équilibre *ay·kee·lee·bruh m* balance; **perdre son équilibre** *pehr·druh soñ nay·kee·lee·bruh* to lose one's balance; **tenir* en équilibre** *tuh·neer oñ nay·kee·lee·bruh* to balance; **l'équilibre des forces** *ay·kee·lee·bruh day fors* balance of power

s'équilibrer *say·kee·lee·bray vr* balance

équipage *ay·kee·pazh m* crew (*of ship, plane*)

équipe *ay·keep f* team; shift (*of workmen*)

équipements *ay·keep·moñ mpl* facilities

équitable *ay·kee·ta·bluh adj* fair (*just*)

équitation *ay·kee·ta·syoñ f* horseriding

équivalent(e) *ay·kee·va·loñ(·loñt) adj* equivalent; **équivalent(e) à** *ay·kee·va·loñ(·loñt) a* equivalent to

érotique *ay·ro·teek adj* erotic

errer *eh·ray vi* wander

erreur *eh·rur f* mistake; error; **faire* une erreur** *fehr ōōn eh·rur* to make a mistake; **par erreur** *par eh·rur* in error; by mistake

éruption *ay·rōōp·syoñ f* rash

escabeau *es·ka·bō m* stepladder

escale *es·kal f* stopover (*air travel*)

escalier *es·ka·lyay m* stairs; flight of steps; staircase; **l'escalier roulant** *es·ka·lyay roo·loñ* escalator; **l'escalier de secours** *es·ka·lyay duh suh·koor* fire escape

escalope *es·ka·lop f* escalope

escargot *es·kar·gō m* snail

esclave *es·klav m/f* slave

escorte *es·kort f* escort

escorter *es·kor·tay vt* escort

espace *es·pas m* space

Espagne *es·pa·nyuh f* Spain

espagnol *es·pa·nyol m* Spanish □ *adj* espagnol(e) *es·pa·nyol* Spanish; **il est Espagnol** *eel eh tes·pa·nyol* he's Spanish; **elle est Espagnole** *el eh tes·pa·nyol* she's Spanish

espèce *es·pes f* sort; **les espèces** *es·pes* cash

espéranto *es·pay·roñ·tō m* Esperanto

espérer* *es·pay·ray vi* hope □ *vt* hope for; **je l'espère** *zhuh les·pehr* I hope so; **j'espère que non** *zhes·pehr kuh noñ* I hope not

espion *es·pyoñ m* spy

espionne *es·pyon f* spy

espoir *es·pwahr m* hope

esprit *es·pree m* mind; spirit (*soul*)

essai *eh·say m* trial; test; essay; **l'essai sur route** *eh·say sōōr root* road test; **l'essai de route** *eh·say duh root* test-drive; **faire* un essai de route à une voiture** *fehr fehr uñ neh·say duh root à ōōn vwah·tōōr* to test-drive a car

essayer *eh·say·yay vt* test (*product*); try; attempt; **essayer de faire quelque chose** *eh·say·yay duh fehr kel·kuh shōz* to try to do something; **essayer une robe** *eh·say·yay ōōn rob* to try on a dress

essence *eh·soñs f* petrol; gas(oline)

essentiel(le) *eh·soñ·syel adj* essential (*necessary*)

essentiellement *eh·soñ·syel·moñ adv* basically

essieu *eh·syuh m* axle

essor *eh·sor m* rapid expansion

essorer *eh·so·ray vt* spin(-dry); wring (*clothes*)

essuie-glace *eh·swee·glas m* windscreen wiper; windshield wiper

essuyer *eh·swee·yay vt* wipe

est *est m* east; **à l'est** *a lest* in/to the east; **de l'est** *duh lest* eastern

estimation *es·tee·ma·syoñ f* estimate

estimer *es·tee·may vt* estimate

estomac *es·to·ma m* stomach

estrade *es·trad f* platform (*in hall*)

et *ay conj* and

établi *ay·ta·blee m* bench (*work table*)

établir *ay·ta·bleer vt* establish

étage *ay·tazh m* storey; **le premier étage** *pruh·myeh ray·tazh* 1st floor; **à étages** *a ay·tazh* multi-storey

étagère *ay·ta·zhehr f* shelf

étain *ay·tañ m* tin (*substance*)

étaler *ay·ta·lay vt* spread

étang *ay·toñ m* pond (*natural*)

étape *ay·tap f* stage (*point*); **par étapes** *par ay·tap* in stages

état *ay·ta m* state (*condition*); **l'État** *ay·ta* the State; **être* en état de marche** *eh·truh oñ nay·ta duh marsh* to be in working order

États-Unis (d'Amérique) *ay·ta·zōō·nee (da·may·reek) mpl* United States (of America)

etc *et say·tuh·ra abbrev* etc

été *ay·tay m* summer

éteindre* *ay·tañ·druh vt* turn off; switch off

éteint(e) *ay·tañ(·tañt) adj* off (*light*)

étendre *ay·toñ·druh vt* spread (out); **s'étendre** *say·toñ·druh* spread; stretch

éternuement *ay·tehr·nōō·moñ m* sneeze

éternuer *ay·tehr·nōō·ay vi* sneeze

ethnique *et·neek adj* ethnic

étinceler* *ay·tañ·suh·lay vi* sparkle

étincelle *ay·tañ·sel f* spark

étiqueter* *ay·teek·tay vt* label

étiquette *ay·tee·ket f* label; tab; tag

s'étirer *say·tee·ray vr* stretch

étoffe *ay·tof f* fabric

étoile *ay·twahl f* star

étole *ay·tōl f* stole (*wrap*)

étonnant(e) *ay·to·noñ(·noñt) adj* amazing

étonner *ay·to·nay vt* surprise

étourdir *ay·toor·deer vt* stun

étrange *ay·troñzh adj* strange

étranger *ay·troñ·zhay m* stranger; foreigner; **à l'étranger** *a lay·troñ·zhay* overseas; abroad; **aller* à l'étranger** *a·lay a lay·troñ·zhay* to go abroad □ *adj* foreign

étrangère *ay·troñ·zhehr f* stranger; foreigner □ *adj* foreign

étrangler *ay·troñ·glay vt* strangle

être* *eh·truh vi* be; **je suis** *zhuh swee* I am; **j'étais** *zhay·teh* I was; **il est** *eel eh* he is; **il était** *eel ay·teh* he was; **nous sommes** *noo som* we are; **nous étions** *noo zay·tyoñ* we were; **vous êtes** *voo zet* you are; **vous étiez** *voo zay·tyay* you were; **ils sont** *eel soñ* they are; **ils étaient** *eel zay·teh* they were; **il est médecin** *eel eh mayd·sañ* he is a doctor; **qu'est-ce que c'est?** *kes·kuh seh* what is that?

étroit(e) *ay·trwah(·trwat) adj* narrow; tight

étude *ay·tōōd f* study; **l'étude de marché** *ay·tōōd duh mar·shay* market research; **aimer bien ses études** *ay·may byañ say zay·tōōd* to enjoy one's studies

étudiant(e) *ay·tōō·dyoñ(·dyoñt)* m/f
student; undergraduate

étudier *ay·tōō·dyay* vt/i study

Europe *uh·rop* f Europe; **l'Europe
continentale** *uh·rop koñ·tee·noñ·tal*
the Continent

européen(ne) *uh·ro·pay·yañ(·yen)* adj
European

eux *uh* pron them

eux-mêmes *uh·mem* pron themselves

évaluer *ay·va·lōō·ay* vt value

évanoui(e) *ay·va·nwee* adj unconscious

s'évanouir *say·va·nweer* vr faint

s'évaporer *say·va·po·ray* vr evaporate

événement *ay·ven·moñ* m occasion;
event

éventail *ay·voñ·tye* m fan (folding)

éventaire *ay·voñ·tehr* m stall; stand

éventé(e) *ay·voñ·tay* adj flat (beer)

évêque *ay·vek* m bishop

évidemment *aý·vee·da·moñ* adv obviously

évident(e) *ay·vee·doñ(·doñt)* adj obvious

évier *ay·vyay* m sink (basin)

éviter *ay·vee·tay* vt avoid

évolution *ay·vo·lōō·syoñ* f evolution

ex- *eks* pref ex-

exact(e) *eg·zakt* adj exact; correct; accurate

exactement *eg·zak·tuh·moñ* adv exactly

exagération *eg·za·zhay·ra·syoñ* f exaggeration

exagérer* *eg·za·zhay·ray* vt exaggerate

examen *eg·za·mañ* m examination; test

examiner *eg·za·mee·nay* vt examine;
test (sight, hearing)

excédent de bagages *ek·say·doñ duh
ba·gazh* m excess baggage

excellent(e) *ek·say·loñ(·loñt)* adj excellent

excentrique *ek·soñ·treek* adj eccentric

exception *ek·sep·syoñ* f exception

exceptionnel(le) *ek·sep·syo·nel* adj exceptional

excès *ek·seh* m excess; **l'excès de vitesse** *ek·seh duh vee·tes* speeding (in
car)

excessif(ive) *ek·seh·seef(·seev)* adj unreasonable (demand, price)

excitation *ek·see·ta·syoñ* f excitement

excité(e) *ek·see·tay* adj excited

s'exclamer *seks·kla·may* vr exclaim

exclure *eks·klōōr* vt exclude

exclusif(ive) *eks·klōō·zeef(·zeev)* adj
exclusive

exclusivité *eks·klōō·zee·vee·tay* f exclusive rights

excursion *ek·skōōr·syoñ* f trip; outing;
excursion; **faire* une excursion au
bord de la mer** *fehr ōōn ek·skōōr·
syoñ ō bor duh la mehr* to go on a
trip to the seaside; **les excursions à
pied** *ek·skōōr·syoñ za pyay* hiking

excuse *eks·kōōz* f excuse (pretext); **les
excuses** *eks·kōōz* apologies

excuser *eks·kōō·zay* vt excuse; **s'excuser** *sek·skōō·zay* apologize; **excusez-
moi** *ek·skōō·zay·mwah* (I'm) sorry

exécuter *eg·zay·kōō·tay* vt execute
(kill); **exécuter un ordre** *eg·zay·kōō·
tay uñ nor·druh* to carry out an order

exemplaire *eg·zoñ·plehr* m copy (of
book etc)

exemple *eg·zoñ·pluh* m example; **par
exemple** *par eg·zoñ·pluh* e.g.; for example

exempt(e) d'impôts *eg·zoñ(·zoñt) dañ·
pō* adj tax-free

s'exercer* *seg·zehr·say* vr practise;
s'exercer* au piano *seg·zehr·say ō
pya·nō* to practise the piano

exercice *eg·zehr·sees* m exercise

exigence *eg·zee·zhoñs* f requirement

exiger* *eg·zee·zhay* vt demand; insist
on

existence *eg·zees·toñs* f existence

exister *eg·zees·tay* vi exist

exotique *eg·zo·teek* adj exotic

expédier *ek·spay·dyay* vt dispatch

expéditeur *ek·spay·dee·tur* m sender

expédition *ek·spay·dee·syoñ* f expedition

expérience *ek·spay·ryoñs* f experiment; experience; **avoir* de l'expérience pratique** *a·vwahr duh lek·
spay·ryoñs pra·teek* to have practical
experience

expérimenté(e) *ek·spay·ree·moñ·tay*
adj experienced

expert *ek·spehr* m expert

expert-comptable *ek·spehr koñ·ta·bluh*
m chartered accountant; auditor

expirer *ek·spee·ray* vi expire

explication *ek·splee·ka·syoñ* f explanation

expliquer *ek·splee·kay* vt explain

explorer *ek·splo·ray* vt explore

exploser *ek·splō·zay* vi explode

explosion *ek·splō·zyoñ* f explosion;
blast

exportateur *ek·spor·ta·tur* m exporter

exportation *ek·spor·ta·syoñ* f export

exporter *ek·spor·tay* vt export

exposé *ek·spō·zay* m talk (lecture)

exposition *ek·spo·zee·syoñ* f exhibition; exposure (photographic)

exprès *ek·spreh* adv on purpose; deliberately □ m expédier quelque chose
par exprès *ek·spay·dyay kel·kuh shōz
par ek·spres* to send something express

express *ek·spres* m espresso (coffee);
express train

expression *ek·spreh·syoñ* f expression;
phrase

exprimer *ek·spree·may* vt express

extérieur *ek·stay·ryur* m outside □ adj
extérieur(e) *ek·stay·ryur* exterior; **le
mur extérieur** *luh mōōr ek·stay·ryur*
the outside wall; **à l'extérieur de la
maison** *a lek·stay·ryur duh la meh·
zoñ* outside the house

externe *ek·stern* adj external

extincteur *ek·stañk·tur* m fire extinguisher

extraordinaire *ek·stra·or·dee·nehr* adj
extraordinary

extravagant(e) *ek·stra·va·goñ(·goñt)*
adj extravagant

extrêmement *ek·streh·muh·moñ* adv
extremely

Extrême-Orient *ek·strem o·ryoñ* m the
Far East

eye-liner *eye·lye·nehr* m eyeliner

F

fabricant *fa·bree·koñ* m manufacturer

fabrication *fa·bree·ka·syoñ* f manufacturing; **fabrication en série** *fa·
bree·ka·syoñ oñ say·ree* mass production

fabriquer *fa·bree·kay* vt manufacture;
fabriquer en série *fa·bree·kay oñ say·
ree* mass-produce

en face de *oñ fas duh* prep facing; opposite □ adv **en face** *oñ fas* opposite;
la maison d'en face *la meh·zoñ doñ
fas* the house opposite

facile *fa·seel* adj easy

facilement *fa·seel·mon̄* adv easily

façon *fa·son̄* f way (*manner*); d'une autre façon *dōon̄ ō·truh fa·son̄* (in) a different way; de toute façon *duh toot fa·son̄* anyway (*nonetheless*)

facteur *fak·tur* m factor; mailman; postman

facture *fak·tōōr* f invoice

faculté *fa·kool·tay* f faculty (*university*)

faible *feh·bluh* adj weak (*person*); dim (*light*); slack (*business*); faint (*sound etc*)

faillite *fa·yeet* f bankruptcy; en faillite *on̄ fa·yeet* bankrupt; faire* faillite *fehr fa·yeet* to go bankrupt

faim *fan̄* f hunger; avoir* faim *a·vwahr fan̄* to be hungry

faire* *fehr* vt make; do; ça ne fait rien *sah nuh feh ree·an̄* never mind; it doesn't matter; faire* faire quelque chose *fehr fehr kel·kuh shōz* to have something done; faire* les lits *fehr lay lee* to make the beds; il fait chaud *eel feh shō* it is hot; je le ferai *zhuh luh fuh·ray* I shall do it; faire* avec quelque chose *fehr a·vek kel·kuh shōz* to make do with something

faisan *fuh·zon̄* m pheasant

fait *feh* m fact; en fait *on̄ feh* in fact; actually

fait(e) *feh (fet)* adj mature (*cheese*); ripe

falaise *fa·lez* f cliff

falloir* *fal·war* vi to be necessary; il faut faire *eel fō fehr* I/you etc must do

familier(ère) *fa·meel·yay(·yehr)* adj familiar; l'animal familier *a·nee·mal fa·meel·yay* pet

famille *fa·meey* f family; household

se faner *fa·nay* vr fade

fantaisie *fon̄·tay·zee* adj fancy

farce *fars* f farce; dressing; stuffing (in chicken etc)

farci(e) *far·see* adj stuffed (*chicken etc*)

farine *fa·reen* f flour

fascinant(e) *fa·see·non̄(·non̄t)* adj fascinating

fatigué(e) *fa·tee·gay* adj tired

faubourg *fō·boor* m suburb

fauché(e) *fō·shay* adj broke (*penniless*)

fausse *fōs* adj fake; (*name etc*); wrong; les fausses dents *fōs don̄* false teeth

faut see falloir

faute *fōt* f fault; mistake; la faute d'impression *fōt dan̄·preh·syon̄* misprint; à qui la faute? *a kee la fōt* whose fault is it?; ce n'est pas de ma faute *suh neh pa duh ma fōt* it's not my fault

fauteuil *fō·tuhy* m armchair; seat (*in front of theatre*); le fauteuil roulant *fō·tuhy roo·lon̄* wheelchair

fauve *fōv* adj fawn

faux *fō* m forgery (*copy*) □ adj fake; wrong; false (*name etc*)

favori(te) *fa·vo·ree(·reet)* adj favo(u)rite

fédéral(e) *fay·day·ral* adj federal

fée *fay* f fairy

feed-back *feed·bak* m feedback

fêler *feh·lay* vt crack; le verre s'est fêlé *luh vehr seh feh·lay* the glass cracked

félicitations *fay·lee·see·ta·syon̄* fpl congratulations; félicitations! *fay·lee·see·ta·syon̄* congratulations!

féliciter *fay·lee·see·tay* vt congratulate; féliciter quelqu'un de quelque chose *fay·lee·see·tay kel·kun̄ duh kel·kuh*

shōz to congratulate someone on something

femelle *fuh·mel* adj female (*animal*)

féminin(e) *fay·mee·nan̄(·neen)* adj feminine; le sexe féminin *seks fay·mee·nan̄* the female sex

femme *fam* f woman; wife; la femme de ménage de chambre *fam duh may·nazh/duh shon̄·bruh* cleaner (of house etc); la femme politique *fam po·lee·teek* politician

femme-agent *fam·a·zhon̄* f policewoman

fenêtre *fuh·neh·truh* f window

fente *fon̄t* f crack (*split*); slot

fer *fehr* m iron (*material, golf club*); le fer à repasser *fehr a ruh·pa·say* iron (*for clothes*)

ferme *fehrm* adj firm; buoyant (*market*) □ f la ferme *fehrm* farmhouse; farm

fermer *fehr·may* vt/i close □ vt shut; to turn off (*water*); la porte s'est fermée *la port seh fehr·may* the door closed; à quelle heure ferment les magasins? *a kel ur fehrm lay ma·ga·zan̄* when do the shops close?; fermé(e) *fehr·may* shut; fermer à clé *fehr·may a klay* to lock

fermeture éclair *fehr·muh·tōōr ay·klehr* f zip(-fastener); zipper

fermier *fehr·myay* m farmer

fermoir *fehr·mwahr* m clasp

féroce *fay·ros* adj fierce

ferry *feh·ree* m ferry (*large*)

fertile *fehr·teel* adj fertile (*land*)

festival *fes·tee·val* m festival

fête *fet* f feast day; holiday; fête

fêter *feh·tay* vt celebrate

feu *fuh* m light (*traffic light*); fire; avez-vous du feu? *a·vay·voo dōō fuh* have you got a light?; feu le roi *fuh luh rwah* the late king; les feux *fuh* traffic lights; le feu rouge *fuh roozh* red light; le feu orange *fuh o·ron̄zh* amber; les feux de position *fuh duh pō·zee·syon̄* parking lights; sidelights (on car); le feu de joie *fuh duh zhwah* bonfire; le feu d'artifice *fuh dar·tee·fees* fireworks; la maison est en feu *la meh·zon̄ eh on̄ fuh* the house is on fire; mettre* le feu à *meh·truh luh fuh a* to set fire to

feuille *fuhy* f sheet (*of paper*); leaf

feutre *fuh·truh* m felt (*cloth*); felt-tip pen

février *fay·vree·yay* m February

fiançailles *fee·yon̄·sye* fpl engagement (*betrothal*)

fiancé(e) *fee·yon̄·say* adj engaged (*betrothed*) □ m/f le/la fiancé(e) *fee·yon̄·say* fiancé(e)

fibre *fee·bruh* f grain (*in wood*); fibre; la fibre de verre *fee·bruh duh vehr* fibre-glass

ficeler* *fees·lay* vt tie up

ficelle *fee·sel* f string

fiche *feesh* f slip (*of paper*)

fichier *fee·shyay* m card index; file; le fichier de données *fee·shyay duh do·nay* data file

se fier à *suh fee·ay a* vr trust

fier (fière) *fyehr* adj proud; fier (fière) de *fyehr duh* proud of

fierté *fyehr·tay* f pride

fièvre *fyeh·vruh* f fever; avoir* de la fièvre *a·vwahr duh la fyeh·vruh* to have a temperature

figue *feeg* f fig

figure *fee·gōōr* f face; figure; court-card

fil *feel* m thread; lead (*electrical*); **le fil de coton** *feel duh ko·toñ* cotton (*thread*); **le fil de fer** *feel duh fehr* wire; **le fil électrique** *feel ay·lek·treek* wire; **le fil de fer barbelé** *feel duh fehr bar·buh·lay* barbed wire

file *feel* f lane; row (*behind one another*)

filer *fee·lay* vt spin (*wool*)

filet *fee·lay* m net; fillet (*of meat, fish*); **le filet à provisions** *fee·lay a pro·vee·zyoñ* string bag; **le filet à bagages** *fee·lay a ba·gazh* rack (*for luggage*)

filiale *fee·lyal* f affiliated company; subsidiary (*company*)

fille *feey* f daughter; **la jeune fille** *zhuhn feey* girl (*young woman*)

fillette *fee·yet* f girl (*child*)

film *feelm* m film; movie; **le grand film** *groñ feelm* feature film; **le film d'épouvante** *feelm day·poo·voñt* horror film, horror movie; **le film à suspense** *feelm a sōōs·poñs* thriller

fils *fees* m son

filtre *feel·truh* m filter; **le filtre à huile** *feel·tra weel* oil filter; **le filtre à air** *feel·tra ehr* air filter

fin *fañ* f end □ adj **fin(e)** *fañ (feen)* thin (*material*); fine (*delicate*); **très fin(e)** *treh fañ (feen)* sheer (*stockings*)

final(e) *fee·nal* adj final

finale *fee·nal* f finals (*sports*)

finalement *fee·nal·moñ* adv finally; eventually

finance *fee·noñs* f finance

financer* *fee·noñ·say* vt finance; back (*financially*)

financier(ère) *fee·noñ·syay('·syehr)* adj financial

finir *fee·neer* vt/i end; finish; **quand j'aurai fini mon travail** *koñ zhō·ray fee·nee moñ tra·vye* when I'm through with my work; **le match est fini** *luh matsh eh fee·nee* the match is over

finlandais(e) *fañ·loñ·deh('·dez) adj* Finnish

Finlande *fañ·loñd* f Finland

finnois *fañ·nwah* m Finnish

firme *feerm* f firm

fisc *feesk* m Internal Revenue; Inland Revenue

fiscal(e) *fees·kal* adj fiscal

fixe *feeks* adj fixed

fixer *feek·say* vt arrange (*meeting*); fix; **fixer le prix de** *feek·say luh pree duh* to price (*goods*)

flacon *fla·koñ* m bottle

flamand *fla·moñ* m Flemish □ adj **flamand(e)** *fla·moñ('·moñd)* Flemish

flamber *floñ·bay* vi blaze (*fire*)

flamme *flam* f flame

flan *floñ* m custard tart

flaque *flak* f puddle; pool (*of rain*)

flash *flash* m flash (*on camera*)

flèche *flesh* f arrow

fléchette *flay·shet* f dart (*to throw*); **les fléchettes** *flay·shet* game of darts

fleur *flur* f flower; bloom; **être* en fleur** *eh·troñ flur* to bloom

fleuriste *fluh·reest* m/f florist

fleuve *fluv* m river

flexible *flek·see·bluh* adj flexible

flipper *flee·pehr* m pinball

flirter *flur·tay* vi flirt

flocon *flo·koñ* m flake

flotte *flot* f fleet

flotter *flo·tay* vi float

flotteur *flo·tur* m float (*for swimming, fishing*)

fluor *flōō·or* m fluoride

flûte *flōōt* f flute; long loaf

foi *fwah* f belief; faith

foie *fwah* m liver

foin *fwañ* m hay

foire *fwahr* f fair

fois *fwah* f time; **la première fois** *la pruh·myehr fwah* the first time; **combien de fois?** *koñ·byañ duh fwah* how many times?; **une fois** *ōōn fwah* once; **deux fois** *duh fwah* twice

folle *fol* adj mad (*insane*); crazy

foncé(e) *foñ·say* adj dark (*colour*)

fonction *foñk·syoñ* f duty; function

fonctionnaire *foñk·syoñ·nehr* m/f civil servant

fonctionner *foñk·syo·nay* vi work

fond *foñ* m back (*of hall, room*); bottom

fonder *foñ·day* vt establish (*business*)

fondre *foñ·druh* vi melt; thaw (*ice*); **faire* fondre** *fehr foñ·druh* melt

fonds *foñ* mpl funds; **les fonds de roulement** *foñ duh rool·moñ* working capital

fontaine *foñ·ten* f fountain

fonte *foñt* f cast iron

football *foot·bol* m football (*game*); soccer

footing *foo·teeng* m jogging; **faire* du footing** *fehr dōō foo·teeng* to go jogging

force *fors* f strength; force (*violence*)

forcément *for·say·moñ* adv necessarily

forcer* *for·say* vt force (*compel*)

forêt *fo·reh* f forest

formation *for·ma·syoñ* f training (*for job*); **recevoir* une formation de professeur** *ruh·suh·vwahr ōōn for·ma·syoñ duh pro·feh·sur* to train as a teacher

forme *form* f figure (*of human*); form; shape; **en bonne forme** *oñ bon form* fit (*strong, healthy*); **in good form**

formel(le) *for·mel* adj positive (*definite*)

former *for·may* vt train (*apprentice*)

formidable *for·mee·da·bluh* adj great (*excellent*)

formulaire *for·mōō·lehr* m form (*document*)

fort(e) *for (fort)* adj strong; stout; loud □ adv **fort** for loudly; **mettre* plus fort** *meh·truh plōō for* to turn up (*heat, etc*)

fortune *for·tōōn* f fortune (*wealth*)

fossé *fo·say* m ditch

fou *foo* adj mad (*insane*); crazy

foudre *foo·druh* f lightning

fouet *foo·eh* m whip; whisk

fouetter *foo·eh·tay* vt whip (*cream, eggs*)

fougère *foo·zhehr* f fern; bracken

fouiller *foo·yay* vt search

foulard *foo·lar* m scarf

foule *fool* f crowd

se fouler la cheville *suh foo·lay la shuh·veey* vr to sprain one's ankle

four *foor* m oven; **le four à microondes** *foor a mee·krō·oñd* microwave oven

fourchette *foor·shet* f fork

fourgon *foor·goñ* m baggage car

fourmi *foor·mee* f ant

fournir *foor·neer* vt provide; supply (*goods*); **fournir des capitaux** *foor·neer day ka·pee·tō* to put up capital; **fournir quelque chose à quelqu'un** *foor·neer kel·kuh shōz a kel·kuñ* to provide someone with something; **fournir quelqu'un en quelque chose**

foor·neer kel·kuñ oñ kel·kuh shōz to supply someone with something

fourre-tout *foor·too m* holdall

fourrure *foo·rōōr f* fur

foyer *fwah·yay m* hostel; hearth; le foyer de jeunes *fwah·yay duh zhuhn* youth club

fracas *fra·ka m* crash (*noise*)

fracture *frak·tōōr f* fracture (*of arm etc*)

fragile *fra·zheel adj* fragile; handle with care (*on parcel*)

fraîche *fresh adj* fresh; cool; wet (*paint*)

frais *freh adj* fresh; cool □ *mpl* les frais *freh* costs (*of production etc*); expenses; les frais généraux *freh zhay·nay·rō* business expenses; overheads; rentrer dans ses frais *roñ·tray doñ say freh* to break even; les frais de banque *freh duh boñk* bank charges; les frais d'exploitation *freh dek·splwah·ta·syoñ* running costs

fraise *frez f* strawberry

framboise *froñ·bwahz f* raspberry

français *froñ·seh m* French; en français *oñ froñ·seh* in French

français(e) *froñ·seh(·sez) adj* French; il est Français *eel eh froñ·seh* he's French; elle est Française *el eh froñ·sez* she's French

France *froñs f* France; en France *oñ froñs* in/to France

franchir *froñ·sheer vt* get over

frange *froñzh f* fringe; bangs

frapper *fra·pay vt* hit; strike; knock; frapper légèrement *fra·pay lay·zhehr·moñ* tap; frapper à la porte *fra·pay a la port* to knock (at) the door

frein *froñ m* brake; le frein à main *froñ a mañ* handbrake; le frein à pyed *a pyay* footbrake; les freins à disque *froñ a deesk* disc brakes; le liquide de frein *lee·keed duh froñ* brake fluid

freiner *freh·nay vi* to put on the brakes; brake

frêne *frehn m* ash (*tree*)

fréquemment *fray·ka·moñ adv* frequently

fréquent(e) *fray·koñ(·koñt) adj* frequent

frère *frehr m* brother

fret *freh m* freight (*goods*)

friand *free·oñ m* sausage roll

frigidaire *free·zhee·dehr m* fridge; ice-box

frire *freer vt/i* fry

frisé(e) *free·zay adj* curly

frissonner *free·so·nay vi* shiver

frit(e) *free(t) adj* fried

frites *freet fpl* french fried potatoes, french fries; chips

froid(e) *frwah (frwahd) adj* cold; j'ai froid *zhay frwah* I'm cold; servir quelque chose froid *sehr·veer kel·kuh shōz frwah* to serve something chilled

froissé(e) *frwah·say adj* creased

froisser *frwah·say vt* crease; strain (*muscle*)

frôler *frō·lay vt* brush against

fromage *fro·mazh m* cheese; le fromage blanc *fro·mazh bloñ* cottage cheese; le fromage frais *fro·mazh freh* cream cheese

froncé(e) *froñ·say adj* gathered

front *froñ m* forehead; le front de mer *froñ duh mehr* front (*seaside*)

frontière *froñ·tyehr f* border (*of country*); frontier; boundary

frotter *fro·tay vt* rub; strike (*match*)

fruit *frwee m* fruit; les fruits de mer *frwee duh mehr* shellfish (*on menu*); seafood

fuir *fweer vi* leak

fuite *fweet f* leak

fumé(e) *foo·may adj* smoked (*salmon etc*)

fumée *foo·may f* smoke

fumer *foo·may vt/i* smoke

fumeur *foo·mur m* smoker (*person*)

furieux(euse) *foo·ree·uh(·uhz) adj* mad (*angry*)

furoncle *foo·roñ·kluh m* boil (*on skin*)

fuseau *foo·zō m* ski pants; le fuseau horaire *foo·zō o·rehr* time zone

fusée *foo·zay f* rocket

fusible *foo·zee·bluh m* fuse

fusil *foo·zee m* gun; rifle

fusionnement *foo·zyo·mon m* merger

fusionner *foo·zyo·nay vi* merge

G

gâcher *gah·shay vt* spoil

gadget *gad·zhet m* gadget

gagnant(e) *ga·nyoñ(·nyoñt) m* winner

gagner *ga·nyay vi* win □ *vt* win; earn; gain; gagner £25 de l'heure *ga·nyay £25 duh lur* to earn £25 per hour; gagner sa vie *ga·nyay sa vee* to earn one's living

gai(e) *gay adj* merry; gay

gain *gañ m* earnings

gaine *gen f* girdle (*corset*)

gala *ga·la m* gala

galerie *gal·ree f* gallery; roof rack; art gallery (*commercial*); la galerie marchande *gal·ree mar·shoñd* arcade

gallois(e) *gal·wah(·wahz) adj* Welsh □ *m* le gallois *gal·wah* Welsh

galop *ga·lō m* gallop

galoper *ga·lo·pay vi* gallop

gamme *gam f* scale (*music*); la gamme des prix *gam day pree* price range

gangster *goñ·stehr m* gangster

gant *goñ m* glove; le gant de toilette *goñ duh twah·let* flannel; facecloth

garage *ga·razh m* garage

garantie *ga·roñ·tee f* guarantee; warrant(y)

garantir *ga·roñ·teer vt* underwrite (*finance*); guarantee

garçon *gar·soñ m* waiter; boy

garçon d'honneur *gar·soñ don·nur m* best man

garde *gard m* guard (*sentry*) □ *f* la garde *gard* guard (*soldiers*); de garde *duh gard* on duty (*doctor*); le garde du corps *gard dōō kor* bodyguard (*person*)

garde-boue *gard·boo m* mudguard

garde-côte *gard·kōt m* coastguard

garde-manger *gard·moñ·zhay m* larder

garder *gar·day vt* keep; guard; garder les enfants *gar·day lay zoñ·foñ* to babysit; garder quelque chose pour plus tard *gar·day kel·kuh shōz poor plōō tar* to keep something till later; garder quelque chose dans le frigo *gar·day kel·kuh shōz doñ luh free·gō* to keep something in the fridge; gardez la monnaie! *gar·day la mo·neh* keep the change!

garderie d'enfants *gar·duh·ree doñ·foñ f* crèche

garde-robe *gard·rob f* wardrobe (*furniture*)

gardien *gar·dyañ m* caretaker; le gardien de nuit *gar·dyañ duh nwee* night porter

gare *gar f* railway station; la gare rou-

tière gar roo·tyehr terminal (buses);
la gare de jonction gar duh zhoñk·
syoñ junction (railway)
garer ga·ray vt park
se gargariser suh gar·ga·ree·zay vr
gargle
garni(e) gar·nee adj served with vegetables
garnir gar·neer vt trim (decorate)
garniture de piston gar·nee·tōōr duh
pees·toñ f gasket
gas-oil gaz·oyl m diesel fuel
gaspillage gas·pee·yazh m waste
gaspiller gas·pee·yay vt waste
gâteau gah·tō m cake; gateau; le gâteau sec gah·tō sek cookie; le gâteau
de Savoie gah·tō duh sa·vwah sponge
(cake)
gâter gah·tay vt spoil; se gâter suh gah·
tay to go bad (food)
gauche gōsh adj, n left; à gauche a
gōsh to/on the left; le côté gauche
luh kō·tay gōsh the left side
gaucher(ère) gō·shay(·shehr) adj left-
handed
gaufre gō·fruh f waffle
gaufrette gō·fret f wafer
gaz gaz m gas; les gaz d'échappement
gaz day·shap·moñ exhaust (fumes)
gaze gaz f gauze
gazeux(euse) ga·zuh(·zuhz) adj sparkling (wine etc)
gazon ga·zoñ m grass
géant zhay·oñ m giant
gel zhel m frost
gelée zhuh·lay f jello, jelly
geler* zhuh·lay vi freeze
gémir zhay·meer vi moan; groan
gémissement zhay·mees·moñ m moan;
groan
gencive zhoñ·seev f gum (of teeth)
gendarme zhoñ·darm m policeman
gêné(e) zheh·nay adj embarrassed
gêner zheh·nay vt bother; la chaleur ne
me gêne pas la sha·lur nuh muh zhen
pah I don't mind the heat
général zhay·nay·ral m general (soldier); en général oñ zhay·nay·ral in
general
général(e) zhay·nay·ral adj general
généralement zhay·nay·ral·moñ adv
generally
générateur zhay·nay·ra·tur m generator (electrical)
génération zhay·nay·ra·syoñ f generation
généreux(euse) zhay·nay·ruh(·ruhz)
adj generous (person)
Genève zhuh·nev f Geneva
genou zhuh·noo m knee; se mettre* à
genoux suh meh·tra zhuh·noo to
kneel down; s'asseoir* sur les genoux
de quelqu'un sa·swahr sōōr lay zhuh·
noo duh kel·kuñ to sit on someone's
knee; les genoux zhuh·noo lap (of
person)
genre zhoñ·ruh m kind (type); gender
gens zhoñ mpl people
gentil(le) zhoñ·teey adj kind; nice (person); pas gentil(le) pa zhoñ·teey unkind
géographie zhay·o·gra·fee f geography
géologie zhay·o·lo·zhee f geology
géométrie zhay·o·may·tree f geometry
géranium zhay·ra·nyum m geranium
gérer* zhay·ray vt manage (business)
geste zhest m gesture
gestion zhes·tyoñ f management (of
business)
ghetto geh·tō m ghetto
gibier zhee·byay m game (hunting)

gifle zhee·fluh f smack
gifler zhee·flay vt smack
gigot d'agneau zhee·gō da·nyō m leg of
lamb
gilet zhee·leh m waistcoat; cardigan; le
gilet de sauvetage zhee·leh duh sōv·
tazh life preserver (jacket); life
jacket
gin djeen m gin (drink)
gingembre zhan·zhoñ·bruh m ginger
gitan(e) zhee·toñ(·tan) m/f gypsy
glaçage gla·sazh m icing (on cake)
glace glas f ice; ice cream; la glace à la
vanille glas a la va·neey vanilla ice
cream
glacé(e) gla·say adj glacé
glaçon gla·soñ m ice cube; avec des
glaçons a·vek day gla·soñ on the
rocks (with ice)
gland gloñ m acorn
glande gloñd f gland
glissant(e) glee·soñ(·soñt) adj slippery
glissement de terrain glees·moñ duh
teh·rañ m landslide
glisser glee·say vi glide; slide; slip
glissière glee·syehr f crash barrier
global(e) glo·bal adj inclusive (costs);
global
globe glob m globe (map)
glycérine glee·say·reen f glycerin(e)
golf golf m golf
gomme gom f eraser
gonflable goñ·fla·bluh adj inflatable
gonfler goñ·flay vt inflate
gorge gorzh f throat
goudron goo·droñ m tar
goulache goo·lash f goulash
goulot d'étranglement goo·lō day·trañ·
gluh·moñ m bottleneck
gourmand(e) goor·moñ(·moñd) adj
greedy
gourmet goor·meh m gourmet
gousse d'ail goos dye f clove of garlic
goût goo m flavo(u)r; taste; ça a un
goût de poisson sa a uñ goo duh
pwah·soñ it tastes like fish; de mauvais goût duh mō·veh goo in poor
taste; de bon goût duh boñ goo in
good taste
goûter goo·tay m afternoon tea □ vt
taste (try)
goutte goot f drip; drop (of liquid)
goutter goo·tay vi drip
gouttière goo·tyehr f gutter (on building)
gouvernail goo·vehr·nye m rudder
gouvernante goo·vehr·noñt f housekeeper
gouvernement goo·vehr·nuh·moñ m
government
gouverner goo·ver·nay vt rule; govern
gouverneur goo·vehr·nur m governor
(of colony)
grâce à grahs a prep thanks to
gracieux(euse) gra·syuh(·syuhz) adj
graceful
grade grad m degree (stage); grade
grain grañ m grain (cereal crops)
graine gren f seed; les graines de soja
gren duh so·ya soya beans
graisse gres f grease; la graisse de rognon gres duh ro·nyoñ suet
graisseux(euse) greh·suh(·suhz) adj
greasy (surface)
grammaire gra·mehr f grammar; le livre de grammaire lee·vruh duh gra·
mehr grammar (book)
gramme gram m gramme; gram
grand(e) groñ (groñd) adj great; high
(speed, number); big; tall; wide

(range); **le Grand Prix** *groñ pree* Grand Prix

Grande-Bretagne *groñd·bruh·tan·yuh* f Great Britain

grandir *groñ·deer* vi grow *(child)*

grand-mère *groñ·mehr* f grandmother

grand-père *groñ·pehr* m grandfather

grand'route *groñ·root* f highway

grange *groñzh* f barn

graphique *gra·feek* m graph

gras *gra* m fat □ adj **gras(se)** *gra (gras)* fat; greasy *(food)*

gratte-ciel *grat·syel* m skyscraper

gratuit(e) *gra·twee(·tweet)* adj free of charge

grave *grav* adj serious; deep *(voice)*

gravier *gra·vyay* m gravel

gravillon *gra·vee·yoñ* m grit

gravure *gra·voôr* f print

grec *grek* adj Greek

Grèce *gres* f Greece

grêle *grel* f hail

grêler *grel·ay* vi hail

grenade *gruh·nad* f pomegranate

grenier *gruh·nyay* m loft; attic

grenouille *gruh·noo·yuh* f frog

greque *grek* adj Greek

grève *grev* f strike *(industrial)*; **la grève du zèle** *grev dōō zel* work-to-rule; **la grève sauvage** *grev sō·vazh* unofficial strike; **la grève perlée** *grev pehr·lay* go-slow; **la grève-surprise** *grev·sôôr·preez* walkout; **en grève** *oñ grev* on strike; **immobilisé(e) par une grève** *ee·mo·bee·lee·zay par ōōn grev* strikebound; **faire* grève** *fehr grev* to strike

gréviste *gray·veest* m/f striker

griffer *gree·fay* vt scratch

gril *greel* m grill *(gridiron)*

grill *greel* m grillroom

grille *greey* f railings; **la grille de foyer** *greey duh fwah·yay* grate

grille-pain *greey·pañ* m toaster

griller *gree·yay* vt grill

grimace *gree·mas* f grimace

grimper *grañ·pay* vi climb

grippe *greep* f flu

gris(e) *gree (greez)* adj grey

grogner *gro·nyay* vi growl; grunt

grondement *groñ·duh·moñ* m rumble; roar *(of engine)*; boom *(noise)*

gronder *groñ·day* vi rumble; roar *(engine)*

groom *groom* m bellboy; pageboy

gros(se) *grō (grōs)* adj fat *(person)*; big *(sum of money)*; large; **en gros** *oñ grō* in bulk *(in large quantities)*; wholesale; **de gros** *duh grō* wholesale *(price)*

groseille à maquereau *grō·zay a ma·kuh·rō* f gooseberry; **la groseille rouge** *grō·zay roozh* red currant

grosse *grōs* f gross

grosseur *grō·sur* f size; growth *(on body)*

grossier(ère) *gro·syay(·syehr)* adj coarse *(texture, material)*

grossiste *grō·seest* m/f wholesaler

grotesque *gro·tesk* adj grotesque

groupe *groop* m group; **le groupe de pression** *groop duh pre·syoñ* pressure group

grue *grōō* f crane *(machine)*

grumeau *grōō·mō* m lump *(in sauce)*

gué *gay* m ford

guérir *gay·reer* vt cure

guerre *gehr* f war; **la guerre mondiale** *gehr moñ·dyal* world war; **la guerre civile** *gehr see·veel* civil war

gueule *guhl* f mouth *(of animal)*; la

---

gueule de bois *guhl duh bwah* hangover; **avoir* la gueule de bois** *a·vwahr la guhl duh bwah* to have a hangover

guichet *gee·sheh* m ticket office; **le guichet de location** *gee·sheh duh lo·ka·syoñ* advance booking office

guide *geed* m/f guide □ m guidebook

guidon *gee·doñ* m handlebar(s)

guitare *gee·tar* f guitar

gymnase *zheem·naz* m gym(nasium)

gymnastique *zheem·nas·teek* f gymnastics

H

habiller *a·bee·yay* vt dress *(child)*; **s'habiller** *sa·bee·yay* dress; dress oneself; **nous nous sommes habillés** *noo noo som za·bee·yay* we dressed ourselves

habit *a·bee* m outfit; tailcoat

habitant(e) *a·bee·toñ(·toñt)* m/f inhabitant

habiter *a·bee·tay* vi live *(reside)* □ vt live in

habitude *a·bee·tōōd* f habit; **nous avions l'habitude d'y aller** *noo za·vyoñ la·bee·tōōd dee a·lay* we used to; **d'habitude** *da·bee·tōōd* usually

habituel(le) *a·bee·tōō·el* adj usual; regular

habituellement *a·bee·tōō·el·moñ* adv usually

s'habituer à *sa·bee·tōō·ay* a vr get used to

hache *ash* f axe

hacher *a·shay* vt mince; chop *(food)*

hachis *a·shee* m minced beef

hachoir *ash·wahr* m mincer

haie *ay* f hedge

haine *en* f hatred

haïr* *ye·eer* vt hate

haleine *a·len* f breath

haleter* *al·tay* vi pant

halles *al* fpl central food market

hamac *ha·mak* m hammock

hamburger *am·bur·gur* m hamburger

hameçon *a·muh·soñ* m hook *(fishing)*

hanche *oñsh* f hip

handicap *oñ·dee·kap* m handicap

hardi(e) *ar·dee* adj bold

hardware *ard·wehr* m hardware *(computing)*

hareng *ha·roñ* m herring

haricots *a·ree·kō* mpl beans; haricot beans; **les haricots rouges** *a·ree·kō roozh* kidney beans; **les haricots à rame** *a·ree·kō a ram* runner beans

harnais *ar·neh* m harness

harpe *arp* f harp

hasard *a·zar* m chance; **par hasard** *par a·zar* by chance; **au hasard** *ō a·zar* at random; **à tout hasard** *a too ta·zar* just in case

hâte *aht* f haste

se hâter *suh ah·tay* vr hurry

hausse *ōs* f rise

hausser *ō·say* vt raise; **hausser les épaules** *ō·say lay zay·pōl* shrug

haut *ō* m top *(of ladder)*; **en haut** *oñ ō* high up; upstairs; **du haut** *dōō ō* top; **vers le haut** *ver luh ō* upwards

haut(e) *ō (ōt)* adj high; tall; **à haute voix** *a ōt vwah* aloud; **haut(e) de 6 mètres** *ō (ōt) duh 6 meh·truh* 6 metres high; **plus haut(e)** *plōō ō (ōt)* higher; **à hauts talons** *a ō ta·loñ* high-heeled

haut-de-forme *ō·duh·form* m top hat

hauteur *ō·tur* f height *(of object)*

haut-parleur ō·par·lur m loudspeaker

la Haye la ay f Hague (the)

hayon (arrière) ay·yoñ (a·ryehr) m tailgate (of car)

hebdomadaire eb·do·ma·dehr adj weekly □ m l'hebdomadaire eb·do·ma·dehr weekly (periodical)

hélicoptère ay·lee·kop·tehr m helicopter

hémorroïdes ay·muh·ro·eed fpl h(a)emorrhoids

herbe ehrb f grass; les fines herbes feen zehrb herbs; la mauvaise herbe mō·vez ehrb weed

hériter de ay·ree·tay duh vt inherit

hermétique ehr·may·teek adj airtight

hermine ehr·meen f ermine (fur)

hernie ehr·nee f hernia; l'hernie discale ehr·nee dees·kal slipped disc

hésiter ay·zee·tay vi hesitate; hésiter à faire quelque chose ay·zee·tay a fehr kel·kuh shōz to hesitate to do something

hêtre eh·truh m beech

heure ur f hour; à l'heure a lur on time; punctual; on schedule; quelle heure est-il? kel ur eh·teel what's the time?; il est 5 heures eel eh 5 ur it's 5 o'clock; à 3 heures a 3 ur at 3 o'clock; les heures de travail ur tra·vye business hours; les heures supplémentaires ur sōō·play·moñ·tehr overtime; faire* des heures supplémentaires fehr day zur sōō·play·moñ·tehr to work overtime; l'heure du déjeuner ur dōō day·zhuh·nay lunch hour; les heures de bureau ur duh bōō·rō office hours; les heures d'affluence ur da·flōō·oñs rush hour; les heures de pointe ur duh pwañt peak hours; les heures de travail ur duh tra·vye working hours; se lever* de bonne heure suh luh·vay duh bon ur to get up early; toutes les heures toot lay zur hourly

heureusement uh·ruz·moñ adv fortunately

heureux(euse) uh·ruh(·ruhz) adj happy; fortunate

heurter uhr·tay vt hit

hi-fi ee·fee adj hi-fi

histoire ees·twahr f history; story; les histoires ees·twahr fuss; faire* des histoires fehr day zees·twahr to make a fuss

hiver ee·vehr m winter

hockey o·kay m hockey

hold-up old·up m raid (by criminals)

hollandais o·loñ·deh m Dutch □ adj hollandais(e) o·loñ·deh(·dez) Dutch; il est Hollandais eel o·loñ·deh he's Dutch; elle est Hollandaise el o·loñ·dez she's Dutch

Hollande o·loñd f Holland

homard o·mar m lobster

homme om m man; l'homme politique om po·lee·teek politician

homogénéisé(e) o·mo·zhay·nay·ee·zay adj homogenized

Hongrie oñ·gree f Hungary

hongrois oñ·grwah m Hungarian □ adj hongrois(e) oñ·grwah(·grwahz) Hungarian

honnête o·net adj honest

honneur o·nur f honour

honoraires o·no·rehr mpl fee

honte oñt f shame; avoir* honte (de) a·vwahr oñt (duh) to be ashamed (of)

hôpital o·pee·tal m hospital; l'hôpital

psychiatrique o·pee·tal psee·kee·a·treek mental hospital

hoquet o·kay m hiccup; avoir* le hoquet a·vwahr luh o·kay to have (the) hiccups

horaire o·rehr m timetable (for trains etc); schedule; l'horaire des départs o·rehr day day·par departure board

horizon o·ree·zoñ m horizon

horizontal(e) o·ree·zoñ·tal adj horizontal; level

horloge or·lozh f clock; l'horloge de parquet or·lozh duh par·keh grandfather clock

horrible o·ree·bluh adj horrible

hors-bord or·bor m speedboat □ adj outboard

hors de or duh prep out of

hors d'œuvre or duh·vruh m hors d'œuvre

hors-saison or·say·zoñ adj off-season

hors-taxe or·taks adj duty-free (shop)

hospitalité os·pee·ta·lee·tay f hospitality

hot-dog ot·dog m hot dog

hôte ōt m host; guest; hôte payant ōt pay·yoñ paying guest

hôtel ō·tel m hotel

hôtel de ville ō·tel duh veel m town hall

hôtesse ō·tes f hostess; stewardess; l'hôtesse de l'air ō·tes duh lehr flight attendant; air hostess

hublot ōō·blō m porthole

huile weel f oil (edible, for car); l'huile d'olive weel do·leev olive oil; l'huile de ricin weel duh ree·sañ castor oil; l'huile solaire weel so·lehr suntan oil

huit weet num eight

huitième wee·tyem adj eighth

huître wee·truh f oyster

humain(e) ōō·mañ(·men) adj human

humeur ōō·mur f mood; de mauvaise humeur duh mō·vez ōō·mur in a bad temper; de bonne humeur duh bon ōō·mur in a good mood

humide ōō·meed adj damp; wet (road)

hurlement ōōr·luh·moñ m roar

hurler ōōr·lay vi roar (person)

hygiénique ee·zhay·neek adj hygienic

hymne national eem na·syoñ·nal m national anthem

hypermarché ee·pehr·mar·shay m superstore; hypermarket

hypermétrope ee·pehr·may·trop adj long-sighted

hypothèque ee·po·tek f mortgage

hypothéquer* ee·po·tay·kay vt mortgage

hystérique ees·tay·reek adj hysterical

I

ici ee·see adv here; par ici s'il vous plaît par ee·see see voo play this way please; venez ici vuh·nay zee·see come (over) here; il est en vacances ici eel eh toñ va·koñs ee·see he's (over) here on holiday

idéal(e) ee·day·al adj ideal

idée ee·day f idea

identifier ee·doñ·tee·fyay vt identify

identique ee·doñ·teek adj identical

identité ee·doñ·tee·tay f identity

idiot(e) ee·dyō(·dyot) adj stupid □ m/f idiot

ignorant(e) ee·nyo·roñ(·roñt) adj ignorant

ignorer ee·nyo·ray vt ignore; not to know

il eel pron he; it; il y a eel ya there is/

are; **il y a 4 ans** *eel ya 4 oň* 4 years ago; **il pleut** *eel pluh* it's raining

île *eel f* island

illégal(e) *ee·lay·gal adj* illegal

illégitime *ee·lay·zhee·teem adj* illegitimate

illimité(e) *ee·lee·mee·tay adj* unlimited

illuminations *ee·lōō·mee·na·syoň fpl* illuminations

illuminé(e) *ee·lōō·mee·nay adj* floodlit

illustration *ee·lōō·stra·syoň f* illustration

ils *eel pron* they

image *ee·mazh f* picture (drawing)

imagination *ee·ma·zhee·na·syoň f* imagination

imaginer *ee·ma·zhee·nay vt* imagine

imbattable *aň·ba·ta·bluh adj* unbeatable

imbécile *aň·bay·seel m/f* idiot

imiter *ee·mee·tay vt* imitate

immangeable *ee·moň·zha·bluh adj* inedible

immédiat(e) *ee·may·dya(·dyat) adj* immediate; instant

immédiatement *ee·may·dyat·moň adv* immediately

immeuble *ee·muh·bluh m* block of flats, apartment block; **l'immeuble de bureaux** *ee·muh·bluh duh bōō·rō* office-block

immigrant(e) *ee·mee·groň(·groňt) m/f* immigrant

immobile *ee·mo·beel adj* still (motionless)

immobilier *ee·mo·bee·lyay m* real estate

immobiliser *ee·mo·bee·lee·zay vt* tie up (capital)

impair(e) *aň·pehr adj* odd (number)

impartial(e) *aň·par·syal adj* unbiased

impasse *aň·pas f* blind alley; dead end

impatient(e) *aň·pa·syoň(·syoňt) adj* impatient; eager; **être* impatient de faire quelque chose** *eh·traň·pa·syoň duh fehr kel·kuh shōz* to be eager to do something

imperméable *aň·pehr·may·a·bluh adj* waterproof □ *m* **l'imperméable** *aň·pehr·may·a·bluh* mack(intosh); raincoat

impersonnel(le) *aň·pehr·so·nel adj* impersonal

impoli(e) *aň·po·lee adj* rude

importance *aň·por·toňs f* importance

important(e) *aň·por·toň(·toňt) adj* important; sizeable

importateur *aň·por·ta·tur m* importer

importation *aň·por·ta·syoň f* import

importer *aň·por·tay vt/i* import; matter

imposable *aň·pō·za·bluh adj* taxable

imposer *aň·pō·zay vt* tax (income)

impossible *aň·po·see·bluh adj* impossible

impôt *aň·pō m* tax; **les impôts indirects** *aň·pō aň·dee·rekt* indirect taxation/ taxes; **l'impôt sur le revenu** *aň·pō sōōr luh ruh·vuh·nōō* income tax

impôts *aň·pō mpl* taxation; tax (on income)

impression *aň·preh·syoň f* impression

impressionnant(e) *aň·preh·syo·noň (·noňt) adj* impressive

impressionner *aň·preh·syo·nay vt* impress (win approval)

imprimer *aň·pree·may vt* print (book, newspaper)

imprimeur *aň·pree·mur m* printer

incapable *aň·ka·pa·bluh adj* unable; **être* incapable de faire quelque chose** *eh·truh aň·ka·pa·bluh duh fehr kel·*

kuh shōz to be unable to do something

incassable *aň·kas·sa·bluh adj* unbreakable

incendie *aň·soň·dee m* fire (accident); blaze

incertain(e) *aň·sehr·taň(·ten) adj* uncertain (fact)

inchangé(e) *aň·shoň·zhay adj* unchanged

incident *aň·see·doň m* incident (event)

incinérateur *aň·see·nay·ra·tur m* incinerator

incliner *aň·klee·nay vt* tip (tilt)

inclure* *aň·klōōr vt* include; **du 6 au 12 inclus** *dōō 6 ō 12 aň·klōō* from 6th to 12th inclusive

incomplet(ète) *aň·koň·pleh(·plet) adj* incomplete

inconditionnel(le) *aň·koň·dee·syo·nel adj* unconditional (offer)

inconfortable *aň·koň·for·ta·bluh adj* uncomfortable

inconnu(e) *aň·ko·nōō adj* unknown; strange □ *m/f* stranger

inconvenant(e) *aň·koň·vuh·noň(·noňt) adj* indecent

incorrect(e) *aň·ko·rekt adj* incorrect

incroyable *aň·krwah·ya·bluh adj* incredible

Inde *aňd f* India

indépendance *aň·day·poň·doňs f* independence

indépendant(e) *aň·day·poň·doň(·doňt) adj* independent; self-contained (apartment)

index *aň·deks m* index (in book)

indexé(e) *aň·dek·say adj* index-linked (interest rates etc)

indications *aň·dee·ka·syoň fpl* instructions; directions (to a place)

indice *aň·dees m* index (financial)

indien(ne) *aň·dyaň(·dyen) adj* Indian □ *m/f* **l'Indien(ne)** *aň·dyaň(·dyen)* Indian

indigeste *aň·dee·zhest adj* indigestible

indigestion *aň·dee·zhes·tyoň f* indigestion

indiquer *aň·dee·kay vt* point out; show

indirect(e) *aň·dee·rekt adj* indirect

individu(el)(le) *aň·dee·vee·dōō·el adj* individual

individuellement *aň·dee·vee·dōō·el·moň adv* individually

industrie *aň·dōōs·tree f* industry; **l'industrie du service** *aň·dōōs·tree dōō sehr·vees* service industry; **l'industrie légère** *aň·dōōs·tree lay·zhehr* light industry

industriel(le) *aň·dōōs·tryel adj* industrial

inefficace *een·eh·fee·kas adj* inefficient; ineffective

inévitable *een·ay·vee·ta·bluh adj* inevitable; unavoidable

infection *aň·fek·syoň f* infection

inférieur(e) *aň·fay·ryur adj* inferior; lower; **de qualité inférieure** *duh ka·lee·tay aň·fay·ryur* inferior

infirme *aň·feerm adj* disabled

infirmière *aň·feer·myehr f* nurse

inflammable *aň·fla·ma·bluh adj* inflammable

inflammation *aň·fla·ma·syoň f* inflammation

inflation *aň·fla·syoň f* inflation (economic)

influence *aň·flōō·oňs f* influence

information *aň·for·ma·syoň f* piece of information

informations *an̄·for·ma·syon̄* **fpl** news; information

informatique *an̄·for·ma·teek* **f** data processing; computer science

infusion *an̄·fŌŌ·zyon̄* **f** herbal tea

ingénieur *an̄·zhay·nyur* **m** engineer

ingénieux(euse) *an̄·zhay·nyuh(·nyuhz)* **adj** clever (*plan*)

ingrédients *an̄·gray·dyon̄* **mpl** ingredients

initiales *ee·nee·syal* **fpl** initials

injuste *an̄·zhŌŌst* **adj** unfair

innocent(e) *ee·no·son̄(·son̄t)* **adj** innocent

inoculation *ee·no·kŌŌ·la·syon̄* **f** inoculation

inoffensif(ive) *ee·no·fon̄·seef(·seev)* **adj** harmless

inondation *ee·non̄·da·syon̄* **f** flood

inoxydable *een·ok·see·da·bluh* **adj** rustproof; stainless (*steel*)

input *in·poot* **m** input (*computing*)

inquiet(ète) *an̄·kyay(·kyet)* **adj** worried

inquiéter* *an̄·kyay·tay* **vt** worry

insecte *an̄·sekt* **m** insect

insigne *an̄·see·nyuh* **m** badge (*of metal*)

insignifiant(e) *an̄·see·nyee·fyon̄(·fyon̄t)* **adj** trivial; insignificant

insistance *an̄·sees·ton̄s* **f** stress (*emphasis*)

insister *an̄·sees·tay* **vi** insist; keep trying

insolation *an̄·so·la·syon̄* **f** sunstroke

insolent(e) *an̄·so·lon̄(·lon̄t)* **adj** insolent

inspecter *an̄·spek·tay* **vt** inspect

inspecteur *an̄·spek·tur* **m** inspector

installer *an̄·sta·lay* **vt** install; put (in); **s'installer** *san̄·sta·lay* to settle in

instant *an̄·ston̄* **m** instant; moment; **il est arrivé à l'instant** *eel eh ta·ree·vay a lan̄·ston̄* he arrived just now

instantané(e) *an̄·ston̄·ta·nay* **adj** instant (*product*)

institut *an̄·stee·tŌŌ* **m** institute

instituteur *an̄·stee·tŌŌ·tur* **m** teacher (*primary school*)

institutrice *an̄·stee·tŌŌ·trees* **f** teacher (*primary school*)

instruire* *an̄·strweer* **vt** teach; educate

instrument *an̄·strŌŌ·mon̄* **m** instrument

insuline *an̄·sŌŌ·leen* **f** insulin

insulte *an̄·sŌŌlt* **f** insult

insulter *an̄·sŌŌl·tay* **vt** insult

insupportable *an̄·sŌŌ·por·ta·bluh* **adj** unbearable

intelligence *an̄·teh·lee·zhon̄s* **f** intelligence

intelligent(e) *an̄·teh·lee·zhon̄(·zhon̄t)* **adj** intelligent; clever; bright

intendant *an̄·ton̄·don̄* **m** steward (*at club*)

intention *an̄·ton̄·syon̄* **f** intention; **avoir l'intention de faire** *a·vwahr lan̄·ton̄·syon̄ duh fehr* to mean to do; intend to do

interdire* *an̄·ter·deer* **vt** prohibit; ban

interdit *an̄·tehr·dee* **m** ban □ **adj** interdit(e) *an̄·tehr·dee(·deet)* forbidden

intéressant(e) *an̄·tay·reh·son̄(·son̄t)* **adj** interesting

intéressé(e) *an̄·tay·reh·say* **adj** interested

intéresser *an̄·tay·reh·say* **vt** interest; **s'intéresser à** *san̄·tay·reh·say a* to be interested in

intérêt *an̄·tay·reh* **m** interest; **les intérêts composés** *an̄·tay·reh kon̄·pō·zay* compound interest

intérieur *an̄·tay·ryur* **m** inside □ **adj** intérieur(e) *an̄·tay·ryur* interior; inside; inner; **le mur intérieur** *mōōr an̄·tay·ryur* the inside wall; **à l'intérieur de la boîte** *a lan̄·tay·ryur duh la bwaht* inside the box; **être* à l'intérieur** *eh·tra lan̄·tay·ryur* to be inside/indoors

international(e) *an̄·tehr·na·syo·nal* **adj** international

interne *an̄·tehrn* **adj** internal

interphone *an̄·tehr·fon* **m** intercom

interprétation *an̄·tehr·pray·ta·syon̄* **f** performance (*of actor*)

interprète *an̄·tehr·pret* **m/f** interpreter; **servir* d'interprète** *sehr·veer dan̄·tehr·pret* interpret

interpréter* *an̄·tehr·pray·tay* **vt** interpret

interrompre* *an̄·teh·ron̄·pruh* **vt** interrupt

intersection *an̄·tehr·sek·syon̄* **f** junction (*on road*)

interurbain(e) *an̄·tehr·ōōr·ban̄(·ben)* **adj** long-distance (*phone call*)

intoxication alimentaire *an̄·tok·see·ka·syon̄ a·lee·mon̄·tehr* **f** food poisoning

intrigue *an̄·treeg* **f** plot (*in play*)

inutile *ee·nŌŌ·teel* **adj** useless; unnecessary

invalide *an̄·va·leed* **m/f** disabled person

inventaire *an̄·von̄·tehr* **m** inventory; stocktaking

inventer *an̄·von̄·tay* **vt** invent

invention *an̄·von̄·syon̄* **f** invention

investir *an̄·ves·teer* **vt** invest

investissement *an̄·ves·tees·mon̄* **m** investment

invisible *an̄·vee·zee·bluh* **adj** invisible

invitation *an̄·vee·ta·syon̄* **f** invitation

invité(e) *an̄·vee·tay* **m/f** guest

inviter *an̄·vee·tay* **vt** invite

iode *yod* **m** iodine

Irak *ee·rak* **m** Iraq

Iran *ee·ron̄* **m** Iran

irlandais(e) *eer·lon̄·deh(·dez)* **adj** Irish

Irlande *eer·lon̄d* **f** Ireland

Islande *ees·lon̄d* **f** Iceland

Israël *ees·ra·el* **m** Israel

Italie *ee·ta·lee* **f** Italy

italien(ne) *ee·ta·lyan̄* **m** Italian □ **adj** italien(ne) *ee·ta·lyan̄(·lyen)* Italian; **il est Italien** *eel eh tee·ta·lyan̄* he's Italian; **elle est Italienne** *el eh tee·ta·lyen* she's Italian

itinéraire *ee·tee·nay·rehr* **m** route; **l'itinéraire touristique** *ee·tee·nay·rehr too·rees·teek* scenic route

ivoire *ee·vwar* **m** ivory

ivre *ee·vruh* **adj** drunk

J

jaloux(ouse) *zha·loo(·looz)* **adj** jealous

jamais *zha·meh* **adv** never; ever; **êtes-vous jamais allé à Londres?** *et·voo zha·meh za·lay a lon̄·druh* have you ever been to London?; **je ne suis jamais allé à...** *zhuh nuh swee zha·meh za·lay a* I've never been to...

jambe *zhon̄b* **f** leg (*of person*)

jambon *zhon̄·bon̄* **m** ham

janvier *zhon̄·vyay* **m** January

Japon *zha·pon̄* **m** Japan

japonais(e) *zha·po·neh* **m** Japanese □ **adj** japonais(e) *zha·po·neh(·nez)* Japanese; **il est Japonais** *eel eh zha·po·neh* he's Japanese; **elle est Japonaise** *el eh zha·po·nez* she's Japanese

jardin *zhar·dan̄* **m** garden; **les jardins botaniques** *zhar·dan̄ bo·ta·neek* botanical gardens

jardinier *zhar·dee·nyay* **m** gardener

jarretelles *zhar·tel* fpl suspenders (*for stockings*)

jauge *zhozh* f gauge (*device*); **la jauge de niveau d'huile** *zhozh duh nee·vô dweel* dipstick

jaune *zhôn* adj yellow

jazz *jaz* m jazz

je, j' *zhuh* pron I

jean *jeen* m jeans

jeep *jeep* f jeep

jersey *zhehr·zay* m jersey (*fabric*)

jet *zhay* m spray (*of liquid*); **le jet d'eau** *zhay dô* fountain

jetée *zhuh·tay* f pier

jeter* *zhuh·tay* vt throw; throw away; **à jeter** *a zhuh·tay* disposable

jeton *zhuh·toñ* m chip (*in gambling*); counter; token (*for machine*)

jeu *zhuh* m set (*collection*); pack (*of cards*); gambling; game; **être* en jeu** *eh·troñ zhuh* to be at stake; **le jeu de dames** *zhuh duh dam* checkers, draughts; **le jeu de cartes** *zhuh duh kart* card game

jeu-concours *zhuh·koñ·koor* m quiz

jeudi *zhuh·dee* m Thursday

jeune *zhuhn* adj young

jeunesse *zhuh·nes* f youth (*period*)

jockey *zho·kay* m jockey

joie *zhwah* f joy

joindre* *zhwañ·druh* vt join; enclose

joker *zho·kehr* m joker (*cards*)

joli(e) *zho·lee* adj pretty

jonquille *zhoñ·keey* f daffodil

joue *zhoo* f cheek

jouer *zhoo·ay* vi gamble □ *vt/i* play; **jouer à pile ou face** *zhoo·ay a peel oo fas* to toss a coin; **jouer le rôle de Hamlet** *zhoo·ay luh rôl duh Hamlet* to act Hamlet; **jouer au football** *zhoo·ay ô foot·bal* to play football; **jouer du violon** *zhoo·ay doo vee·o·loñ* to play the violin; **jouer avec** *zhoo·ay a·vek* to play with; **jouer franc-jeu** *zhoo·ay froñ·zhuh* to play fair

jouet *zhoo·eh* m toy

joueur *zhoo·ur* m gambler; player (*in sport*); **le/la joueur(euse) de golf** *zhoo·uhr(·uhz) duh golf* golfer

joueuse *zhoo·uz* f player (*in sport*)

jour *zhoor* m day; **le jour de Noël** *zhoor duh no·el* Christmas Day; **le jour de l'An** *zhoor duh loñ* New Year's Day; **le jour férié** *zhoor fay·ree·ay* holiday (*day*); **le jour de semaine** *zhoor duh suh·men* weekday; **mettre* à jour** *meh·tra zhoor* update; **tous les jours** *too lay zhoor* every day; **de jour en jour** *duh zhoor oñ zhoor* day by day; **dès qu'il a fait jour** *deh keel a feh zhoor* as soon as it was light; **un jour** *uñ zhoor* one day; **de nos jours** *duh nô zhoor* nowadays

journal *zhoor·nal* m newspaper; diary; **le journal du soir** *zhoor·nal dôô swahr* evening paper

journaliste *zhoor·na·leest* m/f reporter (*press*); journalist

journée *zhoor·nay* f day (*length of time*); **toute la journée** *toot la zhoor·nay* all day long

jubilé *zhôô·bee·lay* m jubilee

judo *zhôô·dô* m judo

juge *zhôôzh* m judge

juger* *zhôô·zhay* vt try (*in law*); judge

Juif *zhweef* m Jew □ adj **juif** *zhweef* Jewish

juillet *zhwee·yeh* m July

juin *zhwañ* m June

juive *zhweev* adj Jewish

juke-box *jook·boks* m jukebox

jumbo-jet *jum·bo·jet* m jumbo jet

jumeaux *zhôô·mô* mpl twins

jumelles *zhôô·mel* fpl twins; binoculars; field glasses

jupe *zhôôp* f skirt

jupon *zhôô·poñ* m petticoat; underskirt

jurer *zhôô·ray* vi swear

jus *zhôô* m juice; **le jus de pamplemousse** *zhôô duh poñ·pluh·moos* grapefruit juice; **le jus de citron** *zhôô duh see·troñ* lemon juice; **le jus d'orange** *zhôô do·roñzh* orange juice; **le jus de viande** *zhôô duh vyoñd* gravy

jusqu'à *zhôô·ska* prep until; till; **jusqu'à maintenant** *zhôô·ska mañ·tuh·noñ* up till now; **jusqu'à 6** *zhôô·ska 6* up to 6; **jusqu'à ce qu'il vienne** *zhôô·ska suh keel vyen* until he comes; **jusqu'à la gare** *zhôôs·ka la gar* as far as the station; **jusqu'à l'aube** *zhôô·ska lôb* till dawn

juste *zhôôst* adj fair; right; tight □ adv **j'ai tout juste réussi à le faire** *zhay too zhôôst ryôô·see a luh fehr* I just managed it; **juste au-dessus du coude** *zhôôst ô·duh·sôô dôô kood* just above the elbow; **juste ici** *zhôôst ee·see* just here

de justesse *duh zhôôs·tes* adv only just

justice *zhôôs·tees* f justice

K

karaté *ka·ra·tay* m karate

kascher *ka·shehr* adj kosher

kayac *kye·yak* m canoe; **faire* du kayac** *fehr dôô kye·yak* to go canoeing

kébab *kay·bab* m kebab

Kenya *ken·ya* m Kenya

ketchup *ke·chup* m ketchup

kidnapper *keed·na·pay* vt kidnap

kilo *kee·lô* m kilo; **F3 le kilo** *F3 luh kee·lô* F3 per kilo

kilogramme *kee·lô·gram* m kilogram(me)

kilométrage *kee·lô·may·trazh* m ≈ mileage

kilomètre *kee·lô·meh·truh* m kilometer, kilometre; **kilomètres à l'heure** *kee·lô·meh·truh a lur* ≈ miles per hour, m.p.h.

kilowatt *kee·lô·wat* m kilowatt

kilt *keelt* m kilt

kiosque *kee·osk* m kiosk; **le kiosque à journaux** *kee·osk a zhoor·nô* newsstand

kirsch *keersh* m kirsch

klaxon *klak·soñ* m horn (*of car*)

klaxonner *klak·so·nay* vi hoot (*horn*); sound one's horn

L

la, l' *la* pron her; it; **la voici** *la vwah·see* here she is □ *art* **la femme** *la fam* the woman

là *la* adv there; **là-haut** *la·ô* up there; **est-ce qu'il est là?** *es·keel eh la* is he there/here/in?

là-bas *la·ba* adv over there

laboratoire *la·bo·ra·twahr* m laboratory; **le laboratoire de langues** *la·bo·ra·twahr duh loñg* language laboratory

lac *lak* m lake

lacet *la·seh* m shoelace

lâche *lahsh m/f* coward □ *adj* slack (*loose*)

lâcher *lah·shay vi* fail (*brakes*) □ *vt* let go

laid(e) *leh* (*led*) *adj* ugly (*object, person*)

laine *len f* wool; **la laine d'agneau** *len da·nyō* lambswool; **de laine** *duh len* wool(l)en

laisse *les f* leash

laisser *leh·say vt* leave; let (*allow*); **laisser quelqu'un faire quelque chose** *leh·say kel·kuñ fehr kel·kuh shōz* to let someone do something; **laissez-moi entrer** *leh·say·mwah oñ·tray* let me in; **laissez votre manteau ici** *leh·say vo·truh moñ·tō ee·see* leave your coat here; **laisser un message** *leh·say uñ meh·sazh* to leave a message; **ils l'ont laissé partir** *eel loñ leh·say par·teer* they let him go

laisser-passer *leh·say·pa·say m* pass (*permit*)

lait *leh m* milk; **le lait en poudre** *luh leh oñ poo·druh* dried milk; **le lait parfumé fouetté** *leh par·fōō·may fweh·tay* milkshake; **le lait écrémé** *leh ay·kray·may* skim(med) milk; **le lait caillé** *leh kye·yay* junket; **le lait condensé** *leh koñ·doñ·say* condensed milk; **le lait concentré** *leh koñ·soñ·tray* evaporated milk

laitier *lay·tyay m* milkman

laitue *lay·tōō f* lettuce

en lambeaux *loñ·bō adj* ragged (*clothes*)

lame *lam f* blade (*of knife*); **la lame de rasoir** *lam duh ra·zwahr* razor blade

lampadaire *loñ·pa·dehr m* standard lamp

lampe *loñp f* light; lamp; **la lampe à rayons ultraviolets** *loñp a ray·yoñ zōōl·tra·vyo·leh* sunlamp; **la lampe de poche** *loñp duh posh* flashlight; torch

lancer* *loñ·say vt* throw; launch

langage *loñ·gazh m* language (*way one speaks*)

langouste *loñ·goost f* crawfish, crayfish (*saltwater*)

langoustines *loñ·goos·teen fpl* scampi

langue *loñg f* tongue; language

lanoline *la·no·leen f* lanolin

lapin *la·pañ m* rabbit

laque *lak f* hair spray

laquelle *la·kel pron* which one; **la chaise sur laquelle** *la shez sōōr la·kel* the chair on which

large *larzh adj* wide; broad; **4 cm. de large** *4 cm. duh larzh* 4 cm. wide

largeur *lar·zhur f* width

larme *larm f* tear; **en larmes** *oñ larm* in tears

laryngite *la·rañ·zheet f* laryngitis

latin *la·tañ m* Latin □ *adj* **latin(e)** *la·tañ(·teen)* Latin

lavable *la·va·bluh adj* washable

lavabo *la·va·bō m* washbasin

laver *la·vay vt* wash; bathe (*wound etc*); **se laver** *suh la·vay* to wash (*oneself*); **je me suis lavé les mains** *zhuh muh swee la·vay lay mañ* I washed my hands

laverie automatique *la·vree ō·tō·ma·teek f* launderette

lavette *la·vet f* dishcloth

lave-vaisselle *lav·veh·sel m* dishwasher

laxatif *lak·sa·teef m* laxative

le, l' *luh pron* him; it; **prenez-le** *pruh·*

nay·luh* take it □ *art* **le garçon *luh gar·soñ* the boy; **le jeudi** *luh zhuh·dee* on Thursdays

lécher* *lay·shay vt* lick

lèche-vitrines *lesh·vee·treen m* window shopping

leçon *luh·soñ f* lesson

lecture *lek·tōōr f* reading

légal(e) *lay·gal adj* legal

léger(ère) *lay·zhay(·zhehr) adj* light (*not heavy*); minor (*injury*); weak (*tea*)

légumes *lay·gōōm mpl* vegetables

lendemain *loñ·duh·mañ m* the next day

lent(e) *loñ* (*loñt*) *adj* slow

lentement *loñt·moñ adv* slowly

lentille *loñ·teey f* lens (*of glasses*)

lentilles *loñ·teey fpl* lentils

lequel *luh·kel pron* which one; **je ne sais pas lequel prendre** *zhuh nuh seh pa luh·kel proñ·druh* I don't know which to take

les *lay pron* them; **achetez-les** *ash·tay·lay* buy them □ *art* **les livres** *lay lee·vruh* the books

lessive *leh·seev f* soap powder; washing powder; washing (*clothes*); **faire* la lessive** *fehr la leh·seev* to do the washing

lettre *leh·truh f* letter; **la lettre explicative** *leh·truh ek·splee·ka·teev* covering letter; **la lettre exprès** *leh·trek·spres* express letter; **la lettre recommandée** *leh·truh ruh·ko·moñ·day* registered letter; **la lettre par avion** *leh·truh par a·vyoñ* air letter

leur(s) *lur adj* their □ *pron* montrez-leur les livres *moñ·tray·lur lay lee·vruh* show them the books; **il leur a parlé** *eel lur a par·lay* he spoke to them; **le/la leur** *luh/la lur* theirs; **les leurs** *lay lur* theirs (*plural*)

levé *luh·vay m* survey (*of land*)

levée *luh·vay f* trick (*in cards*); collection (*of mail*)

lever* *luh·vay vt* raise; **il n'est pas encore levé** *eel neh pa zoñ·kor luh·vay* he isn't up yet (*out of bed*); **se lever*** *suh luh·vay* to get up; rise (*person, sun*)

lever du soleil *luh·vay dōō so·lay m* sunrise

levier *luh·vyay m* lever; **le levier de vitesse** *luh·vyay duh vee·tes* gear lever, gearshift

lèvre *leh·vruh f* lip

levure *luh·vōōr f* yeast

lexique *lek·zeek m* vocabulary (*list of words*)

libérer* *lee·bay·ray vt* release (*prisoner*)

liberté *lee·behr·tay f* freedom

librairie *lee·breh·ree f* bookshop

libre *lee·bruh adj* free; vacant (*seat, toilet*); clear (*not blocked*)

libre-service *lee·bruh·sehr·vees adj* self-service

Libye *lee·bee f* Libya

licencier *lee·soñ·syay vt* lay off (*workers*); dismiss; pay off

Liechtenstein *leekh·ten·shtine m* Liechtenstein

liège *lyezh m* cork

lier *lee·ay vt* tie up

lieu *lyuh m* place; **au lieu de** *ō lyuh duh* instead of

lièvre *lee·eh·vruh m* hare

ligne *lee·nyuh f* line; service; route (*transport*); **la ligne de changement de date** *lee·nyuh duh shoñ·zhuh·moñ* *duh dat* date line; **les grandes lignes** *grond lee·nyuh* outline (*summary*); **la ligne pointillée** *lee·nyuh pwañ·tee·yay* dotted line

limande-sole *lee·moñd·sôl f* lemon sole

lime *leem f* file (*tool*); **la lime à ongles** *leem a oñ·gluh* emery board; nailfile

limitation de vitesse *lee·mee·ta·syoñ duh vee·tes f* speed limit

limite *lee·meet f* limit; boundary; **dans les limites de** *doñ lay lee·meet duh* within the scope of

limiter *lee·mee·tay vt* limit; restrict

limonade *lee·mo·nad f* lemonade

limousine *lee·moo·zeen f* limousine

lin *lañ m* linen (*cloth*)

linge *lañzh m* linen (*for bed, table*); underwear; laundry (*clothes*)

linoléum *lee·no·lay·yum m* lino(leum)

lion *lee·yoñ m* lion

liquidation *lee·kee·da·syoñ f* liquidation

liquide *lee·keed m* liquid □ *adj* liquid

liquidités *lee·kee·dee·tay fpl* liquid assets

lire* *leer vt/i* read

lis *lee m* lily

lisse *lees adj* smooth

listage *lees·tazh m* printout

liste *leest f* list; **dresser une liste de** *dreh·say ōōn leest duh* to list; **la liste d'adresses** *leest da·dres* mailing list; **la liste des prix** *leest day pree* price list

liste d'attente *leest da·toñt f* waiting list

lit *lee m* bed; **un lit d'une personne** *uñ lee dōōn pehr·son* a single bed; **le grand lit** *groñ lee* double bed; **le lit d'enfant** *lee doñ·foñ* cot; crib; **le lit de camp** *lee duh koñ* camp-bed; **les lits superposés** *lee sōō·pehr·pō·zay* bunk beds; **les lits jumeaux** *lee zhōō·mō* twin beds; **au lit** *ō lee* in bed

literie *lee·tuh·ree f* bedding

litre *lee·truh m* litre, liter

littérature *lee·tay·ra·tōōr f* literature

livraison *lee·vreh·zoñ f* delivery (*of goods*); **la livraison des bagages** *lee·vreh·zoñ day ba·gazh* baggage claim

livre *lee·vruh f* pound; **la livre sterling** *lee·vruh stehr·leeng* sterling

livre *lee·vruh m* book; **le livre de poche** *lee·vruh duh posh* paperback; **le grand livre** *groñ lee·vruh* ledger

livrer *lee·vray vt* deliver (*goods*)

livret de banque *lee·vray duh boñk m* bankbook

local(e) *lo·kal adj* local

locataire *lo·ka·tehr m/f* tenant; lodger

location *lo·ka·syoñ f* rental; **le bureau de location** *boo·rō duh lo·ka·syoñ* box office; booking office

locaux *lo·kō mpl* premises

locomotive *lo·ko·mo·teev f* engine (*of train*)

logement *lozh·moñ m* accommodation; housing

loger* *lo·zhay vt* accommodate □ *vi* **loger* chez des amis** *lo·zhay shay day za·mee* to stay with friends

logiciel *lo·zhee·syel m* software

loi *lwah f* law

loin *lwañ adv* far; **au loin** *ō lwañ* in the distance; **plus loin** *plōō lwañ* farther; **c'est loin** *seh lwañ* it's a long way; **de loin** *duh lwañ* far (*much*)

loisir *lwah·zeer m* leisure

Londres *loñ·druh m* London

long(ue) *loñ (loñg) adj* long; **le long de la rue** *luh loñ duh la rōō* along the

street; **long de 6 mètres** *loñ duh 6 meh·truh* 6 metres long

longtemps *loñ·toñ adv* a long time; long; **je n'en ai pas pour longtemps** *zhuh noñ nay pa poor loñ·toñ* I shan't be long

longueur *loñ·gur f* length; **quelle est la longueur de la rivière?** *kel eh la loñ·gur duh la ree·vyehr* how long is the river?

loquet *lo·keh m* latch

lorsque *lor·skuh conj* when

lot *lō m* prize; lot (*at auction*)

loterie *lo·tree f* lottery

lotion *lō·syoñ f* lotion; **la lotion après-rasage** *lō·syoñ a·preh ra·zazh* after-shave (lotion)

lotissement *lo·tees·moñ m* plot (*of land*)

louche *loosh f* ladle

louer *loo·ay vt* let; hire; rent; **à louer** *a loo·ay* to let (*house etc*)

loukoum *loo·koom m* Turkish delight

loup *loo m* wolf

lourd(e) *loor (loord) adj* heavy; close (*stuffy*); **trop lourd(e)** *trō loor (loord)* overweight (*baggage*)

loyer *lwah·yay m* rent

lubrifiant *lōō·bree·fyoñ m* grease (*lubricant*)

lui *lwee pron* him; he; her; it; **donnez-le-lui** *do·nay·luh·lwee* give it to him/her; **c'est lui** *seh lwee* it's him

lui-même *lwee·mem pron* himself; **il l'a fait lui-même** *eel la feh lwee·mem* he did it himself

lumière *lōō·myehr f* light

lundi *luñ·dee m* Monday

lune *lōōn f* moon; **la lune de miel** *lōōn duh myel* honeymoon

lunettes *lōō·net fpl* glasses; **les lunettes de soleil** *lōō·net duh so·lay* sunglasses; shades; **les lunettes protectrices** *lōō·net pro·tek·trees* goggles

lutte *lōōt f* wrestling; struggle

lutter *lōō·tay vi* struggle (*physically*)

luxe *lōōks m* luxury; **de luxe** *duh lōōks* de luxe; luxury

Luxembourg *lōōk·soñ·boor m* Luxembourg

luxueux(euse) *lōōk·sōō·uh(·uhz) adj* luxurious

lycée *lee·say m* secondary school; high school

M

ma *ma adj* my; **ma mère** *ma mehr* my mother

macadam *ma·ka·dam m* tarmac

macaronis *ma·ka·ro·nee mpl* macaroni

mâcher *mah·shay vt* chew

machine *ma·sheen f* machine; **la machine à coudre** *ma·sheen a koo·druh* sewing machine; **la machine à écrire** *ma·sheen a ay·kreer* typewriter; **la machine à sous** *ma·sheen a soo* one-armed bandit; slot machine; **la machine à laver** *ma·sheen a la·vay* washing machine

machinerie *ma·sheen·ree f* machinery

mâchoire *mash·wahr f* jaw

Madame *ma·dam f* Mrs; Ms; **Dear Madam**; **madame** *ma·dam* madam

Mademoiselle *mad·mwah·zel f* Miss

madère *ma·dehr m* Madeira (*wine*)

Madrid *ma·dreed f* Madrid

magasin *ma·ga·zañ m* store; shop; **faire* les magasins** *fehr lay ma·ga·zañ* to go round the shops; **le magasin de jouets** *ma·ga·zañ duh zhoo·eh* toyshop; **le magasin de chaussures** *ma·ga·zañ duh shō·sōōr* shoeshop; **le magasin à succursales multiples** *ma·ga·zañ a sŏō·kŏŏr·sal mŏōl·tee·pluh* multiple store; chain store; **le grand magasin** *groñ ma·ga·zañ* department store

magazine *ma·ga·zeen m* magazine (*journal*)

magie *ma·zhee f* magic

magique *ma·zheek adj* magic

magnétophone *ma·nyay·to·fon m* tape recorder; **le magnétophone à cassettes** *ma·nyay·to·fon a ka·set* cassette-recorder

magnétoscope *man·yay·to·skop m* videocassette recorder

magnifique *ma·nyee·feek adj* magnificent

mai *may m* May

maigre *meh·gruh adj* thin (*person*); lean (*meat*)

maigrir *may·greer vi* reduce (*lose weight*)

maille *mye f* stitch; **la maille filée** *mye fee·lay* ladder (*in stocking*)

maillet *mye·yay m* mallet

maillot de bain *mye·yō duh bañ m* swimsuit; **le maillot de corps** *mye·yō duh kor* undershirt

main *mañ f* hand; **fait(e) à la main** *feh (fet) a la mañ* handmade; **à la main à** *la mañ* by hand

main-d'œuvre *mañ·duh·vruh f* labo(u)r; manpower; work force

maintenant *mañ·tuh·noñ adv* now

maintenir* *mañ·tuh·neer vt* maintain; support

maire *mehr m* mayor

mairie *meh·ree f* city hall; town hall

mais *meh conj* but

maïs *ma·ees m* maize; **le maïs doux** *ma·ees doo* sweet corn

maison *meh·zoñ f* house; home; firm; **la maison de campagne** *meh·zoñ duh koñ·pa·nyuh* villa (*country house*); **à la maison à** *la meh·zoñ* at home; **la Maison Blanche** *meh·zoñ bloñsh* White House; **aux frais de la maison** *ō freh duh la meh·zoñ* on the house

maître *meh·truh m* master

maîtresse *meh·tres f* mistress

maîtriser *meh·tree·zay vt* control

maïzena *ma·ee·zeh·na f* cornflour; cornstarch

majorité *ma·zho·ree·tay f* majority; **élu avec une majorité de 5 voix** *ay·lōō a·vek ōōn ma·zho·ree·tay duh 5 vwah* elected by a majority of 5

majuscule *ma·zhōō·skŏōl f* capital letter; **en majuscules** *oñ ma·zhōō·skŏōl* in capitals; **A majuscule** *A ma·zhōō·skŏōl* capital A

mal *mal adv* badly; **faire* mal** *fehr mal* hurt □ *m* **se donner du mal pour quelque chose** *suh do·nay dōō mal poor kel·kuh shōz* to take trouble over something; **le mal au ventre** *mal ō voñ·truh* stomach ache; **j'ai mal au ventre** *zhay mal ō voñ·truh* I have (a) stomach ache; **j'ai mal au cœur** *zhay mal ō kur* I feel sick; **je me trouve mal** *zhuh muh troov mal* I feel faint; **vous vous êtes fait mal** *voo voo zet feh mal* you've hurt yourself; **le mal d'oreille** *mal do·ray* earache; **avoir* mal à l'oreille** *a·vwahr mal a lo·ray* to have earache; **le mal de tête** *mal duh tet* headache; **avoir* mal à la tête** *a·vwahr mal a la tet* to have a headache; **avoir* le mal de mer** *a·*

vwahr luh mal duh mer to be seasick; **avoir* le mal du pays** *a·vwahr luh mal dōō pay·yee* to be homesick; **le mal de dents** *mal duh doñ* toothache; **avoir* mal aux dents** *a·vwahr mal ō doñ* to have toothache; **il y en a pas mal** *eel yoñ na pa mal* there are quite a few

malade *ma·lad m/f* invalid; patient □ *adj* ill

maladie *ma·la·dee f* sickness; disease; illness

maladroit(e) *ma·la·drwah(·drwaht) adj* clumsy (*person*)

malchance *mal·shoñs f* bad luck

malchanceux(euse) *mal·shoñ·suh (·suhz) adj* unlucky

mâle *mahl adj* male

malgré *mal·gray prep* despite

malheureusement *mal·uh·ruz·moñ adv* unfortunately

malheureux(euse) *mal·uh·ruh(·ruhz) adj* unhappy; miserable; unfortunate (*event*)

malhonnête *mal·o·net adj* dishonest

malle *mal f* trunk (*for clothes etc*)

malt *malt m* malt

Malte *malt f* Malta

maman *ma·moñ f* mum(my); mom(my)

manche *moñsh f* sleeve; **la Manche** *moñsh* the Channel □ *m* **le manche** *moñsh* handle (*of knife*)

manchette *moñ·shet f* headline; cuff (*of shirt*)

mandarine *moñ·da·reen f* tangerine

mandat *moñ·da m* money order; **le mandat postal** *moñ·da pos·tal* postal order

manège *ma·nezh m* merry-go-round; roundabout (*fairground*)

manger* *moñ·zhay vt/i* eat

manière *ma·nyehr f* manner

manières *ma·nyehr fpl* manners

manifestation *ma·nee·fes·ta·syoñ f* demonstration (*political*)

manifeste *ma·nee·fest adj* definite (*distinct*)

mannequin *man·kañ m* model (*mannequin*)

manœuvre *ma·nuh·vruh m* labo(u)rer

manquant(e) *moñ·koñ(·koñt) adj* missing (*object*)

manque *moñk m* shortfall

manquer *moñ·kay vt* miss (*target, train*) □ *vi* **manquer de personnel** *moñ·kay duh pehr·so·nel* to be short-staffed; **il y a des pages qui manquent** *eel ya day pazh kee moñk* some pages are missing; **ma mère me manque** *ma mehr muh moñk* I miss my mother

manteau *moñ·tō m* coat; **le manteau de vison** *moñ·tō duh vee·zoñ* mink coat; **le manteau de fourrure** *moñ·tō duh foo·rŏŏr* fur coat

manuel *ma·nwel m* manual (*book*); handbook; textbook □ *adj* manuel(le) *ma·nwel* manual

maquereau *ma·krō m* mackerel

maquillage *ma·kee·yazh m* make-up

se maquiller *suh ma·kee·yay vr* to make (oneself) up

marais *ma·reh m* swamp

marbre *mar·bruh m* marble (*material*)

marc *mar m* grounds (*of coffee*)

marchand *mar·shoñ m* dealer; merchant; **le marchand de légumes** *mar·shoñ duh lay·gŏōm* greengrocer; **le marchand de journaux** *mar·shoñ duh zhoor·nō* newsagent

marchandage *mar·shoñ·dazh* m bargaining (*negotiation*)

marchandises *mar·shoñ·deez* fpl goods; **le train de marchandises** *trañ duh mar·shoñ·deez* freight train

marche f step; stair; march; **la marche arrière** *marsh a·ryehr* reverse (*gear*); **en marche arrière** *oñ marsh a·ryehr* in reverse (gear); **en marche** *oñ marsh* on (*machine*)

marche à pied *marsh a pyay* f walking

marché *mar·shay* m market; **le jour de marché** *zhoor duh mar·shay* market-day; **le Marché Commun** *mar·shay ko·muñ* Common Market; **le marché noir** *mar·shay nwahr* black market; **le marché des changes** *mar·shay day shoñzh* foreign exchange market; **le marché aux puces** *mar·shay ō pōōs* flea market; **bon marché** *boñ mar·shay* inexpensive; **conclure* un marché** *koñ·klōōr uñ mar·shay* to make a bargain; **le marché global** *mar·shay glo·bal* package deal

marcher *mar·shay* vi walk; go (*clock, machine*); work (*clock, mechanism*); run (*machine, engine*); **marcher au pas** *mar·shay ō pah* march; **faire* marcher** *fehr mar·shay* operate (*machine*); **cette voiture marche au gas-oil** *set vwah·tōōr marsh ō gaz·oil* this car runs on diesel

mardi *mar·dee* m Tuesday

mardi gras *mar·dee gra* m Shrove Tuesday

marée *ma·ray* f tide; **la marée haute** *ma·ray ōt* high tide; **la marée basse** *ma·ray bas* low tide; **c'est la marée haute/basse** *seh la ma·ray ōt/bas* the tide is in/out

margarine *mar·ga·reen* f margarine

marge *marzh* f margin (*on page*); **la marge bénéficiaire** *marzh bay·nay·fee·see·ehr* profit margin

mari *ma·ree* m husband

mariage *ma·ree·azh* m wedding; marriage

marié *ma·ryay* m bridegroom □ adj **marié(e)** *ma·ryay* married

mariée *ma·ryay* f bride

se marier *suh ma·ryay* vr marry; **ils se sont mariés hier** *eel suh soñ ma·ryay ee·ehr* they were married yesterday

marin *ma·rañ* m sailor

marina *ma·ree·na* f marina

marine *ma·reen* f navy

marjolaine *mar·zho·len* f marjoram

mark *mark* m mark (*currency*)

marketing *mar·ke·ting* m marketing

Maroc *ma·rok* m Morocco

marocain(e) *ma·ro·kañ(·ken)* adj Moroccan

marque *mark* f make (*of product*); brand; brand name; mark; **la marque déposée** *mark day·pō·zay* registered trademark; **la marque de fabrique** *mark duh fa·breek* trademark

marquer *mar·kay* vt mark; score (*goal*)

marraine *ma·ren* f godmother

marron *ma·roñ* m chestnut □ adj brown

mars *mars* m March

marteau *mar·tō* m hammer

martini *mar·tee·nee* m martini (*Brit*)

mascara *mas·ka·ra* m mascara

masculin(e) *mas·kōō·lañ(·leen)* adj masculine

masque *mask* m mask

masquer *mas·kay* vt mask

massage *ma·sazh* m massage

masse *mas* f earth (*electrical*); une

masse de fleurs *ōōn mas duh flur* a mass of blossom

masser *ma·say* vt massage

masseur *ma·sur* m masseur

masseuse *ma·suhz* f masseuse

mât *mah* m pole (*wooden*); mast (*ship's*); **le mât de tente** *mah duh toñt* tent pole

match *matsh* m match (*sport*)

matelas *mat·la* m mattress; **le matelas pneumatique** *mat·la pnuh·ma·teek* air mattress; air bed

matériel *ma·tay·ryel* m tackle (*gear*); equipment; kit (*sports*); plant (*equipment*)

maternité *ma·tehr·nee·tay* f maternity hospital

mathématiques *ma·tay·ma·teek* fpl mathematics

matière *ma·tyehr* f subject (*in school*); material; **les matières premières** *ma·tyehr pruh·myehr* raw material

matin *ma·tañ* m morning

maussade *mō·sad* adj dull (*day, weather*)

mauvais(e) *mo·veh(·vez)* adj nasty; evil; bad; **le plus mauvais livre** *luh plōō mō·veh lee·vruh* the worst book; **la mauvaise route/réponse** *la mō·vez root/ray·poñs* the wrong road/answer

mauve *mōv* adj mauve

maximum *mak·see·mum* m maximum □ adj maximum; **au maximum** *ō mak·see·mum* at the most; as much as possible

mayday *may·day* m Mayday

mayonnaise *ma·yo·nez* f mayonnaise

mazout *ma·zoot* m oil (*for heating*)

me, m' *muh* pron me, myself; **il me l'a donné** *eel muh la do·nay* he gave it to me

mécanicien *may·ka·nee·syañ* m mechanic

mécanisme *may·ka·neez·muh* m works (*mechanism*)

méchant(e) *may·shoñ(·shoñt)* adj unkind (*remark*); naughty; wicked

mèche *mesh* f wick (*of cigarette lighter*)

médecin *mayd·sañ* m doctor; **le médecin généraliste** *mayd·sañ zhay·nay·ra·leest* general practitioner, G.P.

média *may·dya* mpl media

médical(e) *may·dee·kal* adj medical

médicament *may·dee·ka·moñ* m medicine (*pills etc*); drug

médiocre *may·dyo·kruh* adj poor (*mediocre*)

Méditerranée *may·dee·teh·ra·nay* f the Mediterranean (*sea*)

méditerranéen(enne) *may·dee·teh·ra·nay·añ(·en)* adj Mediterranean

méduse *may·dōōz* f jellyfish

meeting *mee·ting* m rally (*political*)

meilleur(e) *may·yur* adj best; better; **c'est lui le meilleur** *seh lwee luh may·yur* he's the best

mélange *may·loñzh* m mixture; blend

mélanger* *may·loñ·zhay* vt blend; mix; **se mélanger*** *suh may·loñ·zhay* mix

mélasse *may·las* f molasses; treacle; **la mélasse raffinée** *may·las ra·fee·nay* (golden) syrup

mêler *meh·lay* vt mix; **se mêler à** *suh meh·lay* a interfere with

mélodieux(euse) *may·lo·dyuh(·dyuz)* adj sweet (*music*)

melon *muh·loñ* m melon

membre *moñ·bruh* m member; **devenir* membre de** *duh·vuh·neer moñ·bruh duh* to join (*club*); **être* mem-**

bre d'un club *eh·truh moñ·bruh duñ klub* to belong to a club
même *mem adj* same; **le même** *luh mem* the same (one); **tout de même** *too duh mem* all the same; **la même chose, s'il vous plaît** *la mem shōz seel voo pleh* (the) same again please!
□ *adv* **même un enfant pourrait le faire** *mem uñ noñ·foñ poo·reh luh fehr* even a child could do it
mémoire *may·mwahr f* memory
menace *muh·nas f* threat
menacer* *muh·na·say vt* threaten
ménage *may·nazh m* housework; **la femme de ménage** *fam duh may·nazh* cleaner
ménagère *may·na·zhehr f* housewife
mendiant(e) *moñ·dyoñ(·dyoñt) m/f* beggar
mendier *moñ·dyay vi* beg
mener* *muh·nay vt* lead; **cette porte mène au jardin** *set port men ō zhar·dañ* this door leads into the garden
menottes *muh·not fpl* handcuffs
mensonge *moñ·soñzh m* lie (*untruth*)
mensuel(le) *moñ·swel adj* monthly
menthe *moñt f* mint (*herb*); **la menthe à l'eau** *moñt a lō* peppermint cordial
mentholé(e) *moñ·to·lay adj* mentholated
mention *moñ·syoñ f* reference (*mention*)
mentionner *moñ·syo·nay vt* mention
mentir* *moñ·teer vi* lie (*tell a lie*)
menton *moñ·toñ m* chin
menu *muh·nü m* menu
mer *mehr f* sea; **la mer du Nord** *mehr dōō nor* North Sea; **la mer des Antilles** *mehr day zoñ·teey* Caribbean (Sea)
mercerie *mehr·suh·ree f* haberdashery
merci *mehr·see excl* thank you
mercredi *mehr·kruh·dee m* Wednesday
mère *mehr f* mother
meringue *muh·rañg f* meringue
mériter *may·ree·tay vt* deserve
merlan *mehr·loñ m* whiting
merle *mehrl m* blackbird
merveilleux(euse) *mehr·vay·yuh (·yuhz) adj* wonderful; marvellous
mes *may adj* my; **mes frères/sœurs** *may frehr/sur* my brothers/sisters
message *meh·sazh m* message
messager *meh·sa·zhay m* messenger
messe *mes f* mass (*church*)
mesure *muh·zōōr f* measurement; **prendre* des mesures pour faire quelque chose** *proñ·druh day muh·zōōr poor fehr kel·kuh shōz* to take steps to do something; **fait(e) sur mesure** *feh (fet) sōōr muh·zōōr* made-to-measure; custom-made
mesurer *muh·zōō·ray vt/i* measure; **combien mesurez-vous?** *koñ·byañ muh·zōō·ray·voo* how tall are you?
mesures *muh·zōōr fpl* measurements
métal *may·tal m* metal
météo *may·tay·ō f* weather forecast
méthode *may·tod f* method
méthodiste *may·to·deest m/f* Methodist
métier *may·tyay m* trade; occupation (*job*); craft
mètre *meh·truh m* meter (*measure*); metre; **le mètre à ruban** *meh·tra rōō·boñ* tape measure
métrique *may·treek adj* metric
métro *may·tro m* underground railway; subway; **aller* en métro** *a·lay oñ may·tro* to go by underground
mets *meh m* dish (*food*)

metteur en scène *meh·tur oñ sen m* producer (*play*)
mettre* *meh·truh vt* put; put on; set (*alarm*); place; switch on (*TV*); **mettre* au point** *meh·trō pwañ* to focus; **mettez-le sur mon compte** *meh·tay· luh sōōr moñ koñt* charge it to my account; **mettre* en marche** *meh·troñ marsh* to switch on (*engine*); **mettre* K.O.** *meh·truh ka·ō* to knock out; **se mettre* à faire** *suh meh·truh a fehr* to begin to do; **se mettre* à un sport** *suh meh·tra uñ spor* to take up a sport; **mettre* une robe** *meh·trōōn rob* to put on a dress; **mettre* le couvert** *meh·truh luh koo·vehr* to lay the table; **mettre* en cave** *meh·troñ kav* to lay down (*wine*)
meuble *muh·bluh m* piece of furniture
meubler *muh·blay vt* furnish (*room etc*)
meubles *muh·bluh mpl* furniture
meurtre *mur·truh m* murder
mexicain(e) *mek·see·kañ(·ken) adj* Mexican
Mexique *mek·seek m* Mexico
à mi-chemin *a mee·shuh·mañ adv* halfway
microbe *mee·krob m* germ
microfiche *mee·krō·feesh f* microfiche
microfilm *mee·krō·feelm m* microfilm
micro-ordinateur *mee·krō·or·dee·na· tur m* microcomputer
microphone *mee·krō·fon m* microphone
microplaquette *mee·krō·pla·ket f* microchip
microprocesseur *mee·krō·pro·seh·sur m* microprocessor
midi *mee·dee m* midday; noon
miel *myel m* honey
le mien *luh myañ pron* mine; **la mienne** *la myen* mine; **les miens** *lay myañ* mine (*plural*); **les miennes** *lay myen* mine (*plural*)
miette *myet f* crumb
mieux *myuh adv* better; best; **de mieux en mieux** *duh myuh zoñ myuh* better and better; **il le fait le mieux** *eel luh feh luh myuh* he can do it best; **il chante mieux que vous** *eel shoñt myuh kuh voo* he sings better than you; **le mieux serait…** *luh myuh suh· reh* the best thing would be…
mignon(ne) *mee·nyoñ(·nyon) adj* sweet (*cute, pretty*)
migraine *mee·gren f* migraine
mijoter *mee·zho·tay vi* simmer
milieu *mee·lyuh m* environment; middle; **en plein milieu** *oñ plañ mee·lyuh* right in the middle; **au beau milieu** *ō bō mee·lyuh* right in the middle; **au milieu de la nuit** *ō mee· lyuh duh la nwee* in the middle of the night
militaire *mee·lee·tehr adj* military; **l'école militaire** *ay·kol mee·lee·tehr* military academy
mille *meel num* thousand
milliard *meel·yar m* billion
millième *mee·lyem adj* thousandth
milligramme *mee·lee·gram m* milligram(me)
millilitre *mee·lee·lee·truh m* millilitre
millimètre *mee·lee·meh·truh m* millimetre
million *mee·lyoñ m* million
millionième *mee·lyo·nyem adj* millionth
millionnaire *mee·lyo·nehr m* millionaire

mince *mañs adj* slim; thin (*line*)

mine *meen f* expression; mine (*for coal etc*); lead (*in pencil*)

minestrone *mee·neh·stron f* min-estrone (soup)

mineur *mee·nur m* miner; □ *adj* mi-neur(e) *mee·nur* under age

minibus *mee·nee·bōōs m* minibus

minijupe *mee·nee·zhōōp f* miniskirt

minimum *mee·nee·mum m* minimum □ *adj* minimum

miniordinateur *mee·nee·or·dee·na·tur m* minicomputer

ministère *mee·nee·stehr m* ministry (*government*); le ministère des Fi-nances *mee·nee·stehr day fee·noñs* Treasury

ministre *mee·nee·struh m* minister (*in government*); le ministre des finances *mee·nee·struh day fee·noñs* Finance Minister; le premier ministre *pruh·myay mee·nee·struh* prime minister; le ministre des Affaires Étrangères *mee·nee·struh day za·fehr ay·troñ·zhehr* secretary of state

minitaxi *mee·nee·tak·see m* minicab

minorité *mee·no·ree·tay f* minority

minuit *mee·nwee m* midnight; à minuit *a mee·nwee* at midnight

minute *mee·nōōt f* minute; une minute *ōōn mee·nōōt* just a minute

miroir *mee·rwahr m* mirror

mise en plis *meez oñ plee f* set

mise en scène *meez oñ sen f* produc-tion (*of play*)

mi-temps *mee·toñ f* half-time

mixer *meek·sehr m* mixer

mixte *meekst adj* mixed (*co-ed*)

mode *mod f* fashion; la dernière mode *la der·nyehr mod* the latest fashions; à la mode *a la mod* fashionable

mode d'emploi *mod doñ·plwah m* di-rections for use

modèle *mo·del m* model

modéliste *mo·day·leest m/f* designer (*of clothes*)

moderne *mo·dehrn adj* modern

moderniser *mo·dehr·nee·zay vt* mod-ernize

modeste *mo·dest adj* modest

modification *mo·dee·fee·ka·syoñ f* modification

modifier *mo·dee·fyay vt* modify

mohair *mo·ehr m* mohair

moi *mwah pron* me; donnez-le-moi *do·nay·luh·mwah* give it to me; c'est moi *seh mwah* it's me

moi-même *mwah·mem pron* myself; je l'ai fait moi-même *zhuh lay feh mwah·mem* I did it myself

moindre *mwañ·druh adj* least

moine *mwan m* monk

moineau *mwah·nō m* sparrow

moins *mwañ prep* minus; à moins 2 de-grés *a mwañ 2 duh·gray* at minus 2 degrees; une heure moins cinq *ōōn ur mwañ sañk* five to one □ *adv, pron* less; moins de viande *mwañ duh vee·yoñd* less meat; il en a moins *eel oñ na mwañ* he has less; il a le moins *eel a luh mwañ* he has the least; moins que *mwañ kuh* less than; le moins d'argent *luh mwañ dar·zhoñ* the least money; moins d'un kilomè-tre *mwañ duñ kee·lo·meh·truh* under a kilometre; le moins cher *luh mwañ shehr* the least expensive; les enfants de moins de 10 ans *lay zoñ·foñ duh mwañ duh 10 añ* children under 10; au moins *ō mwañ* at least; à moins

que nous ne venions *a mwañ koo nuh vuh·nyoñ* unless we come

mois *mwah m* month

moisson *mwah·soñ f* harvest (*of grain*)

moissonner *mwah·so·nay vt* harvest (*grain*)

moitié *mwah·tyay f* half; à moitié *a mwah·tyay* half; réduire* de moitié *ray·dweer duh mwah·tyay* to halve (*reduce by half*); à moitié prix *a mwah·tyay pree* half-price

molécule *mo·lay·kōōl f* molecule

molle *mol adj* soft (*not hard*)

moment *mo·moñ m* while; moment; point (*in time*); en ce moment *oñ suh mo·moñ* at the moment; at present; pour le moment *poor luh mo·moñ* for the time being; les moments de loisir *mo·moñ duh lwah·zeer* spare time

mon *moñ adj* my; mon père *moñ pehr* my father

Monaco *mo·na·kō f* Monaco

monastère *mo·nas·tehr m* monastery

monde *moñd m* world; le monde du spectacle *moñd dōō spek·ta·kluh* show business

monétaire *mo·nay·tehr adj* monetary

moniteur *mo·nee·tur m* instructor; coach; monitor (*TV*)

monitrice *mo·nee·trees f* instructress; coach

monnaie *mo·nay f* currency; change (*money*); faire* de la monnaie *fehr duh la mo·nay* to get change

mono *mo·nō adj* mono; en mono *oñ mo·nō* in mono

monopole *mo·no·pol m* monopoly

monorail *mo·no·rye m* monorail

Monsieur *muh·syuh m* Mr; Dear Sir (*on letter*); monsieur *muh·syuh* sir; le monsieur *muh·syuh* gentleman

monstre *moñ·struh m* monster

montagne *moñ·ta·nyuh f* mountain

montant *moñ·toñ m* amount (*total*)

monter *moñ·tay vi* go up; rise; monter à cheval *moñ·tay a shuh·val* to ride a horse; monter à bicyclette *moñ·tay a bee·see·klet* to ride a bicycle; monter dans *moñ·tay doñ* to board (*train, bus*); monter à bord de *moñ·tay a bor duh* to board (*ship*); monter sur *moñ·tay sōōr* to climb (*tree, wall*); mount □ *vt* take up; bring up; as-semble (*parts of machine*); monter une colline *moñ·tay ōōn ko·leen* to go up a hill

montre *moñ·truh f* watch

montrer *moñ·tray vt* show

monture *moñ·tōōr f* frames (*of glasses*)

monument *mo·nōō·moñ m* monument

se moquer de *suh mo·kay duh vr* laugh at

moquette *mo·ket f* wall-to-wall car-pet(ing)

moral(e) *mo·ral adj* moral

morceau *mor·sō m* piece; bit; cut (*of meat*); scrap; le morceau de sucre *mor·sō duh sōō·kruh* lump of sugar

mordre *mor·druh vt* bite

morsure *mor·sōōr f* bite (*by animal*)

mort(e) *mor (mort) adj* dead □ *f* la mort *mor* death

mortel(le) *mor·tel adj* fatal

morue *mo·rōō f* cod

Moscou *mos·koo m* Moscow

moselle *mo·zel f* moselle (*wine*)

mosquée *mos·kay f* mosque

mot *mō m* note (*letter*); word; mot à mot *mō ta mō* word for word

motel *mo·tel m* motel

moteur *mo·tur m* motor; engine; **le moteur diesel** *mo·tur dyeh·zel* diesel engine

motif *mo·teef m* pattern

moto *mo·tô f* motorbike

motocycliste *mo·tô·see·kleest m/f* motorcyclist

mou *moo adj* soft (*not hard*)

mouche *moosh f* fly; **la mouche à viande** *moosh a vyoñd* bluebottle

se moucher *suh moo·shay vr* to blow one's nose

moucheron *moo·shuh·roñ m* gnat

mouchoir *moo·shwahr m* handkerchief; **le mouchoir en papier** *moo·shwahr oñ pa·pyay* tissue (*handkerchief*); kleenex

moudre* *moo·druh vt* grind; mill

moufle *moo·fluh f* mitt(en)

mouillé(e) *moo·yay adj* wet

se mouiller *suh moo·yay vr* to get wet

moule *mool f* mussel; mould; tin

moulin *moo·lañ m* mill; **le moulin à vent** *moo·lañ a voñ* windmill

moulu(e) *moo·lōō adj* ground (*coffee*)

mourir* *moo·reer vi* die; **mourir* de** *moo·reer duh* to die of

mousse *moos f* foam; moss; mousse

mousseux(euse) *moo·suh(·suhz) adj* sparkling (*wine*)

moustache *moo·stash f* moustache

moustiquaire *moo·stee·kehr f* mosquito net

moustique *moo·steek m* mosquito

moutarde *moo·tard f* mustard

mouton *moo·toñ m* sheep; mutton

mouvement *moov·moñ m* motion; movement

moyen(ne) *mwah·yañ(·yen) adj* average; medium □ *m* **les moyens** *mwah·yañ* means; **au moyen de** *ô mwah·yañ duh* by means of; **avoir* les moyens pour s'acheter une nouvelle voiture** *a·vwahr lay mwah·yañ poor sash·tay ōōn noo·vel vwah·tōōr* to be able to afford a new car

moyenne *mwah·yen f* average

Moyen-Orient *mwah·yañ nô·ree·oñ m* Middle East

muet(te) *mōō·eh(·et) adj* dumb

multinational(e) *mōōl·tee·na·syo·nal adj* multinational

multiplication *mōōl·tee·plee·ka·syoñ f* multiplication

multiplier *mōōl·tee·plyay vt* multiply; **multiplier 9 par 4** *mōōl·tee·plyay 9 par 4* to multiply 9 by 4

municipal(e) *mōō·nee·see·pal adj* municipal

municipalité *mōō·nee·see·pa·lee·tay f* borough

mur *mōōr m* wall

mûr(e) *mōōr adj* mature (*wine*); ripe (*fruit*); **pas mûr(e)** *pa mōōr* unripe

mûre *mōōr f* blackberry

muscle *mōōs·kluh m* muscle

musée *mōō·zay m* museum; art gallery

musicien *mōō·zee·syañ m* musician

musicienne *mōō·zee·syen f* musician

musique *mōō·zeek f* music

musulman(e) *mōō·zōōl·moñ(·man) adj* Muslim □ *m/f* **le/la musulman(e)** *mōō·zōōl·moñ(·man)* Muslim

myope *myop adj* shortsighted

mystère *mee·stehr m* mystery

N

nage *nazh f* swimming; stroke

nager* *na·zhay vi* swim

naissance *nay·soñs f* birth

naître* *neh·truh vi* to be born

nappe *nap f* tablecloth

natation *na·ta·syoñ f* swimming

nation *na·syoñ f* nation

national(e) *na·syo·nal adj* national

nationaliser *na·syo·na·lee·zay vt* nationalize

nationalité *na·syo·na·lee·tay f* nationality

Nations Unies *na·syoñ zōō·nee fpl* United Nations Organization

natte *nat f* plait (*of hair etc*)

naturalisé(e) *na·tōō·ra·leez·zay adj* naturalized

nature *na·tōōr f* nature

naturel(le) *na·tōō·rel adj* natural

naturellement *na·tōō·rel·moñ adv* naturally (*of course*)

naufrage *nô·frazh m* wreck (*ship*)

nausée *nô·zay f* sickness; nausea

navet *na·veh m* turnip

navigation *na·vee·ga·syoñ f* sailing; **faire* de la navigation de plaisance** *fehr duh la na·vee·ga·syoñ duh pleh·zoñs* to go yachting

navire *na·veer m* ship

ne *see* **pas, jamais** *etc* ; **il ne vient jamais** *eel nuh vyañ zha·meh* he never comes; **il n'y a que 4** *eel nya kuh 4* there are only 4

né(e) *nay adj* born

nécessaire *nay·seh·sehr adj* necessary □ *m* **le nécessaire** *nay·seh·sehr* bag; kit

nef *nef f* nave

négatif *nay·ga·teef m* negative (*of photo*)

négociable *nay·go·sya·bluh adj* negotiable

négociant *nay·go·syoñ m* merchant

négociations *nay·go·sya·syoñ fpl* negotiations

négocier *nay·go·syay vi* negotiate

neige *nezh f* snow; **la neige fondue** *nezh foñ·dōō* sleet

neiger *neh·zhay vi* snow; **il neige** *eel nezh* it's snowing

nerf *nehr m* nerve

nerveux(euse) *nehr·vuh(·vuhz) adj* nervous (*person*)

n'est-ce pas *nes pa* don't I/isn't it etc; **vous le connaissez n'est-ce pas?** *voo luh ko·neh·say nes pa* you know him, don't you?; **il n'est pas venu n'est-ce pas?** *eel neh pa vuh·nōō nes pa* he didn't come, did he?

net(te) *net adj* clear; neat; net (*income, price*)

nettoyer *neh·twah·yay vt* clean; **nettoyer à sec** *neh·twah·yay a sek* dryclean; **faire* nettoyer un costume** *fehr neh·twah·yay uñ kos·tōōm* to have a suit cleaned

neuf *nuf adj* new □ *num* nine

neutre *nuh·truh adj* neutral

neuve *nuv adj* new

neuvième *nuh·vyem adj* ninth

neveu *nuh·vuh m* nephew

nez *nay m* nose

ni ... ni *nee ... nee conj* neither ~ nor; **ni l'un ni l'autre** *nee luñ nee lô·truh* neither

nid *nee m* nest

nièce *nyes f* niece

nier *nee·yay vt* deny

n'importe *nañ·port adv* any...; **donnez-moi n'importe quel livre** *do·nay mwah nañ·port kel lee·vruh* give me any book

niveau *nee·vô m* level; standard; **le ni-**

veau de la mer *nee·vō duh la mehr* sea level; le niveau de vie *nee·vō duh vee* standard of living

Noël *no·el m* Christmas

nœud *nuh m* knot; bow (*ribbon*); faire* un nœud *fehr un* nuh to tie a knot; le nœud papillon *nuh pa·pee·yoñ* bow tie

noir(e) *nwahr adj* black; il fait noir *eel feh nwahr* it's dark; un café noir *un ka·fay nwahr* a black coffee

noix *nwah f* walnut; la noix de coco *nwah duh ko·kō* coconut

nom *noñ m* name; le nom de jeune fille *noñ duh zhuhn feey* maiden name; au nom de *ō noñ duh* on behalf of; le nom de famille *noñ duh fa·meey* surname

nombre *noñ·bruh f* number

nomination *no·mee·na·syoñ f* appointment (*to job*)

nommer *no·may vt* name; appoint

non *noñ adv* no; not; je n'étais pas là et lui non plus *zhuh nay·teh pa la ay lwee noñ plōō* I wasn't there and neither was he

non- *noñ- pref* non-

non-alcoolisé(e) *noñ·al·ko·lee·zay adj* nonalcoholic

non-fumeur *noñ·fōō·mur m* nonsmoker

non-prioritaire *noñ·pree·o·ree·tehr adj* minor (*road*)

nord *nor m* north; au nord *ō nor* in/to the north; du nord *dōō nor* northern

nord-est *nor·est m* northeast

nord-ouest *nor·west m* northwest

normal(e) *nor·mal adj* normal; standard (*size*); regular (*ordinary*) □ f la normale du parcours *nor·mal dōō par·koor* par (*golf*)

normalement *nor·mal·moñ adv* normally (*usually*)

nos *nō adj* our; nos frères/sœurs *nō frehr/sur* our brothers/sisters

notaire *no·tehr m* solicitor

note *not f* memo(randum); note (*music*); bill (*account*); mark (*in school*)

noter *no·tay vt* write down; record

notre *no·truh adj* our

le/la nôtre *luh/la nō·truh* pron ours; les nôtres *lay nō·truh* ours (*plural*); soyez des nôtres *swah·yay day nō·truh* do join us

nouer *noo·ay vt* knot; tie (*string, ribbon*)

nougat *noo·ga m* nougat

nouilles *noo·yuh fpl* noodles

nourrir *noo·reer vt* feed

nourriture *noo·ree·tōōr f* food

nous *noo pron* us; we

nous-mêmes *noo·mem pron* ourselves

nouveau *noo·vō adj* new; de nouveau *duh noo·vō* again

nouvelle *noo·vel adj* new

nouvelles *noo·vel fpl* news

novembre *no·voñ·bruh m* November

noyau *nwah·yō m* stone (*in fruit*)

se noyer *suh nwah·yay vr* drown

nu(e) *nōō adj* naked; bare (*person, head*); nude; marcher pieds nus *mar·shay pyay nōō* to go barefoot

nuage *nōō·azh m* cloud

nuageux(euse) *nōō·azh·uh(·uhz) adj* cloudy

nucléaire *nōō·klay·yehr adj* nuclear (*energy, war*)

nuisible *nwee·zee·bluh adj* harmful

nuit *nwee f* night; bonne nuit! *bon nwee* good night!; cette nuit *set nwee* last night

nul(le) *nōōl adj* void (*contract*); nul(le) et non avenu(e) *nōōl ay noñ nav·uh·nōō* null and void; nulle part *nōōl par* nowhere; je ne le vois nulle part *zhuh nuh luh vwah nōōl par* I can't see it anywhere

numéro *nōō·may·rō m* number; act (*at circus etc*); issue (*of magazine*); le numéro d'immatriculation *nōō·may·rō dee·ma·tree·kōō·la·syoñ* registration number (*on car*); le numéro de téléphone *nōō·may·rō duh tay·lay·fon* telephone number; le numéro d'annonce *nōō·may·rō da·noñs* box number

nylon *nee·loñ m* nylon

O

obéir *o·bay·eer vi* obey; obéir à quelqu'un *o·bay·eer a kel·kuñ* to obey someone

obéissant(e) *o·bay·ee·soñ(·soñt) adj* obedient

objectif *ob·zhek·teef m* objective; target (*sales etc*); lens (*of camera*); l'objectif grand-angulaire *ob·zhek·teef groñ·ton·gōō·lehr* wide-angle lens

objet *ob·zhay m* article (*thing*); object

obligation *o·blee·ga·syoñ f* obligation

obliger* *o·blee·zhay vt* oblige; obliger* quelqu'un à faire quelque chose *o·blee·zhay kel·kuñ a fehr kel·kuh shōz* to make someone do something

oblong(ue) *o·bloñ(·loñg) adj* oblong

obscur(e) *op·skōōr adj* dark; obscure

obsession *op·ses·syoñ f* obsession

obstacle *op·sta·kluh m* obstacle

obstruction *op·strōōk·syoñ f* blockage

obtenir* *op·tuh·neer vt* obtain; get; win (*contract*)

obturateur *op·tōō·ra·tur m* shutter (*in camera*)

occasion *o·ka·zyoñ f* occasion; bargain (*cheap buy*); opportunity; d'occasion *do·ka·zyoñ* used (*car etc*); secondhand

Occident *ok·see·doñ m* the West

occidental(e) *ok·see·doñ·tal adj* western

occupé(e) *o·kōō·pay adj* engaged; taken; busy (*person, telephone*)

s'occuper de *so·kōō·pay duh vr* look after; take care of (*children etc*)

océan *ō·say·oñ m* ocean

octobre *ok·to·bruh m* October

odeur *o·dur f* smell; scent

œil *uhy m pl*: yeux eye; l'œil au beurre noir *uhy ō bur nwahr* black eye

œillet *uh·yeh m* carnation

œuf *uhf m* egg; un œuf sur le plat *un nuhf sōōr luh pla* a fried egg; l'œuf de Pâques *uhf duh pak* Easter egg; un œuf à la coque *un nuhf a la kok* a soft-boiled egg

œuvre *uh·vruh f* work (*art, literature*); l'œuvre d'art *uh·vruh dar* work of art

officiel(le) *o·fee·syel adj* official

officier *o·fee·syay m* officer (*in army etc*)

officieux(euse) *o·fee·syuh(·syuhz) adj* unofficial

offrant(e) *o·froñ m* bidder

offre *o·fruh f* offer; l'offre publique d'achat *o·fruh pōō·bleek da·sha* take-over bid; faire* une offre pour quelque chose *fehr ōōn o·fruh poor kel·kuh shōz* to bid for something; l'offre et la demande *lo·fruh ay la duh·moñd* supply and demand

offrir* *o·freer vt* offer; give; bid

(amount); **je ne peux pas me l'offrir** zhuh nuh puh pah muh lo·freer I can't afford it

oie wah f goose

oignon o·nyoñ m onion

oiseau wa·zō m bird

olive o·leev f olive

ombre oñ·bruh f shade; shadow; **l'ombre à paupières** oñ·bra pō·pyehr eyeshadow

omelette om·let f omelette

omettre* o·meh·truh vt leave out (omit)

on oñ pron one; **on dit que...** oñ dee kuh they say that... (people in general); **on devrait...** oñ duh·vreh one should...

oncle oñ·kluh m uncle

ondes courtes oñd koort fpl short wave; **les ondes moyennes** oñd mwah·yen medium wave; **les grandes ondes** groñd zoñd long wave

ondulation oñ·dōō·la·syoñ f wave (in hair)

ondulé(e) oñ·dōō·lay adj wavy (hair)

ongle oñ·gluh m nail (human)

onguent oñ·goñ m ointment

onze oñz num eleven

onzième oñz·yem adj eleventh

OPEP o·pep f OPEC

opéra o·pay·ra m opera; opera house

opération o·pay·ra·syoñ f operation; **l'opération bénigne** o·pay·ra·syoñ bay·nee·nyuh minor operation

opinion o·pee·nyoñ f opinion

opposé(e) o·po·zay adj opposite

opposition o·po·zee·syoñ f opposition; **faire* opposition à un chèque** fehr o·po·zee·syoñ a uñ shek to stop a cheque

opticien op·tee·syañ m optician

optimiste op·tee·meest adj optimistic

option op·syoñ f option

or or m gold; **en or** oñ nor gold(en)

orage o·razh m thunderstorm

orageux(euse) o·ra·zhuh(·zhuhz) adj stormy

orange o·roñzh f orange □ adj orange

orangeade o·roñ·zhad f orangeade

orchestre or·kes·truh m orchestra; band (musical); stalls (in theatre)

ordinaire or·dee·nehr adj ordinary

ordinateur or·dee·na·tur m computer

ordonnance or·do·noñs f prescription

ordonné(e) or·do·nay adj tidy (person)

ordre or·druh m order; **l'ordre du jour** or·druh dōō zhoor agenda; **l'ordre public** or·druh pōō·bleek law and order

ordures or·dōōr fpl rubbish; garbage

oreille o·ray f ear

oreiller o·ray·yay m pillow

oreillons o·ray·yoñ mpl mumps

organigramme or·ga·nee·gram m flow chart

organisation or·ga·nee·za·syoñ f organization

organiser or·ga·nee·zay vt organize; plan

orgue org m organ (instrument)

Orient o·ryoñ m the East

oriental(e) o·ryoñ·tal adj oriental

s'orienter so·ryoñ·tay vr to take one's bearings

original o·ree·zhee·nal m original □ adj

original(e) o·ree·zhee·nal original (creative)

origine o·ree·zheen f origin; **à l'origine** a lo·ree·zheen originally (at first)

originel(le) o·ree·zhee·nel adj original (earliest)

orme orm m elm

ornement or·nuh·moñ m ornament

orphelin(e) or·fuh·lañ(·leen) m/f orphan

os os m bone

oser ō·zay vi dare

osier ō·zee·ay m wicker

otage ō·tazh m hostage; **prendre* quelqu'un comme otage** proñ·druh kel·kuñ kom ō·tazh to take someone hostage

où oo conj where; **d'où êtes-vous?** doo et·voo where are you from?; **c'est par où Londres?** seh par oo loñ·druh which is the way to London?; **je vous amènerai où vous voudrez** zhuh voo za·men·uh·ray oo voo voo·dray I'll take you anywhere you like; **le jour où nous...** luh zhoor oo noo the day when we...

ou oo conj or; **ou ... ou** oo ... oo either ... or

oublier oo·blee·ay vt forget; miss out; **j'ai oublié de faire...** zhay oo·blee·ay duh fehr I forgot to do...

ouest west m west; **à l'ouest** a lwest in/to the west

oui wee adv yes

ouragan oo·ra·goñ m hurricane

ourlet oor·leh m hem

ours oors m bear

outil oo·teey m tool

outre-mer oo·truh mehr adv overseas

ouvert(e) oo·vehr(·vehrt) adj open; on (water supply)

ouverture oo·vehr·tōōr f overture; opening

ouvrable oo·vra·bluh adj working (day)

ouvre-boîte oo·vruh·bwaht m can-opener

ouvreuse oo·vruz f usherette

ouvrier oo·vree·ay m workman; worker □ adj **ouvrier(ère)** oo·vree·ay(·ehr) working-class

ouvrière oo·vree·ehr f worker

ouvrir* oo·vreer vt open; turn on; unlock □ vi open (store, bank)

ovale o·val adj oval

oxygène ok·see·zhen m oxygen

P

Pacifique pa·see·feek m Pacific Ocean

pagaie pa·gay f paddle (oar)

page pazh f page

paiement pay·moñ m payment; **paiement à la livraison** pay·moñ a la leev·reh·zoñ cash on delivery

paillasson pye·ya·soñ m doormat

paille pye f straw

paillettes de savon pye·yet duh sa·voñ fpl soap-flakes

pain pañ m bread; loaf (of bread); **le petit pain** puh·tee pañ roll (bread); **le pain grillé** pañ gree·yay toast; **le pain d'épices** pañ day·pees gingerbread; **le pain complet** pañ koñ·pleh wholemeal bread

pair pehr m par (business); **au-dessus du pair** ō·duh·sōō dōō pehr above par □ adj **un nombre pair** uñ noñ·bruh pehr an even number

paire pehr f pair; **paire de chaussures** pehr duh shō·sōōr pair of shoes; **paire de ciseaux** pehr duh see·zō pair of scissors

paisible pay·zee·bluh adj peaceful

paix peh f peace

Pakistan pa·kee·stoñ m Pakistan

pakistanais(e) *pa·kee·sta·neh(·nez)* adj Pakistani

palais *pa·leh* m palace

pâle *pahl* adj pale

Palestine *pa·les·teen* f Palestine

palestinien(ienne) *pa·les·tee·nyañ (·nyen)* adj Palestinian

palier *pa·lyay* m landing (on stairs)

palmes *palm* fpl flippers (for swimming)

palmier *pal·myay* m palm-tree

pamplemousse *poñ·pluh·moos* m grapefruit

panaché(e) *pa·na·shay* adj mixed □ le **panaché** *pa·na·shay* shandy

panais *pa·neh* m parsnip

pancarte *poñ·kart* f notice (sign)

panier *pa·nyay* m basket; hamper

panique *pa·neek* f panic; pris(e) de **panique** *pree (preez) duh pa·neek* in a panic

paniquer *pa·nee·kay* vi panic

panne *pan* f breakdown (of car); tomber en **panne** *toñ·bay oñ pan* to go wrong (machine); to break down (car); en **panne** *oñ pan* on tow; out of order (machine)

panneau *pa·nō* m sign (notice); le **panneau d'affichage** *pa·nō da·fee·shazh* notice board

panneau de signalisation *pa·nō duh seen·ya·lee·za·syoñ* m road sign

pansement *poñs·moñ* m bandage; plaster (for wound)

pantalon *poñ·ta·loñ* m trousers; pants; slacks

pantoufle *poñ·too·fluh* f slipper

papa *pa·pa* m dad(dy)

pape *pap* m Pope

paperasserie *pa·puh·ra·suh·ree* f red tape

papeterie *pap·tree* f stationer's (shop)

papier *pa·pyay* m paper; le **papier hygiénique** *pa·pyay ee·zhyay·neek* toilet paper; le **papier peint** *pa·pyay pañ* wallpaper; le **papier de soie** *pa·pyay duh swah* tissue paper; le **papier carbone** *pa·pyay kar·bon* carbon paper; le **papier d'aluminium** *pa·pyay da·lōō·mee·nyum* foil (for food); le **papier à lettres** *pa·pyay a let·truh* writing paper; le **papier d'emballage** *pa·pyay doñ·bal·lazh* wrapping paper; les **papiers** *pa·pyay* papers (passport etc)

papillon *pa·pee·yoñ* m butterfly; le **papillon de nuit** *pa·pee·yoñ duh nwee* moth

paprika *pa·pree·ka* m paprika

paquebot *pak·bō* m liner (ship)

Pâques *pak* fpl Easter; à **Pâques** *a pak* at Easter

paquet *pa·kay* m package; pack; packet; bundle

par *par* prep by; per; passer par Londres *pa·say par loñ·druh* to go by London (via); **par personne** *par pehr·son* per person; **par jour** *par zhoor* per day; **£40 par jour** *£40 par zhoor* twice a day; **£40 par semaine** *£40 par suh·men* £40 a week; **par ici** *par ee·see* about here; this way

parachute *pa·ra·shōōt* m parachute

paragraphe *pa·ra·graf* m paragraph

paraître* *pa·reh·truh* vi appear

parallèle *pa·ra·lel* adj parallel

paralysé(e) *pa·ra·lee·zay* adj paralysed

parapluie *pa·ra·plwee* m umbrella

parasol *pa·ra·sol* m parasol; umbrella (on table)

paravent *pa·ra·voñ* m screen (partition)

parc *park* m park; le **parc automobile** *park ō·tō·mo·beel* fleet of vehicles; le **parc d'attractions** *park da·trak·syoñ* amusement park; le **parc pour bébé** *park poor bay·bay* playpen

parce que *pars kuh* conj because

parc-mètre *park·meh·truh* m parking meter

parcourir* *par·koo·reer* vt cover (distance)

pardessus *par·duh·sōō* m overcoat (man's)

pardon *par·doñ* excl sorry; **pardon?** *par·doñ* pardon me?, (I beg your) pardon?

pardonner *par·do·nay* vt forgive

pare-boue *par·boo* m mud-flap

pare-brise *par·breez* m windscreen; windshield

pare-chocs *par·shok* m bumper (on car); fender

pareil(le) *pa·ray* adj the same; similar

parent(e) *pa·roñ(t)* m/f relation; relative; le **parent le plus proche** *pa·roñ luh plōō prosh* next of kin

parenthèse *pa·roñ·tez* f bracket (in writing)

parents *pa·roñ* mpl parents

paresseux(euse) *pa·reh·suh(·suhz)* adj lazy

parfait(e) *par·feh(·fet)* adj perfect

parfum *par·fuñ* m perfume; scent; flavour

pari *pa·ree* m bet

parier *pa·ryay* vi bet; **parier sur** *pa·ryay sōōr* back (bet on)

Paris *pa·ree* m Paris

parisien(ne) *pa·ree·zyañ(·zyen)* adj Parisian; le/la **parisien(ne)** *pa·ree·zyañ(·zyen)* Parisian

parka *par·ka* m parka

parking *par·keeng* m car-park

parlement *par·luh·moñ* m parliament

parler *par·lay* vt/i speak; talk; **parlez-vous anglais?** *par·lay voo zoñ·gleh* do you speak English?; **parler de quelque chose à quelqu'un** *par·lay duh kel·kuh shōz a kel·kuñ* to speak to someone about something; **parler de quelque chose** *par·lay duh kel·kuh shōz* to talk about something

parmesan *par·muh·zoñ* m Parmesan

parmi *par·mee* prep among(st)

parole *pa·rol* f word (spoken); speech

parrain *pa·rañ* m godfather

part *par* f share (part); autre **part** *ō·truh par* somewhere else

partager* *par·ta·zhay* vt share (money, room)

partenaire *par·tuh·nehr* m/f partner (dancing)

parterre *par·tehr* m flowerbed

parti *par·tee* m party (political)

participation *par·tee·see·pa·syoñ* f participation; la **participation aux bénéfices** *par·tee·see·pa·syoñ ō bay·nay·fees* profit-sharing

participer *par·tee·see·pay* vi participate

particulier(ière) *par·tee·kōō·lyay (·lyehr)* adj private; particular; la **leçon particulière** *luh·soñ par·tee·kōō·lyehr* private lesson; en **particulier** *oñ par·tee·kōō·lyay* in particular

particulièrement *par·tee·kōō·lyehr·moñ* adv particularly; especially

partie *par·tee* f part; round (in competition); une **partie de tennis** *ōōn par·tee duh teh·nees* a game of tennis; en **partie** *oñ par·tee* partly

partir* *par·teer* vi leave; go; come out (*stain*); set off; **il est parti pour une semaine** *eel eh par·tee poor ōōn suh·men* he's away for a week; **tout notre argent est parti** *too no·trar·zhoñ eh par·tee* all our money's gone

partisan de *par·tee·zoñ duh* adj in favour of

partout *par·too* adv everywhere

pas *pa* adv not; **il ne l'a pas fait** *eel nuh la pa feh* he didn't do it; **pas du tout** *pa dōō too* not at all; **pas de voitures** *pa duh vwa·tōōr* no cars; **nous n'en avons pas** *noo noñ na·voñ pa* we haven't any

pas *pa* m step; pace; **le pas de porte** *pa duh port* doorstep

passage *pa·sazh* m passage; **le passage clouté** *pa·sazh kloo·tay* crosswalk; pedestrian crossing; **le passage à niveau** *pa·sazh a nee·vō* grade crossing; level crossing; **le passage souterrain** *pa·sazh soo·tay·rañ* underpass (*for pedestrians*); **le passage inférieur** *pa·sazh añ·fay·ryur* underpass (*for cars*)

passager *pa·sa·zhay* m passenger

passagère *pa·sa·zhehr* f passenger

passé(e) *pa·say* adj past □ m **le passé** *pa·say* past

passe-partout *pas·par·too* m master key

passe-plats *pas·pla* m hatch (*for serving*)

passeport *pas·por* m passport

passer *pa·say* vt spend (*time*); pass (*time, object*); strain (*tea etc*); show (*movie*); **passez-moi le sucre s'il vous plaît** *pa·say·mwah luh sookr seel voo pleh* please pass the sugar; **passer un examen** *pa·say uñ neg·za·mañ* to take an exam; **passer une dette aux profits et pertes** *pa·say ōōn det ō pro·fee ay pehrt* to write off a debt; **passez-moi M. X** *pa·say mwah muh·syuh X* put me through to Mr X (*on phone*); **passer la nuit** *pa·say la nwee* to stay the night; **passer une commande à quelqu'un** *pa·say ōōn ko·moñd a kel·kuñ* to place an order with someone; **passer en courant** *pa·say choo·roñ* □ vi **les trains passent toutes les heures** *lay trañ pass toot lay zur* the trains pass every hour; **passer devant** *pa·say duh·voñ* to pass (*place*); **la route passe devant la maison** *la root pass duh·voñ la may·zoñ* the road runs past the house; **un avion est passé** *uñ na·vyoñ eh pa·say* a plane flew by; **passer prendre un ami** *pa·say proñ·drü·n na·mee* to pick up a friend; **quand passe le film?** *koñ pas luh feelm* when is the film on? □ vr **se passer** *suh pa·say* happen; **comment ça s'est passé?** *ko·moñ sa seh pa·say* how did it go?; **se passer de** *suh pa·say duh* to go without

passerelle *pa·suh·rel* f gangway (*bridge*)

passe-temps *pas·toñ* m interest (*hobby*)

passe-thé *pas·tay* m tea strainer

passif *pa·seef* m liabilities (*on balance sheet*)

passion *pa·syoñ* f passion

passionnant(e) *pa·syo·noñ(·noñt)* adj exciting

passoire *pa·swahr* f strainer; colander

pastèque *pas·tek* f watermelon

pasteur *pas·tur* m minister (*of religion*)

pasteurisé(e) *pas·tuh·ree·zay* adj pasteurized

pastille *pas·teey* f pastille; **la pastille de menthe** *pas·teey duh moñt* peppermint (*confectionery*); **les pastilles pour la toux** *pas·teey poor la too* cough drops

patate douce *pa·tat doos* f sweet potato

pâte *paht* f dough; pastry; **la pâte d'amandes** *paht da·moñd* marzipan; **la pâte dentifrice** *paht doñ·tee·frees* toothpaste

pâté *pah·tay* m meat paste; pâté

pâte à frire *paht a freer* f batter (*for frying*)

patère *pa·tehr* f peg (*for coat*)

pâtes *paht* fpl pasta

patience *pa·syoñs* f patience

patient(e) *pa·syoñ(·syoñt)* adj patient □ m/f **le/la patient(e)** *pa·syoñ(·syoñt)* patient

patin *pa·tañ* m skate; **les patins à roulettes** *pa·tañ a roo·let* roller skates

patiner *pa·tee·nay* vi skate

patinoire *pa·tee·nwahr* f skating rink

patio *pa·tyō* m patio

pâtisserie *pah·tees·ree* f cake shop; pastry (*cake*)

patron *pa·troñ* m boss; pattern (*dressmaking, knitting*)

patronne *pa·tron* f boss

patte *pat* f leg (*of animal*); paw; foot

paume *pōm* f palm (*of hand*)

paupière *pō·pyehr* f eyelid

pause *pōz* f pause; break; **faire* une pause** *fehr ōōn pōz* to pause

pause-café *pōz·ka·fay* f coffee break

pauvre *pōv·ruh* adj poor

pavillon *pa·vee·yoñ* m detached house

payable *pay·ya·bluh* adj payable

payé(e) *pay·yay* adj paid (*vacation*); **payé(e) d'avance** *pay·yay da·voñs* prepaid

payer *pay·yay* vt pay; pay for; **faire* payer quelque chose** *fehr pay·yay kel·kuh shōz* to make a charge for something; **je vous paierai une glace** *zhuh voo pay·uh·ray ōōn glas* I'll treat you to an ice cream

pays *pay·yee* m land; country; **du pays** *dōō pay·yee* local

paysage *pay·ee·zazh* m scenery

Pays Bas *pay·yee ba* mpl Low Countries

Pays de Galles *pay·yee duh gal* m Wales

péage *pay·yazh* m toll (*on road etc*)

peau *pō* f hide (*leather*); skin; **la peau de mouton** *pō duh moo·toñ* sheepskin; **la peau de porc** *pō duh por* pigskin

pêche *pesh* f peach; fishing; **aller* à la pêche** *a·lay a la pesh* to go fishing

pêcheur *peh·shur* m angler

pédale *pay·dal* f pedal

pédalo *pay·da·lō* m pedalo

pédiatre *pay·dya·truh* m/f p(a)ediatrician

pédicure *pay·dee·kōōr* m/f chiropodist

peigne *peh·nyuh* m comb

peigner *peh·nyay* vt comb; **mal peigné** *mal peh·nyay* untidy (*hair*)

peignoir *peh·nywahr* m dressing gown; housecoat; robe

peindre* *pañ·druh* vt paint; decorate

peine *pen* f sorrow; bother (*effort*); **ce n'est pas la peine** *suh neh pa la pen* it's not worth it; **à peine** *a pen* scarcely

peintre *pañ·truh* m painter

peinture *pan·tōōr* f paint

peler* *puh·lay* vi peel (*person*)

pelle *pel* f spade; shovel; **la pelle à poussière** *pel a poo·syehr* dustpan

pellicule *peh·lee·kōōl* f film (*for camera*); **les pellicules** *peh·lee·kōōl* dandruff

pelote *puh·lot* f ball (*of string, wool*)

pelouse *puh·looz* f lawn (*grass*)

pencher *poñ·shay* vi lean; **se pencher** *suh poñ·shay* lean (over)

pendant *poñ·doñ* prep during; **pendant que** *poñ·doñ kuh* while; **pendant une heure** *mar·shay poñ·doñ ōōn ur* to walk for an hour; **pendant ce temps** *poñ·doñ suh toñ* meanwhile; **pendant qu'il dormait** *poñ·doñ keel dor·meh* as he was asleep (*while*)

pendre *poñ·druh* vt/i hang

pendule *poñ·dōōl* f clock

pénétrant(e) *pay·nay·troñ(·troñt)* adj sharp (*intelligent*)

pénétrer* *pay·nay·tray* vt penetrate

péniche *pay·neesh* f barge

pénicilline *pay·nee·see·leen* f penicillin

pénis *pay·nees* m penis

pensée *poñ·say* f thought

penser *poñ·say* vi think; **penser à quelque chose** *poñ·say a kel·kuh shōz* to think of something; **penser à quelqu'un** *poñ·say a kel·kuñ* to think about someone; **je pense que oui** *zhuh poñs kuh wee* I think so

pension *poñ·syoñ* f pension (*from State*); guest-house; boarding house; **la pension complète** *poñ·syoñ koñ·plet* full board; **la pension de retraite** *poñ·syoñ duh ruh·tret* superannuation

pente *poñt* f slope

Pentecôte *poñt·kōt* f Whitsun

pénurie *pay·nōō·ree* f shortage

pépinière *pay·pee·nyehr* f garden centre

percer* *pehr·say* vt pierce; drill (*hole*)

perceuse *pehr·suhz* f drill (*tool*)

percolateur *pehr·ko·la·tur* m percolator

perdre *pehr·druh* vt lose; **se perdre** *suh pehr·druh* to lose one's way; **perdre son temps** *per·druh soñ toñ* to waste one's time

perdrix *pehr·dree* f partridge

père *pehr* m father; **oui, mon père** *wee moñ pehr* yes, Father (*priest*)

performance *pehr·for·moñs* f performance (*of car*)

périmé(e) *pay·ree·may* adj out of date

période *pay·ryod* f period (*of time*); **pendant la période où il exerçait ses fonctions** *poñ·doñ la pay·ryod oo eel eg·zehr·seh say foñk·syoñ* during his term of office; **la période des vacances** *la pay·ryod day va·koñs* the holiday season

périphérique *pay·ree·fay·reek* m ring road

perle *pehrl* f bead; pearl

permanent(e) *pehr·ma·noñ(·noñt)* adj permanent; **de façon permanente** *duh fa·soñ pehr·ma·noñt* permanently

permanente *pehr·ma·noñt* f perm

permettre* *pehr·meh·truh* vt permit (*something*); **permettre* à quelqu'un de partir** *pehr·meh·tra kel·kuñ duh par·teer* to allow someone to go

permis *pehr·mee* m permit; **le permis de sortie** *luh pehr·mee duh sor·tee* exit permit; **le permis de séjour** *pehr·mee* duh say·zhoor residence permit; **le permis de conduire** *pehr·mee duh koñ·dweer* driver's license, driving licence

permission *pehr·mee·syoñ* f permission; **en permission** *oñ pehr·mee·syoñ* on leave

perruque *peh·rōōk* f wig

persan(e) *pehr·zoñ(·zan)* adj Persian

persil *pehr·see* m parsley

personnalité *pehr·so·na·lee·tay* f personality (*character*)

personne *pehr·son* pron nobody; **je ne vois personne** *zhuh nuh vwah pehr·son* I can't see anybody □ f la personne *pehr·son* person; **en personne** *oñ pehr·son* in person

personnel *pehr·so·nel* m staff; personnel □ adj personnel(elle) *pehr·so·nel* personal

personnellement *pehr·so·nel·moñ* adv personally

perspective *pehr·spek·teev* f outlook; prospect

persuader *pehr·swa·day* vt persuade; **persuader quelqu'un de faire quelque chose** *pehr·swa·day kel·kuñ duh fehr kel·kuh shōz* to persuade someone to do something

perte *pehrt* f loss

pertinent(e) *pehr·tee·noñ(·noñt)* adj relevant

peser* *puh·zay* vt weigh

pessimiste *peh·see·meest* adj pessimistic

pétard *pay·tar* m cracker (*paper toy*)

pétillant(e) *pay·tee·yoñ(·yoñt)* adj fizzy

petit(e) *puh·tee(·teet)* adj little; small; slight; short (*person*)

petite-fille *puh·teet·feey* f granddaughter

petite friture *puh·teet free·tōōr* f whitebait

petit-fils *puh·tee·fees* m grandson

pétrole *pay·trol* m oil (*petroleum*); kerosene; paraffin

pétrolier *pay·trol·yay* m oil tanker; **le pétrolier géant** *pay·trol·yay zhay·oñ* supertanker

peu *puh* adv, pron little; **peu de** *puh duh* few; little; **un peu (de)** *uñ puh duh* a little; **il y en a très peu** *eel yoñ na treh puh* there are very few

peuplier *puh·plee·ay* m poplar

peur *pur* f fear; **avoir* peur de quelque chose** *a·vwahr pur duh kel·kuh shōz* to be afraid of something

peut-être *puh·teh·truh* adv perhaps; possibly; **peut-être qu'il viendra** *puh·teh·truh keel vyañ·dra* perhaps he'll come

phare *far* m headlamp; headlight; lighthouse; **le phare antibrouillard** *far oñ·tee·broo·yar* fog-lamp

pharmacie *far·ma·see* f pharmacy; drugstore

pharmacien *far·ma·syañ* m pharmacist; druggist

photo *fo·tō* f photo

photocopie *fo·to·ko·pee* f photocopy

photocopier *fo·to·ko·pyay* vt photocopy

photographe *fo·to·graf* m/f photographer

photographie *fo·to·gra·fee* f photography; photograph

photographier *fo·to·gra·fyay* vt photograph

photomètre *fō·tō·meh·truh* m light meter

phrase *fraz* f sentence

plombier

physique *fee·zeek adj* physical □ *f* la physique *fee·zeek* physics
piano *pya·nō m* piano; **le piano à queue** *pya·nō a kuh* grand piano
pichet *pee·shay m* jug
pièce *pyes f* room (*in house*); patch (*of material*); coin; play (*theatrical*); component (*for car etc*); **la pièce de rechange** *pyes duh ruh·shonzh* spare (part)
pied *pyay m* foot (*of person*); **faire* 10 km à pied** *fehr 10 km a pyay* to walk 10 km
piège *pyezh m* trap
pierre *pyehr f* stone; **la pierre précieuse** *pyehr pray·syuhz* gem; **la pierre à briquet** *pyehr a bree·keh* flint (*in lighter*)
pierreux(euse) *pyeh·ruh(·ruhz) adj* stony
piéton *pyay·toñ m* pedestrian
pigeon *pee·zhoñ m* pigeon
pile *peel f* pile; battery (*for radio etc*)
pilier *pee·lyay m* pillar
pilon *pee·loñ m* drumstick (*of chicken*)
pilote *pee·lot m* pilot
pilule *pee·lōōl f* pill; **prendre* la pilule** *proñ·druh la pee·lōōl* to be on the pill
piment *pee·moñ m* chili
pin *pañ m* pine
pince *pañs f* pliers; dart (*on clothes*); **la pince à épiler** *pañs a ay·pee·lay* tweezers; **la pince à linge** *pañs a lañzh* clothes-peg; **la pince à cheveux** *pañs a shuh·vuh* hairpin
pinceau *pañ·sō m* brush (*for painting*)
pincée *pañ·say f* pinch (*of salt etc*)
pincer* *pañ·say vt* pinch
pinces *pañs fpl* pliers
ping-pong *peeng·pong m* table tennis; ping-pong
pintade *pañ·tad f* guinea fowl
pioche *pyosh f* pickaxe
pipe *peep f* pipe (*for smoking*)
pipeau *pee·pō m* pipe (*musical*)
pipe-line *peep·leen m* pipeline
pique *peek m* spades (*cards*)
pique-nique *peek·neek m* picnic; **aller* faire un pique-nique** *a·lay fehr uñ peek·neek* to go on a picnic
piquer *pee·kay vt* prick; sting
piquet *pee·kay m* peg; **le piquet de tente** *pee·kay duh toñt* tent peg; **le piquet de grève** *pee·kay duh grev* picket
piqûre *pee·kōōr f* bite (*by insect*); injection; sting
pirate de l'air *pee·rat duh lehr m* hijacker
pire (que) *peer (kuh) adj* worse (than); **le/la pire** *luh/la peer* the worst; **faire* quelque chose de pire** *fehr kel·kuh shōz duh peer* to do something worse
pis *pee adv* worse; worst
piscine *pee·seen f* swimming pool
piste *peest f* race track; track (*of animal*); **la piste d'atterrissage** *peest da·tay·ree·sazh* landing strip; runway; **la piste de ski** *peest duh skee* ski run; **la piste pour débutants** *peest poor day·bōō·toñ* nursery slope
piston *pees·toñ m* piston
pitié *pee·tyay f* pity
pittoresque *pee·tor·esk adj* quaint
pizza *pee·tsa f* pizza
placard *pla·kar m* cupboard; closet
place *plas f* square (*in town*); seat; space (*room*); place; **la place du marché** *plas dōō mar·shay* market-

place; **en place** *oñ plas* in place; **sur place** *sōōr plas* on the spot
placement *plas·moñ m* investment
placer* *pla·say vt* place; **placer* son argent dans** *pla·say soñ nar·zhoñ doñ* to invest in
plafond *pla·foñ m* ceiling
plage *plazh f* beach; track (*on record*)
se plaindre* *suh plañ·druh vr* complain; **se plaindre de** *suh plañ·druh duh* to complain about
plaine *plen f* plain
plainte *plañt f* complaint (*dissatisfaction*)
plaire* *plehr vi* please; **cela me plaît** *suh·la muh pleh* I like it
plaisanterie *play·zoñ·tuh·ree f* joke
plaisir *play·zeer m* pleasure; pleasure; **un petit plaisir** *uñ puh·tee play·zeer* a little treat
plan *ploñ m* map (*of town*); plan (*map, drawing*); **faire* les plans de** *fehr lay ploñ duh* to plan
planche *ploñsh f* board (*of wood*); plank; **la planche de surf** *ploñsh duh surf* surf board; **la planche à roulettes** *ploñsh a rōō·let* skateboard; **la planche à voile** *ploñsh a vwal* windsurfing; **faire* de la planche à voile** *fehr duh la ploñsh à vwal* to go windsurfing
plancher *ploñ·shay m* floor
planétarium *pla·nay·ta·ree·oom m* planetarium
planète *pla·net f* planet
planeur *pla·nur m* glider
planification *pla·nee·fee·ka·syoñ f* planning (*economic*)
plante *ploñt f* sole (*of foot*); plant
planter *ploñ·tay vt* plant
plaque *plak f* plate (*of glass, metal*); **la plaque chauffante** *plak shō·foñt* hotplate; **la plaque d'immatriculation** *plak dee·ma·tree·kōō·la·syoñ* license plate
plaqué(e) or *pla·kay or adj* gold-plated
plaquer *pla·kay vt* tackle (*in sports*)
plastique *plas·teek m* plastic; **en plastique** *oñ plas·teek* plastic
plat *pla m* dish; course (*of meal*)
plat(e) *pla (plat) adj* level (*surface*); flat; **à plat** *a pla* flat (*battery*)
platane *pla·tan m* plane (*tree*)
plateau *pla·tō m* tray
plate-forme *plat·form f* platform (*of oil-rig*); **la plate-forme pétrolière** *plat·form pay·tro·lyehr* oil-rig
platine *pla·teen m* platinum
plâtre *plah·truh m* plaster; **le plâtre de Paris** *plah·truh duh pa·ree* plaster of Paris
plein(e) *plañ (plen) adj* full; solid (*not hollow*); **plein(e) de** *plañ (plen) duh* full of; **de plein fouet** *duh plañ foo·eh* head-on; **à plein temps** *a plañ toñ* full-time; **faites le plein!** *fet luh plañ* fill it up! (*car*)
pleurer *pluh·ray vi* cry
pleuvoir* *pluh·vwahr vi* rain; **il pleut** *eel pluh* it's raining
plexiglas *plek·see·glas m* plexiglas; Perspex
pli *plee m* crease; **sous pli séparé** *soo plee say·pa·ray* under separate cover
pliant *plee·oñ m* folding chair
plier *plee·yay vt* bend (*arm, leg*); fold
plissé(e) *plee·say adj* pleated
plomb *ploñ m* lead
plombage *ploñ·bazh m* filling (*in tooth*)
plombier *ploñ·byay m* plumber

plongeoir *ploñ·zhwahr* m divingboard

plongeon *ploñ·zhoñ* m dive

plonger* *ploñ·zhay* vi dive

pluie *plōō·ee* f rain

plume *plōōm* f feather

plupart *plōō·par* f majority; **la plupart des gens** *la plōō·par day zhoñ* most people

plus *plōōs* prep plus □ adv, pron more; **ne … plus** *nuh … plōō* no longer (*in time*); **plus de lait** *plōō duh leh* more milk; **nous n'avons plus de lait** *nōō na·voñ plōō duh leh* we've no more milk; **plus dangereux que** *plōō dañ·zhuh·ruh kuh* more dangerous than; **plus de 10** *plōō duh 10* more than 10; **le plus beau** *luh plōō bō* the most beautiful; **plus ou moins** *plōō zōō mwañ* more or less; **le plus grand nombre de voitures** *luh plōō groñ noñ·bruh duh vwa·tōōr* the most cars; **il a le plus** *eel a luh plōō* he has the most; **tout au plus** *tōō tō plōō* at the most; **en plus** *oñ plōōs* extra; **en plus de lui** *oñ plōōs duh lwee* besides him

plusieurs *plōō·zyur* adj several; **plusieurs d'entre nous** *plōō·zyur doñ·truh nōō* several of us

plutôt *plōō·tō* adv rather

pluvieux(euse) *plōō·vyuh(·vyuhz)* adj rainy; wet (*weather, day*)

pneu *pnuh* m tyre; tire

pneumonie *pnuh·mo·nee* f pneumonia

poche *posh* f pocket

poché(e) *po·shay* adj poached

poêle *pwahl* f fry(ing) pan □ m **le poêle** *pwahl* stove

poêlon *pwah·loñ* m skillet

poème *po·em* m poem

poésie *po·ay·zee* f poetry

poids *pwah* m weight (*mass*); **le poids net** *pwah net* net weight

poignard *pwah·nyar* m dagger

poignarder *pwa·nyar·day* vt stab

poignée *pwah·nyay* f handle; **la poignée de porte** *pwah·nyay duh port* door handle, doorknob

poignet *pwah·nyay* m wrist

poinçon *pwañ·soñ* m hallmark

poinçonner *pwañ·so·nay* vt punch (*ticket etc*)

poing *pwañ* m fist; **le coup de poing** *koo duh pwañ* punch (*blow*); **donner un coup de poing à** *do·nay uñ koo duh pwañ a* to punch

point *pwañ* m stitch (*sewing*); dot; point (*sport: in score*); full stop; period (*punctuation*); point (*subject, idea*); **le point de côté** *pwañ duh kō·tay* stitch (*pain*); **à point** *a pwañ* medium done; **être* sur le point de faire quelque chose** *eh·truh sōōr luh pwañ duh fehr kel·kuh shōz* to be about to (do something); **il lui a répondu point par point** *eel lwee a ray·poñ·dōō pwañ par pwañ* he answered him point by point; **le point de vue** *pwañ duh vōō* point of view; **le point de repère** *pwañ duh ruh·pehr* landmark

point d'interrogation *pwañ dañ·tehr·ro·ga·syoñ* m question mark

pointe *pwañt* f point (*tip*); **les heures de pointe** *lay zur duh pwañt* rush hour

point mort *pwañ mor* m neutral (*gear*)

pointure *pwañ·tōōr* f size (*of shoes*)

poire *pwahr* f pear

poireau *pwah·rō* m leek

pois *pwah* m spot (*dot*); **les petits pois** *puh·tee pwah* peas

poison *pwah·zoñ* m poison

poisseux(euse) *pwah·suh(·suhz)* adj sticky

poisson *pwah·soñ* m fish; **le poisson rouge** *pwah·soñ roozh* goldfish

poissonnier *pwah·so·nyay* m fishmonger

poitrine *pwah·treen* f breast; bust; chest (*of body*)

poivre *pwah·vruh* m pepper

poivré(e) *pwah·vray* adj peppery

poivrière *pwah·vree·ehr* f pepperpot

poivron *pwah·vroñ* m pepper (*capsicum*); **le poivron vert/rouge** *pwah·vroñ vehr/roozh* green/red pepper

poker *po·ker* m poker (*card game*)

polaroïd *po·la·ro·eed* adj Polaroid

Pôle Nord *pōl nor* m North Pole

Pôle Sud *pōl sōōd* m South Pole

poli(e) *po·lee* adj polite

police *po·lees* f policy (*insurance*); police; **la police d'assurance** *po·lees da·sōō·roñs* insurance policy

polio *po·lyo* f polio

politique *po·lee·teek* adj political □ f **la politique** *po·lee·teek* politics; policy; **la politique extérieure** *po·lee·teek ek·stay·ryur* foreign policy

pollution *po·lōō·syoñ* f pollution

polo *po·lo* m polo

Pologne *po·lon·yuh* f Poland

polonais *po·lo·neh* m Polish □ adj **polonais(e)** *po·lo·neh(·nez)* Polish; **le/la Polonais(e)** *po·lo·neh(·nez)* Pole

polyester *po·lee·es·tehr* m polyester

polyéthylène *po·lee·ay·tee·len* m polythene

polyglotte *po·lee·glot* adj multilingual

pomme *pom* f apple

pomme de terre *pom duh tehr* f potato

pommier *pom·yay* m apple tree

pompe *poñp* f pump; **la pompe à essence** *poñp a eh·soñs* petrol pump; fuel pump

pomper *poñ·pay* vt pump

pompier *poñ·pyay* m fireman

ponctuel(le) *poñk·tōō·el* adj punctual (*person*)

poney *po·nay* m pony

pont *poñ* m deck (*of ship*); ramp (*in garage*); bridge; **le pont à péage** *poñ a pay·yazh* toll bridge; **le pont autoroutier** *poñ ō·tō·roo·tyay* overpass; **le pont en dos d'âne** *poñ oñ dō dan* humpback bridge

pop *pop* adj pop (*music, art*); **le groupe pop** *groop pop* pop group

pop-corn *pop·korn* m popcorn

popeline *pop·leen* f poplin

populaire *po·pōō·lehr* adj popular

population *po·pōō·la·syoñ* f population

porc *por* m pork; pig

porcelaine *por·suh·len* f porcelain; china

porche *porsh* m porch

port *por* m harbo(u)r; port (*for ships*); **franco de port** *froñ·kō duh por* carriage free or paid

portail *por·tye* m gate (*of garden*)

portatif(ive) *por·ta·teef(·teev)* adj portable

porte *port* f gate (*of building*); door

porte-bagages *port·ba·gazh* m luggage rack (*in train*)

porte-bébé *port·bay·bay* m carry-cot

porte-cigarettes *port·see·ga·ret* m cigarette case

porte-clés *port·klay* m key ring

portée *por·tay f* range (*of missile*); **hors de portée** *or duh por·tay* out of reach

portefeuille *por·tuh·fuhy m* portfolio; pocketbook; wallet

portemanteau *port·moñ·tō m* coat hanger; hat stand

porte-monnaie *port·mo·nay m* purse (*for money*)

porte-parapluies *port·pa·ra·plwee m* umbrella stand

porteparole *port·pa·rol m* spokesman

porter *por·tay vt* bear (*weight*); carry (*in hands, arms*); wear (*clothes*); **portez ceci à la poste** *por·tay suh·see a la post* take this to the post office

porteur *por·tur m* porter (*for luggage*)

portier *por·tyay m* doorman (*in hotel*)

portion *por·syoñ f* helping; portion

porto *por·tō m* port (*wine*)

portugais *por·tōō·geh m* Portuguese □ *adj* **portugais(e)** *por·tōō·geh(·gez)* Portuguese

Portugal *por·tōō·gal m* Portugal

poser *pō·zay vt* stand (*put*); lay down; **poser une question** *pō·zay ōōn kes·tyoñ* to ask a question; **poser une affiche** *pō·zay ōōn a·feesh* to put up a notice; **poser un paquet** *pō·zay uñ pa·kay* to put down a parcel

positif(ive) *po·zee·teef(·teev) adj* positive

position *po·zee·syoñ f* position

posologie *pō·zo·lō·zhee f* dosage

posséder *po·say·day vt* own (*possess*)

possession *po·seh·syoñ f* ownership

possibilité *po·see·bee·lee·tay f* possibility

possible *po·see·bluh adj* possible; **faire tout son possible** *fehr too soñ po·see·bluh* to do all one possibly can

postal(e) *pos·tal adj* postal

postdater *post·da·tay vt* postdate

poste *post m* (*radio/TV*) set; extension (*phone*); **le poste vacant** *post va·koñ* vacant (*job*) □ *f* **la poste** *la post* post; **poste restante** *post res·toñt* poste restante; **le service des postes** *ser·vees day post* the Post Office; **je dois aller à la poste** *zhuh dwah za·lay a la post* I must go to the post office; **mettre à la poste** *meh·truh a la post* to post

pot *pō m* pot(ty); pot (*for jam, for plant*); carton (*of yogurt etc*)

poteau *po·tō m* post (*pole*); **le poteau indicateur** *po·tō añ·dee·ka·tur* signpost

poterie *po·tree f* pottery

potiron *po·tee·roñ m* pumpkin

poubelle *poo·bel f* trash can; dustbin

pouce *poos m* thumb

poudre *poo·druh f* powder; **en poudre** *oñ poo·druh* powdered

poule *pool f* hen

poulet *poo·leh m* chicken

poumon *poo·moñ m* lung

poupée *poo·pay f* doll

pour *poor prep* for; **pour toujours** *poor too·zhoor* forever; **20 pour cent** *poor soñ* 20 per cent; **il fait bon pour mars** *eel feh boñ poor mars* it's warm for March; **partir pour Londres** *par·teer poor loñ·druh* to leave for London; **pour faire quelque chose** *poor fehr kel·kuh shōz* in order to do something; **il l'a fait pour que je parte** *eel la feh poor kuh zhuh part* he did it so that I would go

pourboire *poor·bwahr m* tip (*money given*)

pourcentage *poor·soñ·tazh m* percentage

pourparlers *poor·par·lay mpl* talks (*negotiations*)

pourquoi *poor·kwah adv* why

pourri(e) *poor·ree adj* rotten (*wood etc*)

pourrir *poo·reer vi* rot

poursuivre *poor·swee·vruh vt* chase; **poursuivre en justice** *poor·swee·vroñ zhōōs·tees* to sue

pourtant *poor·toñ conj* however; **il est pourtant heureux** *eel eh poor·toñ uh·ruh* he's happy, though

pourvoir à *poor·vwahr a vi* provide for

pourvu que *poor·vōō kuh conj* provided, providing; as long as (*provided that*); **pourvu qu'il vienne** *poor·vōō keel vyen* provided (that) he comes

pousser *poo·say vi* grow (*plant, hair*) □ *vt* push; **faire pousser** *fehr poo·say* grow (*plants*)

poussette *poo·set f* stroller; push-chair

poussière *poo·syehr f* dust

poussiéreux(euse) *poo·syay·ruh(·ruhz) adj* dusty

poutre *poo·truh f* beam (*of wood*)

pouvoir *poo·vwahr m* power (*authority*) □ *vi* **pouvoir** *poo·vwar* be able; **pouvoir faire quelque chose** *poo·vwahr fehr kel·kuh shōz* to be able to do something; **il pourrait pleuvoir** *eel poo·reh pluh·vwahr* it might rain; **nous pourrions tout aussi bien y aller** *noo poo·ryoñ too·tō see byañ ee a·lay* we might as well go; **nous pourrions le faire** *noo poo·ryoñ luh fehr* we could do it; **est-ce que je pourrais avoir… es·kuh zhuh poo·reh za·vwahr* could I have…; **je peux** *zhuh puh* I can; **vous pouvez** *voo poo·vay* you can; **il/elle peut** *eel/el puh* he/she can; **nous pouvons** *noo poo·voñ* we can; **puis-je entrer?** *pweezh oñ·tray* may I come in?; **je n'y peux rien** *zhuh nee puh ryañ* I can't help it

Prague *prag f* Prague

praire *prehr f* clam

pratique *pra·teek adj* handy (*convenient*); practical; **pas pratique** *pa·pra·teek* inconvenient

précédent(e) *pray·say·doñ(·doñt) adj* previous

précepteur *pray·sep·tur m* tutor

préceptrice *pray·sep·trees f* tutor

précieux(euse) *pray·syuh(·syuz) adj* precious (*jewel etc*)

se précipiter *suh pray·see·pee·tay vr* rush

précis(e) *pray·see(·seez) adj* precise; exact (*detailed*); precise

préciser *pray·see·zay vt* specify

précision *pray·see·zyoñ f* precision

prédiction *pray·deek·syoñ f* prediction

prédire *pray·deer vt* predict

préfecture de police *pray·fek·tōōr duh po·lees f* police headquarters

préférer *pray·fay·ray vt* prefer

préjugé *pray·zhōō·zhay m* prejudice

prélèvement *pray·lev·moñ m* specimen (*medical*)

préliminaire *pray·lee·mee·nehr adj* preliminary

premier(ère) *pruhm·yay(·yehr) adj* first; top (*in rank*); **les premiers secours** *pruhm·yay suh·koor* first aid; **en première** *oñ pruhm·yehr* in first (*gear*); **de premier ordre** *duh pruhm·*

yehr or druh high-class; **de première classe** *duh pruhm·yehr klas* first-class (*work etc*); **voyager* en première** *vwa·ya·zhay oñ pruhm·yehr* to travel first class

première *pruhm·yehr f* première

prendre* *proñ·druh vt* take; get; have (*meal, shower, drink*); **s'y prendre* avec** *see proñ·dra·vek* handle (*deal with*); **il me l'a pris** *eel muh la pree* he took it from me; **prendre* froid** *proñ·druh frwah* to catch cold

prénom *pray·noñ m* first name; forename; Christian name

préparatifs *pray·pa·ra·teef mpl* preparations (*for trip*)

préparation *pray·pa·ra·syoñ f* preparation

préparer *pray·pa·ray vt* prepare; fix; **se préparer** *suh pray·pa·ray* to get ready; **il se prépare à partir** *eel suh pray·par a par·teer* he's preparing to leave; **préparer le feu** *pray·pa·ray luh fuh* to lay the fire

près *preh adv* near; **près de** *preh duh* close to; **tout près** *too preh* close by; **à peu près** *a puh preh* roughly (*approximately*); **près de la maison** *preh duh la meh·zoñ* near (*to*) the house; **près de Noël** *preh duh no·el* near (*to*) Christmas

presbytérien(ne) *prez·bee·tay·ree·añ (·en) adj* Presbyterian

présent(e) *pray·zoñ(·zoñt) adj* present

présentation *pray·zoñ·ta·syoñ f* presentation; introduction (*social*)

présenter *pray·zoñ·tay vt* present (*give*); introduce (*person*); **se présenter à l'enregistrement** *suh pray·zoñ·tay a loñ·ruh·zhee·struh·moñ* to check in (*at airport*)

préservatif *pray·zehr·va·teef m* sheath (*contraceptive*)

président *pray·zee·doñ m* chairman; president (*of country*)

président-directeur général (PDG) *pray·zee·doñ dee·rek·tur zhay·nay·ral (pay day zhay) m* president (*of company*)

presque *pres·kuh adv* almost; nearly

presse *pres f* press

pressé(e) *preh·say adj* in a hurry

presse-citron *pres·see·troñ m* lemon-squeezer

presser *preh·say vt* press; squeeze (*lemon*); **se presser** *suh preh·say* hurry

pressing *preh·seeng m* dry cleaner's

pression *pre·syoñ f* pressure; **la pression de la vie moderne** *la pre·syoñ duh la vee mo·dern* the pressures of modern life; **il était sous pression** *eel ay·teh soo pre·syoñ* he was under pressure

prestidigitateur *pres·tee·dee·zhee·ta·tur m* conjuror

prestige *pres·teezh m* prestige

prêt *preh m* loan

prêt(e) *preh (pret) adj* ready; **prêt(e) à faire quelque chose** *preh (pret) a fehr kel·kuh shōz* willing to do something; ready to do something

prêt-à-porter *preh·ta·por·tay adj* ready-to-wear

prêter *preh·tay vt* loan; lend

prêtre *preh·truh m* priest

preuve *pruhv f* evidence; proof

prévision *pray·vee·zyoñ f* forecast

prier *pree·ay vi* pray; **je vous en prie** *zhuh voo zoñ pree* don't mention it

prière *pree·ehr f* prayer

primaire *pree·mehr adj* primary (*education*)

prime *preem f* bonus (*on salary*); premium

prince *prañs m* prince

princesse *prañ·ses f* princess

principal(e) *prañ·see·pal adj* main; major

principalement *prañ·see·pal·moñ adv* mainly

printemps *prañ·toñ m* spring (*season*)

prioritaire *pree·o·ree·tehr adj* with right of way

priorité *pree·o·ree·tay f* right of way (*on road*); **céder* la priorité** *say·day la pree·o·ree·tay* to give way (*traffic*)

prise *preez f* plug (*electric*); outlet; **en prise** *oñ preez* in gear; **la prise multiple** *preez mōōl·tee·pluh* adapter, adaptor (*electrical*); **la prise de (courant)** *preez (duh koo·roñ)* point (*electric outlet*)

prison *pree·zoñ f* jail; prison; **en prison** *oñ pree·zoñ* in jail; in prison

prisonnier *pree·zo·nyay m* prisoner

prisonnière *pree·zo·nyehr f* prisoner

privé(e) *pree·vay adj* private; **en privé** *oñ pree·vay* in private

prix *pree m* price; prize; **le prix de catalogue** *pree duh ka·ta·log* list price; **à prix réduit** *a pree ray·dwee* cut-price; **le prix du billet** *pree dōō bee·yeh* fare; **le prix de la course** *pree duh la koors* fare (*in taxi*); **le prix minimum** *pree mee·nee·mam* reserve price; **le prix coûtant** *pree koo·toñ* cost price; **acheter* quelque chose au prix coûtant** *ash·tay kel·kuh shōz ō pree koo·toñ* to buy something at cost; **le prix d'entrée** *pree doñ·tray* entrance fee; **acheter* quelque chose à prix réduit** *ash·tay kel·kuh shōz a pree ray·dwee* to buy something at a reduction

probable *pro·ba·bluh adj* probable; likely; **peu probable** *puh pro·ba·bluh* unlikely

probablement *pro·ba·bluh·moñ adv* probably

problème *pro·blem m* problem

procédé *pro·say·day m* process (*method*)

procédure *pro·say·dōōr f* procedure

procès *pro·seh m* trial (*in law*)

processus *pro·seh·sōōs m* process

procès-verbal *pro·seh·vehr·bal m* parking-ticket

prochain(e) *pro·shañ(·shen) adj* next (*stop, station, week*)

proche *prosh adj* close (*near*)

producteur *pro·dōōk·tur m* producer

production *pro·dōōk·syoñ f* production

productivité *pro·dōōk·tee·vee·tay f* productivity

produire* *pro·dweer vt* produce; **se produire*** *suh pro·dweer* occur (*happen*)

produit *pro·dwee m* product; commodity

produits *pro·dwee mpl* produce (*products*)

professeur *pro·fe·sur m* professor; teacher (*secondary school*)

profession *pro·fe·syoñ f* profession

professionnel(le) *pro·fe·syo·nel adj* professional

profit *pro·fee m* profit

profiter de *pro·fee·tay duh vt* take advantage of

profiterole *pro·fee·trol f* profiterole

profond(e) *pro·foñ(·fond) adj* deep (*water, hole*); **peu profond(e)** *puh pro·foñ(·fond)* shallow

profondeur *pro·foñ·dur f* depth

programmation *pro·gra·ma·syoñ f* computer programming

programme *pro·gram m* program(me) (*brochure, computer*); syllabus; schedule

programmer *pro·gra·may vt* program(me)

programmeur *pro·gra·mur m* programmer (*person*)

programmeuse *pro·gra·muhz f* programmer (*person*)

progrès *pro·greh m* progress; **faire* des progrès** *fehr day pro·greh* to make progress

progressif(ive) *pro·greh·seef(·seev) adj* gradual

progressivement *pro·greh·seev·moñ adv* gradually

projecteur *pro·zhek·tur m* floodlight; spotlight; projector

projet *pro·zheh m* project; plan; scheme; **le projet directeur** *pro·zheh dee·rek·tur* blueprint

promenade *pro·muh·nad f* walk; promenade (*by sea*); ride (*in vehicle*); **faire* une promenade** *fehr ōon pro·muh·nad* to go for a walk; **la promenade en voiture** *pro·muh·nad oñ vwah·tōor* run (*outing*); **faire* une promenade en voiture** *fehr ōon pro·muh·nad oñ vwah·tōor* to go for a drive

se promener *suh pro·muh·nay vr* walk (*for pleasure, exercise*)

promesse *pro·mes f* promise

promettre* *pro·meh·truh vt* promise

promotion *pro·mo·syoñ f* promotion

promouvoir* *pro·moo·vwahr vt* promote

prononcer* *pro·noñ·say vt* pronounce

prononciation *pro·noñ·sya·syoñ f* pronunciation

proportion *pro·por·syoñ f* ratio

propos *pro·pō m* talk; **à propos a pro·pō** by the way; **à propos de** *a pro·pō duh* about

proposer* *pro·pō·zay vt* propose (*suggest*); **proposer de faire quelque chose** *pro·pō·zay duh fehr kel·kuh shōz* to offer to do something

proposition *pro·pō·zee·syoñ f* proposition; proposal (*suggestion*)

propre *pro·pruh adj* clean; own

propriétaire *pro·pree·ay·tehr m/f* owner

propriété *pro·pree·ay·tay f* property

prospectus *pros·pek·tōos m* prospectus; leaflet

prospère *pros·pehr adj* successful (*businessman*); prosperous

protéger* *pro·tay·zhay vt* protect

protéine *pro·tay·een f* protein

protestant(e) *pro·tes·toñ(·toñt) adj* Protestant

protestation *pro·tes·ta·syoñ f* protest

protester *pro·tes·tay vi* protest

prototype *pro·to·teep m* prototype

prouver *proo·vay vt* prove

province *pro·vañs f* province (*region*)

provincial(e) *pro·vañ·syal adj* provincial

provision *pro·vee·zyoñ f* supply (*stock*); funds

provisions *pro·vee·zyoñ fpl* groceries

prudent(e) *prōo·doñ(·doñt) adj* careful (*cautious*); wise (*decision*)

prune *prōon f* plum

pruneau *prōo·nō m* prune

P.-S. *pay·es abbrev* P.S.

psychiatre *psee·kya·truh m/f* psychiatrist

psychiatrique *psee·kya·treek adj* psychiatric

psychologie *psee·ko·lo·zhee f* psychology

psychologique *psee·ko·lo·zheek adj* psychological

psychologue *psee·ko·log m/f* psychologist

public *pōo·bleek m* public; audience; **en public** *oñ pōo·bleek* in public

public(ique) *pōo·bleek adj* public

publicité *pōob·lee·see·tay f* advertising; commercial (*ad*); publicity; **l'agence de publicité** *a·zhoñs duh pōob·lee·see·tay* advertising agency; **faire* de la publicité pour** *fehr duh la pōob·lee·see·tay poor* advertise (*product*)

public-relations *pōo·bleek·ruh·la·syoñ m* public relations officer

publier *pōo·blyay vt* publish

puce *pōos f* flea

puis *pwee adv* then

puisque *pwees·kuh conj* since

puissance *pwee·soñs f* power; **la puissance mondiale** *pwee·soñs moñ·dyal* world power

puissant(e) *pwee·soñ(·soñt) adj* powerful

puits *pwee m* well (*for water*)

pull *pōol m* sweater

pull-over *pōol·o·vehr m* pullover

punaise *pōo·nez f* bug (*insect*); thumbtack; drawing pin

punch *puñch m* punch (*drink*)

punir *pōo·neer vt* punish

punition *pōo·nee·syoñ f* punishment

pur(e) *pōor adj* pure

purée *pōo·ray f* purée; **faire* une purée de** *fehr ōon pōo·ray duh* mash; **la purée de pommes de terre** *pōo·ray duh pom duh tehr* mashed potatoes

puzzle *puh·zuhl m* jigsaw (*puzzle*)

P.-V. *pay·vay m* parking ticket

pyjama *pee·zha·ma m* pajamas; pyjamas

pyramide *pee·ra·meed f* pyramid

Pyrénées *pee·ray·nay fpl* Pyrenees

Q

quai *kay m* platform (*in station*); wharf; quay; quayside

qualifié(e) *ka·lee·fyay adj* skilled (*workers*); qualified

se qualifier pour *suh ka·lee·fyay poor vr* qualify for (*in sports*)

qualité *ka·lee·tay f* quality; **les articles de qualité** *ar·tee·kluh duh ka·lee·tay* quality goods

quand *koñ conj* when

quand même *koñ mem adv* even so

quant à *koñ·tee·tay f* quantity

quantité *koñ·tee·tay f* quantity

quarantaine *ka·roñ·ten f* about forty; quarantine; **mettre* un chien en quarantaine** *meh·truñ shyañ oñ ka·roñ·ten* to put a dog in quarantine

quarante *ka·roñt num* forty

quart *kar m* quarter; **un quart d'heure** *uñ kar dur* a quarter of an hour; **4 heures moins le quart** *4 ur mwañ luh kar* (a) quarter to 4; **4 heures et quart** *4 ur ay kar* (a) quarter past 4

quartier *kar·tyay m* neighbo(u)rhood; district (*of town*); **les magasins du quartier** *lay ma·ga·zañ dōo kar·tyay* the local shops; **le quartier réservé** *kar·tyay ray·zehr·vay* red light district

quartz *kwarts* m quartz

quatorze *ka·torz* num fourteen

quatre *ka·truh* num four

quatre-vingt-dix *ka·truh·vañ·dees* num ninety

quatre-vingts *ka·truh·vañ* num eighty; **les années quatre-vingts** *lay za·nay ka·truh·vañ* the eighties (*decade*)

quatrième *ka·tryem* adj fourth; **la quatrième vitesse** *ka·tryem vee·tes* top (*gear*)

que *kuh* conj that; than □ *pron* whom; that; what; **mieux que lui** *myuh kuh lwee* better than him; **j'ai vu ce que vous avez fait** *zhay voo suh kuh voo za·vay feh* I saw what you did; **l'homme que vous voyez** *lom kuh voo vwah·yay* the man whom you see; **la photo que je vous ai donnée** *la fo·tô kuh zhuh voo zay do·nay* the photo that I gave you; **j'espère que…** *zhes·pehr kuh* I hope that…; **qu'est-ce qui s'est passé?** *kes kee seh pa·say* what's happened?; **que voulez-vous?** *kuh voo·lay voo* what do you want?; **n'était qu'une erreur** *suh nay·teh kōōn eh·rur* it was just a mistake

quel(le) *kel* adj which; what; **quel livre?** *kel lee·vruh* which book?; **quelles langues?** *kel loñg* which languages?; **quel désordre!** *kel day·zor·druh* what a mess! (*in room*)

quelque *kel·kuh* adj some

quelque chose *kel·kuh shōz* pron something; **quelque chose de plus grand** *kel·kuh shōz duh plōō groñ* something bigger; **est-ce que vous voyez quelque chose?** *es·kuh voo vwah·yay kel·kuh shōz* can you see anything?

quelquefois *kel·kuh·fwah* adv sometimes

quelque part *kel·kuh par* adv somewhere

quelques *kel·kuh* adj a few; **quelques livres** *kel·kuh lee·vruh* a few books

quelqu'un *kel·kuñ* pron somebody, someone; **est-ce que vous voyez quelqu'un?** *es·kuh voo vwah·yay kel·kuñ* can you see anybody?; **quelqu'un d'autre** *kel·kuñ dō·truh* someone else

querelle *kuh·rel* f quarrel

question *kes·tyoñ* f question; issue (*matter*); **hors de question** *or duh kes·tyoñ* out of the question; **poser une question** *pô·zay ōōn kes·tyoñ* to ask a question

questionnaire *kes·tyo·nehr* m questionnaire

queue *kuh* f tail; line (*people waiting*); queue; **faire* la queue** *fehr la kuh* to stand in line; queue

qui *kee* pron who; which; **je sais à qui c'est** *zhuh seh a kee seh* I know whose it is; **à qui est ce livre?** *a kee eh suh lee·vruh* whose book is this?; **le garçon avec qui…** *luh gar·soñ a·vek kee* the boy with whom…; **n'importe qui** *nañ·port kee* anybody at all; **j'ai vu ce qui s'est passé** *zhay voo suh kee seh pa·say* I saw what happened; **le livre, qui est long** *luh lee·vruh kee eh loñ* the book, which is long

quiche *keesh* f quiche

quincailler *kañ·kye·yay* m ironmonger

quincaillerie *kañ·kye·yuh·ree* f hardware

quinze *kañz* num fifteen

quitter *kee·tay* vt quit; leave (*room, club, school*); **ne quittez pas!** *nuh kee·tay pa* hold on! (*on phone*)

quoi *kwa* pron what; **n'importe quoi** *nañ·port kwa* anything at all; **après quoi** *a·preh kwah* after which

quota *kô·ta* m quota (*of goods*)

quotidien(ne) *ko·tee·dyañ(·dyen) adj* daily

R

rabais *ra·beh* m reduction; **au rabais** *ō ra·beh* at a reduction; **3% de rabais** *3% duh ra·beh* 3% off

rabat *ra·ba* m flap

rabbin *ra·bañ* m rabbi

rabot *ra·bô* m plane (*tool*)

raccourci *ra·koor·see* m short cut

raccourcir *ra·koor·seer* vt shorten

raccrocher *ra·kro·shay* vi ring off; hang up (*phone*)

race *ras* f race

racial(e) *ra·syal* adj racial

racine *ra·seen* f root

raconter *ra·koñ·tay* vt tell; **raconter quelque chose à quelqu'un** *ra·koñ·tay kel·kuh shōz a kel·kuñ* to tell someone something

radar *ra·dar* m radar

radiale *ra·dyal* adj radial(-ply)

radiateur *ra·dya·tur* m heater; radiator

radio *ra·dyô* f radio; X-ray (*photo*); **à la radio** *a la ra·dyô* on the radio

radiographier *ra·dyo·gra·fyay* vt X-ray

radis *ra·dee* m radish

rafale *ra·fal* f squall; gust

raffiné(e) *ra·fee·nay* adj sophisticated (*person*)

raffiner *ra·fee·nay* vt refine

raffinerie *ra·fee·nuh·ree* f refinery

rafle *ra·fluh* f raid (*by police*)

rafraîchir *ra·fray·sheer* vt chill (*wine, food*)

rafraîchissements *ra·freh·shees·moñ* mpl refreshments

rage *razh* f rabies

ragoût *ra·goo* m stew; casserole (*food*)

raid *red* m raid (*military*)

raide *red* adj steep; tight (*rope*); stiff; straight

raie *ray* f parting (*in hair*); skate (*fish*); stripe; streak

rails *rye* mpl rails (*for train*)

raisin *reh·zañ* m grape; **le raisin sec** *reh·zañ sek* sultana; raisin; currant

raison *ray·zoñ* f reason; sense (*common sense*); **avoir* raison** *a·vwar ray·zoñ* to be right; **à raison de** *a reh·zoñ duh* at the rate of

raisonnable *reh·zo·na·bluh* adj sensible; reasonable

ralentir *ra·loñ·teer* vi slow down

rallye *ra·lee* m rally (*sporting*)

ramasser *ra·ma·say* vt pick up (*object*)

rampe *roñp* f handrail (*on stairs*); ramp (*slope*)

ramper *roñ·pay* vi crawl

rancune *roñ·kōōn* f spite

randonnée *roñ·do·nay* f hike; **faire* une randonnée** *fehr ōōn roñ·do·nay* to go for a hike

rang *roñ* m row; rank (*status*)

ranger* *roñ·zhay* vt to put away; **bien rangé(e)** *byañ roñ·zhay* tidy (*room, papers*)

ranimer *ra·nee·may* vt revive (*person*)

râpe *rahp* f grater

râper *rah·pay* vt grate (*food*)

rapide *ra·peed* m express train □ *adj* quick; fast

rapidement *ra·peed·moñ* adv quickly

rappeler* *ra·puh·lay* vt remind; ring back; **rappeler* quelque chose à quelqu'un** *ra·puh·lay kel·kuh shōz a kel·kuñ* to remind someone of something; **se rappeler*** *suh ra·puh·lay* remember

rapport *ra·por* m report; record (*register*); relationship; return (*profit*); **qui a rapport à** *kee a ra·por* a relevant to; **les rapports entre les races** *ra·por oñ·truh lay ras* race relations; **les rapports sexuels** *ra·por sek·sōō·el* sexual intercourse

rapporter *ra·por·tay* vt bring back; yield (*investment*)

raquette *ra·ket* f racket (*tennis*); bat (*table tennis etc*); **la raquette de tennis** *ra·ket duh teh·nees* tennis racket

rare *rar* adj rare; scarce; unusual

rarement *rar·moñ* adv seldom

raser *ra·zay* m razor; **le rasoir électrique** *ra·zwahr ay·lek·treek* shaver

rassembler *ra·soñ·blay* vt gather (*assemble*); **se rassembler** *suh ra·soñ·blay* gather (*crowd*)

rassis(e) *ra·see(·seez)* adj stale (*bread*)

rat *ra* m rat

raté(e) *ra·tay* m/f failure (*person*); **avoir* des ratés** *av·wahr day ra·tay* knock; pink (*engine*)

râteau *ra·tō* m rake

rationalisation *ra·syo·na·lee·za·syoñ* f rationalization

rationaliser *ra·syo·na·lee·zay* vt rationalize

ravi(e) *ra·vee* adj delighted

ravioli *ra·vyo·lee* mpl ravioli

rayon *ray·yoñ* m shelf; department (*in store*); ray; beam (*of light*); **le rayon hommes** *ray·yoñ om* menswear (*department*)

réacteur *ray·ak·tur* m reactor

réaction *ray·ak·syoñ* f reaction

réalisateur *ray·a·lee·za·tur* m director (*of film*)

réaliser *ray·a·lee·zay* vt carry out; realize (*assets*)

réalité *ray·a·lee·tay* f reality

rebondir *ruh·boñ·deer* vi bounce (*ball*)

récemment *ray·sa·moñ* adv lately; recently

récent(e) *ray·soñ(·soñt)* adj recent; **plus récent(e)** *plōō ray·soñ(·soñt)* later (*version*)

récepteur *ray·sep·tur* m receiver (*phone*)

réception *ray·sep·syoñ* f reception; desk (*reception*); **accuser réception de** *a·kōō·zay ray·sep·syoñ duh* acknowledge (*letter*)

réceptionniste *ray·sep·syo·neest* m/f receptionist (*in hotel*)

récession *ray·se·syoñ* f recession

recette *ruh·set* f recipe; **les recettes** *ruh·set* receipts (*income*)

receveur *ruh·suh·vur* m conductor (*on bus*)

recevoir* *ruh·suh·vwahr* vt receive; get; entertain (*give hospitality*)

rechapé *ruh·sha·pay* adj retread

réchauffer *ray·shō·fay* vt warm

recherche *ruh·shersh* f research

rechercher *ruh·shehr·shay* vt look for; retrieve (*data*)

récipient *ray·see·pyoñ* m container

réclame *ray·klam* f advertisement

récolte *ray·kolt* f crop (*harvest*)

recommander *ruh·ko·moñ·day* vt recommend; register

récompense *ray·koñ·poñs* f reward

reconduire* *ruh·koñ·dweer* vt take back

reconnaissant(e) *ruh·ko·neh·soñ (·soñt)* adj grateful

reconnaître* *ruh·ko·neh·truh* vt recognize

record *ruh·kor* m record (*in sports*) □ *adj* record (*production, crop etc*)

recrue *ruh·krōō* f recruit

recrutement *ruh·kroo·tuh·moñ* m recruitment

recruter *ruh·krōō·tay* vt recruit (*personnel*)

reçu *ruh·sōō* m receipt

recueil *ruh·kuhy* m collection; **le recueil d'expressions** *ruh·kuhy dek·spreh·syoñ* phrase book

recueillir* *ruh·kuh·yeer* vt collect (*donations*)

recyclage *ruh·see·klazh* m retraining

recycler *ruh·see·klay* vt retrain; **se recycler** *suh ruh·see·klay* retrain

redistribuer *ruh·dees·tree·bōō·ay* vt redistribute

redistribution *ruh·dees·tree·bōō·syoñ* f redistribution

redouter *ruh·doo·tay* vt dread

réduction *ray·dōōk·syoñ* f reduction

réduire* *ray·dweer* vt cut; reduce

références *ray·fay·roñs* fpl reference (*testimonial*)

réfléchir *ray·flay·sheer* vt/i reflect; bien **réfléchir à quelque chose** *byañ ray·flay·sheer a kel·kuh shōz* to think something over

réflecteur *ruh·flek·tur* m reflector (*on cycle, car*)

refléter* *ruh·flay·tay* vt reflect

refroidissement *ruh·frwah·dees·moñ* m cooling

refuge *ruh·fōōzh* m hut (*on mountain*); **le refuge pour piétons** *ruh·fōōzh poor pyay·toñ* island (*traffic*)

refus *ruh·fōō* m refusal

refuser *ruh·fōō·zay* vt reject; refuse; **refuser de faire quelque chose** *ruh·fōō·zay duh fehr kel·kuh shōz* to refuse to do something

regard *ruh·gar* m look

regarder *ruh·gar·day* vi look □ *vt* watch; look at; **regarder fixement** *ruh·gar·day feeks·moñ* stare (at); **ça ne vous regarde pas** *sa nuh voo ruh·gard pa* that doesn't concern you

régate *ray·gat* f regatta

régime *ray·zheem* m diet (*slimming*); **suivre* un régime** *swee·vruñ ray·zheem* to be on a diet

région *ray·zhyoñ* f region; area

registre *ruh·zhee·struh* m register; **le registre du personnel** *ruh·zhee·struh dōō pehr·so·nel* payroll

règle *reh·gluh* f rule; ruler (*for measuring*); **la règle à calcul** *reh·gla kal·kōōl* slide rule

règlement *reh·gluh·moñ* m rule (*regulation*); **arriver à un règlement à l'amiable** *a·ree·vay a uñ reh·gluh·moñ a la·mya·bluh* to settle out of court

régler* *ray·glay* vt tune (*engine*); direct (*traffic*); adjust; settle

règles *reh·gluh* fpl period (*menstruation*)

réglisse *ray·glees* f licorice

regretter *ruh·gre·tay* vt regret; miss; **je regrette, mais ce n'est pas possible**

*zhuh ruh·gret meh suh neh pah po·
see·bluh* I'm afraid not
régulier(ère) *ray·gōō·lyay(·lyehr)* adj
regular; steady (pace)
rein *rañ* m kidney (of person); **le mal
de reins** *mal duh rañ* backache
reine *ren* f queen
rejoindre* *ruh·zhwan·druh* vt rejoin
se réjouir de *suh ray·zhoo·eer duh* vr
to be delighted about
relatif(ive) *re·la·teef(·teev)* adj relative
relations publiques *ruh·la·syoñ pōō·
bleek* fpl public relations
relier *ruh·lyay* vt connect (join)
religieuse *ruh·lee·zhee·uhz* f nun
religieux(euse) *ruh·lee·zhee·uh(·uhz)*
adj religious (person)
religion *ruh·lee·zhee·oñ* f religion
remarquable *ruh·mar·ka·bluh* adj remarkable
remarque *ruh·mark* f comment; remark
remarquer *ruh·mar·kay* vt notice
remblai *roñ·blay* m embankment
rembourré(e) *roñ·boo·ray* adj stuffed
(cushion etc)
remboursement *roñ·boor·suh·moñ* m
refund
rembourser *roñ·boor·say* vt pay back
(money); repay; refund
remède *ruh·med* m remedy; **un remède
contre** *uñ ruh·med koñ·truh* a remedy for
remercier *ruh·mehr·syay* vt thank
remettre* *ruh·meh·truh* vt put back;
replace; **remettre à plus tard** *ruh·
meh·tra plōō tar* to postpone; **se re-
mettre*** *suh ruh·meh·truh* to get better (from illness)
remise *ruh·meez* f shed; discount
remonte-pente *ruh·moñt·poñt* m ski
lift
remonter *ruh·moñ·tay* vt wind up
(clock)
remorque *ruh·mork* f trailer (for
goods)
remorquer *ruh·mor·kay* vt tow (trailer)
remplaçant(e) *roñ·pla·soñ(·soñt)* m/f
substitute
remplacement *roñ·plas·moñ* m replacement
remplacer* *roñ·pla·say* vt replace (substitute)
remplir *roñ·pleer* vt fill; fill in/out/up;
remplir une fiche d'hôtel *roñ·pleer
ōōn feesh dō·tel* to check in (at hotel)
remporter *roñ·por·tay* vt win (prize)
remuer *ruh·mōō·ay* vt wag (tail); toss
(salad); stir
renard *ruh·nar* m fox
rencontrer *roñ·koñ·tray* vt meet (encounter); **nous nous sommes déjà
rencontrés** *noo noo som day·zha roñ·
koñ·tray* we've met before
rendement *roñ·duh·moñ* m output;
yield
rendez-vous *roñ·day·voo* m date; appointment
rendre *roñ·druh* vt give back; return;
se rendre compte de *suh roñ·druh
koñt duh* to realize; **rendre quelqu'un
triste** *roñ·druh kel·kuñ treest* to
make someone sad
rène *ren* f rein
renforcer* *ruh·for·say* vt strengthen
renoncer* *ruh·noñ·say* vi give up
(abandon hope); **renoncer* à fumer**
ruh·noñ·say a fōō·may to give up
smoking
renouveler* *ruh·noo·vuh·lay* vt renew
(subscription, passport)

renseignement *roñ·seh·nyuh·moñ* m
piece of information
renseignements *roñ·seh·nyuh·moñ* mpl
information; **le bureau de renseignements** *bōō·rō duh roñ·seh·nyuh·moñ*
information desk/office
rentabilité *roñ·ta·bee·lee·tay* f profitability
rentable *roñ·ta·bluh* adj profitable;
peu rentable *puh roñ·ta·bluh* uncon-
omic; unprofitable
rentes *roñt* fpl unearned income
rente viagère *roñt vya·zhehr* f annuity
rentrer *roñ·tray* vi go in; **rentrer à la
maison** *roñ·tray a la meh·zoñ* to go
home
renverser *roñ·vehr·say* vt spill; knock
down/over
renvoyer *roñ·vwah·yay* vt return (send
back); **renvoyer quelqu'un** *roñ·vwah·
yay kel·kuñ* to fire someone (dismiss)
réorganisation *ray·or·ga·nee·za·syoñ* f
reorganization
réorganiser *ray·or·ga·nee·zay* vt reorganize
répandre *ray·poñ·druh* vt spread
(news); **se répandre** *suh ray·poñ·
druh* spill; spread
réparer *ray·pa·ray* vt repair; mend
repas *ruh·pah* m meal
repassage *ruh·pa·sazh* m ironing
repasser *ruh·pa·say* vt press; iron
répercussions *ray·pehr·kōō·syoñ* fpl
backlash
répéter* *ray·pay·tay* vt repeat; **est-ce
que vous pouvez répéter cela?** *es·kuh
voo poo·vay ray·pay·tay suh·la* could
you say that again?
répétition *ray·pay·tee·syoñ* f rehearsal;
repetition
répondre *ray·poñ·druh* vi reply; answer; **répondre à** *ray·poñ·druh a*
meet (demand); **répondre à une
question** *ray·poñ·dra ōōn kes·tyoñ* to
answer a question; **répondre au téléphone** *ray·poñ·drō tay·lay·fon* to answer the phone
réponse *ray·poñs* f answer; reply
reportage *ruh·por·tazh* m report (in
press)
repos *ruh·pō* m rest (repose); **la maison de repos** *la meh·zoñ duh ruh·pō*
nursing home
se reposer *suh ruh·pō·zay* vr rest
représentant(e) *ruh·pray·zoñ·toñ(t)*
m/f representative (deputy, agent)
représentation *ruh·pray·zoñ·ta·syoñ* f
performance (of play)
représenter *ruh·pray·zoñ·tay* vt stand
for (signify); represent
reprise *ruh·preez* f trade-in
repriser *ruh·pree·zay* vt darn
républicain(e) *ray·pōō·blee·kañ(·ken)*
adj republican
république *ray·pōō·bleek* f republic
réputation *ray·pōō·ta·syoñ* f reputation
requin *ruh·kañ* m shark
réservation *ray·zehr·va·syoñ* f reservation (of seats, rooms etc); booking;
la réservation de groupe *ray·zehr·va·
syoñ duh groop* block booking
réserve *ray·zehrv* f reservation
(doubt); store room; stock (supply);

mettre* en réserve *meh·troñ ray· zehrv* store; **sous réserve de** *soo ray· zehrv duh* subject to

réserver *ray·zehr·vay* vt reserve (*seat, room*); book (*seat*)

réserves *ray·zehrv* fpl reserves

réservoir *ray·zehr·vwahr* m tank (*of car*)

résidence *ray·zee·doñs* f residence; **la résidence universitaire** *ray·zee·doñs ōō·nee·vehr·see·tehr* hall of residence (*of college*)

résidentiel(le) *ray·zee·doñ·syel* adj residential (*area*)

résistance *ray·zees·toñs* f resistance

résister à *ray·zees·tay* a vi resist

résoudre* *ray·zoo·druh* vt solve (*problem*)

respect *res·peh* m respect

respectable *res·pek·ta·bluh* adj respectable

respecter *res·pek·tay* vt respect

respirer *res·pee·ray* vi breathe

resplendir *reh·sploñ·deer* vi blaze (*lights*)

responsabilité *res·poñ·sa·bee·lee·tay* f responsibility

responsable *res·poñ·sa·bluh* adj responsible; **être* le responsable** *eh· truh luh res·poñ·sa·bluh* to be to blame; **responsable de** *res·poñ·sa· bluh duh* responsible for

ressembler à *ruh·soñ·blay* a vi resemble; look like; **il ressemble à son père** *eel ruh·soñ·bluh a soñ pehr* he resembles his father

ressort *ruh·sor* m spring (*coil*); **en dernier ressort** *oñ dehr·nyay ruh·sor* in the last resort

ressortir* *ruh·sor·teer* vi stand out

ressources *ruh·soors* fpl resources

restaurant *res·to·roñ* m restaurant

reste *rest* m rest

rester *res·tay* vi remain; stay; **rester à la maison** *res·tay a la meh·zoñ* to stay in; **il reste de la crème** *eel rest duh la krem* there's some cream left

restriction *res·treek·syoñ* f restriction; **les restrictions de crédit** *res·treek· syoñ duh kray·dee* credit squeeze

résultat *ray·zōōl·ta* m result

résumé *ray·zōō·may* m summary

se rétablir *suh ray·ta·bleer* vr recover (*from illness*)

retard *ruh·tar* m delay (*to train, plane*); **en retard** *oñ ruh·tar* late (*not on time*); **le train a pris du retard** *luh trañ a pree dōō ruh·tar* the train has been delayed; **avoir* du retard** *a· vwahr dōō ruh·tar* to be behind schedule

retarder *ruh·tar·day* vi lose (*clock, watch*) □ vt delay (*hold up*)

retirer *ruh·tee·ray* vt withdraw (*money*); **se retirer d'une affaire** *suh ruh·tee·ray dōōn a·fehr* to pull out of a deal

retour *ruh·toor* m return (*going/coming back*)

retournement *ruh·toor·nuh·moñ* m upturn (*in business*)

retourner *ruh·toor·nay* vi return; go back □ vt **retourner quelque chose** *ruh·toor·nay kel·kuh shōz* to turn something over; to turn something round; **il s'est retourné** *eel seh ruh· toor·nay* he turned (round)

retraite *ruh·tret* f retirement; pension (*from company*); **prendre* sa retraite** *proñ·druh sa ruh·tret* to retire

retraité(e) *ruh·treh·tay* adj retired □

m/f le/la retraité(e) *ruh·treh·tay* old-age-pensioner

rétrécir *ray·tray·seer* vi shrink

rétrécissement *ray·tray·sees·moñ* m shrinkage

rétrospectivement *ray·tro·spek·teev· moñ* adv in retrospect

retrouver *ruh·troo·vay* vt find; meet (*by arrangement*)

rétroviseur *ray·trō·vee·zur* m rear-view mirror

réunion *ray·ōō·nyoñ* f meeting

réussir *ray·ōō·seer* vi succeed; **réussir à** *ray·ōō·seer* a succeed in; pass (*exam*); **les oignons ne me réussissent pas** *lay zo·nyoñ nuh muh ray·ōō·sees pah* onions don't agree with me; **il a réussi à le faire** *eel a ray·ōō·see a luh fehr* he succeeded in doing it

revanche *rev* m dream

réveil *ray·vay* m alarm (*clock*)

réveiller *ray·vay·yay* vt wake; **se réveiller** *suh ray·vay·yay* to wake up; **réveillez-moi à 7 heures** *ray·vay·yay mwah à 7 ur* call me at 7 a.m. (*in hotel etc*)

revenant *ruh·vuh·noñ* m ghost

revendre *ruh·voñ·druh* vt resell

revenir* *ruh·vuh·neer* vi return; go back; come back; **revenir* en arrière** *ruh·vuh·neer oñ na·ryehr* to turn back; **revenez chez nous** *ruh·vuh·nay shay noo* come back to our place

revente *ruh·voñt* f resale

revenu *ruh·vuh·nōō* m revenue; income; **le revenu national brut** *ruh· vuh·nōō na·syo·nal brōōt* gross national product

rêver *reh·vay* vi dream; **rêver de** *reh· vay duh* to dream of

réverbère *ray·vehr·behr* m lamppost; streetlamp

révérence *ray·vay·roñs* f bow; **faire* une révérence** *fehr ōōn ray·vay·roñs* to bow

réviser *ray·vee·zay* vt revise; service

révision *ray·vee·zyoñ* f service (*for car*)

révolution *ray·vo·lōō·syoñ* f revolution (*political*)

revue *ruh·vōō* f revue; review; **passer en revue** *pa·say oñ ruh·vōō* to review; **la revue mensuelle** *ruh·vōō moñ·swel* monthly

rez-de-chaussée *ray·duh·shō·say* m ground floor

Rhin *rañ* m Rhine

Rhône *rōn* m Rhone

rhubarbe *rōō·barb* f rhubarb

rhum *rom* m rum

rhumatisme *rōō·ma·teez·muh* m rheumatism

rhume *rōōm* m cold (*illness*); **le rhume des foins** *rōōm day fwañ* hay fever

riche *reesh* adj wealthy; rich

richesses *ree·shes* fpl wealth

ride *reed* f wrinkle

rideau *ree·dō* m curtain; drape

ridicule *ree·dee·kōōl* adj ridiculous

rien *ryañ* pron nothing; **de rien** *duh ryañ* not at all (*don't mention it*); **je ne vois rien** *zhuh nuh vwah ryañ* I can't see anything

rinçage *rañ·sazh* m rinse (*hair conditioner*)

rincer* *rañ·say* vt rinse

rire* *reer* vi laugh □ m **le rire** *reer* laugh; laughter

risotto *ree·zo·tō* m risotto

risque *reesk* m risk

risquer *rees·kay* vt risk

rivage *ree·vazh m* shore (*of sea*)
rival(e) *ree·val m/f* rival
rive *reev f* shore
rivière *ree·vyehr f* river
riz *ree m* rice
robe *rob f* gown; dress; **la robe de chambre** *rob duh shoñ·bruh* dressing gown; **la robe de mariage** *rob duh ma·ree·azh* wedding dress; **la robe de soirée** *rob duh swah·ray* evening dress (*woman's*); **la robe bain de soleil** *rob bañ duh so·lay* sun dress; **la robe de grossesse** *rob duh grō·ses* maternity dress
robe-chasuble *rob·sha·zōō·bluh f* pinafore (*dress*)
robinet *ro·bee·neh m* tap (*for water*); faucet; **l'eau du robinet** *lō dōō ro·bee·neh* tap water; **le robinet d'arrêt** *ro·bee·neh da·reh* stopcock
robot *rō·bō m* robot
roche *rosh f* rock (*substance*)
rocher *ro·shay m* rock (*boulder*)
rock 'n' roll *rok un rol m* rock ('n' roll)
roder *ro·day vt* run in (*engine, car*)
rognon *ro·nyoñ m* kidney (*to eat*)
roi *rwah m* king
rôle *rōl m* part (*in play*)
romain(e) *ro·mañ(·men) adj* Roman
roman *ro·moñ m* novel (*book*); **les romans** *ro·moñ* fiction; **le roman à suspense** *ro·moñ a sōōs·poñs* thriller
romantique *ro·moñ·teek adj* romantic
Rome *rom f* Rome
rompre *roñ·pruh vt* break
romsteak *roñ·stek m* rump steak
ronchonner *roñ·sho·nay vi* grumble
rond *roñ m* ring (*circle*) □ *adj* **rond(e)** *roñ (roñd)* round; **le chiffre rond** *shee·fruh roñ* round figure/number
rondelet(te) *roñ·duh·lay(·let) adj* plump
rond-point *roñ·pwañ m* roundabout
ronfler *roñ·flay vi* snore
rosbif *ros·beef m* roast beef; roasting beef
rose *rōz adj* pink □ *f* **la rose** *rōz* rose
rosé *rō·zay m* rosé
rôti *rō·tee m* roast meat; joint (*of meat*)
rôtir *rō·teer vt* roast
rôtisserie *rō·tee·suh·ree f* steakhouse
roue *roo f* wheel; **la roue de secours** *roo duh suh·koor* spare wheel
rouge *roozh adj* red; **le rouge à lèvres** *roozh a leh·vruh* lipstick
rougeole *roo·zhol f* measles
rougeoyer *roo·zhwah·yay vi* glow
rougir *roo·zheer vi* blush
rouille *roo·yuh f* rust □ *adj* **rouillé(e)** *roo·yay* rusty
rouiller *roo·yay vi* rust
rouleau *roo·lō m* roll
rouleau à pâtisserie *roo·lō a pa·tees·ree m* rolling pin
roulement *roo·luh·moñ m* turnover (*in goods*)
rouler *roo·lay vi* roll; run; go (*car*) □ *vt* roll; roll up; roll out
roulette *roo·let f* roulette
roumain *roo·mañ m* Rumanian (*language*) □ *adj* **roumain(e)** *roo·mañ (·men)* Rumanian
Roumanie *roo·ma·nee f* Rumania
round *rawnd m* round (*in boxing*)
rousse *roos adj* red-haired
route *root f* road; route; **en route** *oñ root* on the way; **la route nationale** *root na·syo·nal* trunk-road; **la route de délestage** *root duh day·les·tazh* relief road; **la route de contournement**

root duh koñ·toorn·moñ bypass; **la route à quatre voies** *root a ka·truh vwah* dual carriageway
routier *roo·tyay m* lorry driver; **la carte routière** *kart roo·tyehr* road map
routine *roo·teen f* routine
roux *roo adj* red-haired
royal(e) *rwah·yal adj* royal
Royaume-Uni *rwah·yōm·ōō·nee m* United Kingdom, U.K.
R.S.V.P. *abbrev* R.S.V.P.
ruban *rōō·boñ m* tape; ribbon
rubis *rōō·bee m* ruby
rudement *rōō·duh·moñ adv* roughly
rue *rōō f* street; **la rue à sens unique** *rōō a soñs ōō·neek* one-way street; **la grande rue** *groñd rōō* high street; **3 rues plus loin** *3 rōō ploo lwañ* 3 blocks away
ruée *rōō·ay f* rush
ruelle *rōō·el f* lane (*in town*); alley
rugby *rug·bee m* rugby
rugir *rōō·zheer vi* roar (*lion*)
rugissement *rōō·zhees·moñ m* roar (*of lion*)
rugueux(euse) *rōō·guh(·guhz) adj* rough (*surface*)
ruine *rōō·een f* ruin
ruiner *rōō·ee·nay vt* wreck (*plans*); ruin
ruines *rōō·een fpl* ruins
ruisseau *rwee·sō m* stream; gutter
rumsteck *rum·stek m* rump steak
rural(e) *rōō·ral adj* rural
ruse *rōōz f* trick (*clever act*)
russe *rōōs adj* Russian (*language*) □ *adj* Russian; **il est Russe** *eel eh rōōs* he's Russian; **elle est Russe** *el eh rōōs* she's Russian
Russie *rōō·see f* Russia
rutabaga *rōō·ta·ba·ga m* swede
rythme *reet·muh m* rhythm; rate

S

S.A. *es·a abbrev* Ltd; plc
sa *sa adj* his; her; its; **sa mère** *sa mehr* her mother; his mother
sable *sa·bluh m* sand; **de sable** *duh sa·bluh* sandy (*beach*)
sablé *sa·blay m* shortbread
sabot *sa·bō m* clog; **le sabot de frein** *sa·bō duh fraň* brake shoe
sac *sak m* bag; sack; **le sac à dos** *sak a dō* rucksack; **le sac en plastique** *sak oñ plas·teek* plastic bag; **le sac à main** *sak a mañ* handbag, purse; **le sac de couchage** *sak duh koo·shazh* sleeping bag; **le sac de toilette** *sak duh twah·let* sponge-bag
saccharine *sa·ka·reen f* saccharin(e)
sachet *sa·shay m* sachet; **le sachet de thé** *sa·shay duh tay* tea bag
sage *sazh adj* good (*well-behaved*); wise (*person*)
sage-femme *sazh·fam f* midwife
saignant(e) *say·nyoñ(·nyoñt) adj* rare (*steak*)
saignement de nez *sen·yuh·moñ duh nay m* nosebleed
saigner *say·nyay vi* bleed
saindoux *sañ·doo m* lard
saint(e) *sañ (sañt) adj* holy □ *m/f* saint
Saint-Sylvestre *sañ seel·ves·truh f* New Year's Eve
saisir *seh·zeer vt* snatch; grab; seize; grip
saison *seh·zoñ f* season; **les fraises sont de saison** *lay frez soñ duh seh·zoñ* strawberries are in season; **la pleine saison** *plen seh·zoñ* high season

salade *sa·lad f* lettuce; salad; green salad; **la salade de fruits** *sa·lad duh frwee* fruit salad

salaire *sa·lehr m* wage, wages; salary; pay; **le salaire net** *sa·lehr net* take-home pay

salarié(e) *sa·la·ree·ay m/f* wage earner

sale *sal adj* dirty

salé(e) *sa·lay adj* salty; savo(u)ry (*not sweet*)

saleté *sal·tay f* dirt

salière *sa·lyehr f* salt cellar

salive *sa·leev f* saliva

salle *sal f* lounge (*at airport*); hall (*room*); ward (*in hospital*); auditorium; **la salle d'eau** *sal dō* shower room; **la salle de départ** *sal duh day·par* departure lounge; **la salle de séjour** *sal duh say·zhoor* living room; **la salle à manger** *sal a moñ·zhay* dining room; **la salle d'exposition** *sal dek·spo·zee·syoñ* showroom; **la salle d'attente** *sal da·toñt* waiting room (*at station*); **la salle de bains** *sal duh bañ* bathroom

salon *sa·loñ m* sitting room; lounge; **le salon de thé** *sa·loñ duh tay* tea-shop; **le salon de l'automobile** *sa·loñ duh lō·tō·mō·beel* motor show

salopette *sa·lo·pet f* dungarees

salutation *sa·lōō·ta·syoñ f* greeting

samedi *sam·dee m* Saturday

sanatorium *sa·na·to·ryum m* sanatorium

sanctions *soñk·syoñ fpl* sanctions

sandale *soñ·dal f* sandal

sandwich *soñd·weech m* sandwich; **un sandwich au jambon** *uñ soñd·weech ō zhoñ·boñ* a ham sandwich

sang *soñ m* blood

sanguin *soñ·gañ adj* blood (*group*)

sans *soñ prep* without; **sans eau** *soñ zō* neat (*liquor*); **sans essence** *e·truh soñs eh·soñs* to be out of petrol

santé *soñ·tay f* health; **à votre santé!** *a vo·truh soñ·tay* cheers!; **en bonne santé** *oñ bon soñ·tay* healthy (*person*)

sapeurs-pompiers *sa·pur·poñ·pyay mpl* fire brigade

sapin *sa·pañ m* fir (*tree*)

sarcastique *sar·kas·teek adj* sarcastic

Sardaigne *sar·deh·nyuh f* Sardinia

sardine *sar·deen f* sardine

satellite *sa·teh·leet m* satellite

satin *sa·tañ m* satin

satire *sa·teer f* satire

satisfaire* *sa·tees·fehr vt* satisfy

satisfaisant(e) *sa·tees·fuh·zoñ(·zoñt) adj* satisfactory

saturer *sa·tōō·ray vt* saturate (*market*)

sauce *sōs f* sauce; **la sauce de soja** *sōs duh·so·ya* soy(a) sauce; **la sauce tartare** *sōs tar·tar* tartar sauce

saucisse *sō·sees f* sausage

saucisson *sō·see·soñ m* slicing sausage; **le saucisson à l'ail** *sō·see·soñ a lye* garlic sausage

sauf *sōf prep* except (for), except(ing); **tous sauf lui** *toos sōf lwee* all but him

sauge *sōzh f* sage (*herb*)

saumon *sō·moñ m* salmon

sauna *sō·na m* sauna

sauté(e) *sō·tay adj* sauté

sauter *sō·tay vi* jump; blow (*fuse*); **sauter par-dessus un mur** *sō·tay par·duh·sōō uñ mōōr* to jump (over) a wall; **sauter à cloche-pied** *sō·tay a klosh·pyay* hop □ *vt* **sauter quelque**

chose *sō·tay kel·kuh shōz* to jump over something

sauvage *sō·vazh adj* wild

sauvegarde *sōv·gard f* safeguard

sauver *sō·vay vt* save (*person*); rescue; **se sauver** *suh sō·vay* to run away

sauvetage *sōv·tazh m* rescue

savoir* *sa·vwahr vt* know (*fact*); **savoir* faire quelque chose** *sa·vwahr fehr kel·kuh shōz* to know how to do something

savon *sa·voñ m* soap; **le savon à barbe** *sa·voñ a barb* shaving soap

savonnette *sa·vo·net f* bar of soap

scandinave *skoñ·dee·nav adj* Scandinavian

Scandinavie *skoñ·dee·na·vee f* Scandinavia

scarabée *ska·ra·bay m* beetle

scène *sen f* scene; stage (*in theatre*); **mettre* en scène** *meh·troñ sen* produce (*play*)

Schweppes *shweps m* tonic water

science *see·oñs f* science

science-fiction *see·oñs·feek·syoñ f* science fiction

scientifique *see·oñ·tee·feek adj* scientific □ *m/f* **le/la scientifique** *see·oñ·tee·feek* scientist

scooter *skoo·tehr m* scooter

score *skor m* score

scotch *skotch m* sellotape; Scotch (*liquor*)

scrutin *skrōō·tañ m* ballot

sculpture *skōōl·tōōr f* sculpture

se *suh pron* oneself; himself; herself; itself; themselves; **ils se lavent** *eel suh lav* they wash themselves

séance *say·oñs f* meeting; performance; **lever* la séance** *luh·vay la say·oñs* to adjourn

seau *sō m* bucket; pail

sec *sek adj* dried (*fruit, beans*); dry

sèche *sesh adj* dried (*fruit, beans*); dry

sèche-cheveux *sesh·shuh·vuh m* hairdrier

sécher* *say·shay vt* blot (*ink*); dry (*hair*); **faire* sécher** *fehr say·shay* dry (*clothes*)

sécheresse *say·shuh·res f* drought

séchoir *say·shwahr m* drier; **le séchoir à linge** *say·shwahr a lañzh* clotheshorse

secondaire *suh·goñ·dehr adj* secondary

second(e) *suh·goñ(·goñd) adj* second

seconde *suh·goñd f* second; second class

secouer *suh·koo·ay vt* shake

secours *suh·koor m* help; **au secours!** *ō suh·koor* help!

secret *suh·kreh m* secret □ *adj* **secret(ète)** *suh·kreh(·kret)* secret

secrétaire *suh·kray·tehr m/f* secretary; **le secrétaire particulier** *suh·kray·tehr par·tee·kōō·lyay* personal assistant, P.A.; **le secrétaire général** *suh·kray·tehr zhay·nay·ral* company secretary

secteur *sek·tur m* sector (*economy*); **le secteur postal** *sek·tur pos·tal* postal district; **le secteur privé** *sek·tur pree·vay* private sector; **le secteur public** *sek·tur pōō·bleek* public sector

sécurité *say·kōō·ree·tay f* security; safety; **la sécurité sociale** *say·kōō·ree·tay so·syal* social security; **en sécurité** *oñ say·kōō·ree·tay* safe (*out of danger*)

sédatif *say·da·teef m* sedative

séduisant(e) *say·dwee·zoñ(·zoñt) adj* seductive; attractive; glamorous

seigle *seh·gluh m* rye; **le pain de seigle** *pañ duh seh·gluh* rye bread
sein *sañ m* breast
seize *sez num* sixteen
seizième *seh·zyem adj* sixteenth
séjour *say·zhoor m* stay (period); visit
séjourner *say·zhoor·nay vi* stay (reside)
sel *sel m* salt; **sans sel** *soñ sel* unsalted (butter)
sélection *say·lek·syoñ f* selection
selle *sel f* saddle
selon *suh·loñ prep* according to
semaine *suh·men f* week; **chaque semaine** *shak suh·men* weekly
semblable *soñ·bla·bluh adj* like; similar; alike; **semblable à** *soñ·bla·bluh a* similar to
semblant *soñ·bloñ m* semblance; **faire* semblant de faire quelque chose** *fehr soñ·bloñ duh fehr kel·kuh shōz* to pretend to do something
sembler *soñ·blay vi* seem; look (appear)
semelle *suh·mel f* sole (of shoe)
sénat *say·na m* senate (political)
sénateur *say·na·tur m* senator
sens *soñs m* sense (feeling); meaning; direction; **le sens de l'humour** *soñs duh lōō·moor* sense of humour; **sens interdit** *soñs añ·tehr·dee* no entry (road); **sens unique** *soñs ōō·neek* one-way street; **avoir* du sens** *a·vwahr dōō soñs* to make sense
sensation *soñ·sa·syoñ f* sensation; feeling
sensible *soñ·see·bluh adj* sensitive
sentier *soñ·tyay m* footpath
sentiment *soñ·tee·moñ m* feeling (emotion)
sentir* *soñ·teer vt/i* smell □ *vt* taste; feel; **ça sent fort** *sa soñ for* it has a strong smell; **cette pièce sent le renfermé** *set pyes soñ luh roñ·fehr·may* the room smells stale; **je me sens mieux** *zhuh muh soñ myuh* I feel better; **sentir* l'ail** *soñ·teer lye* to smell of garlic
séparé(e) *say·pa·ray adj* separate
séparément *say·pa·ray·moñ adv* apart (separately)
séparer *say·pa·ray vt* separate; **se séparer** *suh say·pa·ray* separate; divide
sept *set num* seven
septembre *sep·toñ·bruh m* September
septième *seh·tyem adj* seventh
sergé *sehr·zhay m* twill
série *say·ree f* series; set; round (of talks)
sérieux *say·ryuh m* reliability (of person) □ *adj* **sérieux(euse)** *say·ryuh (·ryuhz)* serious; reliable
serpent *sehr·poñ m* snake
serpenter *sehr·poñ·tay vi* twist (road)
serre *sehr f* greenhouse
serré(e) *seh·ray adj* tight
serrer *seh·ray vt* grip; squeeze (hand); **serrer dans ses bras** *seh·ray doñ say bra* to hug; **serrer la main à quelqu'un** *seh·ray la mañ a kel·kuñ* to shake hands with someone; **serrer à droite** *seh·ray a drwat* keep to the right
serrure *seh·rōōr f* lock (on door); **le trou de la serrure** *troo duh la seh·rōōr* keyhole
serveuse *sehr·vuhz f* waitress; barmaid
service *sehr·vees m* service; service charge; favour; **les services sociaux** *sehr·vees so·syō* social services; **le service de la comptabilité** *sehr·vees*

duh la koñ·ta·bee·lee·tay accounts department; **le service de navette** *sehr·vees duh na·vet* shuttle (service) (airline); **le service du personnel** *sehr·vees dōō pehr·so·nel* personnel department; **rendre service à quelqu'un** *roñ·druh sehr·vees a kel·kuñ* to do someone a favour
serviette *sehr·vyet f* towel; briefcase; serviette; **la serviette hygiénique** *sehr·vyet ee·zhay·neek* sanitary towel
servir* *sehr·veer vt* dish up; serve □ *vi* **cela ne sert à rien** *suh·la nuh sehr a ryañ* it's no use □ *vr* **se servir* de** *suh sehr·veer duh* to use; **servez-vous** *sehr·vay·voo* help yourself
ses *say adj* his; its; her; **ses sœurs/frères** *say sur/frehr* her sisters/brothers; his sisters/brothers
set de table *set duh ta·bluh m* place mat
seul(e) *suhl adj* alone; lonely (person); **la seule femme présente** *la suhl fam pray·zoñt* the only woman there; **un seul** *uñ suhl* only one □ *adv* **seul** *suhl* alone; **il l'a fait tout seul** *eel la feh too suhl* he did it on his own
seulement *suhl·moñ adv* only; non seulement *noñ suhl·moñ* not only; **si seulement je pouvais... je pouvais...** *see suhl·moñ zhuh poo·veh* I wish I could...
sévère *say·vehr adj* harsh (severe); drastic
sexe *seks m* sex
sexy *sek·see adj* sexy
shampooing *shoñ·pwañ m* shampoo
shérif *shay·reef m* sheriff
sherry *sheh·ree m* sherry
short *short m* shorts
si *see conj* if; whether □ *adv* yes (in answer to negative question); **si content que... je** *see koñ·toñ kuh* so pleased that...
Sicile *see·seel f* Sicily
siècle *syeh·kluh m* century
siège *syezh m* seat; head office
le sien *luh syañ pron* his; hers; **la sienne** *la syen* his; hers; **les siens** *lay syañ* his; hers; **les siennes** *lay syen* his; hers
sieste *syest f* siesta
sifflement *see·fluh·moñ m* whistle (sound)
siffler *see·flay vi* whistle
sifflet *see·fleh m* whistle (object)
signal *see·nyal m* signal
signaler *see·nya·lay vt* report
signature *see·nya·tōōr f* signature
signe *see·nyuh m* sign
signer *see·nyay vt* sign (document)
signifier *see·nyee·fyay vt* mean (signify)
silence *see·loñs m* silence
silencieusement *see·loñ·syuhz·moñ adv* quietly (walk, work)
silencieux *see·loñ·syuh m* silencer (on car) □ *adj* **silencieux(euse)** *see·loñ·syuh(·syuhz)* silent
s'il vous plaît *seel voo pleh adv* please
simple *sañ·pluh adj* simple; single (not double)
sincère *sañ·sehr adj* sincere
singe *sañzh m* monkey; ape
sinon *see·noñ adv* otherwise; if not
sirène *see·ren f* siren
sirop *see·rō m* syrup; **le sirop pour la toux** *see·rō poor la too* cough medicine
site *seet m* site (of building)
situation *see·tōō·a·syoñ f* situation; position (job)

situé(e) *see·tōō·ay adj* located; **bien situé(e) pour les magasins** *byañ see·tōō·ay poor lay ma·ga·zañ* convenient for shops

six *sees num* six

sixième *see·zyem adj* sixth

ski *skee m* ski; skiing; **faire⋆ du ski** *fehr dōō skee* to ski; to go skiing

skieur *skee·ur m* skier

skieuse *skee·uhz f* skier

ski nautique *skee nō·teek m* waterskiing; **faire⋆ du ski nautique** *fehr dōō skee nō·teek* to go water-skiing

Slave *slav m/f* Slav

slip *sleep m* underpants; panties; briefs

slogan *slō·gon m* slogan

smoking *smo·keeng m* tuxedo; dinner jacket

snack *snak m* diner; snack bar

snob *snob m/f* snob □ *adj* snobbish

social(e) *so·syal adj* social

socialisme *so·sya·leez·muh m* socialism

socialiste *so·sya·leest m/f* socialist □ *adj* socialist

société *so·syay·tay f* corporation (*firm*); company; society; **la société anonyme** *so·syay·tay a·no·neem* private limited company; **la société par actions** *so·syay·tay par ak·syoñ* joint-stock company

S.O.S. *es·ō·es m* SOS

souci *soo·see m* concern (*anxiety*); worry

se soucier de *suh soo·syay duh vr* care about

soucoupe *soo·koop f* saucer

soudain *soo·dañ adv* suddenly □ *adj* **soudain(e)** *soo·dañ(·den)* sudden

soude *sood f* soda (*chemical*)

souder *soo·day vt* solder; weld

soufflé *soo·flay m* soufflé

souffler *soo·flay vi* blow

souffrir⋆ *soo·freer vi* suffer

soulagement *soo·lazh·moñ m* relief (*from pain, anxiety*)

soulager⋆ *soo·la·zhay vt* ease (*pain*)

soulever⋆ *soo·luh·vay vt* lift

soulier *soo·lyay m* shoe

souligner *soo·lee·nyay vt* underline; emphasize

soumettre⋆ *soo·meh·truh vt* submit (*proposal*)

soupape *soo·pap f* valve (*in machine*)

soupe *soop f* soup

souper *soo·pay m* supper

soupirer *soo·pee·ray vi* sigh

source *soors f* source; spring (*of water*)

sourcil *soor·seey m* eyebrow

sourd(e) *soor (soord) adj* deaf

sourire⋆ *soo·reer m* smile □ *vi* **sourire⋆** *soo·reer* smile; grin

souris *soo·ree f* mouse

sous *soo prep* underneath; under; **sous la pluie** *soo la plwee* in the rain

sous-comité *soo·ko·mee·tay m* subcommittee

souscripteur *soo·skreep·tur m* underwriter

souscrire⋆ *soo·skreer vt* underwrite (*insurance*)

sous-développé(e) *soo·day·vuh·lo·pay adj* underdeveloped (*country*)

sous-estimer *soo·zes·tee·may vt* under-value

sous-exposé(e) *soo·zek·spō·zay adj* underexposed

sous-marin *soo·ma·rañ m* submarine

sous-payé(e) *soo·pay·yay adj* underpaid

sous-sol *soo·sol m* basement

sous-titre *soo·tee·truh m* subtitle (*of movie*)

soustraire⋆ *soos·trehr vt* subtract

sous-traitant *soo·treh·toñ m* subcontractor

son *soñ adj* his; her; its; **son père** *soñ pehr* her father; his father

son *soñ m* sound

sonner *so·nay vt/i* ring; **la pendule a sonné trois heures** *la poñ·dōōl a so·nay trwah zur* the clock struck three

sonnerie *so·nuh·ree f* bell (*electric*)

sonnette *so·net f* bell (*on door*); **la sonnette d'alarme** *so·net da·larm* communication cord

sophistiqué(e) *so·fees·tee·kay adj* sophisticated

sorbet *sor·bay m* water ice

sorcière *sor·syehr f* witch

sorte *sort f* kind

sorti(e) *sor·tee adj* out (*not at home*)

sortie *sor·tee f* exit; **la sortie de secours** *sor·tee duh suh·koor* emergency exit

sortir⋆ *sor·teer vt* take out; release (*book, film*) □ *vi* come out; go out; **il est sorti de la maison en courant** *eel eh sor·tee duh la meh·zoñ oñ koo·roñ* he ran out of the house; **sortir⋆ avec quelqu'un** *sor·teer a·vek kel·kuñ* to go out with somebody

soie *swah f* silk; **une robe de soie** *ōōn rob duh swah* a silk dress

soif *swahf f* thirst; **avoir⋆ soif** *a·vwahr swahf* to be thirsty

soigné(e) *swah·nyay adj* neat (*appearance*)

soigner *swah·nyay vt* treat; nurse (*patient*)

soi-même *swah·mem pron* oneself

soin *swañ m* care (*carefulness*); **aux bons soins de** *ō boñ swañ duh* care of, c/o; **le soin des mains** *swañ day mañ* manicure

soir *swahr m* evening; **le soir** *luh swahr* in the evening; **ce soir** *suh swahr* tonight

soirée *swah·ray f* evening; party (*celebration*)

soixante *swah·soñt num* sixty

soixante-dix *swah·soñt·dees num* seventy

sol *sol m* ground; soil

solaire *so·lehr adj* solar

soldat *sol·da m* soldier

solde *sold m* balance (*remainder owed*) □ *f* pay

solder *sol·day vt* balance (*accounts*)

soldes *sold pl* sales (*cheap prices*)

sole *sōl f* sole (*fish*)

soleil *so·lay m* sunshine; sun; **prendre⋆ un bain de soleil** *proñ·druñ bañ duh so·lay* to sunbathe

solide *so·leed adj* solid (*not liquid, strong*); tough (*material*); strong (*structure, material*); durable (*fabric, article*); reliable (*car*); hard-wearing

solidité *so·lee·dee·tay f* strength (*of girder, rope etc*); reliability (*of car*)

solution *so·lōō·syoñ f* solution

sombre *soñ·bruh adj* dark; dim (*room*)

somme *som f* sum (*total amount*); **le petit somme** *puh·tee som* nap (*sleep*); **la somme totale** *som to·tal* sum total

sommeil *so·may m* sleep; **avoir⋆ sommeil** *a·vwar so·may* to be sleepy

sommeiller *so·may·yay vi* doze

sommelier *so·muh·lyay m* wine waiter

sommet *so·meh m* top (*of mountain*)

somnifère *som·nee·fehr m* sleeping pill

sous-traité *soo·treh·tay* m subcontract
sous-vêtements *soo·vet·moñ* mpl underwear; underclothes
soutenir* *soo·tuh·neer* vt support
souterrain(e) *soo·tay·rañ*(·ren) adj underground (pipe etc)
soutien *soo·tyañ* m backing; support (moral, financial)
soutien-gorge *soo·tyañ·gorzh* m bra
souvenir *soo·vuh·neer* m souvenir; un de mes souvenirs *uñ duh may soo·vuh·neer* one of my memories
se souvenir* de *suh soo·vuh·neer duh* vr remember
souvent *soo·voñ* adv often
soviétique *so·vyay·teek* adj Soviet
spaghettis *spa·geh·tee* mpl spaghetti
sparadrap *spa·ra·dra* m sticking-plaster; bandaid
spatule *spa·tool* f spatula
spécial(e) *spay·syal* adj special
spécialisé(e) *spay·sya·lee·zay* adj specialized
se spécialiser *suh spay·sya·lee·zay* vr specialize; se spécialiser en *suh spay·sya·lee·zay oñ* to specialize in
spécifications *spay·see·fee·ka·syoñ* fpl specifications
spécimen *spay·see·men* m specimen
spectacle *spek·ta·kluh* m scene (sight); show (in theatre); entertainment; le spectacle de variétés *spek·ta·kluh duh va·ree·ay·tay* variety show; le spectacle de cabaret *spek·ta·kluh duh ka·ba·reh* cabaret
spectateurs *spek·ta·tur* mpl audience (in theatre)
spiritueux *spee·ree·tôö·uh* m liquor □ mpl les spiritueux *spee·ree·tôö·uh* spirits (alcohol)
splendide *sploñ·deed* adj splendid
sport *spor* m sport; les sports d'hiver *spor dee·vehr* winter sports
squash *skwosh* m squash (sport)
stable *sta·bluh* adj stable; steady
stade *stad* m stadium
stagiaire *sta·zhee·ehr* m/f trainee
standard *stoñ·dar* m switchboard □ adj standard (model); regular (size)
standardiste *stoñ·dar·deest* m/f switchboard operator
starter *star·tehr* m choke (of car)
station *sta·syoñ* f station; la station d'essence *sta·syoñ deh·soñs* filling station; la station thermale *sta·syoñ tehr·mal* spa; la station balnéaire *sta·syoñ bal·nay·ehr* seaside resort; la station de taxis *sta·syoñ duh tak·see* taxi rank
stationnement *sta·syon·moñ* m parking; le stationnement en double file *sta·syon·moñ oñ doo·bluh feel* double-parking
stationner *sta·syo·nay* vi park
station-service *sta·syoñ·sehr·vees* f service station
statistique *sta·tees·teek* adj statistical □ f la statistique *sta·tees·teek* statistics
statue *sta·tôö* f statue
sténodactylo *stay·no·dak·tee·lo* m/f shorthand typist; stenographer
sténographie *stay·no·gra·fee* f shorthand
stéréo *stay·ray·ô* f stereo(phonic); en stéréo *oñ stay·ray·ô* in stereo
stéréophonique *stay·ray·ô·fo·neek* adj stereo(phonic)
stérile *stay·reel* adj sterile
stériliser *stay·ree·lee·zay* vt sterilize (disinfect)

steward *stôö·ar* m steward
stipulation *stee·pôö·la·syoñ* f stipulation
stipuler *stee·pôö·lay* vt stipulate
stock *stok* m stock (in shop); en stock *oñ stok* in stock
stockiste *sto·keest* m stockist
store *stor* m blind (at window); window shade
strict(e) *streekt* adj strict
strip-tease *streep·teez* m striptease
strip-teaseuse *streep·tee·zuhz* f stripper
structure *strôök·tôör* f structure
studio *stôö·dyô* m studio; one-room flat
stupide *stôö·peed* adj stupid; silly
style *steel* m style
styliste *stee·leest* m/f designer
stylo *stee·lô* m pen; fountain pen
subalterne *sôö·bal·tehrn* adj subordinate
subir *sôö·beer* vt suffer (pain, grief)
subordonné(e) *sôö·bor·do·nay* m/f subordinate
suborner *sôö·bor·nay* vt bribe
subsidiaire *sôöp·see·dyehr* adj subsidiary
subsistance *sôöb·zee·stoñs* f keep
subsister *sôöb·zees·tay* vi survive (custom)
substance *sôöp·stoñs* f substance; stuff
substantiel(le) *sôöp·stoñ·syel* adj filling (food)
subtil(e) *sôöp·teel* adj subtle
subvention *sôöb·voñ·syoñ* f subsidy; grant (to institution)
subventionner *sôöb·voñ·syo·nay* vt subsidize
succès *sôök·seh* m success; couronné(e) de succès *koo·ro·nay duh sôök·seh* successful (venture)
succursale *sôö·kôör·sal* f branch (of store, bank etc)
sucer* *sôö·say* vt/i suck
sucette *sôö·set* f lollipop
sucre *sôö·kruh* m sugar □ adj sucré(e) *sôö·kray* sweet (taste, food)
sucrier *sôö·kree·ay* m sugar bowl
sud *sôöd* m south; au sud ô *sôöd* in/to the south; du sud *dôö sôöd* southern
sud-africain(e) *sôöd·a·free·kañ*(·ken) adj South African
sud-américain(e) *sôöd·a·may·ree·kañ*(·ken) adj South American
sud-est *sôöd·est* m southeast
sud-ouest *sôöd·west* m southwest
Suède *swed* f Sweden
suédois *sway·dwah* m Swedish □ m/f le/la Suédois(e) *sway·dwah*(·dwaz) Swede □ adj suédois(e) *sway·dwah* (·dwaz) Swedish
suer *sôö·ay* vi sweat
sueur *sôö·ur* f sweat
suffire* *sôö·feer* vi be enough; merci, ça suffit *mehr·see sa sôö·fee* thank you, that's plenty
suggérer* *sôög·zhay·ray* vt suggest
suggestion *sôög·zhes·tyoñ* f suggestion
suicide *sôö·ee·seed* m suicide
suisse *swees* adj Swiss; elle/il est Suisse *el/eel eh swees* (s)he's Swiss
Suisse *swees* f Switzerland; en Suisse *oñ swees* in/to Switzerland
suite *sweet* f series; continuation; tout de suite *too duh sweet* at once; comme suite à votre lettre *kom sweet a vo·truh le·truh* with reference to your letter
suivant(e) *swee·voñ*(·voñt) adj following
suivre* *swee·vruh* vt follow; faire* sui-

vre *fehr swee·vruh* readdress; forward (*letter*)

sujet *sōō·zheh* m topic; subject

superficie *sōō·pehr·fee·see* f area (*of surface*)

supérieur(e) *sōō·pay·ryur* adj upper; higher; superior (*quality*) □ m/f le/la supérieur(e) *sōō·pay·ryur* superior

supermarché *sōō·pehr·mar·shay* m supermarket

superstition *sōō·pehr·stee·syoñ* f superstition

suppléant(e) *sōō·play·oñ(·oñt)* adj acting

supplémentaire *sōō·play·moñ·tehr* adj extra

support *sōō·por* m support; les supports visuels *sōō·por vee·zōō·el* visual aids

supporter *sōō·por·tay* vt support; bear (*endure*); stand □ m le supporter *sōō·por·tehr* fan (*supporter*)

supposer *sōō·po·zay* vt suppose; assume; je suppose qu'il viendra *zhuh sōō·pōz keel vyañ·dra* I suppose he'll come

suppositoire *sōō·po·zee·twahr* m suppository

sur *sōōr* prep on; onto; on top of; upon; 2 sur 10 *2 sōōr 10* 2 out of 10; 3 mètres sur 3 *3 meh·truh sōōr 3* 3 metres square

sûr(e) *sōōr* adj sure (*person*); ça marchera à coup sûr *sa mar·shuh·ra a koo sōōr* it's sure to work; il est sûr de venir *eel eh sōōr duh vuh·neer* he's sure to come

surcharge *sōōr·sharzh* f surcharge

surdose *sōōr·dōz* f overdose

sûrement *sōōr·moñ* adv surely; il va sûrement venir *eel va sōōr·moñ vuh·neer* he's sure to come

surexposé(e) *sōōr·ek·spō·zay* adj overexposed (*photo*)

surf *surf* m surfing; faire* du surf *fehr dōō surf* to go surfing

surface *sōōr·fas* f surface

surplus *sōōr·plōō* m surplus

surprendre* *sōōr·proñ·druh* vt surprise

surpris(e) *sōōr·pree(·preez)* adj surprised; surpris(e) par *sōōr·pree (·preez) par* surprised at

surprise *sōōr·preez* f surprise

surtout *sōōr·too* adv especially

surveillant(e) *sōōr·vay·yoñ(·yoñt)* m/f supervisor; le surveillant de plage *sōōr·vay·yoñ duh plazh* lifeguard

surveiller *sōōr·vay·yay* vt watch (*spy on*); guard (*prisoner*); supervise

survêtement *sōōr·vet·moñ* m track suit

survivre* *sōōr·vee·vruh* vi survive

suspendre* *sōōs·poñ·druh* vt suspend (*worker*)

suspension *sōōs·poñ·syoñ* f suspension (*on car*)

sweat-shirt *swet·shirt* m sweatshirt

syllabe *see·lab* f syllable

symbole *sañ·bol* m symbol

symbolique *sañ·bo·leek* adj symbolic; nominal (*fee*)

symétrique *see·may·treek* adj symmetrical

sympathique *sañ·pa·teek* adj nice; pleasant

symphonie *sañ·fo·nee* f symphony

symposium *sañ·pō·zyum* m symposium

symptôme *sañp·tōm* m symptom

synagogue *see·na·gog* f synagogue

synchronisation *sañ·kro·nee·za·syoñ* f synchromesh

syndicat *sañ·dee·ka* m trade union; syndicate

syndicat d'initiative *sañ·dee·ka dee·nee·sya·teev* m tourist office

synthétique *sañ·tay·teek* adj synthetic

Syrie *see·ree* f Syria

syrien(ne) *see·ree·añ(·en)* adj Syrian

systématique *sees·tay·ma·teek* adj systematic

système *sees·tem* m system

T

ta *ta* adj your (*familiar form*); ta mère *ta mehr* your mother

tabac *ta·ba* m tobacconist's (shop); tobacco; le marchand de tabac *mar·shoñ duh ta·ba* tobacconist; le tabac à priser *ta·ba a pree·zay* snuff

table *ta·bluh* f table; la table basse *ta·bluh bas* coffee table; la table pliante *ta·bluh plee·oñt* folding table; la table des matières *ta·bluh day ma·tyehr* contents (*table in book*); le set de table *set duh ta·bluh* place mat

tableau *ta·blō* m painting; picture; chart (*diagram, table*); le tableau de bord *ta·blō duh bor* dashboard

tablette de chocolat *ta·blet duh sho·kō·lah* f bar of chocolate

tablier *ta·blee·ay* m apron

tabouret *ta·boo·reh* m stool

tache *tash* f spot; patch; blot; stain

tâche *tash* f job; task

tacher *ta·shay* vt mark; stain

tactique *tak·teek* f tactics

taie d'oreiller *tay do·ray·yay* f pillowcase, pillowslip

taille *tye* f height (*of person*); size (*of clothes*); waist; grande taille *groñd tye* outsize (*clothes*)

tailler *tye·yay* vt trim (*hedge*)

tailleur *tye·yur* m tailor; suit (*women's*)

tailleur-pantalon *tye·yur·poñ·ta·loñ* m pant(s) suit

se taire *suh tehr* vr be silent; taisez-vous! *teh·zay·voo* be quiet!

talc *talk* m talc(um powder)

talent *ta·loñ* m talent

talon *ta·loñ* m heel; stub (*counterfoil*); les talons aiguilles *ta·loñ zay·gwee* stiletto heels

tambour *toñ·boor* m drum

tamis *ta·mee* m sieve; passer au tamis *pa·say ō ta·mee* to sieve

tamiser *ta·mee·zay* vt sieve

tampon *toñ·poñ* m pad; plug; tampon; le tampon abrasif *toñ·poñ a·bra·zeef* scourer

tango *toñ·gō* m tango

tanguer *toñ·gay* vi sway (*building, bridge*)

tant *toñ* adv so many/much; tant de *toñ duh* such a lot of, so much/many

tante *toñt* f aunt(ie)

taper *ta·pay* vt slam; taper à la machine *ta·pay a la ma·sheen* type (*letter*)

tapis *ta·pee* m carpet; le petit tapis *puh·tee ta·pee* rug; mat; le tapis de sol *ta·pee duh sol* groundsheet

tapisser *ta·pee·say* vt paper (*wall*)

tard *tar* adv late; tard dans la journée *tar doñ la zhoor·nay* late in the day; plus tard *plōō tar* later

tarif *ta·reef* m rate (*price*); tariff (*list of charges*); le tarif douanier *ta·reef dwa·nyay* tariff (*tax*)

tartan *tar·toñ* m tartan

tarte *tart* f flan; tart

tas *ta m* heap

tasse *tas f* cup; mug; **la tasse à café** *tas a ka·fay* coffee cup; **la tasse à thé** *tas a tay* teacup

taureau *to·rō m* bull

taux *tō m* rate; **le taux du change** *tō dōō shoñzh* exchange rate; **le taux de l'inflation** *tō duh lañ·fla·syoñ* rate of inflation; **le taux fixe** *tō feeks* flat rate; **le taux d'intérêt** *tō dañ·tay·reh* interest rate

taxe *taks f* duty; tax (*on goods*); **la taxe à la valeur ajoutée** *taks a la va·lur a·zhoo·tay* value-added tax

taxer *tak·say vt* tax (*goods*)

taxi *tak·see m* taxi; **aller* en taxi** *a·lay oñ tak·see* to go by taxi

Tchécoslovaquie *che·ko·slō·va·kee f* Czechoslovakia

tchèque *chek adj* Czech(oslovakian)

te, t' *tuh pron* you (*familiar form*)

technicien *tek·nee·syañ m* technician

technicienne *tek·nee·syen f* technician

technique *tek·neek f* technique □ *adj* technical

technologie *tek·no·lo·zhee f* technology

technologique *tek·no·lo·zheek adj* technological

tee *tee m* tee (*in golf*)

tee-shirt *tee·shurt m* T-shirt

teindre *tañ·druh vt* dye

teint *tañ m* complexion; **bon teint** *boñ tañ* fast (*dye*)

teinture *tañ·tōōr f* dye

teinturerie *tañ·tōō·ruh·ree f* dry-cleaner's

tel(le) *tel adj* such; **un tel livre** *uñ tel lee·vruh* such a book; **de tels livres** *duh tel lee·vruh* such books; **une telle gentillesse** *ōōn tel zhoñ·tee·yes* such kindness

télé *tay·lay f* TV

télécommande *tay·lay·ko·moñd f* remote control

télécommunications *tay·lay·ko·mōō·nee·ka·syoñ fpl* telecommunications

télégramme *tay·lay·gram m* telegram

télégraphier *tay·lay·gra·fyay vt* telegraph

télémètre *tay·lay·meh·truh m* range finder (*on camera*)

téléobjectif *tay·lay·ob·zhek·teef m* telephoto lens

téléphone *tay·lay·fon m* telephone; **être* au téléphone** *eh·trō tay·lay·fon* to be on the telephone; **par téléphone** *par tay·lay·fon* by telephone

téléphoner *tay·lay·fo·nay vi* telephone; **téléphoner à** *tay·lay·fo·nay a* telephone (*person*); **téléphoner en P.C.V.** *tay·lay·fo·nay oñ pay·say·vay* to reverse the charges

téléphoniste *tay·lay·fo·neest m/f* telephonist; operator

télescope *tay·leh·skop m* telescope

télésiège *tay·lay·syezh m* chair-lift

téléviser *tay·lay·vee·zay vt* televise; broadcast (*on television*)

téléviseur *tay·lay·vee·zur m* television (*set*)

télévision *tay·lay·vee·zyoñ f* television; video; **la télévision en circuit fermé** *tay·lay·vee·zyoñ oñ seer·kwee fehr·may* closed circuit television; **la télévision en couleur** *tay·lay·vee·zyoñ oñ koo·lur* colo(u)r TV; **à la télévision** *a la tay·lay·vee·zyoñ* on television; on video

télex *tay·leks m* telex; **par télex** *par tay·leks* by telex

tellement *tel·moñ adv* so (much)

témoignage *tay·mwah·nyazh m* evidence (*of witness*)

témoin *tay·mwañ m* witness

température *toñ·pay·ra·tōōr f* temperature; **prendre* la température de quelqu'un** *proñ·druh la toñ·pay·ra·tōōr duh kel·kuñ* to take someone's temperature

tempête *toñ·pet f* storm; **la tempête de neige** *toñ·pet duh nezh* snowstorm

temple *toñ·pluh m* church; temple (*building*)

temporaire *toñ·po·rehr adj* temporary

temps *toñ m* weather; time; **peu de temps** *puh duh toñ* a short time; **dans le temps** *doñ luh toñ* in times past; **de temps en temps** *duh toñ zoñ toñ* occasionally; from time to time; **juste à temps** *zhōōst a toñ* just in time; **à temps partiel** *a toñ par·syel* part-time

tendance *toñ·doñs f* tendency; trend; **avoir* tendance à faire quelque chose** *a·vwahr toñ·doñs a fehr kel·kuh shōz* to tend to do something

tendre *toñ·druh adj* tender (*meat, vegetables*) □ *vt* stretch (*fabric etc*); **il a tendu la main** *eel a toñ·dōō la mañ* he put out his hand

tendu(e) *toñ·dōō adj* tense

tenir* *tuh·neer vt* hold; **tenez-le tranquille** *tuh·nay·luh troñ·keel* hold him still; **tiens-toi bien!** *tyañ·twah byañ* behave yourself!; **tenir* quelque chose au chaud** *tuh·neer kel·kuh shōz ō shō* to keep something hot

tennis *teh·nees m* tennis; **le tennis sur gazon** *teh·nees sōōr ga·zoñ* lawn tennis; **les tennis** *teh·nees* gym shoes, sneakers

tension *toñ·syoñ f* blood pressure; voltage; **la tension nerveuse** *toñ·syoñ nehr·vuhz* stress

tentative *toñ·ta·teev f* attempt

tente *toñt f* tent

tenter *toñ·tay vt* tempt

tenue *tuh·nōō f* clothes, dress; **tenue de soirée** *tuh·nōō duh swa·ray* evening dress

tergal *tehr·gal m* terylene

terme *tehrm m* term (*word*); **les termes** *lay tehrm* terms (*of contract*); **à long terme** *a loñ tehrm* long-term

terminal *tehr·mee·nal m* terminal (*computer*)

terminer *tehr·mee·nay vt* end

terne *tehrn adj* drab

terrain *teh·rañ m* ground; land; field (*for football etc*); course (*for golf*); **le terrain de sport** *teh·rañ duh spor* playing field; **le terrain de camping** *teh·rañ duh koñ·ping* camping site

terrasse *tay·ras f* terrace

terre *tehr f* land (*opposed to sea*); earth; ground; **à terre** *a tehr* ashore

terrible *teh·ree·bluh adj* terrible

territoire *teh·ree·twahr m* territory

terrorisme *teh·ro·reez·muh m* terrorism

terroriste *teh·ro·reest m/f* terrorist

tes *tay adj* your (*familiar form*); **tes sœurs** *tay sur* your sisters

test *test m* test (*in school etc*)

testament *tes·ta·moñ m* will (*testament*)

tête *tet f* head; **être* en tête** *eh·troñ tet* to lead (*in contest*)

tétine *tay·teen f* dummy; teat, nipple (*for bottle*)

têtu(e) *teh·tōō adj* stubborn

texte *tekst m* text

textiles *tek·steel* mpl textiles

texture *tek·stoor* f texture

thé *tay* m tea

théâtre *tay·ah·truh* m drama (art); theater, theatre; **aller* au théâtre** *a·lay o tay·ah·truh* to go to the theatre

théière *tay·yehr* f teapot

théorie *tay·o·ree* f theory

thermomètre *tehr·mo·meh·truh* m thermometer

thermos *tehr·mos* f Thermos (flask)

thon *toñ* m tuna(-fish)

thym *tañ* m thyme

tibia *tee·bya* m shin

ticket *tee·keh* m ticket (for bus, metro)

le tien *luh tyañ* pron yours (familiar form); **la tienne** *la tyen* yours; **où sont les tiens?** *oo soñ lay tyañ* where are yours?

tiers *tyehr* m third party; **l'assurance au tiers** *a·sōō·roñs ō tyehr* third party insurance

Tiers-Monde *tyehr·moñd* m Third World

tige *teezh* f stem

tigre *tee·gruh* m tiger

timbre *tañ·bruh* m stamp

timbre-prime *tañ·bruh·preem* m trading stamp

timbrer *tañ·bray* vt stamp (letter)

timide *tee·meed* adj shy

tire-bouchon *teer·boo·shoñ* m corkscrew

tirer *tee·ray* vi shoot □ vt/i pull; **tirer la chasse d'eau** *tee·ray la shas dō* to flush the toilet; **tirer des bords** *tee·ray day bor* to tack (sailing)

tiret *tee·reh* m dash (in writing)

tiroir *tee·rwahr* m drawer

tisane *tee·zan* f herbal tea

tisser *tee·say* vt weave

tissu *tee·sōō* m material; fabric; **le tissu écossais** *tee·sōō ay·ko·seh* plaid; **le tissu ouaté** *tee·sōō wa·tay* lint

titre *tee·truh* m title; **les titres** *tee·truh* securities; qualifications

toast *tōst* m toast; **porter un toast à quelqu'un** *por·tay uñ tōst a kel·kuñ* to propose a toast to someone

toboggan *to·bo·goñ* m flyover (road); slide (chute)

toi *twah* pron you

toile *twahl* f canvas; **la toile de jean** *twahl duh jeen* denim

toilette *twah·let* f washing; getting ready; **faire* sa toilette** *fehr sa twah·let* to get washed

toilettes *twah·let* fpl toilet; powder room; washroom

toi-même *twah·mem* pron yourself (familiar form)

toit *twah* m roof; **le toit ouvrant** *twah oo·vroñ* sunroof

tôle ondulée *tōl oñ·dōō·lay* f corrugated iron

tomate *to·mat* f tomato

tombe *toñb* f grave; tomb

tomber *toñ·bay* vi fall (over/down); drop; **faire* tomber** *fehr toñ·bay* to knock over; **tomber amoureux(euse)** *toñ·bay a·moo·ruh(·ruhz)* to fall in love; **laisser tomber** *leh·say toñ·bay* to drop (let fall)

ton *toñ* m tone □ adj your (familiar form); **ton père** *toñ pehr* your father

tonalité *to·na·lee·tay* f dial(ling) tone; **la tonalité occupé** *to·na·lee·tay o·kōō·pay* engaged/busy signal

tondeuse *toñ·duhz* f mower; **la tondeuse à gazon** *toñ·duhz a ga·zoñ* lawn mower

tondre *toñ·druh* vt mow

tonique *to·neek* m tonic (medicine)

tonne *ton* f tonne; ton

tonneau *to·nō* m barrel (for beer)

tonnerre *to·nehr* m thunder

topinambour *to·pee·noñ·boor* m Jerusalem artichoke

torchon *tor·shoñ* m tea-cloth

tordre *tor·druh* vt twist

tordu(e) *tor·dōō* adj crooked

tornade *tor·nad* f whirlwind

tort *tor* m fault; **vous avez tort** *voo za·vay tor* you're wrong

torticolis *tor·tee·ko·lee* m stiff neck

tôt *tō* adv early; **plus tôt** *plōō tō* earlier; **il est venu trop tôt** *eel eh vuh·nōō trō tō* he came too soon

total *to·tal* m total; **le total partiel** *to·tal par·syel* subtotal

total(e) *to·tal* adj total

touche *toosh* f key (of piano, typewriter)

toucher *too·shay* vt feel; touch; **toucher à** *too·shay* a handle (touch) □ m **c'est doux au toucher** *seh doo ō too·shay* it feels soft

toujours *too·zhoor* adv always; still

toupet *too·peh* m cheek (impudence)

tour *toor* f tower; **la tour de contrôle** *toor duh koñ·trōl* control tower; **la tour d'habitation** *toor da·bee·ta·syoñ* high-rise (block)

tour *toor* m trip; walk; ride; trick (malicious); **aller* faire un tour** *a·lay fehr uñ toor* to go for a stroll etc; **faire* un tour en voiture** *fehr uñ toor oñ vwah·tōōr* to go for a ride (by car); **faire* le tour d'un champ** *fehr luh toor duñ shoñ* to go round a field; **le tour de poitrine** *toor duh pwah·treen* bust measurements; **le tour de piste** *toor duh peest* lap (of track); **à tour de rôle** *a toor duh rōl* in turn

tourbière *toor·byehr* f bog

tourbillon *toor·bee·yoñ* m whirlpool

tourisme *too·reez·muh* m tourism; tourist trade; sightseeing

touriste *too·reest* m/f tourist; **la classe touriste** *klas too·reest* tourist class

tournant *toor·noñ* m turn (bend in road)

tourné(e) *toor·nay* adj sour (milk); off

tourner *toor·nay* vt turn □ vi turn (person, car); spin (rotate)

tournevis *toor·nuh·vees* m screwdriver

tourte *toort* f pie

tous *too* adj all (with plural noun); **tous les passagers** *too lay pa·sa·zhay* all the passengers; **tous les deux jours** *too lay duh zhoor* every other day; **tous les six jours** *too lay see zhoor* every 6th day

tous *toos* pron all (plural); **ils savent tous que...** *eel sav toos kuh* all of them know that...

tousser *too·say* vi cough

tout *too* pron everything; all (singular); **tout ce qu'il vous faut** *too suh keel voo fō* all you need □ adv tout de même *too duh mem* still (nevertheless); **pas du tout** *pa dōō too* not at all; **le tout dernier** *luh too dehrn·yay* the very last; **tout droit** *too drwah* straight ahead; **tout seul** *too sul* all alone

tout à fait *toot a feh* adv quite (absolutely)

tout de suite *too duh sweet* adv straight away

tout(e) *too (toot)* adj all (with singular noun); **tout le pain** *luh pañ* all the bread; **toute la journée** *toot la zhoor·nay* all day

toutes *toot adj* all (with plural noun); **toutes les tables** *toot lay ta·bluh* all the tables □ *pron* all (plural)

tout le monde *too luh moñd pron* everybody, everyone

toux *too f* cough

toxicomane *tok·see·ko·man m/f* addict

trace *tras f* trace (mark)

tracteur *trak·tur m* tractor

traction avant *trak·syoñ a·voñ f* front-wheel drive; **la traction arrière** *trak·syoñ a·ryehr* rear-wheel drive

tradition *tra·dee·syoñ f* tradition

traduction *tra·dōōk·syoñ f* translation

traduire* *tra·dweer vt* translate

train *trañ m* train; **par le train** *par luh trañ* by train

train auto-couchettes *trañ ō·tō·koo·shet m* car-sleeper train

traîne *tren f* train (on dress)

traineau *treh·nō m* sleigh; sledge

trainer *treh·nay vt* drag □ *vi* **des affaires qui trainent un peu partout** *day za·fehr kee tren uñ puh par·too* things lying around

trait *treh m* line; **le trait d'union** *treh dōō·nyoñ* hyphen

traite *tret f* draft (financial); bank bill

traitement *tret·moñ m* treatment; course of treatment; **le traitement des données** *tret·moñ day dō·nay* data processing

traiter *treh·tay vt* treat □ *vi* **traiter avec une firme** *treh·tay a·vek ōōn feerm* to deal with a firm; **traiter d'un sujet** *treh·tay duñ sōō·zheh* to deal with a subject

traits *treh mpl* features

trajet *tra·zhay m* journey; **ce n'est qu'un petit trajet** *suh neh kuñ puh·tee tra·zhay* it's only a short ride

tramway *tram·way m* streetcar; tram(car)

tranchant *troñ·shoñ m* edge (of blade) □ *adj* **tranchant(e)** *troñ·shoñ(·shoñt)* sharp (knife)

tranche *troñsh f* slice; **couper en tranches** *koo·pay oñ troñsh* to slice

tranquille *troñ·keel adj* quiet

tranquillisant *troñ·kee·lee·zoñ m* tranquillizer

transaction *troñ·zak·syoñ f* transaction

transatlantique *troñ·zat·loñ·teek adj* transatlantic

transférer* *troñs·fay·ray vt* transfer (money)

transistor *troñ·zees·tor m* transistor

en transit *oñ troñ·zeet adv* in transit

transmetteur *troñz·meh·tur m* transmitter

transmission *troñz·mees·yoñ f* transmission (of car)

transparent(e) *troñ·spa·roñ(·roñt) adj* transparent

transpirer *troñ·spee·ray vi* perspire

transport *troñ·spor m* transport; **le transport par avion** *troñ·spor par a·vyoñ* air freight

transporter *troñ·spor·tay vt* carry; transport; ship (goods)

travail *tra·vye m* work; **du bon travail** *dōō boñ tra·vye* a good piece of work; **le travail à la pièce** *tra·vye a la pyes* piecework; **aller* au travail** *a·lay ō tra·vye* to go to work; **le travail de manœuvre** *tra·vye duh ma·nuh·vruh* unskilled labo(u)r

travailler *tra·vye·yay vi* work

travaux *tra·vō mpl* road works

à travers *a tra·vehr prep* through

travers de porc *tra·vehr duh por m* spare rib

traversée *tra·vehr·say f* crossing (voyage)

traverser *tra·vehr·say vt* cross (road, sea); **traverser la Manche à la nage** *tra·vehr·say la moñsh a la nazh* to swim the Channel; **nous avons traversé la France en voiture** *noo za·voñ tra·vehr·say la froñs oñ vwah·tōōr* we drove across France

traversin *tra·vehr·sañ m* bolster

trébucher *tray·bōō·shay vi* trip (stumble)

trèfle *treh·fluh m* clubs (in cards)

treize *trez num* thirteen

treizième *treh·zyem adj* thirteenth

tremblement de terre *troñ·bluh·moñ duh tehr m* earthquake

trembler *troñ·blay vi* tremble

tremper *troñ·pay vt* dip (into liquid); **faire* tremper** *fehr troñ·pay* soak (washing)

trente *troñt num* thirty

trente-trois tours *troñt·trwah toor m* L.P.

trentième *troñ·tyem adj* thirtieth

trépied *tray·pyay m* tripod

très *treh adv* very; much

trésor *tray·zor m* treasure

triangle *tree·oñ·gluh m* triangle

tribu *tree·bōō f* tribe

tricher *tree·shay vi* cheat

tricot *tree·kō m* knitting; jersey (sweater); **le tricot de corps** *tree·kō duh kor* vest (undergarment); **les tricots** *tree·kō* knitwear

tricoter *tree·ko·tay vt/i* knit

trictrac *treek·trak m* backgammon

trimestre *tree·mes·truh m* term (of school etc)

tringle *trañ·gluh f* rod (metallic)

tripes *treep fpl* tripe

triste *treest adj* sad

trois *trwah num* three

troisième *trwah·zyem adj* third; **la troisième vitesse** *trwah·zyem vee·tes* third (gear)

trombone *troñ·bon m* paper clip

tromper *troñ·pay vt* deceive

trompette *troñ·pet f* trumpet

tronc *troñ m* trunk (of tree)

trop *trō adv* too; too much; **il est trop grand** *eel eh trō groñ* he's too big; **trop de livres** *trō duh lee·vruh* too many books

tropical(e) *tro·pee·kal adj* tropical

tropiques *tro·peek mpl* tropics

trotter *tro·tay vi* trot (horse)

trottoir *tro·twahr m* pavement, sidewalk; **le trottoir roulant** *tro·twahr roo·loñ* moving walkway

trou *troo m* gap; pit; hole

troubles *troo·bluh mpl* trouble (medical disorder); **les troubles dans ce pays** *lay troo·bluh doñ suh pay·yee* the troubles in this country

troupe *troop f* troop

troupeau *troo·pō m* flock

trousse de pharmacie *troos duh far·ma·see f* first-aid kit; **la trousse à ongles** *troos a oñ·gluh* manicure set

trouver *troo·vay vt* find; **se trouver** *suh troo·vay* to be; **je trouve que... zhuh troov kuh** I feel that...

truffe *trōōf f* truffle (fungus)

truite *trweet f* trout

trust *trust m* trust (company)

T-shirt *tee·shurt m* tee shirt

T.S.V.P. *abbrev* P.T.O.

tu *tōō pron* you (*familiar form*)
tuba *tōō·ba m* snorkel
tube *tōōb m* tube; **le tube fluorescent** *tōōb flōō·o·reh·soñ* fluorescent light
tuer *tōō·ay vt* kill
tuile *tweel f* tile (*on roof*)
tulipe *tōō·leep f* tulip
tunique *tōō·neek f* tunic (*of uniform*)
Tunisie *tōō·nee·zee f* Tunisia
tunisien(ne) *tōō·nee·zyañ(·zyen) adj* Tunisian
tunnel *tōō·nel m* tunnel
turbot *tōōr·bō m* turbot
turc *toork adj* Turkish
turque *toork adj* Turkish
Turquie *tōōr·kee f* Turkey
turquoise *tōōr·kwahz adj* turquoise
tuteur *tōō·tur m* guardian
tutrice *tōō·trees f* guardian
tuyau *twee·yō m* pipe (*tube*); hose (*pipe*); **le tuyau d'écoulement** *twee·yō day·kool·moñ* drainpipe; **le tuyau d'échappement** *twee·yō day·shap·moñ* exhaust
T.V.A. *tay·vay·a f* V.A.T.
type *teep m* type; fellow
typique *tee·peek adj* typical

U

ulcère *ōōl·sehr m* ulcer
ultérieur(e) *ōōl·tay·ryur adj* later (*date etc*)
ultimatum *ōōl·tee·ma·tum m* ultimatum
ultra-courtes *ōōl·tra·koort fpl* V.H.F.
ultra-rapide *ōōl·tra·ra·peed adj* high-speed
un(e) *uñ (ōōn) num* one □ *art* an; a □ *pron* **l'un (l'une) de vous deux** *luñ (lōōn) duh voo duh* either of you; **l'un(e) l'autre** *luñ (lōōn) lō·truh* one another
unanime *ōō·na·neem adj* unanimous (*decision*)
Unesco *ōō·ne·skō f* UNESCO
uni(e) *ōō·nee adj* plain (*not patterned*)
uniforme *ōō·nee·form m* uniform
unilatéral(e) *ōō·nee·la·tay·ral adj* unilateral
union *ōō·nyoñ f* union
Union Soviétique *ōō·nyoñ so·vyay·teek f* Soviet Union
unique *ōō·neek adj* unique; single
unir *ōō·neer vt* unite
unisexe *ōō·nee·seks adj* unisex
unitaire *ōō·nee·tehr adj* unit (*price*)
unité *ōō·nee·tay f* unit (*of measurement*)
univers *ōō·nee·vehr m* universe
universel(le) *ōō·nee·vehr·sel adj* universal
université *ōō·nee·vehr·see·tay f* university
urbain(e) *ōōr·bañ(·ben) adj* urban
urgence *ōōr·zhoñs f* urgency; emergency; **d'urgence** *dōōr·zhoñs* urgently
urgent(e) *ōōr·zhoñ(·zhoñt) adj* urgent
U.R.S.S. *ōō·ehr·es·es f* U.S.S.R.
usage *ōō·zazh m* use; **en usage** *oñ nōō·zazh* in use
usé(e) *ōō·zay adj* worn; **complètement usé(e)** *koñ·plet·moñ ōō·zay* worn-out (*object*)
user *ōō·zay vt* wear out; **s'user** *sōō·zay* wear (out) (*fabric*)
usine *ōō·zeen f* factory; plant; works
usure *ōō·zōōr f* wear and tear
utérus *ōō·tay·rōōs m* womb
utile *ōō·teel adj* useful

utiliser *ōō·tee·lee·zay vt* use

V

vacances *va·koñs fpl* holiday (*period*); vacation; **en vacances** *oñ va·koñs* on holiday; on vacation
vacancier *va·koñ·syay m* holiday-maker, vacationer
vacarme *va·karm m* row (*noise*)
vaccination *vak·see·nas·yoñ f* vaccination
vache *vash f* cow
vague *vag f* wave (*in sea*) □ *adj* vague
en vain *oñ vañ adv* in vain
vaincre* *vañ·kruh vt* defeat
vaisselle *veh·sel f* crockery; **faire* la vaisselle** *fehr la veh·sel* to wash up
valable *va·la·bluh adj* valid
valet *va·leh m* jack (*cards*); **le valet de chambre** *va·leh duh shoñ·bruh* valet (*in hotel*)
valeur *va·lur f* value; **les valeurs** *va·lur* stocks (*financial*); **les valeurs vedettes** *va·lur vuh·det* blue chips; **prendre* de la valeur** *proñ·druh duh la va·lur* to appreciate (*in value*); **de grande valeur** *duh groñd va·lur* valuable; **les objets de valeur** *ob·zhay duh va·lur* valuables; **la valeur marchande** *va·lur mar·shoñd* market value
valise *va·leez f* suitcase; grip (*case*); **faire* sa valise** *fehr sa va·leez* to pack one's case
vallée *va·lay f* valley
vallonné(e) *va·lo·nay adj* hilly
valoir* *va·lwahr vt* to be worth; **ça en vaut la peine** *sa oñ vō la pen* it's worth it; **il vaut mieux faire** *eel vō myuh fehr* it's better to do
valse *vals f* waltz
valve *valv f* valve (*holding in air*)
vandale *voñ·dal m/f* vandal
vanille *va·neey f* vanilla
vaniteux(euse) *va·nee·tuh(·tuhz) adj* conceited; vain
se vanter *suh voñ·tay vr* boast
vapeur *va·pur m* steamer (*ship*) □ *f* **la vapeur** *va·pur* steam; **cuire* à la vapeur** *kweer a la va·pur* to steam (*food*)
vaporisateur *va·po·ree·za·tur m* spray (*container*)
vaporiser *va·po·ree·zay vt* spray (*liquid*)
variable *va·ree·a·bluh adj* variable □ *f* **la variable** *va·ree·a·bluh* variable
variation *va·ree·a·syoñ f* variation
varicelle *va·ree·sel f* chicken pox
varier *va·ree·ay vi* vary
variété *va·ree·ay·tay f* variety
variole *va·ryol f* smallpox
Varsovie *var·so·vee f* Warsaw
vase *vaz m* vase
vaseline *vas·leen f* vaseline; petroleum jelly
Vatican *va·tee·koñ m* Vatican
veau *vō m* calf; veal
vedette *vuh·det f* star (*celebrity*); launch
végétarien(ne) *vay·zhay·tay·ree·añ (·en) adj* vegetarian
véhicule *vay·ee·kōōl m* vehicle
veille *vay f* the day before; **la veille** *la vay* on the previous day; **la veille de Noël** *vay duh no·el* Christmas Eve
veilleuse *vay·yuhz f* pilot light (*gas*)
veine *ven f* vein
velours *vuh·loor m* velvet; **le velours côtelé** *vuh·loor kōt·lay* corduroy

venaison *vuh·nay·zoñ* f venison

vendange *voñ·doñzh* f harvest (of grapes)

vendanger* *voñ·doñ·zhay* vt harvest (grapes)

vendeur *voñ·duhr* m vendor; clerk (in store); sales assistant

vendeuse *voñ·duhz* f clerk (in store); sales assistant

vendre *voñ·druh* vt sell; market (product); les X se vendent bien *lay X suh voñd byañ* there is a good market for X; vendre quelque chose 400 francs *voñ·druh kel·kuh shôz 400 froñ* to sell something for 400 francs

vendredi *voñ·druh·dee* m Friday; venez vendredi *vuh·nay voñ·druh·dee* come on Friday; le Vendredi Saint *voñ·druh·dee sañ* Good Friday

vénéneux(euse) *vay·nay·nuh(·nuhz) adj* poisonous (substance)

venimeux(euse) *vuh·nee·muh(·muhz) adj* poisonous (snake)

venir* *vuh·neer* vi come; elle viendrait si... *el vyañ·dreh see* she would come if...; il vient de partir *eel vyañ duñ par·teer* he's just left; nous venons demain? *noo vuh·noñ duh·mañ* shall we come tomorrow?; venir* de Londres *vuh·neer duh loñ·druh* to come from London

Venise *vuh·neez* f Venice

vent *voñ* m wind (breeze); exposé(e) au vent *ek·spô·zay ô voñ* windy (place); il y a du vent *eel ya dōō voñ* it's windy

vente *voñt* f sale; la vente aux enchères *voñt ô zoñ·shehr* auction; la vente à crédit *voñt a kray·dee* hire purchase; la vente au détail *voñt ô day·tye* retail; la vente en gros *voñt oñ grô* wholesale

ventilateur *voñ·tee·la·tur* m fan (electric); ventilator

ventre *voñ·truh* m stomach

ver *vehr* m worm

véranda *vay·roñ·da* f veranda

verbal(e) *vehr·bal adj* verbal (agreement)

verdict *vehr·deekt* m verdict

verger *vehr·zhay* m orchard

verglas *vehr·gla* m black ice

vérification *vay·ree·fee·ka·syoñ* f check(ing); la vérification ponctuelle *vay·ree·fee·ka·syoñ poñk·tōō·el* spot check

vérifier *vay·ree·fyay* vt audit; check

vérité *vay·ree·tay* f truth

vermouth *vehr·moot* m vermouth

vernis *vehr·nee* m varnish; le vernis à ongles *vehr·nee a oñ·gluh* nail polish, nail varnish

verre *vehr* m glass; le verre à vin *vehr a vañ* wineglass; les verres de contact *vehr duh koñ·takt* contact lenses; le petit verre d'alcool *puh·tee vehr dal·kol* short drink

verrerie *veh·ruh·ree* f glass (glassware)

verrou *veh·roo* m bolt

verrouiller *veh·roo·yay* vt bolt (door, gate)

verrue *veh·rōō* f wart

vers *vehr* prep toward(s); about; vers le haut *vehr luh ô* upward(s)

versement *vehrs·moñ* m payment; instal(l)ment

verser *vehr·say* vt pour; pay

version *vehr·syoñ* f version

vert(e) *vehr (vehrt) adj* green

vertical(e) *vehr·tee·kal adj* vertical

vertige *vehr·teezh* f dizzy spell; pris(e) de vertige *pree (preez) duh vehr·teezh* dizzy (person)

vessie *veh·see* f bladder

veste *vest* f jacket; la veste de sport *vest duh spor* sports coat, sports jacket

vestiaire *ves·tyehr* m cloakroom

veston *ves·toñ* m jacket

vêtement *vet·moñ* m garment

vêtements *vet·moñ* mpl clothes; les vêtements de sport *vet·moñ duh spor* casual clothes, casual wear; sportswear

vétérinaire *vay·tay·ree·nehr* m/f vet(erinary surgeon)

veto *vay·tô* m veto; opposer son veto à *o·pô·zay soñ vay·tô a* to veto

veuf *vuhf* m widower

veuve *vuhv* f widow

via *vee·a* prep via

viaduc *vee·a·dōōk* m viaduct

viande *vyoñd* f meat

vice-président *vees·pray·zee·doñ* m vice chairman; vice president

vice versa *vee·sa vehr·sa adv* vice versa

vichy *vee·shee* m gingham

victime *veek·teem* f victim

victoire *veek·twar* f victory

vide *veed adj* empty

vider *vee·day* vt empty; drain (sump, pool)

vie *vee* f life; à vie *a vee* for life

vieille *vyay adj* old

Vienne *vyen* f Vienna

vieux *vyuh adj* old

vigne *veen·yuh* f vine

vignoble *veen·yo·bluh* m vineyard

vilain(e) *vee·lañ(·len) adj* naughty; ugly

villa *vee·la* f villa (vacation home)

village *vee·lazh* m village

ville *veel* f town; les villes jumelées *veel zhōō·muh·lay* twin towns; aller* en ville *a·lay oñ veel* to go to town

vin *vañ* m wine; le vin du Rhin *vañ dōō rañ* hock

vinaigre *vee·nay·gruh* m vinegar

vinaigrette *vee·nay·gret* f vinaigrette (sauce); salad dressing

vingt *vañ* num twenty

vingt-et-un *vañ·tay·uñ* m blackjack; pontoon

vinyle *vee·neel* m vinyl

violence *vee·o·loñs* f violence

violet(te) *vee·o·lay(·let) adj* purple

violon *vee·o·loñ* m violin

violoncelle *vee·o·loñ·sel* m cello

V.I.P. *vay·ee·pay* m V.I.P.

vipère *vee·pehr* f adder (snake)

virage *vee·razh* m bend (in road); curve; corner; le virage sans visibilité *vee·razh soñ vee·zee·bee·lee·tay* blind corner; le virage en S *vee·razh oñ es* double bend; le virage en épingle à cheveux *vee·razh oñ nay·pañ·gla shuh·vuh* hairpin bend; prendre* un virage *proñ·druh vee·razh* to corner

virement *veer·moñ* m transfer; l'ordre de virement bancaire *or·druh duh veer·moñ boñ·kehr* banker's order

virgule *veer·gōōl* f comma; decimal point; 3 virgule 4 *3 veer·gōōl 4* 3 point 4

vis *vees* f screw

visa *vee·za* m visa, visé; le visa de transit *vee·za duh troñ·zeet* transit visa

visage *vee·zazh* m face

viser *vee·zay* vt stamp (visa) □ vi aim

visible *vee·zee·bluh adj* visible

visière *vee·zyehr* f peak (of cap); sun visor (in car)

visite *vee·zeet* f visit; consultations (of

doctor); **rendre visite à** *roñ·druh vee·zeet a* to visit (*person*); **la visite d'expert** *vee·zeet dek·spehr* survey (*of building*); **la visite guidée** *vee·zeet gee·day* guided tour

visiter *vee·zee·tay vt* to visit (*place*); tour (*town*); **visiter la ville** *vee·zee·tay la veel* to see the sights

visiteur *vee·zee·tur m* visitor

visiteuse *vee·zee·tuhz f* visitor

vison *vee·zoñ m* mink (*fur*)

vital(e) *vee·tal adj* vital (*essential*)

vitamine *vee·ta·meen f* vitamin

vite *veet adv* quickly; fast

vitesse *vee·tes f* gear (*of car*); speed; **deuxième/troisième vitesse** *duh·zyem/ trwah·zyem vee·tes* 2nd/3rd gear; **quatrième/première vitesse** *ka·tryem/ pruh·myehr vee·tes* top/bottom gear; **la vitesse surmultipliée** *vee·tes sōōr· mōōl·tee·plyay* overdrive; **aller* à la même vitesse que** *a·lay a la mem vee· tes kuh* to keep pace with

vitrail *vee·trye m* —**aux** stained glass window

vitre *vee·truh f* pane; window (*in car, train*)

vitrine *vee·treen f* shop window; **qui a fait la vitrine** *kee a feh la vee·treen* shop-soiled

vivant(e) *vee·voñ(·voñt) adj* lively; alive

vivre* *vee·vruh vi* live; **faire* vivre** *fehr vee·vruh* to keep (*feed and clothe*)

vocabulaire *vo·ka·bōō·lehr m* vocabulary

vodka *vod·ka f* vodka

vœu *vuh m* wish; **meilleurs vœux** *may· yur vuh* with best wishes (*on gift*)

voici *vwah·see prep* here is/here are; **la voici qui arrive** *la vwah·see kee a· reev* here she comes

voie *vwah f* lane (*of road*); line; track (*for trains*); **la voie de gauche** *la vwah duh gōsh* the outside lane (*in road*); **la voie express** *vwah ek·spres* expressway

voilà *vwah·la prep* there is/are; **le/la voilà!** *luh/la vwah·la* there he/she is!

voile *vwahl m* veil □ *f* **la voile** *vwahl* sail; **faire* de la voile** *fehr duh la vwahl* to sail

voilier *vwah·lyay m* yacht; sail(ing) boat

voir* *vwahr vt/i* see; **se voir*** *suh vwahr* show (*be visible*); **je ne vois pas la différence entre eux** *zhuh nuh vwah pas la dee·fay·roñs oñ·truh* I can't tell the difference between them

voisin *vwah·zañ m* neighbo(u)r

voisine *vwah·zeen f* neighbo(u)r

voiture *vwah·tōōr f* car; auto(mobile); coach (*of train*); **la voiture de sport** *vwah·tōōr duh spor* sports car; **la voiture de location** *vwah·tōōr duh lo· ka·syoñ* hire car; rental car; **prendre* quelqu'un en voiture** *proñ·druh kel· kuñ oñ vwah·tōōr* to give somebody a lift; **aller* en ville en voiture** *a·lay oñ veel oñ vwah·tōōr* to drive to town; **la voiture de pompiers** *vwah· tōōr duh poñ·pyay* fire engine; **la voiture de police** *vwah·tōōr duh po· lees* police car; **la voiture automatique** *vwah·tōōr ō·to·ma·teek* automatic; **la voiture d'enfant** *vwah·tōōr doñ·foñ* pram, baby buggy, baby carriage

voix *vwah f* voice; vote

vol *vol m* flight; robbery; **le vol régulier** *vol ray·gōō·lyay* scheduled

flight; **le vol plané** *vol pla·nay* gliding (*sport*); **le vol à l'étalage** *vol a lay·ta· lazh* shoplifting; **prendre* un vol direct pour Venise** *proñ·druñ vol dee· rekt poor vuh·neez* to fly to Venice direct

volaille *vo·lye f* poultry

volant *vo·loñ m* steering-wheel

vol-au-vent *vol·ō·voñ m* vol-au-vent

volcan *vol·koñ m* volcano

voler *vo·lay vi* fly □ *vt* steal; **voler quelque chose à quelqu'un** *vo·lay kel·kuh shōz a kel·kuñ* to steal something from someone

volet *vo·leh m* shutter (*on window*)

voleur *vo·lur m* thief

volley-(ball) *vo·lay(·bol) m* volleyball

volonté *vo·loñ·tay f* will; **des circonstances indépendantes de notre volonté** *day seer·koñ·stoñs añ·day·poñ· doñt duh no·truh vo·loñ·tay* circumstances beyond our control

volume *vo·lōōm m* volume

vomir *vo·meer vi* to be sick; vomit

vos *vō adj* your (*polite form, plural form*)

vote *vot m* vote

voter *vo·tay vi* vote

votre *vo·truh adj* your (*polite, plural form*)

le/la vôtre *luh/la vō·truh pron* yours

vouloir* *voo·lwahr vt* want (*wish for*); **vouloir* faire quelque chose** *voo· lwahr fehr kel·kuh shōz* to want to do something; **vous voulez que je le fasse?** *voo voo·lay kuh zhuh luh fas* shall I do it?

vous *voo pron* you; to you (*polite, plural form*)

vous-même *voo·mem pron* yourself (*polite form*); **vous l'avez fait vous-même** *voo la·vay feh voo·mem* you did it yourself

vous-mêmes *voo·mem pron* yourselves

voûte *voot f* arch

voyage *vwah·yazh m* trip; journey; **le voyage d'affaires** *vwah·yazh da·fehr* business trip; **les voyages** *vwah·yazh* travel; **le voyage aller-retour** *vwah· yazh a·lay·ruh·toor* round trip; **en voyage de noces** *oñ vwah·yazh duh nos* on one's honeymoon; **le voyage organisé** *vwah·yazh or·ga·nee·zay* package holiday

voyager *vwah·ya·zhay vi* travel

voyageur *vwah·ya·zhur m* travel(l)er

voyants *vwah·yoñ mpl* stoplights

en vrac *oñ vrak adv* in bulk (*unpackaged*)

vrai(e) *vray adj* real; true; **c'est un vrai problème** *set uñ vray pro·blem* it's a real problem

vraiment *vray·moñ adv* really

vue *vōō f* view; sight; eyesight; **avoir* une mauvaise vue** *a·vwahr ōōn mō· vez vōō* to have poor sight

W

wagon *va·goñ m* car (*of train*); wag(g)on (*rail*); **le wagon fumeurs** *va·goñ fōō·mœr* smoker (*compartment*)

wagon-couchettes *va·goñ·koo·shet m* sleeping car

wagon-lit *va·goñ·lee m* wagon-lit

wagon-restaurant *va·goñ·res·tō·roñ m* dining car

watt *wat m* watt

w-c *vay·say mpl* toilet

week-end *week·end m* weekend

western *wes·tern* **m** western (*movie*)
whisky *wee·skee* **m** whisky; **le whisky de malt** *wee·skee duh malt* malt (whisky); **un whisky soda** *uñ wee·skee so·da* a whisky and soda; **le whisky américain** *wee·skee a·may·ree·kañ* rye (whisky)
whist *weest* **m** whist

Y

y *ee* **adv** there; on it; in it; **il y est allé** *eel ee eh ta·lay* he went there
yacht *yot* **m** yacht; **le yacht à moteur** *yot a mo·tur* cabin cruiser
yachting *yo·ting* **m** yachting
yaourt *ya·oort* **m** yoghurt; **le yaourt nature** *ya·oor na·tōōr* plain yoghurt
yeux *yuh* **mpl** eyes

yoga *yo·ga* **m** yoga
yougoslave *yoo·go·slav* **adj** Yugoslav(ian)
Yougoslavie *yoo·go·sla·vee* **f** Yugoslavia
youyou *yoo·yoo* **m** dinghy

Z

zèbre *zeh·bruh* **m** zebra
zéro *zay·rō* **m** nought; zero; nil
zinc *zañk* **m** zinc
zona *zō·na* **m** shingles (*illness*)
zone *zōn* **f** zone; **la zone piétonnière** *zōn pyay·ton·yehr* pedestrian precinct; **la zone industrielle** *zōn añ·dōōs·tree·yel* trading estate
zoo *zō* **m** zoo
zoom *zoom* **m** zoom lens

ENGLISH–FRENCH DICTIONARY

a *art* un(e) uñ *(ōōn)*; **twice a day** deux fois par jour *duh fwah par zhoor*; **$40 a week** $40 par semaine *$40 par suh·men*

abbey *n* l'abbaye (f) *a·bay·ee*

abbreviation *n* l'abréviation (f) *a·bray·vya·syoñ*

abdomen *n* l'abdomen (m) *ab·do·men*

ability *n* la compétence *koñ·pay·toñs*

able *adj* □ **to be able to do something** pouvoir* faire quelque chose *poo·vwahr fehr kel·kuh shōz*

aboard *adv* □ **to go aboard** aller* à bord *a·lay a bor* □ *prep* **aboard the ship** à bord du bateau *a bor dōō ba·tō*

abolish *vt* abolir *a·bo·leer*

about *prep* □ **about $10** environ $10 *oñ·vee·roñ $10*; **about here** par ici *par ee·see*; **to talk about something** parler de quelque chose *par·lay duh kel·kuh shōz* □ *adv* **things lying about** des affaires qui traînent un peu partout *day za·fehr kee tren uñ puh par·too*; **to look about** regarder autour de soi *ruh·gar·day ō·toor duh swah*; **to be about to do something** être* sur le point de faire quelque chose *eh·truh sōōr luh pwañ duh fehr kel·kuh shōz*

above *prep* □ **the house is above the valley** la maison est au-dessus de la vallée *la meh·zoñ eh tō·duh·sōō duh la va·lay* □ *adv* **above, you can see...** au-dessus vous voyez... *ō·duh·sōō voo vwah·yay*

abroad *adv* à l'étranger *a lay·troñ·zhay*; **to go abroad** aller* à l'étranger *a·lay a lay·troñ·zhay*

abrupt *adj* (person) brusque *brōōsk*; (slope) abrupt(e) *a·brōōpt*

abscess *n* l'abcès (m) *ap·seh*

absent *adj* absent(e) *ap·soñ(·soñt)*

absenteeism *n* l'absentéisme (m) *ap·soñ·tay·eez·muh*

absolute *adj* absolu(e) *ap·so·lōō*

absorb *vt* (fluid) absorber *ap·sor·bay*; (shock) amortir *a·mor·teer*

absorbent *adj* absorbant(e) *ap·sor·boñ(·boñt)*

absorbent cotton *n* le coton hydrophile *ko·toñ ee·dro·feel*

abstain *vi* (in voting) s'abstenir* *sap·stuh·neer*

abstract *adj* abstrait(e) *ap·streh(·stret)*

absurd *adj* absurde *ap·sōōrd*

academy *n* □ **academy of music** le conservatoire *koñ·sehr·va·twahr*; **military academy** l'école militaire (f) *ay·kol mee·lee·tehr*

accelerate *vi* accélérer* *ak·say·lay·ray*

accelerator *n* l'accélérateur (m) *ak·say·lay·ra·tur*

accent *n* l'accent (m) *ak·soñ*

accept *vt* accepter *ak·sep·tay*

acceptance *n* l'acceptation (f) *ak·sep·ta·syoñ*

access *n* l'accès (m) *ak·seh*

accessible *adj* accessible *ak·seh·seh·bluh*

accessories *pl* les accessoires (mpl) *ak·seh·swahr*

accident *n* l'accident (m) *ak·see·doñ*; **by accident** accidentellement *ak·see·doñ·tel·moñ* I12, Ea4

accidental *adj* accidentel(le) *ak·see·doñ·tel*

accommodation *n* le logement *lozh·moñ*

accompany *vt* (go with) accompagner *a·koñ·pa·nyay*

according to *prep* selon *suh·loñ*

account *n* (at bank) le compte *koñt* M29

accountancy *n* la comptabilité *koñ·ta·bee·lee·tay*

accountant *n* le/la comptable *koñ·ta·bluh*

accounts department *n* le service de la comptabilité *sehr·vees duh la koñ·ta·bee·lee·tay*

accrue *vi* s'accroître* *sa·krwah·truh*

accumulate *vi* s'accumuler *sa·kōō·mōō·lay*

accurate *adj* exact(e) *eg·zakt*

accuse *vt* accuser *a·kōō·zay*

ace *n* (cards) l'as (m) *ahs*

ache *n* la douleur *doo·lur* □ *vi* faire* mal *fehr mal*

acid *n* l'acide (m) *a·seed*

acknowledge *vt* (letter) accuser réception de *a·kōō·zay ray·sep·syoñ duh*

acne *n* l'acné (m) *ak·nay*

acorn *n* le gland *gloñ*

acquaintance *n* la connaissance *ko·neh·soñs*

acquire *vt* acquérir* *a·kay·reer*

acquisition *n* l'acquisition (f) *a·kee·zee·syoñ*

acre *n* ≈ le demi-hectare *duh·mee ek·tar*

across *prep* □ **to walk across the road** traverser la route *tra·vehr·say la root*; **I saw him** (from) **across the road** je l'ai vu de l'autre côté de la rue *zhuh lay vōō duh lō·truh kō·tay duh la rōō*; **we drove across France** nous avons traversé la France en voiture *noo za·voñ tra·vehr·say la froñs oñ vwah·tōōr*

acrylic *adj* acrylique *a·kree·leek*

act *n* (of play) l'acte (m) *akt*; (at circus etc) le numéro *nōō·may·rō* □ *vi* (behave) agir *a·zheer* □ *vt* **to act Hamlet** jouer le rôle de Hamlet *zhoo·ay luh rōl duh Hamlet*; **to act as X** servir* de X *sehr·veer duh X*

acting *adj* suppléant(e) *sōō·play·oñ (·oñt)*

action *n* l'action (f) *ak·syoñ*

active *adj* (energetic) actif(ive) *ak·teef(·teev)*; (volcano) en activité *oñ nak·tee·vee·tay*

activity *n* l'activité (f) *ak·tee·vee·tay*

actor *n* l'acteur (m) *ak·tur*

actress *n* la comédienne *ko·may·dyen*

actually *adv* en fait *oñ feh*

acute accent *n* l'accent aigu (m) *ak·soñ ay·gōō*

adapt *vt* adapter *a·dap·tay*

adapter, adaptor *n* (electrical) la prise multiple *preez mōōl·tee·pluh*

add *vt* (comment) ajouter *a·zhoo·tay*; **add (up)** (numbers) additionner *a·dee·syo·nay*

adder *n* (snake) la vipère *vee·pehr*

addict *n* le/la toxicomane *tok·see·ko·man*

addition *n* l'addition (f) *ad·dee·syoñ*

address n l'adresse (f) a·dres □ vt (letter) adresser a·dre·say T91, F2, S27
adjourn vi lever* la séance luh·vay la say·oñs
adjournment n l'ajournement (m) a·zhoor·nuh·moñ
adjust vt régler* ray·glay
administration n l'administration (f) ad·mee·nee·stra·syoñ
admire vt admirer ad·mee·ray
admission n l'entrée (f) oñ·tray L15
admission fee n le prix d'entrée pree doñ·tray
adopt vt adopter a·dop·tay
Adriatic (Sea) n l'Adriatique (f) a·dree·a·teek
adult n l'adulte (m/f) a·dōōlt □ adj (movie etc) pour adultes poor a·dōōlt
advance vt/i avancer* a·voñ·say □ n (loan) l'avance (f) a·voñs; **in advance** à l'avance a la·voñs M10
advance booking office n le guichet de location gee·shay duh lo·ka·syoñ
advantage n l'avantage (m) a·voñ·tazh
adventure n l'aventure (f) a·voñ·tōōr
advertisement n la réclame ray·klam; (in small ads) l'annonce (f) a·noñs
advertise vt (product) faire* de la publicité pour fehr duh la pōōb·lee·see·tay poor □ vi to advertise for a secretary faire* paraître une annonce pour trouver une secrétaire fehr pa·reh·truh ōōn a·noñs poor troo·vay ōōn suh·kray·tehr
advertisement n la réclame ray·klam
advertising n la publicité pōōb·lee·see·tay Bm19
advertising agency n l'agence de publicité a·zhoñs duh pōōb·lee·see·tay
advice n le conseil koñ·say
advice note n l'avis (m) a·vee
advise vt conseiller koñ·say·yay; **to advise someone to do something** conseiller à quelqu'un de faire quelque chose koñ·say·yay a kel·kuñ duh fehr kel·kuh shōz
aerial n l'antenne (f) oñ·ten
aeroplane n l'avion (m) a·vyoñ
aerosol n la bombe boñb
affair n (matter) l'affaire (f) a·fehr; **affairs** les affaires (fpl) a·fehr
affect vt affecter a·fek·tay
affection n l'affection (f) a·fek·syoñ
affectionate adj affectueux(euse) a·fek·tōō·uh(·uhz)
affiliated company n la filiale fee·lyal
afford vt □ **I can't afford it** je ne peux pas me l'offrir zhuh nuh puh pah muh lo·freer; **to be able to afford a new car** avoir* les moyens pour s'acheter une nouvelle voiture a·vwahr lay mwah·yañ poor sash·tay ōōn noo·vel vwah·tōōr
afraid adj □ **to be afraid of something** avoir* peur de quelque chose a·vwahr pur duh kel·kuh shōz; **I'm afraid not** je regrette, mais ce n'est pas possible zhuh ruh·gret meh suh neh pah po·see·bluh; **I'm afraid I can't do it** je suis désolé mais je ne peux pas le faire zhuh swee day·zo·lay meh zhuh nuh puh pah luh fehr
Africa n l'Afrique (f) a·freek
African adj africain(e) a·free·kañ (·ken)
after prep, adv après a·preh; **to come after someone/something** suivre* quelqu'un/quelque chose swee·vruh kel·kuñ/kel·kuh shōz; **4 years after** 4 ans plus tard 4 oñ plōō tar □ conj

after après que a·preh kuh; **after we had left** après notre départ a·preh no·truh day·par
afternoon n l'après-midi (m) a·preh·mee·dee
after-sales service n le service après-vente sehr·vees a·preh·voñt
aftershave (lotion) n la lotion après-rasage lō·syoñ a·preh ra·zazh
afterward(s) adv après a·preh
again adv encore une fois oñ·kor ōōn fwah; **de nouveau** duh noo·vō
against prep contre koñ·truh
age n (of person) l'âge (m) ahzh; (era) l'époque (f) ay·pok; **under age** mineur(e) mee·nur
agency n (office) l'agence (f) a·zhoñs
agenda n l'ordre du jour (m) or·druh dōō zhoor
agent n l'agent (m) a·zhoñ; **the Renault agent** le concessionnaire Renault koñ·seh·syo·nehr ruh·nō
aggressive adj agressif(ive) a·greh·seef(·seev)
agile adj agile a·zheel
ago adv □ **4 years ago** il y a 4 ans eel ya 4 oñ
agony n la douleur atroce doo·lur a·tros
agree vt/i □ **to agree with somebody** être* d'accord avec quelqu'un eh·truh da·kor a·vek kel·kuñ; **to agree on** (price) se mettre* d'accord sur suh meh·truh da·kor sōōr; **onions don't agree with me** les oignons ne me réussissent pas lay zo·nyoñ nuh muh ray·ōō·sees pah
agreement n l'accord (m) a·kor
agricultural adj agricole a·gree·kol
agriculture n l'agriculture (f) a·gree·kōōl·tōōr
ahead adv □ **to see something ahead** voir* quelque chose plus loin devant soi vwahr kel·kuh shōz plōō lwañ duh·voñ swah; **to plan ahead** faire* des projets à l'avance fehr day pro·zhay za la·voñs; **to think ahead** penser à l'avenir poñ·say a la·vuh·neer □ prep **ahead of the others** en avance sur les autres oñ na·voñs sōōr lay zō·truh
aim vt (gun etc) braquer bra·kay; **to aim a gun at someone** braquer un fusil sur quelqu'un bra·kay uñ fōō·zee sōōr kel·kuñ □ vi aim viser vee·zay □ n (intention) le but bōōt
air n l'air (m) ehr; **by air** par avion par a·vyoñ □ vt air (room, clothes) aérer* a·eh·ray
air bed n le matelas pneumatique ma·tuh·la pnuh·ma·teek
air bus n l'airbus (m) ehr·bōōs
air-conditioned adj climatisé(e) klee·ma·tee·zay
air-conditioning n la climatisation klee·ma·tee·za·syoñ
aircraft n l'avion (m) a·vyoñ
air filter n le filtre à air feel·tra ehr
air force n l'armée de l'air (f) ar·may duh lehr
air freight n le transport par avion troñs·por par a·vyoñ
air hostess n l'hôtesse de l'air (f) ō·tes duh lehr
air letter n la lettre par avion leh·truh par a·vyoñ
airline n la compagnie d'aviation koñ·pa·nyee da·vya·syoñ
air mail n □ **by air mail** par avion par a·vyoñ

air-mattress *n* le matelas pneumatique *ma·tuh·la pnuh·ma·teek*
airplane *n* l'avion (*m*) *a·vyoñ*
airport *n* l'aéroport (*m*) *a·eh·ro·por*
airtight *adj* hermétique *ehr·may·teek*
air travel *n* le voyage par avion *vwah·yazh par a·vyoñ*
à la carte *adv* à la carte *a la kart*
alarm *n* (*signal, apparatus*) l'alarme (*f*) *a·larm* □ *vt* alarmer *a·lar·may*
alarm (clock) *n* le réveil *ray·vay*
album *n* l'album (*m*) *al·bum*
alcohol *n* l'alcool *al·kol*
alcoholic *adj* (*drink*) alcoolisé(e) *al·ko·lee·zay* □ *n* l'alcoolique (*m/f*) *al·ko·leek*
alcove *n* l'alcôve (*f*) *al·kôv*
Algeria *n* l'Algérie (*f*) *al·zhay·ree*
Algerian *adj* algérien(ne) *al·zhay·ryañ(·ryen)*
Algiers *n* Alger (*m*) *al·zhay*
alike *adj* semblable *soñ·bla·bluh*
alive *adj* vivant(e) *vee·voñ(·voñt)*
all *adj* (*with singular noun*) tout(e) *too* (*toot*); (*with plural noun*) tous *too*, toutes *toot*; **all day** toute la journée *toot la zhoor·nay*; **all the tables** toutes les tables *toot lay ta·bluh*; **all the bread** tout le pain *too luh pañ*; **all passengers** tous les passagers *too lay pa·sa·zhay* □ *pron* all (*singular*) tout *too*; (*plural*) tous *toos*, toutes *toot*; **all you need** tout ce qu'il vous faut *too suh keel voo fô*; **all of them know that...** ils savent tous que... *eel sav toos kuh*
Allah *n* Allah (*m*) *a·lah*
allergic to *adj* allergique à *a·lehr·zheek a*
allergy *n* l'allergie (*f*) *a·lehr·zhee*
alley *n* la ruelle *rõõ·el*
alliance *n* l'alliance (*f*) *a·lyoñs*
allocate *vt* (*funds*) allouer *a·loo·ay*; (*duties*) attribuer *a·tree·bõõ·ay*
allow *vt* □ to allow someone to go permettre* à quelqu'un de partir *pehr·meh·tra kel·kuñ duh par·teer*; **we will allow £10** nous prévoyons £10 *noo pray·vwah·yoñ £10*; **allow 10 minutes to get there** comptez 10 minutes pour y aller *koñ·tay 10 mee·nõõt poor ee a·lay*
allowance *n* (*state payment*) l'allocation (*f*) *a·lo·ka·syoñ*
alloy *n* l'alliage (*m*) *a·lee·azh*
all right *adv* (*yes*) entendu *oñ·toñ·dõõ*; **he's all right** (*safe, fit*) il va bien *eel va byañ*; **he did it all right** (*satisfactorily*) il l'a bien fait *eel la byañ feh*
almond *n* l'amande (*f*) *a·moñd*
almond paste *n* la pâte d'amandes *paht da·moñd*
almost *adv* presque *pres·kuh*
alone *adj* seul(e) *suhl*
along *prep* □ along the street le long de la rue *luh loñ duh la rõõ*
aloud *adv* (*read*) à haute voix *a ôt vwah*
alphabet *n* l'alphabet (*m*) *al·fa·beh*
alpine *adj* des Alpes *day zalp*
Alps *pl* les Alpes (*fpl*) *alp*
already *adv* déjà *day·zha*
also *adv* aussi *ô·see*
altar *n* l'autel (*m*) *ô·tel*
alter *vt* changer* *shoñ·zhay*
alternator *n* (*in car*) l'alternateur (*m*) *al·tehr·na·tur*
although *conj* bien que *byañ kuh*
altitude *n* l'altitude (*f*) *al·tee·tõõd*
aluminium, aluminum *n* l'aluminium (*m*) *a·lõõ·mee·nyum*

always *adv* toujours *too·zhoor*
am *vi* □ I am je suis *zhuh swee*
a.m. *adv* du matin *dõõ ma·tañ*
amalgamation *n* l'amalgamation (*f*) *a·mal·ga·ma·syoñ*
amateur *n* l'amateur (*m*) *a·ma·tur*
ambassador *n* l'ambassadeur (*m*) *oñ·ba·sa·dur*
amber *n* (*traffic light*) le feu orange *fuh o·roñzh*
ambition *n* (*aim*) l'ambition (*f*) *oñ·bee·syoñ*
ambitious *adj* ambitieux(euse) *oñ·bee·syuh(·syuhz)*
ambulance *n* l'ambulance (*f*) *oñ·bõõ·loñs* I13
amenities *pl* les agréments (*mpl*) *a·gray·moñ*
America *n* l'Amérique (*f*) *a·may·reek*
American *adj* américain(e) *a·may·ree·kañ(·ken)*; **he's American** il est Américain *eel eh ta·may·ree·kañ*; **she's American** elle est Américaine *el eh ta·may·ree·ken*
amethyst *n* l'améthyste (*f*) *a·may·teest*
among(st) *prep* parmi *par·mee*
amount *n* (*total*) le montant *moñ·toñ*; **a large amount of X** beaucoup de X *bô·koo duh X*; **a small amount of X** peu de X *puh duh X* □ *vi* it amounts to F400 ça s'élève à F400 *sa say·lev a F400*
amp *n* l'ampère (*m*) *oñ·pehr*
amplifier *n* l'amplificateur (*m*) *oñ·plee·fee·ka·tur*
amuse *vt* amuser *a·mõõ·zay*
amusement park *n* le parc d'attractions *park da·trak·syoñ*
an *art* un (*õõn*)
anaemic *adj* anémique *a·nay·meek*
anaesthetic *n* l'anesthésique (*m*) *a·nes·tay·zeek*
analyse *vt* analyser *a·na·lee·zay*
analysis *n* l'analyse (*f*) *a·na·leez*
ancestor *n* l'ancêtre (*m*) *oñ·seh·truh*
anchor *n* l'ancre (*f*) *oñ·kruh*
anchovy *n* l'anchois (*m*) *oñ·shwah*
and *conj* et *ay*; **better and better** de mieux en mieux *duh myuh zoñ myuh*; **to go and buy** aller* acheter *a·lay ash·tay*
anemic *adj* anémique *a·nay·meek*
anesthetic *n* l'anesthésique (*m*) *a·nes·tay·zeek*
angel *n* l'ange (*m*) *oñzh*
anger *n* la colère *ko·lehr*
angler *n* le pêcheur *peh·shur*
angling *n* la pêche *pesh*
angora *n* (*fabric*) l'angora (*m*) *oñ·go·ra*
angry *adj* (*person*) en colère *oñ ko·lehr*; **to be angry with someone** être* en colère contre quelqu'un *eh·troñ ko·lehr koñ·truh kel·kuñ*
animal *n* l'animal (*m*) *a·nee·mal*
ankle *n* la cheville *shuh·veey*
anniversary *n* l'anniversaire (*m*) *a·nee·vehr·sehr*
announce *vt* annoncer* *a·noñ·say*
annoy *vt* agacer* *a·ga·say*
annual *adj* annuel(le) *a·nõõ·el*
annual general meeting, AGM *n* l'assemblée générale annuelle (*f*) *a·soñ·blay zhay·nay·ral a·nõõ·el*
annuity *n* la rente viagère *roñt vya·zhehr*
anorak *n* l'anorak (*m*) *a·no·rak*
another *adj* □ another beer please! encore une bière s'il vous plaît *oñ·kor õõn byehr seel voo play*; **I want to see another shirt** je voudrais voir une

autre chemise *zhuh voo·dreh vwahr ōōn ō·truh shu·meez*

answer *n* la réponse *ray·poñs* □ *vi* répondre *ray·poñ·druh* □ *vt* to answer a question répondre à une question *ray·poñ·dra ōōn kes·tyoñ*; to answer the phone répondre au téléphone *ray·poñ·dr·tay·lay·fon*

ant *n* la fourmie *foor·mee*

Antarctic *n* l'Antarctique (m) *oñ·tark·teek*

antenna *n* l'antenne (f) *oñ·ten*

antibiotic *n* l'antibiotique (m) *oñ·tee·byo·teek*

antifreeze *n* l'antigel (m) *oñ·tee·zhel*

antihistamine *n* l'antihistaminique (m) *oñ·tee·ee·sta·mee·neek*

antique *n* l'objet d'art ancien (m) *ob·zhay dar oñ·syañ*; (furniture) le meuble ancien *muh·bluh oñ·syañ* S85

antique dealer *n* l'antiquaire (m/f) *oñ·tee·kehr*

antiseptic *n* l'antiseptique (m) *oñ·tee·sep·teek*

any *adj* □ give me any book donnez-moi n'importe quel livre *do·nay mwah nañ·port kel lee·vruh*; we haven't any bread nous n'avons pas de pain *noo na·voñ pah duh pañ*; have you any bread? avez-vous du pain? *a·vay voo dōō pañ*; is there any more soup? est-ce qu'il y a encore de la soupe? *es·keel ya oñ·kor duh la soop* □ *pron* we haven't any nous n'en avons pas *noo noñ na·voñ pah*; can any of you sing? est-ce que l'un d'entre vous sait chanter? *es·kuh luñ doñ·truh voo seh shoñ·tay*

anybody, anyone *pron* □ can you see anybody? est-ce que vous voyez quelqu'un? *es·kuh voo vwah·yay kel·kuñ*; I can't see anybody je ne vois personne *zhuh nuh vwah pehr·son*; anybody at all n'importe qui *nañ·port kee*

anything *pron* □ can you see anything? est-ce que vous voyez quelque chose? *es·kuh voo vwah·yay kel·kuh shōz*; I can't see anything je ne vois rien *zhuh nuh vwah ree·añ*; anything at all n'importe quoi *nañ·port kwah*

anyway *adv* (nonetheless) de toute façon *duh toot fa·soñ*

anywhere *adv* □ I'll take you anywhere you like je vous amènerai où vous voudrez *zhuh voo za·men·uh·ray oo voo voo·dray*; I can't see it anywhere je ne le vois nulle part *zhuh nuh luh vwah nōōl par*

apart *adv* (separately) séparément *say·pa·ray·moñ*

apartment *n* l'appartement (m) *a·par·tuh·moñ*

ape *n* le singe *sañzh*

aperitif *n* l'apéritif (m) *a·pay·ree·teef*

apologize *vi* s'excuser *sek·skōō·zay*

apparently *adv* apparemment *a·pa·ra·moñ*

appear *vi* apparaître• *a·pa·reh·truh*; he appears ill il a l'air malade *eel a lehr ma·lad*; it appears that... il paraît que... *eel pa·reh kuh*

appendicitis *n* l'appendicite (f) *a·pañ·dee·seet*

appetite *n* l'appétit (m) *a·pay·tee*

appetizer *n* l'amuse-gueule (m) *a·mōōz·gul*

applause *n* les applaudissements (mpl) *a·plō·dees·moñ*

apple *n* la pomme *pom* S31

apple tree *n* le pommier *pom·yay*

appliance *n* l'appareil (m) *a·pa·ray*

application *n* (for job) la demande *duh·moñd*

apply *vi* □ to apply for a job faire• une demande d'emploi *fehr ōōn duh·moñd doñ·plwah*

appoint *vt* nommer *no·may*

appointment *n* (rendezvous) le rendez-vous *roñ·day·voo*; (to job) la nomination *no·mee·na·syoñ* Sn39, Bm9

appreciate *vt* apprécier *a·pray·see·ay* □ *vi* (in value) prendre• de la valeur *proñ·druh duh la va·lur*

apprentice *n* l'apprenti(e) (m/f) *a·proñ·tee*

approach *vi* (person) s'approcher *sa·pro·shay*; (season) approcher *a·pro·shay* □ *vt* to approach a place s'approcher d'un endroit *sa·pro·shay duñ noñ·drwah*

approval *n* l'approbation (f) *a·pro·ba·syoñ*; on approval sous condition *soo koñ·dee·syoñ*

approve of *vt* approuver *a·proo·vay*

approximate *adj* approximatif(ive) *a·prok·see·ma·teef(·teev)*

apricot *n* l'abricot (m) *ab·ree·kō*

April *n* avril (m) *a·vreel*

apron *n* le tablier *ta·blee·ay*

aquarium *n* l'aquarium (m) *a·kwa·ryum*

Arab *n* l'Arabe (m/f) *a·rab*

Arabic *adj* arabe *a·rab* □ *n* l'arabe (m) *a·rab*

arcade *n* la galerie marchande *gal·ree mar·shoñd*

arch *n* la voûte *voot*

architect *n* l'architecte (m) *ar·shee·tekt*

architecture *n* l'architecture (f) *ar·shee·tek·tōōr*

Arctic *n* l'Arctique (m) *ark·teek*

are *vi* □ we are nous sommes *noo som*; you are vous êtes *voo zet*; they are ils (elles) sont *eel (el) soñ*

area *n* (of surface) la superficie *sōō·pehr·fee·see*; (region) la région *ray·zhoñ*

Argentina *n* l'Argentine (f) *ar·zhoñ·teen*

Argentine *adj* argentin(e) *ar·zhoñ·tañ(·teen)*

argue *vi* (quarrel) se disputer *suh dees·pōō·tay*

argument *n* (quarrel) la dispute *dees·pōōt*

arithmetic *n* l'arithmétique (f) *a·reet·may·teek*

arm *n* (of person) le bras *brah* I24

armchair *n* le fauteuil *fō·tuhy*

arms *pl* les armes (fpl) *arm*

army *n* l'armée (f) *ar·may*

around *adv* □ to look around regarder autour de soi *ruh·gar·day ō·toor duh swah*; things lying around des affaires qui traînent un peu partout *day za·fehr kee tren uñ puh par·too* □ *prep* to go around the world aller• autour du monde *a·lay ō·toor dū moñd*; the scarf around her neck l'écharpe autour de son cou *lay·sharp ō·toor duh soñ koo*; around $10 environ $10 *oñ·vee·roñ $10*

arrange *vt* (flowers, furniture) arranger• *a·roñ·zhay*; (meeting) fixer *feek·say*

arrears *pl* l'arriéré (m) *a·ree·eh·ray*; to be in arrears with a payment avoir• de l'arriéré dans ses paiements *a·vwahr duh la·ree·eh·ray doñ say pay·moñ*

arrest *vt* arrêter *a·reh·tay*

arrival n l'arrivée (f) a·ree·vay

arrive vi arriver a·ree·vay

arrow n la flèche flesh

art n l'art (m) ar

artery n l'artère (f) ar·tehr

art gallery n le musée môö·zay; (commercial) la galerie gal·ree

arthritis n l'arthrite (f) ar·reet

artichoke n l'artichaut (m) ar·tee·shô; Jerusalem artichoke le topinambour to·pee·noñ·boor

article n (in newspaper) l'article (m) ar·tee·kluh; (thing) l'objet (m) ob·zhay

artificial adj artificiel(le) ar·tee·fee·syel

artist n l'artiste (m/f) ar·teest

as conj □ as he was asleep (because) comme il dormait kom eel dor·meh; (while) pendant qu'il dormait poñ·doñ keel dor·meh; he arrived as we left il est arrivé comme nous partions eel et a·ree·vay kom noo par·tyoñ; do as I say faites comme je vous dis fet kom zhuh voo dee; as big as aussi grand que ô·see groñ kuh; as for this quant à ceci koñ ta suh·see; as if, as though comme si kom see; as well (too) aussi ô·see; as much/many as autant que ô·toñ kuh

asbestos n l'amiante (f) a·myoñt

ash n (tree) le frêne frehn; (cinders) la cendre soñ·druh

ashamed adj □ to be ashamed (of) avoir* honte (de) a·vwahr oñt (duh)

ashcan n la poubelle poo·bel A71

ashore adv à terre a tehr

ashtray n le cendrier soñ·dree·ay A41

Asia n l'Asie (f) azee

Asian adj asiatique a·zya·teek

ask vt/i demander duh·moñ·day; to ask a question poser une question pô·zay öön tes·tyoñ; to ask someone the time demander l'heure à quelqu'un duh·moñ·day lur a kel·kuñ; to ask for something demander quelque chose duh·moñ·day kel·kuh shôz; to ask the price demander le prix duh·moñ·day luh pree

asleep adj endormi(e) oñ·dor·mee

asparagus n l'asperge (f) as·pehrzh

aspirin n l'aspirine (f) as·pee·reen

assemble vt (parts of machine) monter moñ·tay

assembly line n la chaîne de montage shen duh moñ·tazh

asset n (financial) l'actif (m) ak·teef

assistant n (in shop) le vendeur voñ·dur, la vendeuse voñ·duhz

associate n l'associé(e) (m/f) a·so·syay

association n l'association (f) a·so·sya·syoñ

assorted adj assorti(e) a·sor·tee

assume vt (suppose) supposer söö·po·zay

asthma n l'asthme (m) as·muh

at prep □ at 4 o'clock à 4 heures a 4 ur; at my house chez moi shay mwah; at school à l'école a lay·kol; to stop at London s'arrêter à Londres sa·reh·tay a loñ·druh; to throw something at someone jeter* quelque chose à quelqu'un zhuh·tay kel·kuh shôz a kel·kuñ; not at all pas du tout pah döö too; at once tout de suite too duh sweet

Athens n Athènes (f) a·ten

athlete n l'athlète (m/f) at·let

Atlantic Ocean n l'Atlantique (m) at·loñ·teek

atlas n l'atlas (m) at·las

attach vt attacher a·ta·shay

attack vt attaquer a·ta·kay □ n l'attaque (f) a·tak

attempt vt essayer eh·say·yay □ n la tentative toñ·ta·teev

attend vt (meeting etc) assister à a·sees·tay a

attic n le grenier gruh·nyay

attitude n l'attitude (f) a·tee·tööd

attorney n l'avoué (m) a·voo·ay

aubergine n l'aubergine (f) ô·behr·zheen

auction n la vente aux enchères voñt ô zoñ·shehr

audience n (in theatre) les spectateurs (mpl) spek·ta·tur

audio-guide n le guide-audio portatif geed·ô·dyô por·ta·teef

audio-visual adj audio-visuel(le) ô·dyô·vee·zöö·el

audit vt vérifier vay·ree·fyay

auditor n l'expert-comptable (m) ek·spehr·koñ·ta·bluh

auditorium n la salle sal

au gratin adj au gratin ô gra·tañ

August n août (m) oo

aunt(ie) n la tante toñt

Australia n l'Australie (f) os·tra·lee

Australian adj australien(ne) os·tra·lyañ(·lyen); he's Australian il est Australien eel eh tos·tra·lyañ; she's Australian elle est Australienne el eh tos·tra·lyen

Austria n l'Autriche (f) ô·treesh

Austrian adj autrichien(ne) ô·tree·shyañ(·shyen); he's Austrian il est Autrichien eel eh tô·tree·shyañ; she's Austrian elle est Autrichienne el eh tô·tree·shyen

author n l'auteur (m) ô·tur

automatic adj automatique ô·to·ma·teek □ n (car) la voiture automatique vwah·töör ô·to·ma·teek

automatically adv automatiquement ô·to·ma·teek·moñ

automation n l'automatisation (f) ô·to·ma·tee·za·syoñ

auto(mobile) n la voiture vwah·töör

autumn n l'automne (m) ô·ton

available adj disponible dees·po·nee·bluh

avalanche n l'avalanche (f) a·va·loñsh

avenue n l'avenue (f) a·vuh·nöö

average adj moyen(ne) mwah·yañ (·yen) □ n la moyenne mwah·yen

aviation n l'aviation (f) a·vya·syoñ

avocado (pear) n l'avocat (m) a·vo·ka

avoid vt éviter ay·vee·tay

away adv □ away from home absent(e) de chez soi ap·soñ(t) duh shay swah; he's away for a week il est parti pour une semaine eel eh par·tee poor öön suh·men; 30 kilometres away à 30 kilomètres a 30 kee·lo·meh·truh

awful adj affreux(euse) a·fruh(·fruhz)

axe n la hache ash

axle n l'essieu (m) eh·syuh

B

baby n le bébé bay·bay C11, 17

baby buggy, baby carriage n la voiture d'enfant vwah·töör doñ·foñ

babysit vi garder les enfants gar·day lay zoñ·foñ

baby-sitter n le baby-sitter bay·bee·see·tehr C5

baccarat n le baccara ba·ka·rah

bachelor n le célibataire say·lee·ba·tehr

back n le dos dô; (of chair) le dossier

dō·syay; (of hall, room) le fond foñ; (in sports) l'arrière (m) a·ryehr □ adv (backwards) en arrière oñ na·ryehr; to come back revenir* ruh·vuh·neer; to go back retourner ruh·toor·nay □ vt back (support) soutenir* soo·tuh·neer; (financially) financer* fee·noñ·say; (bet on) parier sur pa·ryay sōōr; to back the car faire* marche arrière fehr marsh a·ryehr
backache n le mal de reins mal duh rañ
backdate vt antidater oñ·tee·da·tay
backer n le commanditaire ko·moñ·dee·tehr
backgammon n le trictrac treek·trak
background n l'arrière-plan (m) ar·yehr·ploñ
backing n le soutien soo·tyañ
backlash n les répercussions (fpl) ray·pehr·kōō·syoñ
backlog n □ backlog of work l'accumulation de travail (f) a·kōō·mōō·la·syoñ duh tra·vye
back pack n le sac à dos sak a dō
backward adj (glance) en arrière oñ na·ryehr; (child) arriéré(e) a·ryeh·ray
backwards adv en arrière oñ na·ryehr
bacon n le bacon ba·koñ
bad adj mauvais(e) mō·veh(·vez); (naughty) vilain(e) vee·lañ(·len); to go bad (food) se gâter suh gah·tay; a bad debt une mauvaise créance ōōn mō·vez kray·oñs
badge n (of metal) l'insigne (m) añ·seeñ·yuh; (of cloth) l'écusson (m) ay·kōō·soñ
badly adv mal mal; to want something badly avoir* grande envie de quelque chose a·vwahr groñ doñ·vee duh kel·kuh shōz
badminton n le badminton bad·meen·ton
bag n (of paper) le sac sak; bags (luggage) les bagages (mpl) ba·gazh B75, T22f, S25
baggage n les bagages (mpl) ba·gazh
baggage car n le fourgon foor·goñ
baggage check n le bulletin de consigne bōōl·tañ duh koñ·seeñ
baggage claim n la livraison des bagages lee·vray·zoñ day ba·gazh
baggage room n la consigne koñ·see·nyuh T25, 33
bail n (for prisoner) la caution kō·syoñ; on bail sous caution soo kō·syoñ
bait n (in fishing) l'appât (m) a·pah
bake vt faire* cuire au four fehr kweer ō foor
baker n le boulanger boo·loñ·zhay S29
bakery n la boulangerie boo·loñ·zhuh·ree
balance n l'équilibre (m) ay·kee·lee·bruh; (remainder owed) le solde sold; balance of power l'équilibre des forces ay·kee·lee·bruh day fors; balance of payments la balance des paiements ba·loñs day pay·moñ; balance of trade la balance commerciale ba·loñs ko·mehr·syal; to lose one's balance perdre son équilibre pehr·druh soñ nay·kee·lee·bruh □ vt balance tenir* en équilibre tuh·neer oñ nay·kee·lee·bruh; (accounts) solder sol·day □ vi s'équilibrer say·kee·lee·bray
balance sheet n le bilan bee·loñ
balcony n le balcon bal·koñ
bald adj chauve shōv

ball n la balle bal; (inflated) le ballon ba·loñ; (of string, wool) la pelote puh·lot; (dance) le bal bal
ballet n le ballet ba·lay
balloon n le ballon ba·loñ
ballot n le scrutin skrōō·tañ
bamboo n le bambou boñ·boo
ban vt interdire* añ·tehr·deer □ n l'interdit (m) añ·tehr·dee
banana n la banane ba·nan
band n (musical) l'orchestre (m) or·kes·truh
bandage n le pansement poñs·moñ
bandaid n le sparadrap spa·ra·dra
bang n (of gun etc) la détonation day·to·na·syoñ; (of door) le claquement klak·moñ; (blow) le coup koo □ vt (door) claquer kla·kay; to bang one's head se cogner la tête suh ko·nyay la tet □ vi bang (gun etc) détoner day·to·nay
bangs pl la frange froñzh
bank n (of river, lake) la rive reev; (finance) la banque boñk □ vt (money) déposer en banque day·pō·zay oñ boñk □ vi to bank with Smiths avoir* un compte à la Smiths a·vwahr uñ koñt a la Smiths M28f
bank account n le compte en banque koñt oñ boñk
bank balance n le solde sold
bank bill n la traite tret
bankbook n le livret de banque lee·vray duh boñk
bank charges pl les frais de banque (mpl) fray duh boñk
banker n le banquier boñ·kyay
banker's card n la carte d'identité bancaire kart dee·doñ·tee·tay boñ·kehr
banker's order n l'ordre de virement bancaire (m) or·druh duh veer·moñ boñ·kehr
bank holiday n le jour férié zhoor fay·ryay
bank loan n l'emprunt bancaire (m) oñ·pruñ boñ·kehr
bank manager n le directeur de banque dee·rek·tur duh boñk
bank note n le billet de banque bee·yay duh boñk
bankrupt adj en faillite oñ fa·yeet; to go bankrupt faire* faillite fehr fa·yeet
bankruptcy n la faillite fa·yeet
banner n la bannière ba·nyehr
banquet n le banquet boñ·kay
baptism n le baptême ba·tem
Baptist n le baptiste bap·teest
bar n (metal) la barre bar; (counter) le comptoir koñ·twahr; (drinking establishment) le bar bar; bar of soap la savonnette sa·vo·net; bar of chocolate la tablette de chocolat (a·tablet duh sho·kō·lah
barbecue n le barbecue bar·buh·kōō
barbed wire n le fil de fer barbelé feel duh fehr bar·buh·lay
barber n le coiffeur kwah·fur
bare adj (person, head) nu(e) nōō; to go barefoot marcher pieds nus mar·shay pyay nōō
bargain n (cheap buy) l'occasion (f) o·ka·zyoñ; to make a bargain conclure* un marché koñ·klōōr uñ mar·shay
bargaining n (negotiation) le marchandage mar·shoñ·dazh
barge n la péniche pay·neesh
bark n (of tree) l'écorce (f) ay·kors; (of dog) l'aboiement (m) a·bwah·moñ □ vi aboyer a·bwah·yay
barmaid n la serveuse sehr·vuhz

barman n le barman *bar·man*
barn n la grange *gronzh*
barracks pl la caserne *ka·zehrn*
barrel n (for beer) le tonneau *to·nō*
barrier n (fence) la barrière *ba·ryehr*
barrister n l'avocat (m) *a·vo·kah*
bartender n le barman *bar·man*
base n la base *bahz* □ vt baser *bah·zay*
baseball n le base-ball *bays·bol*
basement n le sous-sol *soo·sol*
basic adj de base *duh bahz*
basically adv essentiellement *eh·soñ·syel·moñ*
basin n (dish) le bol *bol*; (for washing) le lavabo *la·va·bō*
basis n la base *bahz*
basket n la corbeille *kor·bay*
basketball n le basket-ball *bas·ket·bol*
bat n (table tennis etc) la raquette *ra·ket*; (animal) la chauve-souris *shōv·soo·ree*
bath n le bain *bañ*; (tub) la baignoire *bay·nwahr* A4
bathe vi se baigner *suh bay·nyay* □ vt (wound etc) laver *la·vay*
bathing cap n le bonnet de bain *bo·nay duh bañ*
bathing suit n le maillot de bain *mye·yō duh bañ*
bathroom n la salle de bains *sal duh bañ*; (lavatory) les toilettes (fpl) *twah·let* A17
batter n (for frying) la pâte à frire *paht a freer*
battery n (for radio etc) la pile *peel*; (in car) la batterie *ba·tree* T182, S48
battle n la bataille *ba·tye*
bay n (on coast) la baie *bay*
bazaar n le bazar *ba·zar*
be vi être* *eh·truh*; I am je suis *zhuh swee*; you are vous êtes *voo zet*; he is il est *eel eh*; we are nous sommes *noo som*; they are ils sont *eel soñ*; how are you? comment ta·lay·voo; I am hungry j'ai faim *zhay fañ*; what is that? qu'est-ce que c'est? *kes kuh seh*; how much is it? combien ça coûte? *koñ·byañ sa koot*; is it hot? il fait chaud *eel feh shō*; we are going to the beach nous allons à la plage *noo za·loñ za la plazh*; we have been to Paris nous sommes allés à Paris *noo som za·lay a pa·ree*; he is a doctor il est médecin *eel eh mayd·sañ*
beach n la plage *plazh* L20
bead n (of wood) la perle *pehrl*
beam n (of wood) la poutre *poo·truh*; (of light) le rayon *ray·yoñ*
beans pl les haricots (mpl) *lay a·ree·kō*
bear n l'ours (m) *oors* □ vt (weight) porter *por·tay*; (endure) supporter *sōō·por·tay*
beard n la barbe *barb*
bearings pl (in car) les coussinets (mpl) *koo·see·neh*; to take one's bearings s'orienter *so·ryoñ·tay*
beat vt/i battre* *ba·truh*
beautiful adj beau *bō*, belle *bel*
beauty n la beauté *bō·tay*
because conj parce que *pars kuh*; because of à cause de *a kōz duh*
become vi devenir* *duh·vuh·neer*
bed n le lit *lee*; in bed au lit *ō lee*; to go to bed aller* se coucher *a·lay suh koo·shay* I52
bedclothes pl les couvertures (fpl) *koo·vehr·toor*
bedding n la literie *lee·tuh·ree* A68
bedroom n la chambre *shoñ·bruh*
bee n l'abeille (f) *a·bay*

beech n le hêtre *eh·truh*
beef n le bœuf *buhf*
beer n la bière *byehr* E55
beetle n le scarabée *ska·ra·bay*
beetroot n la betterave *bet·rahv*
before prep (in time) avant *a·voñ*; before noon avant midi *a·voñ mee·dee*; before the king (in space) devant le roi *duh·voñ luh rwah* □ adv before avant *a·voñ*; we've met before nous nous sommes déjà rencontrés *noo noo som day·zha roñ·koñ·tray* □ conj before avant que *a·voñ kuh*; before I go to bed avant de me coucher *a·voñ duh muh koo·shay*
beg vi mendier *moñ·dyay*
beggar n le/la mendiant(e) *moñ·dyoñ (·dyoñt)*
begin vt/i commencer* *ko·moñ·say*
beginner n le/la débutant(e) *day·bōō·toñ(·toñt)*
behalf n □ on behalf of au nom de *ō noñ duh*
behave vi se comporter *suh koñ·por·tay*; behave yourself! tiens-toi bien! *tyañ·twah byañ*
behavio(u)r n le comportement *koñ·port·moñ*
behind adv derrière *deh·ryehr*; to look behind regarder en arrière *ruh·gar·day oñ na·ryehr*; to stand behind se tenir* derrière *suh tuh·neer deh·ryehr* □ prep behind the wall derrière le mur *deh·ryehr luh mōōr*; to be behind schedule avoir* du retard *a·vwahr dōō ruh·tar*
beige adj beige *bayzh*
belief n (faith) la foi *fwah*; (tenet) la conviction *koñ·veek·syoñ*
believe vt/i croire* *krwahr*; to believe in croire* en *krwahr oñ*
bell n la cloche *klosh*; (on door) la sonnette *so·net*; (electric) la sonnerie *so·nuh·ree*
bellboy n le groom *groom*
belong vi □ to belong to someone appartenir* à quelqu'un *a·par·tuh·neer a kel·kuñ*; to belong to a club être* membre d'un club *eh·truh moñ·bruh duñ klub*
belongings pl les affaires (fpl) *a·fehr*
below adv en dessous *oñ duh·soo*; to look below regarder en dessous *ruh·gar·day oñ duh·soo*; to stand below se tenir* en bas *suh tuh·neer oñ bah* □ prep to put one's case below the chair mettre* sa valise en dessous de la chaise *meh·truh sa va·leez oñ duh·soo duh la shez*; my room is below his ma chambre est en dessous de la sienne *ma shoñ·bruh eh toñ duh·soo duh la syen*
belt n (for waist) la ceinture *sañ·tōōr* S79
bench n (seat) le banc *boñ*; (work table) l'établi (m) *ay·ta·blee*
bend n (in pipe, wire etc) le coude *kood*; (in road) le virage *vee·razh* □ vt courber *koor·bay*; (arm, leg) plier *plee·yay* □ vi (person) se courber *suh koor·bay*; (road) faire* un coude *fehr uñ kood* T210
beneath = **below**
benefit n l'avantage (m) *a·voñ·tazh*; it's of no benefit (to us) ça ne nous aide pas *sa nuh noo zed pah*
Benelux n le Bénélux *bay·nay·lōōks*
berry n la baie *bay*
berth n la couchette *koo·shet*
beside prep à côté de *a kō·tay duh*
besides adv (moreover) d'ailleurs *dye*

yur □ *prep* **besides** him en plus de lui
oñ plōōs duh lwee

best *adj* meilleur(e) *may·yur* □ *n* he's
the best c'est lui le meilleur *seh luh
luh may·yur* □ *adv* he can do it best il
le fait le mieux *eel luh feh luh myuh*

best man *n* le garçon d'honneur *gar·
soñ don·nur*

bet *vt/i* parier *pa·ryay* □ *n* le pari *pa·
ree*

better *adj* meilleur(e) *may·yur* □ *adv*
he sings better than you il chante
mieux que vous *eel shoñt myuh kuh
voo*; **to get better** (*from illness*) se remettre* *suh ruh·meh·truh*; **they are
better off** than us (*richer*) ils ont plus
d'argent que nous *eel zoñ plōō dar·
zhoñ kuh noo*

between *prep* entre *oñ·truh*

beyond *prep* au-delà de *ō·duh·lah duh*;
beyond my reach hors de ma portée
or duh ma por·tay; **beyond his means**
au-dessus de ses moyens *ō·duh·sōō
duh say mwah·yañ*

Bible *n* la Bible *bee·bluh*

bicycle *n* la bicyclette *bee·see·klet*

bid *vt* (*amount*) offrir* *o·freer* □ *vi* to
bid for something faire* une offre
pour quelque chose *fehr ōōn o·fruh
poor kel·kuh shōz* □ *n* l'enchère (*f*)
(*f*) *oñ·shehr*

bidder *n* l'offrant (*m*) *o·froñ*

big *adj* (*person, house*) grand(e) groñ
(groñd); (*sum of money*) gros(se)
grō (grōs)

bikini *n* le bikini *bee·kee·nee*

bilingual *adj* bilingue *bee·lañg*

bill *n* (*account*) la note *not*; (*bank
note*) le billet de banque *bee·yay duh
boñk* M14, A21

billiards *n* le billard *bee·yar*

billion *n* le milliard *meel·yar*

bin *n* (*for refuse*) la poubelle *poo·bel*

binoculars *pl* les jumelles (*fpl*) *zhōō·
mel*

biology *n* la biologie *bee·o·lo·zhee*

birch *n* (*tree*) le bouleau *boo·lō*

bird *n* l'oiseau (*m*) *wa·zō* L35

birth *n* la naissance *nay·soñs*

birth certificate *n* l'acte de naissance
(*m*) *akt duh nay·soñs*

birthday *n* l'anniversaire (*m*) *a·nee·
vehr·sehr*

biscuit *n* (*sweet*) le biscuit *bees·kwee*;
(*savoury*) le biscuit salé *bees·kwee
sa·lay*

bishop *n* l'évêque (*m*) *ay·vek*

bit *n* (*piece*) le morceau *mor·sō*; **a bit
of** un peu de *uñ puh duh*

bite *n* mordre* *mor·druh* □ *n* (*by animal*) la morsure *mor·sōōr*; (*by insect*) la piqûre *pee·kōōr*; (*of food*) la
bouchée *boo·shay*

bitter *adj* amer *a·mehr*, amère *a·mehr*
□ *n* (*beer*) la bière brune *byehr
brōōn*

black *adj* noir(e) *nwahr*; **a black coffee**
un café noir *uñ ka·fay nwahr*

blackberry *n* la mûre *mōōr*

blackbird *n* le merle *mehrl*

blackcurrant *n* le cassis *ka·sees*

black eye *n* l'œil au beurre noir (*m*)
uhy ō bur nwahr

blackjack *n* le vingt-et-un *vañ·tay·uñ*

black market *n* le marché noir *mar·
shay nwahr*

bladder *n* la vessie *veh·see*

blade *n* (*of knife*) la lame *lam*

blame *vt* (*reproach*) blâmer *blah·may*;

to be to blame être* le responsable
eh·truh luh reh·spoñ·sa·bluh

blank *adj* blanc *bloñ*, blanche *bloñsh*;
blank cheque le chèque en blanc
shek oñ bloñ; **please leave blank** laissez en blanc s'il vous plaît *leh·say oñ
bloñ seel voo pleh*

blanket *n* la couverture *koo·vehr·tōōr*
A41

blast *n* (*explosion*) l'explosion (*f*) *ek·
splō·zyoñ*

blaze *n* (*fire*) l'incendie (*m*) *añ·soñ·dee*
□ *vi* (*fire*) flamber *floñ·bay*; (*lights*)
resplendir *reh·sploñ·deer*

blazer *n* le blazer *bla·zehr*

bleed *vi* saigner *say·nyay*

blend *vt* mélanger* *may·loñ·zhay* □ *n*
le mélange *may·loñzh*

bless *vt* bénir *bay·neer*

blind *adj* (*person*) aveugle *a·vuh·gluh*
□ *n* (*at window*) le store *stor*

blind alley *n* l'impasse (*f*) *añ·pas*

blind corner *n* le virage sans visibilité
vee·razh soñ vee·zee·bee·lee·tay

blink *vi* cligner des yeux *klee·nyay day
zyuh*

blister *n* (*on skin*) l'ampoule (*f*) *oñ·
pool*

blizzard *n* la tempête de neige *toñ·pet
duh nezh*

block *n* (*of stone*) le bloc *blok*; **3
blocks away** (*streets*) 3 rues plus loin
3 rōō plōō lwañ; **block of flats, apartment block** l'immeuble (*m*) *ee·muh·
bluh* □ *vt* **block** (*road*) bloquer *blo·
kay*; (*pipe*) boucher *boo·shay*; **block
letters** les majuscules (*fpl*) *ma·zhōō·
skōōl*; **block booking** la réservation
de groupe *ray·zehr·va·syoñ duh
groop*

blockage *n* l'obstruction (*f*) *ob·strōōk·
syoñ*

blond(e) *adj* blond(e) *bloñ* (bloñd)

blood *n* le sang *soñ*

blood group *n* le groupe sanguin *groop
soñ·gañ*

blood poisoning *n* l'empoisonnement
du sang (*m*) *oñ·pwah·zon·moñ dōō
soñ*

blood pressure *n* la tension *toñ·syoñ*

bloom *n* (*flower*) la fleur *flur* □ *vi*
être* en fleur *eh·troñ flur*

blossom *n* les fleurs (*fpl*) *flur*

blot *n* la tache *tash* □ *vt* (*ink*) sécher*
say·shay

blouse *n* le chemisier *shuh·mee·zyay*
S19

blow *n* (*knock*) le coup *koo* □ *vi*
(*wind*) souffler *soo·flay*; (*fuse*) sauter *sō·tay* □ *vt* **to blow one's nose** se
moucher *suh moo·shay*

blow-dry *n* le brushing *bruh·sheeng*

blow-out *n* l'éclatement (*m*) *ay·klat·
moñ*

blue *adj* bleu(e) *bluh*

bluebottle *n* la mouche à viande
moosh a vyoñd

blue chips *pl* les valeurs vedettes (*fpl*)
va·lur vuh·det

blueprint *n* le projet directeur *pro·
zhay dee·rek·tur*

blunt *adj* (*knife*) émoussé(e) *ay·moo·
say*

blush *vi* rougir *roo·zheer*

board *n* (*of wood*) la planche *ploñsh*;
(*for notices*) le panneau d'affichage
pa·nō da·fee·shazh; (*of directors*) le
conseil d'administration *koñ·say
dad·mee·nee·stra·syoñ*; **on board**
(*ship, plane*) à bord *a bor*; **full board**
la pension complète *poñ·syoñ koñ·*

plet; **half board** la demi-pension *duh·mee·poñ·syoñ* □ **vt board** *(train, bus)* monter dans *moñ·tay doñ;* *(ship)* monter à bord de *moñ·tay a bor duh*

boarding house *n* la pension *poñ·syoñ*

boarding pass *n* la carte d'embarquement *kart doñ·bar·kuh·moñ*

boast *vi* se vanter *suh voñ·tay*

boat *n* le bateau *ba·tō*

bobby pin *n* la pince à cheveux *pañs a shuh·vuh*

body *n* le corps *kor;* *(corpse)* le cadavre *ka·da·vruh*

bodyguard *n (person)* le garde du corps *gard dōō kor*

bog *n* la tourbière *toor·byehr*

boil *vi* hardi(e) *boo·yeer* □ **vt** *(water)* faire* bouillir *fehr boo·yeer* □ *n (on skin)* le furoncle *fōō·roñ·kluh*

bold *adj* hardi(e) *ar·dee*

bolster *n* le traversin *tra·vehr·sañ*

bolt *n* le verrou *veh·roo* □ *vt (door, gate)* verrouiller *veh·roo·yay*

bomb *n* la bombe *boñb*

bone *n* l'os *(m) os;* *(of fish)* l'arête *(f) a·ret*

bonfire *n* le feu de joie *fuh duh zhwah*

bonnet *n (on car)* le capot *ka·pō*

bonus *n (on salary)* la prime *preem*

book *n* le livre *le·vruh* □ *vt (seat)* réserver *ray·zehr·vay*

booking *n* la réservation *ray·zehr·va·syoñ*

booking office *n* le bureau de location *bōō·rō duh lo·ka·syoñ*

boom *n (noise)* le grondement *groñ·duh·moñ;* *(economic)* le boom *boom* □ *vi* **business is booming** les affaires sont en plein essor *lay za·fehr soñ toñ plañ neh·sor*

boost *vt (sales)* augmenter *ōg·moñ·tay*

boot *n* la botte *bot;* *(of car)* le coffre *ko·fruh*

booth *n (telephone)* la cabine *ka·been* Sn18

border *n (edge)* le bord *bor;* *(of country)* la frontière *froñ·tyehr*

bored *adj* □ **I'm bored** je m'ennuie *zhuh moñ·nwee*

boring *adj* ennuyeux(euse) *oñ·nwee·yuh(·yuhz)*

born *adj* né(e) *nay;* **to be born** naître* *neh·truh*

borough *n* la municipalité *mōō·nee·see·pa·lee·tay*

borrow *vt* emprunter *oñ·pruñ·tay;* **to borrow something from someone** emprunter quelque chose à quelqu'un *oñ·pruñ·tay kel·kuh shōz a kel·kuñ*

boss *n* le patron *pa·troñ,* la patronne *pa·tron*

botanical gardens *pl* les jardins botaniques *(mpl) zhar·dañ bo·ta·neek*

both *adj* les deux *lay duh;* **both girls** les deux filles *lay duh feey* □ *pron* **both** *(of them)* tous (toutes) les deux *too (toot) lay duh*

bother *vt (annoy)* ennuyer *oñ·nwee·yay* □ *vi* **please don't bother** ce n'est pas la peine *suh neh pa la pen* □ *n* **bother** *(nuisance)* l'ennui *(m) oñ·nwee;* *(effort)* la peine *pen*

bottle *n* la bouteille *boo·tay;* *(baby's)* le biberon *bee·buh·roñ* E12, C3

bottleneck *n* le goulot d'étranglement *goo·lō day·troñ·gluh·moñ*

bottle opener *n* le décapsuleur *day·kap·sōō·lur*

bottom *n* le fond *foñ;* *(of page, list)* le bas *bah;* *(of person)* le derrière *deh·ryehr* □ *adj* du bas *dōō bah*

bounce *vi (ball)* rebondir *ruh·boñ·deer;* *(cheque)* être* sans provision *eh·truh soñ pro·vee·zyoñ*

bound *adj* □ **bound for** *(ship)* à destination de *a des·tee·na·syoñ duh* □ **out of bounds** dont l'accès est interdit *doñ lak·seh eh tañ·tehr·dee*

boundary *n* la frontière *froñ·tyehr*

bourbon *n* le bourbon *boor·boñ*

boutique *n* la boutique *boo·teek*

bow¹ *vi* faire* une révérence *fehr ōōn ray·vay·roñs* □ *n* la révérence *ray·vay·roñs*

bow² *n (ribbon)* le nœud *nuh*

bowl *n (for food)* le bol *bol;* *(for washing)* la cuvette *kōō·vet*

bowler hat *n* le chapeau melon *sha·pō muh·loñ*

bow tie *n* le nœud papillon *nuh pa·pee·yoñ*

box *n* la boîte *bwat;* *(cardboard)* le carton *kar·toñ*

boxing *n* la boxe *boks*

box number *n* le numéro d'annonce *nōō·may·rō da·noñs*

box office *n* le bureau de location *boo·rō duh lo·ka·syoñ*

boy *n* le garçon *gar·soñ* S108

boycott *vt* boycotter *boy·ko·tay*

boyfriend *n* le petit ami *puh·tee ta·mee*

bra *n* le soutien-gorge *soo·tyañ·gorzh*

bracelet *n* le bracelet *bras·lay*

bracken *n* la fougère *foo·zhehr*

bracket *n (in writing)* la parenthèse *pa·roñ·tez*

brain *n* le cerveau *sehr·vō;* **brains** *(as food)* la cervelle *sehr·vel*

braised *adj* braisé(e) *breh·zay*

brake *n* le frein *frañ* □ *vi* freiner *freh·nay* T176, 214

brake fluid *n* le liquide de frein *lee·keed duh frañ*

branch *n (of tree)* la branche *broñsh;* *(of store, bank etc)* la succursale *sōō·kōōr·sal*

brand *n (of product)* la marque *mark*

brand name *n* la marque *mark*

brandy *n* le cognac *ko·nyak* E58

brass *n* le cuivre jaune *kwee·vruh zhōn*

brave *adj* courageux(euse) *koo·ra·zhuh(·zhuz)*

bread *n* le pain *pañ* E29

break *n (pause)* la pause *pōz* □ *vt (object)* casser *ka·say;* *(contract)* rompre* *roñ·pruh;* *(record)* battre* *ba·truh;* **to break one's arm** se casser le bras *suh ka·say luh brah* □ *vi* **break** se casser *suh ka·say;* **to break down** *(car)* tomber en panne *toñ·bay oñ pan*

breakdown *n (of car)* la panne *pan* B71, T167f

breakdown van *n* la dépanneuse *day·pa·nuhz*

break even *vi* rentrer dans ses frais *roñ·tray doñ say freh*

breakfast *n* le petit déjeuner *puh·tee day·zhuh·nay* A9, 26

breast *n* le sein *sañ;* *(chest)* la poitrine *pwah·treen;* *(of poultry)* le blanc *bloñ*

breath *n* l'haleine *(f) a·len*

breathe *vi* respirer *res·pee·ray*

breeze *n* la brise *breez*

brewery *n* la brasserie *bra·suh·ree*

bribe *vt* suborner *sōō·bor·nay*

brick *n* la brique *breek*

bride *n* la mariée *ma·ree·ay*

bridegroom *n* le marié *ma·ree·ay*

bridge *n* le pont *poñ;* *(game)* le bridge *bridge*

bridle n la bride breed

brief adj bref bref, brève brev

briefcase n la serviette sehr·vyet

briefs pl le slip sleep

bright adj brillant(e) bree·yoñ(·yoñt); (clever) intelligent(e) añ·teh·lee·zhoñ(·zhoñt)

bring vt (thing) apporter a·por·tay; (person) amener* a·muh·nay; **to bring in** (profit) rapporter ra·por·tay

Britain n la Grande-Bretagne groñd·bruh·tan·yuh

British adj britannique bree·ta·neek; **he's British** il est Britannique eel eh bree·ta·neek; **she's British** elle est Britannique el eh bree·ta·neek

broad adj large larzh

broadcast n vt (on radio) diffuser dee·fōō·zay; (on television) téléviser tay·lay·vee·zay □ n l'émission (f) ay·mee·syoñ

broccoli n le brocoli bro·ko·lee

brochure n le dépliant day·plee·yoñ A6

broil vt faire* cuire sur le gril fehr kweer sōōr luh greel

broke adj (penniless) fauché(e) fō·shay

broker n le courtier koor·tyay

bronchitis n la bronchite broñ·sheet

bronze n le bronze broñz

brooch n la broche brosh S86

broom n le balai ba·lay

brother n le frère frehr

brother-in-law n le beau-frère bō·frehr

brown adj brun(e) bruñ (brōōn); (hair) châtain shah·tañ

bruise n le bleu bluh

brush n la brosse bros; (for painting) le pinceau pañ·sō □ vt brosser bro·say

Brussels n Bruxelles (f) brōō·sel

Brussels sprouts pl les choux de Bruxelles (mpl) shoo duh brōō·sel

bubble n la bulle bōōl

bucket n le seau sō

buckle n la boucle boo·kluh

bud n le bourgeon boor·zhoñ

budget n le budget bōōd·zhay

buffet n (snackbar) le buffet bōō·fay

bug n (insect) la punaise pōō·nez

build vt (house) construire* koñ·strweer

building n le bâtiment bah·tee·moñ L12

building society n la société de crédit immobilier so·syay·tay duh cray·dee ee·mo·bee·lyay

bulb n le bulbe bōōlb; (light) l'ampoule (f) oñ·pool

bulk n □ **in bulk** (in large quantities) en gros oñ grō; (unpackaged) en vrac oñ vrak; **bulk buying** l'achat en gros (m) a·sha oñ grō

bull n le taureau to·rō

bulldozer n le bulldozer bōōl·dō·zehr

bullet n la balle bal

bulletin n le bulletin bōōl·tañ

bullfight n la course de taureaux koors duh to·rō

bump n (knock) le choc shok; (lump) la bosse bos □ vt cogner ko·nyay

bumper n (on car) le pare-chocs par·shok

bun n le petit pain au lait puh·tee pañ ō lay

bunch n (of flowers) le bouquet boo·kay

bundle n le paquet pa·kay

bungalow n le bungalow buñ·ga·lō

bunk n la couchette koo·shet; **bunk beds** les lits superposés lee sōō·pehr·pō·zay

buoy n la bouée boo·ay

buoyant adj (market) ferme fehrm

bureau n (office) le bureau bōō·rō

burglar n le cambrioleur koñ·bree·o·lur

burn vt brûler brōō·lay; **I've burnt my arm** je me suis brûlé le bras zhuh muh swee brōō·lay luh brah

burst vi éclater ay·kla·tay □ vt crever* kruh·vay

bury vt (person) enterrer oñ·teh·ray

bus n l'autobus (m) ō·tō·bōōs; (long distance) le car kar T4, 78f

bush n le buisson bwee·soñ

business n (dealings, work) les affaires (fpl) a·fehr; (firm) le commerce ko·mehrs; **on business** pour affaires poor a·fehr; **to do business with someone** faire* des affaires avec quelqu'un fehr day za·fehr a·vek kel·kuñ E6, Bm13

business expenses pl les frais généraux (mpl) freh zhay·nay·rō

business hours pl les heures de travail (fpl) ur duh tra·vye

businessman n l'homme d'affaires (m) om da·fehr

business trip le voyage d'affaires vwah·yazh da·fehr

businesswoman n la femme d'affaires fam da·fehr

bus service n le service d'autobus sehr·vees dō·tō·bōōs

bus stop n l'arrêt d'autobus (m) a·reh dō·tō·bōōs

bust n le buste bōōst

busy adj (person, telephone) occupé(e) o·kōō·pay; (place) animé(e) a·nee·may

busy signal n la tonalité occupé to·na·lee·tay o·kōō·pay

but conj mais meh; **not this, but that** non pas ceci mais cela noñ pah suh·see meh suh·la □ prep all but him tous sauf lui toos sōf lwee

butcher n le boucher boo·shay; **butcher's** (shop) la boucherie boo·shuh·ree S29

butter n le beurre bur E30, S30

butterfly n le papillon pa·pee·yoñ

button n le bouton boo·toñ Sn80

buy vt acheter* ash·tay; **to buy out** (partner etc) désintéresser day·zañ·tay·reh·say S6

buyer n l'acheteur (m) ash·tur, l'acheteuse (f) ash·tuhz

by prep (next to) près de preh duh; **to go by London** (via) passer par Londres pa·say par loñ·druh; **by air** par avion pa·a·vyoñ; **by train/car** en train/voiture oñ trañ/vwah·tōōr; **we'll be there by 4 o'clock** nous y serons avant 4 heures noo zee suh·roñ a·voñ 4 ur □ adv **a plane flew by** un avion est passé uñ na·vyoñ eh pa·say

bypass n la route de contournement root duh koñ·toorn·moñ

C

cab n (taxi) le taxi tak·see

cabaret n le spectacle de cabaret spek·ta·kluh duh ka·ba·reh

cabbage n le chou shoo

cabin n (in ship) la cabine ka·been

cabin cruiser n le yacht à moteur yot a mo·tur

cable n le câble kah·bluh

cactus n le cactus kak·tōōs

caddie n le caddie *ka·dee*

café n le café *ka·fay*

cafeteria n la cafétéria *ka·fay·tay·rya*

cage n la cage *kazh*

cake n le gâteau *gah·tō*

calcium n le calcium *kal·syum*

calculate vt calculer *kal·kōō·lay*

calculator n la calculatrice *kal·kōō·la·trees*

calendar n le calendrier *ka·loñ·dryay*

calf n le veau *vō*

call n (shout) l'appel (m) *a·pel*; (on phone) le coup de téléphone *koo duh tay·lay·fon* □ vt/i appeler · *a·puh·lay* □ vt (telephone) téléphoner à *tay·lay·fo·nay a*; **call me at 7 a.m.** (in hotel etc) réveillez-moi à 7 heures *ray·vay·yay mwah a 7 ur*; **to be called** s'appeler* *sa·puh·lay*

call box n la cabine téléphonique *ka·been tay·lay·fo·neek*

call girl n la call-girl *kar·geerl*

Calor gas n le butagaz *bōō·ta·gaz*

calorie n la calorie *ka·lo·ree*

camel n le chameau *sha·mō*

camera n l'appareil-photo (m) *a·pa·ray·fo·tō*; (TV) la caméra *ka·may·ra* S47f

camp vi camper *koñ·pay* A81f

campaign n la campagne *koñ·pa·nyuh*

camp-bed n le lit de camp *lee duh koñ*

camping n le camping *koñ·ping*; **to go camping** aller* camper *a·lay koñ·pay*

camp(ing) site n le camping *koñ·ping*

camshaft n l'arbre à cames (m) *ar·bra kam*

can¹ n (container) la boîte *bwaht* S33, T168

can² vi pouvoir* *poo·vwar*; **I can** je peux *zhuh puh*; **you can** vous pouvez *voo poo·vay*; **he/she can** il/elle peut *eel/el puh*; **we can** nous pouvons *noo poo·voñ*

Canada n le Canada *ka·na·da*

Canadian adj canadien(ne) *ka·na·dyañ(·dyen)*; **he's Canadian** il est Canadien *eel eh ka·na·dyañ*; **she's Canadian** elle est Canadienne *el eh ka·na·dyen*

canal n le canal *ka·nal*

canasta n la canasta *ka·na·sta*

cancel vt (reservation) annuler *a·nōō·lay*; (appointment) décommander *day·ko·moñ·day*

cancer n le cancer *koñ·sehr*

candidate n (for election) le/la candidat(e) *koñ·dee·da(·dat)*

candle n la bougie *boo·zhee*

candy n les bonbons (mpl) *boñ·boñ*

cane n (walking stick) la canne *kan*

canned adj en boîte *oñ bwaht*

cannon n le canon *ka·noñ*

canoe n le kayac *kye·yak*

canoeing n □ **to go canoeing** faire* du kayac *fehr dō kye·yak*

can-opener n l'ouvre-boîte (m) *oo·vruh·bwaht*

canteen n la cantine *koñ·teen*

canvas n la toile *twahl*

cap n (hat) la casquette *kas·ket*

capable adj capable *ka·pa·bluh*; **capable of** capable de *ka·pa·bluh duh*

cape n la cape *kap*

capital n (city) la capitale *ka·pee·tal*; (finance) le capital *ka·pee·tal*; **in capitals** en majuscules *oñ ma·zhōō·skōōl*; **capital A** A majuscule *A ma·zhōō·skōōl*

capital goods pl les biens d'équipement (mpl) *byañ day·keep·moñ*

capitalism n le capitalisme *ka·pee·ta·leez·muh*

capitalist n le/la capitaliste *ka·pee·ta·leest*

capital letter n la majuscule *ma·zhōō·skōōl*

capsule n (of medicine) la capsule *kap·sōōl*

captain n le capitaine *ka·pee·ten*

capture vt capturer *kap·tōō·ray*

car n la voiture *vwah·tōōr*; (of train) le wagon *va·goñ* T101f

carafe n la carafe *ka·raf* E12

caramel n le caramel *ka·ra·mel*

carat n le carat *ka·ra*

caravan n la caravane *ka·ra·van*

carbon n le carbone *kar·bon*

carbon copy n le carbone *kar·bon*

carbon paper n le papier carbone *pa·pyay kar·bon*

carburet(t)or n le carburateur *kar·bōō·ra·tur*

card n (post) la carte postale *kart pos·tal*; (playing card) la carte *kart*; **to play cards** jouer aux cartes *zhoo·ay ō kart* Bm2, A23

cardboard n le carton *kar·toñ*

card game n le jeu de cartes *zhuh duh kart*

cardigan n le cardigan *kar·dee·goñ*

card index n le fichier *fee·shyay*

care n (carefulness) le soin *swañ* □ vi **I don't care** ça m'est bien égal *sa meh byañ nay·gal*; **to take care of** (children etc) s'occuper de *so·kōō·pay duh*

career n la carrière *ka·ryehr*

careful adj (cautious) prudent(e) *prōō·doñ(·doñt)*; **be careful!** faites attention! *fet a·toñ·syoñ*

care of, c/o prep aux bons soins de *ō boñ swañ duh*

caretaker n le gardien *gar·dyañ*

car-ferry n le ferry *feh·ree*

cargo n la cargaison *kar·geh·zoñ*

Caribbean (Sea) n la mer des Antilles *mehr day zoñ·teey*

carnation n l'œillet (m) *uh·yeh*

carnival n le carnaval *kar·na·val*

carol n le chant de Noël *shoñ duh no·el*

car-park n le parking *par·keeng*

carpenter n le charpentier *shar·poñ·tyay*

carpet n le tapis *ta·pee*

carport n l'auvent pour voiture (m) *ō·voñ poor vwah·tōōr*

carriage n (railway) la voiture *vwah·tōōr*; **carriage free** or **paid** franco de port *froñ·kō duh por*

carriageway n (of road) la chaussée *shō·say*

carrot n la carotte *ka·rot*

carry vt (in hands, arms) porter *por·tay*; (transport) transporter *troñs·por·tay*; **to carry out an order** exécuter un ordre *eg·zay·kōō·tay uñ nor·druh*

carry-cot n le porte-bébé *port·bay·bay*

carry-out adj (food) à emporter *a oñ·por·tay*

cart n la charrette *sha·ret*

cartel n le cartel *kar·tel*

carton n (box) le carton *kar·toñ*; (yogurt etc) le pot *pō*

cartoon n le dessin humoristique *deh·sañ ōō·mō·rees·teek*; (animated) le dessin animé *deh·sañ a·nee·may*

cartridge n (for gun) la cartouche *kar·toosh*; (for camera) le chargeur *shar·zhur*; (of tape) la cassette *ka·set*

carve vt (meat) découper day·koo·pay

case n la valise va·leez; (of wine) la caisse kes; (instance) le cas kah; (lawsuit) l'affaire (f) a·fehr; just in case à tout hasard a too ta·zar; in case of en cas de oñ kah duh; in any case en tout cas oñ too kah

cash vt (cheque) encaisser oñ·keh·say □ l'argent (m) ar·zhoñ; to pay cash for something payer quelque chose en argent comptant pay·yay kel·kuh shōz oñ nar·zhoñ koñ·toñ; cash on delivery paiement à la livraison pay·moñ a la leev·reh·zoñ

cashdesk n la caisse kes

cash flow n le cash-flow kash·flō

cashier n le caissier keh·syay, la caissière keh·syehr

cashmere n le cachemire kash·meer

casino n le casino ka·zee·nō

casserole n (food) le ragoût ra·goo; (dish) la cocotte ko·kot

cassette n la cassette ka·set

cassette-recorder n le magnétophone à cassettes ma·nyeh·to·fon a ka·set

cast n (of play) les acteurs (mpl) ak·tur

cast iron n la fonte foñt

castle n le château shah·tō F6

castor oil n l'huile de ricin (f) weel duh ree·sañ

casual clothes, casual wear n les vêtements de sport (mpl) vet·moñ duh spor

cat n le chat sha

catalog(ue) n le catalogue ka·ta·log Bm20

catch vt attraper a·tra·pay; to catch cold prendre* froid proñ·druh frwah

cathedral n la cathédrale ka·tay·dral F3

catholic adj catholique ka·to·leek

cattle pl le bétail bay·tye

cauliflower n le chou-fleur shoo·flur

cause n la cause kōz □ vt causer kō·zay

cave n la caverne ka·vehrn

caviar(e) n le caviar ka·vyar

cedar n le cèdre seh·druh

cedilla n la cédille say·deey

ceiling n le plafond pla·foñ

celebrate vi célébrer* say·lay·bray □ vt fêter feh·tay

celeriac n le céleri-rave say·luh·ree·rav

celery n le céleri say·luh·ree

cell n (in prison) la cellule seh·lōōl

cellar n la cave kav

cello n le violoncelle vyo·loñ·sel

cellophane n le cellophane seh·lo·fan

Celsius adj Celsius sel·syōōs

cement n le béton bay·toñ

cemetery n le cimetière seem·tyehr

cent n le cent sent

centenary n le centenaire soñ·tuh·nehr

center n le centre soñ·truh

centigrade adj centigrade soñ·tee·grad

centilitre n le centilitre soñ·tee·lee·truh

centimetre n le centimètre soñ·tee·meh·truh

central adj central(e) soñ·tral

central heating n le chauffage central shō·fazh soñ·tral

central reservation n la bande médiane boñd may·dyan

centre n le centre soñ·truh

century n le siècle syeh·kluh

cereal n (breakfast) les céréales (fpl) say·ray·al

ceremony n la cérémonie say·ray·mo·nee

certain adj certain(e) sehr·tañ(·ten)

certainly adv certainement sehr·ten·moñ

certificate n le certificat sehr·tee·fee·ka

certified mail n l'envoi recommandé (m) oñ·vwah ruh·ko·moñ·day

chain n la chaîne shen

chain store n le magasin à succursales multiples ma·ga·zañ a sōō·kōōr·sal mōōl·tee·pluh

chair n la chaise shez; (armchair) le fauteuil fō·tuhy

chair-lift n le télésiège tay·lay·syezh

chairman n le président pray·zee·doñ

chalet n le chalet sha·leh

chalk n la craie kray

Chamber of Commerce n la Chambre de Commerce shoñ·bruh duh ko·mehrs

champagne n le champagne shoñ·pa·nyuh

champion n le champion shoñ·pyoñ, la championne shoñ·pyon

chance n □ by chance par hasard par a·zar; he has a good chance of… il a de fortes chances de… eel a duh fort shoñis duh

chancellor n (in Germany, Austria) le chancelier shoñ·suh·lyay

Chancellor of the Exchequer n le Chancelier de l'Échiquier shoñ·suh·lyay duh lay·shee·kyay

change vi se changer* suh shoñ·zhay □ vt changer* shoñ·zhay; (substitute) changer* de shoñ·zhay duh; (exchange) échanger* ay·shoñ·zhay; to change one's clothes changer* de vêtements shoñ·zhay duh vet·moñ; to change trains at Marseilles changer* de train à Marseille shoñ·zhay duh trañ a mar·say □ n change (transformation) le changement shoñ·zhuh·moñ; (money) la monnaie mo·nay; a change in the weather un changement de temps shoñ·zhuh·moñ duh toñ T100, M15

Channel n la Manche moñsh

chapel n la chapelle sha·pel

chapter n le chapitre sha·pee·truh

character n (nature) le caractère ka·rak·tehr

charge n (accusation) l'accusation (f) a·kōō·za·syoñ; to make a charge for something payer quelque chose fehr pay·yay kel·kuh shōz; free of charge gratuit(e) gra·twee(·tweet); to be in charge of être* responsable de eh·truh res·poñ·sa·bluh duh □ vt charge (money) faire* payer fehr pay·yay; charge it to my account mettez-le sur mon compte meh·tay·luh sōōr moñ koñt B60

charm n le charme sharm

charming adj charmant(e) shar·moñ(·moñt)

chart n (map) la carte kart; (diagram, table) le tableau ta·blō

charter vt (plane, bus) affréter* a·fray·tay

chartered accountant n l'expert-comptable (m) ek·spehr koñ·ta·bluh

charter flight n le charter shar·tehr

chase vt poursuivre* poor·swee·vruh

chassis n le chassis shah·see

chauffeur n le chauffeur shō·fur

cheap adj bon marché boñ mar·shay

cheat vi tricher tree·shay

check n (banking) le chèque shek; (bill) l'addition (f) a·dee·syoñ □ vt vérifier vay·ree·fyay; (passport, ticket) contrôler koñ·trō·lay; to check in (at hotel) remplir une fiche d'hôtel *roň·pleer ōōn feesh dō·tel*; (*at airport*) se présenter à l'enregistrement *suh pray·zoň·tay a loň·ruh·zhee·struh·moň*; **to check out** régler* sa note *ray·glay sa not* M25

checkbook *n* le carnet de chèques *kar·nay duh shek*

check(er)ed *adj* (*patterned*) à carreaux *a ka·rō*

checkers *pl* le jeu de dames *zhuh duh dam*

checking account *n* le compte courant *koňt koo·roň*

checkout *n* (*in store*) la caisse *kes*

checkroom *n* la consigne *koň·see·nyuh*

cheek *n* la joue *zhoo*; (*impudence*) le toupet *too·peh*

cheeky *adj* effronté(e) *eh·froň·tay*

cheer *vt* acclamer *a·kla·may*; **cheers!** à votre santé! *a vo·truh soň·tay*

cheese *n* le fromage *fro·mazh* E25, 72, S30

cheesecake *n* le flan au fromage blanc *floň ō fro·mazh bloň*

chef *n* le chef *shef*

chemical *adj* chimique *shee·meek*

chemist *n* (*pharmacist*) le pharmacien *far·ma·syaň*; **chemist's shop** la pharmacie *far·ma·see*

chemistry *n* la chimie *shee·mee*

cheque *n* le chèque *shek* A21

cheque-book *n* le carnet de chèques *kar·nay duh shek*

cheque card *n* la carte d'identité bancaire *kart dee·doň·tee·tay boň·kehr*

cherry *n* la cerise *suh·reez*; (*tree*) le cerisier *suh·ree·zee·ay*

chess *n* les échecs (*mpl*) *ay·shek*

chest *n* (*of body*) la poitrine *pwah·treen*

chestnut *n* la châtaigne *shah·teh·nyuh*

chew *vt* mâcher *mah·shay*

chewing gum *n* le chewing-gum *shwing·gum*

chicken *n* le poulet *poo·leh*

chicken pox *n* la varicelle *va·ree·sel*

chicory *n* (*for coffee*) la chicorée *shee·ko·ray*; (*vegetable*) les endives (*fpl*) *oň·deev*

chief *n* (*boss*) le chef *shef*

child *n* (*m/f*) *oň·foň* C1f

Chile *n* le Chili *shee·lee*

chili *n* le piment *pee·moň*

chill *vt* (*wine, food*) faire* rafraîchir *fehr ra·fray·sheer*; **to serve something chilled** servir quelque chose froid *sehr·veer kel·kuh shōz frwah*

chimney *n* la cheminée *shuh·mee·nay*

chin *n* le menton *moň·toň*

china *n* la porcelaine *por·suh·len*

China *n* la Chine *sheen*

Chinese *adj* chinois(e) *shee·nwah* (·*nwahz*); **he's Chinese** il est Chinois *eel eh shee·nwah*; **she's Chinese** elle est Chinoise *el eh shee·nwahz* □ *n* **Chinese** (*language*) le chinois *shee·nwah*

chip *n* (*electronics*) la microplaquette *mee·kro·pla·ket*; (*in gambling*) le jeton *zhuh·toň*

chips *pl* les frites (*fpl*) *freet*

chiropodist *n* le/la pédicure *pay·dee·koōr*

chives *pl* la ciboulette *see·boo·let*

chocolate *n* le chocolat *sho·kō·la*

choice *n* le choix *shwah*

choir *n* le chœur *kur*

choke *n* (*of car*) le starter *star·tehr*

cholesterol *n* le cholestérol *ko·le·stay·rol*

choose *vt* choisir *shwah·zeer*

chop *vt* (*food*) hacher *a·shay* □ *n* pork chop la côtelette de porc *kōt·let duh por*

chopsticks *pl* les baguettes (*fpl*) *ba·get*

Christian *n* le chrétien *kray·tyaň*, la chrétienne *kray·tyen*

Christian name *n* le prénom *pray·noň*

Christmas *n* Noël (*m*) *no·el*

Christmas card la carte de Noël *kart duh no·el*

Christmas Day *n* le jour de Noël *zhoor duh no·el*

Christmas Eve *n* la veille de Noël *vay duh no·el*

Christmas tree *n* l'arbre de Noël (*m*) *ar·bruh duh no·el*

chrome *n* le chrome *krōm*

chrysanthemum *n* le chrysanthème *kree·zoň·tem*

church *n* l'église (*f*) *ay·gleez* Sn91

churchyard *n* le cimetière (autour d'une église) *seem·tyehr* (*ō·toor dōōn ay·gleez*)

cider *n* le cidre *see·druh*

cigar *n* le cigare *see·gar*

cigarette *n* la cigarette *see·ga·ret* Mc37

cigarette case *n* le porte-cigarettes *port·see·ga·ret*

cigarette lighter *n* le briquet *bree·keh*

cine-camera *n* la caméra *ka·may·ra*

cinema *n* le cinéma *see·nay·ma*

cinnamon *n* la cannelle *ka·nel*

circle *n* le cercle *sehr·kluh*; (*in theatre*) le balcon *bal·koň*

circuit *n* (*electric*) le circuit *seer·kwee*

circumflex (accent) *n* l'accent circonflexe (*m*) *ak·soň seer·koň·fleks*

circumstances *pl* les circonstances (*fpl*) *seer·koň·stoňs*

circus *n* le cirque *seerk*

city *n* la cité *see·tay*; **city centre** le centre ville *soň·truh veel*

city hall *n* la mairie *meh·ree*

civilization *n* la civilisation *see·vee·lee·za·syoň*

civil servant *n* le/la fonctionnaire *foňk·syoň·nehr*

civil service *n* l'administration (*f*) *ad·mee·nee·stra·syoň*

civil war *n* la guerre civile *gehr see·veel*

claim *vt* (*lost property, baggage*) demander *duh·moň·day*

clam *n* la praire *prehr*

clap *vi* applaudir *a·plo·deer*

claret *n* le bordeaux *bor·dō*

clasp *n* le fermoir *fehr·mwahr*

class *n* la classe *klas*; **to travel first class** voyager* en première *vwah·ya·zhay oň prum·yehr*; **a second class ticket** un billet de deuxième classe *uň bee·yeh duh duz·yem klas*

classical *adj* (*music, art*) classique *kla·seek*

clause *n* (*in contract*) la clause *klōz*

clay *n* l'argile (*f*) *ar·zheel*

clean *adj* propre *pro·pruh* □ *vt* nettoyer *neh·twah·yay*; **to have a suit cleaned** faire* nettoyer un costume *fehr neh·twah·yay uň kos·tōōm*

cleaner *n* (*of house etc*) la femme de ménage *fam duh may·nazh*

cleaner's *n* la teinturerie *taň·tōō·ruh·ree*

clear *adj* (*transparent*) transparent(e) *troň·spa·roň*(·*roňt*); (*distinct*) clair(e) *klehr*; (*not blocked*) libre *lee·bruh* □ *vt* (*road*) dégager* *day·ga·zhay*; (*pipe*) déboucher *day·boo·shay*

clerk *n* (*in office*) l'employé(e) de bureau (*m/f*) *oň·plwah·yay duh boō·rō*;

(*in store*) le vendeur *voñ·dur*, la vendeuse *voñ·duhz*

clever *adj* (*person*) intelligent(e) *añ·teh·lee·zhoñ(·zhoñt*); (*plan*) ingénieux(euse) *añ·zhay·nyuh(·nyuhz*)

client *n* le/la client(e) *klee·oñ(·oñt*)

cliff *n* la falaise *fa·lez*

climate *n* le climat *klee·ma*

climb *vt* (*tree, wall*) monter sur *moñ·tay sōōr*; **to climb over something** franchir quelque chose *froñ·sheer kel·kuh shōz*

clinic *n* le centre médical *soñ·truh may·dee·kal*

cloak *n* la grande cape *groñd kap*

cloakroom *n* le vestiaire *ves·tyehr*

clock *n* (*large*) l'horloge (*f*) *or·lozh*; (*small*) la pendule *poñ·dōōl*

closed circuit television *n* la télévision en circuit fermé *tay·lay·vee·zyoñ oñ seer·kwee fehr·may*

close[1] *adj* (*near*) proche *prosh*; (*stuffy*) lourd(e) *loor* (*loord*); **close to** près de *preh duh*; **close by** tout près *too preh*

close[2] *vt* fermer *fehr·may* □ *vi* **the door closed** la porte s'est fermée *la port seh fehr·may*; **when do the shops close?** à quelle heure ferment les magasins? *a kel ur fehrm lay ma·ga·zañ* T201, A29

closet *n* le placard *pla·kar*

cloth *n* (*cleaning*) la lavette *la·vet*

clothes *pl* les vêtements (*mpl*) *vet·moñ* A53, S77

clotheshorse *n* le séchoir à linge pliant *say·shwahr a lañzh plee·yoñ*

clothesline *n* la corde à linge *kord a lañzh*

clothes-peg *n* la pince à linge *pañs a lañzh*

cloud *n* le nuage *nōō·azh*

cloudy *adj* nuageux(euse) *nōō·azh·uh(·uhz*)

clove *n* le clou de girofle *kloo duh zhee·ro·fluh*; **clove of garlic** la gousse d'ail *goos dye*

clown *n* le clown *kloon*

club *n* (*society*) le club *klub*; **clubs** (*in cards*) le trèfle *treh·fluh*

clumsy *adj* (*person*) maladroit(e) *ma·la·drwah(·drwaht*)

clutch *n* (*of car*) l'embrayage (*m*) *oñ·bray·yazh*

coach *n* (*of train*) la voiture *vwah·tōōr*; (*bus*) le car *kar*; (*instructor*) le moniteur *mo·nee·tur*, la monitrice *mo·nee·trees*

coal *n* le charbon *shar·boñ*

coarse *adj* (*texture, material*) grossier(ère) *gro·syay(·syehr*)

coast *n* la côte *kōt*

coastguard *n* le garde-côte *gard·kōt*

coat *n* le manteau *moñ·tō*

coat hanger *n* le cintre *sañ·truh*

cock(erel) *n* le coq *kok*

cockle *n* la coque *kok*

cocktail *n* (*drink*) le cocktail *kok·tel*; **prawn cocktail** le cocktail de crevettes *kok·tel duh kruh·vet*

cocoa *n* le cacao *ka·ka·ō*

coconut *n* la noix de coco *nwah duh ko·kō*

cod *n* la morue *mo·rōō*

codeine *n* la codéine *ko·day·een*

coffee *n* le café *ka·fay*; **black coffee** le café noir *ka·fay nwahr*; **white coffee** le café au lait *ka·fay ō leh* B51, S31

coffee break *n* la pause-café *pōz·ka·fay*

coffee cup *n* la tasse à café *tas a ka·fay*

coffeepot *n* la cafetière *kaf·tyehr*

coffee table *n* la table basse *ta·bluh bas*

coffin *n* le cercueil *sehr·kuhy*

cognac *n* le cognac *ko·nyak*

coin *n* la pièce *pyes*

coincide *vi* coïncider *ko·añ·see·day*

coincidence *n* la coïncidence *ko·añ·see·doñs*

colander *n* la passoire *pas·wahr*

cold *adj* froid(e) *frwah* (*frwahd*); **I'm cold** j'ai froid *zhay frwah* □ *n* **cold** (*illness*) le rhume *rōōm* E35, S40

coleslaw *n* la salade de chou cru *sa·lad duh shoo krōō*

colic *n* la colique *ko·leek*

collaborate *vi* collaborer *ko·la·bo·ray*

collapse *vi* (*person*) s'écrouler *say·kroo·lay*

collar *n* le col *kol*; (*for dog*) le collier *ko·lyay*

colleague *n* le/la collègue *ko·leg*

collect *vt* (*stamps etc*) collectionner *ko·lek·syo·nay*; (*donations*) recueillir *ruh·kuh·yeer*

collect call *n* la communication en P.C.V. *ko·mōō·nee·ka·syoñ oñ pay·say·vay*

collection *n* (*of mail*) la levée *luh·vay*

college *n* le collège *ko·lezh*

collide *vi* entrer en collision *oñ·tray oñ ko·lee·zyoñ*

collision *n* la collision *ko·lee·zyoñ*

cologne *n* l'eau de Cologne (*f*) *ō duh ko·lon·yuh*

colo(u)r *n* la couleur *koo·lur*; **colo(u)r TV** la télévision en couleur *tay·lay·vee·zyoñ oñ koo·lur*

colo(u)red *adj* (*person*) de couleur *duh koo·lur*

comb *n* le peigne *peh·nyuh* □ *vt* peigner *peh·nyay*

come *vi* (*arrive*) venir* *vuh·neer*; **to come from London** venir* de Londres *vuh·neer duh loñ·druh*; **to come in** entrer *oñ·tray*; **to come off** se détacher *suh day·ta·shay*; **to come out** (*person, sun*) sortir* *sor·teer*; (*stain*) partir* *par·teer*; **to come round** (*recover*) reprendre* connaissance *ruh·proñ·druh ko·neh·soñs*

comedian *n* le comique *ko·meek*

comedy *n* la comédie *ko·may·dee*

comfort *n* (*ease*) le confort *koñ·for*

comfortable *adj* confortable *koñ·for·ta·bluh*

comfort station *n* les toilettes (*fpl*) *twah·let*

comic *n* le comic *ko·meek*

comma *n* la virgule *veer·gōōl*

command *n* l'ordre (*m*) *or·druh*

comment *n* la remarque *ruh·mark*

commerce *n* le commerce *ko·mehrs*

commercial *adj* commercial(e) *ko·mehr·syal* □ *n* (*ad*) la publicité *pōō·blee·see·tay*

commercialized *adj* (*resort*) commercialisé(e) *ko·mehr·sya·lee·zay*

commission *n* (*sum received*) la commission *ko·mee·syoñ*

commit *vt* (*crime*) commettre* *ko·meh·truh*

committee *n* le comité *ko·mee·tay*

commodity *n* le produit *pro·dwee*

common *adj* (*ordinary, frequent*) fréquent(e) *fray·koñ(·koñt*)

Common Market *n* le Marché Commun *mar·shay ko·muñ*

communicate *vi* □ **to communicate with someone** communiquer avec quelqu'un *ko·mōō·nee·kay a·vek kel·kuñ*

communication cord *n* la sonnette d'alarme *so·net da·larm*

Communist *n* le/la communiste *ko·mōō·neest* □ *adj* communiste *ko·mōō·neest*

commutation ticket *n* la carte d'abonnement *kart da·bon·moñ*

commuter *n* le/la banlieusard(e) *boñ·lyuh·zar(·zard)*

company *n* (*firm*) la société *so·syay·tay*

company secretary *n* le secrétaire général *suh·kray·tehr zhay·nay·ral*

compare *vt* □ to **compare something with something** comparer quelque chose avec quelque chose *koñ·pa·ray kel·kuh shōz a·vek kel·kuh shōz*

compartment *n* (*on train*) le compartiment *koñ·par·tee·moñ*

compass *n* la boussole *boo·sol*

compensation *n* la compensation *koñ·poñ·sa·syoñ*

competent *adj* compétent(e) *koñ·pay·toñ(·toñt)*

competition *n* la compétition *koñ·pay·tee·syoñ*

competitor *n* le/la concurrent(e) *koñ·kōō·roñ(·roñt)*

complain *vi* se plaindre* *suh plañ·druh*; to **complain about** se plaindre de *suh plañ·druh duh*

complaint *n* (*dissatisfaction*) la plainte *plañt*

complete *adj* achevé(e) *ash·vay* □ *vt* achever* *ash·vay*

completely *adv* complètement *koñ·plet·moñ*

complex *adj* complexe *koñ·pleks*

complexion *n* le teint *tañ*

complicated *adj* compliqué(e) *koñ·plee·kay*

compliment *n* le compliment *koñ·plee·moñ*

component *n* (*for car etc*) la pièce *pyes*

composer *n* le compositeur *koñ·po·zee·tur*

compound interest *n* les intérêts composés (*mpl*) *añ·tay·reh koñ·pō·zay*

comprehensive insurance *n* l'assurance tous-risques (*f*) *a·sōō·roñs too reesk*

computer *n* l'ordinateur (*m*) *or·dee·na·tur*

computerize *vt* (*system*) automatiser *ō·to·ma·tee·zay*

computer programming *n* la programmation *pro·gra·ma·syoñ*

conceited *adj* vaniteux(euse) *va·nee·tuh(·tuhz)*

concern *n* (*anxiety*) le souci *soo·see* □ *vt* (*be important to*) concerner *koñ·sehr·nay*; **that doesn't concern you** ça ne vous regarde pas *sa nuh voo ruh·gard pa*

concert *n* le concert *koñ·sehr* L39

concrete *n* le béton *bay·toñ* □ *adj* en béton *oñ bay·toñ*

condemn *vt* condamner *koñ·da·nay*

condensed milk *n* le lait condensé *leh koñ·doñ·say*

condiments *pl* les condiments (*mpl*) *koñ·dee·moñ*

condition *n* la condition *koñ·dee·syoñ*; **on condition that…** à condition que… *a koñ·dee·syoñ·kuh*

conditioner *n* (*for hair*) la crème démêlante *krem day·meh·loñt*

conductor *n* (*on bus*) le receveur *ruh·suh·vur*; (*of orchestra*) le chef d'orchestre *shef dor·kes·truh*; (*on train*) le chef de train *shef duh trañ*

cone *n* (*for ice cream*) le cornet *kor·nay*

confectioner *n* le confiseur *koñ·fee·zur*

confectionery *n* la confiserie *koñ·fee·zuh·ree*

conference *n* (*meeting*) la réunion *ray·ōō·nyoñ*

confess *vt* confesser *koñ·feh·say* □ *vi* se confesser *suh koñ·feh·say*; to **confess to something** avouer quelque chose *a·voo·ay kel·kuh shōz*

confession *n* la confession *koñ·feh·syoñ*

confidence *n* (*trust*) la confiance *koñ·fyoñs*; **confidence in** la confiance en *koñ·fyoñs oñ*; **in confidence** en confidence *oñ koñ·fee·doñs*

confident *adj* assuré(e) *a·sōō·ray*

confidential *adj* confidentiel(le) *koñ·fee·doñ·syel*

confirm *vt* (*reservation etc*) confirmer *koñ·feer·may*

confuse *vt* confondre *koñ·foñ·druh*; to **confuse one thing with another** confondre quelque chose avec quelque chose d'autre *koñ·foñ·druh kel·kuh shōz a·vek kel·kuh shōz dō·truh*

confused *adj* (*muddled*) confus(e) *koñ·fōō(·fōōz)*

congratulate *vt* félciter *fay·lee·see·tay*; to **congratulate someone on something** féliciter quelqu'un de quelque chose *fay·lee·see·tay kel·kuñ duh kel·kuh shōz*

congratulations *pl* les félicitations (*fpl*) *fay·lee·see·ta·syoñ*; **congratulations!** félicitations! *fay·lee·see·ta·syoñ*

conjuror *n* le prestidigitateur *preh·stee·dee·zhee·ta·tur*

connect *vt* (*join*) relier *ruh·lyay*; **this train connects with the 16.45** ce train assure la correspondance avec le train de 16.45 *suh trañ a·sōōr la ko·res·poñ·doñs a·vek luh trañ duh 16.45*

connection *n* (*train etc*) la correspondance *ko·res·poñ·doñs*

connoisseur *n* le connaisseur *ko·neh·sur*

conscience *n* la conscience *koñ·syoñs*

conscious *adj* conscient(e) *koñ·syoñ(·syoñt)*

consequence *n* (*result*) la conséquence *koñ·say·koñs*

conservative *adj* conservateur *koñ·sehr·va·tur*, conservatrice *koñ·sehr·va·trees*

conservatory *n* (*greenhouse*) la serre *sehr*

consider *vt* considérer *koñ·see·day·ray*

consist of *vt* consister en *koñ·sees·tay oñ*

consommé *n* le consommé *koñ·so·may*

constipated *adj* constipé(e) *koñ·stee·pay*

construct *vt* construire* *koñ·strweer*

consul *n* le consul *koñ·sōōl*

consulate *n* le consulat *koñ·sōō·la* Sn90

consult *vt* consulter *koñ·sōōl·tay*

consultant *n* (*doctor*) le médecin consultant *mayd·sañ koñ·sōōl·toñ*; (*other specialist*) le consultant *koñ·sōōl·toñ*

consulting room *n* le cabinet de consultation *ka·bee·neh duh koñ·sōōl·ta·syoñ*

consumer *n* le consommateur *koñ·so·ma·tur*, la consommatrice *koñ·so·ma·trees*

consumer goods *pl* les biens de consommation (*mpl*) *byañ duh koñ·som·ma·syoñ*

contact *vt* se mettre* en contact avec *suh met·troñ koñ·takt a·vek*

contact lenses *pl* les verres de contact (*mpl*) *vehr duh koñ·takt*

contagious *adj* contagieux(euse) *koñ·ta·zhyuh(·zhyuhz)*

contain *vt* contenir* *koñ·tuh·neer*

container *n* le récipient *ray·see·pyoñ*; (*for shipping etc*) le container *koñ·tay·nehr*

contemporary *adj* (*modern*) contemporain(e) *koñ·toñ·po·rañ(·ren)*

content(ed) *adj* content(e) *koñ·toñ (·toñt)*

contents *pl* le contenu *koñ·tuh·nōō*; (*table in book*) la table des matières *ta·bluh day ma·tyehr*

contest *n* (*competition*) le concours *koñ·koor*

contestant *n* le/la concurrent(e) *koñ·kōō·roñ(·roñt)*

continent *n* le continent *koñ·tee·noñ*; **the Continent** l'Europe continentale (*f*) *uh·rop koñ·tee·noñ·tal*

continental *adj* continental(e) *koñ·tee·noñ·tal*

continental breakfast *n* le petit déjeuner *puh·tee day·zhuh·nay*

continental quilt *n* la couette *kwet*

continual *adj* continuel(le) *koñ·tee·nōō·el*

continue *vt/i* continuer *koñ·tee·nōō·ay*; **to continue to do** continuer de faire *koñ·tee·nōō·ay duh fehr*

continuous *adj* continu(e) *koñ·tee·nōō*

continuously *adv* sans cesse *soñ ses*

contraband *n* la contrebande *koñ·truh·boñd*

contraceptive *n* le contraceptif *koñ·tra·sep·teef*

contract *n* le contrat *koñ·tra*

contractor *n* l'entrepreneur (*m*) *oñ·truh·pruh·nur*

contrary *n* □ **on the contrary** au contraire *ô koñ·trehr*

contribute *vi* contribuer *koñ·tree·bōō·ay*

control *vt* maîtriser *may·tree·zay* □ *n* **circumstances beyond our control** des circonstances indépendantes de notre volonté *day seer·koñ·stoñs añ·day·poñ·doñt duh no·truh vo·loñ·tay*

controls *pl* les commandes (*fpl*) *ko·moñd* T113

control tower *n* la tour de contrôle *toor duh koñ·trôl*

conurbation *n* la conurbation *ko·nōōr·ba·syoñ*

convalescence *n* la convalescence *koñ·va·leh·soñs*

convenient *adj* commode *ko·mod*; **convenient for shops** bien situé(e) pour les magasins *byañ see·tōō·ay poor lay ma·ga·zañ*

convent *n* le couvent *koo·voñ*

conversation *n* la conversation *koñ·vehr·sa·syoñ*

convertible *n* (*car*) la décapotable *day·ka·po·ta·bluh*

convince *vt* convaincre* *koñ·vañ·kruh*

cook *vt* faire* cuire *fehr kweer* □ *vi* cuire* *kweer* □ *n* le cuisinier *kwee·zee·nyay*, la cuisinière *kwee·zee·nyehr*

cooker *n* la cuisinière *kwee·zee·nyehr*

cookie *n* le gâteau sec *gah·tô sek*

cooking *n* la cuisine *kwee·zeen*

cool *adj* frais *freh*, fraîche *fresh*

cooling system *n* le système de refroidissement *see·stem duh ruh·frwah·dees·moñ*

co-operate *vi* coopérer* *kô·o·pay·ray*

co-operative *n* la coopérative *kô·o·pay·ra·teev*

Copenhagen *n* Copenhague (*f*) *ko·pen·hag*

copper *n* (*metal*) le cuivre *kwee·vruh*

copy *n* (*of book etc*) l'exemplaire (*m*) *eg·zoñ·plehr*; (*imitation*) la copie *ko·pee* □ *vt* copier *ko·pyay*

copyright *n* les droits d'auteur (*mpl*) *drwah dō·tur*

coral *n* le corail *ko·rye*

cord *n* (*twine*) la corde *kord*; (*fabric*) le velours côtelé *vuh·loor kôt·lay*

cordial *n* le cordial *kor·dyal*

corduroy *n* le velours côtelé *vuh·loor kôt·lay*

cork *n* le liège *lyezh*; (*of bottle*) le bouchon *boo·shoñ*

corkscrew *n* le tire-bouchon *teer·boo·shoñ*

corn *n* (*cereals*) le blé *blay*; (*on foot*) le cor *kor*

corned beef *n* le corned-beef *kor·nud·beef*

corner *n* (*of streets*) le coin *kwañ*; (*bend in road*) le virage *vee·razh* □ *vi* prendre* un virage *proñ·druñ vee·razh*

cornet *n* (*of ice cream*) le cornet *kor·nay*

cornflakes *pl* les cornflakes (*fpl*) *korn·flakes*

cornflour *n* la maïzena *ma·ee·zeh·na*

corn-on-the-cob *n* l'épi de maïs (*m*) *ay·pee duh ma·ees*

cornstarch *n* la maïzena *ma·ee·zeh·na*

coronation *n* le couronnement *koo·ro·nuh·moñ*

corporation *n* (*firm*) la société *so·syay·tay*; (*of town*) le conseil municipal *koñ·say mōō·nee·see·pal*

corporation tax *n* l'impôt sur les bénéfices (*m*) *añ·pô sōōr lay bay·nay·fees*

correct *adj* (*accurate*) exact(e) *eg·zakt*; (*proper*) correct(e) *ko·rekt* □ *vt* corriger* *ko·ree·zhay*

correction *n* (*alteration*) la correction *ko·rek·syoñ*

correspondence *n* (*mail*) la correspondance *ko·res·poñ·doñs*

correspondence course *n* le cours par correspondance *koor par ko·res·poñ·doñs*

corridor *n* le couloir *koo·lwahr*

corrode *vt* corroder *ko·ro·day*

corrugated iron *n* la tôle ondulée *tôl oñ·dōō·lay*

corrugated paper *n* le carton ondulé *kar·toñ oñ·dōō·lay*

corrupt *adj* corrompu(e) *ko·roñ·pōō*

corruption *n* la corruption *ko·rōōp·syoñ*

corset *n* le corset *kor·seh*

Corsica *n* la Corse *kors*

cosmetics *pl* les cosmétiques (*mpl*) *kos·may·teek*

cosmetic surgery *n* la chirurgie esthétique *shee·rōōr·zhee es·tay·teek*

cosmopolitan *adj* cosmopolite *kos·mo·po·leet*

cost *n* le coût *koo*; **to buy something at cost** acheter* quelque chose au prix coûtant *ash·tay kel·kuh shôz ô pree*

koo·toñ □ *vt* cost coûter koo·tay S4,
Bm25f

cost of living *n* le coût de la vie koo
duh la vee

cost price *n* le prix coûtant pree koo·
toñ

costs *pl* (*of production etc*) les frais
(*mpl*) freh

costume *n* (*theatrical*) le costume kos·
tōōm

costume jewellery *n* les bijoux (de)
fantaisie (*mpl*) bee·zhoo (duh) foñ·
tay·zee

cot *n* le lit d'enfant lee doñ·foñ

cottage *n* la petite maison puh·teet
meh·zoñ

cottage cheese *n* ≈ le fromage blanc
fro·mazh bloñ

cotton *n* (*fabric*) le coton ko·toñ;
(*thread*) le fil de coton feel duh
ko·toñ

cotton wool *n* le coton hydrophile ko·
toñ ee·dro·feel

couch *n* le canapé ka·na·pay

couchette *n* la couchette koo·shet

cough *n* la toux too □ *vi* tousser too·
say S40

cough drops *pl* les pastilles pour la
toux (*fpl*) pas·teey poor la too

cough medicine *n* le sirop pour la toux
see·rō poor la too

could *vi* □ **we could do it** nous pourrions le faire noo poo·reeoñ luh fehr;
could I have... est-ce que je pourrais
avoir... es·kuh zhuh poo·reh za·
vwahr

council *n* (*of town*) le conseil municipal koñ·say mōō·nee·see·pal

count *vt* (*objects, people*) compter
koñ·tay □ *vi* **to count up to 10** compter jusqu'à 10 koñ·tay zhōōs·ka 10

counter *n* (*in shop*) le comptoir koñ·
twahr; (*gambling*) le jeton zhuh·toñ

counterfoil *n* le talon ta·loñ

country *n* (*land*) le pays pay·yee; (*not
town*) la campagne koñ·pa·nyuh; **in
the country** à la campagne a la koñ·
pa·nyuh Mc55

countryside *n* la campagne koñ·pa·
nyuh

county *n* le comté koñ·tay

coup d'état *n* le coup d'état koo day·ta

coupé *n* (*car*) le coupé koo·pay

couple *n* (*persons*) le couple koo·pluh;
a couple of (*a few*) quelques kel·kuh

coupon *n* le coupon koo·poñ

courage *n* le courage koo·razh

courgettes *pl* les courgettes (*fpl*) koor·
zhet

courier *n* le guide geed

course *n* (*lessons*) le cours koor; (*of
meal*) le plat plah; (*for golf*) le terrain teh·rañ; **course of treatment** le
traitement tret·moñ

court *n* (*law*) la cour koor; (*tennis etc*)
le court koor

court-card *n* la figure fee·gōōr

courtyard *n* la cour koor

cousin *n* le/la cousin(e) koo·zañ(·zeen)

cover *n* la couverture koo·vehr·tōōr;
under separate cover sous pli séparé
soo plee say·pa·ray □ *vt* couvrir•
koo·vreer; (*distance*) parcourir• par·
koo·reer

cover charge *n* le couvert koo·vehr

covering letter *n* la lettre explicative
leh·truh ek·splee·ka·teev

cow *n* la vache vash

coward *n* le/la lâche lahsh

cowboy *n* le cow-boy kow·boy

crab *n* le crabe krab

crack *n* (*split*) la fente foñt; (*noise*) le
craquement krak·moñ □ *vt* **to crack
a glass** fêler un verre feh·lay uñ vehr
□ *vi* **the glass cracked** le verre s'est
fêlé luh vehr seh feh·lay

cracker *n* (*crisp wafer*) le biscuit salé
bees·kwee sa·lay; (*paper toy*) le pétard pay·tar

cradle *n* le berceau behr·sō

craft *n* le métier may·tyay

craftsman *n* (*m*) (*pl -men*) l'artisan (*m*) ar·tee·zoñ

cramp *n* la crampe kroñp

cranberry *n* la canneberge kan·behrzh

crane *n* (*machine*) la grue grōō

crash *n* (*noise*) le fracas fra·ka; (*collision*) la collision ko·lee·zyoñ □ *vt* **to
crash one's car** avoir• une collision
avec sa voiture a·vwahr ōōn ko·lee·
zyoñ a·vek sa vwah·tōōr □ *vi* **to crash
into something** percuter quelque
chose pehr·kōō·tay kel·kuh shōz

crash barrier *n* la glissière glee·syehr

crash course *n* le cours intensif koor
añ·toñ·seef

crash helmet *n* le casque protecteur
kask pro·tek·tur

crash-landing *n* l'atterrissage en catastrophe (*m*) a·teh·ree·sazh oñ ka·tas·
trof

crate *n* la caisse kes

crawfish, crayfish *n* (*freshwater*) l'écrevisse (*f*) ay·kruh·vees; (*saltwater*) la
langouste loñ·goost

crawl *vi* ramper roñ·pay □ *n* (*swimming*) le crawl krol

crayon *n* le crayon de couleur kray·
yoñ duh koo·lur

crazy *adj* fou foo, folle fol

cream *n* la crème krem □ *adj* crème
krem

cream cheese *n* le fromage frais fro·
mazh freh

creamy *adj* (*texture*) crémeux(euse)
kray·muh(·muz)

crease *n* le pli plee

creased *adj* froissé(e) frwah·say

create *vt* créer kray·ay

crèche *n* la garderie d'enfants gar·duh·
ree doñ·foñ

credit *n* le crédit kray·dee; **on credit** à
crédit a kray·dee; **to give somebody
credit** faire• crédit à quelqu'un fehr
kray·dee a kel·kuñ □ *vt* **to credit
F5000 to someone's account** créditer
le compte de quelqu'un de F5000
kray·dee·tay luh koñt duh kel·kuñ
duh F5000

credit card *n* la carte de crédit kart
duh kray·dee T165, M13

creditor *n* le créancier kray·oñ·syay, la
créancière kray·oñ·syehr

credit squeeze *n* les restrictions de crédit ray·streek·syoñ duh kray·dee

crème de menthe *n* la crème de
menthe krem duh moñt

cress *n* le cresson kreh·soñ

Crete *n* la Crète kret

crew *n* (*of ship, plane*) l'équipage (*m*)
ay·kee·pazh

crib *n* (*baby's*) le lit d'enfant lee doñ·
foñ

cricket *n* (*sport*) le cricket kree·ket

crime *n* le crime kreem

criminal *adj* criminel(le) kree·mee·nel

cripple *n* l'invalide (*m/f*) añ·va·leed

crisis *n* la crise kreez

crisp *adj* croustillant(e) kroos·tee·yoñ
(·yoñt) □ *pl* **crisps** les chips (*fpl*)
sheeps

criticize *vt* critiquer kree·tee·kay

crockery *n* la vaisselle veh·sel

crocodile n le crocodile kro·ko·deel
crocus n le crocus kro·kŏŏs
croissant n le croissant krwah·soñ
crooked adj tordu(e) tor·dŏŏ
crop n (harvest) la récolte ray·kolt; (whip) la cravache kra·vash
croquet n le croquet kro·keh
croquette n la croquette kro·ket
cross n la croix krwah □ vt (road, sea) traverser tra·vehr·say; (cheque) barrer ba·ray; **to cross out** barrer ba·ray
crossing n (voyage) la traversée tra·vehr·say
crossroads n le carrefour kar·foor
crosswalk n le passage clouté pa·sazh kloo·tay
croupier n le croupier kroo·pyay
crouton n le croûton kroo·toñ
crowd n la foule fool
crowded adj bondé(e) boñ·day
crown n la couronne koo·ron
crude adj (oil etc) brut(e) brŏŏt
cruel adj cruel(le) krŏŏ·el
cruise n la croisière krwah·zyehr; **to go on a cruise** faire* une croisière fehr ōŏn krwah·zyehr
crumb n la miette myet
crush vt écraser ay·kra·zay
crust n la croûte kroot
crutch n la béquille bay·keey
cry vi pleurer pluh·ray □ n le cri kree
crystal n (glass) le cristal kree·stal
Cuba n le Cuba kōŏ·ba
Cuban adj cubain(e) kōŏ·bañ(·ben)
cube n le cube kōŏb
cubicle n la cabine ka·been
cucumber n le concombre koñ·koñ·bruh
cuddle vt caresser ka·reh·say
cuff n (of shirt) la manchette moñ·shet
cuff link n le bouton de manchette boo·toñ duh moñ·shet
cuisine n la cuisine kwee·zeen
cul-de-sac n le cul-de-sac kōŏ·duh·sak
cultivate vt cultiver kōŏl·tee·vay
culture n la culture kōŏl·tōŏr
cup n la tasse tas; (trophy) la coupe koop
cupboard n le placard pla·kar
curb n le bord du trottoir bor dōŏ tro·twahr
cure vt guérir gay·reer
curious adj curieux(euse) kōŏ·ryuh (·ryuhz)
curl n la boucle boo·kluh
curler n (for hair) le bigoudi bee·goo·dee
curly adj frisé(e) free·zay
currant n le raisin sec reh·zañ sek
currency n la monnaie mo·nay; **foreign currency** les devises étrangères (fpl) duh·veez ay·troñ·zhehr
current n (of water, air) le courant koo·roñ
current account n le compte courant koñt koo·roñ
curry n le curry kōŏ·ree
curry powder n la poudre de curry poo·druh duh kōŏ·ree
curtain n le rideau ree·dō
curve n la courbe koorb; (in road) le virage vee·razh
cushion n le coussin koo·sañ
custard n la crème anglaise krem oñ·glez
custom n la coutume koo·tōŏm
customer n le/la client(e) klee·oñ(·oñt)
custom-made adj fait(e) sur mesure feh (fet) sōŏr muh·zōŏr
customs n la douane dwan

customs duty n les droits de douane (mpl) drwah duh dwan
customs officer n le douanier dwa·nyay
cut vt couper koo·pay; (reduce) réduire* ray·dweer; (dilute) couper koo·pay; **to cut oneself** se couper suh koo·pay □ n cut (wound) la coupure koo·pōŏr; (of meat) le morceau mor·sō
cute adj (pretty) mignon(ne) mee·nyoñ(·nyon)
cutlery n les couverts (mpl) koo·vehr
cutlet n la côtelette kōt·let
cut-price adj à prix réduit a pree ray·dwee
cycle vi faire* de la bicyclette fehr duh la bee·see·klet
cycling n le cyclisme see·klees·muh; **to go cycling** faire* de la bicyclette fehr duh la bee·see·klet
cyclist n le/la cycliste see·kleest
cylinder n le cylindre see·lañ·druh
Cyprus n la Chypre shee·pruh
Czechoslovakia n la Tchécoslovaquie che·ko·slō·va·kee
Czech(oslovakian) adj tchèque chek

D

dacron n le tergal tehr·gal
dad(dy) n le papa pa·pa
daffodil n la jonquille zhoñ·keey
dagger n le poignard pwah·nyar
daily adj quotidien(ne) ko·tee·dyañ (·dyen) □ n (newspaper) le journal zhoor·nal
dainty adj délicat(e) day·lee·ka(·kat)
dairy (store) n la crémerie kray·muh·ree
dam n le barrage ba·razh
damage n les dégâts (mpl) day·ga; **damages** les dommages-intérêts (mpl) do·mazh·zañ·tay·reh □ vt damage abîmer a·bee·may
damp adj humide ōŏ·meed
dance vi danser doñ·say □ n la danse doñs; (ball) le bal bal L38
dandruff n les pellicules (fpl) peh·lee·kōŏl
danger n le danger doñ·zhay
dangerous adj dangereux(euse) doñ·zhuh·ruh(·ruhz)
Danish adj danois(e) da·nwah (·nwahz); **he's Danish** il est Danois eel eh da·nwah; **she's Danish** elle est Danoise el eh da·nwahz □ n Danish le danois da·nwah
dare vi □ **to dare to do something** oser faire quelque chose ō·zay fehr kel·kuh shōz
dark adj sombre soñ·bruh; (colour) foncé(e) foñ·say; (hair) brun(e) bruñ (brōōn); **it's dark** il fait noir eel feh nwahr
darling n le/la chéri(e) shay·ree
darn vt repriser ruh·pree·zay
dart n (to throw) la fléchette flay·shet; (on clothes) la pince pañs; **game of darts** les fléchettes (fpl) flay·shet
dash n (in writing) le tiret tee·reh
dash(board) n le tableau de bord ta·blō duh bor
data pl les données (fpl) do·nay
data bank, **data base** n la banque de données boñk duh do·nay
data file n le fichier de données fee·shyay duh do·nay
data processing n le traitement des données tret·moñ day do·nay
date n (day) la date dat; (appointment)

le rendez-vous *roñ·day·voo;* (*fruit*) la datte *dat;* **what's the date today?** le combien sommes-nous aujourd'hui? *luh koñ·byañ som·noo ō·zhoor·dwee;* **out of date** périmé(e) *pay·ree·may*

date line n la ligne de changement de date *lee·nyuh duh shoñ·zhuh·moñ duh dat*

daughter n la fille *feey* C16

daughter-in-law n la belle-fille *bel·feey*

dawn n l'aube (*f*) *ōb*

day n le jour *zhoor;* (*length of time*) la journée *zhoor·nay;* **every day** tous les jours *too lay zhoor;* **day by day** de jour en jour *duh zhoor oñ zhoor;* **the day before** la veille *la vey;* **the next** or **following day** le lendemain *luh loñ·duh·mañ* T104

day nursery n la crèche *kresh* C5

day-return n le billet aller-retour valable pour la journée *bee·yeh a·lay·ruh·toor va·la·bluh poor la zhoor·nay*

dazzle vt éblouir *ay·bloo·eer*

dead adj (*person*) mort(e) *mor* (*mort*); (*battery*) à plat *a pla;* **the line is dead** (*phone*) on n'entend rien sur la ligne *oñ noñ·toñ ryañ sōōr la lee·nyuh*

dead end n l'impasse (*f*) *añ·pas*

deaf adj sourd(e) *soor* (*soord*)

deal n l'affaire (*f*) *a·fehr* □ vt **to deal with a firm** traiter avec une firme *treh·tay a·vek ōōn feerm;* **to deal with a subject** traiter d'un sujet *treh·tay duñ sōō·zheh;* **to deal in something** faire* le commerce de quelque chose *fehr luh ko·mehrs duh kel·kuh shōz*

dealer n le marchand *mar·shoñ;* (*cards*) le donneur *do·nur*

dear adj cher (chère) *shehr;* **Dear Sir** Monsieur *muh·syuh;* **Dear Madam** Madame *ma·dam;* **Dear Mr. Smith** Cher Monsieur Smith *shehr muh·syuh Smith*

death n la mort *mor*

death certificate n l'acte de décès (*m*) *akt duh day·seh*

debate n le débat *day·ba*

debit n le débit *day·bee* □ vt **to debit $50 to someone's account** porter $50 au débit de quelqu'un *por·tay $50 ō day·bee duh kel·kuñ*

debt n la dette *det;* **to be in debt** avoir* des dettes *a·vwahr day det*

decade n la décennie *day·seh·nee*

decaffeinated adj décaféiné(e) *day·ka·fay·ee·nay*

decanter n la carafe *ka·raf*

deceive vt tromper *troñ·pay*

December n décembre (*m*) *day·soñ·bruh*

decent adj (*moral*) convenable *koñ·vuh·na·bluh;* (*respectable*) décent(e) *day·soñ(·soñt)*

decide vi (*between alternatives*) se décider *suh day·see·day;* **to decide to do something** décider de faire quelque chose *day·see·day duh fehr kel·kuh shōz*

decimal adj décimal(e) *day·see·mal* □ n la décimale *day·see·mal*

decimal point n la virgule *veer·gōōl*

decision n la décision *day·see·zyoñ*

deck n (*of ship*) le pont *poñ;* (*of cards*) le jeu *zhuh*

deck chair n la chaise longue *shez loñg*

declare vt déclarer *day·kla·ray;* **nothing to declare** rien à déclarer *ryañ na day·kla·ray*

decorate vt (*adorn*) décorer *day·ko·ray;* (*paint*) peindre* *pañ·druh*

decorations pl les décorations (*fpl*) *day·ko·ra·syoñ*

decrease vt diminuer *dee·mee·nōō·ay*

deduct vt déduire* *day·dweer*

deep adj (*water, hole*) profond(e) *pro·foñ(·foñd);* (*voice*) grave *grav*

deep freeze n le congélateur *koñ·zhay·la·tur*

deer n le cerf *sehr*

defeat vt vaincre* *vañ·kruh* □ n la défaite *day·fet*

defect n le défaut *day·fō*

defective adj défectueux(euse) *day·fek·tōō·uh(·uhz)*

defence n la défense *day·foñs*

defend vt défendre* *day·foñ·druh*

deficit n le déficit *day·fee·see*

definite adj (*distinct*) manifeste *ma·nee·fest;* (*certain*) certain(e) *sehr·tañ(·ten)*

definitely adv certainement *sehr·ten·moñ;* **he's definitely ill** c'est certain qu'il est malade *seh sehr·tañ keel eh ma·lad*

deflation n la déflation *day·fla·syoñ*

deformed adj difforme *dee·form*

defrost vt (*food*) décongeler* *day·koñ·zhuh·lay;* (*refrigerator*) dégivrer *day·zhee·vray*

degree n (*stage*) le grade *grad;* (*unit of measurement*) le degré *duh·gray;* (*university*) le diplôme universitaire *dee·plōm ōō·nee·vehr·see·tehr*

de-ice vt dégivrer *day·zhee·vray*

delay vt (*hold up*) retarder *ruh·tar·day;* (*postpone*) différer *dee·fay·ray;* **the train has been delayed** le train a pris du retard *luh trañ a pree dōō ruh·tar* □ n **delay** (*to train, plane*) le retard *ruh·tar*

delegate vt déléguer* *day·lay·gay*

delegation n la délégation *day·lay·ga·syoñ*

deliberate adj délibéré(e) *day·lee·bay·ray*

deliberately adv exprès *ek·spreh*

delicate adj délicat(e) *day·lee·ka(·kat)*

delicatessen n l'épicerie fine (*f*) *ay·pee·suh·ree feen*

delicious adj délicieux(euse) *day·lee·syuh(·syuhz)*

delighted adj ravi(e) *ra·vee*

deliver vt (*mail*) distribuer *dees·tree·bōō·ay;* (*goods*) livrer *lee·vray*

delivery n (*of mail*) la distribution *dees·tree·bōō·syoñ;* (*of goods*) la livraison *lee·vreh·zoñ*

de luxe adj de luxe *duh lōōks*

demand vt exiger* *eg·zee·zhay* □ n (*for goods*) la demande *duh·moñd*

demister n le dispositif anti-buée *dees·po·zee·teef oñ·tee·bōō·ay*

demonstrate vt (*appliance etc*) faire* une démonstration de *fehr ōōn day·moñ·stra·syoñ duh*

demonstration n la démonstration *day·moñ·stra·syoñ;* (*political*) la manifestation *ma·nee·fes·ta·syoñ*

denim n la toile de jean *twahl duh jeen*

Denmark n le Danemark *dan·mark*

dense adj (*fog etc*) dense *doñs*

dent n la bosse *bos*

dentist n le/la dentiste *doñ·teest* I58

dentures pl le dentier *doñ·tyay* I68

deny vt nier *nee·yay*

deodorant n le déodorant *day·ō·do·roñ*

department n (*in store*) le rayon *ray·yoñ*

department store *n* le grand magasin *groñ ma·ga·zañ*

departure board *n* l'horaire des départs *(m) o·rehr day day·par*

departure lounge *n* la salle de départ *sal duh day·par*

depend *vi* □ it depends ça dépend *sa day·poñ*; to depend on dépendre de *day·poñ·druh duh*

deposit *n* (*down payment*) l'acompte *(m) a·koñt*; (*for key etc*) la caution *kō·syoñ* □ *vt* (*money*) déposer *day·pō·zay*

deposit account *n* le compte de dépôt *koñt duh day·pō*

depot *n* le dépôt *day·pō*

depressed *adj* (*person*) déprimé(e) *day·pree·may*

depth *n* la profondeur *pro·foñ·dur*

deputy *n* (*second-in-command*) l'adjoint(e) *(m/f) ad·zhwañ('zhwañt)*

describe *vt* décrire* *day·kreer*

description *n* la description *deh·skreep·syoñ*

desert *n* le désert *day·zehr*

deserve *vt* mériter *may·ree·tay*

design *n* le dessin *deh·sañ* □ *vt* dessiner *deh·see·nay*

designer *n* le/la styliste *stee·leest*; (*of clothes*) le/la modéliste *mo·day·leest*

desire *n* le désir *day·zeer*

desk *n* (*in office*) le bureau *bōō·rō*; (*cash desk*) la caisse *kes*; (*reception*) la réception *ray·sep·syoñ*

desperate *adj* désespéré(e) *day·zes·pay·ray*

despite *prep* malgré *mal·gray*

dessert *n* le dessert *day·sehr*

dessertspoon *n* la cuiller à dessert *kwee·yehr a deh·sehr*

destination *n* la destination *des·tee·na·syoñ*

destroy *vt* détruire* *day·trweer*

detached house *n* le pavillon *pa·vee·yoñ*

detail *n* le détail *day·tye*; in detail en détail *oñ day·tye* Bm2

detailed *adj* détaillé(e) *day·tye·yay*

detective *n* l'agent de la sûreté *(m) a·zhoñ duh la sōōr·tay*

detergent *n* le détergent *day·tehr·zhoñ*

determined *adj* déterminé(e) *day·tehr·mee·nay*; to be determined to do something être* décidé à faire quelque chose *eh·truh day·see·day a fehr kel·kuh shōz*

detour *n* le détour *day·toor*; to make a detour faire* un détour *fehr uñ day·toor*

devaluation *n* la dévaluation *day·va·lōō·a·syoñ*

devalue *vt* (*currency*) dévaluer *day·va·lōō·ay*

develop *vi* se développer *suh day·vuh·lo·pay* □ *vt* (*photo*) développer *day·vuh·lo·pay*

developing country *n* le pays en voie de développement *pay·yee oñ vwah duh day·vuh·lop·moñ*

diabetes *n* le diabète *dya·bet*

diabetic *n* le/la diabétique *dya·bay·teek*

diagnosis *n* le diagnostic *dyag·nos·teek*

diagonal *adj* diagonal(e) *dya·go·nal*

diagram *n* le diagramme *dya·gram*

dial *vt* (*number*) composer *koñ·pō·zay*

dialect *n* le dialecte *dya·lekt*

dial(ling) tone *n* la tonalité *to·na·lee·tay*

diameter *n* le diamètre *dya·meh·truh*

diamond *n* le diamant *dya·moñ*; **diamonds** (*cards*) le carreau *ka·rō*

diaper *n* la couche *koosh* C18

diarrh(o)ea *n* la diarrhée *dya·ray*

diary *n* l'agenda *(m) a·zhañ·da*

dice *n* le dé *day*

dictate *vt* (*letter*) dicter *deek·tay*

dictionary *n* le dictionnaire *deek·syo·nehr*

die *vi* mourir* *moo·reer*

diesel *n* le diesel *dyeh·zel*

diesel engine *n* le moteur diesel *mo·tur dyeh·zel*

diesel fuel *n* le gas-oil *gaz·oil*

diet *n* (*slimming*) le régime *ray·zheem*; to be on a diet suivre* un régime *swee·vruñ ray·zheem*

difference *n* la différence *dee·fay·roñs*

different *adj* différent(e) *day·fay·roñ (·roñt)*; different from différent de *dee·fay·roñ duh*

difficult *adj* difficile *dee·fee·seel*

difficulty *n* la difficulté *dee·fee·kōōl·tay*

dig *vt* (*ground*) bêcher *beh·shay*; (*hole*) creuser *kruh·zay*; to dig up déterrer *day·teh·ray*

digital *adj* digital(e) *dee·zhee·tal*

dike *n* la digue *deeg*

dilute *vt* diluer *dee·lōō·ay*

dim *adj* (*light*) faible *feh·bluh*; (*room*) sombre *soñ·bruh*

dimensions *pl* les dimensions *(fpl) dee·moñ·syoñ*

diner *n* le snack *snak*

dinghy *n* le youyou *yoo·yoo*; (*inflatable*) le canot pneumatique *ka·nō pnuh·ma·teek*

dining car *n* le wagon-restaurant *va·goñ·res·tō·roñ*

dining room *n* la salle à manger *sal a moñ·zhay*

dinner *n* le dîner *dee·nay* E6

dinner jacket *n* le smoking *smō·keeng*

dinner party *n* le dîner *dee·nay*

dip *vt* (*in liquid*) tremper *troñ·pay*; (*headlights*) mettre* en code *meh·troñ kod*

diploma *n* le diplôme *dee·plōm*

diplomat *n* le diplomate *dee·plo·mat*

dipstick *n* la jauge de niveau d'huile *zhōzh duh nee·vō dweel*

dip-switch *n* le basculeur de phares *bas·kōō·lur duh far*

direct *adj* direct(e) *dee·rekt* □ *adv* to fly to Venice direct prendre* un vol direct pour Venise *proñ·druñ vol dee·rekt poor vuh·neez* □ *vt* direct (*traffic*) régler* *ray·glay*

direction *n* la direction *dee·rek·syoñ*; **directions** (*to a place*) les indications *(fpl) añ·dee·ka·syoñ*; directions for use le mode d'emploi *mod doñ·plwah*

director *n* (*of firm*) le directeur *dee·rek·tur*; (*of film*) le réalisateur *ray·a·lee·za·tur* Bm3

directory *n* l'annuaire *(m) a·nōō·ehr* Sn29

dirt *n* la saleté *sal·tay*

dirty *adj* sale *sal* A49

disabled *adj* infirme *añ·feerm*

disadvantage *n* le désavantage *day·za·voñ·tazh*; at a disadvantage désavantagé(e) *day·za·voñ·ta·zhay*

disagree *vi* □ to disagree with somebody ne pas être* d'accord avec quelqu'un *nuh pa zeh·truh da·kor a·vek kel·kuñ*; eggs disagree with me les œufs ne me conviennent pas *lay zuh nuh muh koñ·vyen·pa*

disagreement n le désaccord *day·za·kor*

disappear vi disparaître* *dees·pa·reh·truh*

disappointed adj déçu(e) *day·sōō*

disapprove vi □ to disapprove of something désapprouver quelque chose *day·za·proo·vay kel·kuh shōz*

disaster n le désastre *day·zas·truh*

disc n le disque *deesk*; **slipped disc** l'hernie discale (f) *ehr·nee dees·kal*

disc brakes pl les freins à disque (mpl) *fraň a deesk*

discipline n la discipline *dee·see·pleen*

disc jockey n le disc-jockey *deesk·jo·kay*

disco(thèque) n la disco *dees·kō*

discount n la remise *ruh·meez*; **at a discount** au rabais *ō ra·beh* M5

discouraged adj découragé(e) *day·koo·ra·zhay*

discover vt découvrir* *day·koo·vreer*

discreet adj discret(ète) *dees·kreh (·kret)*

discrimination n (racial etc) la discrimination *dees·kree·mee·na·syoň*

discuss vt discuter *dees·kōō·tay*

disease n la maladie *ma·la·dee*

disguise n le déguisement *day·geez·moň*; **in disguise** déguisé(e) *day·gee·zay*

disgust n le dégoût *day·goo*

disgusted adj dégoûté(e) *day·goo·tay*

dish n le plat *pla*; (food) le mets *meh* E18

dishcloth n la lavette *la·vet*

dishonest adj malhonnête *mal·o·net*

dish up vt servir* *sehr·veer*

dishwasher n le lave-vaisselle *lav·veh·sel*

disinfect vt désinfecter *day·zaň·fek·tay*

disinfectant n le désinfectant *day·zaň·fek·toň*

dislocate vt disloquer *dees·lo·kay*

dismiss vt (from job) licencier *lee·soň·syay*

disobedient adj désobéissant(e) *day·zo·bay·ee·soň(·soňt)*

disobey vt désobéir à *day·zo·bay·yeer a*

dispatch vt expédier *ek·spay·dyay*

disposable adj à jeter *a zhuh·tay*

dispute n (fact) contester *koň·tes·tay* □ n la dispute *dees·pōōt*; (industrial) le conflit *koň·flee*

disqualify vt disqualifier *dees·ka·lee·fyay*

dissolve vt dissoudre* *dee·soo·druh* □ vi se dissoudre* *suh dee·soo·druh*

distance n la distance *dees·toňs*; **in the distance** au loin *ō lwaň*

distant adj distant(e) *dees·toň(·toňt)*

distilled water n l'eau distillée (f) *ō dees·tee·lay*

distillery n la distillerie *dees·teel·luh·ree*

distinct adj (clear) distinct(e) *dees·taň(·taňkt)*

distinguish vt distinguer *dees·taň·gay*; **to distinguish something from something** distinguer quelque chose de quelque chose *dees·taň·gay kel·kuh shōz duh kel·kuh shōz*

distract vt distraire* *dees·trehr*

distress n la détresse *day·tres*; **a ship in distress** un navire en perdition *uň na·veer oň pehr·dee·syoň*

distributor n (in car) le distributeur *dees·tree·bōō·tur*; (commercial) le concessionnaire *koň·seh·syo·nehr*

district n (of town) le quartier *kar·*

tyay; (in country) la région *ray·zhyoň*; (administrative) l'arrondissement (m) *a·roň·dees·moň*

disturb vt (interrupt) déranger* *day·roň·zhay*

ditch n le fossé *fo·say*

divan n le divan *dee·voň*

dive vi plonger* *ploň·zhay* □ n le plongeon *ploň·zhoň*

diversify vt/i diversifier *dee·vehr·see·fyay*

diversion n (traffic) la déviation *day·vya·syoň*

divert vt (stream) dévier *day·vyay*; (traffic) détourner *day·toor·nay*

divide vt (separate) séparer *say·pa·ray*; (apportion) diviser *dee·vee·zay*; **to divide 8 by 4** diviser 8 par 4 *dee·vee·zay 8 par 4*

divided highway n la route à quatre voies *root a ka·truh vwah*

dividend n le dividende *dee·vee·doňd*

diving board n le plongeoir *ploň·zhwahr*

divorce n le divorce *dee·vors*

divorced adj divorcé(e) *dee·vor·say*

dizzy adj (person) pris(e) de vertige *pree (preez) duh vehr·teezh*

do vt/i faire* *fehr*; **will it do?** (be enough) est-ce que ça ira? *es·kuh sa ee·ra*; (be suitable) est-ce que ça convient? *es·kuh sa koň·vyaň*; **you know him, don't you?** vous le connaissez n'est-ce pas? *voo luh ko·neh·say nes pa*; **he didn't come, did he?** il n'est pas venu n'est-ce pas? *eel neh pa vuh·nōō nes pa*

dock n le dock *dok*

doctor n le médecin *mayd·saň*; **it's Doctor Smith** c'est le docteur Smith *seh luh dok·tur Smith* B50, I7f, Ea6

doctor's office n le cabinet de consultation *ka·bee·neh duh koň·sōōl·ta·syoň*

document n le document *do·kōō·moň* Bm24

dog n le chien *shyaň*

do-it-yourself n le bricolage *bree·ko·lazh*

doll n la poupée *poo·pay*

dollar n le dollar *do·lar*

dollar bill n le billet d'un dollar *bee·yeh duň do·lar*

donate vt (funds) faire* don de *fehr doň duh*

donation n (money) le don *doň*

done adj (cooked) cuit(e) *kwee (kweet)*

donkey n l'âne (m) *an*

door n la porte *port* A60

doorbell n la sonnette *so·net*

door handle, doorknob n la poignée de porte *pwah·nyay duh port*

doorman n (in hotel) le portier *por·tyay*

doormat n le paillasson *pye·ya·soň*

doorstep n le pas de porte *pa duh port*

door-to-door salesman n le représentant à domicile *ruh·pray·zoň·toň a do·mee·seel*

dormitory n (room) le dortoir *dor·twahr*; (of college) la résidence universitaire *ray·zee·doňs ōō·nee·vehr·see·tehr*

dosage n la posologie *pō·zo·lō·zhee*

dose n la dose *dōz*

dot n le point *pwaň*

dotted line n la ligne pointillée *lee·nyuh pwaň·tee·yay*

double vt doubler *doo·blay* □ adv **to cost double** coûter le double *koo·tay luh doo·bluh* □ adj double *doo·bluh*

doo·bluh; **a double whisky** un double whisky *uñ doo·bluh wees·kee*
double bed *n* le grand lit *groñ lee*
double bend *n* le virage en S *vee·razh oñ es*
double-parking *n* le stationnement en double file *sta·syon·moñ oñ doo· bluh feel*
double room *n* la chambre pour deux personnes *shoñ·bruh poor duh pehr· son*
doubt *n* le doute *doot*; **no doubt** sans doute *soñ doot*; **without (a) doubt** sans aucun doute *soñ zō·kuñ doot* □ *vt* **doubt** douter de *doo·tay duh*; **I doubt it** j'en doute *zhoñ doot*
doubtful *adj* douteux(euse) *doo·tuh (·tuhz)*
dough *n* la pâte *paht*
doughnut *n* le beignet *beh·nyeh*
dove *n* la colombe *ko·loñb*
down *n* (*fluff*) le duvet *dōō·veh* □ *adv* **to come/go down** descendre *deh·soñ· druh*
downhill *adv* □ **to go downhill** descendre *deh·soñ·druh*
down payment *n* l'acompte (*m*) *a·koñt*
downstairs *adv* en bas *oñ ba*
downstream *adv* en aval *oñ na·val*
downtown *adv* en ville *oñ veel* □ *adj* **downtown Chicago** le centre de Chicago *luh soñ·truh duh shee·ka·gō*
downward(s) *adv* vers le bas *vehr luh ba*
doze *vi* sommeiller *so·may·yay*
dozen *n* la douzaine *doo·zen*; **4 dozen eggs** 4 douzaines d'œufs *4 doo·zen duh*
drab *adj* terne *tehrn*
draft *n* (*wind*) le courant d'air *koo·roñ dehr*; (*financial*) la traite *tret*; (*rough outline*) le brouillon *broo·yoñ*
draft beer *n* la bière à la pression *byehr a la preh·syoñ*
draftsman *n* le dessinateur *deh·see·na· tur*
drag *vt* traîner *treh·nay*
drain *n* l'égout (*m*) *ay·goo* □ *vt* (*land*) drainer *dreh·nay*; (*vegetables*) égoutter *ay·goo·tay*; (*sump, pool*) vider *vee·day*
drainboard, draining-board *n* l'égouttoir (*m*) *ay·goo·twahr*
drain pipe *n* le tuyau d'écoulement *twee·yō day·kool·moñ*
drama *n* (*art*) le théâtre *tay·ah·truh*
dramatic *adj* dramatique *dra·ma·teek*
drape *n* le rideau *ree·dō*
drastic *adj* sévère *say·vehr*
draught *n* (*wind*) le courant d'air *koo· roñ dehr*
draught beer *n* la bière à la pression *byehr a la preh·syoñ*
draughts *pl* les dames (*fpl*) *dam*
draughtsman *n* le dessinateur *deh·see· na·tur*
draw *vt* (*picture*) dessiner *deh·see·nay*; **to draw out** (*money*) retirer *ruh·tee· ray*; **to draw up** (*document*) dresser *dreh·say*
drawer *n* le tiroir *tee·rwahr*
drawing *n* le dessin *deh·soñ*
drawing pin *n* la punaise *pōō·nez*
dread *vt* redouter *ruh·doo·tay*
dream *n* le rêve *rev* □ *vi* rêver *reh·vay*; **to dream of** *or* **about** rêver de *reh· vay duh*
dress *n* la robe *rob* □ *vt* (*child*) habiller *a·bee·yay* □ *vi* (*oneself*) s'habiller *sa· bee·yay* S57

dress circle *n* le premier balcon *pruh· myay bal·koñ*
dressing *n* (*salad*) l'assaisonnement (*m*) *a·seh·zon·moñ*; (*stuffing*) la farce *fars*
dressing gown *n* le peignoir *peh· nywahr*
dressing table *n* la coiffeuse *kwah·fuhz*
dried *adj* (*fruit, beans*) sec *sek*, sèche *sesh*; **dried milk** le lait en poudre *luh leh oñ poo·druh*
drift *vi* (*boat*) aller* à la dérive *a·lay a la day·reev*
drill *n* (*tool*) la perceuse *pehr·suhz* □ *vt* (*hole*) percer* *pehr·say*
drink *vt* boire* *bwahr* □ *n* la boisson *bwah·soñ*; **have a drink!** buvez donc quelque chose! *bōō·vay doñk kel· kuh shōz* L48
drinking water *n* l'eau potable (*f*) *ō po·ta·bluh*
drip *n* la goutte *goot* □ *vi* goutter *goo· tay*
drip-dry *vt* laisser s'égoutter *leh·say say·goo·tay* (*shirt etc*) qui ne nécessite aucun repassage *kee nuh nay·seh·seet ō·kuñ ruh·pa·sazh*
drive *vt/i* (*car etc*) conduire* *koñ· dweer*; **do you drive?** savez-vous conduire? *sa·vay·voo koñ·dweer*; **to drive to town** aller* en ville en voiture *a·lay oñ veel oñ vwah·tōōr* □ *n* drive (*journey*) le trajet en voiture *tra·zheh oñ vwah·tōōr*; (*driveway*) l'allée (*f*) *a·lay*; **to go for a drive** faire* une promenade en voiture *fehr ōōn pro·muh·nad oñ vwah·tōōr*; **left-hand drive** la conduite à gauche *koñ·dweet a gōsh*; **front-wheel drive** la traction avant *trak·syoñ a·voñ*
driver *n* (*of car*) le conducteur *koñ· dōōk·tur*, la conductrice *koñ·dōōk· trees*; (*of taxi, bus*) le chauffeur *shō· fur*
driver's license, driving licence *n* le permis de conduire *pehr·mee duh koñ·dweer* T10
drizzle *n* la bruine *brōō·een*
drop *n* (*of liquid*) la goutte *goot* □ *vt* (*let fall*) laisser tomber *leh·say toñ· bay* □ *vi* (*fall*) tomber *toñ·bay*
drought *n* la sécheresse *say·shuh·res*
drown *vi* se noyer *suh nwah·yay*
drug *n* (*medicine*) le médicament *may· dee·ka·moñ*; (*narcotic*) la drogue *drog* 147
druggist *n* le pharmacien *far·ma·syañ*
drugstore *n* la pharmacie *far·ma·see*
drum *n* le tambour *toñ·boor*
drumstick *n* (*of chicken*) le pilon *pee· loñ*
drunk *adj* ivre *ee·vruh*
dry *adj* sec *sek*, sèche *sesh* □ *vt* (*hair*) sécher* *say·shay*; (*clothes*) faire* sécher *fehr say·shay*
dry-clean *vt* nettoyer à sec *neh·twah· yay a sek*
dry-cleaner's *n* la teinturerie *tañ·tōō· ruh·ree*
dual carriageway *n* la route à quatre voies *la root a ka·truh vwah*
duck *n* le canard *ka·nar*
due *adj* (*owing*) dû (due) *dōō*; **when is the train due?** quand est-ce que le train doit arriver? *koñ tes·kuh luh trañ dwah ta·ree·vay*
duke *n* le duc *dōōk*
dull *adj* (*day, weather*) maussade *mō· sad*; (*boring*) ennuyeux(euse) *oñ· nwee·yuh(·yuhz)*

dumb *adj* muet(te) *mōō·eh(·et)*; *(stupid)* bête *bet*

dummy *n (baby's)* la tétine *tay·teen*

dump *n (for rubbish)* la décharge publique *day·sharzh pōō·bleek*

dumping *n (of goods)* le dumping *duñ·peeng*

dumpling *n* la boulette *boo·let*

dune *n* la dune *dōōn*

dungarees *pl* la salopette *sa·lo·pet*

dungeon *n* le cachot *ka·shō*

durable *adj (fabric, article)* solide *so·leed*

during *prep* pendant *poñ·doñ*

dusk *n* le crépuscule *kray·pōōs·kōōl*

dust *n* la poussière *poo·syehr* □ *vt (furniture)* épousseter* *ay·poos·tay*

dustbin *n* la poubelle *pōō·bel* A71

dustpan *n* la pelle à poussière *pela a poo·syehr*

dusty *adj* poussiéreux(euse) *poo·syay·ruh(·ruhz)*

Dutch *adj* hollandais(e) *o·loñ·deh (·dez)*; *he's Dutch* il est Hollandais *eel eh o·loñ·deh*; *she's Dutch* elle est Hollandaise *el eh o·loñ·dez* □ *n Dutch* le hollandais *o·loñ·deh*

duty *n (obligation)* le devoir *duh·vwahr*; *(function)* la fonction *foñk·syoñ*; *(tax)* la taxe *taks*; *on duty (doctor)* de garde *duh gard*; *off duty* libre *lee·bruh*

duty-free *adj (goods)* exempté de douane *egzoñ·tay duh dwan*; *(shop)* hors-taxe *or·taks* T42

duvet *n* la couette *kwet*

dye *n* la teinture *tañ·tōōr* □ *vt* teindre* *tañ·druh*

dyke *n* la digue *deeg*

dynamic *adj (person)* dynamique *dee·na·meek*

dynamo *n* la dynamo *dee·na·mō*

E

each *adj* chaque *shak* □ *pron* chacun(e) *sha·kuñ(·kōōn)*; *each of them* chacun d'entre eux *sha·kuñ doñ·truh*

eager *adj* impatient(e) *añ·pa·syoñ (·syoñt)*; *to be eager to do something* être* impatient de faire quelque chose *eh·trañ·pa·syoñ duh fehr kel·kuh shōz*

eagle *n* l'aigle *m* *eh·gluh*

ear *n* l'oreille *(f)* *o·ray*

earache *n* le mal d'oreille *mal do·ray*; *to have earache* avoir* mal à l'oreille *a·vwahr mal a lo·ray*

earlier *adj* antérieur(e) *oñ·tay·ree·ur* □ *adv* plus tôt *plōō tō*

early *adj* □ *you're early* vous arrivez en avance *voo za·ree·vay oñ na·voñs*; *the early train* le premier train *luh prum·yay trañ* □ *adv* early tôt *tō*; *to get up early* se lever* de bonne heure *suh luh·vay duh bon ur*

earn *vt* gagner *ga·nyay*

earnings *pl* les gains *(mpl)* *gañ*

earplugs *pl* les boules Quiès *(fpl)* *bool kyes*

earring *n* la boucle d'oreille *boo·kluh do·ray*

earth *n* la terre *tehr*; *(electrical)* la masse *mas*

earthquake *n* le tremblement de terre *troñ·bluh·moñ duh tehr*

ease *vt (pain)* soulager* *soo·la·zhay*

easily *adv* facilement *fa·seel·moñ*

east *n* l'est *(m)* *est*; *the East* l'Orient *(m)* *o·ryoñ* □ *adv east* à l'est *a lest*

Easter *n* Pâques *(fpl)* *pak*; *at Easter* à Pâques *a pak*

Easter egg *n* l'œuf de Pâques *(m)* *uhf duh pak*

eastern *adj* de l'est *duh lest*

East Germany *n* l'Allemagne de l'Est *(f)* *al·ma·nyuh duh lest*

easy *adj* facile *fa·seel*

eat *vt* manger* *moñ·zhay*

eau-de-Cologne *n* l'eau de Cologne *(f)* *ō duh ko·lo·nyuh*

eccentric *adj* excentrique *ek·soñ·treek*

echo *n* l'écho *(m)* *ay·kō*

éclair *n* l'éclair *(m)* *ay·klehr*

economic *adj* économique *ay·ko·no·meek*

economical *adj (use, method)* économique *ay·ko·no·meek*

economics *n* l'économie politique *(f)* *ay·ko·no·mee po·lee·teek*

economist *n* l'économiste *(m/f)* *ay·ko·no·meest*

economy *n (of country)* l'économie *(f)* *ay·ko·no·mee*

eczema *n* l'eczéma *(m)* *eg·zay·ma*

edge *n* le bord *bor*; *(of blade)* le tranchant *troñ·shoñ*

edition *n* l'édition *(f)* *ay·dee·syoñ*

educate *vt* instruire* *añ·strweer*

education *n* l'enseignement *(m)* *oñ·seh·nyuh·moñ*

E.E.C. *n* la C.E.E. *say·uh·uh*

eels *pl* les anguilles *(fpl)* *oñ·geey*

effect *n (result)* l'effet *(m)* *eh·feh*; *to take effect* prendre* effet *proñ·dreh·feh*

effective *adj (remedy etc)* efficace *eh·fee·kas*

efficient *adj* efficace *eh·fee·kas*

effort *n* l'effort *(m)* *eh·for*

e.g. *abbrev* par exemple *par eg·zoñ·pluh*

egg *n* l'œuf *(m)* *uhf*; *eggs* les œufs *lay zuh* S31

egg cup *n* le coquetier *kok·tyay*

eggplant *n* l'aubergine *(f)* *ō·behr·zheen*

Egypt *n* l'Égypte *(f)* *ay·zheept*

Egyptian *adj* égyptien(ne) *ay·zheep·syañ(·syen)*

eiderdown *n* l'édredon *(m)* *ay·druh·doñ*

eight *num* huit *weet*

eighteen *num* dix-huit *deez·weet*

eighth *adj* huitième *wee·tyem*

eighties *pl (decade)* les années quatre-vingts *lay za·nay ka·truh·vañ*

eighty *num* quatre-vingts *ka·truh·vañ*

either *pron* □ *of you (l'une)* de vous deux *luñ (lōōn) duh voo duh*; *which one?* - either lequel? - l'un ou l'autre *luh·kel · luñ oo lō·truh* □ *adj* on either side des côtés *day duh kō·tay* □ *conj* either ... or ou ... ou *oo ... oo*

elaborate *adj* compliqué(e) *koñ·plee·kay*

elastic *n* l'élastique *(m)* *ay·las·teek*

elastic band *n* l'élastique *(m)* *ay·las·teek*

elbow *n* le coude *kood*

elder *adj* aîné(e) *ay·nay*

eldest *adj* aîné(e) *ay·nay*

elect *vt* élire* *ay·leer*

election *n* l'élection *(f)* *ay·lek·syoñ*

electric(al) *adj* électrique *ay·lek·treek*

electric blanket *n* la couverture chauffante *koo·vehr·tōōr shō·foñt*

electrician *n* l'électricien *(m)* *ay·lek·tree·syañ*

electricity *n* l'électricité *(f)* *ay·lek·tree·see·tay*

electronic adj électronique ay·lek·tro·neek

electronics n l'électronique (f) ay·lek·tro·neek

elegant adj élégant(e) ay·lay·goñ (·goñt)

element n l'élément (m) ay·lay·moñ

elephant n l'éléphant (m) ay·lay·foñ

elevator n l'ascenseur (m) a·soñ·sur A30

eleven num onze oñz

eleventh adj onzième oñz·yem

elm n l'orme (m) orm

else adj □ somewhere else autre part ō·truh par; someone else quelqu'un d'autre kel·kuñ dō·truh

embankment n le remblai roñ·blay

embargo n l'embargo (m) oñ·bar·gō

embark vi embarquer oñ·bar·kay

embarrassed adj gêné(e) zhay·nay

embassy n l'ambassade (f) oñ·ba·sad

embrace vt embrasser oñ·bra·say

embroidered adj brodé(e) bro·day

embroidery n la broderie bro·duh·ree

emerald n l'émeraude (f) ay·muh·rōd

emergency n le cas urgent ka ōōr·zhoñ Ea8

emergency exit n la sortie de secours sor·tee duh suh·koor

emergency landing n l'atterrissage forcé (m) a·tay·ree·sazh for·say

emery board n la lime à ongles leem a oñ·gluh

emigrate vi émigrer ay·mee·gray

emotion n l'émotion (f) ay·mō·syoñ

emotional adj (person) très sensible treh soñ·see·bluh

emperor n l'empereur (m) oñ·puh·rur

emphasis n l'accent (m) ak·soñ; emphasis on something l'accent sur quelque chose lak·soñ sōōr kel·kuh shōz

emphasize vt souligner soo·lee·nay; (syllable etc) accentuer ak·soñ·tōō·ay

empire n l'empire (m) oñ·peer

employ vt (worker) employer oñ·plwah·yay

employee n l'employé(e) (m/f) oñ·plwah·yay

employer n l'employeur (m) oñ·plwah·yur

employment n l'emploi (m) oñ·plwah

empty adj vide veed □ vt vider vee·day

enamel n l'émail (m) ay·mye

enclosure n (in letter) l'annexe (f) a·neks

encore n le bis bees; encore! bis! bees

encyclop(a)edia n l'encyclopédie (f) oñ·see·klo·pay·dee

end n la fin fañ; (of street, table) le bout boo □ vt terminer tehr·mee·nay □ vi finir fee·neer

endive n (smooth) l'endive (f) oñ·deev; (curly) la chicorée shee·ko·ray

endorse vt (document) endosser oñ·dō·say

enemy n l'ennemi(e) (m/f) eh·nuh·mee

energetic adj énergique ay·nehr·zheek

energy n l'énergie (f) ay·nehr·zhee

engaged adj (betrothed) fiancé(e) fee·yoñ·say; (busy) occupé(e) o·kōō·pay

engagement n (betrothal) les fiançailles (fpl) fee·yoñ·sye

engagement ring n la bague de fiançailles bag duh fee·yoñ·sye

engine n (motor) le moteur mo·tur; (of train) la locomotive lo·ko·mo·teev T183

engineer n l'ingénieur (m) añ·zhay·nyur

England n l'Angleterre (f) oñ·gluh·tehr

English adj anglais(e) oñ·gleh(·glez); he's English il est Anglais eel eñ toñ·gleh; she's English elle est Anglaise el eñ toñ·glez □ n l'anglais (m) oñ·gleh; in English en anglais oñ noñ·gleh

enjoy vt (concert, outing) aimer ay·may; to enjoy oneself s'amuser sa·mōō·zay

enjoyment n le plaisir play·zeer

enlarge vt agrandir a·groñ·deer

enormous adj énorme ay·norm

enough pron assez a·say; have you enough? vous en avez assez? voo zoñ na·vay a·say □ adj enough time assez de temps a·say duh toñ; enough books assez de livres a·say duh lee·vruh □ adv big enough assez grand(e) a·say groñ (groñd)

ensemble n (clothes) l'ensemble (m) oñ·soñ·bluh

enter vt (room) entrer dans oñ·tray doñ □ vi entrer oñ·tray

enterprise n l'entreprise (f) oñ·truh·preez

entertain vt (amuse) amuser a·mōō·zay; (give hospitality) recevoir* ruh·suh·vwahr

entertainment n (show) le spectacle spek·ta·kluh

enthusiasm n l'enthousiasme (m) oñ·too·zyaz·muh

enthusiastic adj enthousiaste oñ·too·zyast

entrance n (way in) l'entrée (f) oñ·tray

entrance fee n le prix d'entrée pree doñ·tray

entrée n l'entrée (f) oñ·tray

entry n (way in) l'entrée (f) oñ·tray

envelope n l'enveloppe (f) oñ·vuh·lop S92

envious adj envieux(euse) oñ·vyuh (·vyuhz)

environment n le milieu mee·lyuh

envy vt envier oñ·vyay □ n l'envie (f) oñ·vee

epidemic n l'épidémie (f) ay·pee·day·mee

epilepsy n l'épilepsie (f) ay·pee·lep·see

equal adj égal(e) ay·gal

equator n l'équateur (m) ay·kwa·tur

equipment n le matériel ma·tay·ryel L30

equivalent adj équivalent(e) ay·kee·va·loñ(·loñt); equivalent to quelque chose à ay·kee·va·loñ(·loñt) a

erase vt effacer* eh·fa·say

eraser n la gomme gom

ermine n (fur) l'hermine (f) ehr·meen

erotic adj érotique ay·ro·teek

errand n la course koors; to do or run an errand faire* une course fehr ōōn koors

error n l'erreur (f) eh·rur; in error par erreur par eh·rur

escalator n l'escalier roulant (m) es·ka·lyay roo·loñ

escalope n l'escalope (f) es·ka·lop

escape vi (person) s'échapper say·sha·pay; (liquid, gas) échapper ay·sha·pay

escort vt escorter es·kor·tay □ n l'escorte (f) es·kort

especially adv particulièrement par·tee·kōō·lyehr·moñ

Esperanto n l'espéranto (m) es·pay·roñ·tō

espresso (coffee) n l'express (m) ek·spres

essay n l'essai (m) eh·say

essential adj (necessary) essentiel(le) eh·soñ·syel

establish vt établir ay·ta·bleer; (business) fonder foñ·day

estate n (property) le domaine do·men; (housing) la cité see·tay

estate agent n l'agent immobilier (m) a·zhoñ ee·mo·bee·lyay

estate (car) n le break brek

estimate vt estimer es·tee·may □ n l'estimation (f) es·tee·ma·syoñ M9, Bm25

etc abbrev etc et·say·tuh·ra

ethical adj moral(e) mo·ral

ethnic adj ethnique et·neek

etiquette n les convenances (fpl) koñ·vuh·noñs

Europe n l'Europe (f) uh·rop

European adj européen(ne) uh·ro·pay·yañ(·yen)

evaporate vi s'évaporer say·va·po·ray

evaporated milk n le lait concentré leh koñ·soñ·tray

even adj égal(e) ay·gal; an even number un nombre pair uñ noñ·bruh pehr □ adv even faster encore plus vite oñ·kor plŏō veet; even a child could do it même un enfant pourrait le faire mem uñ noñ·foñ poo·reh luh fehr; even so quand même koñ mem

evening n le soir swahr; in the evening le soir luh swahr

evening dress n (woman's) la robe de soirée rob duh swah·ray; (man's) le smoking smo·keeng

evening paper n le journal du soir zhoor·nal dŏō swahr

event n l'événement (m) ay·ven·moñ

eventually adv finalement fee·nal·moñ

ever adv jamais zha·may; have you ever been to London? êtes-vous jamais allé à Londres? et·voo zha·meh za·lay a loñ·druh; ever since he... depuis qu'il... duh·pwee keel; he's been there ever since il est là depuis ce temps-là eel ehl a duh·pwee suh toñ·la

every adj chaque shak; every other day tous les deux jours too lay duh zhoor; every 6th day tous les six jours too lay see zhoor

everybody, **everyone** pron tout le monde too luh moñd

everything pron tout too

everywhere adv partout par·too

evidence n (proof) la preuve pruhv; (of witness) le témoignage tay·mwah·nyazh

evil adj mauvais(e) mō·veh(·vez)

evolution n l'évolution (f) ay·vo·lŏō·syoñ

ex- pref ex- eks

exact adj (correct) exact(e) eg·zakt; (detailed) précis(e) pray·see(·seez)

exactly adv exactement eg·zak·tuh·moñ

exaggerate vt/i exagérer* eg·za·zhay·ray

exaggeration n l'exagération (f) eg·za·zhay·ra·syoñ

examination n l'examen (m) eg·za·mañ

examine vt (inspect) examiner eg·za·mee·nay

example n l'exemple (m) eg·zoñ·pluh; for example par exemple par eg·zoñ·pluh

exceed vt dépasser day·pa·say

excellent adj excellent(e) ek·say·loñ(·loñt)

except (for), **except(ing)** prep sauf sŏf

exception n l'exception (f) ek·sep·syoñ

exceptional adj exceptionnel(le) ek·sep·syo·nel

excess n l'excès (m) ek·seh

excess baggage n l'excédent de bagages (m) ek·say·doñ duh ba·gazh

exchange vt échanger* ay·shoñ·zhay; **to exchange something for something** échanger* quelque chose contre quelque chose ay·shoñ·zhay kel·kuh shōz koñ·truh kel·kuh shōz □ n **exchange** (between currencies) le change shoñzh; (telephone) le central soñ·tral

exchange rate n le taux du change tō dŏō shoñzh

excise duties pl les impôts indirects (m) añ·pō añ·dee·rekt

excited adj excité(e) ek·see·tay

excitement n l'excitation (f) ek·see·ta·syoñ

exciting adj passionnant(e) pa·syo·noñ(·noñt)

exclaim vi s'exclamer seks·kla·may

exclude vt exclure* eks·klŏōr

exclusive adj exclusif(ive) eks·klŏō·zeef(·zeev); **exclusive rights** l'exclusivité (f) eks·klŏō·zee·vee·tay; **exclusive of...** ...non compris noñ koñ·pree

excursion n l'excursion (f) eks·kŏōr·syoñ; **to go on an excursion** faire* une excursion fehr ōōn eks·kŏōr·syoñ

excuse vt excuser eks·kŏō·zay □ n (pretext) l'excuse (f) eks·kŏōz

ex-directory adj qui ne figure pas à l'annuaire kee nuh fee·gŏōr pa za la·nŏō·ehr

execute vt (kill) exécuter eg·zay·kŏō·tay

executive n le cadre ka·druh

exercise n l'exercice (m) eg·zehr·sees

exercise book n le cahier ka·yay

exhaust n (fumes) les gaz d'échappement (mpl) gaz day·shap·moñ; (pipe) le tuyau d'échappement twee·yō day·shap·moñ

exhausted adj épuisé(e) ay·pwee·zay

exhibition n l'exposition (f) ek·spo·zee·syoñ

exist vi exister eg·zees·tay

existence n l'existence (f) eg·zees·toñs

exit n la sortie sor·tee

exit permit n le permis de sortie pehr·mee duh sor·tee

exotic adj exotique eg·zo·teek

expand vt (material) dilater dee·la·tay; (business) développer day·vuh·lo·pay □ vi (material) se dilater suh dee·la·tay; (business) se développer suh day·vuh·lo·pay

expect vt (anticipate) espérer* es·pay·ray; **I expect he'll come** je suppose qu'il viendra zhuh sŏō·pōz keel vyañ·dra; **I expect so** je crois que oui zhuh krwah kuh wee; **she's expecting a baby** elle attend un bébé el a·toñ uñ bay·bay

expedition n l'expédition (f) eks·pay·dee·syoñ

expenditure n les dépenses (fpl) day·poñs

expense n (cost) les frais (mpl) freh; **expenses** les frais (mpl) freh

expense account n les frais de représentation (mpl) freh duh ruh·pray·zoñ·ta·syoñ

expensive adj coûteux(euse) koo·tuh(·tuhz)

experience n l'expérience (f) ek·spay·ryoñs

experienced adj expérimenté(e) ek·spay·ree·moñ·tay

experiment n l'expérience (f) ek·spay·ryoñs

expert n l'expert (m) ek·spehr

expire vi expirer ek·spee·ray

explain vt expliquer ek·splee·kay

explanation n l'explication (f) ek·splee·ka·syoñ

explode vi exploser ek·splo·zay

explore vt explorer ek·splo·ray

explosion n l'explosion (f) ek·splo·zyoñ

export n l'exportation (f) ek·spor·ta·syoñ □ vt exporter ek·spor·tay

exporter n l'exportateur (m) ek·spor·ta·tur

express vt exprimer ek·spree·may □ adv to send something express expédier quelque chose par exprès ek·spay·dyay kel·kuh shōz par ek·spres

expression n l'expression (f) ek·spreh·syoñ

express letter n la lettre exprès leh·trek·spres

express train n le rapide ra·peed

expressway n la voie express vwah ek·spres

extension n (building) l'agrandissement (m) a·groñ·dees·moñ; (phone) le poste post

exterior adj extérieur(e) ek·stay·ryur

external adj externe ek·stern

extra adj supplémentaire sōō·play·moñ·tehr; postage extra les frais de port en sus lay freh duh por oñ sōōs □ adv extra en plus oñ plōōs M3,A18

extraordinary adj extraordinaire ek·stra·or·dee·nehr

extravagant adj extravagant(e) ek·stra·va·goñ(·goñt)

extremely adv extrêmement ek·streh·muh·moñ

eye n l'œil (m) uhy; eyes les yeux (mpl) yuh

eyebrow n le sourcil soor·seey

eyelash n le cil seel

eyelid n la paupière pō·pyehr

eyeliner n l'eye-liner (m) eye·lye·nehr

eyeshadow n l'ombre à paupières (f) oñ·bra pō·pyehr

eyesight n la vue vōō

F

fabric n le tissu tee·sōō Sn72

face n le visage vee·zazh

facecloth n le gant de toilette goñ duh twah·let

face cream n la crème pour le visage krem poor luh vee·zazh

facilities n/pl les équipements (mpl) ay·keep·moñ

facing prep en face de oñ fas duh

fact n le fait feh; in fact en fait oñ feh

factor n le facteur fak·tur

factory n l'usine (f) ōō·zeen

faculty n (university) la faculté fa·kōōl·tay

fade vi s'affaiblir sa·feh·bleer; (colour) se faner suh fa·nay

Fahrenheit adj Fahrenheit

fail vi échouer ay·shoo·ay; (brakes) lâcher lah·shay □ vt (exam) échouer à ay·shoo·ay a □ n without fail à coup sûr a koo sōōr

failure n l'échec (m) ay·shek; (person) le/la raté(e) ra·tay; (mechanical) la défaillance day·fye·yoñs

faint vi s'évanouir say·va·nweer □ adj (sound etc) faible feh·bluh; I feel faint je me trouve mal zhuh muh troov mal

fair adj (just) équitable ay·kee·ta·bluh; (hair) blond(e) bloñ (bloñd); (average) assez bon(ne) a·say boñ (bon) □ adv to play fair jouer franc-jeu zhoo·ay froñ·zhuh □ n fair (funfair) la foire fwahr; (commercial) la foire fwahr

fairground n le champ de foire shoñ duh fwahr

fairly adv (rather) assez a·say

fairy n la fée fay

faith n la foi fwah

faithfully adv □ yours faithfully veuillez agréer mes salutations distinguées vuh·yay za·gray·yay may sa·lōō·ta·syoñ dee·stañ·gay

fake adj faux fō, fausse fōs

fall vi (person) tomber toñ·bay; (prices etc) baisser beh·say; to fall down tomber toñ·bay; to fall in love tomber amoureux(euse) toñ·bay a·moo·ruh(·ruhz) □ n fall la chute shōōt; (decrease) la baisse bes; (season) l'automne (m) ō·ton

false adj (name etc) faux fō, fausse fōs; false teeth les fausses dents (fpl) fōs doñ

familiar adj (impertinent) familier(ère) fa·meel·yay(·yehr); to be familiar with something bien connaître* quelque chose byañ ko·neh·truh kel·kuh shōz

family n la famille fa·meey A2

famous adj célèbre say·leh·bruh

fan n (folding) l'éventail (m) ay·voñ·tye; (electric) le ventilateur voñ·tee·la·tur; (supporter) le supporter sōō·por·tehr

fanbelt n la courroie de ventilateur koor·wah duh voñ·tee·la·tur

fancy adj fantaisie foñ·tay·zee

fancy dress n le déguisement day·geez·moñ

far adv loin lwañ; (much) de loin de loin lwañ; how far is it to...? combien y a·t·il jusqu'à...? koñ·byañ ee·a·teel zhōōs·ka; as far as the station jusqu'à la gare zhōōs·ka la gar; as far as I know pour autant que je sache poor ō·toñ kuh zhuh sash; the Far East l'Extrême-Orient (m) ek·strem o·ryoñ

farce n la farce fars

fare n le prix du billet pree dōō bee·yeh; (in taxi) le prix de la course pree duh la koors

farm n la ferme fehrm

farmer n le fermier fehr·myay

farmhouse n la ferme fehrm

farmyard n la cour de ferme koor duh fehrm

farther adv plus loin plōō lwañ

farthest adv le (la) plus éloigné(e) luh (la) plōō zay·lwañ·nyay

fascinating adj fascinant(e) fa·see·noñ(·noñt)

fashion n la mode mod; the latest fashions la dernière mode la der·nyehr mod

fashionable adj à la mode a la mod

fast adj (speedy) rapide ra·peed; (dye) bon teint boñ tañ; my watch is fast ma montre avance ma moñ·truh a·voñs □ adv fast vite veet; to be fast asleep être* profondément endormi(e) eh·truh pro·foñ·day·moñ oñ·dor·mee T203

fasten vt attacher a·ta·shay; **fasten seat belts** attachez vos ceintures a·ta·shay vô sañ·tōōr

fat adj (person) gros(se) grō (grōs) □ n le gras grah

fatal adj mortel(le) mor·tel

father n le père pehr; **yes, Father** (priest) oui, mon père wee moñ pehr

father-in-law n le beau-père bō·pehr

faucet n le robinet ro·bee·neh

fault n (defect) le défaut day·fō; (blame) la faute fōt; **whose fault is it?** à qui la faute? a kee la fōt; **it's not my fault** ce n'est pas de ma faute suh neh pa duh ma fōt

faulty adj défectueux(euse) day·fek·tōō·uh(·uhz)

favo(u)r n le service sehr·vees; **to do someone a favour** rendre service à quelqu'un roñ·druh sehr·vees a kel·kuñ; **I'm not in favour of that idea** je ne suis pas partisan de cette idée zhuh nuh swee pa par·tee·zoñ duh set ee·day

favo(u)rite adj favori(te) fa·vo·ree(·reet)

fawn adj fauve fōv

fear n la peur pur

feasibility n la possibilité po·see·bee·lee·tay

feasibility study n l'étude des possibilités (f) ay·tōōd day po·see·bee·lee·tay

feast n le banquet boñ·keh

feather n la plume plōōm

feature film n le grand film groñ feelm

features pl les traits (mpl) treh

February n février fay·vree·yay

federal adj fédéral(e) fay·day·ral

fed up adj □ **I'm fed up** j'en ai assez zhoñ nay a·say

fee n les honoraires (mpl) o·no·rehr

feed vt nourrir noo·reer □ vi manger* moñ·zhay

feedback n le feed-back feed·bak

feel vt (touch) toucher too·shay; **I feel that... je** touche que... zhuh troov kuh □ vi **it feels soft** c'est doux au toucher seh doo ō too·shay; **I feel hungry** j'ai faim zhay fañ; **I feel better** je me sens mieux zhuh muh soñ myuh; **I feel like a beer** j'ai envie d'une bière zhay oñ·vee dōōn byehr

feeling n la sensation soñ·sa·syoñ; (emotion) le sentiment soñ·tee·moñ

fellow n le type teep; **fellow countryman** le compatriote koñ·pa·tree·yot

felt n (cloth) le feutre fuh·truh

felt-tip pen n le feutre fuh·truh

female adj (animal) femelle fuh·mel; **the female sex** le sexe féminin seks fay·mee·nañ

feminine adj féminin(e) fay·mee·nañ (·neen)

fence n la barrière ba·ryehr

fender n (on car) le pare-chocs par·shok

fern n la fougère foo·zhehr

ferry n (small) le bac bak; (large) le ferry fai·ree

fertile adj (land) fertile fehr·teel

festival n le festival fes·tee·val

fetch vt aller* chercher a·lay shehr·shay

fête n la fête fet

fever n la fièvre fyeh·vruh

few adj peu de puh duh; **a few books** quelques livres kel·kuh lee·vruh □ pron **there are very few** il y en a très peu eel yoñ na treh puh; **there are quite a few** il y en a pas mal eel yoñ na pa mal

fiancé(e) n le/la fiancé(e) fee·yoñ·say

fibre n la fibre fee·bruh

fibre-glass n la fibre de verre fee·bruh duh vehr

fiction n les romans (mpl) ro·moñ

field n le champ shoñ; (for football etc) le terrain teh·rañ

field glasses pl les jumelles (fpl) zhōō·mel

fierce adj féroce fay·ros

fifteen num quinze kañz

fifth adj cinquième sañ·kyem

fifty num cinquante sañ·koñt

fig n la figue feeg

fight n **to fight** se battre* suh ba·truh □ n la bagarre ba·gar

figure n (of human) la forme form; (number) le chiffre shee·fruh; **to have a nice figure** être* bien faite eh·truh byañ fet □ vt **figure** (suppose) supposer sōō·pō·zay

file n (tool) la lime leem; (dossier) le dossier dō·syay

filing cabinet n le classeur kla·sur

fill vt remplir roñ·pleer; **to fill in/out/up** remplir roñ·pleer; **fill it up!** (car) faites le plein! fet luh plañ

fillet n (of meat, fish) le filet fee·leh

filling adj (food) substantiel(le) sōōp·stoñ·syel □ n (in tooth) le plombage ploñ·bazh 162

filling station n la station d'essence sta·syoñ deh·soñs

film n (movie) le film feelm; (for camera) la pellicule peh·lee·kōōl

filter n le filtre feel·truh L39, S47f

final adj final(e) fee·nal

finally adv finalement fee·nal·moñ

finals pl (sports) la finale fee·nal

finance n la finance fee·noñs □ vt financer* fee·noñ·say

Finance Minister n le ministre des finances mee·nee·struh day fee·noñs

financial adj financier(ère) fee·noñ·syay(·syehr)

find vt trouver troo·vay; **to find out** découvrir* day·koo·vreer

fine adj (delicate) fin(e) fañ (feen); (weather) beau bō, belle bel; **(that's) fine!** très bien! treh byañ □ n **fine** l'amende (f) a·moñd

finger n le doigt dwah

finish vt/i finir fee·neer

Finland n la Finlande fañ·loñd

Finnish adj finlandais(e) fañ·loñ·deh (·dez) □ n le finnois fañ·nwah

fire n le feu fuh; (accident) l'incendie (m) añ·soñ·dee; **the house is on fire** la maison est en feu la meh·zoñ eh toñ fuh; **to set fire to** mettre* le feu à meh·truh luh fuh a □ vt **to fire a gun** tirer un coup de feu tee·ray uñ koo duh fuh; **to fire someone** (dismiss) renvoyer quelqu'un roñ·vwah·yay kel·kuñ

fire alarm n l'avertisseur d'incendie (m) a·vehr·tee·sur dañ·soñ·dee

firearm n l'arme à feu (f) arm a fuh

fire brigade n les sapeurs-pompiers (mpl) sa·pur·poñ·pyay

fire engine n la voiture de pompiers vwah·tōōr duh poñ·pyay

fire escape n l'escalier de secours (m) es·ka·lyay duh suh·koor

fire extinguisher n l'extincteur (m) ek·stañk·tur

fireman n le pompier poñ·pyay

fireplace n la cheminée shuh·mee·nay

fire station n la caserne de pompiers ka·zehrn duh poñ·pyay

fireworks *pl* le feu d'artifice *fuh dar·tee·fees*

firm *n* la compagnie *koñ·pa·nyee* □ *adj* ferme *fehrm*

first *adj* premier(ère) *pruhm·yay (·yehr)* □ *adv* le premier *luh pruhm·yay*, la première *la pruhm·yehr* □ *n* in first (gear) en première *oñ pruhm·yehr*; at first d'abord *da·bor*

first aid *n* les premiers secours (*mpl*) *pruhm·yay suh·koor*

first-aid kit *n* la trousse de pharmacie *troos duh far·ma·see*

first-class *adj* (work etc) de première classe *duh pruhm·yehr klas*; to travel first class voyager* en première *vwa·ya·zhay oñ pruhm·yehr*

first floor *n* le premier étage *pruhm·yeh ray·tazh*

first name *n* le prénom *pray·noñ*

fir (tree) *n* le sapin *sa·pañ*

fiscal *adj* fiscal(e) *fees·kal*

fiscal year *n* l'année budgétaire (*f*) *a·nay bōōd·zheh·tehr*

fish *n* le poisson *pwah·soñ* E27

fishing *n* la pêche *pesh*; to go fishing aller* à la pêche *a·lay a la pesh* L29

fishing rod *n* la canne à pêche *kan a pesh*

fishmonger *n* le poissonnier *pwah·so·nyay*

fist *n* le poing *pwañ*

fit *adj* (strong, healthy) en bonne forme *oñ bon form*; (suitable) convenable *koñ·vuh·na·bluh*; it fits (me) ça me va *sa muh va* □ *vt/i* il fit (seizure) l'accès (*m*) *ak·seh*

five *num* cinq *sañk*

fix *vt* fixer *feek·say*; (mend) réparer *ray·pa·ray*; (prepare) préparer *pray·pa·ray*

fizzy *adj* pétillant(e) *pay·tee·yoñ(·yoñt)*

flag *n* le drapeau *dra·pō*

flake *n* l'écaille (*f*) *ay·kye*; (of snow) le flocon *flo·koñ*

flame *n* la flamme *flam*

flan *n* la tarte *tart*

flannel *n* (facecloth) le gant de toilette *goñ duh twah·let*

flap *n* le rabat *ra·ba* □ *vi* (sail) claquer *kla·kay*

flash *n* l'éclair (*m*) *ay·klehr*; (on camera) le flash *flash* □ *vi* (light) briller *bree·yay* S56

flashbulb *n* l'ampoule de flash (*f*) *oñ·pool duh flash*

flash cube *n* le cube-flash *kōōb·flash*

flashlight *n* la lampe de poche *loñp duh posh*

flask *n* la thermos *tehr·mos*

flat *adj* plat(e) *pla (plat)*; (deflated) crevé(e) *kruh·vay*; (battery) à plat *a pla*; (beer) éventé(e) *ay·voñ·tay*; B flat (music) le si bémol *see bay·mol*; flat rate le taux fixe *tō feeks* □ *n* flat (apartment) l'appartement (*m*) *a·par·tuh·moñ*

flavo(u)r *n* le goût *goo*

flea *n* la puce *pōōs*

flea market *n* le marché aux puces *mar·shay ō pōōs*

fleet *n* la flotte *flot*; fleet of vehicles le parc automobile *park ō·tō·mo·beel*

Flemish *adj* flamand(e) *fla·moñ (·moñd)* □ *n* le flamand *fla·moñ*

flesh *n* la chair *shehr*

flexible *adj* flexible *flek·see·bluh*

flight *n* le vol *vol*; (of steps) l'escalier (*m*) *es·ka·lyay* T2f, T38

flight attendant *n* l'hôtesse de l'air (*f*) *ō·tes duh lehr*

flint *n* (in lighter) la pierre à briquet *pyehr a bree·keh*

flippers *pl* (for swimming) les palmes (*fpl*) *palm*

flirt *vi* flirter *flur·tay*

float *vi* flotter *flo·tay* □ *n* (for swimming, fishing) le flotteur *flo·tur*

flock *n* le troupeau *troo·pō*

flood *n* l'inondation (*f*) *ee·noñ·da·syoñ*

floodlight *n* le projecteur *pro·zhek·tur*

floodlit *adj* illuminé(e) *ee·lōō·mee·nay*

floor *n* le plancher *ploñ·shay*; 1st floor (Brit) le premier étage *pruh·myeh ray·tazh*; 2nd floor (US) le premier étage *pruh·myeh ray·tazh*

florist *n* le/la fleuriste *fluh·reest*

flour *n* la farine *fa·reen*

flow *vi* couler *koo·lay*; (traffic) circuler *seer·kōō·lay*

flow chart *n* l'organigramme (*m*) *or·ga·nee·gram*

flower *n* la fleur *flur* L35

flowerbed *n* le parterre *par·tehr*

flu *n* la grippe *greep*

fluent *adj* □ he speaks fluent French il parle le français couramment *eel parl luh froñ·seh koo·ra·moñ*

fluorescent light *n* le tube fluorescent *tōōb flōō·ō·reh·soñ*

fluoride *n* le fluor *flōō·or*

flush *vt* □ to flush the toilet tirer la chasse d'eau *tee·ray la shas dō*

flute *n* la flûte *flōōt*

fly *n* la mouche *moosh* □ *vi* voler *vo·lay*; (passengers) voyager* en avion *vwah·ya·zhay oñ na·vyoñ*

flying *n* l'aviation (*f*) *a·vya·syoñ*; to like flying aimer l'avion *ay·may la·vyoñ*

flyover *n* (road) le toboggan *to·bo·goñ*

foam *n* la mousse *moos*

focus *vt* mettre* au point *meh·trō pwañ*

fog *n* le brouillard *broo·yar*

foggy *adj* brumeux(euse) *brōō·muh (·muhz)*; it's foggy il y a du brouillard *eel ya dōō broo·yar*

fog-lamp *n* le phare antibrouillard *far oñ·tee·broo·yar*

foil *n* (for food) le papier d'aluminium *pa·pyay da·lōō·mee·nyum*

fold *vt* plier *plee·ay*

folding chair *n* le pliant *plee·oñ*

folding table *n* la table pliante *ta·bluh plee·oñt*

folk dance *n* la danse folklorique *doñs folk·lo·reek*

folk song *n* la chanson folklorique *shoñ·soñ folk·lo·reek* L38

follow *vt/i* suivre* *swee·vruh*

following *adj* suivant(e) *swee·voñ (·voñt)*

food *n* la nourriture *noo·ree·tōōr*

food poisoning *n* l'intoxication alimentaire (*f*) *añ·tok·see·ka·syoñ a·lee·moñ·tehr*

foot *n* (of person) le pied *pyay*; (of animal) la patte *pat*; (measurement) ≈ .300 m

football *n* (game) le football *foot·bol*; (ball) le ballon *ba·loñ*

footbrake *n* le frein à pied *frañ a pyay*

footpath *n* le sentier *soñ·tyay*

for *prep* pour *poor*; to sell something for 400 francs vendre quelque chose 400 francs *voñ·druh kel·kuh shōz 400 froñ*; to leave for London partir* pour Londres *par·teer poor loñ·druh*; to walk for an hour marcher pendant une heure *mar·shay poñ·doñ ōōn ur*; what's the French for "dog"? comment est-ce qu'on dit "dog" en français? *ko·moñ es·koñ dee dog oñ froñ·seh*; it's warm for March il fait bon pour mars *eel feh boñ poor mars*

forbid vt défendre *day·foñ·druh*; **to forbid someone to do something** défendre à quelqu'un de faire quelque chose *day·foñ·dra kel·kuñ duh fehr kel·kuh shōz*

force n (violence) la force *fors* □ vt (compel) forcer* *for·say*

ford n le gué *gay*

forecast n la prévision *pray·vee·zyoñ*; (weather) le bulletin météorologique *bōōl·tañ may·tay·o·ro·lo·zheek*

forehead n le front *froñ*

foreign adj étranger(ère) *ay·troñ·zhay(·zhehr)*

foreigner n l'étranger (m) *ay·troñ·zhay*, l'étrangère (f) *ay·troñ·zhehr* T194

foreign exchange market n le marché des changes *mar·shay day shoñzh*

foreign policy n la politique extérieure *po·lee·teek ek·stay·ryur*

foreman n le contremaître *koñ·truh·meh·truh*

forename n le prénom *pray·noñ*

forest n la forêt *fo·reh*

forever adv pour toujours *poor too·zhoor*

forgery n (copy) le faux *fō*

forget vt oublier *oo·blee·ay*

forgive vt pardonner *par·do·nay*

fork n la fourchette *foor·shet*; (in road) la bifurcation *bee·fōōr·ka·syoñ*

form n la forme *form*; (document) le formulaire *for·mōō·lehr*; **in good form** en bonne forme *oñ bon form*

formal adj officiel(le) *o·fee·syel*

fortnight n les quinze jours (mpl) *kañz zhoor*

fortune n (wealth) la fortune *for·tōōn*

forty num quarante *ka·roñt*

forward vt (letter) faire* suivre *fehr swee·vruh*

forward(s) adv en avant *oñ na·voñ*; **too far forward** trop en avant *trō poñ na·voñ*

fountain n la fontaine *foñ·ten*; (for drinking) le jet d'eau potable *zhay dō po·ta·bluh*

fountain pen n le stylo *stee·lō*

four num quatre *ka·truh*

fourteen num quatorze *ka·torz*

fourth adj quatrième *ka·tryem*

fox n le renard *ruh·nar*

fracture n (of arm etc) la fracture *frak·tōōr*

fragile adj fragile *fra·zheel*

frame n (of picture) le cadre *ka·druh*; **frames** (of glasses) la monture *moñ·tōōr*

France n la France *froñs*; **in/to France** en France *oñ froñs*

free adj libre *lee·bruh*; (costing nothing) gratuit(e) *gra·twee(·tweet)* Bm11

freeway n l'autoroute (f) *ō·tō·root*

freeze vi geler* *zhuh·lay* □ vt (food) congeler* *koñ·zhuh·lay*

freezer n le congélateur *kon·zhay·la·tur*

freight n (goods) le fret *freh*

freight train n le train de marchandises *trañ duh mar·shoñ·deez*

French adj français(e) *froñ·seh(·sez)*; he's French il est Français *eel eh froñ·seh*; she's French elle est Française *el eh froñ·sez* □ n French le français *froñ·seh*; **in French** en français *oñ froñ·seh*

french fried potatoes, french fries pl les frites (fpl) *freet*

frequent adj fréquent(e) *fray·koñ (·koñt)*

fresh adj frais *freh*, fraîche *fresh*; (impudent) trop libre *trō lee·bruh*

Friday n vendredi (m) *voñ·druh·dee*

fridge n le frigidaire *free·zhee·dehr*

fried adj frit(e) *free(t)*; **a fried egg** un œuf sur le plat *uñ nuhf sōōr luh pla*

friend n l'ami(e) (m/f) *a·mee*

friendly adj amical(e) *a·mee·kal*

frighten vt effrayer *eh·fray·yay*

fringe n la frange *froñzh*

fritter n le beignet *beh·nyeh*

frog n la grenouille *gruh·noo·yuh*

frogs legs pl les cuisses de grenouille (fpl) *kwees duh gruh·noo·yuh*

from prep de *duh*; from London de Londres *duh loñ·druh*; **from 8 o'clock** de 8 heures *duh 8 ur*; **a letter from Mary** une lettre de Mary *ōōn leh·truh duh Mary*; **water from the tap** l'eau du robinet *lō dōō ro·bee·neh*

front adj de devant *duh duh·voñ* □ n (foremost part) le devant *duh·voñ*; (seaside) le front de mer *froñ duh mehr*; **at the front** à l'avant *a la·voñ*; **to sit in front** s'asseoir* devant *sa·swahr duh·voñ*

frontier n la frontière *froñ·tyehr*

front-wheel drive n la traction avant *trak·syoñ na·voñ*

frost n le gel *zhel*

frozen adj (food) congelé(e) *koñ·zhuh·lay*

fruit n le fruit *frwee*

fruit salad n la salade de fruits *sa·lad duh frwee*

fry vt faire* frire *fehr freer*

fry(ing) pan n la poêle *pwahl*

fuel n le combustible *koñ·bōōs·tee·bluh*

fuel pump n la pompe à essence *poñp a e·soñs*

full adj plein(e) *plañ (plen)*; **full of** plein(e) de *plañ (plen) duh*; **full up** (bus etc) complet(ète) *koñ·pleh (·plet)*

full stop n le point *pwañ*

full-time adj, adv à plein temps *a plañ toñ*

fun n □ it was great fun c'était très amusant *say·teh trez za·mōō·zoñ*

funds pl les fonds (mpl) *foñ*

funeral n l'enterrement (m) *oñ·tehr·moñ*

funny adj (amusing) drôle *drōl*; (strange) curieux(euse) *kōō·ryuh (·ryuhz)*

fur n la fourrure *foo·rōōr*

fur coat n le manteau de fourrure *moñ·tō duh foo·rōōr*

furnish vt (room etc) meubler *muh·blay*

furniture n les meubles (mpl) *muh·bluh*

further adv plus loin *plōō lwañ*

furthest adv le (la) plus éloigné(e) *luh (la) plōō zay·lwañ·nyay*

fuse n le fusible *fōō·zee·bluh* A75, T185

fuss n les histoires (fpl) *ees·twahr*; **to make a fuss** faire* des histoires *fehr day zees·twahr*

future n l'avenir (m) *a·vuh·neer*

G

gadget n le gadget *gad·zhet* S15

gain vt (obtain) gagner ga·nyay □ vi
(clock) avancer* a·voń·say

gala n le gala ga·la

gale n le coup de vent koo duh voń

gallery n la galerie ga·luh·ree; (in
theatre) le dernier balcon dehr·nyay
bal·koń

gallon n le gallon ga·loń

gallop vi galoper ga·lo·pay □ n le ga·
lop ga·lō

gamble vi jouer zhoo·ay

gambler n le joueur zhoo·ur

gambling n le jeu zhuh

game n le jeu zhuh; (hunting) le gibier
zhee·byay; **a game of tennis** une par·
tie de tennis ōoń par·tee duh teh·nees

gang n la bande bońd

gangster n le gangster goń·stehr

gangway n (passage) l'allée (f) a·lay;
(bridge) la passerelle pa·suh·rel

gap n le trou troo

garage n le garage ga·razh

garbage n les ordures (fpl) or·dōōr

garbage can n la poubelle poo·bel

garden n le jardin zhar·dań

garden centre n la pépinière pay·pee·
nyehr

gardener n le jardinier zhar·dee·nyay

gargle vi se gargariser suh gar·ga·ree·
zay

garlic n l'ail (m) eye

garlic sausage n le saucisson à l'ail sō·
see·soń a lye

garment n le vêtement vet·moń

gas n le gaz gaz; **gas cooker** la cuisi·
nière à gaz kwee·zee·nyehr a gaz

gasket n la garniture de piston gar·nee·
tōōr duh pees·toń

gas(oline) n l'essence (f) eh·sońs

gas station n la station d'essence sta·
syoń deh·sońs

gate n (of garden) le portail por·tye;
(of building) la porte port

gateau n le gâteau gah·tō

gather vt (assemble) rassembler ra·
soń·blay □ vi (crowd) se rassembler
suh ra·soń·blay

gathered adj froncé(e) froń·say

gauge n (device) la jauge zhōzh

gauze n la gaze gaz

gay adj (merry) gai(e) gay

gear n (equipment) le matériel ma·tay·
ryel; (of car) la vitesse vee·tes; **in
gear** en prise oń preez; **2nd/3rd gear**
deuxième/troisième vitesse duh·
zyem/trwah·zyem vee·tes; **top/bottom
gear** quatrième/première vitesse ka·
tryem/pruh·myehr vee·tes

gearbox n la boîte de vitesse bwaht
duh vee·tes

gear lever, gear shift n le levier de vi·
tesse luh·vyay duh vee·tes

gem n la pierre précieuse pyehr pray·
syuhz

gender n le genre zhoń·ruh

general adj général(e) zhay·nay·ral
□ n (soldier) le général zhay·nay·ral;
in general en général oń zhay·nay·ral

general election n les élections législa·
tives (fpl) ay·lek·syoń lay·zhee·sla·
teev

general knowledge n la culture géné·
rale kōōl·tōōr zhay·nay·ral

generally adv généralement zhay·nay·
ral·moń

general practitioner, G.P. n le méde·
cin généraliste mayd·sań zhay·nay·
ra·leest

generation n la génération zhay·nay·
ra·syoń

generator n (electrical) le générateur
zhay·nay·ra·tur

generous adj (person) généreux(euse)
zhay·nay·ruh(·ruhz)

Geneva n Genève (f) zhuh·nev

gentle adj doux doo, douce doos

gentleman n le monsieur muh·syuh

genuine adj authentique ō·toń·teek

geography n la géographie zhay·o·gra·
fee

geology n la géologie zhay·o·lo·zhee

geometry n la géométrie zhay·o·may·
tree

geranium n le géranium zhay·ra·nyum

germ n le microbe mee·krob

German adj allemand(e) al·moń
(·mońd); **he's German** il est Alle·
mand eel eh tal·moń; **she's German**
elle est Allemande el eh tal·mońd
□ n German l'allemand (m) al·moń

Germany n l'Allemagne (f) al·ma·
nyuh; **in/to Germany** en Allemagne
oń nal·ma·nyuh

gesture n le geste zhest

get vt (obtain) obtenir* op·tuh·neer;
(fetch) aller* chercher a·lay shehr·
shay; (receive) recevoir* ruh·suh·
vwahr; (prepare: food) préparer
pray·pa·ray; (catch: illness) attraper
a·tra·pay; **to have got(ten)** (possess)
avoir* a·vwahr; **to get tired** devenir*
fatigué(e) duh·vuh·neer fa·tee·gay;
to get ready se préparer suh pray·pa·
ray; **how do we get there?** comment
est-ce que nous y allons? ko·moń es·
kuh noo zee a·loń; **to get home** ren·
trer à la maison roń·tray a la meh·
zoń; **get off the grass** ne marchez pas
sur la pelouse nuh mar·shay pa sū̄r
la puh·looz; **to get one's hair cut** se
faire* couper les cheveux suh fehr
koo·pay lay shuh·vuh; **to get away**
(escape) échapper ay·sha·pay; **how
are you getting on?** comment ça va?
ko·moń sa va; **to get onto a road** re·
joindre* une route ruh·zhwan·druh
ōōn root; **to get through** (on phone)
obtenir* la communication op·tuh·
neer la ko·mōō·nee·ka·syoń; **to get
up** se lever* suh luh·vay

gherkin n le cornichon kor·nee·shoń

ghetto n le ghetto geh·tō

ghost n le revenant ruh·vuh·noń

giant n le géant zhay·oń

gift n le cadeau ka·dō; (ability) le don
doń

gifted adj doué(e) doo·ay

gift token n le chèque-cadeau shek·ka·
dō

gift-wrap vt faire* un paquet-cadeau
de fehr uń pa·keh ka·dō duh

gin n (drink) le gin djeen

ginger n le gingembre zhań·zhoń·bruh

ginger ale n la boisson gazeuse au gin·
gembre bwah·soń ga·zuhz ō zhań·
zhoń·bruh

gingerbread n le pain d'épices pań
day·pees

gingham n le vichy vee·shee

gipsy n le/la gitan(e) zhee·toń(·tan)

girdle n (corset) la gaine gen

girl n (child) la fillette fee·yet; (young
woman) la jeune fille zhuhn feey
S108

girlfriend n la petite amie puh·teet a·
mee

giro n (post office) les comptes chè·
ques postaux koń·t shek po·stō; **bank
giro (system)** le système de virement
bancaire see·stem duh veer·moń boń·
kehr

give *vt* donner *do·nay*; **to give someone something** donner quelque chose à quelqu'un *do·nay kel·kuh shōz a kel·kuñ*; **to give away** donner *do·nay*; **to give back** rendre* *roñ·druh*; **to give in** (*yield*) céder* *say·day*; **to give up** (*abandon hope*) renoncer* *ruh·noñ·say*; **to give up smoking** renoncer* à fumer *ruh·noñ·say a fōō·may*; **to give way** (*traffic*) céder* la priorité *say·day la pree·o·ree·tay*

glacé *adj* glacé(e) *gla·say*

glad *adj* heureux(euse) *uh·ruh(·ruhz)*; **I was glad to hear...** j'ai été content d'apprendre... *zhay ay·tay koñ·toñ da·proñ·druh*

glamorous *adj* séduisant(e) *say·dwee·zoñ(·zoñt)*

glance *n* le coup d'œil *koo duhy* □ *vi* **to glance at** jeter* un coup d'œil à *zhuh·tay uñ koo duhy a*

gland *n* la glande *gloñd*

glare *n* (*of light*) la lumière éclatante *lōō·myehr ay·kla·toñt*

glass *n* le verre *vehr*; (*glassware*) la verrerie *veh·ruh·ree* B72, E14

glasses *pl* les lunettes (*fpl*) *lōō·net* B74

glide *vi* glisser *glee·say*

glider *n* le planeur *pla·nur*

gliding *n* (*sport*) le vol plané *vol pla·nay*

global *adj* global(e) *glo·bal*

globe *n* (*map*) le globe *glob*

globe artichoke *n* l'artichaut (*m*) *ar·tee·shō*

glove *n* le gant *goñ*

glove compartment *n* la boîte à gants *bwaht a goñ*

glow *vi* rougeoyer *roo·zhwah·yay*

glue *n* la colle *kol* □ *vt* coller *ko·lay*

glycerin(e) *n* la glycérine *glee·say·reen*

gnat *n* le moucheron *moo·shuh·roñ*

go *vi* aller* *a·lay*; (*leave*) partir* *par·teer*; (*clock, machine*) marcher *mar·shay*; **to go shopping** faire* les courses *fehr lay koors*; **to go bad** s'avarier *sa·va·ryay*; **how did it go?** comment ça s'est passé? *ko·moñ sa seh pa·say*; **the books go here** les livres se mettent ici *lay lee·vruh suh met·teñ tee·see*; **it won't go in** ça n'entre pas *sa noñ·truh pa*; **all our money's gone** tout notre argent est parti *too no·trar·zhoñ eh par·tee*; **I'm going to do it** je vais le faire *zhuh veh luh fehr*; **go ahead!** allez-y! *a·lay·zee*; **to go away** s'en aller* *soñ na·lay*; **to go back to** venir* *ruh·vuh·neer*; **to go down** descendre *deh·soñ·druh*; **to go in** entrer *roñ·tray*; **to go out** sortir* *sor·teer*; **to go out with somebody** sortir* avec quelqu'un *sor·teer a·vek kel·kuñ*; **this goes with your dress** ceci va avec votre robe *suh·see va a·vek vo·truh rob*; **we will have to go without milk** nous devrons nous passer de lait *noo duh·vroñ noo pa·say duh leh*

goal *n* le but *bōō*

goat *n* la chèvre *sheh·vruh*

god *n* le dieu *dyuh*; **God** Dieu (*m*) *dyuh*

godfather *n* le parrain *pa·rañ*

godmother *n* la marraine *ma·ren*

goggles *pl* les lunettes protectrices (*fpl*) *lōō·net pro·tek·trees*

gold *n* l'or (*m*) *or* □ *adj* en or *oñ nor*; **gold-plated** plaqué(e) or *pla·kay or* S89

golden *adj* doré(e) *do·ray*

goldfish *n* le poisson rouge *pwah·soñ roozh*

golf *n* le golf *golf* L27

golf ball *n* la balle de golf *bal duh golf*

golf club *n* le club de golf *klub duh golf*

golf course *n* le terrain de golf *teh·rañ duh golf*

golfer *n* le/la joueur(euse) de golf *zhoo·uhr(·uhz) duh golf*

good *adj* bon(ne) *boñ (bon)*; (*weather*) beau *bō*, belle *bel*; (*well-behaved*) sage *sazh*; **to be good at golf** jouer bien au golf *zhoo·ay byañ ō golf*; **spinach is good for you** les épinards sont bons pour la santé *lay zay·pee·nar soñ boñ poor la soñ·tay*; **it'll do you good** ça vous fera du bien *sa voo fuh·ra dōō byañ*; **good morning/afternoon!** bonjour! *boñ·zhoor*; **good evening!** bonsoir! *boñ·swahr*; **good night!** bonne nuit! *bon nwee*

goodbye *excl* au revoir *ō ruh·vwahr*

Good Friday *n* le Vendredi Saint *voñ·druh·dee sañ*

goods *pl* les marchandises (*fpl*) *mar·shoñ·deez*

goose *n* l'oie (*f*) *wah*

gooseberry *n* la groseille à maquereau *grō·zay a ma·kuh·rō*

go-slow *n* la grève perlée *grev pehr·lay*

gossip *vi* bavarder *ba·var·day* □ *n* (*chatter*) le bavardage *ba·var·dazh*

goulash *n* la goulache *goo·lash*

gourmet *n* le gourmet *goor·meh*

govern *vt* (*country*) gouverner *goo·vehr·nay*

government *n* le gouvernement *goo·vehr·nuh·moñ*

governor *n* (*of colony*) le gouverneur *goo·vehr·nur*; (*of institution*) le directeur *dee·rek·tur*

gown *n* la robe *rob*

grab *vt* saisir *seh·zeer*

graceful *adj* gracieux(euse) *gra·syuh(·syuhz)*

grade *n* le grade *grad*; (*class*) la classe *klas*

grade crossing *n* le passage à niveau *pa·sazh a nee·vō*

grade school *n* l'école primaire (*f*) *ay·kol pree·mehr*

gradual *adj* progressif(ive) *pro·greh·seef(·seev)*

gradually *adv* progressivement *pro·greh·seev·moñ*

graduate *n* (*from university*) le/la diplômé(e) d'université *dee·plō·may dōō·nee·vehr·see·tay* □ *vi* obtenir* son diplôme *op·tuh·neer soñ dee·plōm*

grain *n* (*cereal crops*) le grain *grañ*; (*in wood*) la fibre *fee·bruh*

gram *n* le gramme *gram*

grammar *n* la grammaire *gra·mehr*; **grammar** (*book*) le livre de grammaire *lee·vruh duh gra·mehr*

gramme *n* le gramme *gram*

grand *adj* splendide *sploñ·deed*

grandchild *n* le/la petit(e) enfant *puh·tee(·teet) oñ·foñ*

granddaughter *n* la petite-fille *puh·teet·feey*

grandfather *n* le grand-père *groñ·pehr*

grandfather clock *n* l'horloge de parquet (*f*) *or·lozh duh par·keh*

grandmother *n* la grand-mère *groñ·mehr*

grand piano *n* le piano à queue *pya·nō a kuh*

Grand Prix *n* le Grand Prix *groñ pree*

grandson *n* le petit-fils *puh·tee·fees*

grant *n* (*to student*) la bourse *boors*;

(to institution) la subvention *sōōb·voñ·syoñ* □ *vt (wish)* accorder *a·kor·day*

grape *n* le raisin *reh·zañ*

grapefruit *n* le pamplemousse *poñ·pluh·moos*

grapefruit juice *n* le jus de pamplemousse *zhōō duh poñ·pluh·moos*

graph *n* le graphique *gra·feek*

grasp *vt (seize)* saisir *seh·zeer*

grass *n* l'herbe *(f) ehrb*

grate *n* la grille de foyer *greey duh fwah·yay* □ *vt (food)* râper *rah·pay*

grateful *adj* reconnaissant(e) *ruh·ko·neh·soñ(·soñt)*

grater *n* la râpe *rahp*

grave *n* la tombe *toñb*

grave (accent) *n* l'accent grave *(m) ak·soñ grav*

gravel *n* le gravier *gra·vyay*

graveyard *n* le cimetière *seem·tyehr*

gravy *n* le jus de viande *zhōō duh vyoñd*

gray *adj* gris(e) *gree (greez)*

graze *vi* l'écorchure *(f) ay·kor·shōōr* □ *vt (skin)* écorcher *ay·kor·shay*

grease *n* la graisse *gres*; *(lubricant)* le lubrifiant *lōō·bree·fyoñ*

greasy *adj (surface)* graisseux(euse) *greh·suh(·suhz)*; *(food)* gras(se) *gra (gras)*

great *adj* grand(e) *groñ (groñd)*; *(excellent)* formidable *for·mee·da·bluh*

Great Britain *n* la Grande Bretagne *groñd bruh·ta·nyuh*

Greece *n* la Grèce *gres*

greedy *adj* gourmand(e) *goor·moñ (·moñd)*

Greek *adj* grec *grek*, grecque *grek*

green *adj* vert(e) *vehr (vehrt)*

green card *n* la carte verte *kart vehrt*

greengrocer *n* le marchand de légumes *mar·shoñ duh lay·gōōm*

greenhouse *n* la serre *sehr*

green salad *n* la salade *sa·lad*

greet *vt* accueillir¹ *a·kuh·yeer*

greeting *n* la salutation *sa·lōō·ta·syoñ*

greetings card *n* la carte de vœux *kart duh vuh*

grey *adj* gris(e) *gree (greez)*

grief *n* le chagrin *sha·grañ*

grill *n (gridiron)* le gril *greel* □ *vt* griller *gree·yay*

grillroom *n* le grill *greel*

grimace *n* la grimace *gree·mas*

grin *vi* sourire¹ *soo·reer* □ *n* le sourire *soo·reer*

grind *vt* moudre¹ *moo·druh*

grip *vt* saisir *seh·zeer* □ *n (case)* la valise *va·leez*

grit *n* le gravillon *gra·vee·yoñ*

groan *vi* gémir *zhay·meer* □ *n* le gémissement *zhay·mees·moñ*

grocer *n* l'épicier *(m) ay·pee·syay*

groceries *pl* les provisions *(fpl) pro·vee·zyoñ*

grocery shop *n* l'épicerie *(f) ay·pee·suh·ree*

gross *n* la grosse *grōs* □ *adj (before deductions)* brut(e) *brōōt*

gross national product, GNP *n* le revenu national brut *ruh·vuh·nōō na·syo·nal brōōt*

grotesque *adj* grotesque *gro·tesk*

ground *n* la terre *tehr* □ *adj (coffee)* moulu(e) *moo·lōō*; **ground beef** le biftek haché *beef·tek ah·shay*

ground floor *n* le rez-de-chaussée *ray·duh·shō·say*

groundnut *n* l'arachide *(f) a·ra·sheed*

grounds *pl (land)* le domaine *do·men*; *(of coffee)* le marc *mar*

groundsheet *n* le tapis de sol *ta·pee duh sol*

group *n* le groupe *groop*

grouse *n (bird)* le coq de bruyère *kok duh brōō·yehr*

grow *vi (child)* grandir *groñ·deer*; *(plant, hair)* pousser *poo·say* □ *vt (plants)* faire¹ pousser *fehr poo·say*; **to grow up** devenir¹ adulte *duh·vuh·neer a·dōōlt*

growl *vi* grogner *gro·nyay*

grown-up *adj* adulte *a·dōōlt* □ *n* l'adulte *(m/f) a·dōōlt*

growth *n* la croissance *krwah·soñs*; *(in amount etc)* l'augmentation *(f) ōg·moñ·ta·syoñ*; *(anatomical)* la grosseur *grō·sur*

grumble *vi* ronchonner *roñ·sho·nay*

grunt *vi* grogner *gro·nyay*

guarantee *n* la garantie *ga·roñ·tee* □ *vt* garantir *ga·roñ·teer*

guard *vt (prisoner)* surveiller *sōōr·vay·yay*; *(protect)* protéger¹ *pro·tay·zhay* □ *n (sentry)* le garde *gard*; *(soldiers)* la garde *gard*; *(on train)* le chef de train *shef duh trañ*

guardian *n* le tuteur *tōō·tur*, la tutrice *tōō·trees*

guess *vt/i* deviner *duh·vee·nay*

guest *n* l'invité *(m/f) añ·vee·tay*; *(at hotel)* le/la client(e) *klee·oñ(·oñt)*

guest-house *n* la pension *poñ·syoñ*

guest-room *n* la chambre d'amis *shoñ·bruh da·mee*

guide *n* le guide *geed*

guidebook *n* le guide *geed* L4

guide dog *n* le chien d'aveugle *shyañ da·vuh·gluh*

guided tour *n* la visite guidée *vee·zeet gee·day* L6f

guilt *n* la culpabilité *kōōl·pa·bee·lee·tay*

guilty *adj* coupable *koo·pa·bluh*

guinea fowl *n* la pintade *pañ·tad*

guitar *n* la guitare *gee·tar*

gum *n (of teeth)* la gencive *zhoñ·seev*; *(chewing gum)* le chewing-gum *shwing·gum* 167

gun *n* le fusil *fōō·zee*

gunman *n* le bandit armé *boñ·dee ar·may*

gust *n* la rafale *ra·fal*

gusty *adj (wind)* **it's** il souffle en rafales *kee soo·floñ ra·fal*

gutter *n (in street)* le caniveau *ka·nee·vō*; *(on building)* la gouttière *goo·tyehr*

gym(nasium) *n* le gymnase *zheem·naz*

gymnastics *n* la gymnastique *zheem·nas·teek*

gypsy *n* le/la gitan(e) *zhee·toñ(·tan)*

H

haberdashery *n* la mercerie *mehr·suh·ree*

habit *n* l'habitude *(f) a·bee·tōōd*

haddock *n* l'églefin *(m) ay·gluh·fañ*

haemorrhoids *pl* les hémorroïdes *(fpl) ay·muh·ro·eed*

Hague (the) *n* la Haye *la ay*

hail *n* la grêle *grel* □ *vi* **it's hailing** il grêle *eel grel*

hair *n* les cheveux *(mpl) shuh·vuh*; *(single strand)* le cheveu *shuh·vuh* Sn41

hairbrush *n* la brosse à cheveux *bros a shuh·vuh*

haircut *n (style)* la coupe de cheveux

koop duh shuh·vuh; **to have a hair-cut** se faire* couper les cheveux *suh fehr koo·pay lay shuh·vuh*

hairdresser n le coiffeur *kwah·fur*, la coiffeuse *kwah·fuhz*

hair-drier n le sèche-cheveux *sesh·shuh·vuh*

hairpin n la pince à cheveux *pañs a shuh·vuh*

hairpin bend n le virage en épingle à cheveux *vee·razh oñ nay·pañ·gla shuh·vuh*

hair spray n la laque *lak*

hair-style n la coiffure *kwah·fōōr*

half n la moitié *mwah·tyay*; **half an hour** une demi-heure *ōōn duh·mee·ur*; **two and a half** deux et demi *duh ay duh·mee*; **to cut something in half** couper quelque chose en deux *koo·pay kel·kuh shōz oñ duh* □ adj **a half dozen** une demi-douzaine *ōōn duh·mee·doo·zen*; **three and a half kilometers** trois kilomètres et demi *trwah kee·lo·meh·tray duh·mee* □ adv **half** à moitié *a mwah·tyay*; **half open** à demi ouvert *a duh·mee oo·vehr*

half-fare n le demi-tarif *duh·mee·ta·reef*

half holiday n la demi-journée de congé *duh·mee zhoor·nay duh koñ·zhay*

half-hour n la demi-heure *duh·mee·ur*

half-price adj à moitié prix *a mwah·tyay pree*

half-time n la mi-temps *mee·toñ*

half way adv à mi-chemin *a mee·shuh·mañ*

hall n (entrance) l'entrée (f) *oñ·tray*; (room) la salle *sal*

hallmark n le poinçon *pwañ·soñ*

halve vt (divide in two) partager* en deux *par·ta·zhay oñ duh*; (reduce by half) réduire* de moitié *ray·dweer duh mwah·tyay*

ham n le jambon *zhoñ·boñ* E72, S31

hamburger n le hamburger *am·bur·gur*

hammer n le marteau *mar·tō*

hammock n le hamac *ha·mak*

hamper n le panier *pa·nyay*

hand n la main *mañ*; (of clock) l'aiguille (f) *ay·gwee*) □ vt **to hand the main à la mañ** □ vt **to hand someone something** donner quelque chose à quelqu'un *do·nay kel·kuh shōz a kel·kuñ*

handbag n le sac à main *sak a mañ*

handbook n le manuel *ma·nōō·el*

hand-brake n le frein à main *frañ a mañ*

hand cream n la crème pour les mains *krem poor lay mañ*

handcuffs pl les menottes (fpl) *muh·not*

handicap n le handicap *oñ·dee·kap*

handkerchief n le mouchoir *moo·shwahr*

handle n la poignée *pwah·nyay*; (of cup) l'anse (f) *oñs*; (of knife) le manche *moñsh* □ vt (touch) toucher à *too·shay a*; (deal with) s'y prendre* avec *see proñ·dra·vek*; **handle with care** (on parcel) fragile *fra·zheel*

handlebar(s) n le guidon *gee·doñ*

hand-luggage n les bagages à main (mpl) *ba·gazh a mañ*

handmade adj fait(e) à la main *feh (fet) a la mañ* S109

handrail n (on stairs) la rampe *roñp*

handsome adj (person) beau *bō*

handy adj (convenient) pratique *pra·teek*

hang vt accrocher *a·kro·shay*; (criminal) pendre *poñ·druh* □ vi pendre *poñ·druh*; **hang on!** (on phone) ne quittez pas *nuh kee·tay pa*; **to hang up** (phone) raccrocher *ra·kro·shay*

hangover n la gueule de bois *guhl duh bwah*; **to have a hangover** avoir* la gueule de bois *a·vwahr la guhl duh bwah*

happen vi arriver *a·ree·vay*; **what happened to him?** qu'est-ce qui lui est arrivé? *kes·kee lwee eh ta·ree·vay*

happiness n le bonheur *bon·ur*

happy adj heureux(euse) *uh·ruh (·ruhz)*

harbo(u)r n le port *por*

harbo(u)r master n le capitaine de port *ka·pee·ten duh por*

hard adj dur(e) *dōōr*; (difficult) difficile *dee·fee·seel*

hard-boiled adj dur(e) *dōōr*

hard shoulder n l'accotement stabilisé (m) *a·kot·moñ sta·bee·lee·zay*

hardware n la quincaillerie *kañ·kye·yuh·ree*; (computing) le hardware *ard·wehr*

hard-wearing adj solide *so·leed*

hare n le lièvre *lee·eh·vruh*

haricot beans pl les haricots (mpl) *a·ree·kō*

harmful adj nuisible *nwee·zee·bluh*

harmless adj inoffensif(ive) *ee·no·foñ·seef(·seev)*

harness n le harnais *ar·neh*

harp n la harpe *arp*

harsh adj (severe) sévère *say·vehr*

harvest n (of grain) la moisson *mwah·soñ*; (of grapes) la vendange *voñ·doñzh* □ vt (grain) moissonner *mwah·so·nay*; (grapes) vendanger* *voñ·doñ·zhay*

haste n la hâte *aht*

hat n le chapeau *sha·pō* S12

hatch n (for serving) le passe-plats *pas·pla*

hatchback n (car) la berline avec hayon arrière *behr·leen a·vek eye·yoñ a·ryehr*

hate vt haïr *ye·eer*

hatred n la haine *en*

hat stand n le portemanteau *port·moñ·tō*

have vt avoir* *a·vwahr*; (meal, shower, drink) prendre* *proñ·druh*; **she has to do it** elle doit le faire *el dwah luh fehr*; **to have something done** faire* faire quelque chose *fehr fehr kel·kuh shōz*

hay n le foin *fwañ*

hay fever n le rhume des foins *rōōm day fwañ* S40

he pron il *eel*; **here he is!** le voilà *luh vwah·la*

head n la tête *tet*; (chief) le chef *shef*

headache n le mal de tête *mal duh tet*; **to have a headache** avoir* mal à la tête *a·vwahr mal a la tet* S40

headlamp, headlight n le phare *far*

headline n la manchette *moñ·shet*

headmaster n le directeur *dee·rek·tur*

headmistress n la directrice *dee·rek·trees*

head office n le bureau central *bōō·rō soñ·tral*

head-on adj de plein fouet *duh plañ foo·eh*

headphones pl le casque à écouteurs *cask a ay·koo·tur*

headrest n l'appui-tête (m) *a·pwee·tet*

heal vi (wound) se cicatriser *suh see·ka·tree·zay*

health n la santé *soñ·tay*

health food n les aliments naturels (mpl) *a·lee·moñ na·tōō·rel*

health service n la Sécurité Sociale *say·kŌŌ·ree·tay so·syal*

healthy adj (person) en bonne santé *oñ bon soñ·tay*

heap n le tas *ta*

hear vt/i entendre *oñ·toñ·druh*; **I can't hear (you)** je ne vous entends pas *zhuh nuh voo zoñ·toñ pa*

hearing aid n l'appareil acoustique (m) *a·pa·ray a·koos·teek*

heart n le cœur *kur*; **by heart** par cœur *par ku*r; **hearts** (cards) le cœur *kur*

heart attack n la crise cardiaque *kreez kar·dyak*

heartburn les brûlures d'estomac (fpl) *brŌō·lŌōr des·to·ma*

hearth n le foyer *fwah·yay*

heat n la chaleur *sha·lur*; (sports) l'éliminatoire (f) *ay·lee·mee·na·twahr*

heater n le radiateur *ra·dya·tur*

heating n le chauffage *shō·fazh* A44, 66

heavy adj lourd(e) *loor (loord)*

hedge n la haie *ay*

heel n le talon *ta·loñ*

height n (of object) la hauteur *ō·tur*; (of person) la taille *tye*

helicopter n l'hélicoptère (m) *ay·lee·kop·tehr*

hello excl bonjour *boñ·zhoor* B4, 5

helmet n le casque *kask*

help n l'aide (f) *ed*; **help!** au secours! *ō suh·koor* □ vt help aider *ay·day*; **help yourself** servez-vous *sehr·vay·voo*; **I can't help it** je n'y peux rien *zhuh nee puh ryañ*

helping n la portion *por·syoñ*

hem n l'ourlet (m) *oor·leh* Sn80

hemorrhoids pl les hémorroïdes (fpl) *ay·muh·ro·eed*

hen n la poule *pool*

her pron la *la*; **it's her** c'est elle *seh tel*; **give it to her** donnez-le-lui *do·nay·luh·lwee* □ adj her son *soñ*, sa *sa*, ses *say*; **her father** son père *soñ pehr*; **her mother** sa mère *sa mehr*; **her sisters/brothers** ses sœurs/frères *say sur/frehr*

herbs pl les fines herbes (fpl) *feen zehrb*

here adv ici *ee·see*; **here's my sister** voici ma sœur *vwah·see ma sur*; **here she comes** la voici qui arrive *la vwah·see kee a·reev*

hernia n la hernie *ehr·nee*

herring n le hareng *ha·loñ·rō·tō·stop·pur*, l'autostoppeuse (f) *ō·tō·stop·puhz*

hers pron le sien *luh syañ*, la sienne *la syen*; (plural) les siens *lay syañ*, les siennes *lay syen*

herself pron elle-même *el·mem*; **she did it herself** elle l'a fait elle-même *el la feh el·mem*; **she dressed herself** elle s'est habillée *el seh ta·bee·yay*

hesitate vi hésiter *ay·zee·tay*; **to hesitate to do something** hésiter à faire quelque chose *ay·zee·tay a fehr kel·kuh shōz*

hiccup n le hoquet *o·kay*; **to have (the) hiccups** avoir* le hoquet *a·vwahr luh o·kay*

hide n (leather) la peau *pō* □ vt cacher *ka·shay* □ vi se cacher *suh ka·shay*

hi-fi adj hi-fi *ee·fee* □ n la chaîne hi-fi *shen ee·fee*

high adj (mountain, building) haut(e) *ō (ōt)*; (speed, number) grand(e)

groñ (groñd); (price, temperature) élevé(e) *ay·luh·vay*; (pitch, voice) aigu(ë) *ay·gŌō* □ adv en haut *oñ ō*; **6 metres high** haut(e) de 6 mètres *ō (ōt) duh 6 meh·truh*

highchair n la chaise haute *shez ōt* C4

high-class adj de premier ordre *duh pruh·myehr ordr*

higher adj plus haut(e) *plŌō ō (ōt)*

high-heeled adj à hauts talons *a ō ta·loñ*

high-rise (block) n la tour d'habitation *toor da·bee·ta·syoñ*

high school n le lycée *lee·say*

high season n la pleine saison *plen seh·zoñ*

high-speed adj ultra-rapide *ŌŌl·tra·ra·peed*

high street n la grande rue *groñd rŌō*

high tide n la marée haute *ma·ray ōt*

highway n la grand'route *groñ·root*

Highway Code n le code de la route *kod duh la root*

hijack vt détourner *day·toor·nay*

hijacker n le pirate de l'air *pee·rat duh lehr*

hike n la randonnée *roñ·do·nay*; **to go for a hike** faire* une randonnée *fehr Ōōn roñ·do·nay*

hiking n les excursions à pied *ek·skŌōr·syoñ za pyay*

hill n la colline *ko·leen*; (slope) la côte *kōt*

hilly adj vallonné(e) *va·lo·nay*

him pron le *luh*; **it's him** c'est lui *seh lwee*; **give it to him** donnez-le-lui *do·nay·luh·lwee*

himself pron lui-même *lwee·mem*; **he did it himself** il l'a fait lui-même *eel la feh lwee·mem*; **he dresses himself** il s'habille *eel sa·beey*

hip n la hanche *oñsh*

hire vt louer *loo·ay*; **to hire something out** louer quelque chose *loo·ay kel·kuh shōz*

hire car n la voiture de location *vwah·tŌōr duh lo·ka·syoñ*

hire purchase n la vente à crédit *voñt a kray·dee*

his adj son *soñ*, sa *sa*, ses *say*; **his father** son père *soñ pehr*; **his mother** sa mère *sa mehr*; **his brothers/sisters** ses frères/sœurs *say frehr/sur* □ pron his le sien *luh syañ*, la sienne *la syen*; (plural) les siens *lay syañ*, les siennes *lay syen*

history n l'histoire (f) *ees·twahr*

hit vt frapper *fra·pay*; (with car) heurter *uhr·tay* □ n (blow) le coup *koo*

hitchhike vi faire* de l'auto-stop *fehr duh lō·tō·stop*

hitchhiker n l'autostoppeur (m) *ō·tō·stop·pur*, l'autostoppeuse (f) *ō·tō·stop·puhz*

hobby n le passe-temps favori *pas·toñ fa·vo·ree*

hock n le vin du Rhin *vañ dŌō rañ*

hockey n le hockey *o·kay*

hold vt tenir* *tuh·neer*; (contain) contenir* *koñ·tuh·neer*; (support) soutenir* *soo·tuh·neer*; **hold him** tenez-le tranquille *tuh·nay·luh troñ·keel*; **hold on!** (on phone) ne quittez pas! *nuh kee·tay pa*; **to hold up** (delay) retarder *ruh·tar·day*

holdall n le fourre-tout *foor·too*

hold-up n (traffic) l'embouteillage (m) *oñ·boo·tay·yazh*

hole n le trou *troo*

holiday n (day) le jour férié *zhoor fay·ree·ay*; (period) les vacances (fpl) *va·*

koñs; **on holiday** en vacances *oñ va·koñs* Mc22

holiday-maker *n* le vacancier *va·koñ·syay*

Holland *n* la Hollande *o·loñd*

hollow *adj* creux *kruh*, creuse *kruhz*

holy *adj* saint(e) *sañ (sañt)*

home *n* la maison *meh·zoñ*; **at home** à la maison *a la meh·zoñ*; **to go home** rentrer chez soi *roñ·tray shay swah*

home address *n* le domicile permanent *do·mee·seel pehr·ma·noñ*

homesick *adj* □ **to be homesick** avoir* le mal du pays *a·vwahr luh mal dōō pay·yee*

homework *n* les devoirs (*mpl*) *duh·vwahr*

homogenized *adj* homogénéisé(e) *o·mo·zhay·nay·ee·zay*

honest *adj* honnête *o·net*

honey *n* le miel *myel*

honeymoon *n* la lune de miel *lōōn duh myel*; **on one's honeymoon** en voyage de noces *oñ vwah·yazh duh nos*

hood *n* le capuchon *ka·pōō·shoñ*; (*of car*) le capot *ka·pō*

hook *n* le crochet *kro·sheh*; (*fishing*) l'hameçon (*m*) *a·muh·soñ*; **hook and eye** l'agrafe (*f*) *a·graf*

hoop *n* le cerceau *sehr·sō*

hoot *vi* (*horn*) klaxonner *klak·so·nay*

hop *vi* sauter à cloche-pied *sō·tay a klosh·pyay*

hope *n* l'espoir (*m*) *es·pwahr* □ *vi* espérer* *es·pay·ray*; **I hope so** je l'espère *zhuh les·pehr*; **I hope not** j'espère que non *zhes·pehr kuh noñ*

horizon *n* l'horizon (*m*) *o·ree·zoñ*

horizontal *adj* horizontal(e) *o·ree·zoñ·tal*

horn *n* (*of animal*) la corne *korn*; (*of car*) le klaxon *klak·soñ*

horrible *adj* horrible *o·ree·bluh*

horror film, horror movie *n* le film d'épouvante *feelm day·poo·voñt*

hors d'œuvre *n* le hors d'œuvre *or duh·vruh*

horse *n* le cheval *shuh·val*

horse-racing *n* les courses de chevaux (*fpl*) *koors duh shuh·vō*

horse-riding *n* l'équitation (*f*) *ay·kee·ta·syoñ*; **to go horse-riding** faire* du cheval *fehr dōō shuh·val*

hose *n* (*pipe*) le tuyau *twee·yō*

hospital *n* l'hôpital (*m*) *o·pee·tal* I55, Ea7

hospitality *n* l'hospitalité (*f*) *os·pee·ta·lee·tay*

host *n* l'hôte (*m*) *ōt*

hostage *n* l'otage (*m*) *ō·tazh*; **to take someone hostage** prendre* quelqu'un comme otage *proñ·druh kel·kuñ kom ō·tazh*

hostel *n* le foyer *fwah·yay*

hostess *n* l'hôtesse (*f*) *ō·tes*

hot *adj* chaud(e) *shō (shōd)*; (*spicy*) fort(e) *for (fort)*

hot dog *n* le hot-dog *ot·dog*

hotel *n* l'hôtel (*m*) *ō·tel* A5

hotplate *n* la plaque chauffante *plak shō·foñt*

hot-water bottle *n* la bouillotte *boo·yot*

hour *n* l'heure (*f*) *ur*

hourly *adv* toutes les heures *toot lay zur*

house *n* la maison *meh·zoñ*; **on the house** aux frais de la maison *ō freh duh la meh·zoñ* A53

housecoat *n* le peignoir *peh·nywahr*

household *n* la famille *fa·meey*

housekeeper *n* la gouvernante *goo·vehr·noñt*

housewife *n* la ménagère *may·na·zhehr*

housework *n* le ménage *may·nazh*

housing *n* le logement *lozh·moñ*

hovercraft *n* l'aéroglisseur (*m*) *a·eh·ro·glee·sur*

how *adv* comment *ko·moñ*; **how long?** combien de temps? *koñ·byañ duh toñ*; **how long have you been here?** depuis quand êtes-vous ici? *duh·pwee koñ êt·voo zee·see*; **how much/many?** combien? *koñ·byañ*; **how many people?** combien de gens? *koñ·byañ duh zhoñ*

however *conj* pourtant *poor·toñ*

hug *vt* serrer dans ses bras *seh·ray doñ say bra*

hullo *excl* bonjour *boñ·zhoor*

human *adj* humain(e) *ōō·mañ(·men)*

hump *n* (*on road*) la bosse *bos*

humpback bridge *n* le pont en dos d'âne *poñ oñ dō dan*

hundred *num* cent *soñ*; **a hundred (and) eighty five** cent quatre-vingt-cinq *soñ ka·truh·vañ·sañk*; **a hundred people** cent personnes *soñ pehr·son*; **hundreds of books** des centaines de livres *day soñ·ten duh lee·vruh*

hundredth *adj* centième *soñ·tyem*

Hungarian *adj* hongrois(e) *oñ·grwah (·grwahz)* □ *n* le hongrois *oñ·grwah*

Hungary *n* la Hongrie *oñ·gree*

hunger *n* la faim *fañ*

hungry *adj* affamé(e) *a·fa·may*; **to be hungry** avoir* faim *a·vwahr fañ*

hunt *vt* chasser *sha·say*

hurricane *n* l'ouragan (*m*) *oo·ra·goñ*

hurry *vi* se presser *suh preh·say*; **hurry up!** dépêchez-vous! *day·peh·shay·voo* □ *n* **to be in a hurry** être* pressé(e) *eh·truh preh·say* T95

hurt *vi* faire* mal *fehr mal*; **to hurt oneself** se blesser *suh bleh·say*

husband *n* le mari *ma·ree* T108, S105

hut *n* (*shed*) la cabane *ka·ban*; (*on mountain*) le refuge *ruh·fōōzh*

hygienic *adj* hygiénique *ee·zhay·neek*

hymn *n* le cantique *koñ·teek*

hypermarket *n* l'hypermarché (*m*) *ee·pehr·mar·shay*

hyphen *n* le trait d'union *treh dōō·nyoñ*

hysterical *adj* hystérique *ees·tay·reek*

I

I *pron* je *zhuh*

ice *n* la glace *glas*; **with ice** avec des glaçons *a·vek day gla·soñ* A91

icebox *n* le frigidaire *free·zhee·dehr*

ice cream *n* la glace *glas*

ice cube *n* le glaçon *gla·soñ*

Iceland *n* l'Islande (*f*) *ees·loñd*

ice lolly *n* la glace sur un bâtonnet *glas sōōr uñ bah·to·nay*

icing *n* (*on cake*) le glaçage *gla·sazh*

idea *n* l'idée (*f*) *ee·day*

ideal *adj* idéal(e) *ee·day·al*

identical *adj* identique *ee·doñ·teek*

identify *vt* identifier *ee·doñ·tee·fyay*

identity card *n* la carte d'identité *kart dee·doñ·tee·tay*

idiot *n* l'imbécile (*m/f*) *añ·bay·seel*

if *conj* si *see*

ignition *n* (*car*) l'allumage (*m*) *a·lōō·mazh*

ignition key *n* la clef de contact *klay duh koñ·takt*

ignorant *adj* ignorant(e) *ee·nyo·roñ (·roñt)*

ignore *vt* (*person*) ignorer *ee·nyo·ray*

ill *adj* malade *ma·lad*

illegal *adj* illégal(e) *ee·lay·gal*

illegitimate *adj* illégitime *eel·lay·zhee·teem*

illness *n* la maladie *ma·la·dee*

illuminations *pl* les illuminations (*fpl*) *ee·lōō·mee·na·syoñ*

illustration *n* l'illustration (*f*) *eel·lōō·stra·syoñ*

imagination *n* l'imagination (*f*) *ee·ma·zhe·na·syoñ*

imagine *vt* imaginer *ee·ma·zhee·nay*

imitate *vt* imiter *ee·mee·tay*

immediate *adj* immédiat(e) *ee·may·dya(·dyat)*

immediately *adv* immédiatement *ee·may·dyat·moñ*

immersion heater *n* le chauffe-eau *shō·fō*

immigrant *n* l'immigrant(e) (*m/f*) *ee·mee·groñ(·groñt)*

impatient *adj* impatient(e) *añ·pa·syoñ(·syoñt)*

imperfect *adj* défectueux(euse) *day·fek·tōō·uh(·uhz)*

impersonal *adj* impersonnel(le) *añ·pehr·so·nel*

import *n* l'importation (*f*) *añ·por·ta·syoñ* □ *vt* importer *añ·por·tay*

importance *n* l'importance (*f*) *añ·por·toñs*

important *adj* important(e) *añ·por·toñ(·toñt)*

importer *n* l'importateur (*m*) *añ·por·ta·tur*

impossible *adj* impossible *añ·po·see·bluh*

impress *vt* (*win approval*) impressionner *añ·preh·syo·nay*

impression *n* l'impression (*f*) *añ·preh·syoñ*

impressive *adj* impressionnant(e) *añ·preh·syo·noñ(·noñt)*

improve *vt* améliorer *a·may·lyo·ray* □ *vi* s'améliorer *sa·may·lyo·ray*

improvement *n* l'amélioration (*f*) *a·may·lyo·ra·syoñ*

in *prep* dans *doñ*; in May en mai *oñ may*; he did it in 2 days il l'a fait en 2 jours *eel la feh oñ 2 zhoor*; he'll be back in 2 days il sera de retour dans 2 jours *eel sur·ra duh ruh·toor doñ 2 zhoor*; in town/France en ville/France *oñ veel/froñs*; in Portugal au Portugal *ō por·tōō·gal*; in French en français *oñ froñ·seh* □ *adv* is he in? est-ce qu'il est là? *es·keel eh la*

incentive *n* l'encouragement (*m*) *oñ·koo·razh·moñ*

inch *n* le pouce *poos*

incident *n* (*event*) l'incident (*m*) *añ·see·doñ*

incinerator *n* l'incinérateur (*m*) *añ·see·nay·ra·tur*

include *vt* inclure* *añ·klōōr*

including *prep* y compris *ee koñ·pree*

inclusive *adj* (*costs*) global(e) *glo·bal*; from 6th to 12th inclusive du 6 au 12 inclus *dōō 6 ō 12 añ·klōō* □ *adv* inclusive of service service compris *sehr·vees koñ·pree*

income *n* le revenu *ruh·vuh·nōō*

income tax *n* l'impôt sur le revenu (*m*) *añ·pō sōōr luh ruh·vuh·nōō*

incomplete *adj* incomplet(ète) *añ·koñ·pleh(·plet)*

inconvenient *adj* pas pratique *pa·pra·teek*

incorrect *adj* incorrect(e) *añ·ko·rekt*

increase *vt/i* augmenter *ōg·moñ·tay* □ *n* l'augmentation (*f*) *ōg·moñ·ta·syoñ*

incredible *adj* incroyable *añ·krwah·ya·bluh*

indecent *adj* inconvenant(e) *añ·koñ·vuh·noñ(·noñt)*

independence *n* l'indépendance (*f*) *añ·day·poñ·doñs*

independent *adj* indépendant(e) *añ·day·poñ·doñ(·doñt)*

index *n* (*in book*) l'index (*m*) *añ·deks*; (*financial*) l'indice (*m*) *añ·dees*

index-linked *adj* (*interest rates etc*) indexé(e) *añ·dek·say*

India *n* l'Inde (*f*) *añd*

Indian *adj* indien(ne) *añ·dyañ(·dyen)* □ *n* l'Indien(ne) (*m/f*) *añ·dyañ (·dyen)*

indicator *n* (*of car*) le clignotant *klee·nyo·toñ*

indigestible *adj* indigeste *añ·dee·zhest*

indigestion *n* l'indigestion (*f*) *añ·dee·zhes·tyoñ*

indirect *adj* (*route*) indirect(e) *añ·dee·rekt*

individual *adj* individuel(le) *añ·dee·vee·dōō·el*

individually *adv* individuellement *añ·dee·vee·dōō·el·moñ*

indoor *adj* (*games*) pratiqué(e) en salle *pra·tee·kay oñ sal*

indoors *adv* à l'intérieur *a lañ·tay·ryur*

industrial *adj* industriel(le) *añ·dōōs·tryel*

industry *n* l'industrie (*f*) *añ·dōōs·tree*

inedible *adj* immangeable *ee·moñ·zha·bluh*

inefficient *adj* inefficace *een·eh·fee·kas*

inevitable *adj* inévitable *een·ay·vee·ta·bluh*

inexpensive *adj* bon marché *boñ·mar·shay*

infection *n* l'infection (*f*) *añ·fek·syoñ*

infectious *adj* contagieux(euse) *koñ·ta·zhyuh(·zhuhz)*

inferior *adj* de qualité inférieure *duh ka·lee·tay añ·fay·ryur*

inflammable *adj* inflammable *añ·fla·ma·bluh*

inflammation *n* l'inflammation (*f*) *añ·fla·ma·syoñ*

inflatable *adj* gonflable *goñ·fla·bluh*

inflate *vt* gonfler *goñ·flay*

inflation *n* (*economic*) l'inflation (*f*) *añ·fla·syoñ*

influence *n* l'influence (*f*) *añ·flōō·oñs*

inform *vt* avertir *a·vehr·teer*

informal *adj* (*party*) entre amis *oñ·tra·mee*; dress: informal tenue de ville *tuh·nōō duh veel*

information *n* les renseignements (*mpl*) *roñ·seh·nyuh·moñ*

information desk/office *n* le bureau de renseignements *bōō·rō duh roñ·seh·nyuh·moñ*

ingredients *pl* les ingrédients (*mpl*) *añ·gray·dyoñ*

inhabit *vt* habiter *a·bee·tay*

inhabitant *n* l'habitant(e) (*m/f*) *a·bee·toñ(·toñt)*

inherit *vt* hériter de *ay·ree·tay duh*

initials *pl* les initiales (*fpl*) *ee·nee·syal*

injection *n* la piqûre *pee·kōōr*

injure *vt* blesser *ble·say*

injured *adj* blessé(e) *ble·say* I17

injury *n* la blessure *bleh·sōōr*

ink *n* l'encre (*f*) *oñ·kruh*

Inland Revenue *n* le fisc *feesk*

inn *n* l'auberge (*f*) *ō·berzh*

innocent adj innocent(e) ee·no·soñ
(·soñt)

inoculation n l'inoculation (f) ee·no·
kōō·la·syoñ

input n (computing) l'input (m) in·
poot

insect n l'insecte (m) añ·sekt S40

insect repellent n la crème anti-insecte
krem oñ·tee·añ·sekt

inside n l'intérieur (m) añ·tay·ryur
□ **adj the inside wall** le mur intérieur
mōōr añ·tay·ryur □ **prep inside the
box** à l'intérieur de la boîte a lañ·tay·
ryur duh la bwaht □ **adv to be inside**
être* à l'intérieur eh·tra lañ·tay·ryur;
to go inside entrer oñ·tray; **to turn
something inside out** mettre* quelque chose sur l'envers meh·truh kel·
kuh shōz sōōr loñ·vehr

insist vi insister añ·sees·tay; **to insist on
something** exiger* quelque chose eg·
zee·zhay kel·kuh shōz

insolent adj insolent(e) añ·so·loñ
(·loñt)

inspect vt inspecter añ·spek·tay;
(ticket) contrôler koñ·trō·lay

inspector n (police) l'inspecteur de police (m) añ·spek·tur duh po·lees; (of
tickets) le contrôleur koñ·trō·lur

instal(l)ment n le versement vehrs·
moñ

instant adj immédiat(e) ee·may·dya
(·dyat); **instant coffee** le café en
poudre ka·fay oñ poo·druh □ n
instant l'instant (m) añ·stoñ

instead of prep au lieu de ō lyuh duh

institute n l'institut (m) añ·stee·tōō

instructions pl les directives (fpl) dee·
rek·teev; **instructions for use** le mode
d'emploi mod doñ·plwah

instructor n le moniteur mo·nee·tur

instructress n la monitrice mo·nee·trees

instrument n l'instrument (m) añ·
strōō·moñ

insulin n l'insuline (f) añ·sōō·leen

insult n l'insulte (f) añ·sōōlt □ vt insulter añ·sōōl·tay

insurance n l'assurance (f) a·sōō·roñs
T108

insurance company n la compagnie
d'assurances koñ·pan·yee da·sōō·
roñs Sn86, T192

insurance policy n la police d'assurance po·lees da·sōō·roñs

insure vt assurer a·sōō·ray □ vi to insure against something s'assurer contre quelque chose sa·sōō·ray koñ·
truh kel·kuh shōz

insured adj assuré(e) a·sōō·ray

intelligence n l'intelligence (f) añ·te·
lee·zhoñs

intelligent adj intelligent(e) añ·teh·lee·
zhoñ(·zhoñt)

intend vt destiner deh·stee·nay; **to intend to do something** avoir* l'intention de faire quelque chose a·vwahr
lañ·toñ·syoñ duh fehr kel·kuh shōz

intention n l'intention (f) añ·toñ·syoñ

interchange n (on roads) l'échangeur
(m) ay·shoñ·zhur

intercom n l'interphone (m) añ·tehr·
fon

interest n l'intérêt (m) añ·tay·reh;
(hobby) le passe-temps pas·toñ □ vt
intéresser añ·tay·reh·say

interested adj intéressé(e) añ·tay·reh·
say; **to be interested in** s'intéresser à
sañ·tay·reh·say a

interesting adj intéressant(e) añ·tay·
reh·soñ(·soñt)

interest rate n le taux d'intérêt tō dañ·
tay·reh

interfere vi se mêler à suh meh·lay a

interior adj intérieur(e) añ·tay·ryur

internal adj interne añ·tehrn

Internal Revenue n le fisc feesk

international adj international(e) añ·
tehr·na·syo·nal

interpret vt interpréter* añ·tehr·pray·
tay □ vi servir* d'interprète sehr·veer
dañ·tehr·pret

interpreter n l'interprète (m/f) añ·tehr·
pret

interrupt vt/i interrompre* añ·teh·roñ·
pruh

intersection n (of roads) le carrefour
kar·foor

interval n (in performance) l'entracte
(m) oñ·trakt

interview n (for job) l'entrevue (f) oñ·
truh·vōō

into prep dans doñ

introduce vt (person) présenter pray·
zoñ·tay Mc39

introduction n (in book) l'avant-
propos (m) a·voñ·pro·pō; (social) la
présentation pray·zoñ·ta·syoñ

invalid n le/la malade ma·lad

invent vt inventer añ·voñ·tay

invention n l'invention (f) añ·voñ·syoñ

inventory n l'inventaire (m) añ·voñ·
tehr

invest vt investir añ·ves·teer □ vi to invest in placer* son argent dans pla·
say soñ nar·zhoñ doñ

investment n l'investissement (m) añ·
ves·tees·moñ

investor n l'actionnaire (m/f) ak·syo·
nehr

invisible adj invisible añ·vee·zee·bluh

invitation n l'invitation (f) añ·vee·ta·
syoñ

invite vt inviter añ·vee·tay

invoice n la facture fak·tōōr

iodine n l'iode (m) yod

Iran n l'Iran (m) ee·roñ

Iraq n l'Irak (m) ee·rak

Ireland n l'Irlande (f) eer·loñd

Irish adj irlandais(e) eer·loñ·deh(·dez)

iron n (material, golf club) le fer fehr;
(for clothes) le fer à repasser fehr a
ruh·pa·say □ vt repasser ruh·pa·say

ironmonger n le quincaillier kañ·kye·
yay

is vi □ she/he is elle/il est el/eel eh

island n l'île (f) eel; (traffic) le refuge
pour piétons ruh·fōōzh poor pyay·
toñ

Israel n l'Israël (m) ees·ra·el

issue n (matter) la question kes·tyoñ;
(of magazine) le numéro nōō·may·
rō; (of stocks) l'émission (f) ay·mee·
syoñ

it pron □ **it's blue** il/elle est bleu(e)
eel/el eh bluh; **take it** prenez-le/la
pruh·nay·luh/la; **it's me** c'est moi seh
mwah; **it's raining** il pleut eel pluh;
it's 5 kilometres c'est à 5 kilomètres
seh ta 5 kee·lo·me·truh

Italian adj italien(ne) ee·ta·lyañ(·lyen);
he's Italian il est Italien el eh tee·ta·
lyañ; **she's Italian** elle est Italienne el
eh tee·ta·lyen □ n **Italian** l'italien (m)
ee·ta·lyañ

Italy n l'Italie (f) ee·ta·lee

itch n la démangeaison day·moñ·zheh·
zoñ □ vi démanger* day·moñ·zhay

item n l'article (m) ar·tee·kluh

itemized adj (bill etc) détaillé(e) day·
tye·yay

its adj son soñ, sa sa, ses say

ivory n l'ivoire (m) ee·vwar

J

jack n (for car) le cric kreek; (cards) le valet va·leh
jacket n la veste vest
jail n la prison pree·zoñ; **in jail** en prison oñ pree·zoñ
jam vi (machine) se bloquer suh blo·kay □ n la confiture koñ·fee·tōōr; (in traffic) l'embouteillage (m) oñ·boo·tay·yazh
janitor n le concierge koñ·syehrzh
January n janvier (m) zhoñ·vyay
Japan n le Japon zha·poñ
Japanese adj japonais(e) zha·po·neh (·nez); **he's Japanese** il est Japonais eel eh zha·po·neh; **she's Japanese** elle est Japonaise el eh zha·po·nez □ n **Japanese** le japonais zha·po·neh
jar n le bocal bo·kal
jaw n la mâchoire mash·wahr
jazz n le jazz jaz L38
jealous adj jaloux(ouse) zha·loo(·looz)
jeans pl le jean jeen
jeep n la jeep jeep
jello, jelly n la gelée zhuh·lay
jellyfish n la méduse may·dōōz
jerkin n le blouson bloo·zoñ
jersey n (fabric) le jersey zhehr·zay; (sweater) le tricot tree·kō
jet n (plane) l'avion à réaction (m) a·vyoñ na ray·ak·syoñ
jetty n la digue deeg
Jew n le Juif zhweef
jewel n le bijou bee·zhoo
jeweller n le bijoutier bee·zhoo·tyay
jewellery n les bijoux (mpl) bee·zhoo S85
Jewish adj juif zhweef, juive zhweev
jigsaw (puzzle) n le puzzle puh·zuhl
jingle n (advertising) le couplet publicitaire koo·pleh pōōb·lee·see·tehr
job n (employment) l'emploi (m) oñ·plwah; (task) la tâche tash
jockey n le jockey zho·kay
jogging n le footing foo·teeng; **to go jogging** faire* du footing fehr dōō foo·teeng
join vt joindre* zhwañ·druh; (club) devenir* membre de duh·vuh·neer moñ·bruh duh; **do join us** soyez des nôtres swah·yay day nō·truh
joint n (of body) l'articulation (f) ar·tee·kōō·la·syoñ; (of meat) le rôti rō·tee
joint ownership n la copropriété kō·pro·pree·ay·tay
joint-stock company n la société par actions so·syay·tay par ak·syoñ
joke n la plaisanterie play·zoñ·tuh·ree
joker n (cards) le joker zho·kehr
journalist n le/la journaliste zhoor·na·leest
journey n le voyage vwah·yazh
joy n la joie zhwah
jubilee n le jubilé zhōō·bee·lay
judge n le juge zhōōzh □ vt juger* zhōō·zhay
judo n le judo zhōō·dō
jug n la cruche krōōsh
juice n le jus zhōō
jukebox n le juke-box jook·boks
July n juillet (m) zhwee·yeh
jumbo jet n le jumbo-jet jum·bo·jet
jump vt/i sauter sō·tay; **to jump (over) a wall** sauter par-dessus un mur sō·tay par·duh·sōō zuñ mōōr
jumper n (dress) la robe-chasuble rob·

sha·zōō·bluh; (sweater) le pullover pōōl·o·vehr
jump leads pl les câbles (mpl) de raccordement de batterie ka·bluh duh ra·kor·duh·moñ duh ba·tuh·ree
junction n (in road) le carrefour kar·foor; (railway) la gare de jonction gar duh zhoñk·syoñ
June n juin (m) zhwañ
junior adj (class, pupil) de primaire duh pree·mehr
junket n le lait caillé leh kye·yay
just adv □ **just here** juste ici zhōōst ee·see; **he's just left** il vient de partir eel vyañ duh par·teer; **it was just a mistake** ce n'était qu'une erreur suh nay·teh kōōn eh·rur; **I just managed it** j'ai tout juste réussi à le faire zhay too zhōōst ray·ōō·see a luh fehr; **just above the elbow** juste au-dessus du coude zhōōst ō·duh·sōō dōō kood; **it only just missed** ça l'a manqué de justesse sa la moñ·kay duh zhōōs·tes; **he arrived just now** il est arrivé à l'instant eel eh ta·ree·vay a lañ·stoñ
justice n la justice zhōōs·tees

K

karate n le karaté ka·ra·tay
kebab n le kébab kay·bab
keen adj (swimmer, reader) enthousiaste oñ·too·zee·ast
keep n la subsistence sōōb·zee·stoñs; **to earn one's keep** gagner sa vie ga·nyay sa vee □ vt keep (retain) garder gar·day; (feed and clothe) faire* vivre fehr vee·vruh; **to keep something till later** garder quelque chose pour plus tard gar·day kel·kuh shōz poor plōō tar; **to keep something in the fridge** garder quelque chose dans le frigo gar·day kel·kuh shōz doñ luh free·gō; **keep the change!** gardez la monnaie! gar·day la mo·neh; **to keep something tidy** tenir* quelque chose en état tuh·neer kel·kuh shōz oñ nay·ta □ vi milk doesn't keep very well le lait ne se conserve pas bien luh leh nuh suh koñ·serv pah byañ
Kenya n le Kenya ken·ya
kerb n la bordure du trottoir bor·dōōr dōō tro·twahr
kerosene n le pétrole pay·trol
ketchup n le ketchup ke·chup
kettle n la bouilloire boo·yuh·wahr
key n (of piano, typewriter) la clé klay; (of piano, typewriter) la touche toosh B74, T187, A41
keyhole n le trou de la serrure troo duh la seh·rōōr
key ring n la porte-clés port·klay
kick n le coup de pied koo duh pyay □ vt donner un coup de pied à do·nay uñ koo duh pyay a
kid n (leather) le chevreau shuh·vrō
kidnap vt kidnapper keed·na·pay
kidney n (of person) le rein rañ; (to eat) le rognon ro·nyoñ
kidney beans pl les haricots rouges (mpl) a·ree·kō roozh
kill vt tuer tōō·ay
killer n l'assassin (m) a·sa·sañ
kilo n le kilo kee·lō
kilogram(me) n le kilogramme kee·lō·gram
kilometer, kilometre n le kilomètre kee·lō·meh·truh
kilowatt n le kilowatt kee·lō·wat
kilt n le kilt keelt
kind n (type) le genre zhoñ·ruh; **a kind of bean** une sorte de haricot ōōn sort

duh·ree·kō □ *adj* kind gentil(le) zhoñ·teey

king *n* le roi *rwah*

kiosk *n* (for newspapers) le kiosque *kee·osk*; (telephone) la cabine *ka·been*

kirsch *n* le kirsch *keersh*

kiss *vt* embrasser *oñ·bra·say*; to kiss (each other) s'embrasser *soñ·bra·say* □ *n* kiss le baiser *beh·zay*

kit *n* (sports) le matériel *ma·tay·ryel*

kitchen *n* la cuisine *kwee·zeen*

kite *n* le cerf-volant *sehr·vo·loñ*

kleenex *n* le mouchoir en papier *moo·shwahr oñ pa·pyay*

knee *n* le genou *zhuh·noo*; to sit on someone's knee s'asseoir* sur les genoux de quelqu'un *sa·swahr sōōr lay zhuh·noo duh kel·kuñ*

kneel *vi* s'agenouiller *sa·zhuh·noo·yay*; to kneel down se mettre* à genoux *suh·meh·tra zhuh·noo*

knife *n* le couteau *koo·tō*

knit *vt/i* tricoter *tree·ko·tay*

knitting needle *n* l'aiguille à tricoter (f) *ay·gwey a tree·ko·tay*

knitwear *n* les tricots (mpl) *tree·kō*

knob *n* le bouton *boo·toñ*

knock *vt* frapper *fra·pay*; to knock (at) the door frapper à la porte *fra·pay a la port*; to knock down renverser *roñ·vehr·say*; to knock out mettre* K.O. *meh·truh ka·ō* □ *vi* knock (engine) avoir* des ratés *av·wahr day ra·tay*

knot *vt* nouer *noo·ay* □ *n* le nœud *nuh*; to tie a knot faire* un nœud *fehr uñ nuh*

know *vt* (person) connaître* *ko·neh·truh*; (fact) savoir* *sa·vwahr*; (subject, language) connaître* *ko·neh·truh*; to know how to do something savoir* faire quelque chose *sa·vwahr fehr kel·kuh shōz*

knowledge *n* la connaissance *ko·neh·soñs*

knuckle *n* l'articulation des phalanges (f) *ar·tee·kōō·la·syoñ day fa·loñzh*

kohlrabi *n* le chou-rave *shoo·rav*

kosher *adj* kascher *ka·shehr*

L

label *n* l'étiquette (f) *ay·tee·ket* □ *vt* étiqueter* *ay·teek·tay*

laboratory *n* le laboratoire *la·bo·ra·twahr*

labo(u)r *n* la main-d'œuvre *mañ·duh·vruh*

labo(u)rer *n* le manœuvre *ma·nuh·vruh*

labo(u)r force *n* la main-d'œuvre *mañ·duh·vruh*

lace *n* la dentelle *doñ·tel*; (of shoe) le lacet *la·seh*

lacquer *n* (for hair) la laque *lak*

ladder *n* l'échelle (f) *ay·shel*; (in stocking) la maille filée *mye fee·lay*

ladle *n* la louche *loosh*

lady *n* la dame *dam*

lager *n* la bière blonde *byehr bloñd*

lake *n* le lac *lak*

lamb *n* l'agneau (m) *a·nyō* S37

lambswool *n* la laine d'agneau *len da·nyō*

lamp *n* la lampe *loñp*

lamppost *n* le réverbère *ray·vehr·behr*

lampshade *n* l'abat-jour (m) *a·ba·zhoor*

land *n* (opposed to sea) la terre *tehr*; (country) le pays *pay·yee*; (soil) la terre *tehr*; (property) le domaine *do·men* □ *vi* (from ship) débarquer *day·bar·kay*; (plane) atterrir *a·tay·reer*

landing *n* (of plane) l'atterrissage (m) *a·tay·ree·sazh*; (on stairs) le palier *pa·lyay*

landing stage *n* le débarcadère *day·bar·ka·dehr*

landing strip *n* la piste d'atterrissage *peest da·tay·ree·sazh*

landlady *n* la propriétaire *pro·pree·ay·tehr*

landlord *n* le propriétaire *pro·pree·ay·tehr*

landmark *n* le point de repère *pwañ duh ruh·pehr*

landslide *n* le glissement de terrain *glees·moñ duh teh·rañ*

lane *n* (in country) le chemin *shuh·mañ*; (in town) la ruelle *rōō·el*; (of road) la voie *vwah*

language *n* la langue *loñg*; (way one speaks) le langage *loñ·gazh*

language laboratory *n* le laboratoire de langues *la·bo·ra·twahr duh loñg*

lanolin *n* la lanoline *la·no·leen*

lap *n* (of track) le tour de piste *toor duh peest*; (of person) les genoux (mpl) *zhuh·noo*

lard *n* le saindoux *sañ·doo*

larder *n* le garde-manger *gard·moñ·zhay*

large *adj* gros(se) *grō* (grōs)

laryngitis *n* la laryngite *la·rañ·zheet*

last *adj* dernier(ère) *dehr·nyay* (·nyehr); last night cette nuit *set nwee*; last week la semaine dernière *la suh·men dehr·nyehr*; last en dernier *oñ dehr·nyay*; at last enfin *oñ·fañ* □ *vi* last durer *dōō·ray*

latch *n* le loquet *lo·keh*

late *adj* (not on time) en retard *oñ ruh·tar* □ *adv* tard *tar*; late in the day tard dans la journée *tar doñ la zhoor·nay*; the latest news les dernières nouvelles *lay dehr·nyehr noo·vel*; the late king feu le roi *fuh luh rwah*

lately *adv* récemment *ray·sa·moñ*

later *adj* (date etc) ultérieur(e) *ōōl·tay·ryur*; (version) plus récent(e) *plōō ray·soñ(·soñt)* □ *adv* (to come etc) plus tard *plōō tar*

Latin *n* le latin *la·tañ* □ *adj* latin(e) *la·tañ(·teen)*

Latin America *n* l'Amérique latine (f) *a·may·reek la·teen*

Latin American *adj* d'Amérique latine *da·may·reek la·teen*

laugh *vi* rire* *reer*; to laugh at somebody se moquer de quelqu'un *suh mo·kay duh kel·kuñ* □ *n* laugh le rire *reer*

laughter *n* le rire *reer*

launch *n* la vedette *vuh·det* □ *vt* lancer* *loñ·say*

launderette *n* la laverie automatique *la·vree ō·tō·ma·teek*

laundry *n* (place) la blanchisserie *bloñ·shee·suh·ree*; (clothes) le linge *lañzh*

lavatory *n* les toilettes (fpl) *twah·let* T166

law *n* la loi *lwah*; law and order l'ordre public (m) *or·druh pōō·bleek*

lawn *n* (grass) la pelouse *puh·looz*

lawn mower *n* la tondeuse à gazon *toñ·duhz a ga·zoñ*

lawn tennis *n* le tennis sur gazon *teh·nees sōōr ga·zoñ*

lawyer *n* l'avocat (m) *a·vo·ka* Sn89

laxative *n* le laxatif *lak·sa·teef*

lay *vt* poser *pō·zay*; to lay the table

mettre* le couvert *meh·truh luh koo·vehr*; **to lay the fire** préparer le feu *pray·pa·ray luh fuh*; **to lay down** déposer *day·pō·zay*; (*wine*) mettre* en cave *meh·tron kav*; **to lay off** (*workers*) licencier *lee·son·syay*

lay-by *n* l'aire de stationnement *ehr duh sta·syon·mon*

layer *n* la couche *koosh*

lazy *adj* paresseux(euse) *pa·reh·suh (·suhz)*

lead[1] *vt* mener* *muh·nay* □ *vi* (*in contest*) être* en tête *eh·tron tet*; **this door leads into the garden** cette porte mène au jardin *set port men ō zhar·dan* □ *n* **lead** (*electrical*) le fil *feel*; (*dog's*) la laisse *les*

lead[2] *n* le plomb *plon*; (*in pencil*) la mine *meen*

leaf *n* la feuille *fuhy*

leak *n* la fuite *fweet* □ *vi* fuir* *fweer* T184

lean *adj* (*meat*) maigre *meh·gruh* □ *vi* pencher *pon·shay*; **to lean against something** s'appuyer contre quelque chose *sa·pwee·yay kon·truh kel·kuh shōz*

learn *vt* apprendre* *a·pron·druh*

learner(-driver) *n* le conducteur débutant *kon·dōōk·tur day·bōō·ton*

lease *n* le bail *bye*

leash *n* la laisse *les*

least *adj* □ **the least money** le moins d'argent *luh mwan dar·zhon*; **the least amount** la moindre quantité *la mwan·druh kon·tee·tay* □ *adv* **the least expensive** le moins cher *luh mwan shehr* □ *n* **he has the least** il a le moins *eel a luh mwan*; **at least** au moins *ō mwan*; **not in the least** pas du tout *pa dōō too*

leather *n* le cuir *kweer*

leave *n* (*holiday*) le congé *kon·zhay*; **on leave** en permission *on pehr·mee·syon* □ *vi* partir* *par·teer* □ *vt* (*room, club, school*) quitter *kee·tay*; **leave it to me** je m'en charge *zhuh mon sharzh*; **leave your coat here** laissez votre manteau ici *leh·say vo·truh mon·tō ee·see*; **to leave a message** laisser un message *leh·say un meh·sazh*; **to leave out** (*omit*) omettre* *o·meh·truh*

lecture *n* la conférence *kon·fay·rons*

ledger *n* le grand livre *gron lee·vruh*

leek *n* le poireau *pwah·rō*

left *adj* □ **there's some cream left** il reste de la crème *eel rest duh la krem*; **to turn left** tourner à gauche *toor·nay a gōsh* □ *adj* **the left side** le côté gauche *luh kō·tay gōsh* T97

left-handed *adj* gaucher(ère) *gō·shay (·shehr)*

left luggage office *n* la consigne *kon·see·nyuh*

leg *n* (*of person*) la jambe *zhonb*; (*of animal*) la patte *pat*; **leg of lamb** le gigot d'agneau *zhee·gō da·nyō*; **chicken leg** la cuisse de poulet *kwees duh poo·leh* 124

legal *adj* légal(e) *lay·gal*

leisure *n* le loisir *lwah·zeer*

leisure centre *n* le centre de sports et loisirs *son·truh duh spor ay lwah·zeer*

lemon *n* le citron *see·tron*

lemonade *n* la limonade *lee·mo·nad*

lemon juice *n* le jus de citron *zhōō duh see·tron*

lemon sole *n* la limande-sole *lee·mond·sōl*

lemon-squeezer *n* le presse-citron *pres·see·tron*

lend *vt* prêter *preh·tay*

length *n* la longueur *lon·gur*

lens *n* (*of glasses*) la lentille *lon·teey*; (*of camera*) l'objectif (*m*) *ob·zhek·teef*

lentils *pl* les lentilles (*fpl*) *lon·teey*

less *adj* □ **less meat** moins de viande *mwan duh vee·yond* □ *adv* **less quickly** moins vite *mwan veet* □ *n* **he has less** il en a moins *eel on na mwan*; **less than** moins que *mwan kuh*

lesson *n* la leçon *luh·son*

let *vt* (*allow*) laisser *leh·say*; (*rent out*) louer *loo·ay*; **to let someone do something** laisser quelqu'un faire quelque chose *leh·say kel·kun fehr kel·kuh shōz*; **let me in** laissez-moi entrer *leh·say·mwah on·tray*; **let's go** allons-y *a·lon·zee*; **they let him go** ils l'ont laissé partir *eel lon leh·say par·teer*; **to let** (*house etc*) à louer *a loo·ay*; **to let someone down** décevoir* quelqu'un *day·suh·vwahr kel·kun*

letter *n* la lettre *leh·truh* B77, A36, Bm22

letter box *n* la boîte aux lettres *bwat ō leh·truh*

lettuce *n* la laitue *lay·tōō*

level *n* le niveau *nee·vō* □ *adj* (*surface*) plat(e) *pla* (*plat*); (*horizontal*) horizontal(e) *ō·ree·zon·tal*

level crossing *n* le passage à niveau *pa·sazh a nee·vō*

lever *n* le levier *luh·vyay*

Levis *pl* le jean *jeen*

liabilities *pl* (*on balance sheet*) le passif *pa·seef*

library *n* la bibliothèque *bee·blyo·tek*

Libya *n* la Libye *lee·bee*

licence, license *n* (*for driving*) le permis de conduire *pehr·mee duh kon·dweer*

license plate *n* la plaque d'immatriculation *plak dee·ma·tree·kōō·la·syon*

lick *vt* lécher* *lay·shay*

licorice *n* la réglisse *ray·glees*

lid *n* le couvercle *koo·vehr·kluh*

lie *n* (*untruth*) le mensonge *mon·sonzh* □ *vi* être* étendu(e) *eh·truh ay·ton·dōō*; (*tell a lie*) mentir* *mon·teer*; **to lie down** s'allonger* *sa·lon·zhay*

Liechtenstein *n* le Liechtenstein *leekh·ten·shtine*

life *n* la vie *vee*; **for life** à vie *a vee*

lifebelt *n* la bouée de sauvetage *boo·ay duh sōv·tazh*

lifeboat *n* (*on ship*) la chaloupe de sauvetage *sha·loop duh sōv·tazh*; (*from shore*) le canot de sauvetage *ka·nō duh sōv·tazh*

lifeguard *n* le surveillant de plage *sōōr·vay·yon du plazh*

life insurance *n* l'assurance-vie (*f*) *a·sōō·rons·vee*

life jacket *n* le gilet de sauvetage *zhee·leh duh sōv·tazh*

life preserver *n* (*belt*) la bouée de sauvetage *boo·ay duh sōv·tazh*; (*jacket*) le gilet de sauvetage *zhee·leh duh sōv·tazh*

lift *vt* soulever* *soo·luh·vay* □ *n* (*elevator*) l'ascenseur (*m*) *a·son·sur*; **to give somebody a lift** prendre* quelqu'un en voiture *pron·druh kel·kun on vwah·tōōr*

light *vt* (*fire, cigarette*) allumer *a·lōō·may*; **to light up** (*car*) allumer les phares *a·lōō·may lay far* □ *n* **light** la lumière lōō·myehr; (lamp) la lampe lonp; (on car) le phare far; (traffic light) le feu fuh; **have you got a light?** avez-vous du feu? a·vay·voo dōō fuh □ adj **light** (bright, pale) clair(e) klehr; (not heavy) léger(ère) lay·zhay(·zhehr); **light music** la musique légère mōō·zeek lay·zhehr; **as soon as it was light** dès qu'il a fait jour deh keel a feh zhoor

light bulb n l'ampoule (f) oñ·pool

lighter n le briquet bree·keh S103

lighthouse n le phare far

light industry n l'industrie légère añ·dōōs·tree lay·zhehr

lighting n (on road) l'éclairage (m) ay·kleh·razh; **when is lighting-up time?** à quelle heure éclaire-t-on les rues? a kel ur ay·klehr·toñ lay rōō?

light meter n le photomètre fō·tō·meh·truh

lightning la foudre foo·druh

like prep comme kom □ adj semblable soñ·bla·bluh; **what's it like?** comment est-ce? ko·moñ es □ vt **like** aimer ay·may; **I'd like to go** j'aimerais y aller zheh·muh·reh zee a·lay; **I'd like an ice cream** j'aimerais une glace zheh·muh·reh zōōn glas; **what would you like?** kes kuh vooz eh·muh·ryay

likely adj probable pro·ba·bluh; **he's likely to come** il va sûrement venir eel va sōōr·moñ vuh·neer

lily n le lis lee

lime n (fruit) le citron vert see·troñ vehr

lime juice n le jus de citron vert zhōō duh see·troñ vehr

limit n la limite lee·meet

limousine n la limousine lee·moo·zeen

limp vi boiter bwah·tay

line n la ligne lee·nyuh; (railway) la voie vwah; (telephone) la ligne lee·nyuh; (people waiting) la queue kuh; **to stand in line** faire* la queue fehr la kuh

linen n (cloth) le lin lañ; (for bed, table) le linge lañzh

liner n (ship) le paquebot de ligne pak·bō duh lee·nyuh

lining la doublure doo·blōōr

lino(leum) n le linoléum lee·no·lay·yum

lint n le tissu ouaté tee·sōō wa·tay

lion n le lion lee·yoñ

lip n la lèvre leh·vruh

lipstick n le rouge à lèvres roozh a leh·vruh

liqueur la liqueur lee·kur E15

liquid n le liquide lee·keed □ adj liquide lee·keed

liquid assets pl les liquidités (fpl) lee·kee·dee·tay

liquidation n la liquidation lee·kee·da·syoñ; **to go into liquidation** déposer son bilan day·pō·zay soñ bee·loñ

liquor n le spiritueux spee·ree·tōō·uh

list n la liste leest □ vt dresser une liste de dreh·say ōōn leest duh

listen vi écouter ay·koo·tay; **to listen to** écouter ay·koo·tay

list price n le prix de catalogue pree duh ka·ta·log

liter n le litre lee·truh

literature n la littérature lee·tay·ra·tōōr

litre n le litre lee·truh

little adj petit(e) puh·tee(·teet) □ n a little un peu uñ puh

live¹ adj (alive) vivant(e) vee·voñ (·voñt)

live² vi vivre* vee·vruh; (reside) habiter a·bee·tay

lively adj plein(e) d'entrain plañ (plen) doñ·trañ

liver n le foie fwah

living room n la salle de séjour sal duh say·zhoor

load n la charge sharzh □ vt charger* shar·zhay

loaf (of bread) n le pain pañ

loan n le prêt preh □ vt prêter preh·tay

lobby n (entrance) l'entrée (f) oñ·tray

lobster n le homard ō·mar

local adj local(e) lo·kal; **the local shops** les magasins du quartier lay ma·ga·zañ dōō kar·tyay; **a local call** (on phone) une communication urbaine ōōn ko·mōō·nee·ka·syoñ ōōr·behn E9

lock n (on door) la serrure seh·rōōr; (in canal) l'écluse (f) ay·klōōz □ vt fermer à clé fehr·may a klay A47

locker n le casier ka·zyay

lodger n le/la locataire lo·ka·tehr

lodgings pl la chambre shoñ·bruh

loft n le grenier gruh·nyay

log n (of wood) la bûche bōōsh

logbook n (of car) la carte grise kart greez

lollipop n la sucette sōō·set

London n Londres (m) loñ·druh

lonely adj (person) seul(e) suhl

long adj long(ue) oñ (loñg); **how long is the river?** quelle est la longueur de la rivière? kel eh la loñ·gur duh la ree·vyehr; **6 metres long** long de 6 mètres loñ duh 6 meh·truh; **how long is the programme?** le programme dure combien de temps? luh pro·gram dōōr koñ·byañ duh toñ; **6 months long** qui dure 6 mois kee dōōr 6 mwah □ adv long longtemps loñ·toñ; **all day long** toute la journée toot la zhoor·nay; **I shan't be long** je n'en ai pas pour longtemps zhuh noñ nay pa poor loñ·toñ; **as long as** (provided that) pourvu que poor·vōō kuh

long-distance adj (phone call) interurbain(e) añ·tehr·ōōr·bañ(·ben)

long drink n le long drink loñ dreenk

long-sighted adj hypermétrope ee·pehr·may·trop

long-term adj à long terme a loñ tehrm

long wave n les grandes ondes (fpl) groñd zoñd

look n (at something) (appearance) l'air (m) ehr □ vi regarder ruh·gar·day; (appear) sembler soñ·blay; **to look at** regarder ruh·gar·day; **to look like** ressembler à ruh·soñ·blay a; **to look after** s'occuper de so·kōō·pay duh; **to look for** chercher shehr·shay; **to look forward to** attendre avec impatience a·toñ·druh a·vek añ·pa·syoñs; **look out!** attention! a·toñ·syoñ; **to look up** (word) chercher shehr·shay

loop n la boucle boo·kluh

loose adj (knot, screw) desserré(e) deh·seh·ray; (clothing) ample oñ·pluh; (stone) branlant(e) broñ·loñ (·loñt)

lorry n le camion ka·myoñ

lorry driver n le routier roo·tyay

lose vt perdre pehr·druh; **to lose one's way** se perdre suh pehr·druh □ vi lose (clock, watch) retarder ruh·tar·day

loss n la perte pehrt Sn83

lost property office n le bureau des objets trouvés *bōō·rō day zob·zhay troo·vay*

lot *n* (*at auction*) le lot *lō*; **lots of** or **a lot of milk** beaucoup de lait *bō·koo duh leh*; **lots of** or **a lot of people** beaucoup de gens *bō·koo duh zhoñ*; **a lot better** beaucoup mieux *bō·koo myuh*

lotion *n* la lotion *lō·syoñ*

lottery *n* la loterie *lo·tree*

loud *adj* fort(e) *for* (*fort*)

loudly *adv* fort *for*

loudspeaker *n* le haut-parleur *ō·par·lur*

lounge *n* le salon *sa·loñ*; (*at airport*) la salle *sal*

love *vt* aimer *ay·may*; **to love doing something** aimer faire quelque chose *ay·may fehr kel·kuh shōz*; **I'd love to go** j'aimerais bien y aller *zheh·muh·reh byañ ee a·lay* □ *n* love l'amour (*m*) *a·moor*; **in love** amoureux(euse) *a·moo·ruh(·ruhz)*; **love from** (*on letter*) affectueusement *a·fek·tōō·uhz·moñ*

lovely *adj* beau *bō*, belle *bel*; **we had a lovely time** nous nous sommes bien amusés *noo noo som byañ a·mōō·zay*

low *adj* bas(se) *ba* (*bas*)

Low Countries *pl* les Pays Bas (*mpl*) *pay·yee ba*

lower *adj* plus bas(se) *plōō ba* (*bas*)

low tide *n* la marée basse *ma·ray bas*

L.P. *n* le trente-trois tours *troñt·trwah toor*

Ltd *abbrev* S.A. *es·a*

luck *n* la chance *shoñs*; **good luck!** bonne chance! *bon shoñs*; **bad luck** la malchance *mal·shoñs*

lucky *adj* □ **to be lucky** avoir* de la chance *a·vwahr duh la shoñs*

luggage *n* les bagages (*mpl*) *ba·gazh*

luggage rack *n* (*in train*) le porte-bagages *port·ba·gazh*; (*on car*) la galerie *gal·ree*

luggage trolley *n* le chariot à bagages *sha·ryō a ba·gazh*

lump *n* (*on skin*) la grosseur *grō·sur*; (*in sauce*) le grumeau *grōō·mō*; **lump of sugar** le morceau de sucre *mor·sō duh sōō·kruh*

lunch *n* le déjeuner *day·zhuh·nay* A26

lunch hour *n* l'heure du déjeuner (*f*) *ur dōō day·zhuh·nay*

lung *n* le poumon *poo·moñ*

Luxembourg *n* le Luxembourg *luh lōōk·soñ·boor*

luxurious *adj* luxueux(euse) *lōōk·sōō·uh(·uhz)*

luxury *n* le luxe *lōōks* □ *adj* (*car, hotel*) de luxe *duh lōōks*

M

macaroni *n* les macaronis (*mpl*) *ma·ka·ro·nee*

machine *n* la machine *ma·sheen*

machinery *n* la machinerie *ma·sheen·ree*

mackerel *n* le maquereau *ma·krō*

mack(intosh) *n* l'imperméable (*m*) *añ·pehr·may·a·bluh*

mad *adj* (*insane*) fou *foo*, folle *fol*; (*angry*) furieux(euse) *fōō·ree·uh (·uhz)*

madam *n* madame (*f*) *ma·dam*

Madeira *n* (*wine*) le madère *ma·dehr*

made-to-measure *adj* fait(e) sur mesure *feh* (*fet*) *sōōr muh·zōōr*

Madrid *n* Madrid (*f*) *ma·dreed*

magazine *n* (*journal*) le magazine *ma·ga·zeen*

magic *n* la magie *ma·zhee* □ *adj* magique *ma·zheek*

magnet *n* l'aimant (*m*) *eh·moñ*

magnetic tape *n* la bande magnétique *boñd ma·nyay·teek*

magnificent *adj* magnifique *ma·nyee·feek*

mahogany *n* (*tree*) l'acajou (*m*) *a·ka·zhoo*

maid *n* la femme de ménage *fam duh may·nazh* A67

maiden name *n* le nom de jeune fille *noñ duh zhuhn feey*

maid service *n* le service d'une femme de ménage *sehr·vees dōōn fam duh may·nazh*

mail *n* le courrier *koo·ryay* □ *vt* envoyer par la poste *oñ·vwah·yay par la post*

mailbox *n* la boîte aux lettres *bwat ō leh·truh*

mailing list *n* la liste d'adresses *leest da·dres*

mailman *n* le facteur *fak·tur*

mail order *n* □ (*of buy something by mail order*) acheter* quelque chose par correspondance *ash·tay kel·kuh shōz par ko·res·poñ·doñs*

main *adj* principal(e) *prañ·see·pal* □ *n* **to turn the electricity/water off at the mains** couper le courant/l'eau au compteur *kōō·pay luh koo·roñ/lō ō koñ·tur*

mainland *n* le continent *koñ·tee·noñ*

mainly *adv* principalement *prañ·see·pal·moñ*

maintenance *n* l'entretien (*m*) *oñ·truh·tyañ*

maize *n* le maïs *ma·ees*

major *adj* principal(e) *prañ·see·pal*

majority *n* (*of*) la majorité *ma·zho·ree·tay*; **elected by a majority of 5** élu avec une majorité de 5 voix *ay·lōō a·vek ōōn ma·zho·ree·tay duh 5 vwah*

make *n* (*of product*) la marque *la mark* □ *vt* faire* *fehr*; **to make the beds** faire* les lits *fehr lay lee*; **to make someone sad** rendre quelqu'un triste *roñ·druh kel·kuñ treest*; **to make someone do something** obliger* quelqu'un à faire quelque chose *o·blee·zhay kel·kuñ a fehr kel·kuh shōz*; **to make do with something** faire* avec quelque chose *fehr a·vek kel·kuh shōz*; **to make (oneself) up** se maquiller *suh ma·kee·yay*

make-up *n* le maquillage *ma·kee·yazh*

male *adj* mâle *mahl*

mallet *n* le maillet *mye·yay*

malt *n* le malt *malt*

Malta *n* la Malte *malt*

malt (whisky) *n* le whisky de malt *wees·kee duh malt*

man *n* l'homme (*m*) *om*

manage *vt* (*business*) gérer* *zhay·ray*; **can you manage?** vous y arrivez? *voo zee a·ree·vay*; **to manage to do something** arriver à faire quelque chose *a·ree·vay a fehr kel·kuh shōz*

management *n* (*of business*) la gestion *zhes·tyoñ*; (*managers*) la direction *dee·rek·syoñ*

manager *n* le directeur *dee·rek·tur* M32

manageress *n* la directrice *dee·rek·trees*

managing director, M.D. *n* le directeur général *dee·rek·tur zhay·nay·ral*

manicure *n* le soin des mains *swañ day mañ*

manicure set n la trousse à ongles troos a oñ·gluh

man-made adj artificiel(le) ar·tee·fee·syel

manner n la manière ma·nyehr

manners pl les manières (fpl) ma·nyehr

manpower n la main-d'œuvre mañ·duh·vruh

mansion n le château shah·tō

mantelpiece n la cheminée shuh·mee·nay

manual adj manuel(le) ma·nwel □ n (book) le manuel ma·nwel

manufacture vt fabriquer fa·bree·kay

manufacturer n le fabricant fa·bree·koñ

manufacturing n la fabrication fa·bree·ka·syoñ

many pron beaucoup bō·koo □ adj many books beaucoup de livres bō·koo duh leev·ruh

map n (of country) la carte kart; (of town) le plan ploñ F7, L4, S95

marble n (material) le marbre mar·bruh; (ball) la bille beey

March n mars (m) mars

march vi marcher au pas mar·shay ō pah □ n la marche marsh

margarine n la margarine mar·ga·reen

margin n (on page) la marge marzh

marina n la marina ma·ree·na

marjoram n la marjolaine mar·zho·len

mark n la marque mark; (currency) le mark mark; (in school) la note noṭ □ vt marquer mar·kay; (stain) tacher ta·shay

market n le marché mar·shay; there is a good market for X les X se vendent bien X suh voñd byañ ō vt **market** (product) vendre voñ·druh Bm18f

market-day n le jour de marché zhoor duh mar·shay

marketing n le marketing mar·ke·ting

marketing manager n le directeur du marketing dee·rek·tur dōō mar·ke·ting

market-place n la place du marché plas dōō mar·shay

market research n l'étude de marché (f) ay·tōōd duh mar·shay

market value n la valeur marchande va·lur mar·shoñd

marmalade n la confiture d'oranges koñ·fee·tōōr do·roñzh

maroon adj bordeaux bor·dō

marriage n le mariage ma·ryazh

married adj marié(e) ma·ryay; they were married yesterday ils se sont mariés hier eel suh soñ ma·ryay ee·ehr

marrow n (vegetable) la courge koorzh

marry vt épouser ay·poo·zay □ vi se marier suh ma·ryay

martini n (Brit) le martini mar·tee·nee; (US) le martini gin mar·tee·nee jeen

marvellous adj merveilleux(euse) mehr·vay·yuh(·yuhz)

marzipan n la pâte d'amandes paht da·moñd

mascara n le mascara mas·ka·ra

masculine adj masculin(e) mas·kōō·lañ(·leen)

mash vt faire* une purée de fehr ōōn pōō·ray duh

mashed potatoes pl la purée de pommes de terre pōō·ray duh pom duh tehr

mask n le masque mask □ vt masquer mas·kay

mass n (church) la messe mes; a mass of blossom une masse de fleurs ōōn mas duh flur

massage n le massage ma·sazh □ vt masser ma·say

masseur n le masseur ma·sur

masseuse n la masseuse ma·suhz

massive adj énorme ay·norm

mass-produce vt fabriquer en série fa·bree·kay oñ say·ree

mass production n fabrication en série fa·bree·ka·syoñ oñ say·ree

mast n (ship's) le mât mah; (radio) l'antenne oñ·ten

master n le maître meh·truh

master key n le passe-partout pas·par·too

masterpiece n le chef-d'œuvre shay·duh·vruh

mat n le petit tapis puh·tee ta·pee; (place mat) le set de table set duh ta·bluh; (under a glass) le dessous-de-verre duh·soo duh vehr

match n l'allumette (f) a·lōō·met; (sport) le match matsh □ vt aller* bien avec a·lay byañ a·vek S101

matchbox n la boîte d'allumettes bwat da·lōō·met

material n la matière ma·tyehr; (fabric) le tissu tee·sōō S61

maternity dress n la robe de grossesse rob duh grō·ses

maternity hospital n la maternité ma·tehr·nee·tay

mathematics n les mathématiques (fpl) ma·tay·ma·teek

matter n □ what's the matter? qu'est-ce qu'il y a? kes keel ya □ vi it doesn't matter ça ne fait rien sa nuh feh ryañ

mattress n le matelas ma·tuh·lah

mature adj (wine) mûr(e) mōōr; (cheese) fait(e) feh (fet)

mauve adj mauve mōv

maximize vt porter au maximum por·tay ō mak·see·mum

maximum n le maximum mak·see·mum □ adj maximum mak·see·mum

May n mai (m) may

may vi □ may I come in? puis-je entrer? pweezh oñ·tray; it may rain il pourrait bien pleuvoir eel poo·reh byañ pluh·vwahr; we may as well go nous pourrions tout aussi bien y aller noo poo·ryoñ too tō·see byañ ee a·lay

Mayday n le mayday may·day

mayonnaise n la mayonnaise ma·yo·nez

mayor n le maire mehr

me pron me muh; give it to me donnez-le-moi do·nay·luh·mwah; he gave it to me il me l'a donné eel muh la do·nay; it's me c'est moi seh mwah

meal n le repas ruh·pah T43, E47

mean adj (miserly) avare a·var; (unkind) méchant(e) may·shoñ(·shoñt) □ vt (signify) signifier see·nyee·fyay; to mean to do avoir* l'intention de faire av·wahr lañ·toñ·syoñ duh fehr

meaning n le sens soñs

means pl les moyens (mpl) mwah·yañ; by means of au moyen de ō mwah·yañ duh

meanwhile adv pendant ce temps poñ·doñ suh toñ

measles n la rougeole roo·zhol

measure vt/i mesurer muh·zōō·ray

measurements pl les mesures (fpl)

muh·zōōr; **bust measurements** le tour de poitrine *toor duh pwah·treen*
meat *n* la viande *vyoñd*
mechanic *n* le mécanicien *may·ka·nee·syañ* T170
media *pl* les média (*mpl*) *may·dya*
medical *adj* médical(e) *may·dee·kal*
medicine *n* (*pills etc*) le médicament *may·dee·ka·moñ*
Mediterranean *adj* méditerranéen (enne) *may·dee·teh·ra·nay·añ*(·*en*); **the Mediterranean (sea)** la Méditerranée *may·dee·teh·ra·nay*
medium *adj* moyen(ne) *mwah·yañ* (·*yen*); **medium wave** les ondes moyennes (*fpl*) *oñd mwah·yen*
meet *vt* (*encounter*) rencontrer *roñ·koñ·tray*; (*make acquaintance of*) faire* la connaissance de *fehr la ko·neh·soñs duh*; (*by arrangement*) retrouver *ruh·troo·vay*; (*demand*) répondre à *ray·poñ·druh a*; **I'll meet you at the station** (*go to get*) j'irai vous chercher à la gare *zhee·ray voo shehr·shay a la gar*
meeting *n* la réunion *ray·ōō·nyoñ*
melon *n* le melon *muh·loñ*
melt *vi* fondre *foñ·druh* ◻ *vt* faire* fondre *fehr foñ·druh*
member *n* le membre *moñ·bruh* L52
memo(randum) *n* la note *not*
memory *n* la mémoire *may·mwahr*; **one of my memories** un de mes souvenirs *uñ duh may soov·neer*
mend *vt* réparer *ray·pa·ray*
menswear *n* (*department*) le rayon hommes *ray·yoñ om*
mental hospital *n* l'hôpital psychiatrique (*m*) *o·pee·tal psee·kee·a·treek*
mentholated *adj* mentholé(e) *moñ·to·lay*
mention *vt* mentionner *moñ·syo·nay*; **don't mention it** je vous en prie *zhuh voo zoñ pree*
menu *n* le menu *muh·nōō* E8, 16
merchant *n* le marchand *mar·shoñ*
merchant bank *n* la banque d'affaires *boñk da·fehr*
merge *vi* fusionner *fōō·zyo·nay*
merger *n* le fusionnement *fōō·zyon·moñ*
meringue *n* la meringue *muh·rañg*
merry *adj* gai(e) *gay*
merry-go-round *n* le manège *ma·nezh*
mess *n* le désordre *day·zor·druh*; **to make a mess** faire* du désordre *fehr dōō day·zor·druh*; **to make a mess of** (*spoil*) gâcher *gah·shay*
message *n* le message *meh·sazh* B76, A36
messenger *n* le messager *meh·sa·zhay*
metal *n* le métal *may·tal*
meter *n* le compteur *koñ·tur*; (*measure*) le mètre *meh·truh*
method *n* la méthode *may·tod*
Methodist *n* le/la méthodiste *may·to·deest*
methylated spirits *pl* l'alcool à brûler (*m*) *al·kol a brōō·lay*
metre *n* le mètre *meh·truh*
metric *adj* métrique *may·treek*
Mexican *adj* mexicain(e) *mek·see·kañ*(·*ken*)
Mexico *n* le Mexique *mek·seek*
microchip *n* la microplaquette *mee·krō·pla·ket*
microcomputer *n* le micro-ordinateur *mee·krō·or·dee·na·tur*
microfiche *n* la microfiche *mee·krō·feesh*

microfilm *n* le microfilm *mee·krō·feelm*
microphone *n* le microphone *mee·krō·fon*
microprocessor *n* le microprocesseur *mee·krō·pro·seh·sur*
microwave oven *n* le four à micro-ondes *foor a mee·krō·oñd*
midday *n* le midi *mee·dee*; **at midday** à midi *a mee·dee*
middle *n* le milieu *mee·lyuh*; **right in the middle** au beau milieu *ō bō mee·lyuh*; **in the middle of the night** au milieu de la nuit *ō mee·lyuh duh la nwee*
middle-aged *adj* entre deux âges *oñ·truh duh zahzh*
middle-class *adj* bourgeois(e) *boor·zhwah*(·*zhwahz*)
Middle East *n* le Moyen-Orient *mwah·yañ nō·ree·oñ*
middle management *pl* les cadres moyens (*mpl*) *ka·druh mwah·yañ*
midnight *n* le minuit *mee·nwee*; **at midnight** à minuit *a mee·nwee*
midwife *n* la sage-femme *sazh·fam*
might *v* ◻ **it might rain** il pourrait pleuvoir *eel poo·reh pluh·vwahr*; **we might as well go** nous pourrions tout aussi bien y aller *noo poo·ryoñ too tō·see byañ ee a·lay*
migraine *n* la migraine *mee·gren*
mild *adj* doux *doo*, douce *doos*
mile *n* le mile *meel*
miles per hour, m.p.h. ≈ kilomètres à l'heure *kee·lō·meh·truh a lur*
mileage *n* ≈ le kilométrage *kee·lō·may·trazh*
military *adj* militaire *mee·lee·tehr*
milk *n* le lait *leh* E60, S34
milk chocolate *n* le chocolat au lait *sho·kō·la ō leh*
milkman *n* le laitier *lay·tyay*
milkshake *n* le lait parfumé fouetté *leh par·fōō·may fweh·tay*
mill *n* le moulin *moo·lañ* ◻ *vt* moudre* *moo·druh*
milligram(me) *n* le milligramme *mee·lee·gram*
millilitre *n* le millilitre *mee·lee·lee·truh*
millimetre *n* le millimètre *mee·lee·meh·truh*
million *num* le million *mee·lyoñ*
millionaire *n* le millionnaire *mee·lyo·nehr*
millionth *adj* millionième *mee·lyo·nyem*
milometer *n* ≈ le compteur kilométrique *koñ·tur kee·lō·may·treek*
mince *vt* hacher *a·shay* ◻ *n* (*meat*) la viande hachée *vyoñd a·shay*
mincer *n* le hachoir *ash·wahr*
mind *n* l'esprit (*m*) *es·pree*; **to change one's mind** changer* d'avis *shoñ·zhay da·vee*; **to make up one's mind** se décider *suh day·see·day* ◻ *vt* **I don't mind the heat** la chaleur ne me gêne pas *la sha·lur nuh muh zhen pah*; **I don't mind** cela m'est égal *suh·la meh tay·gal*; **never mind** ça ne fait rien *sah nuh feh ree·añ*; **do you mind if …?** cela vous dérange si …? *suh·la voo day·roñzh see*; **mind the step** attention à la marche *a·toñ·syoñ a la marsh*
mine *pron* le mien *luh myañ*, la mienne *la myen*; (*plural*) les miens *lay myañ*, les miennes *lay myen* ◻ *n* (*for coal etc*) la mine *meen*
miner *n* le mineur *mee·nur*

mineral water n l'eau minérale (f) ŏ mee·nay·ral
minestrone (soup) n le minestrone mee·neh·stron
minibus n le minibus mee·nee·bōōs
minicab n le minitaxi mee·nee·tak·see
minicomputer n le miniordinateur mee·nee·or·dee·na·tur
minimum n le minimum mee·nee·mum □ adj minimum mee·nee·mum
miniskirt n la minijupe mee·nee·zhōōp
minister n (in government) le ministre mee·nees·truh; (of religion) le pasteur pas·tur Sn93
ministry n (government) le ministère mee·nee·stehr
mink n (fur) le vison vee·zoñ
mink coat n le manteau de vison moñ·tō duh vee·zoñ
minor adj (road) non-prioritaire noñ·pree·o·ree·tehr; (injury) léger(ère) lay·zhay(·zhehr); **minor operation** l'opération bénigne o·pay·ra·syoñ bay·nee·nyuh
minority n la minorité mee·no·ree·tay
mint n (herb) la menthe moñt; (confectionery) le bonbon à la menthe boñ·boñ a la moñt
minus prep moins mwañ; **at minus 2 degrees** à moins 2 degrés a mwañ 2 duh·gray
minute n la minute mee·nōōt; **just a minute** une minute ōōn mee·nōōt
mirror n le miroir meer·wahr S71
miscarriage n la fausse couche fōs koosh
miserable adj malheureux(euse) ma·luh·ruh(·ruhz)
misprint n la faute d'impression fōt dañ·preh·syoñ
Miss n Mademoiselle (f) mad·mwah·zel
miss vt (target, train) manquer moñ·kay; (signpost) ne pas voir* nuh pah vwahr; **I miss my mother** ma mère me manque ma mehr muh moñk; **to miss out** oublier oo·blee·ay
missing adj (object) manquant(e) moñ·koñ(·koñt); (person) disparu(e) dees·pa·rōō; **some pages are missing** il y a des pages qui manquent eel ya day pazh kee moñk; **my wallet is missing** mon portefeuille a disparu moñ port·fuhy a dees·pa·rōō
mist n la brume brōōm
mistake n l'erreur (f) eh·rur; **by mistake** par erreur par eh·rur; **to make a mistake** faire* une erreur fehr ōōn eh·rur E45
mistress n la maîtresse meh·tres
mitt(en) n la moufle moo·fluh
mix vt mélanger* may·loñ·zhay; **to mix up** (confuse) confondre koñ·foñ·druh □ vi mix se mélanger* suh may·loñ·zhay
mixed adj (co-ed) mixte meekst; **mixed grill** l'assortiment de grillades a·sor·tee·moñ duh gree·yad
mixer n le mixer meek·sehr
mixture n le mélange may·loñzh
moan n le gémissement zhay·mees·moñ □ vi gémir zhay·meer
model n le modèle mo·del; (mannequin) le mannequin man·kañ; **a model railway** un chemin de fer en miniature uñ shuh·mañ duh fehr oñ mee·nya·tōōr
modern adj moderne mo·dern S85
modernize vt moderniser mo·dehr·nee·zay
modest adj modeste mo·dest

modification n la modification mo·dee·fee·ka·syoñ
modify vt modifier mo·dee·fyay
mohair n le mohair mo·ehr
molasses n la mélasse may·las
molecule n la molécule mo·lay·kōōl
moment n le moment mo·moñ; **at the moment** en ce moment oñ suh mo·moñ
mom(my) n la maman ma·moñ
Monaco n la Monaco mo·na·kō
monastery n le monastère mo·nas·tehr
Monday n lundi (m) luñ·dee
monetary adj monétaire mo·nay·tehr
money n l'argent (m) ar·zhoñ; **to make money faire*** de l'argent fehr duh lar·zhoñ M17f
money order n le mandat moñ·da
monitor n (TV) le moniteur mo·nee·tur
monk n le moine mwan
monkey n le singe sañzh
mono adj mono mo·nō; **in mono** en mono oñ mo·nō
monopoly n le monopole mo·no·pol
monorail n le monorail mo·no·rye
monster n le monstre moñ·struh
month n le mois mwah
monthly adj mensuel(le) moñ·swel □ n la revue mensuelle ruh·vōō moñ·swel
monument n le monument mo·nōō·moñ
mood n l'humeur (f) ōō·mur; **in a good mood** de bonne humeur duh bon ōō·mur
moon n la lune lōōn
moor vt amarrer a·ma·ray
mop n le balai à laver ba·lay a la·vay □ vt éponger ay·poñ·zhay
moped n le cyclomoteur see·klō·mo·tur
more adj encore de oñ·kor duh; **more cheese** encore du fromage oñ·kor dōō fro·mazh; **more people** encore du monde oñ·kor dōō moñd □ pron **I'd like (some) more** je voudrais un peu plus zhuh voo·dreh zuñ puh plōō □ adv **more dangerous than** plus dangereux que plōō dañ·zhuh·ruh kuh; **more or less** plus ou moins plōō zoo mwañ
morning n le matin ma·tañ
Moroccan adj marocain(e) ma·ro·kañ(·ken)
Morocco n le Maroc ma·rok
mortgage n le prêt hypothécaire preh tee·po·tay·kehr □ vt hypothéquer* ee·po·tay·kay
Moscow n Moscou (m) mos·koo
moselle n (wine) la moselle mo·zel
mosque n la mosquée mos·kay
mosquito n le moustique moo·steek
mosquito net n la moustiquaire moo·stee·kehr
most adv □ **the most beautiful** le plus beau luh plōō bō, la plus belle la plōō bel □ adj **most people** la plupart des gens la plōō·par day zhoñ; **the most cars** le plus grand nombre de voitures luh plōō groñ noñ·bruh duh vwa·tōōr □ pron **he has the most** il a le plus eel a luh plōō; **at the most** tout au plus too tō plōō; **to make the most of** profiter au maximum de pro·fee·tay ō mak·see·mum duh
motel n le motel mo·tel
moth n le papillon de nuit pa·pee·yoñ duh nwee
mother n la mère mehr

mother-in-law n la belle-mère *bel·mehr*

motion n (*movement*) le mouvement *moov·moñ*

motor n le moteur *mo·tur*

motorbike n la moto *mo·tō*

motorboat n le bateau à moteur *ba·tō a mo·tur*

motorcyclist n le/la motocycliste *mo·tō·see·kleest*

motorist n l'automobiliste (*m/f*) *ō·tō·mō·bee·leest*

motor show n le salon de l'automobile *sa·loñ duh lō·tō·mō·beel*

motorway n l'autoroute (*f*) *ō·tō·root*

mount vt monter sur *moñ·tay sōōr*

mountain n la montagne *moñ·ta·nyuh*

mountaineering n l'alpinisme (*m*) *al·pee·neez·muh*; **to go mountaineering** faire* de l'alpinisme *fehr duh lal·pee·neez·muh*

mouse n la souris *soo·ree*

mousse n la mousse *moos*

mouth n la bouche *boosh*; (*of animal*) la gueule *guhl*

move vt bouger* *boo·zhay* □ vi bouger* *boo·zhay*; (*traffic*) circuler *seer·kōō·lay*; (*move house*) déménager* *day·may·na·zhay*; **to move in** emménager* *oñ·may·na·zhay*; **to move out** déménager* *day·may·na·zhay*

movement n le mouvement *moov·moñ*

movie n le film *feelm*

moving walkway n le trottoir roulant *tro·twahr roo·loñ*

mow vt tondre *toñ·druh*

mower n la tondeuse *toñ·duhz*

Mr n Monsieur (*m*) *muh·syuh*

Mrs n Madame (*f*) *ma·dam*

Ms n Madame (*f*) *ma·dam*

much adv □ **much better** beaucoup mieux *bō·koo myuh*; **much bigger** beaucoup plus grand *bō·koo plōō groñ*; (*of*) **much milk** beaucoup de lait *bō·koo duh leh* □ pron **have you got much?** vous en avez beaucoup? *voo zoñ na·vay bō·koo*; **not much** pas beaucoup *pa bō·koo*

mud n la boue *boo*

muddle n le désordre *day·zor·druh*; **in a muddle** en désordre *oñ day·zor·druh*

muddy adj (*water*) boueux(euse) *boo·uh(·uhz)*; (*clothes*) couvert(e) de boue *koo·ver(t) duh boo*

mud-flap n le pare-boue *par·boo*

mudguard n le garde-boue *gard·boo*

muffler n (*on car*) le silencieux *see·loñ·syuh*

mug n la tasse *tas* □ vt agresser *a·greh·say*

multilingual adj polyglotte *po·lee·glot*

multinational adj multinational(e) *mōōl·tee·na·syo·nal*

multiple store n le magasin à succursales multiples *ma·ga·zañ a sōō·kōōr·sal mōōl·tee·pluh*

multiplication n la multiplication *mōōl·tee·plee·ka·syoñ*

multiply vt multiplier *mōōl·tee·plyay*; **to multiply 9 by 4** multiplier 9 par 4 *mōōl·tee·plyay 9 par 4*

multi-storey adj à étages *a ay·tazh*

mum(my) n la maman *ma·moñ*

mumps n les oreillons (*mpl*) *o·ray·yoñ*

Munich n Munich (*m*) *mōō·neek*

municipal adj municipal(e) *mōō·nee·see·pal*

murder n le meurtre *mur·truh* □ vt assassiner *a·sa·see·nay*

muscle n le muscle *mōōs·kluh*

museum n le musée *mōō·zay* F10, L4

mushroom n le champignon *shoñ·pee·nyoñ*

music n la musique *mōō·zeek* L38

musician n le musicien *mōō·zee·syañ*, la musicienne *mōō·zee·syen*

Muslim adj musulman(e) *mōō·zōōl·moñ(·man)* □ n le/la musulman(e) *mōō·zōōl·moñ(·man)*

mussel n la moule *mool*

must vi □ **I must go** je dois partir *zhuh dwah par·teer*; **you must come** vous devez venir *voo duh·vay vuh·neer*

mustard n la moutarde *moo·tard*

mutton n le mouton *moo·toñ*

my adj mon *moñ*, ma *ma*, mes *may*; **my father** mon père *moñ pehr*; **my mother** ma mère *ma mehr*; **my brothers/sisters** mes frères/sœurs *may frehr/sur*

myself pron moi-même *mwah·mem*; **I washed myself** je me suis lavé *zhuh muh swee la·vay*; **I did it myself** je l'ai fait moi-même *zhuh lay feh mwah·mem*

mystery n le mystère *mee·stehr*

N

nail n (*human*) l'ongle (*m*) *oñ·gluh*; (*metal*) le clou *kloo* □ vt clouer *kloo·ay*

nailbrush n la brosse à ongles *bros a oñ·gluh*

nailfile n la lime à ongles *leem a oñ·gluh*

nail polish, nail varnish n le vernis à ongles *vehr·nee a oñ·gluh*

naked adj nu(e) *nōō*

name n le nom *noñ*; **what is your name?** comment vous appelez-vous? *ko·moñ voo za·play voo*; **my name is Paul** je m'appelle Paul *zhuh ma·pel Paul*

nap n (*sleep*) le petit somme *puh·tee som*

napkin n (*for table*) la serviette *sehr·vyet*

nappy n la couche *koosh*

narrow adj étroit(e) *ay·trwah(·trwat)*

nasty adj mauvais(e) *mo·veh(·vez)*

nation n la nation *na·syoñ*

national adj national(e) *na·syoñ·nal*; **national anthem** l'hymne national (*m*) *eem na·syoñ·nal*; **national dress** le costume national *kos·tōōm na·syoñ·nal*

National Health Service ≈ la Sécurité Sociale *say·kōō·ree·tay so·syal*

nationality n la nationalité *na·syoñ·na·lee·tay*

nationalize vt nationaliser *na·syoñ·na·lee·zay*

native adj du pays *dōō pay·ee*

natural adj naturel(le) *na·tōō·rel*

naturalized adj naturalisé(e) *na·tōō·ra·lee·zay*

naturally adv (*of course*) naturellement *na·tōō·rel·moñ*

nature n la nature *na·tōōr*; (*type, sort*) le genre *zhoñr*

naughty adj vilain(e) *vee·lañ(·len)*

nausea n la nausée *nō·zay*

nave n la nef *nef*

navy n la marine *ma·reen*

navy blue adj bleu marine *bluh ma·reen*

near adv près *preh* □ prep **near (to) the house** près de la maison *preh duh la meh·zoñ*; **near (to) Christmas** près de Noël *preh duh no·el*

nearby *adv* tout près *too preh*

nearly *adv* presque *pres·kuh*

neat *adj* (*appearance*) soigné(e) *swah·nyay*; (*room*) bien rangé(e) *byañ roñ·zhay*; (*liquor*) sans eau *soñ zō*

necessary *adj* nécessaire *nay·seh·sehr*

neck *n* le cou *koo*

necklace *n* le collier *kol·yay*

necktie *n* la cravate *kra·vat*

need *vt* avoir* besoin de *av·wahr buh·zwañ duh*; I need to go je dois aller *zhuh dwah zal·ay*; you needn't come vous n'avez pas besoin de venir *voo na·vay pa buh·zwañ duh vuh·neer* S9

needle *n* l'aiguille (*f*) *ay·gwee*

negative *n* (*of photo*) le négatif *nay·ga·teef*

negotiable *adj* négociable *nay·go·sya·bluh*

negotiate *vi* négocier *nay·go·syay*

negotiations *pl* les négociations (*fpl*) *nay·go·sya·syoñ*

neighbo(u)r *n* le voisin *vwah·zañ*, la voisine *vwah·zeen*

neighbo(u)rhood *n* le quartier *kar·tyay*

neither *pron* ni l'un ni l'autre *nee luñ nee lō·truh* □ *adv* neither ... nor ni ... ni *nee ... nee* □ *conj* I wasn't there and neither was he je n'étais pas là et lui non plus *zhuh nay·teh pa la ay lwee noñ plōō*

nephew *n* le neveu *nuh·vuh*

nerve *n* le nerf *nehr*; (*courage*) le courage *koo·razh*

nervous *adj* (*person*) nerveux(euse) *nehr·vuh(·vuhz)*; nervous breakdown la dépression nerveuse *day·preh·syoñ nehr·vuhz*

nest *n* le nid *nee*

net *n* le filet *fee·lay* □ *adj* (*income, price*) net *net*; net weight le poids net *pwah net*

neutral *adj* neutre *nuh·truh* □ *n* (*gear*) le point mort *pwañ mor*

never *adv* jamais *zha·meh*; he never comes il ne vient jamais *eel nuh vyañ zha·meh*

new *adj* nouveau *noo·vō*, nouvelle *noo·vel*

news *n* les nouvelles (*fpl*) *noo·vel*; (*on radio, TV*) les informations (*fpl*) *añ·for·ma·syoñ*

newsagent *n* le marchand de journaux *mar·shoñ duh zhoor·nō*

newspaper *n* le journal *zhoor·nal* S92

newsstand *n* le kiosque à journaux *kee·osk a zhoor·nō*

New Year's Day *n* le jour de l'An *zhoor duh loñ*

New Year's Eve *n* la Saint-Sylvestre *sañ seel·ves·truh*

next *adj* (*stop, station, week*) prochain(e) *pro·shañ(·shen*); next of kin le parent le plus proche *luh pa·roñ luh plōō prosh*

nice *adj* (*place, holiday*) agréable *a·gray·a·bluh*; (*person*) gentil(le) *zhoñ·teey*; (*dress, picture*) joli(e) *zho·lee*

niece *n* la nièce *nyes*

night *n* la nuit *nwee*

night club *n* la boîte de nuit *bwaht duh nwee*

nightdress *n* la chemise de nuit *shuh·meez duh nwee*

nightmare *n* le cauchemar *kosh·mar*

night porter *n* le gardien de nuit *gar·dyañ duh nwee*

night school *n* les cours (*mpl*) du soir *koor dōō swahr*

nil *n* le zéro *zay·rō*

nine *num* neuf *nuhf*

nineteen *num* dix-neuf *deez·nuhf*

ninety *num* quatre-vingt-dix *ka·truh·vañ·dees*

ninth *adj* neuvième *nuh·vyem*

nipple *n* (*on bottle*) la tétine *tay·teen*

no *adv* (*as answer*) non *noñ*

nobody *pron* personne *pehr·son*; I can see nobody je ne vois personne *zhuh nuh vwa pehr·son*

noise *n* le bruit *brwee*

noisy *adj* bruyant(e) *brwee·yoñ(·yoñt*)

nominal *adj* (*fee*) symbolique *sañ·bo·leek*

non- *pref* non- *noñ-*

nonalcoholic *adj* non-alcoolisé(e) *noñ·al·ko·lee·zay*

none *pron* aucun(e) *ō·kuñ(·kōōn*)

nonsense *n* les absurdités (*fpl*) *ap·sōōr·dee·tay*

nonsmoker *n* (*person*) le non-fumeur *noñ·fōō·mur*; (*compartment*) le compartiment non-fumeur *koñ·par·tee·moñ noñ·fōō·mur*

noodles *pl* les nouilles (*fpl*) *noo·yuh*

noon *n* midi (*m*) *mee·dee*

no one *pron* personne *pehr·son*; I can see no one je ne vois personne *zhuh nuh vwa pehr·son*

normal *adj* normal(e) *nor·mal*

normally *adv* (*usually*) normalement *nor·mal·moñ*

north *n* le nord *nor* □ *adv* au nord *ō nor* □ □ northeast le nord-est *nor·est*; northwest le nord-ouest *nor·west*

North America *n* l'Amérique du Nord (*f*) *a·may·reek dōō nor*

northern *adj* du nord *dōō nor*

North Pole *n* le pôle Nord *pōl nor*

North Sea *n* la mer du Nord *mehr dōō nor*

nose *n* le nez *nay*

nosebleed *n* le saignement de nez *sen·yuh·moñ duh nay*

not *adv* pas *pa*; he did not *or* didn't do it il ne l'a pas fait *eel nuh la pa feh*; not at all pas du tout *pa dōō too*; (*don't mention it*) de rien *duh ryañ*

note *n* (*music*) la note *not*; (*letter*) le mot *mō*; (*banknote*) le billet *bee·yeh* M20J

notepaper *n* le papier à lettres *pa·pyay a leh·truh* A41, S93

nothing *n* rien *ryañ*

notice *n* (*poster*) l'affiche (*f*) *a·feesh*; (*sign*) la pancarte *poñ·kart* □ *vt* remarquer *ruh·mar·kay*

notice board *n* le panneau d'affichage *pa·nō da·fee·shazh*

notions *pl* les articles de mercerie (*mpl*) *ar·tee·kluh duh mehr·suh·ree*

nougat *n* le nougat *noo·ga*

nought *n* le zéro *zay·rō*

novel *n* (*book*) le roman *ro·moñ*

November *n* novembre (*m*) *no·voñ·bruh*

now *adv* maintenant *mañ·tuh·noñ*; now and then, now and again de temps en temps *duh toñ zoñ toñ*

nowadays *adv* de nos jours *duh nō zhoor*

nowhere *adv* nulle part *nōōl par*

nuclear *adj* (*energy, war*) nucléaire *nōō·klay·yehr*

nude *adj* nu(e) *nōō*

nuisance *n* l'ennui (*m*) *oñ·nwee*; he's a nuisance il est assommant *eel eh ta·so·moñ*; it's a nuisance c'est ennuyeux *seh toñ·nwee·yuh*

null and void *adj* nul(le) et non avenu(e) *nōōl ay noñ nav·uh·nōō*

numb *adj* (*with cold*) engourdi(e) *oñ·goor·dee*

number *n* le nombre *noñ·bruh*

numberplate *n* la plaque d'immatriculation *plak dee·ma·tree·kōō·la·syoñ*

nun *n* la religieuse *ruh·lee·zhee·uhz*

nurse *n* l'infirmière (f) *añ·feer·myehr* □ *vt* (*patient*) soigner *swah·nyay*

nursery *n* la chambre d'enfants *shoñ·bruh doñ·foñ*

nursery slope *n* la piste pour débutants *peest poor day·bōō·toñ*

nursing home *n* la maison de repos *meh·zoñ duh ruh·pō*

nylon *n* le nylon *nee·loñ*

O

oak *n* le chêne *shen*

oar *n* l'aviron *a·vee·roñ*

oats *pl* l'avoine (f) *a·vwahn*

obedient *adj* obéissant(e) *o·bay·ee·soñ(·soñt)*

obey *vi* obéir *o·bay·eer* □ *vt* to obey someone obéir à quelqu'un *o·bay·eer a kel·kuñ*

object[1] *n* l'objet (m) *ob·zhay*

object[2] *vi* □ to object to a remark protester contre une remarque *pro·tes·tay koñ·truh ōōn ruh·mark*

objective *n* l'objectif (m) *ob·zhek·teef*

obligation *n* l'obligation (f) *ob·lee·ga·syoñ*

oblong *adj* oblong(ue) *ob·loñ(·loñg)*

obscure *adj* obscur(e) *op·skōōr*

obsession *n* l'obsession (f) *op·ses·syoñ*

obstacle *n* l'obstacle (m) *ob·sta·kluh*

obtain *vt* obtenir* *op·tuh·neer*

obvious *adj* évident(e) *ay·vee·doñ (·doñt)*

obviously *adv* évidemment *ay·vee·da·moñ*

occasion *n* l'occasion (f) *o·ka·zyoñ*; (*special event*) l'événement (m) *ay·ven·moñ*

occasional *adj* (*event*) qui a lieu de temps en temps *kee a lyuh duh toñ zoñ toñ*

occasionally *adv* de temps en temps *duh toñ zoñ toñ*

occupation *n* (*job*) le métier *may·tyay*

occur *vi* (*happen*) se produire* *suh pro·dweer*

ocean *n* l'océan (m) *ō·say·oñ*

o'clock *adv* □ at 3 o'clock à 3 heures *a 3 ur*; it's 4 o'clock il est 4 heures *eel eh 4 ur*

October *n* octobre (m) *ok·to·bruh*

odd *adj* (*number*) impair(e) *añ·pehr*; (*strange*) bizarre *bee·zar*

odds *pl* (*in betting*) la cote *kot*

of *prep* de *duh*; a friend of mine un de mes amis *uñ duh may za·mee*; 3 of them 3 d'entre eux *3 doñ·truh*; 14th of June le quatorze juin *luh ka·torz zhwañ*; made of stone de pierre *duh pyehr*

of course *adv* bien sûr *byañ sōōr*

off *adj* (*machine*) coupé(e) *kōō·pay*; (*radio*) fermé(e) *fehr·may*; (*water supply*) fermé(e) *fehr·may*; (*light*) éteint(e) *ay·tañ·tañt*; (*meat*) avarié(e) *a·va·ryay*; (*milk*) tourné(e) *toor·nay* □ *adv* a day off un jour de congé *uñ zhoor duh koñ·zhay*; 3% off 3% de rabais *3% duh ra·beh*; 6 kilometres off à 6 kilomètres *a 6 kee·lo·meh·truh* □ *prep* to fall off a wall tomber d'un mur *toñ·bay duñ mōōr*; off the main road à l'écart de la

grand-route *a lay·kar duh la groñ·root*

offend *vt* blesser *bleh·say*

offer *vt* offrir* *o·freer*; to offer to do something proposer de faire quelque chose *pro·pō·zay duh fehr kel·kuh shōz* □ *n* offer l'offre (f) *o·fruh*

office *n* le bureau *bōō·rō*; (*doctor's*) le cabinet de consultation *ka·bee·neh duh koñ·sōōl·ta·syoñ* T50

office-block *n* l'immeuble de bureaux (m) *ee·muh·bluh duh bōō·rō*

office hours *pl* les heures de bureau (fpl) *ur duh bōō·rō*

officer *n* (*in army etc*) l'officier (m) *o·fee·syay*; (*police*) l'agent de police (m) *a·zhoñ duh po·lees*

office worker *n* l'employé(e) de bureau (m/f) *oñ·plwah·yay duh bōō·rō*

official *adj* officiel(le) *o·fee·syel*

off-season *adj* hors-saison *or·say·zoñ*

offshore *adj* (*island*) proche du littoral *prosh dōō lee·tō·ral*; offshore sailing la navigation côtière *na·vee·ga·syoñ kō·tyehr*

often *adv* souvent *soo·voñ*

oil *n* (*edible, for car*) l'huile (f) *weel*; (*for heating*) le mazout *ma·zoot*; (*petroleum*) le pétrole *pay·trol* T160

oil filter *n* le filtre à huile *feel·tra weel*

oil pan *n* (*in car*) le carter *kar·tehr*

oil-rig *n* la plate-forme pétrolière *plat·form pay·tro·lyehr*

oil tanker *n* le pétrolier *pay·tro·lyay*

ointment *n* l'onguent (m) *oñ·goñ*

O.K., okay *adv* (*agreement*) d'accord *da·kor*; it's OK ça va *sa va*

old *adj* vieux *vyuh*, vieille *vyay*; how old are you? quel âge avez-vous? *kel azh a·vay·voo*

old-age-pensioner *n* le/la retraité(e) *ruh·treh·tay*

old-fashioned *adj* démodé(e) *day·mo·day*

olive *n* l'olive (f) *o·leev*

olive oil *n* l'huile d'olive (f) *weel do·leev*

omelette *n* l'omelette (f) *om·let*

on *adj* (*machine*) en marche *oñ marsh*; (*light, radio*) allumé(e) *a·lōō·may*; (*water supply*) ouvert(e) *oo·vehr (·vehrt)*; when is the film on? quand passe le film? *koñ pas luh feelm* □ *prep* on sur *sōōr*; on the table sur la table *sōōr la ta·bluh*; on the train dans le train *doñ luh trañ*; on the wall au mur *ō mōōr*; on the left/right à gauche/droite *a gōsh/drwat*; come on Friday venez vendredi *vuh·nay voñ·druh·dee*; on television à la télévision *a la tay·lay·vee·zyoñ*

once *adv* une fois *ōōn fwah*; (*formerly*) autrefois *ō·truh·fwah*; once more encore une fois *oñ·kor ōōn fwah*

one *num* un(e) *uñ (ōōn)*; one day un jour *uñ zhoor* □ *pron* which one lequel *luh·kel*, laquelle *la·kel*; the one on the table celui qui est sur la table *suh·lwee kee eh sōōr la ta·bluh*; this one celui-ci *suh·lwee·see*, celle-ci *sel·see*; one should... on devrait... *oñ duh·vreh*; one another l'un(e) l'autre *luñ (lōōn) lō·truh*

one-armed bandit *n* la machine à sous *ma·sheen a soo*

oneself *pron* soi-même *swah·mem*; to dress oneself s'habiller *sa·bee·yay*

one-way street *n* la rue à sens unique *rōō a soñs ōō·neek*

one-way ticket *n* le billet simple *bee·yeh sañ·pluh*

onion n l'oignon (m) o·nyoñ

only adv seulement suhl·moñ; **there are only 4** il n'y a que 4 eel nya kuh 4 □ adj **the only woman there** la seule femme présente la suhl fam pray·zoñ; **an only child** un enfant unique uñ noñ·foñ ōō·neek; **not only** non seulement noñ suhl·moñ

onto prep sur sōōr

OPEC n l'OPEP (f) o·pep

open adj ouvert(e) oo·vehr(·vehrt) □ vt (window etc) ouvrir* oo·vreer □ vi (store, bank) ouvrir* oo·vreer; (play) commencer* ko·moñ·say

open-air adj en plein air oñ plen ehr

open-plan adj sans cloisons soñ klwah·zoñ

opera n l'opéra (m) o·pay·ra

operate vt (machine) faire* marcher fehr mar·shay

operation n l'opération (f) o·pay·ra·syoñ

operator n le/la téléphoniste tay·lay·fo·neest

opinion n l'opinion (f) o·pee·nyoñ; **in my opinion** à mon avis a moñ na·vee

opportunity n l'occasion (f) o·ka·zyoñ

opposite adv en face oñ fas; **the house opposite** la maison d'en face la meh·zoñ doñ fas; **the opposite sex** l'autre sexe lō·truh seks □ n **opposite** le contraire koñ·trehr □ prep en face de oñ fas duh

optician n l'opticien (m) op·tee·syañ

optimistic adj optimiste op·tee·meest

option n l'option (f) op·syoñ

or conj ou oo

orange n l'orange (f) o·roñzh □ adj orange o·roñzh

orangeade n l'orangeade (f) o·roñ·zhad

orange juice le jus d'orange zhōō do·roñzh

orchard n le verger vehr·zhay

orchestra n l'orchestre (m) or·kes·truh

order n (in series) l'ordre (m) or·druh; (command) l'ordre (m) or·druh; (for goods) la commande ko·moñd; **out of order** (machine) en panne oñ pan; **in order to do something** pour faire quelque chose poor fehr kel·kuh shōz □ vt **order** (goods, meal) commander ko·moñ·day

order-form n le bon de commande boñ duh ko·moñd

ordinary adj ordinaire or·dee·nehr

organ n (instrument) l'orgue (m) org

organization n l'organisation (f) or·ga·nee·za·syoñ

organize vt organiser or·ga·nee·zay

oriental adj oriental(e) o·ryoñ·tal

origin n l'origine (f) o·ree·zheen

original adj (earliest) originel(le) o·ree·zhee·nel; (creative) original(e) o·ree·zhee·nal □ n l'original (m) o·ree·zhee·nal

originally adv (at first) à l'origine a lo·ree·zheen

ornament n l'ornement (m) or·nuh·moñ

orphan n l'orphelin(e) (m/f) or·fuh·lañ(·leen)

other adj autre ō·truh; **the other day** l'autre jour lō·truh zhōōr □ pron **the other** l'autre (m/f) ō·truh S13

otherwise adv autrement ō·truh·moñ; **otherwise engaged** occupé(e) à autre chose o·kōō·pay a ō·truh shōz

ought vi □ **I ought to do it** je devrais le faire zhuh duh·vreh luh fehr; **he ought to win** il devrait gagner eel

duh·vreh ga·nyay; **that ought to do** ça devrait aller sa duh·vreh a·lay

ounce n l'once (f) oñs

our adj no·truh, nos nō; **our father** notre père no·truh pehr; **our mother** notre mère no·truh mehr; **our brothers/sisters** nos frères/sœurs nō frehr/sur

ours pron le/la nôtre luh/la nō·truh; (plural) les nôtres lay nō·truh

ourselves pron nous-mêmes noo·mem; **we dressed ourselves** nous nous sommes habillés noo noo som za·bee·yay

out adv (not at home) sorti(e) sor·tee; (team, player) éliminé(e) ay·lee·mee·nay; **the tide is out** c'est la marée basse seh la ma·ray bas; **the sun is out** le soleil brille luh so·lay breey; **the light is out** la lumière est éteinte la lōō·myehr eh tay·tañt □ prep **out of** (outside) en dehors de oñ duh·or duh; **to be out of petrol** être* sans essence e·truh soñs eh·soñs; **made out of wood** en bois oñ bwah; **he ran out of the house** il est sorti de la maison en courant eel eh sor·tee duh la meh·zoñ oñ koo·roñ

outboard adj hors-bord or·bor

outdoor adj de plein air duh plen ehr

outdoors adv dehors duh·or

outfit n (clothes) la tenue tuh·nōō

outgoings pl les dépenses (fpl) day·poñs

outing n l'excursion (f) ek·skōōr·syoñ

outlet n (electric) la prise preez

outline n (summary) les grandes lignes (fpl) groñd lee·nyuh

outlook n la perspective pehr·spek·teev

out-of-date adj (passport, ticket) périmé(e) pay·ree·may

output n le rendement roñ·duh·moñ

outside n l'extérieur (m) ek·stay·ryur □ adj **the outside wall** le mur extérieur luh mōōr ek·stay·ryur; **the outside lane** (in road) la voie de gauche la vwah duh gōsh □ prep **outside the house** à l'extérieur de la maison a lek·stay·ryur duh la meh·zoñ □ adv **to be outside** être* dehors eh·truh duh·or; **to go outside** sortir* sor·teer

outsize adj (clothes) grande taille groñd tye

outskirts pl la banlieue boñ·lyuh

oval adj ovale o·val

oven n le four foor

over adv □ **to fall over** tomber toñ·bay; **to knock over** faire* tomber fehr toñ·bay; **to turn something over** retourner quelque chose ruh·toor·nay kel·kuh shōz; **come over here** venez ici vuh·nay zee·see; **he's over here on holiday** il est en vacances ici eel eñ toñ va·koñs ee·see; **the match is over** le match est fini luh matsh eh fee·nee □ prep **to jump over something** sauter quelque chose sō·tay kel·kuh shōz; **it weighs over a kilo** ça pèse plus d'un kilo sa pez plōō duñ kee·lō

overall n la blouse blooz

overalls pl les bleus de travail (mpl) bluh duh tra·vye

overcoat n (woman's) le manteau moñ·tō; (man's) le pardessus par·duh·sōō

overdose n la surdose sōōr·dōz

overdraft n le découvert day·koo·vehr

overdrive n la vitesse surmultipliée vee·tes sōōr·mōōl·tee·plyay

overexposed adj (photo) surexposé(e) sōōr·ek·spō·zay

overhead adj (railway) aérien(ne)

a·ay·ryañ(·ryen) □ adv au-dessus
ō·duh·sōō □ n overheads les frais
généraux (mpl) freh zhay·nay·rō
overheat vi (engine) chauffer shó·fay
overnight adj (a stay) d'une nuit dōōn
nwee □ adv (happen) durant la nuit
dōō·roñ la nwee
overpass n le pont autoroutier poñ
ō·tō·roo·tyay
overseas adv à l'étranger a lay·troñ·
zhay □ adj (market) d'outre-mer
doo·truh mehr; (visitor) étranger·
(ère) ay·troñ·zhay(·zhehr)
overtake vt (car) doubler doo·blay
overtime n les heures supplémentaires
(fpl) ur sōō·play·moñ·tehr; to work
overtime faire* les heures supplé·
mentaires fehr day zur sōō·play·
moñ·tehr
overture n l'ouverture (f) oo·vehr·tōōr
overweight adj (baggage) trop lourd(e)
trō loor (loord); (person) trop
gros(se) trō grō (grōs)
owe vt (money) devoir* duh·vwahr; he
owes me £5 il me doit £5 eel muh
dwah £5
own adj propre pro·pruh □ n he did it
on his own il l'a fait tout seul eel la
feh too suhl □ vt own (possess) pos·
séder* po·say·day
owner n le/la propriétaire pro·pree·ay·
tehr
ownership n la possession po·zeh·syoñ
oxygen n l'oxygène (m) ok·see·zhen
oyster n l'huître (f) wee·truh

P

pace n le pas pah; (speed) l'allure (f)
a·lōōr; to keep pace with aller* à la
même vitesse que a·lay a la mem
vee·tes kuh
Pacific Ocean n le Pacifique pa·see·
feek
pacifier n la tétine tay·teen
pack vt (goods) emballer oñ·ba·lay; to
pack one's case faire* sa valise fehr
sa va·leez □ n pack le paquet pa·kay;
(of cards) le jeu zhuh
package n le paquet pa·kay
package deal n le marché global mar·
shay glo·bal
package holiday n le voyage organisé
vwah·yazh or·ga·nee·zay
packet n le paquet pa·kay S97
packing n (material) l'emballage (m)
oñ·ba·lazh
packing case n la caisse d'emballage
kes doñ·ba·lazh
pad n (notepaper) le bloc de papier à
lettres blok duh pa·pyay a leh·truh
paddle n (oar) la pagaie pa·gay □ vi
barboter bar·bo·tay
paddling pool n le petit bassin puh·tee
ba·sañ
padlock n le cadenas kad·na
paediatrician n le/la pédiatre pay·dya·
truh
page n la page pazh □ vt faire* appeler
fehr a·play
pageboy n le groom groom
paid adj (vacation) payé(e) pay·yay
pail n le seau sō
pain n la douleur doo·lur I31
painful adj douloureux(euse) doo·loo·
ruh(·ruhz)
painkiller n le calmant kal·moñ
paint n la peinture pañ·tōōr □ vt pein·
dre* pañ·druh
painter n le peintre pañ·truh
painting n (picture) le tableau ta·blō

pair n la paire pehr; (of people) le cou·
ple kōō·pluh; of shoes paire de
chaussures pehr duh shó·sōōr; pair
of scissors paire de ciseaux pehr duh
see·zō; pair of trousers le pantalon
poñ·ta·loñ
pajamas pl le pyjama pee·zha·ma
Pakistan n le Pakistan pa·kee·stoñ
Pakistani adj pakistanais(e) pa·kee·sta·
neh(·nez)
palace n le palais pa·leh
pale adj pâle pahl
Palestine n la Palestine pa·les·teen
Palestinian adj palestinien(ienne) pa·
les·tee·nyañ(·nyen)
palm n (of hand) la paume pôm
palm-tree n le palmier pal·myay
pan n (saucepan) la casserole kas·rol;
(frying pan) la poêle pwahl
pancake n la crêpe krep
pane n la vitre vee·truh
panic n la panique pa·neek; in a panic
pris(e) de panique pree (preez) duh
pa·neek □ vi paniquer pa·nee·
kay
pant vi haleter* al·tay
panties pl le slip sleep
pantomime n le spectacle de Noël
spek·ta·kluh duh no·el
pants pl le pantalon poñ·ta·loñ;
(undergarment: men's) le slip sleep;
(women's) la culotte kōō·lot
pant(s) suit n le tailleur-pantalon tye·
yur·poñ·ta·loñ
panty hose n le collant ko·loñ
paper n le papier pa·pyay; (news·
paper) le journal zhoor·nal; papers
(passport etc) les papiers pa·pyay
□ vt (wall) tapisser a·pee·say
paperback n le livre de poche lee·vruh
duh posh S95
paper clip n le trombone troñ·bon
paprika n le paprika pa·pree·ka
par n (golf) la normale du parcours
nor·mal dōō par·koor; (business) le
pair pehr; above par au-dessus du
pair ō·duh·sōō dōō pehr
parachute n le parachute pa·ra·shōōt
parade n le défilé day·fee·lay
paraffin n le pétrole pay·trol
paragraph n le paragraphe pa·ra·graf
parallel adj parallèle pa·ra·lel
paralysed adj paralysé(e) pa·ra·lee·zay
parasol n le parasol pa·ra·sol
parcel n le colis ko·lee Sn4
pardon excl pardon par·doñ; pardon
me?, (I beg your) pardon? pardon?
par·doñ
parents pl les parents (mpl) pa·roñ
Paris n Paris (m) pa·ree
Parisian adj parisien(ne) pa·ree·zyañ
(·zyen) □ n le/la parisien(ne) pa·ree·
zyañ(·zyen)
park n le parc park □ vt garer ga·ray
□ vi can I park here? est-ce qu'on
peut stationner ici? es·koñ puh sta·
syo·nay ee·see T115f, C10, A28
parka n le parka par·ka
parking disk n le disque de stationne·
ment deesk duh sta·syon·moñ
parking lights pl les feux de position
(mpl) fuh duh pō·zee·syoñ
parking-lot n le parking par·keeng
parking meter n le parc-mètre park·
meh·truh
parking-ticket n le procès-verbal pro·
seh·vehr·bal
parliament n le parlement par·luh·
moñ
Parmesan n le parmesan par·muh·zoñ
parsley n le persil pehr·see

parsnip *n* le panais *pa·neh*

part *n* la partie *par·tee*; *(of machine)* la pièce *pyes*; *(in play)* le rôle *rōl* □ *vt (separate)* séparer *say·pa·ray* T190

participate *vi* participer *par·tee·see·pay*

participation *n* la participation *par·tee·see·pa·syoñ*

particular *adj* particulier(ière) *par·tee·kōō·lyay(·lyehr)* □ *n* in particular en particulier *oñ par·tee·kōō·lyay*

particularly *adv* particulièrement *par·tee·kōō·lyehr·moñ*

parting *n (in hair)* la raie *ray*

partition *n (wall)* la cloison *klwah·zoñ*

partly *adv* en partie *oñ par·tee*

partner *n (in business)* l'associé(e) *(m/f) a·so·syay*; *(dancing)* le/la partenaire *par·tuh·nehr*

partridge *n* la perdrix *pehr·dree*

part-time *adj* à temps partiel *a toñ par·syel*

party *n (celebration)* la soirée *swah·ray*; *(group)* le groupe *groop*; *(political)* le parti *par·tee*

pass *n (permit)* le laisser-passer *leh·say·pa·say*; *(in mountains)* le col *kol* □ *vt (place)* passer devant *pa·say duh·voñ*; *(car)* doubler *dōō·blay*; *(exam)* réussir à *ray·ōō·seer a*; *(time, object)* passer *pa·say*; **please pass the sugar** passez-moi le sucre s'il vous plaît *pa·say·mwah luh sōō·kruh seel voo pleh*

passage *n* le passage *pa·sazh*

passenger *n* le passager *pa·sa·zhay*, la passagère *pa·sa·zhehr*

passenger seat *n* le siège du passager *syezh dōō pa·sa·zhay*

passion *n* la passion *pa·syoñ*

passport *n* le passeport *pas·por* T10f, L59

past *adj* passé(e) *pa·say* □ *n* le passé *pa·say* □ *adv* to run past passer en courant *pa·say oñ koo·roñ*; he ran past me il m'a dépassé en courant *eel ma day·pa·say oñ koo·roñ*; he's past forty il a dépassé la quarantaine *eel a day·pa·say la ka·roñ·ten*

pasta *n* les pâtes *(fpl) paht*

paste *n (glue)* la colle *kol*; **meat paste** le pâté *pah·tay*

pasteurized *adj* pasteurisé(e) *pas·tuh·ree·zay*

pastille *n* la pastille *pas·teey*

pastry *n* la pâte *paht*; *(cake)* la pâtisserie *pah·tees·ree*

pat *vt* caresser *ka·reh·say*

patch *n (of material)* la pièce *pyes*; *(for eye)* le bandeau *boñ·dō*; *(spot)* la tache *tash*

pâté *n* le pâté *pah·tay*

patent *n* le brevet d'invention *bruh·vay doñ·voñ·syoñ*

patent leather *n* le cuir verni *kweer vehr·nee*

path *n* le chemin *shuh·mañ*

patience *n* la patience *pa·syoñs*

patient *adj* patient(e) *pa·syoñ(·syoñt)* □ *n* le/la patient(e) *pa·syoñ(·syoñt)*

patio *n* le patio *pa·tyō*

pattern *n* le motif *mo·teef*; *(dressmaking, knitting)* le patron *pa·troñ*

pause *n* la pause *pōz* □ *vi* faire* une pause *fehr ōōn pōz*

pavement *n (sidewalk)* le trottoir *tro·twahr*; *(roadway)* la chaussée *shō·say*

paw *n* la patte *pat*

pay *n* le salaire *sa·lehr* □ *vt* payer *pay·yay*; **to pay back** *(money)* rembourser *roñ·boor·say*; **to pay for** payer

pay *yay*; **to pay off** *(workers)* licencier *lee·soñ·syay*

payable *adj* payable *pay·ya·bluh*

payee *n* le/la bénéficiaire *bay·nay·fee·syehr*

paying guest *n* l'hôte payant *(m) ōt pay·yoñ*

payment *n* le paiement *pay·moñ*

payroll *n* le registre du personnel *ruh·zhees·truh dōō pehr·so·nel*

peace *n* la paix *peh*; *(calm)* le calme *kalm*

peaceful *adj* paisible *pay·zee·bluh*

peach *n* la pêche *pesh*

peak *n (of cap)* la visière *vee·zyehr*; *(of mountain)* la cime *seem*

peak hours *pl* les heures de pointe *(fpl) ur duh pwañt*

peanut *n* la cacahuète *ka·ka·wet*

pear *n* la poire *pwahr*

pearl *n* la perle *perl*

peas *pl* les petits pois *(mpl) puh·tee pwah*

pebble *n* le caillou *kye·yoo*

peck *vt* donner un coup de bec à *do·nay uñ koo duh bek a*

peculiar *adj (strange)* bizarre *bee·zar*

pedal *n* la pédale *pay·dal*

pedalo *n* le pédalo *pay·da·lō*

pedestrian *n* le piéton *pyay·toñ*

pedestrian crossing *n* le passage clouté *pa·sazh kloo·tay*

pedestrian precinct *n* la zone piétonnière *zōn pyay·ton·yehr*

pediatrician *n* le/la pédiatre *pay·dya·truh*

peel *vt* éplucher *ay·plōō·shay* □ *vi (person)* peler* *puh·lay* □ *n* l'épluchure *(f) ay·plōō·shōōr*; *(of orange, lemon)* l'écorce *(f) ay·kors*

peg *n* le piquet *pee·kay*; *(for coat)* la patère *pa·tehr*; *(clothes peg)* la pince à linge *pañs a lañzh*

pen *n* le stylo *stee·lō* B54, S93

pencil *n* le crayon *kray·yoñ* S8

penetrate *vt* pénétrer* *pay·nay·tray*

penicillin *n* la pénicilline *pay·nee·see·leen*

penis *n* le pénis *pay·nees*

penknife *n* le canif *ka·neef*

pen pal *n* le/la correspondant(e) *ko·re·spoñ·doñ(·doñt)*

pension *n (from State)* la pension *poñ·syoñ*; *(from company)* la retraite *ruh·tret*

pensioner *n* le/la retraité(e) *ruh·treh·tay*

pension fund *n* la caisse de retraite *kes duh ruh·tret*

penthouse *n* l'appartement de grand standing *a·par·tuh·moñ duh groñ stoñ·ding*

people *pl* les gens *(mpl) zhoñ* Mc18, 26

pepper *n* le poivre *pwah·vruh*; *(capsicum)* le poivron *pwah·vroñ*; **green/red pepper** le poivron vert/rouge *pwah·vroñ vehr/roozh*

peppermint *n (confectionery)* la pastille de menthe *pas·teey duh moñt*; *(plant)* la menthe poivrée *moñt pwah·vray*

pepper pot *n* la poivrière *pwah·vree·ehr*

peppery *adj* poivré(e) *pwah·vray*

per *prep* par *par*; **100 km per hour** 100 kilomètres à l'heure *100 kee·lo·meh·truh a lur*; **to earn $25 per hour** gagner $25 de l'heure *gan·yay $25 duh lur*; **$3 per kilo** $3 le kilo *$3 luh kee·lō*; **per person** par personne *par* *pehr*·son; **per day** par jour *par zhoor*; **per annum** par an *par oñ*; **20 per cent** 20 pour cent *20 poor soñ*

percentage *n* le pourcentage *poor·soñ·tazh*

percolate *vt* (*coffee*) passer *pa·say*

percolator *n* le percolateur *pehr·ko·la·tur*

perfect *adj* parfait(e) *par·feh(·fet)*

perform *vi* (*business*) marcher *mar·shay*

performance *n* (*of actor*) l'interprétation (*f*) *añ·tehr·pray·ta·syoñ*; (*of play*) la représentation *ruh·pray·zoñ·ta·syoñ*; (*of car*) la performance *pehr·for·moñs* L47

perfume *n* le parfum *par·fuñ* S44

perhaps *adv* peut-être *puh·teh·truh*; **perhaps he'll come** peut-être qu'il viendra *puh·teh·truh keel vyañ·dra*

period *n* (*of time*) la période *pay·ryod*; (*punctuation*) le point *pwañ*; (*menstruation*) les règles (*fpl*) *reh·gluh* □ *adj* (*furniture*) d'époque *day·pok*

perm *n* la permanente *pehr·ma·noñt*

permanent *adj* permanent(e) *pehr·ma·noñ(·noñt*)

permanently *adv* de façon permanente *duh fa·soñ pehr·ma·noñt*

permanent wave *n* la permanente *pehr·ma·noñt*

permission *n* la permission *pehr·mee·syoñ*

permit *vt* (*something*) permettre* *pehr·meh·truh*; **to permit someone to do something** permettre* à quelqu'un de faire quelque chose *pehr·meh·truh a kel·kuñ duh fehr kel·kuh shōz* □ *n* permit le permis *pehr·mee*

Persian *adj* persan(e) *pehr·zoñ(·zan*)

person *n* la personne *pehr·son*; **in person** en personne *oñ pehr·son*

personal *adj* personnel(elle) *pehr·so·nel*; (*private*) privé(e) *pree·vay*

personal assistant, P.A. *n* le secrétaire particulier *suh·kray·tehr par·tee·kōō·lyay*

personality *n* la personnalité *pehr·so·na·lee·tay*

personally *adv* personnellement *pehr·so·nel·moñ*

personnel *n* le personnel *pehr·so·nel*

personnel department *n* le service du personnel *sehr·vees dōō per·so·nel*

personnel manager *n* le chef du personnel *shef dōō pehr·so·nel*

person-to-person call *n* l'appel en préavis (*m*) *a·pel oñ pray·a·vee*

Perspex *n* le plexiglas *plek·see·glas*

perspire *vi* transpirer *troñ·spee·ray*

persuade *vt* persuader *pehr·swa·day*; **to persuade someone to do something** persuader quelqu'un de faire quelque chose *pehr·swa·day kel·kuñ duh fehr kel·kuh shōz*

peseta *n* la peseta *pay·zay·ta*

pessimistic *adj* pessimiste *peh·see·meest*

pet *n* l'animal familier (*m*) *a·nee·mal fa·mee·lyay*

petrol *n* l'essence (*f*) *eh·soñs* T156, 171, 173

petroleum jelly *n* la vaseline *vaz·leen*

petrol pump *n* la pompe à essence *poñp a eh·soñs*

petrol station *n* la station-service *sta·syoñ·sehr·vees*

petticoat *n* le jupon *zhōō·poñ*

pharmacist *n* le pharmacien *far·ma·syañ*

pharmacy *n* la pharmacie *far·ma·see*

pheasant *n* le faisan *fuh·zoñ*

phone *n* le téléphone *tay·lay·fon*; **he's on the phone** il est au téléphone *eel eh tō tay·lay·fon* □ *vt* phone téléphoner à *tay·lay·fo·nay a*

phone-call *n* le coup de téléphone *koo duh tay·lay·fon*

photo *n* la photo *fo·tō* L17

photocopy *n* la photocopie *fo·to·ko·pee* □ *vt* photocopier *fo·to·ko·pyay* Bm15

photograph *n* la photographie *fo·to·gra·fee* □ *vt* photographier *fo·to·gra·fyay* S51

photographer *n* le/la photographe *fo·to·graf*

photography *n* la photographie *fo·to·gra·fee*

phrase *n* l'expression (*f*) *ek·spreh·syoñ*

phrase book *n* le recueil d'expressions *ruh·kuhy dek·spreh·syoñ*

physical *adj* physique *fee·zeek*

physics *n* la physique *fee·zeek*

piano *n* le piano *pya·nō*

pick *n* (*pickaxe*) la pioche *pyosh* □ *vt* (*flower*) cueillir* *kuh·yeer*; (*choose*) choisir *shwah·zeer*; **to pick up** (*object*) ramasser *ra·ma·say*; **to pick up a friend** passer prendre un ami *pa·say proñ·druñ na·mee*

pickaxe *n* la pioche *pyosh*

picket *n* le piquet de grève *pee·kay duh grev*

pickles *pl* les pickles (*mpl*) *pee·kuhlz*

picnic *n* le pique-nique *peek·neek*; **to go on a picnic** aller* faire un pique-nique *a·lay fehr uñ peek·neek* L34

picture *n* le tableau *ta·blō*; (*drawing*) l'image (*f*) *ee·mazh*; (*photo*) la photo *fo·tō*; (*movie*) le film *feelm*

pie *n* la tourte *toort*

piece *n* le morceau *mor·sō*; **piece of furniture** le meuble *muh·bluh*; **a good piece of work** du bon travail *dōō boñ tra·vye*

piecework *n* le travail à la pièce *tra·vye a la pyes*

pier *n* la jetée *zhuh·tay*

pierce *vt* percer* *pehr·say*

pig *n* le cochon *ko·shoñ*

pigeon *n* le pigeon *pee·zhoñ*

pigskin *n* la peau de porc *pō duh por*

pilchard *n* le célan *say·loñ*

pile *n* la pile *peel* □ *vt* **to pile up** entasser *oñ·ta·say*

pill *n* la pilule *pee·lōōl*; **to be on the pill** prendre* la pilule *proñ·druh la pee·lōōl*

pillar *n* le pilier *pee·lyay*

pillow *n* l'oreiller (*m*) *o·ray·yay* A41

pillowcase, pillowslip *n* la taie d'oreiller *tay do·ray·yay*

pilot *n* le pilote *pee·lot*

pilot light *n* (*gas*) la veilleuse *vay·yuhz*

pimple *n* le bouton *boo·toñ*

pin *n* l'épingle (*f*) *ay·pañ·gluh*; (*drawing-pin*) la punaise *pōō·nez*; (*safety pin*) l'épingle de sûreté (*f*) *ay·pañ·gluh duh sōōr·tay* □ *vt* épingler *ay·pañ·glay*

pinball *n* le flipper *flee·pehr*

pinch *vt* pincer* *pañ·say* □ *n* (*of salt etc*) la pincée *pañ·say*

pine *n* le pin *pañ*

pineapple *n* l'ananas (*m*) *a·na·na*

ping-pong *n* le ping-pong *peeng·pong*

pink *adj* rose *rōz* □ *vi* (*engine*) avoir* des ratés *av·wahr day ra·tay*

pint *n* la pinte *pañt*; **a pint of beer** un demi de bière *uñ duh·mee duh byehr*

pipe *n* (*tube*) le tuyau *twee·yō*; (*for*

smoking) la pipe *peep*; (*musical*) le pipeau *pee·pō*; **(bag)pipes** la cornemuse *kor·nuh·mōōz* A77, S99

pipeline *n* le pipe-line *peep·leen*

piston *n* le piston *pees·toň*

pit *n* le trou *troo*

pitch *vt* (*tent*) dresser *dre·say*

pitcher *n* la cruche *krōōsh*

pity *n* la pitié *pee·tyay*; **what a pity!** quel dommage! *kel do·mazh*

pizza *n* la pizza *pee·tsa*

place *n* l'endroit (*m*) *oň·drwah*; (*seat*) la place *plas*; **in place** en place *oň plas*; **out of place** (*object*) pas à sa place *pa za sa plas*; **come back to our place** revenez chez nous *ruh·vuh·nay shay noo* □ *vt* **place** (*put*) mettre* *meh·truh*; (*a bet*) placer* *pla·say*; **to place an order with someone** passer une commande à quelqu'un *pa·say ōōn ko·moňd a kel·kuň*

place mat *n* le set de table *set duh ta·bluh*

place setting *n* le couvert *koo·vehr*

plaice *n* le carrelet *ka·ruh·lay*

plaid *n* le tissu écossais *tee·sōō ay·ko·seh*

plain *n* la plaine *plen* □ *adj* (*clear*) clair(e) *klehr*; (*simple: cooking etc*) simple *saň·pluh*; (*not patterned*) uni(e) *ōō·nee*; **plain chocolate** le chocolat à croquer *sho·kō·la a kro·kay*; **plain yogurt** le yaourt nature *ya·oor na·tōōr*

plait *n* (*of hair etc*) la natte *nat*

plan *n* (*scheme*) le projet *pro·zhay*; (*map, drawing*) le plan *ploň* □ *vt* organiser *or·ga·nee·zay*; (*make a design*) faire* les plans de *fehr lay ploň duh*

plane *n* l'avion (*m*) *a·vyoň*; (*tree*) le platane *pla·tan*; (*tool*) le rabot *ra·bō*; **by plane** en avion *oň·na·vyoň*

planet *n* la planète *pla·net*

planetarium *n* le planétarium *pla·nay·ta·ree·oom*

plank *n* la planche *ploňsh*

planning *n* (*economic*) la planification *pla·nee·fee·ka·syoň*

plant *n* la plante *ploňt*; (*factory*) l'usine (*f*) *ōō·zeen*; (*equipment*) le matériel *ma·tay·ree·el* □ *vt* planter *ploň·tay*

plaster *n* (*for wall*) le plâtre *plah·truh*; (*for wound*) le pansement *poňs·moň*; (*for limb*) le plâtre *plah·truh*; **plaster of Paris** le plâtre de Paris *plah·truh duh pa·ree*

plastic *n* le plastique *plas·teek* □ *adj* en plastique *oň plas·teek*; **plastic surgery** la chirurgie esthétique *shee·rōōr·zhee·es·tay·teek* S25

plastic bag *n* le sac en plastique *sak oň plas·teek*

plate *n* l'assiette (*f*) *as·yet*; (*of glass, metal*) la plaque *plak*

plated *adj* □ **gold plated** plaqué or *pla·kay or*

platform *n* (*in station*) le quai *kay*; (*in hall*) l'estrade (*f*) *es·trad*; (*of oil-rig*) la plate-forme *plat·form* T63

platinum *n* le platine *pla·teen*

play *vt/i* jouer *zhoo·ay*; **to play football** jouer au football *zhoo·ay ō foot·bal*; **to play the violin** jouer du violon *zhoo·ay dōō vee·o·loň*; **to play with** jouer avec *zhoo·ay a·vek* □ *n* **play** (*theatrical*) la pièce *la pyes*

player *n* (*in sport*) le joueur *zhoo·ur*, la joueuse *zhoo·uz*

playground *n* la cour de récréation *koor duh ray·kray·a·syoň*

play-group *n* la garderie *gar·duh·ree*

playing card *n* la carte à jouer *kart a zhoo·ay*

playing field *n* le terrain de sport *tay·raň duh spor*

play pen *n* le parc pour bébé *park poor bay·bay*

pleasant *adj* agréable *a·gray·a·bluh*; (*person*) aimable *ay·ma·bluh*

please *adv* s'il vous plaît *seel voo pleh*

pleased *adj* content(e) *koň·toň(·toňt)*

pleasure *n* le plaisir *play·zeer*

pleasure boat *n* le bateau de plaisance *ba·tō duh play·zoňs*

pleated *adj* plissé(e) *plee·say*

plenty *n* □ **plenty of milk** beaucoup de lait *bō·koo duh leh*; **thank you, that's plenty** merci, ça suffit *mehr·see sa sōō·fee*

plexiglas *n* le plexiglas *plek·see·glas*

pliers *pl* les pinces (*fpl*) *paňs*

plimsolls *pl* les tennis (*fpl*) *te·nees*

plot *n* (*of land*) le lotissement *lo·tees·moň*; (*in play*) l'intrigue (*f*) *aň·treeg*

plough *n* la charrue *sha·rōō*

plug *n* (*for basin etc*) la bonde *boňd*; (*electric*) la prise *preez*; (*in car*) la bougie *boo·zhee* □ *vt* boucher *boo·shay*; **to plug something in** brancher quelque chose *broň·shay kel·kuh shōz*

plum *n* la prune *prōōn*

plumber *n* le plombier *ploň·byay*

plump *adj* rondelet(te) *roň·duh·lay(·let)*

plus *prep* plus *plōōs*

plywood *n* le contre-plaqué *koň·truh·pla·kay*

p.m. *adv* de l'après-midi *duh la·preh·mee·dee*

pneumonia *n* la pneumonie *pnuh·mo·nee*

poached *adj* poché(e) *po·shay*

P.O. Box *n* la boîte postale *bwaht pos·tal*

pocket *n* la poche *posh*

pocketbook *n* le portefeuille *port·fuhy*

pocketknife *n* le canif *ka·neef*

pocket money *n* l'argent de poche (*m*) *ar·zhoň duh posh*

poem *n* le poème *po·em*

poetry *n* la poésie *po·ay·zee*

point *vt* (*gun*) braquer *bra·kay* □ *vi* **to point at or something** indiquer quelque chose du doigt *aň·dee·kay kel·kuh shōz dōō dwah*; **to point something out** (*show*) montrer quelque chose *moň·tray kel·kuh shōz* □ *n* **point** (*tip*) la pointe *pwaňt*; (*in time*) le moment *mo·moň*; (*in space*) l'endroit (*m*) *oň·drwah*; (*dot*) le point *pwaň*; (*sport: in score*) le point *pwaň*; (*electric outlet*) la prise (de courant) *preez (duh koo·roň)*; (*subject, idea*) le point *pwaň*; **decimal point** la virgule *veer·gōōl*; **3 point 4 3** virgule 4 *3 veer·gōōl 4*; **he answered him point by point** il lui a répondu point par point *eel lwee a ray·poň·dōō pwaň par pwaň*; **what's the point?** à quoi bon? *a kwah boň*

point of view *n* le point de vue *pwaň duh vōō*

poison *n* le poison *pwah·zoň*

poisonous *adj* (*substance*) vénéneux(euse) *vay·nay·nuh(·nuhz)*; (*snake*) venimeux(euse) *vuh·nee·muh(·muhz)*

poker *n* (*card game*) le poker *po·ker*

Poland n la Pologne *po·lon·yuh*
Polaroid adj polaroïd *po·la·ro·eed*
pole n (*wooden*) le mât *mah*
Pole n la Polonais(e) *po·lo·neh* (*·nez*)
police n la police *po·lees* T220, Sn81f
police car n la voiture de police *vwah·tōōr duh po·lees*
policeman n l'agent de police (*m*) *a·zhoñ duh po·lees*
police station n le commissariat de police *ko·mee·sa·ree·a duh po·lees*
policewoman n la femme-agent *fam·a·zhoñ*
policy n la politique *po·lee·teek*; (*insurance*) la police *po·lees*
polio n la polio *po·lyo*
polish n (*for shoes*) le cirage *see·razh*; (*for floor*) la cire *seer* □ vt polish cirer *see·ray*; (*metal*) faire* briller *fehr bree·yay*
Polish adj polonais(e) *po·lo·neh(·nez)*; he's Polish il est Polonais *eel eh po·lo·neh*; she's Polish elle est Polonaise *el eh po·lo·nez* □ n Polish le polonais *po·lo·neh*
polite adj poli(e) *po·lee*
political adj politique *po·lee·teek*
politician n l'homme politique (*m*) *om po·lee·teek*, la femme politique *fam po·lee·teek*
politics n la politique *po·lee·teek*
pollution n la pollution *po·lōō·syoñ*
polo n le polo *po·lō*
polo neck n le col roulé *kol roo·lay*
polyester n le polyester *po·lee·es·tehr*
polythene n le polyethylène *po·lee·ay·tee·len*
polythene bag n le sac en plastique *sak oñ plas·teek*
pomegranate n la grenade *gruh·nad*
pond n (*natural*) l'étang (*m*) *ay·toñ*; (*artificial*) le bassin *ba·sañ*
pontoon n le vingt-et-un *vañ·tay·uñ*
pony n le poney *po·nay*
pool n (*of rain*) la flaque *flak*; (*swimming*) la piscine *pee·seen*; (*game*) la cagnotte *ka·nyot*
poor adj pauvre *pōv·ruh*; (*mediocre*) médiocre *may·dyo·kruh*
pop adj (*music, art*) pop *pop*
pop concert n le concert pop *koñ·sehr pop*
popcorn n le pop-corn *pop·korn*
pope n le pape *pap*
pop group n le groupe pop *groop pop*
poplar n le peuplier *puh·plee·ay*
poplin n la popeline *pop·leen*
popsicle n le bâtonnet glacé *ba·to·nay gla·say*
popular adj populaire *po·pōō·lehr*; (*fashionable*) à la mode *a la mod*
population n la population *po·pōō·la·syoñ*
porcelain n la porcelaine *por·suh·len*
porch n le porche *porsh*
pork n le porc *por*
porridge n le porridge *po·reezh*
port n (*for ships*) le port *por*; (*wine*) le porto *por·tō*
portable adj portatif(ive) *por·ta·teef* (*·teev*)
porter n (*for luggage*) le porteur *por·tur*; (*doorkeeper*) le/la concierge *koñ·syerzh* T26
portfolio n le portefeuille *por·tuh·fuhy*
porthole n le hublot *uh·blō*
portion n la portion *por·syoñ*
Portugal n le Portugal *por·tōō·gal*
Portuguese adj portugais(e) *por·tōō·geh(·gez)*; he's Portuguese il est Por-

tugais *eel eh por·tōō·geh*; she's Portuguese elle est Portugaise *el eh por·tōō·gez* □ n Portuguese le portugais *por·tōō·geh*
position n la position *po·zee·syoñ*; (*job*) la situation *see·tōō·a·syoñ*
positive adj positif(ive) *po·zee·teef* (*·teev*); (*definite*) formel(le) *for·mel*
possibility n la possibilité *po·see·bee·lee·tay*
possible adj possible *po·see·bluh*
possibly adv peut-être *puh·teh·truh*; to do all one possibly can faire* tout son possible *fehr too soñ po·see·bluh*
post n (*pole*) le poteau *po·tō*; (*mail*) le courrier *koo·ryay*; by post par la poste *par la post* □ vt post mettre* à la poste *meh·truh a la post*
postage n l'affranchissement (*m*) *a·froñ·shees·moñ*
postal adj postal(e) *pos·tal*
postal district n le secteur postal *sek·tur pos·tal*
postal order n le mandat postal *moñ·da pos·tal*
post-box n la boîte aux lettres *bwaht ō le·truh*
postcard n la carte postale *kart pos·tal* L18, S96
post-code n le code postal *kod pos·tal*
postdate vt postdater *post·da·tay*
poster n l'affiche (*f*) *a·feesh*
poste restante adv poste restante *post res·toñt*
postman n le facteur *fak·tur*
post office n le bureau de poste *bōō·rō duh post*; the Post Office le service des postes *ser·vees day post*; I must go to the post office je dois aller à la poste *zhuh dwah za·lay a la post* F8
post-office box n la boîte postale *bwaht pos·tal*
postpone vt remettre* à plus tard *ruh·meh·tra plōō tar*
pot n (*for cooking*) la casserole *kas·rol*; (*for jam, for plant*) le pot *pō*
potato n la pomme de terre *pom duh tehr*
pottery n la poterie *po·tree*
pot(ty) n le pot *pō*
poultry n la volaille *vo·lye*
pound n la livre *lee·vruh*
pour vt (*tea, milk*) verser *ver·say* □ vi couler à flots *koo·lay a flō*
powder n la poudre *poo·druh*
powder room n les toilettes (*fpl*) *twah·let*
power n (*of machine*) la puissance *pwee·soñs*; (*authority*) le pouvoir *poo·vwahr*; (*electricity*) le courant *koo·roñ*
power cut n la coupure de courant *koo·pōōr duh koo·roñ*
powerful adj puissant(e) *pwee·soñ* (*·soñt*)
power point n la prise de courant *preez duh koo·roñ*
P.R. n les relations publiques (*fpl*) *ruh·la·syoñ pōō·bleek*
practical adj pratique *pra·teek*; to have practical experience avoir* de l'expérience pratique *a·vwahr duh lek·spay·ryoñs pra·teek*
practise vt/i □ to practise running s'exercer* à courir *seg·zehr·say a koo·reer*; to practise the piano s'exercer* au piano *seg·zehr·say ō pya·nō*
Prague n Prague (*f*) *prag*
pram n la voiture d'enfant *vwah·tōōr doñ·foñ*
prawn n la crevette rose *kruh·vet rōz*

pray *vi* prier *pree·ay*
prayer *n* la prière *pree·ehr*
precinct *n* (*administrative area*) la circonscription *seer·kon·skreep·syon*
precious *adj* (*jewel etc*) précieux(euse) *pray·syuh(·syuz)*
precise *adj* précis(e) *pray·see(·seez)*
precision *n* la précision *pray·see·zyon*
predict *vt* prédire* *pray·deer*
prediction *n* la prédiction *pray·deek·syon*
prefer *vt* préférer* *pray·fay·ray*
preference shares *n* les actions privilégiées (*fpl*) *ak·syon pree·vee·lay·zhyay*
pregnant *adj* enceinte *on·sant* I49
prejudice *n* le préjugé *pray·zhoo·zhay*
preliminary *adj* préliminaire *pray·lee·mee·nehr*
première *n* la première *pruh·myehr*
premises *pl* les locaux (*mpl*) *lo·kō*
premium *n* la prime *preem*
prepaid *adj* payé(e) d'avance *pay·yay da·vons*
preparation *n* la préparation *pray·pa·ra·syon*; **preparations** (*for trip*) les préparatifs (*mpl*) *pray·pa·ra·teef*
prepare *vt* préparer *pray·pa·ray* □ *vi* he's preparing to leave il se prépare à partir *eel suh pray·par a par·teer*
Presbyterian *adj* presbytérien(ne) *prez·bee·tay·ree·añ(·en)*
prescription *n* l'ordonnance (*f*) *or·do·nons*
present *adj* présent(e) *pray·zon(·zont)*; the present king le roi actuel *luh rwah ak·tōō·el* □ *n* present (*gift*) le cadeau *ka·dō*; at present en ce moment *on suh mo·mon* □ *vt* present (*give*) présenter *pray·zon·tay* S6, 105
presentation *n* la présentation *pray·zon·ta·syon*
preserve(s) *n* la confiture *kon·fee·tōōr*
president *n* (*of country*) le président *pray·zee·don*; (*of company*) le président-directeur général (PDG) *pray·zee·don dee·rek·tur zhay·nay·ral (pay day zhay)*
press *n* la presse *pres* □ *vt* presser *pre·say*; (*iron*) repasser *ruh·pa·say*; press the button appuyez sur le bouton *a·pwee·yay sür luh boo·ton*
press-campaign *n* la campagne de presse *kon·pan·yuh duh pres*
press-stud *n* le bouton-pression *boo·ton·pre·syon*
pressure *n* la pression *pre·syon*; the pressures of modern life la pression de la vie moderne *la pre·syon duh la vee mo·dern*; he was under great pressure il était sous pression *eel ay·teh soo pre·syon* T160
pressure cooker *n* la cocotte-minute *ko·kot·mee·nōōt*
pressure group *n* le groupe de pression *groop duh pre·syon*
prestige *n* le prestige *pres·teezh*
pretax *adj* (*profit*) brut(e) *brōōt*
pretend *vi* faire* semblant *fehr son·blon*; **to pretend to do something** faire* semblant de faire quelque chose *fehr son·blon duh fehr kel·kuh shōz*
pretty *adj* joli(e) *zho·lee*
preview *n* l'avant-première (*f*) *a·von·pruh·myehr*
previous *adj* précédent(e) *pray·say·don(·dont)*; **on the previous day** la veille *la vay*
price *n* le prix *pree* □ *vt* (*goods*) fixer

le prix de *feek·say luh pree duh* Bm27
price list *n* la liste des prix *leest day pree*
price range *n* la gamme des prix *gam day pree*
prick *vt* piquer *pee·kay*
pride *n* la fierté *fyehr·tay*
priest *n* le prêtre *preh·truh* Sn93
primary *adj* (*education*) primaire *pree·mehr*
prime minister, P.M. *n* le premier ministre *pruh·myay mee·nee·struh*
prince *n* le prince *prañs*
princess *n* la princesse *prañ·ses*
principal *n* (*of school etc*) le directeur *dee·rek·tur*, la directrice *dee·rek·trees*
print *vt* (*book, newspaper*) imprimer *añ·pree·may*; (*write in block letters*) écrire* en caractères d'imprimerie *ay·kreer on ka·rak·tehr dañ·pree·mree* □ *n* la gravure *gra·vōōr*; (*photographic*) l'épreuve (*f*) *ay·pruhv*; **out of print** épuisé(e) *ay·pwee·zay* S50
printer *n* l'imprimeur (*m*) *añ·pree·mur*
printout *n* le listage *lees·tazh*
prison *n* la prison *pree·zon*; **in prison** en prison *on pree·zon*
prisoner *n* le prisonnier *pree·zo·nyay*, la prisonnière *pree·zo·nyehr*
private *adj* privé(e) *pree·vay*; (*confidential*) confidentiel(le) *kon·fee·don·syel*; **private lesson** la leçon particulière *luh·son par·tee·kōō·lyehr*; **in private** en privé *on pree·vay*
private enterprise *n* l'entreprise privée (*f*) *on·truh·preez pree·vay*
private limited company *n* la société anonyme *so·syay·tay a·no·neem*
private sector *n* le secteur privé *sek·tur pree·vay*
prize *n* le prix *pree*
probable *adj* probable *pro·ba·bluh*
probably *adv* probablement *pro·ba·bluh·mon*
problem *n* le problème *pro·blem* A69
procedure *n* la procédure *pro·say·dōōr*
process *n* le processus *pro·seh·sōōs*; (*method*) le procédé *pro·say·day* □ *vt* traiter *treh·tay*
produce *vt* (*manufacture*) produire* *pro·dweer*; (*play*) mettre* en scène *meh·tron sen*; (*movie*) produire* *pro·dweer* □ *n* (*products*) les produits (*mpl*) *pro·dwee*
producer *n* le producteur *pro·dōōk·tur*; (*of play*) le metteur en scène *meh·tur on sen*; (*of movie*) le ducteur *pro·dōōk·tur*
product *n* le produit *pro·dwee* Bm18
production *n* la production *pro·dōōk·syon*; (*of play*) la mise en scène *meez on sen*
productivity *n* la productivité *pro·dōōk·tee·vee·tay*
profession *n* la profession *pro·fe·syon*
professional *adj* professionnel(le) *pro·fe·syo·nel*
professor *n* le professeur *pro·fe·sur*
profit *n* le profit *pro·fee*
profitability *n* la rentabilité *ron·ta·bee·lee·tay*
profitable *adj* rentable *ron·ta·bluh*
profiterole *n* la profiterole *pro·fee·trol*
profit-making *adj* à but lucratif *a bōō lōō·kra·teef*
profit margin *n* la marge bénéficiaire *marzh bay·nay·fee·see·ehr*
profit-sharing *n* la participation aux

bénéfices *par·tee·see·pa·syoñ ō bay·nay·fees*

program(me) *n (radio, TV)* l'émission *(f) ay·mee·syoñ*; *(brochure, computer)* le programme *pro·gram* □ *vt* programmer *pro·gra·may* L45

programmer *n (person)* le programmeur *pro·gra·mur*, la programmeuse *pro·gra·muhz*

programming *n (computer)* la programmation *pro·gra·ma·syoñ*

progress *n* le progrès *pro·greh*; **to make progress** faire* des progrès *fehr day pro·greh*

prohibit *vt* interdire* *añ·ter·deer*

project *n (plan)* le projet *pro·zheh*; *(venture)* l'entreprise *(f) oñ·truh·preez* Bm30

projector *n* le projecteur *pro·zhek·tur*

promenade *n (by sea)* la promenade *prom·nad*

promise *n* la promesse *pro·mes* □ *vt* promettre* *pro·meh·truh*

promote *vt* promouvoir* *pro·moo·vwahr*

promotion *n* la promotion *pro·mo·syoñ*

pronounce *vt* prononcer* *pro·noñ·say*

pronunciation *n* la prononciation *pro·noñ·sya·syoñ*

proof *n* la preuve *pruhv*; *(of photo)* l'épreuve *(f) ay·pruhv*; **a 70° proof** whisky un whisky qui titre 40° d'alcool *uñ wees·kee kee tee·truh 40 duh·greh dal·kol*

proper *adj (appropriate)* approprié(e) *a·pro·pree·ay*; *(correct)* correct(e) *ko·rekt*; *(respectable)* convenable *koñ·vuh·na·bluh*

properly *adv* correctement *ko·rek·tuh·moñ*

property *n* la propriété *pro·pree·ay·tay*; *(estate)* le domaine *do·men*

proposal *n (suggestion)* la proposition *pro·pō·zee·syoñ*

propose *vt (suggest)* proposer *pro·pō·zay*; **to propose a toast to someone** porter un toast en l'honneur de quelqu'un *por·tay uñ tōst oñ lo·nur duh kel·kuñ*

proposition *n (proposal)* la proposition *pro·pō·zee·syoñ*

prospect *n* la perspective *per·spek·teev*

prospectus *n* le prospectus *pros·pek·tōōs*

prosperous *adj* prospère *pros·pehr*

protect *vt* protéger* *pro·tay·zhay*

protein *n* la protéine *pro·tay·een*

protest *n* la protestation *pro·tes·ta·syoñ* □ *vi* protester *pro·tes·tay*

Protestant *adj* protestant(e) *pro·tes·toñ(·toñt)*

prototype *n* le prototype *pro·to·teep*

proud *adj* fier (fière) *fyehr*; **proud of** fier (fière) de *fyehr duh*

prove *vt* prouver *proo·vay*

provide *vt* fournir *foor·neer*; **to provide someone with something** fournir quelque chose à quelqu'un *foor·neer kel·kuh shōz a kel·kuñ*; **to provide for someone** pourvoir* aux besoins de quelqu'un *poor·vwahr ō buh·zwañ duh kel·kuñ*

provided, providing *conj* pourvu que *poor·vōō keuh*; **provided (that) he comes** pourvu qu'il vienne *poor·vōō keel vyen*

province *n (region)* la province *pro·vañs*

provincial *adj* provincial(e) *pro·vañ·syal*

proviso *n* la condition *koñ·dee·syoñ*

prune *n* le pruneau *prōō·nō*

P.S. *abbrev* P.-S.

psychiatric *adj* psychiatrique *psee·kya·treek*

psychiatrist *n* le/la psychiatre *psee·kya·truh*

psychological *adj* psychologique *psee·ko·lo·zheek*

psychologist *n* le/la psychologue *psee·ko·log*

psychology *n* la psychologie *psee·ko·lo·zhee*

P.T.O. *abbrev* T.S.V.P.

pub *n* le pub *pub*

public *adj* public(ique) *pōō·bleek* □ *n* le public *pōō·bleek*; **in public** en public *oñ pōō·bleek*

public conveniences *pl* les toilettes *(fpl) twah·let*

publicity *n* la publicité *pōō·blee·see·tay*

publicity campaign *n* la campagne de publicité *koñ·pan·yuh duh pōō·blee·see·tay*

public relations *n* les relations publiques *(fpl) ruh·la·syoñ pōō·bleek*

public relations officer *n* le public-relations *pōō·bleek·ruh·la·syoñ*

public school *n (in Britain)* le collège secondaire privé *ko·lezh suh·goñ·dehr pree·vay*

public sector *n* le secteur public *sek·tur pōō·bleek*

publish *vt* publier *pōō·blyay*

publisher *n (man) ay·dee·tur*, l'éditrice *(f) ay·dee·trees*

pudding *n* le dessert *day·sehr*

puddle *n* la flaque (d'eau) *flak (dō)*

pull *vt/i* tirer *tee·ray*; **to pull something out** retirer quelque chose *ruh·tee·ray kel·kuh shōz*; **to pull out of a deal** se retirer d'une affaire *suh ruh·tee·ray dōōn a·fehr*; **the car pulled in** la voiture s'est arrêtée *la vwah·tōōr set a·reh·tay*; **he pulled out to overtake** la car il a débȯité pour doubler *la vwah·tōōr eel a day·bwah·tay poor doo·blay*; **to pull something off** enlever* quelque chose *oñ·luh·vay kel·kuh shōz*

pullover *n* le pull-over *pōōl·o·vehr*

pump *n* la pompe *poñp* □ *vt* pomper *poñ·pay*

pumpkin *n* le potiron *po·tee·roñ*

punch *n (blow)* le coup de poing *koo duh pwañ*; *(drink)* le punch *puñch* □ *vt (with fist)* donner un coup de poing à *do·nay uñ koo duh pwañ a*; *(ticket etc)* poinçonner *pwañ·so·nay*

punctual *adj (person)* ponctuel(le) *poñk·tōō·el*; *(train)* à l'heure *a lur*

puncture *n* la crevaison *kruh·veh·zoñ*

punish *vt* punir *pōō·neer*

punishment *n* la punition *pōō·nee·syoñ*

pupil *n* l'élève *(m/f) ay·lev*

purchase *n* l'achat *(m) a·sha* □ *vt* acheter* *ash·tay*

pure *adj* pur(e) *pōōr*

purée *n* la purée *pōō·ray*

purple *adj* violet(te) *vee·o·lay(·let)*

purpose *n* le but *bōōt*; **on purpose** exprès *ek·spreh*

purse *n (for money)* le porte-monnaie *port·mo·nay*; *(lady's bag)* le sac à main *sak a mañ*

push *vt* pousser *poo·say*; *(button)* appuyer sur *a·pwee·yay sōōr*; *(product)* pousser la vente de *poo·say la vañt duh*; **push it in** enfoncez-le *oñ·foñ·say·luh*

push-chair *n* la poussette *poo·set*

put *vt* mettre* *meh·truh*; **to put a question** poser une question *pō·zay ōōn kes·tyoñ*; **to put one's things away** ranger* *ses affaires roñ·zhay say za·fehr*; **to put back** *(replace)* remettre* *ruh·meh·truh*; **to put down a parcel** poser un paquet *pō·zay uñ pa·kay*; **to put on a dress** mettre* une robe *meh·trōōn rob*; **to put on the light** allumer la lumière *a·lōō·may la lōō·myehr*; ; **to put on the brakes** freiner *freh·nay*; **to put out the light** éteindre* la lumière *ay·tañ·druh la lōō·myehr*; **he put out his hand** il a tendu la main *eel a toñ·dōō la mañ*; **to put someone through** *(on phone)* mettre* quelqu'un en communication *meh·truh kel·kuñ oñ ko·mōō·nee·ka·syoñ*; **to put up a notice** poser une affiche *pō·zay ōōn a·feesh*; **to put up capital** fournir des capitaux *foor·neer day ka·pee·tō*

puzzle *n* le casse-tête *kas·tet*; *(jigsaw)* le puzzle *puz·luh*

pyjamas *pl* le pyjama *pee·zha·ma*

pyramid *n* la pyramide *pee·ra·meed*

Pyrenees *pl* les Pyrénées *(fpl)* *pee·ray·nay*

Q

quail *n* la caille *kye*

quaint *adj* pittoresque *pee·tor·esk*

qualification *n* *(diploma etc)* les titres *(mpl)* *tee·truh*; *(restriction)* la réserve *ray·zehrv*

qualified *adj* qualifié(e) *ka·lee·fyay*

qualify for *vt* *(grant etc)* remplir les conditions requises pour *roñ·pleer lay koñ·dee·syoñ ruh·keez poor*; *(in sports)* se qualifier pour *suh ka·lee·fyay poor*

quality *n* la qualité *ka·lee·tay*; *(characteristic)* la qualité *ka·lee·tay*; **quality goods** les articles de qualité *(mpl)* *ar·tee·kluh duh ka·lee·tay*

quantity *n* la quantité *koñ·tee·tay*

quarantine *n* la quarantaine *ka·roñ·ten*; **to put a dog in quarantine** mettre* un chien en quarantaine *meh·truñ shyañ oñ ka·roñ·ten*

quarrel *n* la querelle *kuh·rel* □ *vi* se disputer *suh dees·pōō·tay*; **to quarrel with somebody** se disputer avec quelqu'un *suh dees·pōō·tay a·vek kel·kuñ*

quarry *n* la carrière *kar·ryehr*

quart *n* ≈ le litre *lee·truh*

quarter *n* le quart *kar*; **a quarter of an hour** un quart d'heure *uñ kar dur*; **(a) quarter to 4** 4 heures moins le quart *4 ur mwañ luh kar*; **(a) quarter past 4** 4 heures et quart *4 ur ay kar*

quartz *n* le quartz *kwarts*

quay *n* le quai *kay*

quayside *n* le quai *kay*

queen *n* la reine *ren*

queer *adj* *(strange)* bizarre *bee·zar*

question *n* la question *kes·tyoñ*; **to ask a question** poser une question *pō·zay ōōn kes·tyoñ*; **it's a question of** il s'agit de *eel sa·zhee duh*; **out of the question** hors de question *or duh kes·tyoñ*

question mark *n* le point d'interrogation *pwañ dañ·tehr·ro·ga·syoñ*

questionnaire *n* le questionnaire *kes·tyo·nehr*

queue *n* la queue *kuh* □ *vi* faire* la queue *fehr la kuh*

quiche *n* la quiche *keesh*

quick *adj* rapide *ra·peed*; **be quick!** dépêchez-vous! *day·peh·shay·voo*

quickly *adv* vite *veet*

quiet *adj* tranquille *troñ·keel*; **be quiet!** taisez-vous! *teh·zay·voo A5*

quietly *adv* *(speak)* doucement *doo·suh·moñ*; *(walk, work)* silencieusement *see·loñ·syuhz·moñ*

quilt *n* l'édredon *(m)* *ay·druh·doñ*; *(duvet)* la couette *kwet*

quit *vt* *(leave)* quitter *kee·tay* □ *vi* *(give up)* renoncer* *ruh·noñ·say*

quite *adv* *(fairly)* assez *a·say*; *(absolutely)* tout à fait *toot a feh*; **quite a few** un assez grand nombre *uñ na·say groñ noñ·bruh*

quiz *n* le jeu-concours *zhuh·koñ·koor*

quota *n* *(of goods)* le quota *kō·ta*

quotation *n* *(passage)* la citation *see·ta·syoñ*; *(price)* le devis *duh·vee*

quote *vt* *(passage)* citer *see·tay*; *(price)* donner *do·nay*

R

rabbi *n* le rabbin *ra·bañ*

rabbit *n* le lapin *la·pañ*

rabies *n* la rage *razh*

race *n* la race *ras*; *(sport)* la course *koors*; **the races** les courses *(fpl)* *koors*

racecourse *n* le champ de courses *shoñ duh koors*

racehorse *n* le cheval de course *shu·val duh koors*

race relations *pl* les rapports entre les races *ra·por oñ·truh lay ras*

race track *n* la piste *peest*

racial *adj* racial(e) *ra·syal*

rack *n* *(for luggage)* le filet à bagages *fee·lay a ba·gazh*; *(for wine)* le casier *ka·zyay*; *(for dishes)* l'égouttoir *(m)* *ay·goo·twahr*

racket *n* *(tennis)* la raquette *ra·ket*

radar *n* le radar *ra·dar*

radar trap *n* le contrôle radar *koñ·trōl ra·dar*

radial(-ply) *adj* à carcasse radiale *a kar·kas ra·dyal*

radiator *n* le radiateur *ra·dya·tur*

radio *n* la radio *ra·dyō*; **on the radio** à la radio *a la ra·dyō*

radish *n* le radis *ra·dee*

rag *n* le chiffon *shee·foñ*

ragged *adj* *(clothes)* en lambeaux *oñ loñ·bō*

raid *n* *(military)* le raid *red*; *(by police)* la rafle *ra·fluh*; *(by criminals)* le hold-up *old·up*

rail *n* *(on stairs)* la rampe *roñp*; *(on bridge, balcony)* la balustrade *ba·lōōs·trad*; *(for train)* les rails *(mpl)* *rye*; **by rail** par chemin de fer *par shuh·mañ duh fehr*

railings *pl* la grille *greey*

railroad, railway *n* le chemin de fer *shuh·mañ duh fehr*

railway station *n* la gare *gar*

rain *n* la pluie *plwee* □ *vi* pleuvoir* *pluh·vwahr*; **it's raining** il pleut *eel pluh*

rainbow *n* l'arc-en-ciel *(m)* *ark·oñ·syel*

raincoat *n* l'imperméable *(m)* *añ·pehr·may·a·bluh*

rainy *adj* pluvieux(euse) *plōō·vyuh (·vyuhz)*

raise *vt* lever* *luh·vay*; *(price)* augmenter *ōg·moñ·tay*; *(family)* élever* *ay·luh·vay* □ *n* l'augmentation *(f)* *ōg·moñ·ta·syoñ*

raisin *n* le raisin sec *ray·zañ sek*

rake *n* le râteau *ra·tŏ*

rally *n* (political) le meeting *mee·ting*; (sporting) le rallye *ra·lee*

ramp *n* (slope) la rampe *roñp*; (in garage) le pont *poñ*

ranch *n* le ranch *roñch*

random *adj* fait(e) au hasard *feh (feht) ŏ a·zar*; at random au hasard *ŏ a·zar*

range *n* (variety) le choix *shwah*; (of mountains) la chaîne *shen*; (of missile) la portée *por·tay* □ *vi* to range from X to Y aller* de X à Y *a·lay duh X a Y*

range finder *n* (on camera) le télémètre *tay·lay·meh·truh*

rank *n* (status) le rang *roñ*; (for taxis) la station de taxis *sta·syoñ duh tak·see*

rare *adj* rare *rar*; (steak) saignant(e) *say·nyoñ(·nyoñt)*

rash *n* l'éruption (f) *ay·rŏŏp·syoñ*

raspberry *n* la framboise *froñ·bwahz*

rat *n* le rat *ra*

rate *n* (price) le tarif *ta·reef*; at the rate of à raison de *a reh·zoñ duh*; rate of inflation le taux de l'inflation *tŏ duh lañ·fla·syoñ*; rate of exchange le taux du change *tŏ dŏŏ shoñzh* Sn25

rates *pl* (local tax) les impôts locaux (mpl) *añ·pŏ lo·kŏ*

rather *adv* (quite) assez *a·say*; I'd rather go to the cinema j'aimerais mieux aller au cinéma *zheh·muh·reh myuh za·lay ŏ see·nay·ma*

ratio *n* la proportion *pro·por·syoñ*

rationalization *n* la rationalisation *ra·syo·na·lee·za·syoñ*

rationalize *vt* rationaliser *ra·syo·na·lee·zay*

ravioli *n* les ravioli (mpl) *ra·vyo·lee*

raw *adj* (uncooked) cru(e) *crŏŏ*; (unprocessed) brut(e) *brŏŏt*

raw material *n* les matières premières (fpl) *ma·tyehr pruh·myehr*

ray *n* le rayon *ray·oñ*

razor *n* le rasoir *ra·zwahr* A42

razor blade *n* la lame de rasoir *lam duh ra·zwahr*

reach *vt* (arrive at) arriver à *a·ree·vay a*; (with hand) atteindre* *a·tañ·druh*; (contact) contacter *koñ·tak·tay* □ *n* out of reach hors de portée *or duh por·tay*; within easy reach of the sea à proximité de la mer *a prok·see·mee·tay duh la mehr*

reaction *n* la réaction *ray·ak·syoñ*

reactor *n* le réacteur *ray·ak·tur*

read *vt/i* lire* *leer*

readdress *vt* faire* suivre *fehr swee·vruh*

reading *n* la lecture *lek·tŏŏr*

ready *adj* prêt(e) *preh (preht)*; ready to do something prêt(e) à faire quelque chose *preh (preht) a fehr kel·kuh shŏz*

ready-cooked *adj* tout cuit *too kwee*, toute cuite *toot kweet*

ready-made *adj* (clothes) de confection *duh koñ·fek·syoñ*

ready-to-wear *adj* prêt-à-porter *preh·ta·por·tay*

real *adj* vrai(e) *vray*; it's a real problem c'est un vrai problème *set uñ vray pro·blem*; in real terms dans la réalité *doñ la ray·a·lee·tay*

real estate *n* l'immobilier (m) *ee·mo·bee·lyay*

realize *vt* se rendre* compte de *suh roñ·druh koñt duh*; (assets) réaliser *ray·a·lee·zay*

really *adv* vraiment *vray·moñ*

realtor *n* l'agent immobilier (m) *a·zhoñ ee·mo·bee·lyay*

rear *adj* (seat) de derrière *duh deh·ryehr*; (wheel) arrière *a·ryehr* □ *vt* (children, cattle) élever* *ay·luh·vay*

rear-view mirror *n* le rétroviseur *ray·trŏ·vee·zur*

reason *n* la raison *ray·zoñ*

reasonable *adj* raisonnable *ray·zo·na·bluh*; (price) acceptable *ak·sep·ta·bluh*

receipt *n* le reçu *ruh·sŏŏ*; (for parcel) l'accusé de réception (m) *a·kŏŏ·zay duh ray·sep·syoñ*; receipts (income) les recettes (fpl) *ruh·set*

receive *vt* recevoir* *ruh·suh·vwahr*

receiver *n* (phone) le récepteur *ray·sep·tur*

recent *adj* récent(e) *ray·soñ(·soñt)*

recently *adv* récemment *ray·sa·moñ*

reception *n* la réception *ray·sep·syoñ*

reception desk *n* le bureau de réception *bŏŏ·rŏ duh ray·sep·syoñ*

receptionist *n* (in hotel) le/la réceptionniste *ray·sep·syo·neest*

recession *n* la récession *ray·se·syoñ*

recipe *n* la recette *ruh·set*

recognize *vt* reconnaître* *ruh·ko·neh·truh*

recommend *vt* recommander *ruh·ko·moñ·day* E17

record *n* (register) le rapport *ra·por*; (file) le dossier *do·syay*; (disk) le disque *deesk*; (in sports) le record *ruh·kor* □ *adj* (production, crop etc) record *ruh·kor* □ *vt* (sound) enregistrer *oñ·ruh·zhee·stray*; (write down) noter *no·tay*

recorded delivery *n* □ by recorded delivery avec avis de réception *a·vek a·vee duh ray·sep·syoñ*

record-player *n* l'électrophone (m) *ay·lek·tro·fon*

recover *vi* (from illness) se rétablir *suh ray·ta·bleer*

recruit *vt* (personnel) recruter *ruh·krŏŏ·tay* □ *n* la recrue *ruh·krŏŏ*

recruitment *n* le recrutement *ruh·kroo·tuh·moñ*

red *adj* rouge *roozh*

red currant *n* la groseille rouge *gro·zay roozh*

red-haired *adj* roux *roo*, rousse *roos*

redirect *vt* (letter) faire* suivre *fehr swee·vruh*

redistribute *vt* redistribuer *ruh·dees·tree·bŏŏ·ay*

redistribution *n* la redistribution *ruh·dees·tree·bŏŏ·syoñ*

red light *n* (traffic light) le feu rouge *fuh roozh*; to go through a red light brûler un feu rouge *brŏŏ·lay uñ fuh roozh*

red light district *n* le quartier réservé *kar·tyay ray·zehr·vay*

red tape *n* la paperasserie *pa·puh·ra·suh·ree*

reduce *vt* réduire* *ray·dweer*; (price) baisser *bay·say* □ *vi* (lose weight) maigrir *may·greer*

reduction *n* la réduction *ray·dŏŏk·syoñ*; (in price) la baisse *bes*; to buy something at a reduction acheter* quelque chose à prix réduit *ash·tay kel·kuh shŏz a pree ray·dwee*

redundant *adj* (worker) mis(e) au chômage *mee (meez) ŏ shŏ·mazh*

referee *n* (sports) l'arbitre (m) *ar·bee·truh*

reference *n* (mention) la mention *moñ·syoñ*; (testimonial) les références *(fpl) ray·fay·roñs*; **his reference to this matter** son allusion à cette affaire *so·na·lōō·zyoñ* a set a fehr; **with reference to your letter** comme suite à votre lettre *kom sweet a vo·truh le·truh*

refer to *vt (allude to)* faire* allusion à *fehr a·lōō·zyoñ* a; *(consult)* consulter *koñ·sōōl·tay*

refine *vt* raffiner *ra·fee·nay*

refinery *n* la raffinerie *ra·fee·nuh·ree*

reflect *vt* refléter* *ruh·flay·tay*

reflector *n (on cycle, car)* le réflecteur *ruh·flek·tur*

refreshments *pl* les rafraîchissements *(mpl) ra·freh·shees·moñ*

refrigerator *n* le frigidaire *free·zhee·dehr*

refund *vt* rembourser *roñ·boor·say* □ *n* le remboursement *roñ·boor·suh·moñ*

refusal *n* le refus *ruh·fōō*

refuse *vt* refuser *ruh·fōō·zay*; **to refuse to do something** refuser de faire quelque chose *ruh·fōō·zay duh fehr kel·kuh shōz*

regarding *prep* en ce qui concerne *oñ suh kee koñ·sern*

regardless of *prep* sans se soucier de *soñ suh soo·syay duh*

regatta *n* la régate *ray·gat*

region *n* la région *ray·zhyoñ* Mc24

register *n* le registre *ruh·zhee·struh*

registered letter *n* la lettre recommandée *le·truh ruh·ko·moñ·day* Sn7

registered trademark *n* la marque déposée *mark day·pō·zay*

registration number *n (on car)* le numéro d'immatriculation *nōō·may·rō dee·ma·tree·kōō·la·syoñ*

regret *vt* regretter *ruh·gre·tay*

regular *adj* régulier(ère) *ray·gōō·lyay(·lyehr)*; *(usual)* habituel(le) *a·bee·tōō·el*; *(ordinary)* normal(e) *nor·mal*; *(size)* standard *stoñ·dar*

regulation *n (rule)* le règlement *reh·gluh·moñ*

rehearsal *n* la répétition *ray·pay·tee·syoñ*

rein *n* la rène *ren*

reject *vt* refuser *ruh·fōō·zay*; *(goods in manufacture)* mettre* au rebut *meh·truh ō ruh·bōō* □ *n* l'article de rebut *(m) ar·tee·kluh duh ruh·bōō*

relation *n* le/la parent(e) *pa·roñ(t)*

relative *n* le/la parent(e) *pa·roñ(t)* □ *adj* relatif(ive) *re·la·teef(·teev)*

relax *vi* se détendre *suh day·toñ·druh*

release *vt (prisoner)* libérer* *lee·bay·ray*; *(book, film)* sortir* *sor·teer*

relevant *adj* pertinent(e) *pehr·tee·noñ(·noñt)*; **relevant to** qui a rapport à *kee a ra·por a*

reliability *n (of person)* le sérieux *say·ree·uh*; *(of car)* la solidité *so·lee·dee·tay*

reliable *adj (person)* de confiance *duh koñ·fyoñs*; *(car)* solide *so·leed*

relief *n (from pain, anxiety)* le soulagement *soo·lazh·moñ*

relief road *n* la route de délestage *root duh day·les·tazh*

relief train *n* le train supplémentaire *trañ sōō·play·moñ·tehr*

religion *n* la religion *ruh·lee·zhee·oñ*

religious *adj (person)* religieux(euse) *ruh·lee·zhee·uh(·uhz)*

rely on *vt (person)* compter sur *koñ·tay sōōr*

remain *vi* rester *res·tay*

remark *n* la remarque *ruh·mark*

remarkable *adj* remarquable *ruh·mar·ka·bluh*

remedy *n* le remède *ruh·med*; **a remedy for** un remède contre *uñ ruh·med koñ·truh*

remember *vt* se souvenir* de *suh soo·vuh·neer duh*

remind *vt* rappeler* *ra·puh·lay*; **to remind someone of something** rappeler* quelque chose à quelqu'un *ra·puh·lay kel·kuh shōz a kel·kuñ*

remittance *n* l'envoi *(m) oñ·vwah*

remote control *n* la télécommande *tay·lay·ko·moñd*

removal van *n* le camion de déménagement *ka·myoñ duh day·may·nazh·moñ*

remove *vt* enlever* *oñ·luh·vay*

renew *vt (subscription, passport)* renouveler* *ruh·noo·vuh·lay*

rent *n* le loyer *lwah·yay* □ *vt* louer *loo·ay* A56, L23

rental *n* la location *lo·ka·syoñ* A61

rental car *n* la voiture de location *vwah·tōōr duh lo·ka·syoñ*

reorder *vt (goods)* commander de nouveau *ko·moñ·day duh noo·vō*

reorganisation *n* la réorganisation *ray·or·ga·nee·za·syoñ*

reorganize *vt* réorganiser *ray·or·ga·nee·zay*

repair *vt* réparer *ray·pa·ray* T189, Sn52

repay *vt* rembourser *roñ·boor·say*

repeat *vt* répéter* *ray·pay·tay*

repeat order *n* l'ordre renouvelé *(m) or·druh ruh·noo·vuh·lay*

repetition *n* la répétition *ray·pay·tee·syoñ*

replace *vt (put back)* remettre* *ruh·meh·truh*; *(substitute)* remplacer* *roñ·pla·say*

replacement *n* le remplacement *roñ·plas·moñ*

reply *vi* répondre *ray·poñ·druh*; **to reply to a question** répondre à une question *ray·poñ·dra ōōn kes·tyoñ* □ *n* la réponse *ray·poñs*

report *vt* signaler *seen·ya·lay* □ *n* le rapport *ra·por*; *(in press)* le reportage *ruh·por·tazh*

reporter *n (press)* le/la journaliste *zhoor·na·leest*

represent *vt* représenter *ruh·pray·zoñ·tay*

representative *n (deputy, agent)* le/la représentant(e) *ruh·pray·zoñ·toñ(t)*; *(for company)* le représentant *ruh·pray·zoñ·toñ* T19, Bm21

republic *n* la république *ray·pōō·bleek*

republican *adj (noun)* républicain(e) *ray·pōō·blee·kañ(·ken)*

reputation *n* la réputation *ray·pōō·ta·syoñ*

request *n* la demande *duh·moñd*

request stop *n* l'arrêt facultatif *(m) a·reh fa·kōōl·ta·teef*

require *vt (need)* avoir* besoin de *a·vwahr buh·zwañ duh*

requirement *n* l'exigence *(f) eg·zee·zhoñs*

reroute *vt* dérouter *day·roo·tay*

resale *n* □ **not for resale** revente interdite *ruh·voñt añ·tehr·deet*

rescue *vt* sauver *sō·vay* □ *n* le sauvetage *sōv·tazh*

research *n* la recherche *ruh·shersh*

resell *vt* revendre *ruh·voñ·druh*

resemble *vt* ressembler à *ruh·soñ·blay* a; **he resembles his father** il ressemble à son père *eel ruh·soñ·bluh a soñ pehr*

reservation *n* (*of seats, rooms etc*) la réservation *ray·zehr·va·syoñ*; (*doubt*) la réserve *ray·zehrv* A57

reserve *vt* (*seat, room*) réserver *ray·zehr·vay* A13, E2

reserve price *n* le prix minimum *pree mee·nee·mum*

reserves *pl* les réserves (*fpl*) *ray·zehrv*

residence *n* la résidence *ray·zee·doñs*

residence permit *n* le permis de séjour *pehr·mee duh say·zhoor*

residential *adj* (*area*) résidentiel(le) *ray·zee·doñ·syel*

resign *vi* démissionner *day·mee·syo·nay*

resignation *n* la démission *day·mee·syoñ*

resist *vt* résister à *ray·zees·tay a*

resistance *n* (*to illness*) la résistance *ray·zees·toñs*

resort *n* le lieu de séjour *lyuh duh say·zhoor*; **in the last resort** en dernier ressort *oñ dehr·nyay ruh·sor* □ *vi* **to resort to** avoir* recours à *a·vwahr ruh·koor a*

resources *pl* les ressources (*fpl*) *ruh·soors*

respect *n* le respect *res·peh* □ *vt* respecter *res·pek·tay*

respectable *adj* respectable *res·pek·ta·bluh*

responsibility *n* la responsabilité *res·poñ·sa·bee·lee·tay*

responsible *adj* responsable *res·poñ·sa·bluh*; **responsible for** responsable de *res·poñ·sa·bluh duh*

rest *vi* se reposer *suh ruh·pō·zay* □ *n* (*repose*) le repos *ruh·pō*; **all the rest** tout le reste *too luh rest*

restaurant *n* le restaurant *res·to·roñ* E1*f*

restaurant car *n* le wagon-restaurant *va·goñ·res·to·roñ*

restrict *vt* limiter *lee·mee·tay*

restriction *n* la restriction *res·treek·syoñ*

restroom *n* les toilettes (*fpl*) *twah·let*

result *n* le résultat *ray·zool·ta*

retail *n* la vente au détail *voñt ō day·tye*; **to sell something retail** vendre quelque chose au détail *voñ·druh kel·kuh shōz ō day·tye* □ *vt* **retail** vendre au détail *voñ·drō day·tye*

retailer *n* le détaillant *day·tye·yoñ*

retail price *n* le prix de détail *pree duh day·tye*

retire *vi* prendre* sa retraite *proñ·druh sa ruh·tret*

retired *adj* retraité(e) *ruh·treh·tay*

retirement *n* la retraite *ruh·tret*

retrain *vt* recycler *ruh·see·klay* □ *vi* se recycler *suh ruh·see·klay*

retraining *n* le recyclage *ruh·see·klazh*

retread *n* le pneu rechapé *pnuh ruh·sha·pay*

retrieve *vt* (*data*) rechercher *ruh·shehr·shay*

retrospect *n* □ **in retrospect** rétrospectivement *ray·tro·spek·teev·moñ*

return *vi* (*come back*) revenir* *ruh·vuh·neer*; (*go back*) retourner *ruh·toor·nay* □ *vt* (*give back*) rendre *roñ·druh*; (*send back*) renvoyer *roñ·vwah·yay* □ *n* (*going/coming back*) le retour *ruh·toor*; (*profit*) le rapport *ra·por*

return ticket *n* le billet aller-retour *bee·yeh a·lay·ruh·toor*

rev *n* (*in engine*) le tour *toor* □ *vt* emballer *oñ·ba·lay*

revenue *n* le revenu *ruh·vuh·nōō*

reverse *n* (*gear*) la marche arrière *marsh ar·yehr*; **in reverse** (*gear*) en marche arrière *oñ marsh ar·yehr* □ *vt* **to reverse the charges** téléphoner en P.C.V. *tay·lay·fo·nay oñ pay·say·vay* □ *vi* **to reverse into the garage** rentrer dans le garage en marche arrière *roñ·tray doñ la·razh oñ marsh ar·yehr*

reversed charge call *n* la communication en P.C.V. *ko·mōō·nee·ka·syoñ oñ pay·say·vay*

review *n* la revue *ruh·vōō*; (*of book etc*) la critique *kree·teek* □ *vt* passer en revue *pa·say oñ ruh·vōō*

revise *vt* réviser *ray·vee·zay*

revive *vt* (*person*) ranimer *ra·nee·may* □ *vi* reprendre* connaissance *ruh·proñ·druh ko·neh·soñs*

revolution *n* (*political*) la révolution *ray·vo·lōō·syoñ*

revue *n* la revue *ruh·vōō*

reward *n* la récompense *ray·koñ·poñs*

rheumatism *n* le rhumatisme *rōō·ma·teez·muh*

Rhine *n* le Rhin *rañ*

Rhone *n* le Rhône *rōn*

rhubarb *n* la rhubarbe *rōō·barb*

rhythm *n* le rythme *reet·muh*

rib *n* la côte *kōt*

ribbon *n* le ruban *rōō·boñ*

rice *n* le riz *ree*

rich *adj* riche *reesh*

ride *n* (*in vehicle*) la promenade *prom·nad*; (*on horse*) la promenade à cheval *prom·nad a shuh·val*; **to go for a ride** (*by car*) faire* un tour en voiture *fehr uñ toor oñ vwah·tōōr*; **to give someone a ride into town** emmener* quelqu'un en ville *oñ·muh·nay kel·kuñ oñ veel*; **it's only a short ride** ce n'est qu'un petit trajet *suh neh kuñ puh·tee tra·zhay* □ *vt* **to ride a horse** monter à cheval *moñ·tay a shuh·val*; **to ride a bicycle** monter à bicyclette *moñ·tay a bee·see·klet*

ridge *n* l'arête (*f*) *a·ret*

ridiculous *adj* ridicule *ree·dee·kōōl*

riding *n* l'équitation (*f*) *ay·kee·ta·syoñ*; **to go riding** faire* du cheval *fehr dōō shuh·val* L28

rifle *n* le fusil *fü·zee*

right *adj* (*correct*) bon *boñ*, bonne *bon*; (*morally good*) bien *byañ*; (*not left*) droit(e) *drwah (drwaht)*; **yes, that's right** oui, c'est ça *wee seh sa* □ *adv* **to turn right** tourner à droite *toor·nay a drwaht*; **right in the middle** en plein milieu *oñ plañ mee·lyuh* □ *n* **right** (*right-hand side*) la droite *drwaht*; (*entitlement*) le droit *drwah*; **on/to the right** à droite *a drwaht* T97, F23

right-handed *adj* droitier(ère) *drwah·tyay(·tyehr)*

right of way *n* (*on road*) la priorité *pree·o·ree·tay*

ring *n* (*on finger*) la bague *bag*; (*circle*) le cercle *sehr·kluh*; (*wedding ring*) l'alliance (*f*) *a·lyoñs* □ *vt* **to ring the** (*door*)**bell** sonner *so·nay* □ *vi* **ring** (*telephone*) sonner *so·nay*; **to ring off** raccrocher *ra·kro·shay*; **to ring back** rappeler* *ra·puh·lay*; **ring me tomorrow** appelez-moi demain *a·puh·lay·mwah duh·mañ* S87

ring road *n* le périphérique *pay·ree·fay·reek*

rink n la patinoire *pa·tee·nwahr*

rinse vt rincer* *rañ·say* □ n *(hair conditioner)* le rinçage *rañ·sazh*

riot n l'émeute (f) *ay·muht*

rip vt déchirer *day·shee·ray* □ vi se déchirer *suh day·shee·ray*

ripe adj *(fruit)* mûr(e) *mōōr*; *(cheese)* fait(e) *feh (feht)*

rise vi *(go up)* monter *moñ·tay*; *(prices)* augmenter *ōg·moñ·tay*; *(person, sun)* se lever* *suh luh·vay* □ n *(in prices, wages)* l'augmentation (f) *ōg·moñ·ta·syoñ*

risk n le risque *reesk* □ vt risquer *rees·kay*

risotto n le risotto *ree·zo·tō*

rival n le/la rival(e) *ree·val*; a rival firm une firme concurrente *ōōn feerm koñ·kōō·roñt*

river n la rivière *ree·vyehr*

Riviera n la Côte d'Azur *kōt da·zōōr*

road n la route *rōōt* T130f, F16f

road block n le barrage routier *ba·razh roo·tyay*

road map n la carte routière *kart roo·tyehr*

road sign n le panneau de signalisation *pa·nō duh seen·ya·lee·za·syoñ*

road test n l'essai sur route (m) *eh·say sōōr root*

road works pl les travaux (mpl) *tra·vō*

roar vi *(person)* hurler *ōōr·lay*; *(lion)* rugir *rōō·zheer*; *(engine)* gronder *groñ·day* □ n *(of person)* le hurlement *ōōr·luh·moñ*; *(of lion)* le rugissement *rōō·zhees·moñ*; *(of engine)* le grondement *groñd·moñ*

roast vt rôtir *rō·teer*; roast meat le rôti *rō·tee*

rob vt dévaliser *day·va·lee·zay*

robbery n le vol *vol*

robe n *(after bath)* le peignoir *peh·nyuh·wahr*

robot n le robot *rō·bō*

rock n *(boulder)* le rocher *ro·shay*; *(substance)* la roche *rosh*; on the rocks *(with ice)* avec des glaçons *a·vek day gla·soñ* □ vt rock bercer* *ber·say*

rocket n la fusée *fōō·zay*

rock ('n' roll) n le rock 'n' roll *rok un rol*

rod n *(metallic)* la tringle *trañ·gluh*; *(fishing)* la canne à pêche *kan a pesh*

roll n le rouleau *roo·lō*; *(bread)* le petit pain *puh·tee pañ* □ vt *(on wheels)* rouler *roo·lay*; to roll up *(newspaper etc)* enrouler *oñ·roo·lay* □ vi roll rouler *roo·lay*

roller skates pl les patins à roulettes (mpl) *pa·tañ a roo·let*

rolling pin n le rouleau à pâtisserie *roo·lō a pa·tees·ree*

Roman adj romain(e) *ro·mañ(·men)*; Roman Catholic catholique *ka·to·leek*

romantic adj romantique *ro·moñ·teek*

Rome n Rome (f) *rom*

roof n le toit *twah*

roof rack n la galerie *gal·ree*

room n *(in house)* la pièce *pyes*; *(in hotel)* la chambre *shoñ·bruh*; *(space)* la place *plas* A4f

room service n le service des chambres *ser·vees day shoñ·bruh*

root n la racine *ra·seen*

rope n la corde *kord*

rose n la rose *rōz*

rosé n le rosé *ro·zay*

rot vi pourrir *poo·reer*

rotten adj *(wood etc)* pourri(e) *poo·ree*

rough n *(golf)* le rough *ruf* □ adj *(surface)* rugueux(euse) *rōō·guh(·guhz)*; *(weather)* mauvais(e) *mo·veh(·vez)*; *(sea)* agité(e) *a·zhee·tay*; *(not gentle)* brutal(e) *brōō·tal*; a rough estimate une approximation *ōōn a·prok·see·ma·syoñ*

roughly adv rudement *rōō·duh·moñ*; *(approximately)* à peu près *a puh preh*

roulette n la roulette *roo·let*

round adj rond(e) *roñ (roñd)* □ n *(circle)* le rond *roñ*; *(in competition)* la partie *par·tee*; *(in boxing)* le round *rawnd*; *(of talks)* la série *say·ree* □ prep to go round a field faire* le tour d'un champ *fehr luh toor duñ shoñ*; we sat round the table nous étions assis autour de la table *noo zay·tyoñ za·see zō·toor duh la ta·bluh*; to go round the shops faire* les magasins *fehr lay ma·ga·zañ*; it's round the corner c'est après le coin *seh ta·preh luh kwañ* □ adv to turn something round retourner quelque chose *ruh·toor·nay kel·kuh shōz*

roundabout n le rond-point *roñ·pwañ*; *(fairground)* le manège *ma·nezh*

round figure/number n le chiffre rond *shee·fruh roñ*

round trip n le voyage aller-retour *vwah·yazh a·lay·ruh·toor*

round trip (ticket) n le billet aller-retour *bee·yeh a·lay·ruh·toor*

route n l'itinéraire (m) *ee·tee·nay·rehr* T126

routine n la routine *roo·teen* □ adj courant(e) *koo·roñ(·roñt)*

row¹ n le rang *roñ*; *(behind one another)* la file *feel* □ vi *(sport)* faire* de l'aviron *fehr duh la·vee·roñ*

row² n *(noise)* le vacarme *va·karm*

rowing n *(sport)* l'aviron (m) *a·vee·roñ*

royal adj royal(e) *rwah·yal*

R.S.V.P. abbrev R.S.V.P.

rub vt frotter *fro·tay*; to rub out effacer* *ay·fa·say*

rubber n *(material)* le caoutchouc *ka·oot·shoo*; *(eraser)* la gomme *gom*

rubber band n l'élastique (m) *ay·las·teek*

rubbish n les ordures (fpl) *or·dōōr*; *(nonsense)* les bêtises (fpl) *bay·teez*

ruby n le rubis *rōō·bee*

rucksack n le sac à dos *sak a dō*

rudder n le gouvernail *goo·vehr·nye*

rude adj impoli(e) *añ·po·lee*

rug n le petit tapis *puh·tee ta·pee*

rugby n le rugby *rug·bee*

ruin n la ruine *rōō·een* □ vt ruiner *rōō·ee·nay*

ruins pl les ruines (fpl) *rōō·een*

rule n *(regulation)* le règlement *reh·gluh·moñ*; *(for measuring)* la règle *reh·gluh* □ vt gouverner *goo·ver·nay*

ruler n *(leader)* le chef *shef*; *(for measuring)* la règle *reh·gluh*

rum n le rhum *rom*

Rumania n la Roumanie *roo·ma·nee*

Rumanian adj roumain(e) *roo·mañ (·men)* □ n *(language)* le roumain *roo·mañ*

rumble vi gronder *groñ·day* □ n le grondement *groñ·duh·moñ*

rump steak n le rumsteck *rum·stek*

run n *(outing)* la promenade en voiture *pro·muh·nad oñ vwah·tōōr*; *(in stocking)* l'échelle (f) *ay·shel* □ vi *(person, animal)* courir* *koo·reer*; *(liquid)* couler *koo·lay*; *(machine, engine)* marcher *mar·shay*; the trains run every hour les trains passent toutes les heures *lay trañ pass toot lay zur*; the road runs past the house la route passe devant la maison *la root pass duh∙voñ la meh∙zoñ*; this car runs on diesel cette voiture marche au gas-oil∙*set vwah∙tōōr marsh ō gaz∙oil*; to run after someone courir* après quelqu'un *koo∙reer a∙preh kel∙kuñ*; to run away se sauver *suh sō∙vay*; to run down or over (*car etc*) renverser *roñ∙ver∙say*; we've run out of milk nous n'avons plus de lait *noo na∙voñ plōō duh leh* □ *vt* run (*a business, country*) diriger* *dee∙ree∙zhay*; to run in (*engine, car*) roder *ro∙day*

runner beans *pl* les haricots à rame (*mpl*) *a∙ree∙kō a ram*

running costs *pl* les frais d'exploitation (*mpl*) *freh dek∙splwah∙ta∙syoñ*

runway *n* la piste d'atterrissage *peest da∙tay∙ree∙sazh*

rural *adj* rural(e) *rōō∙ral*

rush *vi* se précipiter *suh pray∙see∙pee∙tay* □ *vt* (*goods*) envoyer d'urgence *oñ∙vwah∙yay dōōr∙zhoñs* □ *n* la ruée *rōō∙ay*; we had a rush of orders on nous a submergés de commandes *oñ noo za sōōb∙mer∙zhay duh ko∙moñd*

rush hour *n* les heures de pointe (*fpl*) *ur duh pwañt*

Russia *n* la Russie *rōō∙see*

Russian *adj* russe *rōōs*; he's Russian il est Russe *eel eh rōōs*; she's Russian elle est Russe *el eh rōōs* □ *n* Russian (*language*) le russe *rōōs*

rust *n* la rouille *roo∙yuh* □ *vi* rouiller *roo∙yay*

rustproof *adj* inoxydable *een∙ok∙see∙da∙bluh*

rusty *adj* rouillé(e) *roo∙yay*

rye *n* le seigle *seh∙gluh*; rye (whisky) le whisky américain *wees∙kee a∙may∙ree∙kañ*

rye bread *n* le pain de seigle *pañ duh seh∙gluh*

S

saccharin(e) *n* la saccharine *sa∙ka∙reen*

sachet *n* le sachet *sa∙shay*

sack *n* le sac *sak* □ *vt* (*dismiss*) renvoyer *roñ∙vwah∙yay*

sad *adj* triste *treest*

saddle *n* la selle *sel*

safe *adj* (*out of danger*) en sécurité *oñ say∙kōō∙ree∙tay*; (*not dangerous*) sans danger *soñ doñ∙zhay* □ *n* le coffre-fort *ko∙fruh∙for* A34

safeguard *n* la sauvegarde *sōv∙gard*

safety *n* la sécurité *say∙kōō∙ree∙tay*

safety belt *n* la ceinture de sécurité *sañ∙tōōr duh say∙kōō∙ree∙tay*

safety pin *n* l'épingle de nourrice (*f*) *ay∙pañ∙gluh duh noo∙rees*

sage *n* (*herb*) la sauge *sōzh*

sail *n* la voile *vwahl* □ *vi* faire* de la voile *fehr dhu la vwahl* L24

sail(ing) boat *n* le voilier *vwah∙lyay*

sailor *n* le marin *ma∙rañ*

saint *n* le/la saint(e) *sañ* (*sañt*)

sake *n* □ for my sake par égard pour moi *par ay∙gar poor mwah*

salad *n* la salade *sa∙lad* E38

salad cream *n* la mayonnaise *ma∙yon∙nez*

salad dressing *n* la vinaigrette *vee∙nay∙gret*

salary *n* le salaire *sa∙lehr*

sale *n* la vente *voñt*; (*cheap prices*) les soldes (*mpl*) *sold*; on sale or return

vendu(e) avec faculté de retour *voñ∙dōō a∙vek fa∙kōōl∙tay duh ruh∙toor* Bm19

sales *pl* (*cheap prices*) les soldes (*mpl*) sold

sales assistant *n* le vendeur *voñ∙dur*, la vendeuse *voñ∙duhz*

salesman *n* (*rep*) le représentant de commerce *ruh∙pray∙zoñ∙toñ duh ko∙mehrs*

sales manager *n* le directeur commercial *dee∙rek∙tur ko∙mehr∙syal*

saliva *n* la salive *sa∙leev*

salmon *n* le saumon *sō∙moñ*

saloon *n* (*bar*) le bar *bar*; (*car*) la conduite intérieure *koñ∙dweet añ∙tay∙ryur*

salt *n* le sel *sel* S32

salt cellar *n* la salière *sa∙lyehr*

salty *adj* salé(e) *sa∙lay*

same *adj* même *mem*; the same book as (*similar*) le même livre que *luh mem lee∙vruh kuh* □ *pron* all the same tout de même *too duh mem*; (the) same again please! la même chose, s'il vous plaît *la mem shōz seel voo pleh*

sample *n* (*of goods*) l'échantillon (*m*) *ay∙shoñ∙tee∙yoñ* □ *vt* (*wine*) goûter *goo∙tay* Bm23

sanatorium *n* le sanatorium *sa∙na∙to∙ryum*

sanctions *pl* les sanctions (*fpl*) *soñk∙syoñ*

sand *n* le sable *sa∙bluh*

sandal *n* la sandale *soñ∙dal*

sandbank *n* le banc de sable *boñ duh sa∙bluh*

sandwich *n* le sandwich *soñd∙weech*; a ham sandwich un sandwich au jambon *uñ soñd∙weech ō zhoñ∙boñ*

sandy *adj* (*beach*) de sable *duh sa∙bluh*

sanitary towel *n* la serviette hygiénique *sehr∙vyet ee∙zhay∙neek*

sarcastic *adj* sarcastique *sar∙kas∙teek*

sardine *n* la sardine *sar∙deen*

Sardinia *n* la Sardaigne *sar∙deh∙nyuh*

satellite *n* le satellite *sa∙teh∙leet*

satin *n* le satin *sa∙tañ*

satire *n* (*play*) la satire *sa∙teer*

satisfactory *adj* satisfaisant(e) *sa∙tees∙fuh∙zoñ(t)*

satisfy *vt* satisfaire* *sa∙tees∙fehr*

saturate *vt* (*market*) saturer *sa∙tōō∙ray*

Saturday *n* samedi (*m*) *sam∙dee*

sauce *n* la sauce *sōs*

saucepan *n* la casserole *kas∙rol*

saucer *n* la soucoupe *soo∙koop*

sauna *n* le sauna *sō∙na*

sausage *n* la saucisse *sō∙sees*

sausage roll *n* le friand *free∙oñ*

sauté *adj* sauté(e) *sō∙tay*

save *vt* (*person*) sauver *sō∙vay*; (*money*) mettre* de côté *meh∙truh duh kō∙tay*

savings bank *n* la caisse d'épargne *kes day∙par∙nyuh*

savo(u)ry *adj* (*not sweet*) salé(e) *sa∙lay*

say *vt* dire* *deer*; could you say that again? est-ce que vous pouvez répéter cela? *es∙kuh voo poo∙vay ray∙pay∙tay suh∙la*

scab *n* la croûte *kroot*

scald *vt* ébouillanter *ay∙boo∙yoñ∙tay*

scale *n* (*of fish*) l'écaille (*f*) *ay∙kye*; (*on map, thermometer*) l'échelle (*f*) *ay∙shel*; (*music*) la gamme *gam*; scale of charges le barème *ba∙rem*

scales *pl* (*for weighing*) la balance *ba∙loñs*

scallop *n* la coquille Saint-Jacques *ko∙keey sañ∙zhak*

scalp n le cuir chevelu *kweer shuh·vuh·lōō*

scampi n les langoustines (fpl) *loñ·goos·teen*

Scandinavia n la Scandinavie *skoñ·dee·na·vee*

Scandinavian adj scandinave *skoñ·dee·nav*

scar n la cicatrice *see·ka·trees*

scarce adj rare *rar*

scarcely adv à peine *a pen*

scared adj □ **to be scared** avoir* peur *a·vwahr pur*

scarf n l'écharpe (f) *ay·sharp*

scarlet adj écarlate *ay·kar·lat*

scene n la scène *sen*; (sight) le spectacle *spek·ta·kluh*

scenery n le paysage *pay·ee·zazh*

scenic route n l'itinéraire touristique (m) *ee·tee·nay·rehr too·rees·teek*

scent n (smell) l'odeur (f) *o·dur*; (perfume) le parfum *par·fuñ*

schedule n le programme *pro·gram*; (of trains etc) l'horaire (m) *o·rehr*; **on schedule** (train) à l'heure *a lur*

scheduled flight n le vol régulier *vol ray·gōō·lyay*

scheme n (plan) le projet *pro·zhay*

school n l'école (f) *ay·kol*

science n la science *see·oñs*

science fiction n la science-fiction *see·oñs·feek·syoñ*

scientific adj scientifique *see·oñ·tee·feek*

scientist n le/la scientifique *see·oñ·tee·feek*

scissors pl les ciseaux (mpl) *see·zō*

scooter n le scooter *skoo·tehr*

scope n □ **within the scope of** dans les limites de *doñ lay lee·meet duh*

score n le score *skor* □ vt (goal) marquer *mar·kay*

Scot n l'Écossais(e) (m/f) *ay·ko·seh(·sez)*

Scotch (liquor) le scotch *skotch*

Scotland n l'Écosse (f) *ay·kos*

Scottish adj écossais(e) *ay·ko·seh(·sez)*; **he's Scottish** il est Écossais *eel eh tay·ko·seh*; **she's Scottish** elle est Écossaise *el eh tay·ko·sez*

scourer n le tampon abrasif *toñ·poñ a·bra·zeef*

scrap n (bit) le morceau *mor·sō*

scrape vt frôler *frō·lay*

scratch vt griffer *gree·fay*

scream vi crier *kree·yay*

screen n (partition) le paravent *pa·ra·voñ*; (TV, movie) l'écran (m) *ay·kroñ*

screw n la vis *vees*

screwdriver n le tournevis *toor·nuh·vees*

sculpture n la sculpture *skōōl·tōōr*

sea n la mer *mehr*; **to go by sea** aller* par mer *a·lay par mehr*

seafood n les fruits de mer *frwee duh mehr*

seafront n le bord de mer *bor duh mehr*

sea level n le niveau de la mer *nee·vō duh la mehr*

seam n la couture *koo·tōōr*

search vt fouiller *foo·yay*; **to search for** chercher *shehr·shay*

seasick adj □ **to be seasick** avoir* le mal de mer *a·vwahr luh mal duh mehr*

seaside n le bord de la mer *bor duh la mehr*; **seaside resort** la station balnéaire *sta·syoñ bal·nay·ehr*

season n la saison *seh·zoñ*; **the holiday**

season la période des vacances *la pay·ryod day va·koñs*; **strawberries are in season** les fraises sont de saison *lay frez soñ duh seh·zoñ*

seasoning n l'assaisonnement (m) *a·seh·zon·moñ*

season ticket n la carte d'abonnement *kart da·bon·moñ*

seat n la place *plas*; **take a seat** asseyez-vous *a·say·yay·voo* T9, 45, 61f, L40

seat belt n la ceinture de sécurité *sañ·tōōr duh say·kōō·ree·tay*

seaweed n les algues (fpl) *alg*

second (time) la seconde *suh·goñd* □ adj deuxième *duh·zyem*

secondary adj (importance) secondaire *suh·goñ·dehr*

secondary school n le lycée *lee·say*

second-class adj de deuxième classe *duh duh·zyem klas*

second floor n le deuxième étage *duh·zyem ay·tazh*

secondhand adj (car etc) d'occasion *do·ka·zyoñ* S14

secret adj secret(ète) *suh·kreh(·kret)* □ n le secret *suh·kreh*

secretary n le/la secrétaire *suh·kray·tehr* Bm7

secretary of state n le ministre des Affaires Étrangères *mee·nee·struh day za·fehr ay·troñ·zhehr*

sector n (economy) le secteur *sek·tur*; **private sector** le secteur privé *sek·tur pree·vay*; **public sector** le secteur public *sek·tur pōō·bleek*

security n (at airport) la sécurité *say·kōō·ree·tay*; (for loan) la caution *kō·syoñ*

sedative n le sédatif *say·da·teef*

see vt/i voir* *vwahr*; **to see someone off at the station** accompagner quelqu'un à la gare *a·koñ·pa·nyay kel·kuñ a la gar*; **to see someone home** accompagner quelqu'un à la maison *a·koñ·pa·nyay kel·kuñ a la meh·zoñ*; **to see to something** s'occuper de quelque chose *so·kōō·pay duh kel·kuh shōz*

seed n la graine *gren*

seem vi sembler *soñ·blay*

seersucker n le crépon de coton *kray·poñ duh ko·toñ*

seesaw n la bascule *bas·kōōl*

seldom adv rarement *rar·moñ*

selection n la sélection *say·lek·syoñ* Bm23

self-catering adj avec cuisine *a·vek kwee·zeen*

self-contained adj (apartment) indépendant(e) *añ·day·poñ·doñ(·doñt)*

self-employed adj qui travaille à son compte *kee tra·vye a soñ koñt*

selfish adj égoïste *ay·gō·eest*

self-service adj libre-service *lee·bruh·sehr·vees*

sell vt vendre *voñ·druh* S7

sellotape n le scotch *skotch*

semifinal n la demi-finale *duh·mee·fee·nal*

semiskilled adj spécialisé(e) *spay·sya·lee·zay*

senate n (political) le sénat *say·na*

senator n le sénateur *say·na·tur*

send vt envoyer *oñ·vwa·yay*

sender n l'expéditeur (m) *ek·spay·dee·tur*

senior adj (in rank) supérieur(e) *sōō·pay·ryur*; (in age) plus âgé(e) *plōō za·zhay*

sense n (feeling) le sens *soñs*; (com-

mon sense) la raison *reh·zoñ*; **sense of humour** le sens de l'humour *soñs duh lōō·moor*; **to make sense** avoir* du sens *a·vwahr dōō soñs*

sensible *adj* raisonnable *reh·zo·na·bluh*

sentence *n* la phrase *fraz*

separate *adj* séparé(e) *say·pa·ray*

September *n* septembre (*m*) *sep·toñ·bruh*

serious *adj* sérieux(euse) *say·ryuh (·ryuhz)*

serve *vt* servir* *sehr·veer*

service *n* le service *sehr·vees*; (for car) la révision *ray·vee·zyoñ*

service area *n* l'aire de services (*f*) *ehr duh sehr·vees*

service charge *n* le service *sehr·vees*

service industry *n* l'industrie du service (*f*) *añ·dōōs·tree dōō sehr·vees*

service station *n* la station-service *sta·syoñ·sehr·vees* F9

serviette *n* la serviette *sehr·vyet*

set *n* (collection) le jeu *zhuh* □ *vt* (alarm) mettre* *meh·truh*; **to set the table** mettre* le couvert *meh·truh luh koo·vehr*; **to have one's hair set** se faire* faire une mise en plis *suh fehr fehr ōōn meez oñ plee*; **to set out** partir* *par·teer*

settle *vt* régler* *ray·glay* □ *vi* (wine) se déposer *suh day·pō·zay*; **to settle out of court** arriver à un règlement à l'amiable *a·ree·vay a uñ reh·gluh·moñ a la·mya·bluh*; **to settle in** s'installer *sañ·sta·lay*

settled *adj* (weather) au beau fixe *ō bō feeks*

seven *num* sept *set*

seventeen *num* dix-sept *dees·set*

seventeenth *adj* dix-septième *dees·seh·tyem*

seventh *adj* septième *seh·tyem*

seventy *num* soixante-dix *swah·soñt·dees*

several *adj* plusieurs *plōō·zyur* □ *pron* **several of us** plusieurs d'entre nous *plōō·zyur doñ·truh noo*

sew *vi* coudre* *koo·druh*

sewing machine *n* la machine à coudre *ma·sheen a koo·druh*

sex *n* le sexe *seks*

sexual intercourse *n* les rapports sexuels *ra·por sek·sōō·el*

sexy *adj* sexy *sek·see*

shade *n* l'ombre (*f*) *oñ·bruh*; (for lamp) l'abat-jour (*m*) *a·ba·zhoor*

shades *pl* (sunglasses) les lunettes de soleil (*fpl*) *lōō·net duh so·lay*

shadow *n* l'ombre (*f*) *oñ·bruh*

shake *vt* secouer *suh·koo·ay*; **to shake hands with someone** serrer la main à quelqu'un *sehr·ray la mañ a kel·kuñ* □ *vi* shake trembler *troñ·blay*

shall *vi* □ **I shall do it** je le ferai *zhuh luh fuh·ray*; **shall I do it?** vous voulez que je le fasse? *voo voo·lay kuh zhuh luh fas*; **shall we come tomorrow?** nous venons demain? *noo vuh·noñ duh·mañ*

shallot *n* l'échalote (*f*) *ay·sha·lot*

shallow *adj* peu profond(e) *puh pro·foñ(·foñd)*

shame *n* la honte *oñt*; **what a shame!** quel dommage! *kel do·mazh*

shampoo *n* le shampooing *shoñ·pwañ*

shandy *n* le panaché *pa·na·shay*

shape *n* la forme *form*

share *n* (part) la part *par*; (finance) l'action (*f*) *ak·syoñ* □ *vt* (money, room) partager* *par·ta·zhay*

shareholder *n* l'actionnaire (*m/f*) *ak·syo·nehr*

shark *n* le requin *ruh·kañ*

sharp *adj* (knife) tranchant(e) *troñ·shoñ(·shoñt)*; (bend) brusque *brōōsk*; (intelligent) pénétrant(e) *pay·nay·troñ(·troñt)*

sharp practice *n* les procédés malhonnêtes (*mpl*) *prō·say·day mal·o·net*

shave *vi* se raser *suh·ra·zay*

shaver *n* le rasoir électrique *ra·zwahr ay·lek·treek*

shaving brush *n* le blaireau *bleh·rō*

shaving cream *n* la crème à raser *krem a ra·zay*

shaving soap *n* le savon à barbe *sa·voñ a barb*

shawl *n* le châle *shahl*

she *pron* elle *el*; **here she is** la voici *la vwah·see*

sheath *n* (contraceptive) le préservatif *pray·zehr·va·teef*

shed *n* la remise *ruh·meez*

sheep *n* le mouton *moo·toñ*

sheepskin *n* la peau de mouton *pō duh moo·toñ*

sheer *adj* (stockings) très fin(e) *treh fañ (feen)*

sheet *n* le drap *dra*; (of paper) la feuille *fuhy*

shelf *n* l'étagère (*f*) *ay·ta·zhehr*

shell *n* (of egg) la coquille *ko·keey*; (of fish) le coquillage *ko·kee·yazh*

shellfish *n* (on menu) les fruits de mer (*mpl*) *frwee duh mehr*

shelter *n* (for waiting under) l'abri (*m*) *a·bree* □ *vi* (from rain etc) s'abriter *sa·bree·tay*

shelve *vi* (beach) descendre en pente douce *day·soñ·druh oñ poñt doos* □ *vt* (project) mettre* en sommeil *meh·troñ so·may*

sheriff *n* le shérif *shay·reef*

sherry *n* le sherry *sheh·ree*

shift *n* (change) le changement *shoñzh·moñ*; (of workmen) l'équipe (*f*) *ay·keep* □ *vt* **to shift gear** changer* de vitesse *shoñ·zhay duh vee·tes*

shin *n* la tibia *tee·bya*

shine *vi* briller *bree·yay*

shingles *n* (illness) le zona *zō·na*

shiny *adj* brillant(e) *bree·yoñ(·yoñt)*

ship *n* le bateau *ba·tō* □ *vt* (goods) transporter *troñ·spor·tay*

shipbuilding *n* la construction navale *koñ·strōōk·syoñ na·val*

shipment *n* la cargaison *kar·geh·zoñ*

shipping agent *n* l'agent maritime (*m*) *a·zhoñ ma·ree·teem*

shipping company *n* la compagnie de navigation *koñ·pa·nyee duh na·vee·ga·syoñ*

shipyard *n* le chantier naval *shoñ·tyay na·val*

shirt *n* la chemise *shuh·meez* S59, Sn69

shiver *vi* frissonner *free·so·nay*

shock *n* le choc *shok*; (electric) la décharge *day·sharzh*

shock absorber *n* l'amortisseur (*m*) *a·mor·tee·sur*

shoe *n* la chaussure *shō·sōōr*; (of brake) le sabot de frein *sa·bō duh frañ* S11

shoelace *n* le lacet *la·seh*

shoeshop *n* le magasin de chaussures *ma·ga·zañ duh shō·sōōr*

shoot *vt* (injure/kill) blesser/tuer d'un coup de fusil *bleh·say/tōō·ay duñ koo duh fōō·zee* □ *vi* tirer *tee·ray*

shop *n* le magasin *ma·ga·zañ*

shop assistant n le vendeur *voň·dur*, la vendeuse *voň·duhz*

shoplifting n le vol à l'étalage *vol a lay·ta·lazh*

shopping n les achats (mpl) *a·sha*; **to go shopping** faire* des achats *fehr day za·sha*

shopping bag n le cabas *ka·ba*

shopping centre n le centre commercial *soň·truh ko·mehr·syal*

shop-soiled adj qui a fait la vitrine *kee a feh la vee·treen*

shop steward n le/la délégué(e) syndical(e) *day·lay·gay saň·dee·kal*

shop window n la vitrine *vee·treen*

shore n (of sea) le rivage *ree·vazh*; (of lake) la rive *reev*

short adj court(e) à *koor (koort)*; (person) petit(e) *puh·tee(·teet)*; **to be short of something** être* à court de quelque chose *eh·truh a koor duh kel·kuh shōz*; **he gave me short change** il ne m'a pas donné mon dû *eel nuh ma pa do·nay moň dōō*

shortage n la pénurie *pay·nōō·ree*

shortbread n le sablé *sa·blay*

short cut n le raccourci *ra·koor·see* T127

short drink n le petit verre d'alcool *puh·tee vehr dal·kol*

shorten vt raccourcir *ra·koor·seer*

shortfall n le manque *moňk*

shorthand n la sténographie *stay·nō·gra·fee*

shorthand typist n le/la sténodactylo *stay·nō·dak·tee·lō*

short list n la liste des candidats sélectionnés *leest day koň·dee·da say·lek·syo·nay*

shortly adv (soon) bientôt *byaň·tō*

shorts pl le short *short*; (underwear) le slip *sleep*

shortsighted adj myope *myop*

short-staffed adj □ **to be short-staffed** manquer de personnel *moň·kay duh pehr·so·nel*

short term adj à court terme *a koor tehrm*

short wave n les ondes courtes (fpl) *oňd koort*

shot n (from gun) le coup *koo*

should vi □ **we should buy it** nous devrions l'acheter *noo duh·vryoň lash·tay*; **I should like a...** j'aimerais un... *zheh·muh·reh zuň*

shoulder n l'épaule (f) *ay·pōl*

shout n le cri *kree* □ vi crier *kree·ay*

shovel n la pelle *pel*

show n (exhibition) l'exposition (f) *ek·spo·zee·syoň*; (in theatre) le spectacle *spek·ta·kluh* □ vt montrer *moň·tray*; (movie) passer *pa·say*; **to show someone out** reconduire* quelqu'un jusqu'à la porte *ruh·koň·dweer kel·kuň zhōōs·ka la port* □ vi **to show** (be visible) se voir* *suh vwahr*

show business n le monde du spectacle *moňd dōō spek·ta·kluh*

shower n (rain) l'averse (f) *a·vehrs*; (bath) la douche *doosh* A4, 88

showroom n la salle d'exposition *sal dek·spo·zee·syoň*

shrewd adj astucieux(euse) *as·tōō·syuh(·syuhz)*

shrimp n la crevette *kruh·vet*

shrink vi rétrécir *ray·tray·seer*

shrinkage n le rétrécissement *ray·tray·sees·moň*

Shrove Tuesday n le mardi gras *mar·dee gra*

shrub n l'arbrisseau (m) *ar·bree·sō*

shrug vi hausser les épaules *ō·say lay zay·pōl*

shut vt/i fermer *fehr·may* □ adj fermé(e) *fehr·may*

shutter n (on window) le volet *vo·leh*; (in camera) l'obturateur (m) *op·tōō·ra·tur*

shuttle (service) n (airline) le service de navette *sehr·vees duh na·vet*

shy adj timide *tee·meed*

Sicily n la Sicile *see·seel*

sick adj (ill) malade *ma·lad*; **to be sick** (vomit) vomir *vo·meer*; **I feel sick** j'ai mal au cœur *zhay mal ō kur*

sickly adj (cake etc) écœurant(e) *ay·kuh·roň(·roňt)*

sickness n (illness) la maladie *ma·la·dee*; (nausea) la nausée *nō·zay*

side n le côté *kō·tay*; **the right side** (of cloth etc) l'endroit (m) *oň·drwah*; **the wrong side** l'envers (m) *oň·vehr*; **this side up** haut ō

sideboard n le buffet *bōō·feh*

sidelights pl (on car) les feux de position (mpl) *fuh duh pō·zee·syoň*

side-road, side-street n la petite route *puh·teet root*

sidewalk n le trottoir *tro·twahr*

siesta n la sieste *syest*

sieve n le tamis *ta·mee* □ vt tamiser *ta·mee·zay*

sift vt (sieve) passer au tamis *pa·say ō ta·mee*

sigh vi soupirer *soo·pee·ray*

sight n (spectacle) le spectacle *spek·ta·kluh*; **to have poor sight** avoir* une mauvaise vue *a·vwahr ōōn mō·vez vōō*; **to see the sights** visiter la ville *vee·zee·tay la veel*

sightseeing n le tourisme *too·reez·muh* S86

sign n le signe *see·nyuh*; (notice) le panneau *pa·nō* □ vt (document) signer *see·nyay* T195

signal n le signal *see·nyal*

signature n la signature *see·nya·tōōr*

signpost n le poteau indicateur *po·tō aň·dee·ka·tur*

silence n le silence *see·loňs*

silencer n (on car) le silencieux *see·loň·syuh*

silent adj silencieux(euse) *see·loň·syuh(·syuhz)*

silk n la soie *swah*; **a silk dress** une robe de soie *ōōn rob duh swah*

silly adj stupide *stōō·peed*

silver n (metal) l'argent (m) *ar·zhoň*; (money) la monnaie *mo·nay*; (ware) l'argenterie (f) *ar·zhoň·tree*; **a silver bracelet** un bracelet en argent *uň bras·leh oň nar·zhoň* S86

similar adj semblable *soň·bla·bluh*; **similar to** semblable à *soň·bla·bluh a*

simmer vi mijoter *mee·zho·tay*

simple adj simple *saň·pluh*

since prep depuis *duh·pwee*; **I've been here since 4 o'clock** je suis là depuis 4 heures *zhuh swee la duh·pwee 4 ur* □ conj **since we arrived** depuis que nous sommes arrivés *duh·pwee kuh noo som za·ree·vay*; **since he's ill** puisqu'il est malade *pwees·keel eh ma·lad*

sincere adj sincère *saň·sehr*

sincerely adv □ **yours sincerely** je vous prie d'agréer l'expression de mes sentiments les meilleurs *zhuh voo pree da·gray·yay lek·spreh·syoň duh may soň·tee·moň lay may·yur*

sing vt/i chanter *shoň·tay*

single adj (not double) simple *saň·pluh*; (not married) célibataire *say·*

lee·ba·tehr; **a single bed** un lit d'une personne *un leed dōōn pehr·son*; **a single room** une chambre pour une personne *ōōn shoñ·bruh poor ōōn pehr·son*; **a single ticket** un aller simple *uñ na·lay sañ·pluh*

sink n (basin) l'évier (m) *ay·vyay* □ vi (in water) couler *koo·lay*; (currency) baisser *beh·say*

sir n monsieur (m) *muh·syuh*

siren n la sirène *see·ren*

sirloin n l'aloyau (m) *a·lwah·yō*

sister n la sœur *sur*

sister-in-law n la belle-sœur *bel·sur*

sit vi s'asseoir* *sa·swahr*; **we were sitting at the table** nous étions assis à la table *noo zay·tyoñ za·see za la ta·bluh*; **to sit down** s'asseoir* *sa·swahr*

site n (of building) le site *seet*

sitting room n le salon *sa·loñ*

situation n la situation *see·tōō·a·syoñ*

six num six *sees*

sixteen num seize *sez*

sixteenth adj seizième *seh·zyem*

sixth adj sixième *see·zyem*

sixty num soixante *swah·soñt*

size n les dimensions (fpl) *dee·moñ·syoñ*; (of clothes) la taille *tye*; (of shoes) la pointure *pwañ·tōōr*

skate n le patin *pa·tañ*; (fish) la raie *reh* □ vi patiner *pa·tee·nay*

skateboard n la planche à roulettes *ploñsh a roo·let*

skating rink n la patinoire *pa·tee·nwahr*

sketch n (drawing) le croquis *kro·kee* □ vt faire* un croquis de *fehr uñ kro·kee duh*

skewer n la brochette *bro·shet*

ski n le ski *skee* □ vi faire* du ski *fehr dōō skee* L33

ski boot n la chaussure de ski *shō·sōōr duh skee*

skid n le dérapage *day·ra·pazh* □ vi déraper *day·ra·pay*

skier n le skieur *skee·ur*, la skieuse *skee·uhz*

skiing n le ski *skee*; **to go skiing** faire* du ski *fehr dōō skee*

ski lift n le remonte-pente *ruh·moñt·poñt*

skill n l'adresse (f) *a·dres*

skilled adj (workers) qualifié(e) *ka·lee·fyay*

skillet n le poêlon *pwah·loñ*

skim(med) milk n le lait écrémé *leh ay·kray·may*

skin n la peau *pō* S40

ski pants pl le fuseau *fōō·zō*

skirt n la jupe *zhōōp* Sn69

ski run n la piste de ski *peest duh skee*

skull n le crâne *krahn*

sky n le ciel *syel*

skyscraper n le gratte-ciel *grat·syel*

slack adj (loose) lâche *lash*; (business) faible *feh·bluh*

slacks pl le pantalon *poñ·ta·loñ*

slam vt claquer *kla·kay*

slang n l'argot (m) *ar·gō*

slap vt donner une claque à *do·nay ōōn klak a*

slate n l'ardoise (f) *ar·dwaz*

Slav n le/la Slave *slav*

slave n l'esclave (m/f) *es·klav*

sledge n (toboggan) le traîneau *treh·nō*

sleep n le sommeil *so·may* □ vi dormir* *dor·meer* □ vt **the apartment sleeps three** on peut coucher 3 personnes dans l'appartement *oñ puh koo·shay 3 pehr·son doñ la·par·tuh·moñ*

sleeper n (berth) la couchette *koo·shet*; (train) le train-couchettes *trañ·koo·shet*

sleeping bag n le sac de couchage *sak duh koo·shazh*

sleeping car n le wagon-couchettes *va·goñ·koo·shet*

sleeping pill n le somnifère *som·nee·fehr*

sleet n la neige fondue *nezh foñ·dōō*

sleeve n la manche *moñsh*

sleigh n le traîneau *treh·nō*

slice n la tranche *troñsh* □ vt couper en tranches *koo·pay oñ troñsh*

slide vi glisser *glee·say* □ n (chute) le toboggan *to·bo·goñ*; (photo) la diapositive *dya·po·zee·teev*

slide rule n la règle à calcul *reh·gla kal·kōōl*

slight adj (small) petit(e) *puh·tee(·teet)*

slim adj mince *mañs*

sling n (for arm) l'écharpe (f) *ay·sharp*

slip vi glisser *glee·say* □ n (underskirt) la combinaison *koñ·bee·neh·zoñ*; (of paper) la fiche *feesh*

slipper n la pantoufle *poñ·too·fluh*

slippery adj glissant(e) *glee·soñ(·soñt)*

slip-road n la bretelle d'accès *bruh·tel dak·seh*

slogan n le slogan *slō·goñ*

slope n la pente *poñt*

slot n la fente *foñt*

slot machine n la machine à sous *ma·sheen a soo*

slow adj lent(e) *loñ (loñt)*; **my watch is slow** ma montre retarde *ma moñ·truh ruh·tard* □ vi **to slow down** or **up** ralentir *ra·loñ·teer*

slump n l'effondrement (m) *eh·foñ·druh·moñ* □ vi s'effondrer *seh·foñ·dray*

smack vt gifler *zhee·flay* □ n la gifle *zheef·fluh*

small adj petit(e) *puh·tee(·teet)* A15

smallpox n la variole *va·ryol*

smart adj (elegant) élégant(e) *ay·lay·goñ(·goñt)*; (clever) intelligent(e) *añ·teh·lee·zhoñ(·zhoñt)*

smash vt briser *bree·zay*

smell n l'odeur (f) *o·dur* □ vt sentir* *soñ·teer* □ vi **to smell of garlic** sentir* l'ail *soñ·teer lye*

smile n le sourire *soo·reer* □ vi sourire* *soo·reer*

smock n la blouse *blooz*

smoke n la fumée *fōō·may* □ vt/i fumer *fōō·may* Mc36

smoked adj (salmon etc) fumé(e) *fōō·may*

smoker n (person) le fumeur *fōō·mur*; (compartment) le wagon fumeurs *va·goñ fōō·mur*

smooth adj lisse *lees*

smuggle vt passer en contrebande *pa·say oñ koñ·truh·boñd*

snack n le casse-croûte *kas·kroot*

snack bar n le snack *snak*

snail n l'escargot (m) *es·kar·gō*

snake n le serpent *sehr·poñ*

snap vi (break) se casser net *suh ka·say net*

snatch vt saisir *seh·zeer*

sneakers pl les tennis (fpl) *teh·nees*

sneeze n l'éternuement (m) *ay·tehr·nōō·moñ* □ vi éternuer *ay·tehr·nōō·ay*

snob n le/la snob *snob*

snobbish adj snob *snob*

snooker n le jeu de billards *zhuh duh bee·yar*

snore vi ronfler *roñ·flay*

snorkel *n* le tuba *tōō·ba*

snow *n* la neige *nezh* □ *vi* neiger *neh·zhay*; it's snowing il neige *eel nezh*

snowball *n* la boule de neige *bool duh nezh*

snowdrift *n* la congère *koñ·zhehr*

snowman *n* le bonhomme de neige *bo·nom duh nezh*

snowplough, snowplow *n* le chasse-neige *shas·nezh*

snuff *n* le tabac à priser *ta·ba a pree·zay*

so *adv* □ so pleased that... si content que... see *koñ·toñ kuh*; I hope so je l'espère *zhuh les·pehr*; so many/much tant (de) *toñ (duh)* □ *conj* et so we left nous sommes donc partis *noo som doñk par·tee*; so do I moi aussi *mwah ō·see*; so is he lui aussi *lwee ō·see*; he did it so that I would go il l'a fait pour que je parte *eel la feh poor kuh zhuh part*

soak *vt* (washing) faire* tremper *fehr troñ·pay*

soap *n* le savon *sa·voñ* A41

soap-flakes *pl* les paillettes de savon (*fpl*) *pye·yet duh sa·voñ*

soap powder *n* la lessive *leh·seev*

sober *adj* (not drunk) pas ivre *pa zee·vruh*

soccer *n* le football *foot·bal*

social *adj* social(e) *so·syal*

socialism *n* le socialisme *so·sya·leez·muh*

socialist *n* le/la socialiste *so·sya·leest* □ *adj* socialiste *so·sya·leest*

social security *n* la sécurité sociale *say·kōō·ree·tay so·syal*

social services *pl* les services sociaux (*mpl*) *sehr·vees so·syō*

social worker *n* l'assistant(e) social(e) (*m/f*) *a·see·stoñ(·stoñt) so·syal*

society *n* la société *so·syay·tay*; (association) l'association (*f*) *a·so·sya·syoñ*

sock *n* la chaussette *shō·set*

socket *n* (electrical) la prise de courant *preez duh koo·roñ*

soda *n* (chemical) la soude *sood*; a whisky and soda un whisky soda *uñ wee·skee sō·da*

soda water *n* l'eau de Seltz (*f*) *ō duh selts*

sofa *n* le canapé *ka·na·pay*

soft *adj* (not hard) mou *moo*, molle *mol*; (not loud) doux *doo*, douce *doos*; (drink) non alcoolisé(e) *noñ al·kol·ee·zay*

soft-boiled *adj* □ a soft-boiled egg un œuf à la coque *uñ nuhf a la kok*

software *n* le logiciel *lo·zhee·syel*

soil *n* le sol *sol*

solar *adj* solaire *so·lehr*

soldier *n* le soldat *sol·da*

sold out *adj* épuisé(e) *ay·pwee·zay*

sole *n* (of foot) la plante *ploñt*; (of shoe) la semelle *suh·mel*; (fish) la sole *sōl*

solicitor *n* le notaire *no·tehr*

solid *adj* (not hollow) plein(e) *plañ (plen)*; (not liquid, strong) solide *so·leed*; in solid gold en or massif *oñ nor ma·seef*

solution *n* la solution *so·lōō·syoñ*

solve *vt* (problem) résoudre* *ray·zoo·druh*

some *adj* □ some apples des pommes *day pom*; some bread du pain *dōō pañ* □ *pron* some (of it) was left il en restait un peu *eel oñ res·teh tuñ puh*; some (of them) were... certains d'en-

tre eux étaient... *sehr·tañ doñ·truh ay·teh*

somebody, someone *pron* quelqu'un *kel·kuñ*

something *pron* quelque chose *kel·kuh shōz*; something bigger quelque chose de plus grand *kel·kuh shōz duh plōō groñ*

sometimes *adv* quelquefois *kel·kuh·fwah*

somewhere *adv* quelque part *kel·kuh par*

son *n* le fils *fees* Sn88, C12

song *n* la chanson *shoñ·soñ*

son-in-law *n* le beau-fils *bō·fees*

soon *adv* bientôt *byañ·tō*; he came too soon il est venu trop tôt *eel eh vuh·nōō trō tō*

sophisticated *adj* (machine) sophistiqué(e) *sō·fees·tee·kay*; (person) raffiné(e) *ra·fee·nay*

sore *adj* (painful) douloureux(euse) *doo·loo·ruh(·ruhz)*

sorry *adj* désolé(e) *day·zo·lay*; (I'm) sorry excusez-moi *ek·skōō·zay·mwah*

sort *n* (kind) le genre *zhoñ·ruh*

SOS *n* le S.O.S. *es·ō·es*

soufflé *n* le soufflé *soo·flay*

soul *n* l'âme (*f*) *ahm*

sound *n* le son *soñ* □ *vi* it sounds like a car on dirait le bruit d'une voiture *oñ dee·reh luh brwee dōōn vwah·tōōr* □ *vt* to sound one's horn klaxonner *klak·so·nay*

sound track *n* la bande sonore *boñd so·nor*

soup *n* la soupe *soop* E21

sour *adj* (sharp) acide *a·seed*; (milk) tourné(e) *toor·nay*; sour(ed) cream la crème aigre *krem eh·gruh*

source *n* la source *soors*

south *n* le sud *sōōd* □ *adv* au sud *ō sōōd* □ *n* southeast le sud-est *sōōd·est*; southwest le sud-ouest *sōōd·west*

South Africa *n* l'Afrique du Sud (*f*) *a·freek dōō sōōd*

South African *adj* sud-africain(e) *sōōd·a·free·kañ(·ken)*

South America *n* l'Amérique du Sud (*f*) *a·may·reek dōō sōōd*

South American *adj* sud-américain(e) *sōōd·a·may·ree·kañ(·ken)*

southern *adj* du sud *dōō sōōd*

South Pole *n* le Pôle Sud *pōl sōōd*

souvenir *n* le souvenir *soo·vuh·neer*

Soviet *adj* soviétique *so·vyay·teek*

Soviet Union *n* l'Union Soviétique (*f*) *ōō·nyoñ so·vyay·teek*

soya beans *pl* les graines de soja (*fpl*) *gren duh so·ya*

soy(a) sauce *n* la sauce de soja *sōs duh so·ya*

spa *n* la station thermale *sta·syoñ tehr·mal*

space *n* l'espace (*m*) *e·spas*; (room) la place *plas*

spacecraft *n* l'engin spatial (*m*) *oñ·zhañ spa·syal*

spade *n* la bêche *besh*; spades (cards) le pique *peek*

spaghetti *n* les spaghettis (*mpl*) *spa·geh·tee*

Spain *n* l'Espagne (*f*) *es·pa·nyuh*

Spanish *adj* espagnol(e) *es·pa·nyol*; he's Spanish il est Espagnol *eel eh tes·pa·nyol*; she's Spanish elle est Espagnole *el eh tes·pa·nyol* □ *n* Spanish l'espagnol (*m*) *es·pa·nyol*

spanner *n* la clé *klay*

spare *adj* □ spare wheel la roue de secours *roo duh suh·koor*; spare time les moments de loisir *mo·moñ duh lwah·zeer* □ n **spare** (part) la pièce de rechange *pyes duh ruh·shoñzh*

spare rib n le travers de porc *tra·vehr duh por*

spark n l'étincelle (f) *ay·tañ·sel*

sparking plug n la bougie *boo·zhee*

sparkle vi étinceler* *ay·tañ·suh·lay*

sparkling adj (wine) mousseux(euse) *moo·suh(·suhz)*

sparrow n le moineau *mwah·nō*

spatula n la spatule *spa·tool*

speak vt/i parler *par·lay*; **do you speak English?** parlez-vous anglais? *par·lay voo zoñ·gleh*; **to speak to someone about something** parler de quelque chose à quelqu'un *par·lay duh kel·kuh shōz a kel·kuñ*

speaker n (electrical) le haut-parleur *ō·par·lur*

special adj spécial(e) *spay·syal*

specialize vi se spécialiser *suh spay·sya·lee·zay*; **to specialize in** se spécialiser en *suh spay·sya·lee·zay oñ*

specific adj précis(e) *pray·see(·seez)*

specifications pl les spécifications (fpl) *spay·see·fee·ka·syoñ*

specify vt préciser *pray·see·zay*

specimen n le spécimen *spay·see·men*; (medical) le prélèvement *pray·lev·moñ*

speech n la parole *pa·rol*; (oration) le discours *dees·koor*

speed n la vitesse *vee·tes* □ vi **to speed up** accélérer* *ak·say·lay·ray*

speedboat n le hors-bord *or·bor*

speeding n (in car) l'excès de vitesse (m) *ek·seh duh vee·tes*

speed limit n la limitation de vitesse *lee·mee·ta·syoñ duh vee·tes*

speedometer n le compteur *koñ·tur*

spell vt (in writing) écrire* *a·kreer* □ n (period) la courte période *koort pay·ryod*

spend vt (money) dépenser *day·poñ·say*; (time) passer *pa·say*

spice n l'épice (f) *a·pees*

spicy adj épicé(e) *ay·pee·say*

spider n l'araignée (f) *a·reh·nyay*

spill vt renverser *roñ·vehr·say* □ vi se répandre *suh ray·poñ·druh*

spin vi (rotate) tourner *toor·nay* □ vt (wool) filer *fee·lay*

spinach n les épinards (mpl) *ay·pee·nar*

spin(-dry) vt essorer *eh·so·ray*

spine n (backbone) la colonne vertébrale *ko·lon vehr·tay·bral*

spirit n (soul) l'esprit (m) *es·pree*; **spirits** (alcohol) les spiritueux (mpl) *spee·ree·tōō·uh*; **in good spirits** de bonne humeur *duh bon ōō·mur*

spit vi cracher *kra·shay* □ n (for roasting) la broche *brosh*

spite n la rancune *roñ·kōōn*; **in spite of** en dépit de *oñ day·pee duh*

splash n l'éclaboussement (m) *ay·kla·boos·moñ* □ vt éclabousser *ay·kla·boo·say* □ vi barboter *bar·bo·tay*

splint n l'éclisse (f) *a·klees*

splinter n (wood) l'écharde (f) *ay·shard*

split vt (tear) déchirer *day·shee·ray*; (divide, share) partager* *par·ta·zhay* □ vi (tear) se déchirer *suh day·shee·ray* □ n la déchirure *day·shee·rōōr*

spoil vt (damage) abîmer *a·bee·may*; (child) gâter *gah·tay*

spokesman n le porteparole *port·pa·rol*

sponge n l'éponge (f) *ay·poñzh*; (cake) le gâteau de Savoie *gah·tō duh sa·vwah*

sponge-bag n le sac de toilette *sak twah·let*

spoon n la cuiller *kwee·yehr*

spoonful n la cuillerée *kwee·yuh·ray*

sport n le sport *spor* L25, Mc20

sports car n la voiture de sport *vwah·tōōr duh spor*

sports coat, sports jacket n la veste de sport *vest duh spor*

sportswear n les vêtements de sport (mpl) *vet·moñ duh spor*

spot n (patch) la tache *tash*; (dot) le pois *pwah*; (pimple) le bouton *boo·toñ*; (locality) l'endroit (m) *oñ·drwah*; **on the spot** sur place *sōōr plas*

spot check n la vérification ponctuelle *vay·ree·fee·ka·syoñ poñk·tōō·el*

spotlight n le projecteur *pro·zhek·tur*

sprain n l'entorse (f) *oñ·tors* □ vt **to sprain one's ankle** se fouler la cheville *suh foo·lay la shuh·veey*

spray n (of liquid) le jet *zhay*; (container) le vaporisateur *va·po·ree·za·tur* □ vt (liquid) vaporiser *va·po·ree·zay*

spread vt étaler *ay·ta·lay*; (news) répandre *ray·poñ·druh*; **to spread something out** étendre quelque chose *ay·toñ·druh kel·kuh shōz*

spring n (season) le printemps *prañ·toñ*; (coil) le ressort *ruh·sor*; (of water) la source *soors*

spring onion n l'échalote (f) *ay·sha·lot*

sprinkle vt □ **to sprinkle with water** asperger* d'eau *a·spehr·zhay dō*; **to sprinkle with sugar** saupoudrer de sucre *sō·poo·dray duh sōō·kruh*

sprouts pl les choux de Bruxelles (mpl) *shoo duh brōō·sel*

spy n l'espion (m) *es·pyoñ*, l'espionne (f) *es·pyon*

squall n la rafale *ra·fal*

square n (carré) le carré *ka·ray*; (in town) la place *plas*; (math) le carré *ka·ray* □ adj carré(e) *ka·ray*; **a square metre** un mètre carré *uñ meh·truh ka·ray*; **3 metres square** 3 mètres sur 3 3 *meh·truh sōōr 3*

squash vt (crush) écraser *ay·kra·zay* □ n (sport) le squash *skwosh*; (gourd) la courge *koorzh*; **lemon squash** ≈ la citronnade *see·tro·nad*; **orange squash** ≈ l'orangeade (f) *o·roñ·zhad*

squeeze vt (lemon) presser *preh·say*; (hand) serrer *seh·ray* □ n (financial) les restrictions de crédit *ray·streek·syoñ duh kray·dee*

squirrel n l'écureuil (m) *ay·kōō·ruhy*

stab vt poignarder *pwa·nyar·day*

stable n l'écurie (f) *ay·kōō·ree* □ adj stable *sta·bluh*

stadium n le stade *stad*

staff n le personnel *pehr·so·nel*

stage n (in theatre) la scène *sen*; (point) l'étape (f) *ay·tap*; **in stages** par étapes *par ay·tap*

stain n la tache *tash* □ vt tacher *ta·shay* Sn70

stained glass window n le vitrail *vee·trye*

stainless adj (steel) inoxydable *een·ok·see·da·bluh*

stair n la marche *marsh*

staircase n l'escalier (m) *es·ka·lyay* I4

stairs pl l'escalier (m) *es·ka·lyay*

stake n (in gambling) l'enjeu (m) *oñ·*

zhuh; **to be at stake** être* en jeu *eh·troñ zhuh*

stale *adj* (*bread*) rassis(e) *ra·see('seez)*; **the room smells stale** cette pièce sent le renfermé *set pyes soñ luh roñ·fehr·may*

stall *n* (*stand*) l'éventaire (*m*) *ay·voñ·tehr* □ *vi* (*car engine*) caler *ka·lay*

stalls *pl* (*in theatre*) l'orchestre (*m*) *or·kes·truh*

stamp *n* le timbre *tañ·bruh* □ *vt* (*letter*) timbrer *tañ·bray*; (*visa*) viser *vee·zay* Sn2

stand *n* (*stall*) l'éventaire (*m*) *ay·voñ·tehr* □ *vi* être* debout *eh·truh duh·boo*; **to stand up** se mettre* debout *suh·meh·truh duh·boo* □ *vt* **stand** (*put*) poser *pô·zay*; (*bear*) supporter *sôo·por·tay*; **to stand for** (*signify*) représenter *ruh·pray·zoñ·tay*; **to stand out** ressortir* *ruh·sor·teer*

standard *n* le niveau *nee·vô* □ *adj* (*size*) normal(e) *nor·mal*; (*model*) standard *stoñ·dar*

standard lamp *n* le lampadaire *loñ·pa·dehr*

standard of living *n* le niveau de vie *nee·vô duh vee*

standing order *n* le virement automatique *veer·moñ ô·tô·ma·teek*

staple *n* l'agrafe (*f*) *a·graf*

stapler *n* l'agrafeuse (*f*) *a·gra·fuhz*

star *n* l'étoile (*f*) *ay·twahl*; (*celebrity*) la vedette *vuh·det*

starch *n* l'amidon (*m*) *a·mee·doñ*

stare (at) *vt/i* regarder fixement *ruh·gar·day feeks·moñ*

start *vt/i* commencer* *ko·moñ·say* □ *n* (*beginning*) le commencement *ko·moñ·suh·moñ*

starter *n* (*in car*) le démarreur *day·ma·rur*; (*hors d'œuvre*) le hors d'œuvre *or·duh·vruh*

starve *vi* être* affamé(e) *e·truh a·fa·may*; **to be starving** mourir* de faim *moo·reer duh fañ*

state *vt* déclarer *day·kla·ray* □ *n* (*condition*) l'état (*m*) *ay·ta*; **the State** l'État (*m*) *ay·ta*; **the States** les États-Unis (*mpl*) *ay·ta·zôo·nee*

statement *n* la déclaration *day·kla·ra·syoñ*

station *n* la gare *gar*; (*radio*) la station de radio *sta·syoñ duh ra·dyo* F3

stationer's (shop) *n* la papeterie *pap·tree*

stationery *n* le papier à lettres *pa·pyay a leh·truh*

station wagon *n* le break *brek*

statistic *n* la statistique *sta·tees·teek*

statistical *adj* statistique *sta·tees·teek*

statistics *n* la statistique *sta·tees·teek*

statue *n* la statue *sta·tôo*

stay *n* (*period*) le séjour *say·zhoor* □ *vi* rester *res·tay*; (*reside*) séjourner *say·zhoor·nay*; **to stay the night** passer la nuit *pa·say la nwee*; **to stay with friends** loger* chez des amis *lo·zhay shay day za·mee*; **to stay in** rester à la maison *res·tay a la meh·zoñ*; **to stay up** (*at night*) se coucher tard, se coucher *nuh pah suh koo·shay* A2, 55

S.T.D. *n* l'automatique (*m*) *ô·tô·ma·teek*

steady *adj* stable *sta·bluh*; (*pace*) régulier(ière) *ray·gôo·lyay(·lyehr)*

steak *n* le bifteck *beef·tek* E23

steal *vt* voler *vo·lay*; **to steal something from someone** voler quelque chose à quelqu'un *vo·lay kel·kuh shôz a kel·kuñ*

steam *n* la vapeur *va·pur* □ *vt* (*food*) cuire* à la vapeur *kweer a la va·pur*

steamer *n* (*ship*) le vapeur *va·pur*

steel *n* l'acier (*m*) *a·syay*

steep *adj* raide *red*

steer *vt* (*car*) conduire* *koñ·dweer*; (*boat*) diriger* *dee·ree·zhay*

steering *n* (*in car*) la conduite *koñ·dweet*

steering column *n* la colonne de direction *ko·lon duh dee·rek·syoñ*

steering-wheel *n* le volant *vo·loñ*

stem *n* la tige *teezh*

stenographer *n* le/la sténodactylo *stay·nô·dak·tee·lô*

step *n* (*pace*) le pas *pa*; (*stair*) la marche *marsh*; **to take steps to do something** prendre* des mesures pour faire quelque chose *proñ·druh day muh·zôor poor fehr kel·kuh shôz*

stepbrother *n* le demi-frère *duh·mee·frehr*

stepdaughter *n* la belle-fille *bel·feey*

stepfather *n* le beau-père *bô·pehr*

stepladder *n* l'escabeau (*m*) *es·ka·bô*

stepmother *n* la belle-mère *bel·mehr*

stepsister *n* la demi-sœur *duh·mee·sur*

stepson *n* le beau-fils *bô·fees*

stereo(phonic) *adj* stéréophonique *stay·ray·ô·fo·neek* □ *n* la stéréo *stay·ray·ô*; **in stereo** en stéréo *oñ stay·ray·ô*

sterile *adj* stérile *stay·reel*

sterilize *vt* (*disinfect*) stériliser *stay·ree·lee·zay*

sterling *n* la livre sterling *lee·vruh stehr·leeng*

stew *n* le ragoût *ra·goo*

steward *n* le steward *stôo·ar*; (*at club*) l'intendant (*m*) *añ·toñ·doñ*

stewardess *n* l'hôtesse (*f*) *ô·tes*

stick *n* le bâton *bah·toñ* □ *vt* (*with glue etc*) coller *ko·lay*

sticking-plaster *n* le sparadrap *spa·ra·dra*

sticky *adj* poisseux(euse) *pwah·suh(·suhz)*

stiff *adj* raide *red*; **a stiff neck** le torticolis *tor·tee·ko·lee*

stiletto heels *pl* les talons aiguilles (*mpl*) *ta·loñ zay·gweey*

still *adj* (*motionless*) immobile *ee·mo·beel*; (*wine etc*) non gazeux(euse) *noñ ga·zuh(·zuhz)* □ *adv* (*up to this time*) encore *oñ·kor*; (*nevertheless*) tout de même *too duh mem*

sting *vt/i* piquer *pee·kay* □ *n* la piqûre *pee·kôor*

stipulate *vt* stipuler *stee·pôo·lay*

stipulation *n* la stipulation *stee·pôo·la·syoñ*

stir *vt* remuer *ruh·môo·ay*

stitch *n* (*sewing*) le point *pwañ*; (*pain*) le point de côté *pwañ duh kô·tay*

stock *vt* (*have in shop*) avoir* *a·vwahr* □ *n* (*supply*) la réserve *ray·zehrv*; (*in shop*) le stock *stok*; (*for soup etc*) le bouillon *boo·yoñ*; **stocks** (*financial*) les valeurs (*fpl*) *va·lur*; **in stock** en stock *oñ stok*; **out of stock** épuisé(e) *ay·pwee·zay*

stockbroker *n* l'agent de change (*m*) *a·zhoñ duh shoñzh*

stock exchange *n* la Bourse *boors*

stocking *n* le bas *bah*

stockist *n* le stockiste *sto·keest*

stock market *n* la Bourse *boors*

stocktaking *n* l'inventaire (*m*) *añ·voñ·tehr*

stole *n* (*wrap*) l'étole (*f*) *ay·tôl*

stomach *n* l'estomac (*m*) *es·to·ma* S37

stomach ache *n* le mal au ventre *mal ŏ voñ·truh*; **I have (a) stomach ache** j'ai mal au ventre *zhay mal ŏ voñ·truh*

stone *n* la pierre *pyehr*; *(in fruit)* le noyau *nwah·yŏ*; *(weight)* ≈ 6,35 kilo

stony *adj* pierreux(euse) *pyeh·ruh (·ruhz)*

stool *n* le tabouret *ta·boo·reh*

stop *n (bus stop)* l'arrêt *(m) a·reh* □ *vi* s'arrêter *sa·reh·tay*; **to stop doing something** arrêter de faire quelque chose *a·reh·tay duh fehr kel·kuh shŏz* □ *vt* **stop** arrêter *a·reh·tay*; **to stop someone doing something** empêcher quelqu'un de faire quelque chose *añ·peh·shay kel·kuñ duh fehr kel·kuh shŏz*; **to stop a cheque** faire* opposition à un chèque *fehr o·pŏ·zee·syoñ a uñ shek* T82

stopcock *n* le robinet d'arrêt *ro·bee·neh da·reh*

stoplights *pl* les voyants *(mpl) vwah·yoñ*

stopover *n (air travel)* l'escale *(f) es·kal*

stopper *n* le bouchon *boo·shoñ*

stop watch *n* le chronomètre *kro·nŏ·meh·truh*

store *vt* mettre* en réserve *meh·troñ ray·zehrv* □ *(stock)* la réserve *ray·zehrv*; *(shop)* le magasin *ma·ga·zañ*; *(big shop)* le grand magasin *groñ ma·ga·zañ*; *(warehouse)* l'entrepôt *(m) oñ·truh·pŏ*

store room *n* la réserve *ray·zehrv*

storey *n* l'étage *(m) ay·tazh*

storm *n* la tempête *toñ·pet*

stormy *adj* orageux(euse) *o·ra·zhuh (·zhuhz)*

story *n* l'histoire *(f) ees·twahr*

stove *n* le poêle *pwahl*

straight *adj* droit(e) *drwah (drwaht)*; *(drink)* sans eau *soñ zŏ* □ *adv (shoot, write etc)* droit *drwah*; **to go straight home** aller* directement à la maison *a·lay dee·rek·tuh·moñ a la meh·zoñ*; **straight away** tout de suite *too duh sweet* F23

strain *vt (tea etc)* passer *pa·say*; *(muscle)* froisser *frwah·say*

strainer *n* la passoire *pa·swahr*

strange *adj (unknown)* inconnu(e) *añ·ko·nŏŏ*; *(unusual)* étrange *ay·troñzh*

stranger *n* l'étranger *(m) ay·troñ·zhay*, l'étrangère *(f) ay·troñ·zhehr*

strangle *vt* étrangler *ay·troñ·glay*

strap *n* la courroie *koo·rwah*

strapless *adj* sans bretelles *soñ bruh·tel*

straw *n* la paille *pye*

strawberry *n* la fraise *frez*

streak *n* la raie *ray*

stream *n* le ruisseau *rwee·sŏ*

streamlined *adj (car)* aérodynamique *a·ehr·o·dee·na·meek*

street *n* la rue *rŏŏ* F27

streetcar *n* le tramway *tram·way*

streetlamp *n* le réverbère *ray·vehr·behr*

strength *n (of girder, rope etc)* la force *fors*; *(of rope etc)* la solidité *so·lee·dee·tay*

strengthen *vt* renforcer* *roñ·for·say*

stress *n (emphasis)* l'insistance *(f) añ·sees·toñs*; *(tension)* la tension nerveuse *toñ·syoñ nehr·vuhz*

stretch *vt (fabric etc)* tendre *toñ·druh* □ *vi* s'étirer *say·tee·ray*

stretcher *n* le brancard *broñ·kar*

strict *adj* strict(e) *streekt*

strike *vt (hit)* frapper *fra·pay*; *(match)* frotter *fro·tay*; **the clock struck three** la pendule a sonné trois heures *la*

poñ·dŏŏl a so·nay trwah zur □ *vi* **strike** *(workers)* faire* grève *fehr grev* □ *n (industrial)* la grève *grev*; **on strike** en grève *oñ grev*

strikebound *adj* immobilisé(e) par une grève *ee·mo·bee·lee·zay par ŏŏn grev*

strike-breaker *n* le briseur de grève *bree·zur duh grev*

striker *n* le/la gréviste *gray·veest*

string *n* la ficelle *fee·sel*; *(of instrument)* la corde *kord*

string bag *n* le filet à provisions *fee·leh a pro·vee·zyoñ*

strip *n (stripe, length)* la bande *boñd*

stripe *n* la raie *ray*

strip-lighting *n* l'éclairage au néon *(m) ay·kleh·razh ŏ nay·oñ*

stripper *n* la strip-teaseuse *streep·tee·zuhz*

striptease *n* le strip-tease *streep·teez*

stroke *vt* caresser *ka·reh·say* □ *n (swimming)* la nage *nazh*; *(golf)* le coup *koo*; *(illness)* l'attaque d'apoplexie *(f) a·tak da·po·plek·see*

stroll *n* la petite promenade *puh·teet pro·muh·nad*; **to go for a stroll** aller* faire un tour *a·lay fehr uñ toor*

stroller *n* la poussette *poo·set*

strong *adj (person)* fort(e) *for*; *(structure, material)* solide *so·leed*; **it has a strong smell** ça sent fort *sa soñ for*

strongbox *n* le coffre-fort *ko·fruh·for*

strongroom *n* la chambre forte *shoñ·bruh fort*

structure *n* la structure *strŏŏk·tŏŏr*; *(building)* l'édifice *(m) ay·dee·fees*

struggle *n* la lutte *lŏŏt* □ *vi (physically)* lutter *lŏŏ·tay*; **to struggle to do something** se démener* pour faire quelque chose *suh day·muh·nay poor fehr kel·kuh shŏz*

stub *n (counterfoil)* le talon *ta·loñ*

stubborn *adj* têtu(e) *teh·tŏŏ*

stuck *adj* coincé(e) *kwañ·say*

stud *n* le clou *kloo*; *(for collar)* le bouton de col *boo·toñ duh kol*

student *n* l'étudiant(e) *(m/f) ay·tŏŏ·dyoñ(·dyoñt)* M5

studio *n* le studio *stŏŏ·dyŏ*

study *vt/i* étudier *ay·tŏŏ·dyay* □ *n (room)* le bureau *bŏŏ·rŏ*; **to enjoy one's studies** aimer bien ses études *ay·may byañ say zay·tŏŏd*

stuff *n (things)* les affaires *(fpl) a·fehr*; *(substance)* la substance *sŏŏp·stoñs*

stuffed *adj (cushion etc)* rembourré(e) *roñ·boo·ray*; *(chicken)* farci(e) *far·see*

stuffing *n (in chicken etc)* la farce *fars*

stuffy *adj* mal ventilé(e) *mal voñ·tee·lay*

stun *vt* étourdir *ay·toor·deer*

stupid *adj* stupide *stŏŏ·peed*

style *n* le style *steel*

stylish *adj* élégant(e) *ay·lay·goñ(·goñt)*

subcommittee *n* le sous-comité *soo·ko·mee·tay*

subcontract *n* le sous-traité *soo·treh·tay*

subcontractor *n* le sous-traitant *soo·treh·toñ*

subject *n* le sujet *sŏŏ·zheh*; *(in school)* la matière *ma·tyehr* □ *adj* **subject to** sous réserve de *soo ray·zehrv duh*

submarine *n* le sous-marin *soo·ma·rañ*

submit *vt (proposal)* soumettre* *soo·meh·truh*

subordinate *adj* subalterne *sŏŏ·bal·tehrn* □ *n* le/la subordonné(e) *sŏŏ·bor·do·nay*

subscriber *n* l'abonné(e) (*m/f*) *a·bo· nay*

subscribe to *vt* (*periodical*) être* abonné(e) à *eh·truh a·bo·nay a*

subscription *n* (*to periodical*) l'abonnement (*m*) *a·bon·moñ*; (*to club*) la cotisation *ko·tee·za·syoñ*

subsidiary *adj* subsidiaire *sōōp·see· dyehr* □ *n* (*company*) la filiale *feel· yal*

subsidize *vt* subventionner *sōōb·voñ· syo·nay*

subsidy *n* la subvention *sōōb·voñ·syoñ*

substance *n* la substance *sōōp·stoñs*

substandard *adj* inférieur(e) *añ·fay· ryur*

substitute *n* le/la remplaçant(e) *roñ· pla·soñ(·soñt)*

subtitle *n* (*of movie*) le sous-titre *soo· tee·truh*

subtle *adj* subtil(e) *sōōp·teel*

subtotal *n* le total partiel *to·tal par·syel*

subtract *vt* soustraire* *soos·trehr*

suburb *n* le faubourg *fō·boor*; **the suburbs** la banlieue *boñ·lyuh*

suburban *adj* de banlieue *duh boñ· lyuh*

subway *n* (*underground passage*) le passage souterrain *pa·sazh soo·tay· rañ*; (*railway*) le métro *may·trō*

succeed *vi* réussir *ray·ōō·seer*; **he succeeded in doing it** il a réussi à le faire *eel a ray·ōō·see a luh fehr*

success *n* le succès *sōōk·seh*

successful *adj* (*venture*) couronné(e) de succès *koo·ro·nay duh sōōk·seh*; (*businessman*) prospère *pros·pehr*

such *adj* tel(le) *tel*; **such a lot of** tant de *toñ duh*; **such a book** un tel livre *uñ tel lee·vruh*; **such books** de tels livres *duh tel lee·vruh*; **such kindness** une telle gentillesse *ōōn tel zhoñ·tee·yes*

suck *vt* sucer* *sōō·say*

sudden *adj* soudain(e) *soo·dañ(·den)*

suddenly *adv* soudain *soo·dañ*

sue *vt* poursuivre* en justice *poor· swee·vroñ zhōōs·tees*

suede *n* le daim *dañ*

suet *n* la graisse de rognon *gres duh ro·nyoñ*

suffer *vi* souffrir* *soo·freer* □ *vt* (*pain, grief*) subir* *sōō·beer*

sugar *n* le sucre *sōō·kruh* S31

sugar bowl *n* le sucrier *sōō·kree·ay*

suggest *vt* suggérer* *sōōg·zhay·ray*

suggestion *n* la suggestion *sōōg·zhes· tyoñ*

suicide *n* le suicide *sōō·ee·seed*

suit *n* (*men's*) le costume *kos·tōōm*; (*women's*) le tailleur *tye·yur*; (*cards*) la couleur *koo·lur*; (*astronaut, diver*) la combinaison *koñ·bee·neh·zoñ* □ *vt* **that hat suits you** ce chapeau vous va *suh sha·pō voo va*; **does Thursday suit you?** est-ce que jeudi vous convient? *es·kuh zhuh·dee voo koñ·vyañ*

suitable *adj* (*person*) approprié(e) *a·pro·pree· ay*; (*fitting*) convenable *koñ·vuh·na· bluh*

suitcase *n* la valise *va·leez* T31f

sultana *n* le raisin sec *reh·zañ sek*

sum *n* (*total amount*) la somme *som*; (*problem*) le calcul *kal·kōōl*

summary *n* le résumé *ray·zōō·may*

summer *n* l'été (*m*) *ay·tay*

summons *n* l'assignation (*f*) *a·see·nya· syoñ*

sump *n* (*in car*) le carter *kar·tehr*

sum total *n* la somme totale *som to·tal*

sun *n* le soleil *so·lay*

sunbathe *vi* prendre* un bain de soleil *proñ·druñ bañ duh so·lay*

sunburn *n* (*painful*) le coup de soleil *koo duh so·lay* S40

sunburnt *adj* bronzé(e) *broñ·zay*; (*painfully*) brûlé(e) par le soleil *brōō·lay par luh so·lay*

Sunday *n* dimanche (*m*) *dee·moñsh*

sun dress *n* la robe bain de soleil *rob bañ duh so·lay*

sunglasses *pl* les lunettes (*fpl*) de soleil *lōō·net duh so·lay* S7

sun-hat *n* le chapeau de soleil *sha·pō duh so·lay*

sunlamp *n* la lampe à rayons ultraviolets *loñp a ray·yoñ zōōl·tra·vyo·leh*

sunny *adj* ensoleillé(e) *oñ·so·lay·yay*

sunrise *n* le lever du soleil *luh·vay dōō so·lay*

sunroof *n* le toit ouvrant *twah oo·vroñ*

sunset *n* le coucher du soleil *koo·shay dōō so·lay*

sunshade *n* (*over table*) le parasol *pa· ra·sol*

sunshine *n* le soleil *so·lay*

sunstroke *n* l'insolation (*f*) *añ·so·la· syoñ* I36

suntan *n* le bronzage *broñ·zazh*

sun-tanned *adj* bronzé(e) *broñ·zay*

suntan oil *n* l'huile solaire (*f*) *weel so· lehr*

sun visor *n* (*in car*) la visière *vee·zyehr*

superannuation *n* la pension de retraite *poñ·syoñ duh ruh·tret*

superior *adj* (*quality*) supérieur(e) *sōō· pay·ryur* □ *n* le/la supérieur(e) *sōō· pay·ryur*

supermarket *n* le supermarché *sōō· pehr·mar·shay*

superstition *n* la superstition *sōō·pehr· stee·syoñ*

superstore *n* l'hypermarché (*m*) *ee· pehr·mar·shay*

supertanker *n* le pétrolier géant *pay· trol·yay zhay·oñ*

supervise *vt* surveiller *sōōr·vay·yay*

supervisor *n* le/la surveillant(e) *sōōr· vay·yoñ(·yoñt)*

supper *n* (*main meal*) le dîner *dee·nay*; (*snack*) le souper *soo·pay*

supply *vt* (*goods*) fournir* *foor·neer*; **to supply someone with something** fournir quelqu'un en quelque chose *foor· neer kel·kuñ oñ kel·kuh shōz* □ *n* (*stock*) la provision *pro·vee· zyoñ*; **supply and demand** l'offre et la demande *lo·fruh ay la duh·moñd*

support *vt* soutenir* *soo·tuh·neer*; (*financially*) subvenir* aux besoins de *sōōb·vuh·neer ō boh·zwañ duh* □ *n* (*moral, financial*) le soutien *soo·tyañ*

suppose *vt* supposer *sōō·po·zay*; **he's supposed to be an engineer** il est censé être ingénieur *eel eh soñ·say eh·truh añ·zhay·nyur*; **you're supposed to do it today** vous devriez le faire aujourd'hui *voo duh·vree·ay luh fehr ō·zhoor·dwee*

suppository *n* le suppositoire *sōō·po· zee·twahr*

surcharge *n* la surcharge *sōōr·sharzh*

sure *adj* (*person*) sûr(e) *sōōr*; (*fact*) certain(e) *sehr·tañ(·ten)*; **it's sure to work** ça marchera à coup sûr *sa mar· shuh·ra a koo sōōr*; **he's sure to come** il est sûr de venir *eel eh sōōr duh vuh·neer*

surely *adv* sûrement *sōōr·moñ*

surface *n* la surface *sōōr·fas*

surface mail *n* □ **to send something surface mail** envoyer quelque chose par voie de terre *on·vwah·yay kel·kuh shōz par vwah duh tehr*

surf board *n* la planche de surf *plonsh duh surf*

surfing *n* le surf *surf*; **to go surfing** faire* du surf *fehr doo surf*

surgeon *n* le chirurgien *shee·rōor·zhee·an*

surgery *n* (*operation*) la chirurgie *shee·rōor·zhee*; (*place*) le cabinet de consultation *ka·bee·neh duh kon·sōol·ta·syon*

surname *n* le nom de famille *non duh fa·meey*

surplus *n* le surplus *sōor·plōo*

surprise *vt* surprendre* *sōor·pron·druh* □ *n* la surprise *sōor·preez*

surprised *adj* surpris(e) *sōor·pree (·preez)*; **surprised at** surpris(e) par *sōor·pree(·preez) par*

surround *vt* entourer *on·too·ray*

surroundings (*pl* *mpl*) *on·vee·ron*

survey *n* (*of land*) le levé *luh·vay*; (*of building*) la visite d'expert *vee·zeet dek·spehr*

surveyor *n* l'expert (*m*) *ek·spehr*

survive *vi* survivre* *sōor·vee·vruh*; (*custom*) subsister *sōop·sees·tay*

suspend *vt* (*worker*) suspendre* *sōos·pon·druh*

suspenders *pl* (*for stockings*) les jarretelles (*fpl*) *zhar·tel*

suspension *n* (*on car*) la suspension *sōos·pon·syon*

swallow *vt/i* avaler *a·va·lay*

swamp *n* le marais *ma·reh*

swan *n* le cygne *see·nyuh*

sway *vi* (*person*) balancer* *ba·lon·say*; (*building, bridge*) tanguer *ton·gay*

swear *vi* jurer *zhōo·ray*

sweat *n* la sueur *sōo·ur* □ *vi* suer *sōo·ay*

sweater *n* le pull *pōol* S57

sweatshirt *n* le sweat-shirt *swet·shirt*

Swede *n* le/la Suédois(e) *sweh·dwah (·dwaz)*

swede *n* le rutabaga *rōo·ta·ba·ga*

Sweden *n* la Suède *swed*

Swedish *adj* suédois(e) *sway·dwah (·dwaz)* □ *n* le suédois *sway·dwah*

sweep *vt* (*floor*) balayer *ba·lay·yay*

sweet *n* (*candy*) le bonbon *bon·bon*; (*dessert*) le dessert *deh·sehr* □ *adj* (*taste, food*) sucré(e) *sōo·kray*; (*smell*) agréable *a·gray·a·bluh*; (*music*) mélodieux(euse) *may·lo·dyuh(·dyuz)*; (*cute, pretty*) mignon(ne) *mee·nyon(·nyon)*; (*kind*) gentil(le) *zhon·teey*

sweet corn *n* le maïs doux *ma·ees doo*

sweet potato *n* la patate douce *pa·tat doos*

swell (up) *vi* (*limb etc*) enfler *on·flay* I29

swelling *n* (*lump*) l'enflure (*f*) *on·flōor*

swerve *vi* faire* une embardée *fehr ōon on·bar·day*

swim *vi* nager* *na·zhay* □ *vt* **to swim the Channel** traverser la Manche à la nage *tra·vehr·say la monsh a la nazh* L19

swimming *n* la natation *na·ta·syon*; **to go swimming** aller* se baigner *a·lay suh beh·nyay*

swimming pool *n* la piscine *pee·seen* L26

swimming trunks *pl* le caleçon de bain *kal·son duh ban*

swimsuit *n* le maillot de bain *mye·yō duh ban*

swing *n* la balançoire *ba·lon·swahr* □ *vi* se balancer* *suh ba·lon·say* □ *vt* balancer* *ba·lon·say*

Swiss *adj* suisse *swees*; **(s)he's Swiss** elle/il est Suisse *el/eel eh swees*

switch *n* le bouton *boo·ton* □ *vt* **to switch on** (*light*) allumer *a·lōo·may*; (*engine*) mettre* en marche *meh·tron marsh*; (*TV*) mettre* *meh·truh*; **to switch off** éteindre* *ay·tan·druh*; (*engine*) arrêter *a·reh·tay* B72

switchboard *n* le standard *ston·dar*

switchboard operator *n* le/la standardiste *ston·dar·deest*

Switzerland *n* la Suisse *swees*; **in/to Switzerland** en Suisse *on swees*

swollen *adj* enflé(e) *on·flay*

sword *n* l'épée (*f*) *ay·pay*

syllable *n* la syllabe *see·lab*

syllabus *n* le programme *pro·gram*

symbol *n* le symbole *san·bol*

symmetrical *adj* symétrique *see·may·treek*

sympathetic *adj* compatissant(e) *kon·pa·tee·son(·sont)*

sympathy *n* la compassion *kon·pa·syon*

symphony *n* la symphonie *san·fo·nee*

symposium *n* le symposium *san·pō·zyum*

symptom *n* le symptôme *sanp·tōm*

synagogue *n* la synagogue *see·na·gog*

synchromesh *n* la synchronisation *san·kro·nee·za·syon*

syndicate *n* le syndicat *san·dee·ka*

synthetic *adj* synthétique *san·tay·teek*

Syria *n* la Syrie *see·ree*

Syrian *adj* syrien(ne) *see·ree·an(·en)*

syrup *n* le sirop *see·rō*; (*golden*) **syrup** la mélasse raffinée *may·las ra·fee·nay*

system *n* le système *sees·tem*

systematic *adj* systématique *sees·tay·ma·teek*

systems analyst *n* l'analyste-programmeur (*m/f*) *a·na·leest·pro·gra·mur*

T

tab *n* l'étiquette (*f*) *ay·tee·ket*

table *n* la table *ta·bluh*; (*chart*) le tableau *ta·blō* E2f

tablecloth *n* la nappe *nap*

table-mat *n* le dessous-de-plat *duh·soo·duh·pla*

tablespoon *n* la grande cuillère *grond kwee·yehr*; (*measure*) la cuillerée à soupe *kwee·yeh·ray a soop*

tablet *n* (*medicine*) le comprimé *kon·pree·may*

table tennis *n* le ping-pong *peeng·pong*

tack *n* (*nail*) le petit clou *puh·tee kloo* □ *vi* (*sailing*) tirer des bords *tee·ray day bor*

tackle *vt* (*problem*) s'attaquer à *sa·ta·kay a*; (*in sports*) plaquer *pla·kay* □ *n* (*gear*) le matériel *ma·tay·ryel*

tactics *pl* la tactique *tak·teek*

tag *n* l'étiquette (*f*) *ay·tee·ket*

tail *n* la queue *kuh*

tailback *n* le bouchon *boo·shon*

tailcoat *n* l'habit (*m*) *a·bee*

tailgate *n* (*of car*) le hayon (arrière) *ay·yon (a·ryehr)*

tailor *n* le tailleur *tye·yur*

take *vt* prendre* *pron·druh*; (*win: prize*) remporter *ron·por·tay*; **he took it from me** il me l'a pris *eel muh la pree*; **to take someone to the station** conduire* quelqu'un à la gare *kon·dweer kel·kun a la gar*; **take this**

to the post office portez ceci à la poste *por·tay suh·see a la post*; **I'm taking French at school** j'apprends le français à l'école *zha·proñ luh froñ·seh a lay·kol*; **to take an exam** passer un examen *pa·say uñ neg·za·mañ*; **it takes a lot of effort** ça demande un grand effort *sa duh·moñd uñ groñ tef·for*; **to take something away** enlever* quelque chose *oñ·luh·vay kel·kuh shōz*; **to take something back** (*return*) rendre quelque chose *roñ·druh kel·kuh shōz*; **to take off** (*clothes*) enlever* *oñ·luh·vay*; (*plane*) décoller *day·ko·lay*; **to take someone out to the theatre** emmener* quelqu'un au théâtre *oñ·muh·nay kel·kuñ ō tay·ah·truh*; **to have a tooth taken out** se faire* arracher une dent *suh fehr a·ra·shay ōōn doñ*; **to take over a firm** absorber une firme *ap·sor·bay ōōn feerm*; **to take up a sport** se mettre* à un sport *suh meh·tra uñ spor*

take-away *adj* (*food*) à emporter *a oñ·por·tay*

take-home pay *n* le salaire net *sa·lehr net*

takeoff *n* (*of plane*) le décollage *day·ko·lazh*

takeover *n* l'absorption (*f*) *ap·sorp·syoñ*

take-over bid *n* l'offre publique d'achat (*f*) *o·fruh pōō·bleek da·sha*

talc(um powder) *n* le talc *talk*

talent *n* le talent *ta·loñ*

talk *vi* parler *par·lay*; **to talk to someone about something** parler à quelqu'un de quelque chose *par·lay a kel·kuñ duh kel·kuh shōz*; **to talk something over** discuter de quelque chose *dee·skōō·tay duh kel·kuh shōz* □ *vt* **to talk nonsense** dire* des bêtises *deer day beh·teez* □ *n* **talk** (*conversation*) l'entretien (*m*) *oñ·truh·tyañ*; (*lecture*) l'exposé (*m*) *ek·spō·zay*; **talks** (*negotiations*) les pourparlers (*mpl*) *poor·par·lay*

tall *adj* grand(e) *groñ* (*groñd*); **how tall are you?** combien mesurez-vous? *koñ·byañ muh·zōō·ray·voo*

tame *adj* (*animal*) apprivoisé(e) *a·pree·vwah·zay*

tan *adj* brun roux *bruñ roo* □ *n* (*on skin*) le bronzage *broñ·zazh* □ *vi* (*in sun*) bronzer *broñ·zay*

tangerine *n* la mandarine *moñ·da·reen*

tangle *vt* emmêler *oñ·may·lay*

tango *n* le tango *toñ·gō*

tank *n* (*of car*) le réservoir *ray·zehr·vwahr*; (*military*) le char d'assaut *shar da·sō*

tanker *n* (*ship*) le pétrolier *pay·tro·lyay*; (*truck*) le camion-citerne *ka·myoñ·see·tehrn*

tap *n* (*for water*) le robinet *ro·bee·neh* □ *vt* frapper légèrement *fra·pay lay·zhehr·moñ* A31

tape *n* le ruban *rōō·boñ*; (*magnetic*) la bande magnétique *boñd ma·nyay·teek* □ *vt* (*record*) enregistrer *oñ·ruh·zhees·tray*

tape measure *n* le mètre à ruban *meh·tra rōō·boñ*

tape record *vt* enregistrer *oñ·ruh·zhees·tray*

tape recorder *n* le magnétophone *ma·nyay·to·fon*

tap-water *n* l'eau du robinet (*f*) *ō dōō ro·bee·neh*

tar *n* le goudron *goo·droñ*

target *n* la cible *see·bluh*; (*sales etc*) l'objectif (*m*) *ob·zhek·teef*

tariff *n* (*list of charges*) le tarif *ta·reef*; (*tax*) le tarif douanier *ta·reef dwa·nyay*

tarmac *n* le macadam *ma·ka·dam*

tart *n* la tarte *tart*

tartan *n* le tartan *tar·toñ*; **a tartan skirt** une jupe écossaise *ōōn zhōōp ay·ko·sez*

tartar sauce *n* la sauce tartare *sōs tar·tar*

task *n* la tâche *tahsh*

taste *n* le goût *goo*; **in poor taste** de mauvais goût *duh mō·veh goo*; **in good taste** de bon goût *duh boñ goo* □ *vt* **taste** sentir* *soñ·teer*; (*try*) goûter *goo·tay* □ *vi* **it tastes like fish** ça a un goût de poisson *sa a uñ goo duh pwah·soñ*

tax *n* (*on goods*) la taxe *taks*; (*on income*) les impôts (*mpl*) *añ·pō* □ *vt* (*goods*) taxer *tak·say*; (*income*) imposer *añ·pō·zay* A9

taxable *adj* imposable *añ·pō·za·bluh*

taxation *n* les impôts (*mpl*) *añ·pō*

tax-free *adj* exempt(e) d'impôts *eg·zoñ(·zoñt) dañ·pō*

taxi *n* le taxi *tak·see*; **to go by taxi** aller* en taxi *a·lay oñ tak·see*

taxi rank *n* la station de taxis *sta·syoñ duh tak·see*

T-bone steak *n* l'entrecôte (*f*) *oñ·truh·kōt*

tea *n* le thé *tay*; **mint tea** l'infusion de menthe (*f*) *añ·fōō·zyoñ duh moñt* E62

tea bag *n* le sachet de thé *sa·shay duh tay*

tea-break *n* la pause-thé *pōz·tay*

teach *vt* apprendre* *a·proñ·druh*; **to teach someone something** apprendre quelque chose à quelqu'un *a·proñ·druh kel·kuh shōz a kel·kuñ*

teacher *n* (*secondary school*) le professeur *pro·feh·sur*; (*primary school*) l'instituteur (*m*) *añ·stee·tōō·tur*, l'institutrice (*f*) *añ·stee·tōō·trees*

tea-cloth *n* le torchon *tor·shoñ*

teacup *n* la tasse à thé *tas a tay*

team *n* l'équipe (*f*) *ay·keep*

teapot *n* la théière *tay·yehr*

tear[1] *vt* (*rip*) déchirer *day·shee·ray* □ *n* la déchirure *day·shee·rōōr*

tear[2] *n* la larme *larm*; **in tears** en larmes *oñ larm*

tea-shop *n* le salon de thé *sa·loñ duh tay*

teaspoon *n* la petite cuillère *puh·teet kwee·yehr*; (*measure*) la cuillère à café *kwee·yehr a ka·fay*

tea strainer *n* le passe-thé *pas·tay*

teat *n* (*for bottle*) la tétine *tay·teen*

technical *adj* technique *tek·neek*

technician *n* le technicien *tek·nee·syañ*, la technicienne *tek·nee·syen*

technique *n* la technique *tek·neek*

technological *adj* technologique *tek·no·lo·zheek*

technology *n* la technologie *tek·no·lo·zhee*

tee *n* (*in golf*) le tee *tee*

teenager *n* l'adolescent(e) (*m/f*) *a·do·leh·soñ(·soñt)*

tee shirt *n* le T-shirt *tee·shurt*

telecommunications *pl* les télécommunications (*fpl*) *tay·lay·ko·mōō·nee·ka·syoñ*

telegram *n* le télégramme *tay·lay·gram* Sn4

telegraph vt télégraphier *tay·lay·gra· fyay*

telephone n le téléphone *tay·lay·fon*; **to be on the telephone** être* au téléphone *eh·trô tay·lay·fon*; **by telephone** par téléphone *par tay·lay·fon* □ vt **telephone** (person) téléphoner à *tay·lay·fo·nay* à T166, A35, Ea7

telephone booth n la cabine téléphonique *ka·been tay·lay·fo·neek*

telephone call n le coup de téléphone *koo duh tay·lay·fon*

telephone directory n l'annuaire des téléphones (m) *a·nŏŏ·ehr day tay· lay·fon* Sn29

telephone exchange n le central téléphonique *son·tral tay·lay·fo·neek*

telephone number n le numéro de téléphone *nŏŏ·may·rô duh tay·lay· fon*

telephonist n le/la téléphoniste *tay·lay· fo·neest*

telephoto lens n le téléobjectif *tay·lay· ob·zhek·teef*

telescope n le télescope *tay·leh·skop*

televise vt téléviser *tay·lay·vee·zay*

television n la télévision *tay·lay·vee· zyoñ*; (set) le téléviseur *tay·lay·vee· zur*; **on television** à la télévision *a la tay·lay·vee·zyoñ*

telex n le télex *tay·leks*; **by telex** par télex *par tay·leks* □ vt **telex** envoyer par télex *oñ·vwah·yay par tay·leks* A35, Bm22

tell vt raconter *ra·koñ·tay*; **to tell someone something** raconter quelque chose à quelqu'un *ra·koñ·tay kel· kuh shôz a kel·kuñ*; **to tell someone to do something** dire* à quelqu'un de faire quelque chose *deer à kel·kuñ duh fehr kel·kuh shôz*; **I can't tell the difference between them** je ne vois pas la différence entre eux *zhuh nuh vwah pas la dee·fay·roñs oñ·truh ö*

teller n le caissier *keh·syay*, la caissière *keh·syehr*

temper n □ **in a bad temper** de mauvaise humeur *duh mô·vez ŏŏ·mur*; **to lose one's temper** se mettre* en colère *suh meh·troñ ko·lehr*

temperature n la température *toñ·pay· ra·tōōr*; **to have a temperature** (fever) avoir* de la fièvre *a·vwahr duh la fyeh·vruh*; **to take someone's temperature** prendre* la température de quelqu'un *proñ·druh la toñ·pay·ra· tōōr duh kel·kuñ* I34

temple n (building) le temple *toñ·pluh*

temporary adj temporaire *toñ·po·rehr*

tempt vt tenter *toñ·tay*

ten num dix *dees*

tenant n le/la locataire *lo·ka·tehr*

tend vi □ **to tend to do something** avoir* tendance à faire quelque chose *a·vwahr toñ·doñs a fehr kel· kuh shôz*

tender adj (meat, vegetables) tendre *toñ·druh* □ vi **to tender for something** faire* une soumission pour quelque chose *fehr ōōn soo·mee·syoñ poor kel·kuh shôz*

tennis n le tennis *teh·nees* L27

tennis court n le court de tennis *koor duh teh·nees*

tennis racket n la raquette de tennis *ra·ket duh teh·nees*

tense adj tendu(e) *toñ·dōō*

tent n la tente *toñt* A82

tenth adj dixième *dee·zyem*

tent peg n le piquet de tente *pee·keh duh toñt*

tent pole n le mât de tente *mah duh toñt*

term n (of school etc) le trimestre *tree· mes·truh*; (word) le terme *tehrm*; **during his term of office** pendant la période où il exerçait ses fonctions *poñ·doñ la pay·ryod oo eel eg·zehr· seh say foñk·syoñ*; **terms** (of contract) les termes *tehrm*

terminal n (air terminal) l'aérogare (f) *a·eh·ro·gar*; (buses) la gare routière *gar roo·tyehr*; (electricity) la borne *born*; (computer) le terminal *tehr· mee·nal*

terrace n (of café) la terrasse *teh·ras*

terrible adj terrible *teh·ree·bluh*; (weather) épouvantable *ay·poo·voñ· ta·bluh*

territory n le territoire *teh·ree·twahr*

terrorism n le terrorisme *teh·ro·rees· muh*

terrorist n le/la terroriste *teh·ro·reest*

terylene n le tergal *tehr·gal*

test n (trial, check) l'essai (m) *eh·say*; (medical) l'examen (m) *eg·za·mañ*; (in school etc) le test *test*; (driving test) le permis de conduire *pehr·mee duh koñ·dweer* □ vt (product) essayer *eh·say·yay*; (sight, hearing) examiner *eg·za·mee·nay*; (ability) mettre* à l'épreuve *meh·tra luh· pruhv*

test-drive n l'essai de route (m) *eh·say duh root* □ vt **to test-drive a car** faire* faire un essai de route à une voiture *fehr fehr uñ neh·say duh root à ōōn vwah·tōōr*

text n le texte *tekst*

textbook n le manuel *ma·nŏŏ·el*

textiles pl les textiles (mpl) *tek·steel*

texture n la texture *tek·stōōr*

than conj que *kuh*; **better than him** mieux que lui *myuh kuh lwee*; **more than 10** plus de 10 *plōō duh 10*

thank vt remercier *ruh·mehr·syay*; **thank you** merci *mehr·see*; **thanks to** grâce à *grahs a*

that adj ce *suh*, cette *set*; **that boy** ce garçon-là *suh gar·soñ·la*; **that woman** cette femme-là *set fam·la*; **that one** celui-là *suh·lwee·la*, celle-là *sel·la* □ pron **that** ça *sa*; **give me that** donnez-moi ça *do·nay mwah sa*; **that's what I want** c'est ce que je veux *seh suh kuh zhuh vuh*; **what's that?** qu'est-ce que c'est? *kes kuh seh*; **who's that?** qui est-ce? *kee es*; **that is** (to say)... c'est à dire... *seh ta deer*; **the photo that I gave you** la photo que je vous ai donnée *la fo·tô kuh zhuh voo zay do·nay* □ conj **I hope that...** j'espère que... *zhes·pehr kuh*

thaw vi (ice) fondre *foñ·druh*; (frozen food) dégeler *day·zhuh·lay* □ vt (food) faire* dégeler *fehr day·zhuh· lay*

the art □ **the boy** le garçon *luh gar· soñ*; **the woman** la femme *la fam*; **the books** les livres *lay lee·vruh*

theater, theatre n le théâtre *tay·ah· truh*; **to go to the theater** aller* au théâtre *a·lay ō tay·ah·truh*

their adj leur(s) *lur*

theirs pron le/la leur *luh/la lur*; (plural) les leurs *lay lur*

them pron les *lay*; **buy them** achetez-les *ash·tay·lay*; **show them the books** montrez-leur les livres *moñ·tray·lur lay lee·vruh*; **he spoke to them** il leur a parlé *eel lur a par·lay*; **it's them!** ce sont eux! *suh soñ tuh*

themselves *pron* □ they wash themselves ils se lavent *eel suh lav*; they did it themselves ils l'ont fait eux-mêmes *eel loñ feh uh·mem*

then *adv* puis *pwee*; then it must be true alors ce doit être vrai *a·lor suh dwah teh·truh vreh*; from then on dès ce moment-là *deh suh mo·moñ·la*

theory *n* la théorie *tay·o·ree*

there *adv* là *la*; (*distant*) là-bas *la·ba*; there is/are il y a *eel ya*; is there anyone there? il y a quelqu'un? *eel ya kel·kuñ*; he went there il y est allé *eel ee eh ta·lay*; there he/she is! le/la voilà! *luh/la vwah·la*

thermometer *n* le thermomètre *tehr·mo·meh·truh*

Thermos (flask) *n* la thermos *tehr·mos*

these *adj* ces *say* □ *pron* ceux-ci *suh·see*, celles-ci *sel·see*; what are these? qu'est-ce que c'est que ça? *kes·kuh seh kuh sa*

they *pron* ils *eel*, elles *el*; they say that... (*people in general*) on dit que... *oñ dee kuh*; there they are les voilà *lay vwah·la*

thick *adj* épais(se) *ay·peh(·pes)*; 3 metres thick 3 mètres d'épaisseur *3 meh·truh day·peh·sur*

thief *n* le voleur *vo·lur*

thin *adj* (*line*) mince *mañs*; (*person*) maigre *meh·gruh*; (*material*) fin(e) *fañ (feen)*; (*liquid*) peu épais(se) *puh ay·peh(·pes)*

thing *n* la chose *shōz*; the best thing would be... le mieux serait... *luh myuh suh·reh*; where are your things? où sont vos affaires? *oo soñ vō za·fehr*

think *vi* penser *poñ·say*; to think of something penser à quelque chose *poñ·say a kel·kuh shōz*; to think about someone penser à quelqu'un *poñ·say a kel·kuñ*; I think so je pense que oui *zhuh poñs kuh wee*; to think something over bien réfléchir à quelque chose *byañ ray·flay·sheer a kel·kuh shōz*

third *adj* troisième *trwah·zyem* □ *n* third (gear) la troisième vitesse *trwah·zyem vee·tes*

third party insurance *n* l'assurance au tiers (*f*) *a·sōō·roñs ō tyehr*

Third World *n* le Tiers-Monde *tyehr·moñd*

thirsty *adj* qui a soif *kee a swahf*; to be thirsty avoir* soif *a·vwahr swahf*

thirteen *num* treize *trez*

thirteenth *adj* treizième *treh·zyem*

thirtieth *adj* trentième *troñ·tyem*

thirty *num* trente *troñt*

this *adj* ce *suh*, cette *set*; this one celui-ci *suh·lwee·see*, celle-ci *sel·see* □ *pron* this ceci *suh·see*; this is what I want c'est ce que je veux *seh suh kuh zhuh vuh*; what's this? qu'est-ce que c'est? *kes kuh seh*; who's this? qui est-ce? *kee es*

thorough *adj* (*work*) consciencieux (euse) *koñ·syoñ·syuh(·syuhz)*

those *adj* ces *say*; those boys ces garçons-là *say gar·soñ·la*; those women ces femmes-là *say fam·la* □ *pron* those ceux-là *suh·la*, celles-là *sel·la*; what are those? qu'est-ce que c'est que ça? *kes·kuh seh kuh sa*

though *conj, adv* □ though you may think... bien que vous pensiez... *byañ kuh voo poñ·syay*; he's happy, though il est pourtant heureux *eel eh poor·toñ uh·ruh*

thought *n* la pensée *poñ·say*; (*idea*) l'idée (*f*) *ee·day*

thousand *num* mille *meel*

thousandth *adj* millième *mee·lyem*

thread *n* le fil *feel*

threat *n* la menace *muh·nas*

threaten *vt* menacer* *muh·na·say*

three *num* trois *trwah*

thriller *n* (*film*) le film à suspense *feelm a sōōs·poñs*; (*book*) le roman à suspense *ro·moñ a sōōs·poñs*

throat *n* la gorge *gorzh* S40

throttle *n* (*in car*) l'accélérateur (*m*) *ak·say·lay·ra·tur*

through *prep* à travers *a tra·vehr*; through the wood à travers le bois *a tra·vehr luh bwah*; (*all*) through the year durant toute l'année *dōō·roñ toot la·nay*; Monday through Friday de lundi à vendredi *duh luñ·dee a voñ·druh·dee*; I couldn't get through (*on phone*) je n'ai pas pu avoir la communication *zhuh nay pa pōō a·vwahr la ko·mōō·nee·ka·syoñ*; put me through to Mr X passez-moi M. X *pa·say mwah muh·syuh X*; when I'm through with my work quand j'aurai fini mon travail *koñ zhō·ray fee·nee moñ tra·vye*

through train *n* le train direct *trañ dee·rekt*

throw *vt* jeter* *zhuh·tay*; (*rider*) désarçonner *day·zar·so·nay*; to throw a 6 (*dice*) avoir* un 6 *a·vwahr uñ 6*; to throw away jeter* *zhuh·tay*

thumb *n* le pouce *poos* □ *vt* to thumb a lift faire* de l'auto-stop *fehr duh lō·tō·stop*

thumbtack *n* la punaise *pü·nez*

thunder *n* le tonnerre *to·nehr*

thunderstorm *n* l'orage (*m*) *o·razh*

Thursday *n* jeudi (*m*) *zhuh·dee*

thus *adv* (*in this way*) ainsi *añ·see*

thyme *n* le thym *tañ*

tick *n* (*mark*) la coche *kosh* □ *vt* cocher *ko·shay* □ *vi* (*clock*) faire* tic-tac *fehr teek·tak*

ticket *n* le billet *bee·yeh*; (*for bus, metro*) le ticket *tee·keh*; (*label*) l'étiquette (*f*) *ay·tee·ket*; (*parking*) le P.-V. *pay·vay* T58f

ticket office *n* le guichet *gee·sheh* T50

tickle *vt* chatouiller *sha·too·yay*

tide *n* la marée *ma·ray*; the tide is in/out c'est la marée haute/basse *seh la ma·ray ōt/bas* Mc10

tidy *adj* (*person*) ordonné(e) *or·do·nay*; (*room, papers*) bien rangé(e) *byañ roñ·zhay*

tie *n* la cravate *kra·vat* □ *vt* (*string, ribbon*) nouer *noo·ay*; to tie a dog to a post attacher un chien à un poteau *a·ta·shay uñ shyañ a uñ po·tō*; to tie up a parcel ficeler* un paquet *fee·suh·lay uñ pa·keh*; to tie up capital immobiliser des fonds *ee·mo·bee·lee·zay day foñ*

tiger *n* le tigre *tee·gruh*

tight *adj* (*rope*) raide *red*; (*clothes*) ajusté(e) *a·zhōō·stay*; (*schedule*) très chargé(e) *treh shar·zhay*

tights *pl* le collant *ko·loñ*

tile *n* (*on floor, wall*) le carreau *ka·rō*; (*on roof*) la tuile *tweel*

till *prep* jusqu'à *zhōō·ska*; till dawn jusqu'à l'aube *zhōō·ska lōb* □ *conj* till he comes jusqu'à ce qu'il vienne *zhōō·ska suh keel vyen* □ *n* till (*cash register*) la caisse *kes*

time *n* le temps *toñ*; what's the time? quelle heure est-il? *kel ur eh·teel*; the time is 5 o'clock il est 5 heures *eel eh 5 ur*; the first time la première fois *la pruh·myehr fwah*; how many times? combien de fois? *koñ·byañ duh fwah*; a short time peu de temps *puh duh toñ*; a long time longtemps *loñ·toñ*; in times past dans le temps *doñ luh toñ*; to have a good time bien s'amuser *byañ sa·mōō·zay*; for the time being pour le moment *poor luh mo·moñ*; from time to time de temps en temps *duh toñ zoñ toñ*; just in time juste à temps *zhōōst a toñ*; on time à l'heure *a lur* L14, S1, T77

timetable *n* (for trains etc) l'horaire (*m*) *o·rehr*

time zone *n* le fuseau horaire *fōō·zō o·rehr*

tin *n* (substance) l'étain (*m*) *ay·tañ*; (can) la boîte *bwaht* S33

tin foil *n* le papier d'aluminium *pa·pyay da·lōō·mee·nyum*

tinned *adj* (food) en boîte *oñ bwaht*

tin-opener *n* l'ouvre-boîtes (*m*) *oo·vruh·bwaht*

tip *n* (end) le bout *boo*; (money given) le pourboire *poor·bwahr* □ *vt* (tilt) incliner *añ·klee·nay*

tipped *adj* (cigarettes) filtre *feel·truh*

tire *n* le pneu *pnuh*

tired *adj* fatigué(e) *fa·tee·gay*; I'm tired of it j'en ai assez *zho nay a·say*

tissue *n* (handkerchief) le mouchoir en papier *moo·shwahr oñ pa·pyay*

tissue paper *n* le papier de soie *pa·pyay duh swah*

title *n* le titre *tee·truh*

T-junction *n* (on road) l'intersection en T (*f*) *añ·tehr·sek·syoñ oñ tay*

to *prep* à *a*; to the station à la gare *a la gar*; to go to London aller* à Londres *a·lay a loñ·druh*; to France en France *oñ froñs*; to Portugal au Portugal *ō por·tōō·gal*; to school à l'école *a lay·kol*; to town en ville *oñ veel*; give it to me donnez-le-moi *do·nay·luh·mwah*; he wants to leave il veut partir *eel vuh par·teer*; I forgot to do… j'ai oublié de faire… *zhay oo·blyay duh fehr*; the key to my room la clé de ma chambre *la klay duh ma shoñ·bruh*

toast *n* le pain grillé *pañ gree·yay*; to propose a toast to someone porter un toast à quelqu'un *por·tay uñ tōst a kel·kuñ*

toaster *n* le grille-pain *greey·pañ*

tobacco *n* le tabac *ta·ba* S99

tobacconist *n* le marchand de tabac *mar·shoñ duh ta·ba*

tobacconist's (shop) *n* le tabac *ta·ba*

today *adv* aujourd'hui *ō·zhoor·dwee*

toe *n* le doigt de pied *dwah duh pyay*

toffee *n* le caramel *ka·ra·mel*

together *adv* ensemble *oñ·soñ·bluh*

toilet *n* les toilettes (*fpl*) *twah·let* F3, A4

toilet paper *n* le papier hygiénique *pa·pyay ee·zhyay·neek* A51

toiletries *pl* les articles de toilette (*mpl*) *ar·tee·kluh duh twah·let*

toilet water *n* l'eau de toilette (*f*) *ō duh twah·let*

token *n* (voucher) le bon *boñ*; (for machine) le jeton *zhuh·toñ* Sn20

toll *n* (on road etc) le péage *pay·yazh* T132

toll bridge *n* le pont à péage *poñ a pay·yazh*

tomato *n* la tomate *to·mat* S31

tomorrow *adv* demain *duh·mañ* T1, A19

ton *n* la tonne *ton*

tone *n* le ton *toñ*

tongue *n* la langue *loñg*

tonic *n* (medicine) le tonique *to·neek*

tonic water *n* le Schweppes *shweps*

tonight *adv* ce soir *suh swahr*

tonne *n* la tonne *ton*

tonsillitis *n* l'angine (*f*) *oñ·zheen*

too *adv* (also) aussi *ō·see*; he's too big il est trop grand *eel eh trō groñ*; too much trop *trō*; too many books trop de livres *trō duh lee·vruh*

tool *n* l'outil (*m*) *oo·teey*

tooth *n* la dent *doñ* I61

toothache *n* le mal de dents *mal duh doñ*; to have toothache avoir* mal aux dents *a·vwahr mal ō doñ* S40

toothbrush *n* la brosse à dents *bros a doñ*

toothpaste *n* la pâte dentifrice *paht doñ·tee·frees*

top *n* (of mountain) le sommet *so·meh*; (of ladder) le haut *ō*; (of table) le dessus *duh·sōō*; (lid) le couvercle *koo·vehr·kluh*; (of bottle) le bouchon *boo·shoñ*; on top of sur *sōōr*; (of gear) la quatrième vitesse *ka·tryem vee·tes* □ *adj* top du haut *dōō ō*; (in rank) premier(ière) *pruh·myay(·myehr)*; (best) meilleur(e) *may·yur* L16

top hat *n* le haut-de-forme *ō·duh·form*

topic *n* le sujet *sōō·zheh*

torch *n* la lampe de poche *loñp duh posh*

toss *vt* (salad) remuer *ruh·mōō·ay*; to toss a coin jouer à pile ou face *zhoo·ay a peel oo fas*

total *n* le total *to·tal* □ *adj* total(e) *to·tal*

touch *vt* toucher *too·shay* □ *n* in touch with en contact avec *oñ koñ·takt a·vek*

tough *adj* (meat etc) dur(e) *dōōr*; (material) solide *so·leed*

tour *n* le voyage *vwah·yazh* □ *vt* (town) visiter *vee·zee·tay*

tourism *n* le tourisme *too·reez·muh*

tourist *n* le/la touriste *too·reest*

tourist class *n* la classe touriste *klas too·reest*

tourist office *n* le syndicat d'initiative *sañ·dee·ka dee·nee·sya·teev*

tourist trade *n* le tourisme *too·reez·muh*

tow *vt* (trailer) remorquer *ruh·mor·kay*; on tow en panne *oñ pan*

toward(s) *prep* vers *vehr*; his attitude towards others son attitude envers les autres *soñ na·tee·tōōd oñ·vehr lay zō·truh*

tow-bar *n* (on car) l'attache (*f*) *a·tash*

towel *n* la serviette *sehr·vyet* A41

tower *n* la tour *toor*

town *n* la ville *veel*; to go to town aller* en ville *a·lay oñ veel* T92, L4f, Mc33

town hall *n* la mairie *may·ree*

toy *n* le jouet *zhoo·eh*

toyshop *n* le magasin de jouets *ma·ga·zañ duh zhoo·eh*

trace *n* (mark) la trace *tras*

track *n* (of animal) la piste *peest*; (pathway) le chemin *shuh·mañ*; (on record) la plage *plazh*; (for trains) la voie *vwah*; (sports) la piste *peest*

track suit *n* le survêtement *sōōr·vet·moñ*

tractor *n* le tracteur *trak·tur*

trade *n* le commerce *ko·mehrs*

trade-in *n* □ **as a trade-in** en reprise *oñ ruh·preez*

trademark *n* la marque de fabrique *mark duh fa·breek*

trade name *n* la marque déposée *mark day·pô·zay*

trader *n* le/la commerçant(e) *ko·mehr·soñ(·soñt)*

trade union *n* le syndicat *sañ·dee·ka*

trading estate *n* la zone industrielle *zôn añ·dôōs·tree·yel*

trading stamp *n* le timbre-prime *tañ·bruh·preem*

tradition *n* la tradition *tra·dee·syoñ*

traffic *n* (cars) la circulation *seer·kōō·la·syoñ*

traffic jam *n* l'embouteillage (m) *oñ·boo·tay·yazh*

traffic lights *pl* les feux (mpl) *fuh*

traffic warden *n* le/la contractuel(le) *koñ·trak·too·el*

trailer *n* (for goods) la remorque *ruh·mork*; (home on wheels) la caravane *ka·ra·van*

train *n* le train *trañ*; (on dress) la traîne *tren*; **by train** par le train *par luh trañ* □ *vt* **train** (apprentice) former *for·may*; (dog) dresser *dreh·say* □ *vi* (sportsman) s'entraîner *soñ·treh·nay*; **to train as a teacher** recevoir* une formation de professeur *ruh·suh·vwahr ōōn for·ma·syoñ duh pro·feh·sur* T2f, 52f

trainee *n* le/la stagiaire *sta·zhee·ehr*

training *n* (for job) la formation *for·ma·syoñ*; (for sports) l'entraînement (m) *oñ·tren·moñ*

tram(car) *n* le tramway *tram·way*

tramp *n* le/la clochard(e) *klo·shar (·shard)*

tranquillizer *n* le tranquillisant *troñ·kee·lee·zoñ*

transaction *n* la transaction *troñ·zak·syoñ*

transatlantic *adj* transatlantique *troñ·zat·loñ·teek*

transfer *vt* (money) transférer* *troñs·fay·ray*; **to transfer the charges** (on phone) téléphoner en P.C.V. *tay·lay·fo·nay oñ pay·say·vay*

transistor *n* le transistor *troñ·zees·tor*

transit *n* □ **in transit** en transit *oñ troñ·zeet*

transit lounge *n* la salle de transit *sal duh troñ·zeet*

transit visa *n* le visa de transit *vee·za duh troñ·zeet*

translate *vt* traduire* *tra·dweer*

translation *n* la traduction *tra·dōōk·syoñ*

transmission *n* (of car) la transmission *troñz·mees·yoñ*

transmitter *n* le transmetteur *troñz·meh·tur*

transparent *adj* transparent(e) *troñ·spa·roñ(·roñt)*

transport *n* le transport *troñ·spor* □ *vt* transporter *troñ·spor·tay*

transport café *n* le restaurant des routiers *res·tô·roñ day roo·tyay*

trap *n* le piège *pyezh*

trash *n* les ordures (fpl) *or·dōōr*

trash can *n* la poubelle *poo·bel*

travel *n* les voyages (mpl) *vwah·yazh* □ *vi* voyager* *vwah·ya·zhay* □ *vt* (a distance) parcourir* *par·koo·reer*

travel agency *n* l'agence de voyages (f) *a·zhoñs duh vwah·yazh*

travel agent *n* l'agent de voyages (m) *a·zhoñ duh vwah·yazh*

travel(l)er *n* le voyageur *vwah·ya·zhur*

travel(l)er's cheque *n* le chèque de voyage *shek duh vwah·yazh* M12, 22, A21

tray *n* le plateau *pla·tô*

treacle *n* la mélasse *may·las*

treasure *n* le trésor *tray·zor*

Treasury *n* le ministère des Finances *mee·nee·stehr day fee·noñs*

treat *vt* traiter *treh·tay*; **I'll treat you to an ice cream** je vous paierai une glace *zhuh voo pay·uh·ray ōōn glas* □ *n* **a little treat** un petit plaisir *uñ puh·tee play·zeer*

treatment *n* le traitement *tret·moñ*

tree *n* l'arbre (m) *ar·bruh*

trend *n* (tendency) la tendance *toñ·doñs*

trial *n* (test) l'essai (m) *eh·say*; (in law) le procès *pro·seh*

triangle *n* le triangle *tree·oñ·gluh*

tribe *n* la tribu *tree·bōō*

trick *n* (clever act) la ruse *rōōz*; (malicious) le tour *toor*; (in cards) la levée *luh·vay* □ *vt* attraper *a·tra·pay*

trifle *n* (dessert) le diplomate *dee·plo·mat*

trim *vt* (hedge) tailler légèrement *tye·yay lay·zhehr·moñ*; (hair) recouper un peu *ruh·koo·pay uñ puh*; (decorate) garnir *gar·neer*

trip *n* (journey) le voyage *vwah·yazh*; (excursion) l'excursion (f) *ek·skōōr·syoñ*; **to go on a trip** faire* une excursion *fehr ōōn ek·skōōr·syoñ*; **to go on a trip to the seaside** faire* une excursion au bord de la mer *fehr ōōn ek·skōōr·syoñ ô bor duh la mehr* □ *vi* **trip** (stumble) trébucher *tray·bōō·shay*

tripe *n* les tripes (fpl) *treep*

tripod *n* le trépied *tray·pyay*

trivial *adj* insignifiant(e) *añ·see·nyee·fyoñ(·fyoñt)*

trolley *n* le chariot *sha·ryô*

troop *n* la troupe *troop*

tropical *adj* tropical(e) *tro·pee·kal*

tropics *pl* les tropiques (mpl) *tro·peek*

trot *vi* (horse) trotter *tro·tay*

trouble *n* (problems) les problèmes (mpl) *pro·blem*; **the troubles in this country** les troubles dans ce pays *lay troo·bluh doñ suh pay·yee*; **to take trouble over something** se donner du mal pour quelque chose *suh do·nay dōō mal poor kel·kuh shôz*; **stomach trouble** les troubles gastriques (mpl) *troo·bluh gas·treek*; **engine trouble** les ennuis de moteur (mpl) *oñ·nwee duh mo·tur*; **to be in trouble** avoir* des ennuis *a·vwahr day zoñ·nwee* Sn53

trouble-shooter *n* (political) le conciliateur *koñ·see·lee·a·tur*; (technical) l'expert (m) *ek·spehr*

trousers *pl* le pantalon *poñ·ta·loñ* Sn69

trouser-suit *n* le tailleur-pantalon *tye·yur·poñ·ta·loñ*

trout *n* la truite *trweet*

truck *n* (vehicle) le camion *ka·myoñ*

true *adj* vrai(e) *vray*

truffle *n* (fungus) la truffe *trōōf*

truly *adv* □ **yours truly** je vous prie d'agréer l'expression de mes sentiments distingués *zhuh voo pree da·gray·yay lek·spreh·syoñ duh may soñ·tee·moñ dee·stañ·gay*

trump *n* (cards) l'atout (m) *a·too* □ *vt* prendre* avec l'atout *proñ·dra·vek la·too*

trumpet *n* la trompette *troñ·pet*

trunk *n* (of tree) le tronc *troñ*; (for clothes etc) la malle *mal*; (in car) le coffre *ko·fruh*

trunk-call n la communication interurbaine ko·mōō·nee·ka·syoñ añ·tehr·ōōr·ben

trunk-road n la route nationale root na·syo·nal

trust vt avoir* confiance en a·vwahr koñ·fyoñs oñ □ n (company) le trust trust

truth n la vérité vay·ree·tay

try vt essayer eh·say·yay; (in law) juger* zhōō·zhay; to try to do something essayer de faire quelque chose eh·say·yay duh fehr kel·kuh shōz; to try on a dress essayer une robe eh·say·yay ōōn rob

T-shirt n le tee-shirt tee·shurt

tube n le tube tōōb

Tuesday n mardi (m) mar·dee

tulip n la tulipe tōō·leep

tuna(-fish) n le thon toñ

tune n l'air (m) ehr □ vt (engine) régler* ray·glay; (instrument) accorder a·kor·day

tunic n (of uniform) la tunique tōō·neek

Tunisia n la Tunisie tōō·nee·zee

Tunisian adj tunisien(ne) tōō·nee·zyañ(·zyen)

tunnel n le tunnel tōō·nel

turbot n le turbot tōōr·bō

turkey n la dinde dañd

Turkey n la Turquie tōōr·kee

Turkish adj turc toork, turque toork

Turkish delight n le loukoum loo·koom

turn n (bend in road) le tournant toor·noñ; it's your turn c'est à vous seh ta voo; in turn à tour de rôle a toor duh rōl □ vi turn (person, car) tourner toor·nay; he turned (round) il s'est retourné eel seh ruh·toor·nay; to turn back revenir* ruh·vuh·neer oñ na·ryehr; to turn professional devenir* professionnel(le) duh·vuh·neer pro·feh·syo·nel □ vt turn tourner toor·nay; to turn on (light) allumer a·lōō·may; (water) faire* couler fehr koo·lay; to turn off (light) éteindre* ay·tañ·druh; (water) fermer fehr·may; to turn down (heat, etc) baisser beh·say; to turn up (light) mettre* plus fort meh·truh plōō for; to turn something over retourner quelque chose ruh·toor·nay kel·kuh shōz

turnip n le navet na·veh

turnover n (money) le chiffre d'affaires shee·fruh da·fehr; (in goods) le roulement roo·luh·moñ

turnpike n l'autoroute à péage (f) ō·tō·root a pay·yazh

turn signal n le clignoteur klee·nyo·tur

turquoise adj turquoise tōōr·kwahz

turtle soup n le consommé à la tortue koñ·so·may a la tor·tōō

tutor n le précepteur pray·sep·tur, la préceptrice pray·sep·trees

tuxedo n le smoking smo·keeng

TV n la télé tay·lay

tweed n le tweed tweed

tweezers pl la pince à épiler pañs a ay·pee·lay

twelfth adj douzième doo·zyem

twelve num douze dooz

twenty num vingt vañ

twice adv deux fois duh fwah

twig n la brindille brañ·deey

twill n le sergé sehr·zhay

twin beds pl les lits jumeaux (mpl) lee zhōō·mō

twins pl les jumeaux (mpl) zhōō·mō, les jumelles (fpl) zhōō·mel

twin set n le twin-set tween·set

twin towns pl les villes jumelées veel zhōō·muh·lay

twist vt tordre tor·druh □ vi (road) serpenter sehr·poñ·tay

two num deux duh

two-piece n le deux-pièces duh·pyes

tycoon n le gros homme d'affaires grō zom da·fehr

type n (sort) le genre zhoñ·ruh □ vt (letter) taper à la machine ta·pay a la ma·sheen

typewriter n la machine à écrire ma·sheen a ay·kreer

typewritten adj dactylographié(e) dak·tee·lo·gra·fyay

typical adj typique tee·peek

typist n le/la dactylo dak·tee·lō Bm14

tyre n le pneu pnuh T135

U

U-bend n (in road) le coude kood

ugly adj (object, person) laid(e) leh (led)

ulcer n l'ulcère (m) ōōl·sehr

ultimatum n l'ultimatum (m) ōōl·tee·ma·tum

umbrella n le parapluie pa·ra·plwee; (on table) le parasol pa·ra·sol

umbrella stand n le porte-parapluies port·pa·ra·plwee

umpire n l'arbitre (m) ar·bee·truh

unable adj □ to be unable to do something être* incapable de faire quelque chose eh·truh añ·ka·pa·bluh duh fehr kel·kuh shōz

unanimous adj (decision) unanime ōō·na·neem; we were unanimous nous étions tous d'accord noo zay·tyoñ toos da·kor

unarmed adj (person) non armé(e) noñ ar·may

unavoidable adj inévitable ee·nay·vee·ta·bluh

unbearable adj (pain) insupportable añ·sœ·por·ta·bluh

unbeatable adj (offer) imbattable añ·ba·ta·bluh

unbiased adj impartial(e) añ·par·syal

unbreakable adj incassable añ·kas·sa·bluh

uncertain adj (fact) incertain(e) añ·sehr·tañ(·ten)

unchanged adj inchangé(e) añ·shoñ·zhay

uncle n l'oncle (m) oñ·kluh

uncomfortable adj inconfortable añ·koñ·for·ta·bluh

unconditional adj (offer) inconditionnel(le) añ·koñ·dee·syo·nel

unconscious adj évanoui(e) ay·va·nwee

uncover vt découvrir* day·koo·vreer

under prep sous soo; under the table sous la table soo la ta·bluh; under a kilometre moins d'un kilomètre mwañ duñ kee·lo·meh·truh; under repair en cours de réparation oñ koor duh ray·pa·ra·syoñ; children under 10 les enfants de moins de 10 ans lay zoñ·foñ duh mwañ duh 10 añ

underclothes pl les sous-vêtements (mpl) soo·vet·moñ

undercooked adj pas assez cuit(e) pa za·say kwee (kweet)

underdeveloped adj (country) sous-développé(e) soo·day·vuh·lo·pay

underdone adj (steak) saignant(e) seh·nyoñ·(nyoñt); (food in general) pas assez cuit(e) pa za·say kwee (kweet)

underexposed adj sous-exposé(e) soo·zek·spō·zay

undergraduate n l'étudiant(e) (m/f) ay·tōō·dyoñ(·dyoñt)

underground adj (pipe etc) souterrain(e) soo·tay·rañ(·ren); underground railway le métro may·tro; to go by underground aller* en métro a·lay oñ may·tro

underline vt souligner soo·lee·nyay

underneath prep sous soo □ adv it's underneath c'est en dessous seh toñ duh·soo

underpaid adj sous-payé(e) soo·pay·yay

underpants pl le slip sleep

underpass n (for pedestrians) le passage souterrain pa·sazh soo·tay·rañ; (for cars) le passage inférieur pa·sazh añ·fay·ryur

undershirt n le maillot de corps mye·yō duh kor

understand vt/i comprendre* koñ·proñ·druh; we understand that... nous croyons comprendre que... noo krwah·yoñ koñ·proñ·druh kuh

understanding n la compréhension koñ·pray·oñ·syoñ; (agreement) l'accord (m) a·kor

undertake vt entreprendre* oñ·truh·proñ·druh; to undertake to do s'engager à faire soñ·ga·zhay a fehr

undertaking n (enterprise) l'entreprise (f) oñ·truh·preez; (promise) la promesse pro·mes

undervalue vt sous-estimer soo·zes·tee·may

underwear n les sous-vêtements (mpl) soo·vet·moñ

underwrite vt (insurance) souscrire* soo·skreer; (finance) garantir ga·roñ·teer

underwriter n le souscripteur soo·skreep·tur

undo vt défaire* day·fehr

undress vt déshabiller day·za·bee·yay □ vi se déshabiller suh day·za·bee·yay

unearned income n les rentes (fpl) roñt

uneconomic adj peu rentable puh roñ·ta·bluh

uneconomical adj peu économique puh ay·ko·no·meek

unemployed adj en chômage oñ shō·mazh; the unemployed les chômeurs (mpl) shō·mur

unemployment n le chômage shō·mazh

UNESCO n l'Unesco (f) ōō·ne·skō

unfair adj injuste añ·zhōōst; (competition) déloyal(e) day·lwah·yal

unfasten vt défaire* day·fehr

unfold vt déplier day·plee·ay

unfortunate adj (event) malheureux(euse) mal·uh·ruh(·ruhz)

unfortunately adv malheureusement mal·uh·ruhz·moñ

unhappy adj malheureux(euse) mal·uh·ruh(·ruhz)

uniform n l'uniforme (m) ōō·nee·form

unilateral adj unilatéral(e) ōō·nee·la·tay·ral

union n l'union (f) ōō·nyoñ; (trade union) le syndicat sañ·dee·ka

unique adj unique ōō·neek

unisex adj unisexe ōō·nee·seks

unit n (of machinery, furniture) l'élément (m) ay·lay·moñ; (department, squad) le groupe groop; (of measurement) l'unité (f) ōō·nee·tay

unite vt unir ōō·neer

United Kingdom, U.K. n le Royaume-Uni rwah·yōm·ōō·nee

United Nations Organization, UN, UNO n les Nations Unies (fpl) na·syoñ zōō·nee

United States (of America), US(A) n les États-Unis (d'Amérique) (mpl) ay·ta·zōō·nee (da·may·reek)

unit price n le prix unitaire pree ōō·nee·tehr

universal adj universel(le) ōō·nee·vehr·sel

universe n l'univers (m) ōō·nee·vehr

university n l'université (f) ōō·nee·vehr·see·tay

unkind adj (person) pas gentil(le) pa zhoñ·teey; (remark) méchant(e) may·shoñ(·shoñt)

unknown adj inconnu(e) añ·ko·nōō

unless conj □ unless we come à moins que nous ne venions a mwañ kuh noo nuh vuh·nyoñ

unlikely adj peu probable puh pro·ba·bluh

unlimited adj illimité(e) ee·lee·mee·tay

unlined adj (clothes) sans doublure soñ doo·blōōr

unload vt décharger day·shar·zhay

unlock vt ouvrir* oo·vreer

unlucky adj malchanceux(euse) mal·shoñ·suh(·suhz)

unnatural adj anormal(e) a·nor·mal

unnecessary adj inutile ee·nōō·teel

unofficial adj officieux(euse) o·fee·syuh(·syuhz); unofficial strike la grève sauvage grev sō·vazh

unpack vt (case) défaire* day·fehr; (clothes) déballer day·ba·lay

unpaid adj (debt) non acquitté(e) noñ a·kee·tay

unpleasant adj désagréable day·za·gray·a·bluh

unprofitable adj peu rentable puh roñ·ta·bluh

unreasonable adj (demand, price) excessif(ive) ek·seh·seef(·seev)

unripe adj pas mûr(e) pa mōōr

unsalted adj (butter) sans sel soñ sel

unscrew vt dévisser day·vee·say

unskilled labo(u)r n le travail de manœuvre tra·vye duh ma·nuh·vruh

unsuitable adj qui ne convient pas kee nuh koñ·vyañ pa

untidy adj (room) en désordre oñ day·zor·druh; (hair) mal peigné(e) mal peh·nyay

untie vt (parcel) défaire* day·fehr; (animal) détacher day·ta·shay

until prep jusqu'à zhōō·ska □ conj until he comes jusqu'à ce qu'il vienne zhōō·ska suh keel vyen

unusual adj rare rar

unwrap vt défaire* day·fehr

up prep □ to go up a hill monter une colline moñ·tay ōōn ko·leen; up till now jusqu'à maintenant zhōō·ska mañ·tuh·noñ; up to 6 jusqu'à 6 zhōō·ska 6 □ adv up there là-haut la·ō; he isn't up yet (out of bed) il n'est pas encore levé eel neh pa zoñ·kor luh·vay

update vt mettre* à jour meh·tra zhoor

uphill adv vers le haut ver luh ō; to go uphill monter moñ·tay

upkeep n l'entretien (m) oñ·truh·tyañ

upon prep sur sōōr

upper adj supérieur(e) sōō·pay·ryur; the upper class la haute bourgeoisie ōt boor·zhwah·zee

upside down adv à l'envers a loñ·vehr;

to turn something upside down
mettre* quelque chose à l'envers
meh·truh kel·kuh shōz a lon·vehr
upstairs *adv* en haut *on ō*
upturn *n* (*in business*) le retournement
ruh·toor·nuh·mon
upward(s) *adv* vers le haut *vehr luh ō*
urban *adj* urbain(e) *ōōr·bañ(·ben)*
urgent *adj* urgent(e) *ōōr·zhoñ(·zhoñt)*
urgently *adv* d'urgence *dōōr·zhoñs*
us *pron* nous *noo*
use *n* l'emploi (*m*) *oñ·plwah*; in use
en usage *oñ nōō·zazh*; it's no use cela
ne sert à rien *suh·la nuh sehr a ryañ*
□ *vt* use utiliser *ōō·tee·lee·zay*
used *adj* (*car etc*) d'occasion *do·ka·
syoñ*; to get used to s'habituer à *sa·
bee·tōō·ay a* □ *vi* we used to go nous
avions l'habitude d'y aller *noo za·
vyoñ la·bee·tōōd dee a·lay*
useful *adj* utile *ōō·teel*
useless *adj* inutile *ee·nōō·teel*
U.S.S.R. *n* l'U.R.S.S. (*f*) *lōō·ehr·es·es*
usual *adj* habituel(le) *a·bee·tōō·el*
usually *adv* habituellement *a·bee·tōō·
el·moñ*
U-turn *n* (*in car*) le demi-tour *duh·
mee·toor*

V

vacancy *n* (*job*) le poste vacant *post
va·koñ*; (*in hotel etc*) la chambre disponible *shoñ·bruh dees·pō·nee·bluh*;
no vacancies complet *koñ·pleh*
vacant *adj* (*seat, toilet*) libre *lee·bruh*
vacation *n* les vacances (*fpl*) *va·koñs*;
on vacation en vacances *oñ va·koñs*
vacationer *n* le vacancier *va·koñ·syay*,
la vacancière *va·koñ·syehr*
vaccination *n* la vaccination *vak·see·
nas·yoñ*
vacuum cleaner *n* l'aspirateur (*m*) *a·
spee·ra·tur*
vacuum flask *n* la bouteille thermos
boo·tay tehr·mos
vague *adj* vague *vag*
vain *adj* vaniteux(euse) *va·nee·tuh
(·tuhz)*; in vain en vain *oñ vañ*
valet *n* (*in hotel*) le valet de chambre
va·lay duh shoñ·bruh
valid *adj* valable *va·la·bluh*
valley *n* la vallée *va·lay*
valuable *adj* de grande valeur *duh
groñd va·lur*
valuables *pl* les objets de valeur (*mpl*)
ob·zhay duh va·lur
value *n* la valeur *va·lur* □ *vt* évaluer
ay·va·lōō·ay
value-added tax *n* la taxe à la valeur
ajoutée *taks a la va·lur a·zhoo·tay*
valve *n* (*in machine*) la soupape *soo·
pap*; (*holding in air*) la valve *valv*
van *n* la camionnette *kam·yo·net*
vandal *n* le/la vandale *voñ·dal*
vanilla *n* la vanille *va·neey*; vanilla ice
cream la glace à la vanille *glas a la
va·neey*
variable *adj* variable *va·ree·a·bluh* □ *n*
la variable *va·ree·a·bluh*
variation *n* la variation *va·ree·a·syoñ*
variety *n* la variété *va·ree·ay·tay*
variety show *n* le spectacle de variétés
spec·ta·cluh duh va·ree·ay·tay
various *adj* divers(e) *dee·vehr(·vehrs)*
varnish *n* le vernis *vehr·nee*
vary *vi* varier *va·ree·ay*
vase *n* le vase *vaz*
vaseline *n* la vaseline *vas·leen*
V.A.T. *n* la T.V.A. *tay·vay·a*
Vatican *n* le Vatican *va·tee·koñ*

veal *n* le veau *vō*
vegetables *pl* les légumes (*mpl*) *lay·
gōōm* E24
vegetarian *adj* végétarien(ne) *vay·
zhay·tay·ree·añ(·en)*
vehicle *n* le véhicule *vay·ee·kōōl*
veil *n* le voile *vwal*
vein *n* la veine *ven*
velvet *n* le velours *vuh·loor*
vending machine *n* le distributeur
automatique *dees·treeb·bōō·tur ō·tō·
ma·teek*
vendor *n* le vendeur *voñ·duhr*
Venice *n* Venise (*f*) *vuh·neez*
venison *n* la venaison *vuh·nay·zoñ*
ventilator *n* le ventilateur *voñ·tee·la·
tur*
venture *n* l'entreprise (*f*) *oñ·truh·preez*
veranda *n* la véranda *vay·roñ·da*
verbal *adj* (*agreement*) verbal(e) *vehr·
bal*
verdict *n* le verdict *vehr·deekt*
verge *n* le bord *bor*
vermouth *n* le vermouth *vehr·moot*
version *n* la version *vehr·syoñ*
versus *prep* contre *koñ·truh*
vertical *adj* vertical(e) *vehr·tee·kal*
very *adv* très *treh*; the very last le tout
dernier *luh too dehrn·yay*; I like it
very much je l'aime beaucoup *zhuh
lem bō·koo*; I haven't very much je
n'en ai pas beaucoup *zhuh noñ ay
pah bō·koo*
vest *n* (*undergarment*) le tricot de
corps *tree·kō duh kor*
vet(erinary surgeon) *n* le/la vétérinaire
vay·tay·ree·nehr
veto *vt* opposer son veto à *o·pō·zay
soñ vay·tō à* □ *n* le veto *vay·tō*
V.H.F. *abbrev* les ultra-courtes (*fpl*)
ōōl·tra·koort
via *prep* via *vee·a*
viaduct *n* le viaduc *vee·a·dōōk*
vicar *n* le pasteur *pa·stur*
vice chairman *n* le vice-président *vees·
pray·zee·doñ*
vice president *n* le vice-président *vees·
pray·zee·doñ*
vice versa *adv* vice versa *vees vehr·sa*
victim *n* (*of accident etc*) le/la victime
veek·teem
victory *n* la victoire *veek·twar*
video *n* la télévision *tay·lay·vee·zyoñ*;
on video à la télévision *a la tay·lay·
vee·zyoñ*
videocassette *n* la cassette vidéo *ca·set
vee·day·ō*
videocassette recorder *n* le magnétoscope *man·yay·to·skop*
videotape *n* la bande de magnétoscope
boñd duh man·yay·to·skop
Vienna *n* Vienne (*f*) *vee·yen*
view *n* la vue *vōō*; (*opinion*) l'avis (*m*)
a·vee A4
villa *n* (*country house*) la maison de
campagne *meh·zoñ duh koñ·pa·
nyuh*; (*vacation home*) la villa *vee·la*
village *n* le village *vee·lazh*
vinaigrette (sauce) *n* la vinaigrette *vee·
nay·gret*
vine *n* la vigne *veen·yuh*
vinegar *n* le vinaigre *vee·nay·gruh*
vineyard *n* le vignoble *veen·yo·bluh*
vintage *n* l'année (*f*) *a·nay*; a vintage
wine un vin de grand cru *uñ vañ duh
groñ krōō*
vinyl *n* le vinyle *vee·neel*
violence *n* la violence *vee·o·loñs*
violin *n* le violon *vee·o·loñ*
V.I.P. *n* le V.I.P. *vay·ee·pay*
visa, visé *n* le visa *vee·za*

visible *adj* visible *vee·zee·bluh*
visit *vt* (person) rendre visite à *roñ· druh vee·zeet a*; (place) visiter *vee· zee·tay* □ *n* la visite *vee·zeet*; (stay) le séjour *say·zhoor*
visitor *n* le visiteur *vee·zee·tur*, la visiteuse *vee·zee·tuhz*
visual aids *pl* les supports visuels (*mpl*) *sōō·por vee·zoo·el*
vital *adj* (essential) vital(e) *vee·tal*
vitamin *n* la vitamine *vee·ta·meen*
V-neck *n* le décolleté en V *day·col·tay oñ vay*
vocabulary *n* le vocabulaire *vo·ka· bōō·lehr*; (list of words) le lexique *lek·zeek*
vodka *n* la vodka *vod·ka*
voice *n* la voix *vwah*
void *adj* (contract) nul(le) *nōōl*
vol-au-vent *n* le vol-au-vent *vol·ō·voñ*
volcano *n* le volcan *vol·koñ*
volleyball *n* le volley(-ball) *vo·lay (·bol)*
voltage *n* la tension *toñ·syon*
volume *n* le volume *vo·lōōm*
vomit *vi* vomir *vo·meer*
vote *n* le vote *vot* □ *vi* voter *vo·tay*
voucher *n* le bon *boñ*

W

wafer *n* la gaufrette *gō·fret*
waffle *n* la gaufre *gō·fruh*
wag *vt* (tail) remuer *ruh·mōō·ay*
wage, wages *n* le salaire *sa·lehr*
wage earner *n* le/la salarié(e) *sa·la·ree· ay*
wage freeze *n* le blocage des salaires *blo·kazh day sa·lehr*
wag(g)on *n* (rail) le wagon *va·goñ*
wagon-lit *n* le wagon-lit *va·goñ·lee*
waist *n* la taille *tye*
waistcoat *n* le gilet *zhee·lay*
wait *vi* attendre *a·toñ·druh*; to wait for someone attendre quelqu'un *a·toñ· druh kel·kuñ*; to keep someone waiting faire* attendre quelqu'un *fehr a· toñ·druh kel·kuñ*; no waiting (road sign) stationnement interdit *sta· syon·moñ añ·tehr·dee*
waiter *n* le garçon *gar·soñ*
waiting list *n* la liste d'attente *leest da· toñt*
waiting room *n* (at station) la salle d'attente *sal da·toñt*
waitress *n* la serveuse *sehr·vuhz*
wake *vt* réveiller *ray·vay·yay* □ *vi* to wake up se réveiller *suh ray·vay·yay*
Wales *n* le Pays de Galles *pay·yee duh gal*
walk *vi* marcher *mar·shay*; (for pleasure, exercise) se promener *suh pro· muh·nay* □ *vt* to walk 10 km faire* 10 km à pied *fehr 10 km a pyay* □ *n* walk la promenade *pro·muh·nad*; to go for a walk faire* une promenade *fehr ōōn pro·muh·nad* L31
walking *n* la marche à pied *marsh a pyay*
walking stick *n* la canne *kan*
walkout *n* la grève-surprise *grev·sōōr· preez*
wall *n* le mur *mōōr*
wallet *n* le portefeuille *port·fuhy* Sn85
wallpaper *n* le papier peint *pa·pyay pañ*
wall-to-wall carpet(ing) *n* la moquette *mo·ket*
walnut *n* la noix *nwah*
waltz *n* la valse *vals*
wander *vi* errer *eh·ray*

want *vt* (wish for) vouloir* *voo·lwahr*; (need) avoir* besoin de *a·vwahr buh·zwañ duh*; to want to do something faire* vouloir faire quelque chose *voo·lwahr fehr kel·kuh shōz*
war *n* la guerre *gehr*
ward *n* (in hospital) la salle *sal*
wardrobe *n* (furniture) la garde-robe *gard·rob*
warehouse *n* l'entrepôt (*m*) *oñ·truh·pō*
warm *adj* chaud(e) *shō* (*shōd*); it's warm today il fait chaud aujourd'hui *eel feh shō ō·zhoor·dwee*; I'm warm j'ai chaud *zhay shō* □ *vt* warm réchauffer *ray·shō·fay*
warn *vt* avertir *a·vehr·teer*
warrant(y) *n* la garantie *ga·roñ·tee*
Warsaw *n* Varsovie (*f*) *var·so·vee*
wart *n* la verrue *veh·rōō*
was *vi* □ I was j'étais *zhay·teh*; he was il était *eel ay·teh*
wash *vt* laver *la·vay* □ *vi* to wash (oneself) se laver *suh la·vay*; to wash up (dishes) faire* la vaisselle *fehr la vay·sel*
washable *adj* lavable *la·va·bluh* S80
washbasin *n* le lavabo *la·va·bō* A49
washcloth *n* le gant de toilette *goñ duh twah·let*
washing *n* (clothes) la lessive *leh·seev*; to do the washing faire* la lessive *fehr la leh·seev*
washing machine *n* la machine à laver *ma·sheen a la·vay* A94
washing powder *n* la lessive *leh·seev*
washroom *n* les toilettes (*fpl*) *twah·let*
waste *n* le gaspillage *gas·pee·yazh*; (rubbish) les ordures (*fpl*) *or·dōōr* □ *vt* gaspiller *gas·pee·yay*; to waste one's time perdre son temps *per· druh soñ toñ*
waste paper basket *n* la corbeille à papier *kor·bay a pa·pyay*
watch *n* la montre *moñ·truh* □ *vt* regarder *ruh·gar·day*; (spy on) surveiller *sōōr·vay·yay* S87
water *n* l'eau (*f*) *ō* A31, 63, Mc9
watercress *n* le cresson *kreh·soñ*
waterfall *n* la chute d'eau *shōōt dō*
water heater *n* le chauffe-eau *shōf·ō*
water ice *n* le sorbet *sor·bay*
watermelon *n* la pastèque *pas·tek*
waterproof *adj* imperméable *añ·pehr· may·a·bluh*
water-skiing *n* le ski nautique *skee nō· teek*; to go water-skiing faire* du ski nautique *fehr dōō skee nō·teek*
watt *n* le watt *wat*
wave *vi* faire* signe de la main *fehr seen·yuh doh la mañ* □ *n* (in sea) la vague *vag*; (in hair) l'ondulation (*f*) *oñ·dōō·la·syoñ*
wavy *adj* (hair) ondulé(e) *oñ·dōō·lay*
wax *n* la cire *seer*; (in ear) le cérumen *say·rōō·men*
way *n* (manner) la façon *fa·soñ*; (in) a different way d'une autre façon *dōōn ō·truh fa·soñ*; which is the way to London? c'est par où Londres? *seh par oo loñ·druh*; to ask the way to Paris demander le chemin de Paris *duh·moñ·day luh shuh·mañ duh pa· ree*; it's a long way c'est loin *seh lwañ*; to be in the way bloquer le passage *blo·kay luh pa·sazh*; on the way en route *oñ root*; this way please par ici s'il vous plaît *par ee·see seel voo play*; by the way à propos *a pro· pō*; to give way (when driving) céder* la priorité *say·day la pree·o· ree·tay*

we *pron* nous *noo*

weak *adj* (*person*) faible *feh·bluh*; (*tea*) léger(ère) *lay·zhay(·zhehr)*

wealth *n* les richesses (*fpl*) *ree·shes*

wealthy *adj* riche *reesh*

weapon *n* l'arme (*f*) *arm*

wear *vt* (*clothes*) porter *por·tay* □ *vi* (*fabric*) s'user *sŌŌ·zay*; **to wear something out** user quelque chose *ŌŌ·zay kel·kuh shŌz* □ *n* **wear and tear** l'usure (*f*) *ŌŌ·zŌŌr*

weather *n* le temps *toñ*

weather forecast *n* la météo *may·tay·ō*

weave *vt* tisser *tee·say*

wedding *n* le mariage *ma·ree·azh*

wedding dress *n* la robe de mariage *rob duh ma·ree·azh*

wedding present *n* le cadeau de mariage *ka·dō duh ma·ree·azh*

wedding ring *n* l'alliance (*f*) *a·lyoñs*

Wednesday *n* mercredi (*m*) *mehr·kruh·dee*

weed *n* la mauvaise herbe *mō·vez erb*

week *n* la semaine *suh·men* T13, 105

weekday *n* le jour de semaine *zhoor duh suh·men*

weekend *n* le week-end *week·end*

weekly *adv* chaque semaine *shak suh·men* □ *adj* hebdomadaire *eb·dō·ma·dehr* □ *n* (*periodical*) l'hebdomadaire (*m*) *eb·dō·ma·dehr*

weigh *vt* peser *puh·zay*

weight *n* (*mass*) le poids *pwah*

welcome *adj* bienvenu(e) *byañ·vuh·nŌŌ* □ *n* l'accueil (*m*) *ak·kuhy* □ *vt* (*person*) accueillir* *ak·kuh·yeer*; (*event, proposal*) se réjouir de *suh ray·zhoo·eer duh*

weld *vt* souder *soo·day*

well *n* (*for water*) le puits *pwee* □ *adv* bien *byañ*; **to be well** aller* bien *a·lay byañ*; **get well soon** remettez-vous vite *ruh·me·tay·voo veet*; **well!** eh bien! *ay byañ*

wellington boot *n* la botte de caoutchouc *bot duh ka·oot·shoo*

Welsh *adj* gallois(e) *gal·wah(·wahz)* □ *n* le gallois *gal·wah*

were *vi* □ **you were** vous étiez *voo zay·tyay*; **we were** nous étions *noo zay·tyoñ*; **they were** ils étaient *eel zay·teh*

west *n* l'ouest (*m*) *west*; **the West** l'Occident (*m*) *ok·see·doñ* □ *adv* **west** à l'ouest *a lwest*

western *adj* occidental(e) *ok·see·doñ·tal* □ *n* (*movie*) le western *wes·tern*

West Germany *n* l'Allemagne de l'Ouest (*f*) *al·man·yuh duh lwest*

wet *adj* (*clothes*) mouillé(e) *moo·yay*; (*weather, day*) pluvieux(euse) *plŌŌ·vyuh(·vyuhz)*; (*paint*) frais *freh*, fraîche *fresh*; (*climate*) humide *ŌŌ·meed*; **to get wet** se mouiller *suh moo·yay*

whale *n* la baleine *ba·len*

wharf *n* le quai *kay*

what *adj* quel(le) *kel*; **what book?** quel livre? *kel lee·vruh*; **what languages?** quelles langues? *kel loñg* □ *pron* **what** quoi *kwa*; **que** *kuh*; **what's happened?** qu'est-ce qui s'est passé? *kes kee seh pa·say*; **what do you want?** que voulez-vous? *kuh voo·lay voo*; **I saw what happened** j'ai vu ce qui s'est passé *zhay vōō suh keh seh pa·say*; **I saw what you did** j'ai vu ce que vous avez fait *zhay vōō suh kuh voo za·vay feh*; **what's it called?** comment est-ce que ça s'appelle? *ko·moñ es·kuh sa sa·pel*; **what a**

mess! (*in room*) quel désordre! *kel day·zor·druh*; **what?** (*please repeat*) comment? *ko·moñ*

wheat *n* le blé *blay*

wheel *n* la roue *roo*; (*steering wheel*) le volant *vo·loñ*

wheelbarrow *n* la brouette *broo·et*

wheelchair *n* le fauteuil roulant *fō·tuhy roo·loñ* I5

when *conj* quand *koñ*; **the day when we...** le jour où nous... *luh zhoor oo noo*

where *conj* où *oo*; **where are you from?** d'où êtes-vous? *doo et·voo*

whether *conj* si *see*

which *adj* quel(le) *kel*; **which book?** quel livre? *kel lee·vruh*; **which languages?** quelles langues? *kel loñg*; **which one of you?** lequel (laquelle) d'entre vous? *luh·kel (la·kel) doñ·truh voo* □ *pron* **the book, which is** long le livre, qui est long *luh lee·vruh kee eh loñ*; **the apple which you ate** la pomme que vous avez mangée *la pom kuh voo za·vay moñ·zhay*; **I don't know which to take** je ne sais pas lequel prendre *zhuh nuh seh pa luh·kel proñ·druh*; **after which** après quoi *a·preh kwah*; **the chair on which** la chaise sur laquelle *la shez sōōr la·kel*

while *n* le moment *mo·moñ* □ *conj* pendant que *poñ·doñ kuh*

whip *n* le fouet *foo·eh* □ *vt* (*cream, eggs*) fouetter *foo·eh·tay*

whipped cream *n* la crème fouettée *krem foo·eh·tay*

whirlpool *n* le tourbillon *toor·bee·yoñ*

whirlwind *n* la tornade *tor·nad*

whisk *n* le fouet *foo·eh* □ *vt* (*cream, eggs*) fouetter *foo·eh·tay*

whisky *n* le whisky *wee·skee*

whisper *vi* chuchoter *shŌŌ·sho·tay*

whist *n* le whist *weest*

whistle *n* (*sound*) le sifflement *see·fluh·moñ*; (*object*) le sifflet *see·fleh* □ *vi* siffler *see·flay*

white *adj* blanc *bloñ*, blanche *bloñsh*

whitebait *n* la petite friture *puh·teet free·tŌŌr*

White House *n* la Maison Blanche *may·zoñ bloñsh*

whiting *n* le merlan *mehr·loñ*

Whitsun *n* la Pentecôte *poñt·kōt*

Whitsunday *n* le dimanche de Pentecôte *dee·moñsh duh poñt·kōt*

who *pron* qui *kee*

whole *adj* (*complete*) entier(ère) *oñ·tyay(·tyehr)*

wholemeal bread *n* le pain complet *pañ koñ·pleh*

wholesale *n* la vente en gros *voñt oñ grō* □ *adj* (*price*) de gros *duh grō* □ *adv* (*sell*) en gros *oñ grō*

wholesaler *n* le/la grossiste *grō·seest*

whom *pron* que *kuh*; **the man whom you see** l'homme que vous voyez *lom kuh voo vwah·yay*; **the boy with whom...** le garçon avec qui... *luh gar·soñ a·vek kee*

whooping cough *n* la coqueluche *kok·lŌŌsh*

whose *adj* □ **whose book is this?** à qui est ce livre? *a kee eh suh lee·vruh*; **the man, whose son** l'homme dont le fils *lom doñ luh fees*; **I know whose it is** je sais à qui c'est *zhuh seh a kee seh*

why *adv* pourquoi *poor·kwah*

wick *n* (*of cigarette lighter*) la mèche *mesh*

wicked adj méchant(e) may·shoñ (·shoñt)

wicker n l'osier (m) ō·zee·ay

wide adj (broad) large larzh; (range) grand(e) groñ (groñd); **4 cm. wide** 4 cm. de large 4 cm. duh larzh

wide-angle lens n l'objectif grand-angulaire (m) ob·zhek·teef groñ·toñ·gōō·lehr

widow n la veuve vuhv

widower n le veuf vuhf

width n la largeur lar·zhur

wife n la femme fam T108, A2, S105

wig n la perruque peh·rōōk

wild adj sauvage sō·vazh

wildlife n les animaux sauvages (mpl) a·nee·mō sō·vazh

will n (testament) le testament tes·ta·moñ □ vi **he will do it** il le fera eel luh fuh·ra

willing adj □ **willing to do something** prêt(e) à faire quelque chose preh (pret) a fehr kel·kuh shōz

win vi (in match, competition) gagner ga·nyay □ vt (match, competition) gagner ga·nyay; (prize) remporter roñ·por·tay; (contract) obtenir* op·tuh·neer

wind[1] n (breeze) le vent voñ; (in stomach) les vents (mpl) voñ

wind[2] vt enrouler oñ·rōō·lay; **to wind up a clock** remonter une horloge ruh·moñ·tay ōōn or·lozh

windmill n le moulin à vent mōō·lañ a voñ

window n (in house) la fenêtre fuh·neh·truh; (in car, train) la vitre vee·truh; (of shop) la vitrine vee·treen B55, A71

window shade n le store stor

window shopping n le lèche-vitrines lesh·vee·treen

windscreen n le pare-brise par·breez T164

windscreen washer n le lave-glace lav·glas

windscreen wiper n l'essuie-glace (m) eh·swee·glas T178

windshield n le pare-brise par·breez T164

windshield washer n le lave-glace lav·glas

windshield wiper n l'essuie-glace (m) eh·swee·glas

windsurfing n la planche à voile ploñsh a vwal; **to go windsurfing** faire* de la planche à voile fehr duh la ploñsh à vwal

windy adj (place) exposé(e) au vent ek·spō·zay ō voñ; **it's windy** il y a du vent eel ya dōō voñ

wind[1] n (breeze) le vent voñ; **wind** (in stomach) les vents (mpl) voñ

wind[2] vt enrouler oñ·rōō·lay

wine n le vin vañ B53, E9f, S35

wine cellar n la cave à vin kav a vañ

wineglass n le verre à vin vehr a vañ

wine list n la carte des vins kart day vañ

wine waiter n le sommelier so·muh·lyay

wing n l'aile (f) ehl

wink vi faire* un clin d'œil fehr uñ klañ duhy

winner n le/la gagnant(e) ga·nyoñ (·nyoñt)

winter n l'hiver (m) ee·vehr

winter sports pl les sports d'hiver (mpl) spor dee·vehr

wipe vt essuyer eh·swee·yay; **to wipe off** effacer* ay·fa·say

wire n le fil de fer feel duh fehr; (electrical) le fil électrique feel ay·lek·treek; (telegram) le télégramme tay·lay·gram

wise adj (person) sage sazh; (decision) prudent(e) prōō·doñ·(·doñt)

wish n (on gift) **with best wishes** (on gift) meilleurs vœux may·yur vuh; (on letter) bien amicalement byañ a·mee·kal·moñ □ vt/i **I wish I could**... si seulement je pouvais... see suhl·moñ zhuh poo·veh; **to wish for something** souhaiter quelque chose soo·ay·tay kel·kuh shōz

witch n la sorcière sor·syehr

with prep avec a·vek; **the man with the umbrella** l'homme au parapluie lom ō pa·ra·plwee; **red with anger** rouge de colère roozh duh ko·lehr; **filled with water** rempli(e) d'eau roñ·plee dō

withdraw vt (money) retirer ruh·tee·ray

without prep sans soñ

witness n le témoin tay·mwañ □ vt (signature) attester l'authenticité de at·tes·tay lō·toñ·tee·see·tay duh T221

wobble vi (chair etc) branler broñ·lay

wolf n le loup loo

woman n la femme fam

womb n l'utérus (m) ōō·tay·rōōs

wonder vi □ **to wonder whether**... se demander si... suh duh·moñ·day see

wonderful adj merveilleux(euse) mehr·vay·yuh·(·yuhz)

wood n le bois bwah

wooden adj en bois oñ bwah

wool n la laine len

wool(l)en adj de laine duh len

word n le mot mō; (spoken) la parole pa·rol; **word for word** mot à mot mō ta mō

work n le travail tra·vye; (art, literature) l'œuvre (f) uh·vruh; **to go to work** aller* au travail a·lay ō tra·vye □ vi **work** travailler tra·vye·yay; (clock, mechanism) marcher mar·shay; (medicine) agir a·zheer; **to work out** (problem) résoudre* ray·zoo·druh

worker n l'ouvrier (m) oo·vree·ay, l'ouvrière (f) oo·vree·ehr

work force n la main d'œuvre mañ duh·vruh

working capital n les fonds de roulement (mpl) foñ duh rool·moñ

working-class adj ouvrier(ère) oo·vree·ay(·ehr)

working day n le jour ouvrable zhoor oo·vra·bluh

working hours pl les heures de travail (fpl) ur duh tra·vye

working order n □ **to be in working order** être* en état de marche eh·truh oñ nay·ta duh marsh

workman n l'ouvrier (m) oo·vree·ay

work of art n l'œuvre d'art (f) uh·vruh dar

works pl (mechanism) le mécanisme may·ka·neez·muh; (factory) l'usine (f) ōō·zeen

workshop n l'atelier (m) a·tuh·lyay

work-to-rule n la grève du zèle grev dōō zel

world n le monde moñd

world power n la puissance mondiale pwee·soñs moñ·dyal

world war n la guerre mondiale gehr moñ·dyal

worm n le ver vehr

worn adj usé(e) ōō·zay

worn-out adj (object) complètement usé(e) koñ·plet·moñ ōō·zay; (person) épuisé(e) ay·pwee·zay

worried adj inquiet(ète) añ·kyay(·kyet)

worry n le souci soo·see

worse adj □ it's worse (than the other) c'est pire (que l'autre) seh peer (kuh lō·truh) □ adv to do something worse faire° quelque chose de pire fehr kel·kuh shōz duh peer

worst adj □ the worst book le plus mauvais livre luh plōō mō·veh lee·vruh □ adv he did it worst il l'a fait le plus mal eel la feh luh plōō mal

worth adj □ to be worth £5 valoir° £5 va·lwahr £5; 50 francs worth of petrol/gas pour 50 francs d'essence poor 50 froñ deh·soñs; it's worth it ça en vaut la peine sa oñ vō la pen

worthwhile adj (activity) qui en vaut la peine kee oñ vō la pen

would vi □ she would come if... elle viendrait si... el vyañ·dreh see; would you like a cup of coffee? aimeriez-vous un café? ay·muh·ryay voo zuñ ka·fay

wound n (injury) la blessure bleh·sōōr

wrap vt envelopper oñ·vuh·lop·pay; to wrap up a parcel emballer un paquet oñ·bal·lay uñ pa·kay □ n wrap (shawl) le châle shahl

wrapper n (paper) la couverture koo·vehr·tōōr

wrapping paper n le papier d'emballage pa·pyay doñ·bal·lazh

wreck n (ship) l'épave (f) ay·pav □ vt provoquer le naufrage de pro·vo·kay luh nō·frazh duh; (plans) ruiner rōō·ee·nay

wrestling n la lutte lōōt

wring vt (clothes) essorer eh·so·ray

wrinkle n la ride reed

wrist n le poignet pwah·nyay

write vt/i écrire° ay·kreer; to write down noter no·tay; to write off a debt passer une dette aux profits et pertes pa·say duñ det dō pro·fee ay pehrt

writer n l'auteur (m) ō·tur

writing n l'écriture (f) ay·kree·tōōr; in writing par écrit par ay·kree

writing case n le nécessaire de correspondance nay·seh·sehr duh ko·res·poñ·doñs

writing paper n le papier à lettres pa·pyay a leh·truh

wrong adj faux fō, fausse fōs; you're wrong vous avez tort voo za·vay tor; the wrong road/answer la mauvaise route/réponse la mō·vez root/ray·poñs; what's wrong? qu'est-ce qui ne va pas? kes·kee nuh va pa; to go wrong (machine) tomber en panne toñ·bay oñ pan

X

Xerox n la photocopie fo·to·ko·pee □ vt photocopier fo·to·ko·pyay

X-ray n (photo) la radio ra·dyō □ vt radiographier ra·dyo·gra·fyay

Y

yacht n le voilier vwah·lyay

yachting n le yachting yo·ting; to go

yachting faire° de la navigation de plaisance fehr duh la na·vee·ga·syoñ duh pleh·zoñs

yard n (of building) la cour koor; (measure) le yard

yawn vi bâiller bye·yay

year n l'an (m) oñ; (as duration) l'année (f) a·nay

yearly adj annuel(le) a·nōō·el □ adv tous les ans too lay zoñ

yeast n la levure luh·vōōr

yellow adj jaune zhōn

yes adv oui wee; (in answer to negative question) si see

yesterday adv hier yehr

yet adv encore oñ·kor

yield n le rendement roñ·duh·moñ □ vt (investment) rapporter ra·por·tay □ vi (to traffic) céder la priorité say·day la pree·o·ree·tay

yoga n le yoga yo·ga

yoghurt n le yaourt ya·oort

you pron (familiar form) tu tōō; (polite, plural form) vous voo; he's watching you il te/vous regarde eel tuh/voo ruh·gard; milk is good for you le lait vous fait du bien luh leh voo feh dōō byañ

young adj jeune zhuhn

your adj (familiar form) ton toñ, ta ta, tes tay; (polite, plural form) votre vo·truh, vos vō; your father/mother ta/votre père toñ/vo·truh pehr; your mother ta/votre mère ta/vo·truh mehr; your sisters tes/vos sœurs tay/vō sur

yours pron (familiar form) le tien luh tyañ, la tienne la tyen; (polite, plural form) le/la vôtre luh/la vō·truh; where are yours? où sont les tiens/vôtres? oo soñ lay tyañ/vō·truh; these are yours ceux-ci sont à toi/vous suh·see soñ ta twah/voo

yourself pron (familiar form) toi-même twah·mem; (polite form) vous-même voo·mem; you've hurt yourself vous vous êtes fait mal voo voo zet feh mal; you did it yourself vous l'avez fait vous-même voo la·vay feh voo·mem

yourselves pron vous-mêmes voo·mem

youth n (period) la jeunesse zhuh·nes

youth club n le foyer de jeunes fwah·yay duh zhuhn

youth hostel n l'auberge de jeunesse (f) ō·behrzh duh zhuh·nes

Yugoslavia n la Yougoslavie yoo·go·sla·vee

Yugoslav(ian) adj yougoslave yoo·go·slav

Z

zebra n le zèbre zeh·bruh

zero n le zéro zay·rō

zinc n le zinc zañk

zip code n le code postal kod pos·tal

zip(-fastener), zipper n la fermeture éclair fehr·muh·tōōr ay·klehr S79

zone n la zone zōn

zoo n le zoo zō

zoom lens n le zoom zoom

zucchini pl les courgettes (fpl) koor·zhet